FREEDOM AND THE COURT

Freedom and the Court

CIVIL RIGHTS AND LIBERTIES IN THE UNITED STATES

Fifth Edition

Henry J. Abraham

James Hart Professor of
Government and Foreign Affairs
University of Virginia

OXFORD UNIVERSITY PRESS
New York   Oxford
1988

OXFORD UNIVERSITY PRESS

Oxford   New York   Toronto
Delhi   Bombay   Calcutta   Madras   Karachi
Petaling Jaya   Singapore   Hong Kong   Tokyo
Nairobi   Dar es Salaam   Cape Town
Melbourne   Auckland
and associated companies in
Berlin   Ibadan

Copyright © 1967, 1972, 1977, 1982, 1988, by Henry J. Abraham

Published by Oxford University Press, Inc.,
200 Madison Avenue, New York, New York 10016

Oxford is a registered trademark of Oxford University Press

Library of Congress Cataloging-in-Publication Data
Abraham, Henry Julian, 1921–
Freedom and the court: civil rights and liberties in the United
States / by Henry J. Abraham.
p.   cm.   Bibliography: p.   Includes index.
ISBN 0-19-505516-0
1. Civil rights—United States. 2. United States. Supreme Court.
I. Title.   KF4749.A73 1989   342.73'085—dc19   [347.30285]
87-34733   CIP

Printing (last digit): 9 8 7 6 5 4 3
Printed in the United States of America
on acid-free paper

TO
MY MOTHER
AND
THE MEMORY OF MY FATHER

Preface to the Fifth Edition

The more than six years that have elapsed since the publication of this work's fourth edition have witnessed such a plethora of changes that major revisions were demonstrably in order for the fifth. Hence, encouraged and buttressed by a host of formal and informal suggestions from respected and experienced colleagues, the new edition not only updates the developments on the frontiers of civil rights and liberties in our constitutional constellation, it represents a major rewriting and reorganizing of the entire book. Thus, Chapters I and II have been thoroughly recast to reflect the impact of the Supreme Court's response to the ongoing egalitarian revolution, with particular emphasis upon the Court's evolving tiered standards of review under the "new" "equal protection of the laws" jurisprudence. Chapters III and IV manifest the continuing emphasis upon "incorporation" and "nationalization" of the Bill of Rights, and the sundry new developments in the realm of due process of law in criminal justice. Chapter V has been drastically reorganized in order to introduce fundamental considerations relevant to freedom of expression antecedent to the many burgeoning contemporary developments. Chapter VI addresses the numerous recent emotion-charged developments in both the "free exercise" and "separation of Church and State" components, including the 1987 "creationism" decision. The most extensive revisions, however, have been effected regarding race and gender. Chapter VII, which heretofore encompassed both subjects—and the latter rather briefly—now deals exclusively with race. A new Chapter VIII, entitled "Gender and Race Under the New Equal Protection," recounts and analyzes gender discrimination—with a separate section on the abortion controversy— and concludes with a thorough discussion of the very controversial affirmative action/reverse discrimination issue. The book is current as of June 1988.

As has been true of all previous editions of *Freedom and the Court,* the overriding theme of the present edition is "line-drawing"— how to find and draw those elusive and vexatious yet so necessary lines between individual and societal rights and obligations under a written constitution, interpreted by an independent judiciary, with the Supreme Court of the United States at its apex.

While the theme of, and emphasis upon, a particular line may well change from time to time, the need to render judgments is omnipresent. In a democratic society such as ours, lines must be drawn generously, yet not suicidally. In general, the Court has met the challenge. It remains the single most significant safeguard under our system in its role as the ultimate guardian of our fundamental civil rights and liberties.

Once again, I acknowledge with profound appreciation the very generously provided financial research assistance by the Robert W. and Patricia T. Gelfman Fund of the Jewish Communal Fund of New York, and the Mayer and Arlene Mitchell and Abraham A. Mitchell Fund of The Mobile (Alabama) Community Foundation, as well as the many helpful critical suggestions by colleagues and students too numerous to mention. But I wish to tender specific gratitude to a group of ever-faithful graduate research assistants who have so loyally aided in the completion of this latest effort: Gregor Baer, Scott Hill, Linda McClain, Jim Scott, and Kathy Uradnik. My most abiding appreciation goes to Barbara A. Perry, who, first as a graduate student, then as a research assistant, and now as a colleague, has proved to be a truly indispensable, selfless, and treasured associate in the fruition of this enterprise.

Charlottesville, Virginia   H.J.A.
June 1988

Preface to the Fourth Edition

Although the four and a half years that have elapsed since the publication of this work's third edition had brought only one change in the membership of the Supreme Court of the United States—the appointment of Sandra Day O'Connor as of the fall term 1981—far-reaching, indeed seminal, changes informed the Court's interpretations and molding of constitutional law between 1977 and 1981. These developments have brushed or embraced all components and segments of that law; but none has seen such extensive, indeed, dramatic, perhaps even radical, extension or transformation as the "equal protection of the laws" realm of the Fourteenth Amendment, with particular reference to race and gender. This new (fourth) edition of the book, which has continued to be used widely and approvingly, takes account of these and other fundamental alterations in the status of civil rights and liberties in our land, as pronounced by its highest tribunal. Completely updated and thoroughly rewritten, this latest edition is current through the Court's entire 1980–81 term (ending in July of 1981), thus taking account of contemporary holdings of the "Burger Court."

Once again I happily acknowledge the profound debt I owe to a host of colleagues and students whose constructive criticism, aid, and counsel have been as welcome as they have been indispensable. Their encouragement and support are responsible for the present undertaking. I am also deeply grateful for financial research assistance tendered so generously by the Joseph and Rebecca Mitchell Foundation and the Robert W. and Patricia T. Gelfman Fund. A special note of recognition and appreciation goes to my 1979–81 research assistants, Peter M. Dodson, Linda McClain, and Vincent M. Bonventre, whose conscientious, efficient, and loyal labors were essential to the enterprise.

Charlottesville, Virginia   H.J.A.
September 1981

Preface to the Third Edition

The favorable reception accorded to the first and second editions of this book prompted the undertaking of this third. Although the scope and approach of the new work are the same as those of its predecessors, the passage of time—however brief in the annals of constitutional development—has mandated changes, often major, on almost every page, indeed the rewriting as well as enlarging of most chapters. The new edition has been completely updated through 1976, thus taking account of the latest posture of the "Burger Court."

Again, I am profoundly grateful to the numerous colleagues and students whose thoughtfully constructive criticism and support of the first and second editions encouraged me to undertake the third. And I should like to add a special note of gratitude to my 1974–76 research assistant, Bruce Allen Murphy, whose superb, faithful work was essential to the revision's completion.

Keswick, Virginia   H.J.A.
January 1977

Preface to the Second Edition

The favorable reception. accorded to the first edition of this book prompted the undertaking of this second, which appears almost five years later. Although the scope and approach of the new work are the same as that of the original, the passage of time—however brief in the annals of constitutional development— has mandated changes on almost every page and the rewriting as well as enlarging of certain chapters, particularly IV, V, VI, and VII. The new edition has been completely updated through December 1971, thus taking account of the latest posture of the "Burger Court." There are two procedural innovations: the addition of an appendix containing excerpts from the Constitution dealing with civil rights and liberties, and a separate "name" index (alongside "general" and "case" indexes).

I am profoundly grateful to the numerous colleagues and students whose thoughtfully constructive criticism and support of the first edition encouraged me to undertake the second. And I should like to add a special note of gratitude to my 1970–72 research assistants, Norman H. Levine, Mark A. Aronchick, Frank C. Lindgren, Andrew B. Cohn, and Michael E. Marino.

Wynnewood, Pennsylvania H.J.A.
February 1972

Preface to the First Edition

This is essentially a study of the lines that must be drawn by a democratic society as it attempts to reconcile individual freedom with the rights of the community. No single book could cope with the entire field of civil rights and liberties, and no attempt is made to do so here. Rather, it has been my aim to analyze and evaluate the basic problem of drawing lines between individual rights and community rights and to venture some conclusions or suggestions in those spheres that constitute the basic rights and liberties: freedom of religion and the attendant problem of separation of Church and State; freedom of expression; due process of law, particularly procedural safeguards in criminal law; and political and racial equality. The three introductory chapters—the third comprising a thorough analysis of the problem of Amendment Fourteen and "incorporation"—are designed to focus the study and to stress my belief that it is essential to recognize and comprehend the significant role the judicial branch of the United States Government, with the Supreme Court as its apex, has played in defining and strengthening the basic rights and liberties that accrue to us from the principle of a government under constitutionalism, a government that is limited in its impact upon individual freedom.

As usual, I am indebted to many colleagues for stimulation, criticism, and encouragement. I am particularly grateful to Professor Alpheus T. Mason of Princeton, who read the entire manuscript; to Professors David Fellman of Wisconsin and Rocco J. Tresolini of Lehigh, who were generous discussants; and to my departmental colleague, Charles Jasper Cooper, who proved a valued "sounding board" down the hall. My research assistant, Judy F. Lang, was a delightful and industrious aid. Dr. Joan I. Gotwals of the Van Pelt Library kindly provided me with a "secret annex" in which I could work in quiet seclusion. Mrs. Dorothy E. Carpenter typed the manuscript cheerfully and conscientiously. Byron S. Hollinshead, Jr., Helen M. Richardson, and Mary Ollmann of Oxford University Press provided indispensable professional assistance. And my wife, Mildred, and our sons, Philip and Peter, to each of whom earlier books were happily dedicated, made it all worthwhile.

Wynnewood, Pennsylvania   H.J.A.
March 1967

Contents

Freedom and the Court

chapter *I* Introduction

Although, as David Fellman points out, the American people, both in political theory and in public law, have been committed for more than two hundred years to the "primacy of civil liberties in the constellation of human interests,"[1] these civil liberties do not exist in a vacuum or even in anarchy but in a state of society. It is inevitable that the individual's civil rights and those of the community of which he or she is a part come into conflict and need adjudication.[2]

It is easy to state the need for a line between individual rights and the rights of the community, but how, where, and when it is to be drawn are questions that will never be resolved to the satisfaction of the entire community. In John Stuart Mill's perceptive words in his *On Liberty and the Subjection of Women:* "But though the proposition is not likely to be contested in general terms, the practical question, where to place the limits—how to make the fitting adjustment between individual independence and social control—is a subject on which nearly everything remains to be done."[3] Liberty and order are difficult to reconcile, particularly in a democratic society such as ours. We must have *both,* but a happy balance is not easy to maintain. As a constitutional democracy, based upon a government of limited powers under a written con-

[1]*The Limits of Freedom* (Brunswick, N.J.: Rutgers University Press, 1959), from the Foreword (unpaginated).

[2]Although some would object, the terms "rights" and "liberties" are used interchangeably in this book. They are to be distinguished from all the other rights and freedoms individuals may enjoy under law because they are especially protected, in one manner or another, against violations *by governments.* (In Canada, the term "civil rights" refers exclusively to *private* law—the legal relationship between person and person in private life.) See J. A. Corry and Henry J. Abraham, *Elements of Democratic Government,* 4th ed. (New York: Oxford University Press, 1964), pp. 234–39.

[3](New York: Holt, 1898), p. 16.

stitution, and a majoritarianism duly checked by carefully guarded minority rights, we must be generous to the dissenter. Again citing Mill, "all mankind has no right to silence one dissenter . . . [for] all silencing of discussion is an assumption of infallibility." Even near-unanimity under our system does not give society the right to deprive individuals of their constitutional rights. As Judge Jerome Frank observed, "The test of the moral quality of a civilization is its treatment of the weak and powerless."[4] "The worst citizen no less than the best," once wrote Justice Hugo L. Black, dissenting from a Supreme Court reversal of some trespassing convictions, "is entitled to equal protection of the laws of his state and of his nation"[5]—and the citizen of whom he spoke was a defiant racist. Who or what he was is irrelevant, of course; indeed, in Justice Frankfurter's often-quoted words: "It is a fair summary of history to say that safeguards of liberty have been forged in controversies involving not very nice people."[6] The basic issue was memorably phrased by Justice Robert H. Jackson in the *West Virginia Flag Salute* case,[7] in which the Supreme Court struck down, as violating the freedom of religion guarantees of the First and Fourteenth Amendments, a compulsory flag-salute resolution adopted by the West Virginia State Board of Education. As Justice Jackson put it, those "who begin coercive elimination of dissent soon find themselves exterminating dissenters. Compulsory unification of opinion achieves only the unanimity of the graveyard." He elaborated in characteristically beautiful prose:

> If there is any fixed star in our constitutional constellation, it is that no official, high or petty, can prescribe what shall be orthodox in politics, nationalism, religion, or other matters of opinion or force citizens to confess by word or act their faith therein. . . . The very purpose of a Bill of Rights was to withdraw certain subjects from the vicissitudes of political controversy, to place them beyond the reach of majorities and officials and to establish them as legal principles to be applied by the courts. One's right to life, liberty, and property, to free speech, a free press, freedom of worship and

[4]*United States v. Murphy*, 222 F. 2d 698 (1955), at 706.
[5]*Bell v. Maryland*, 378 U.S. 226 (1964), at 328.
[6]*United States v. Rabinowitz*, 339 U.S. 56 (1950), at 69.
[7]*West Virginia State Board of Education v. Barnette*, 319 U.S. 624 (1943). See *infra*, pp. 250–253.

assembly, and other fundamental rights may not be submitted to vote, *they depend on the outcome of no elections.*[8]

While these words raise as many questions as they state valid principles, they nevertheless point out the irreducible basis for our thinking about civil rights and liberties.

ROLE OF THE JUDICIARY

The framers of our Constitution chose a limited majority rule, but majority rule nonetheless; while tyranny by the majority is barred, so also is tyranny by a minority. And the law must be obeyed—until such time as it is validly altered by legislative, judicial, or executive action or by constitutional amendment. Notwithstanding the numerous philosophical arguments to the contrary, disobedience of the law is barred, no matter which valid governmental agency has pronounced it or what small margin has enacted it. *It must be barred.* Liberty is achieved only by a rule of law—which is as the cement of society.[9] Government cannot long endure when any group or class of persons—no matter how just the cause may be or how necessary remedial action may seem to be—is permitted to decide which law it shall obey and which it shall flout. "Dissent and dissenters have no monopoly on freedom. They must tolerate opposition. They must accept dissent from their dissent," as the then Justice Abe Fortas observed well during the student uprisings of the late 1960s.[10] Civil disobedience has often been invoked and will indubitably continue to be invoked—but those who invoke it must be willing to face the consequences. An expert in the philosophy of civil disobedience, Professor of Religious Studies James F. Childress, defined it well as "a public nonviolent *submissive* violation of law as a form of protest."[11] Moreover, in Professor J. A. Corry's words, civil disobedience must be *civil*, not uncivil, disobedience, with the basic

[8]*Ibid.*, at 638, 642. (Italics supplied.)

[9]See Sydney H. Schanberg, "The Rules Are All We've Got," *The New York Times*, July 7, 1981, p. A23.

[10]The phrase also appears in his definitive book on the subject, *Concerning Dissent and Civil Disobedience* (New York: New American Library, 1968), p. 126. (Fortas resigned from the U.S. Supreme Court in mid-1969.)

[11]*Civil Disobedience and Political Obligation: A Study in Christian Social Ethics* (New Haven: Yale University Press, 1973). Italics added.

aim persuasion, not violence.[12] No one knew this and practiced it with more conviction than the assassinated Dr. Martin Luther King, Jr., who once noted tellingly: "I believe in the beauty and majesty of the law so much that when I think a law is wrong, I am willing to go to jail and stay there."[13] And so he did, on numerous occasions.

Under our system of government some agency of course must serve as the arbiter of what is and what is not legal or constitutional. The Founding Fathers did recognize and call for the creation of an arbiter, not only between the states and the national government but also between any level of government and the individual. There was no unanimity on who might arbitrate; and the records of the debates in the Constitutional Convention now available to us demonstrate that nearly every segment of the incipient government framework received at least some consideration for the role of arbiter: the states themselves, Congress, the executive, the judiciary, and several combinations of these. But it was fairly clear that the role would fall to the judiciary and that it should include the power of *judicial review,* which authorizes the Supreme Court to hold unconstitutional, and hence unenforceable, any law, any official action based upon a law, and any other action by a public official that it deems—upon careful reflection and in line with the taught tradition of the law and judicial restraint—to be in conflict with the Constitution.[14]

Scholars continue to argue the authenticity of the power of judicial review. That so many doubts and challenges are raised is due preeminently to the failure of the American Founding Fathers to spell it out in the Constitution *in so many words.* Yet the records of the Philadelphia Constitutional Convention of 1787 indicate that the idea or principle of judicial review was a matter of distinct concern to the framers, who, after all, had little use for unrestrained popular majoritarian government; that judicial review was indeed *known* to the colonists because the British Privy Council had established it over acts passed by colonial

---

[12]See his 1971 CBC Massey Lectures, *The Power of the Law* (Toronto: CBC Learning Systems, 1971), p. 41. The July 1977 looting during New York City's "blackout" is an obvious example of such a totally "uncivil" response.

[13]As quoted in *The New York Times,* October 16, 1966, p. 8E.

[14]See my *The Judicial Process: An Introductory Analysis of the Courts of the United States, England, and France,* 5th ed. (New York: Oxford University Press, 1986), Chapter 7.

legislatures; that at least eight[15] of the ratifying state conventions had expressly discussed *and* accepted the judicial power to pronounce legislative acts void; and that prior to 1789 some eight instances of *state* court judicial review against state legislatures had taken place. The language of both Article Three and the famed "supremacy clause" of Article Six clearly imply the necessary but controversial weapon. Research by constitutional historians such as Charles A. Beard, Edward S. Corwin, and Alpheus T. Mason indicates that between 25 and 32 of the 40 delegates at Philadelphia generally favored the adoption of judicial review.[16] And although it remained for Chief Justice John Marshall to spell it out in 1803 in *Marbury v. Madison*,[17] the issue has been decisively settled by history—the debate over the legitimacy of judicial review is now an academic exercise.

Since the enactment of the "Judges' Bill" in 1925, the Supreme Court has been all but complete master of its docket. The bill gave to the Court absolute discretionary power to choose those cases it would hear on a writ of *certiorari,* a discretionary writ granted only if four Justices agree to do so. Well over five thousand "cert." petitions reach the Court annually, but a mere 2 percent are granted. In theory, certain classes of cases do reach the Court as matter of "right," i.e., those that come to it on writs of *appeal;* but even here ultimate review is not automatic, since the tribunal itself must decide whether the question presented is of a "*substantial* federal nature." Its original jurisdiction docket is so small as to be dismissed for the purpose of this discussion.[18]

Since 1937 the overwhelming majority of judicial vetoes imposed upon the several states and almost *all* of those against the national government have been invoked because they infringed personal liberties, other than those of "property," safeguarded under the Constitu-

---

[15]Virginia, Rhode Island, New York, Connecticut, Massachusetts, New Jersey, North Carolina, and South Carolina.

[16]See particularly Beard's "The Supreme Court—Usurper or Grantee?", 27 *Political Science Quarterly* (1912).

[17]1 Cranch 137.

[18]See Abraham, *op. cit.,* Chapter 5, pp. 178–93, for an overview on matters of jurisdiction. Because of the plethora of appeals to it, all nine members of the current Court favor congressional legislation to provide them with *complete* discretion over the docket, and some have suggested the creation of an additional intermediate appellate court.

tion. This preoccupation with the "basic human freedoms"[19] is amply illustrated by the statistics of the docket of the Supreme Court and the application of its power of judicial review.[20] Well more than half of all cases decided by the Court now fall into this category of "basic human freedoms." Whereas in the 1935–36 term only 2 of 160 written opinions had done so, in the 1979–80 term the ratio had increased to 80 out of 149.[21]

That, indubitably, the contemporary scene has witnessed an unprecedented concern with the identification and strengthening of our basic civil rights and liberties—significantly due to their articulation by the federal judiciary beginning with the late 1920s but not reaching full stride until the F.D.R. era of the 1930s—does not gainsay the continu-

[19]See Chapter II, *infra*. As seen in these pages, they comprise the five enumerated by the First Amendment; the guarantees of procedural due process in the pursuit of criminal justice; and racial, political, ethnic, and sexual equality. (They are also known as the "cultural freedoms.") And the trend of public attitudes in the latter 1960s and evolving 1970s seemed to give fresh emphasis to the concept of privacy, personified by such Supreme Court decisions as those dealing with birth control and abortions. (See especially *Griswold v. Connecticut*, 381 U.S. 479 [1965], *Roe v. Wade*, 410 U.S. 113 [1973] *Doe v. Bolton*, 410 U.S. 179 [1973], and their progeny, including the latter two cases' decisive reaffirmation and extension in a trio of 1983 decisions, written by Justice Powell: *Akron v. Akron Center for Reproductive Health*, 462 U.S. 416; *Planned Parenthood Association of Kansas City, Mo. v. Ashcroft*, 462 U.S. 476; and *Simopoulos v. Virginia*, 462 U.S. 506. Another, less sweeping, reaffirmation came in 1986 in *Thornburgh v. American College of Obstetricians and Gynecologists*, 106 S. Ct. 2169.)

[20]In 1976 a total of 5,320 civil rights suits were brought in *federal* courts against *employers* alone—a 1,500 percent increase from 1970! "I am old enough to know," commented the then seventy-five-year old United States District Court Judge Oren R. Lewis in the fall of 1977 during a discrimination case in his Alexandria, Va., courtroom. "When I first came on the bench [in 1960] I never had a discrimination case. Now that is almost all you have." (*The Washington Post*, November 15, 1977, p. A-1.) The number of federal civil rights suits filed by state prison inmates alone soared from 5,000 in 1973 to 22,000 in 1986.

Another indicator: Between its enactment in 1871 and 1920, only 21 cases were brought under the former year's Civil Rights Act that authorizes suits against "every person" who "under color of law" violates the civil rights of another. In 1976 a total of 17,543 such suits were filed—a figure that has continued to increase steadily. (See A. E. Dick Howard, "I'll See You in Court: The States and the Supreme Court." Monograph published by the National Governors' Association Center for Policy Research, Washington, D.C., 1980.)

[21]Some additional representative statistics: 1965, 39 of 120; 1966, 55 of 132; 1967, 77 of 156; 1968, 70 of 116; 1969, 51 of 105; 1970, 77 of 141; 1971, 82 of 132; 1972, 86 of 164; 1973, 85 of 156; 1974, 63 of 137; 1975, 76 of 144; 1976, 87 of 160; 1977, 84 of 142; 1978, 88 of 138: 1980–81, 71 of 123; 1981–82, 81 of 150; 1982–83, 72 of 162; 1983–84, 85 of 151; 1984–85, 71 of 142; 1985–86, 75 of 147; 1986–87, 91 of 155.

ing need for the appropriate parameters of that ubiquitous line between individual rights and privileges on the one hand, and societal obligations and responsibilities on the other. There are no simple answers, and all too often those answers are subject to the Al Smith aphorism that "it all depends whose ox is being gored." Thus, almost by definition, liberty and equality, *both* of which are cherished constitutional guarantees, find themselves at war, and the current question whether liberty, at least to some extent, has been taking a proverbial licking from equality is just one indication of the delicate and difficult response to where and how to draw the line between personal rights and societal constraints.

There are such troublesome current issues as, for example, the personal right to obtain an abortion *versus* a state's right to regulate, even interdict, it; a racial group's claim to an entitlement for "affirmative action" *versus* another's cry of "reverse discrimination"; the right to freedom of association *versus* that of being judged on the basis of individual merit rather than by characteristics of birth; freedom of the press *versus* a reporter's obligation as a citizen to aid the pursuit of criminal justice; the alleged right of insisting on prayer in the public schools as a constitutionally given element of free exercise of religion *versus* the counterinsistence that such a practice violates that same First Amendment's strictures against the establishment of religion and in favor of the separation of Church and State; an accused's alleged Fourth Amendment right to have illegally obtained evidence barred *versus* society's outcry whether the "culprit shall go free just because the constable blundered?"—a famed Justice Benjamin N. Cardozo question; the presumed First Amendment right to satisfy one's personal, even erotic, tastes in the arts and literature *versus* society's insistence that that right is limited by its right to guard against obscenity (and just how does one define that?); the seemingly logical right of individuals to engage in private, consensual, adult sexual behavior of their choice as an element of privacy *versus* society's age-old rejection and punishment of sodomy (no matter by whom it may be practiced). All these fascinatingly dichotomous, wrenching issues point to the need to find an acceptable line under our commitment of "Equal Justice Under Law," that hallowed creed carved above the portals of the Supreme Court of the United States. It is a creed that emphasizes the need for justice as well as for law; its clarion call is for "equal justice" under "law"— not, as some would have it, "Equal Justice At Any Cost."

It is that fundamental dilemma, a line-drawing of acute complexity—that search for a viable accommodation between our cherished rights and obligations under our governmental system, as ultimately pronounced by the highest tribunal of the land—which *Freedom and the Court* addresses.

chapter *II* The *"Double Standard"*

The just-described fact of the Court's willingness, indeed eagerness, as of some five decades ago, to strike a much bolder blow for basic freedoms and against governmental encroachment in the "cultural" or "non-economic" realm than in the "economic proprietarian" one points to a judicial *fait accompli:* the embrace of a *judicial double standard* that accords a closer, higher level of scrutiny to cases in the cultural/non-economic/civil rights/civil libertarian category than in the economic-proprietarian one. It is a judicially created and drawn line, developed in the 1920s and 1930s, continually refined since, and decidedly in use today, designed to balance individual freedoms and community needs. That such a "double standard" now exists is thus a matter of ongoing record—but so is the collaterally complicating development of an extremely difficult "double standard" *within* a "double standard," under which the higher or privileged category-side of the basic "double standard" is further divided into various subcategories that are judicially accorded separate recognitions of review-entitlement. These categories or classifications range from the top one of "suspect" legislation or executive action to the bottom one of legislation or executive action reviewed by the judiciary on the basis of mere standards or perceptions of "reasonableness." The following pages endeavor to explain the concept of the "double standard," trace its evolution and application, and analyze its justification.

The Evolution of the "Double Standard"

The earliest lines, drawn by the Marshall Court (1801–35), defined and strengthened the young nation, guarding the federal government against the state governments, and furthering its growth and ability to function. They were also drawn to protect the property interests of individuals. From 1836 to 1864 Chief Justice Roger B. Taney's Court sought in a variety of ways to redress the imbalance in part, as it saw it, in favor of the states, while continuing to defend the ownership of land and slaves. The disastrous *Dred Scott*[1] decision bears lasting witness to that posture. The decisions of the next two, arguably rather undistinguished, eras of Chief Justices Salmon P. Chase (1864–74) and Morrison R. Waite (1874–88) were predominantly concerned with confirming state authority over individuals and federal authority over interstate commerce. In general they heralded the broadly proprietarian notions of the next five decades under Chief Justices Melvin W. Fuller (1888–1910), Edward D. White (1910–21), and William Howard Taft (1921–30). The chief concern of this long era was to guard the sanctity of property. Socio-economic experimentation by the legislatures, such as minimum-wage, maximum-hour, and child-labor regulations, was regarded with almost[2] unshakable disapproval by a solid majority of the Court. Again and again the justices struck down, as unconstitutional violations of *substantive* due process of law, legislation that large majorities on both the national and state levels deemed wise and necessary. They reasoned that, because of the *substance* (the nature of the content) of the legislation involved—i.e., what the law was all about— such statutory experimentations deprived "persons" (i.e., property owners, chiefly businessmen) of their liberty and property without due process of law. The "deprivation" of substantive due process was then judicially regarded as proscribed by the wording and command of Amendments Five and Fourteen of the Constitution. "The Justices," as economist John R. Commons wrote in 1924, "spoke as the first authoritative faculty of political economy in the world's history."[3] Admittedly, an occasional enactment would survive—such as maximum hours in hazardous occupations (an eight-hour Utah law for copper

---

[1]*Dred Scott v. Sandford,* 19 Howard 393 (1857).

[2]"Almost," but not quite: cf. fns. 4, 5, and 6 and text on p. 9, *infra.* For a different judgment, see John E. Semonche, *Charting the Future: The Supreme Court Responds to a Changing Society, 1890–1920* (Westport, Conn.: Greenwood Press, 1978). Semonche's thesis is that the Court's "obstacles [placed] in the path of the popular will . . . were relatively . . . few." (At p. 432.)

[3]As quoted by Arthur S. Miller in "The Court Turns Back the Clock," *The Progressive,* October 1976, p. 22.

miners and smelters in 1896);[4] for women in most industrial establishments (an Oregon ten-hour law in 1908);[5] and even one for both men and women (another Oregon ten-hour mill and factory statute, this one in 1917).[6] But until the advent of the "Roosevelt Court" in 1937, the Supreme Court under Chief Justice Charles Evans Hughes (1930–41) continued the substantive due process veto and struck down between 1934 and 1936 a total of sixteen New Deal laws that had been enacted chiefly under the taxing and interstate commerce powers of Congress.[7] Although President Roosevelt lost his battle to "pack" the Court in February of 1937, he was able, within a matter of three months, to win the war with two favorable decisions by the Hughes Court, a political victory often styled as "the switch in time that saved nine."

Here the Chief Justice and Associate Justice Owen J. Roberts—deferring to the legislature and recognizing the political facts of life—joined their colleagues Louis D. Brandeis, Benjamin N. Cardozo, and Harlan F. Stone in upholding a Washington State *minimum-wage law* for women and children—the first time that such a statute was upheld by the Court.[8] (It would be another four years before the Court would have the opportunity to uphold,[9] again for the first time, a *federal child-labor law,* a segment of the Fair Labor Standards Act of 1938, which also provided for minimum wages and maximum hours for all workers in interstate commerce. It had been declared beyond the power of Congress by a lower federal court.) In the other great early spring 1937 "switch-in-time" case, the new 5:4 majority upheld the National Labor Relations Act of 1935 against the challenge that it, too, exceeded the powers of Congress.[10] When Justice Willis van Devanter retired later in 1937 after twenty-six years on the Court, and Democratic Senator Hugo LaFayette Black of Alabama replaced him, the day of resort-

[4]*Holden v. Hardy,* 169 U.S. 366.
[5]*Muller v. Oregon,* 208 U.S. 412. Generally credited to the first use of the "Brandeis Brief."
[6]*Bunting v. Oregon,* 243 U.S. 426.
[7]For explanatory and statistical matter through 1985, see my *The Judicial Process: An Introductory Analysis of the Courts of the United States, England and France,* 5th ed. (New York: Oxford University Press, 1986), pp. 293–308.
[8]*West Coast Hotel Co. v. Parrish,* 300 U.S. 379 (1937).
[9]*United States v. Darby Lumber Co.,* 312 U.S. 100 (1941).
[10]*National Labor Relations Board v. Jones and Laughlin Steel Corporation,* 301 U.S. 1 (1937).

ing to declarations of unconstitutionality on grounds of alleged infringement of economic "substantive due process" had, in effect, passed
beyond recall—while in the future loomed a new and different kind of
substantive due process interest! The post-1937 Court was radically
different from that of the first four decades of the twentieth century—
faced as it was with an agenda of increasingly complex economic,
political, and social pressures and problems, both domestic and international.

Gradually the Court thus embarked upon a policy of paying close
attention to any legislative and executive attempt to curb basic rights
and liberties in the "non-economic" sphere. During the remaining
years of the Hughes Court and continuing through the Stone Court
(1941–46), the Vinson Court (1946–53), and particularly the Warren
Court (1953–69), the chief concern was to find a balance between the
basic civil rights and liberties of the individual and those of the community of which he is a part. That concern continued under the Burger
Court (1969–86), which, with the exception of the criminal justice
sector, did not reveal any clearly demonstrable tendency to chip away at
the legacy of the Warren Court, and indeed charted sundry new rights,
among them those of privacy (including abortion, gender equality, and
"affirmative action"). As of this writing (early 1988) the Rehnquist
Court (1986–) has continued its predecessor Court's jurisprudence.[11]
This post-1937 change in judicial attitude reflects a conviction that
certain fundamental freedoms *ipso facto* require closer judicial scrutiny
lest they be irretrievably lost. A properly lodged complaint with the
Court that legislative or executive action, be it state or national, had
violated the complainant's due process of law, be it substantive or
procedural—and/or the equal protection of the law (applicable to the
state level only)—would be assured at least of judicial interest and
probably of close scrutiny. That this new concern has in effect thereby
created a "double standard" of judicial attitude, whereby governmental
economic experimentation is accorded all but *carte blanche* by the
courts, but alleged violations of individual civil rights and liberties are

[11]For an interesting commentary, contending that once judicially pronounced there has
never been any major policy reversal in the realm of civil rights and liberty on the part of
the Court, see an article by former Associate Justice of the Supreme Court Arthur J.
Goldberg for *The New York Times,* April 12 and 13, 1971, pp. 37c and 37m, respectively.

given meticulous judicial attention, is an issue that will be carefully examined.[12]

Historically, the jurisprudential postures of certain justices have aided in the creation of a double standard.[13] Despite his close adherence to a philosophy of judicial self-restraint, characterized by deference to the legislature, Justice Oliver Wendell Holmes, Jr., spent much of his thirty-year career (1902–32) on the highest bench—which fell in its substantive *economic* due process era—in dissent from judicial vetoes of economic legislation. He did so not because he particularly liked the legislation, but because he was convinced that democracy meant that people had the right to be foolish and unwise. In his own words, he was willing to go so far as "to help my country go to hell if that's what it wants." Yet he nevertheless drew the line and called a firm halt to legislative experimentation when it came to basic "*non*-economic" rights. Prior to Holmes, Justice John Marshall Harlan had been the sole consistent dissenter in the economic substantive due process era. Harlan, grandfather of President Eisenhower's appointee of the same name, served from 1877 until his death in 1911. Though a one-time Kentucky slave-holder, he, as well as Holmes, deserves the title of "great dissenter,"[14] for he believed in a full measure of judicial self-restraint regarding legislative economic-proprietarian enactments. This stance was dramatically illustrated by his solitary dissent in the 1895 case of *United States v. E. C. Knight Co.*,[15] when his eight colleagues on the Court virtually wiped out the hoped-for weapons of the fledgling Sherman Antitrust Act of 1890 by ruling that "commerce succeeds to manufacture and is not a part of it."[16] On the other hand, Harlan's resolute attachment to the role of the Court as the guardian of both the

[12]See especially pp. 18 ff., *infra*.

[13]For contentions as to the latter-day development of a "double standard," or even "double standards," within the original "double standard," consult the Gunther and Wilkinson articles cited on p. 21, footnote 39, *infra*, and the Abraham and Funston articles cited on p. 28, footnote 71.

[14]See my "John Marshall Harlan: A Justice Neglected," 41 *Virginia Law Review* 871 (November 1955). The title of "the" great dissenter will presumably always be the property of Justice Douglas, who in his almost 37 (!) years on the Court (1939–75) dissented no fewer than 795 times. Holmes's dissents numbered 172, placing him fifteenth; Harlan penned 376, third on the list. (Dissents may be written or unwritten.)

[15]156 U.S. 1.

[16]*Ibid.*, majority opinion by Chief Justice Fuller, at 9. (Its impact was not effectively

letter and the spirit of the basic constitutional guarantees of civil rights and liberties is well demonstrated in his lone dissenting opinion in *Plessy v. Ferguson*.[17] In this 1896 decision, the Court, with Justice Henry B. Brown—a native of Massachusetts, a graduate of Harvard and Yale, and a resident of Michigan—delivering the majority opinion of seven, upheld the "separate but equal" doctrine in racial segregation:

> We consider the underlying fallacy of the plaintiff's [Homer Plessy, a Louisianan, seven-eighths white, who had refused to give up his seat in a railroad car reserved for white passengers under an 1890 Louisiana statute] argument to consist in the assumption that the enforced separation of the two races stamped the colored race with a badge of inferiority. If this be so, it is not by reason of anything found in the act, but *solely because the colored race chooses to put that construction on it*.[18]

Thundered Harlan, one of only two Southerners then on the Court:

> *Our Constitution is color-blind, and neither knows nor tolerates classes among citizens.* In respect of civil rights, all citizens are equal before the law. The humblest is the peer of the most powerful. The law regards man as man and takes no account of his surroundings or of his color when his civil rights as guaranteed by the supreme law of the land are involved.[19]

As we shall see below, Harlan was the first Supreme Court jurist to advocate, unsuccessfully during his time of service, the *total* applicability of the federal Bill of Rights to the several states.[20] That he and Holmes were not particularly close personally did not alter their jurisprudential kinship.

---

reversed until the Court's 1937 decision in *National Labor Relations Board v. Jones and Laughlin Steel Corporation*, 301 U.S. 1.)

[17]163 U.S. 537.

[18]*Ibid.*, at 551. (Italics supplied.) Justice David Brewer did not participate in the case.

[19]*Ibid.*, at 559. (Italics supplied.)

[20]E.g., *Hurtado v. California*, 110 U.S. 516 (1884); *Maxwell v. Dow*, 176 U.S. 581 (1900); and *Twining v. New Jersey*, 211 U.S. 78 (1908); to name just three cases. His lone success was the quasi-"incorporation" of the *economic proprietarian* concept of eminent domain in *Chicago Burlington & Quincy RR. v. Chicago*, 166 U.S. 226 (1897), an 8:1 opinion written by him (see pp. 52 ff., *infra*), obviously joined by all except Justice Brewer on the Court because the constitutional protection here conferred dealt with *property* rights as a constituent element of due process of law, although the railroad lost the case on the merits.

However, in this respect Harlan was even closer to Louis Dembitz Brandeis, Woodrow Wilson's close ideological ally whom the President nominated to the highest bench in 1916, five years after Harlan's death and fourteen years after Holmes's appointment to the Court. A pioneering lawyer and crusading supporter of social welfare legislation, a bitter opponent of trusts and monopolies, and the first Jew to be nominated to the Court, Brandeis won a furious and bitter four-month confirmation battle, which was the longest in Court history. He was finally confirmed by a vote of 47 : 22, all but one[21] of the negative votes being cast by the Boston attorney's fellow Republicans![22] Justice Brandeis disappointed neither his nominator nor his "public." He and Holmes, while of widely divergent backgrounds and temperaments, not only became warm friends but were usually on the same side of the Court's decisions, particularly in the interpretation of substantive due process and the double standard. That their reasons for agreement were often quite different affected neither the basic fact of agreement nor the close relationship between them.[23] Holmes did not live to see his position vindicated; he died at ninety-three in 1935, three years after retiring from his beloved bench. He knew, however, that his successor, Cardozo, would follow in his footsteps, and there were ample signs that if the jurisprudential era begun by the Fuller Court had not yet run its course, it was becoming increasingly beleaguered. Brandeis did see the new era dawn. After twenty-three years on the Court, he retired in 1939 at the age of eighty-three, secure in the knowledge that his philosophy would be followed by the post-1937 Court. F.D.R. awarded his seat to a long-time Brandeis admirer, William O. Douglas—who, during his record-setting thirty-six and a half years on the Court,[24] would go far beyond his idol in the furthering of libertarian activism.

---

[21]Democrat Francis G. Newlands of Nevada.

[22]Quite a number either did not vote or were paired, however. See A. L. Todd, *Justice on Trial: The Case of Louis D. Brandeis* (New York: McGraw-Hill Book Co., 1964), for a fascinating account of the confirmation battle. Brandeis was a registered Republican, but he probably voted the Democratic ticket more frequently.

[23] See the fine analysis of the two great justices in Samuel J. Konefsky's *The Legacy of Holmes and Brandeis: A Study in the Influence of Ideas* (New York: The Macmillan Co., 1956). Also available in a later paperback edition (New York: Collier Books, 1961).

[24]He served until late in 1975, when debilitating illness dictated his retirement; he died in 1980.

The Expression and Justification of the Double Standard

In creating the double standard, the *post*-1937 Court came to *assume* as constitutional all legislation in the economic-proprietarian sector *unless* proved to the contrary by a complainant,[25] but to view with a suspicious eye legislative and executive experimentation with other basic human freedoms generally regarded as the "cultural freedoms" guaranteed by the Bill of Rights—among them speech, press, worship, assembly, petition, due process of law in criminal justice, a fair trial. In short, without denying its ultimate responsibility, the Court came to accept legislative action in the economic realm, but kept and, of course, continues to keep, a very close watch over legislative activities described as "basic" or "cultural." What we have then is a judicially recognized area of "preferred freedoms." Any quest for an obvious, clear line between "property rights" and "basic human rights" is, of course, doomed to fail, because by definition and implication *both are guaranteed freedoms* under our national and state constitutions. Property, too, is a "human right," and there is a fundamental interdependence "between the personal right to liberty and the personal right in property," as Justice Stewart wrote in a 1972 opinion for the Court.[26] Committed to that philosophy, the distinguished jurist Learned Hand never failed to reject and challenge any advocacy of the "double standard." A policy urging that the courts, "when concerned with interests other than property . . . should have a wider latitude for enforcing their own predilections than when they were concerned with property itself," was to him a dereliction of the judicial function if not of the oath of office of the Constitution; "just why property itself was not a 'personal right,' "

[25]A major contemporary example is the Court's 8:0 upholding in 1984 of Hawaii's Land Reform Act of 1967, under which the state used its power of eminent domain to break up large estates and transfer land ownership to the estates' tenants. (*Hawaii Housing Authority v. Midkiff*, 467 U.S. 229.) Speaking for the Court, Justice O'Connor found an appropriate "public use" taking rather than a violation of the non-impairment of the obligation of contract safeguard of Article One, Section 10.

[26]*Lynch v. Household Finance Corp.*, 405 U.S. 538 (1972), at 552. At least one student of the problem has attempted to distinguish between "personal" or "individual" and "corporate" or "institutional" property—the former being entitled to double standard inclusion, the latter not. (See Richard H. Rosswurm, "The Double Standard Under Constitution and Supreme Court: An Alternate Model," paper delivered at the 1979 Annual Meeting of the Southern Political Science Association, Gatlinburg, Tenn., November 1–3.)

Hand observed, "nobody took the time to explain."[27] And as Paul Freund, noted scholar of constitutional law and Hand's admirer, has reminded us, it is indeed difficult to "compare the ultimate values of property with those of [for example] free inquiry and expression, or to compare the legislative compromises in the two realms; for laws dealing with libel or sedition or sound trucks or non-political civil service are as truly adjustments and accommodations as are laws fixing prices or making grants of monopolies."[28] However, the values of property are *not* ignored by the judiciary when, in fact, illegal legislative action takes place[29]—or when basic property rights of individuals or groups are adjudged violated beyond the legal or constitutional pale.[30]

Recently, the Court has modified the more traditional "double standard" to give "strict judicial scrutiny" to certain types of equal protection *and* due process cases, especially the former. Depending on the type of legislative statutory classification, the Court now habitually places or views the case before it in different categories or levels, accordingly affecting its treatment of the issue at hand. Thus, for the economic-proprietarian cases (which were discussed earlier in this chapter) the Court still uses the "traditional" equal protection (and due process) test of examining whether the legislature had a "reasonable" or "rational" or "relevant" basis for making its statutory classification. Yet although, ever since the 1937 "switch in time that saved nine," basic civil rights and liberties issues have led to closer scrutiny by the Court, the demonstration of a classification in a law which either

---

[27]"Chief Justice Stone's Conception of the Judicial Function," 46 *Columbia Law Review* 698 (1946).

[28]*The Supreme Court of the United States* (Cleveland: The World Publishing Co., 1961), p. 35.

[29]For example, in 1952 the Supreme Court by an 8 : 1 vote—Justice Burton dissenting—declared as a violation of substantive due process a provision of the Pure Food and Drug Act which provided for federal powers of factory inspection. The Court ruled this provision to be an unconstitutionally vague deprivation of liberty and property safeguarded by the Fifth Amendment. (*United States v. Cardiff,* 344 U.S. 174.)

[30]E.g., *Lloyd v. Tanner,* 407 U.S. 551 (1972), where the Court "balanced" the property rights of a private shopping center with the right of freedom of expression (distribution of leaflets) and found on behalf of the former by a 5 : 4 vote. In the words of Justice Powell's majority opinion: "Although accommodations between [speech and property values] are sometimes necessary, and the courts properly have shown a solicitude for the [First Amendment], this Court has never held that a trespasser of an uninvited guest may exercise general rights of free speech on private property used non-discriminatorily for private purposes only." (At 567–8.)

affects so-styled "fundamental interests" (e.g., voting rights,[31] the right to interstate travel[32]) or touches what has become a "suspect category" of legislation (e.g., race,[33] national origin or alienage "the first cousin of race,"[34] and, as of 1968 but apparently no longer after mid-1976, illegitimacy[35]) has now received an even higher level of Court scrutiny. In some cases the category, while not "suspect," is nonetheless accorded especially close attention—sex, for example, which is second only to race in contemporary equal protection of the laws litigation.[36] Once an issue has accordingly been placed on that special level of scrutiny, the Court in effect shifts the burden of proof of its constitutionality *to the legislature and/or the executive* and requires that *it* demonstrate a "*compelling* state interest" for its legislative classification—as it succeeded in doing, for example, in the *Japanese Evacuation* case of 1944.[37] Once the "fundamental interest" or "suspect"[38] category classification is demonstrated in a case, the "strict

[31]E.g., *Harper v. Virginia Board of Elections*, 383 U.S. 663 (1966).

[32]E.g., *Shapiro v. Thompson*, 394 U.S. 618 (1969)—at least when it involves, as it did here, "a basic necessity of life."

[33]E.g., *Loving v. Virginia*, 388 U.S. 1 (1967). Ironically, the first reference to it was by Justice Black in the Japanese Exclusion case, *Korematsu v. United States*, 323 U.S. 214 (1944): "[All] legal restrictions *which curtail the civil rights of a single racial group are immediately suspect*. This is not to say that all such restrictions are unconstitutional. It is to say that courts must subject them to the most rigid scrutiny. Pressing public necessity may sometimes justify the existence of such restrictions [as a 6:3 Court majority here found]; racial antagonism never can." (At 216. Italics supplied.)

[34]E.g., *Graham v. Richardson*, 403 U.S. 365 (1971). The quoted passage stems from *Trimble v. Gordon*, 430 U.S. 762 (1977), at 777. See *Plyler v. Doe*, 462 U.S. 725 (1983) and *Bernal v. Fainter*, 467 U.S. 216 (1984). But compare *Mathews v. Diaz* 426 U.S. 67 (1976), *Hampton v. Mow Sun Wong*, 426 U.S. 88 (1976), *Ambach v. Norwick*, 441 U.S. 68 (1979), and *Cabell v. Chavez-Salido*, 454 U.S. 432 (1982).

[35]E.g., *Levy v. Louisiana*, 391 U.S. 68 (1968); *Labine v. Vincent*, 401 U.S. 532 (1971); *Weber v. Aetna Casualty Insurance Company*, 406 U.S. 164 (1972). For the "removal decision," see *Norton v. Mathews* and *Mathews v. Lucas*, 427 U.S. 495 (1976).

[36]E.g., *Reed v. Reed*, 404 U.S. 71 (1971), *Frontiero v. Richardson*, 411 U.S. 677 (1973), and *Helgemoe v. Meloon*, 436 U.S. 950 (1978). But compare and contrast those with, e.g., *Kahn v. Shevin*, 416 U.S. 351 (1974), *Schlesinger v. Ballard*, 419 U.S. 498 (1975), and *General Electric Co. v. Gilbert*, 429 U.S. 125 (1976). See Table 8.1, *infra.*, pp. 508 ff., for an updated account.

[37]See fn. 33, *supra*.

[38]The "traditional indices of suspectness," viewed by Justice Stone in his *Carolene* footnote (see pp. 18 ff.) as "discrete and insular minorities," were characterized as follows in Justice Powell's majority opinion in *San Antonio School District v. Rodriquez*, 411 U.S. 1 (1973): "The class [is] saddled with such disabilities, or subjected to such a

judicial scrutiny'' that thereby results leads to considerably greater judicial protection of these rights. In essence, then—as suggested earlier—we see the Court using a complicated double-standard-within-a-double-standard, under which various subcategories are judicially accorded separate recognition of review-entitlement to accomplish this contemporary task[39]—triggering widespread accusations of judicial arrogation of legislative authority (in addition to compounding doctrinal confusion that renders both lay and professional analysis inordinately complex).

Of "Preferred Freedoms"

Although he did not personally use the words until four years later,[40] the articulation of the concept of "preferred freedoms" is appropriately credited to a footnote appended to an opinion for the Court by then Associate Justice Stone in the 1938 case of *United States v. Carolene Products Company*.[41] Stone's Footnote Four probably evolved from the celebrated Cardozo opinion delivered a few months earlier in *Palko v. Connecticut*.[42] In that, his last personally delivered opinion prior to his fatal illness in 1938, Justice Cardozo had established two major categories of rights: those that *are* and those that *are not* "implicit in the concept of ordered liberty." Cardozo justified this distinction, later referred to as the "Honor Roll of Superior Rights," by explaining that ". . . we reach a different plane of social and moral values when we pass to . . . freedom of thought and speech . . . [which] is the matrix, the indispensable condition, of nearly every other form of freedom."[43]

---

history of purposeful unequal treatment, or relegated to such a history of purposeful unequal treatment, or relegated to such a position of political powerlessness as to command extraordinary protection from the majoritarian political process." See also his concurring opinion as well as Justice Brennan's for the majority in *Plyler v. Doe*, 462 U.S. 725 (1982).

[39]For two excellent treatments of this vexatious and complicated issue, see Gerald Gunther, "The Supreme Court: 1971 Term; In Search of Evolving Doctrine on a Changing Court: A Model for a Newer Equal Protection," 86 *Harvard Law Review* 1 (1972), and J. Harvie Wilkinson III, "The Supreme Court, the Equal Protection Clause and the Three Faces of Constitutional Equality," 61 *Virginia Law Review* 945 (1975). Also see this chapter, p. 8, *supra*.

[40]In *Jones v. Opelika*, 316 U.S. 584 (1942), at 608. (See p. 21, *infra*, for further notes on the term's coinage and development.)

[41]304 U.S. 144. Justice McReynolds was the lone dissenter in the 6 : 1 holding (Justices Cardozo and Reed did not participate.)

[42]302 U.S. 319 (1937). (The case will be discussed more fully in Chapter III.)

[43]*Ibid.*, at 326–27.

Stone wrote his opinion in the *Carolene* case with Cardozo's distinction in mind. And, in a very real sense, he took it one step further: he explicitly enunciated the activist doctrine of the "double standard." *Carolene* dealt with an ordinary federal interstate commerce statute, the Filled Milk Act of 1923, which regulated adulterated ("filled") milk— and it would normally have passed into the annals of what the new Court regarded as routine exercise of valid congressional legislative power over interstate commerce. However, addressing himself to the inherent congressional regulatory power, Stone was moved to comment in the body of the opinion that

> the existence of facts supporting the legislative judgment is to be presumed, for regulatory legislation affecting ordinary commercial transactions is not to be pronounced unconstitutional unless in the light of the facts made known or generally assumed, it is of such a character as to preclude the assumption that it rests upon some rational basis within the knowledge and experience of legislators.[44]

This expression of the double standard, from one who had come to the Court from one of the largest New York corporate law offices, is a reminder that Marxian forecasts and interpretations of the attitude of justices on the highest bench are not always accurate!

Having said what he did, Stone then appended his now famous Footnote Four,[45] from which we will examine the following three paragraphs:

1. There may be narrower scope for operation of the presumption of constitutionality when legislation appears on its face to be *within a specific prohibition of the Constitution,* such as those of the first ten amendments, which are deemed equally specific when held to be embraced within the Fourteenth.

---

[44]304 U.S. 144, at 152.

[45]It is now generally accepted that most of the famed footnote was in fact authored by Stone's brilliant law clerk, Louis Lusky, and that Hughes in effect wrote its first paragraph. Hughes was eager to present a formal connection with constitutional text. Stone's concern was with the context of fundamental rights. For the footnote's popularization much credit is due to Professor Alpheus Thomas Mason, long-time McCormick Professor of Jurisprudence at Princeton University. See Lusky's book, *By What Right?* (Charlottesville: The Michie Co., 1975), for a full discussion of Footnote Four.

2. It is unnecessary to consider now whether legislation which restricts *those political processes* which can ordinarily be expected to bring about repeal of undesirable legislation, is to be subjected to more exacting judicial scrutiny under the general prohibitions of the Fourteenth Amendment than are most other types of legislation. . . .

3. Nor need we enquire whether similar considerations enter into review of statutes directed at particular religious . . . or national, . . . or racial minorities . . . ; *whether prejudice against discrete and insular minorities* may be a special condition, which tends seriously to curtail the operation of *those political processes* ordinarily to be relied upon to protect minorities, and which may call for a correspondingly more searching judicial inquiry. . . .[46]

At first glance, the language in paragraph 1 may suggest to some—as it did to Justice Frankfurter[47] that *any* legislation which on its face appears to abridge the constitutional guarantees of the Bill of Rights would have to fall *automatically*. However, as soon became evident, Stone had reference primarily to the five guarantees of the First Amendment (religion, speech, press, assembly, and petition) and secondarily to the proposition that such legislation should simply be *inspected* more critically by the judiciary than where exclusively economic rights are at issue.[48] Stone's colleagues Black, Douglas, Murphy, and Rutledge[49] embraced his position readily—although not necessarily for the same reasons—and their opinion frequently prevailed during their joint ten-

[46]Italics added.

[47]See, for example, his concurring opinion in *Kovacs v. Cooper,* 336 U.S. 77 (1949).

[48]For an interesting analysis of the genesis and application of the "preferred freedom" concept, see Robert B. McKay, "The Preference for Freedom," 34 *New York University Law Review* 1184 (November 1959). He is very critical of the Frankfurter position, on both factual and logical grounds.

[49]Actually it was Rutledge, not Stone, who stated the "preferred freedom" doctrine most clearly, most expressly, and most extremely, in what was the heyday of the avowed utilization of the doctrine, in the 5:4 *Union Organization* case of 1945—in which the now Chief Justice Stone dissented, together with Roberts, Reed, and Frankfurter (*Thomas v. Collins,* 323 U.S. 516, at 529–30 and 540). Rutledge referred to "the preferred place given in our scheme to the great, the indispensable democratic freedoms secured by the First Amendment." He carried his colleagues Black, Douglas, and Murphy, and Jackson concurred to make the majority of five. (Black, uncomfortable with the "preferred" concept, would later "substitute" that of "absolute," which he avowedly adapted, based upon his literalist reading of the Constitution, in 1951, in *Dennis v. United States,* 341 U.S. 494, although he did not formally employ the term "absolute" itself until a few months later in *Carlson v. Landon,* 342 U.S. 524, at 555.)

ure on the Court between 1943 and 1949, sometimes gaining Jackson's vote, occasionally even Frankfurter's or Reed's. Thus at least five votes to carry the day were often available, and a series of memorable decisions was made in behalf of the new concept.[50] And, contrary to some reporting, justices did in fact use the term "preferred position" in majority and minority opinions[51]—and they not only continued to do so but occasionally still do—notwithstanding Frankfurter's angry characterization of it as "a mischievous phrase."[52] However, when Justices Murphy and Rutledge both died in the summer of 1949, their replacements, Tom C. Clark and Sherman Minton, together with Chief Justice Fred M. Vinson (Stone had died on the bench in 1946), consigned the "preferred freedom" doctrine to relative limbo. It remained there until Earl Warren succeeded Vinson on the latter's death in 1953 and the Court renewed its continuing emphasis on civil rights and liberties.

Paragraph 2 calls for a special judicial scrutiny of assaults on "those political processes" which in a very real sense make all other rights in our democratic society possible: equal access to the voting booth, for both nomination and election, and the ability to seek redress of political grievances, wither by striving for public office or by "getting at the rascals" in office. It was this basic requirement of a representative democracy that precipitated the momentous Supreme Court decisions in the *Suffrage* cases of 1941 and 1944. In the first, *United States v. Classic*,[53] the Court overruled precedent[54] and held that the language of the Constitution equated "primaries" with "elections" in races for federal office, and that the former would henceforth be subject to congressional regulation to the same extent and in the same manner as the

---

[50]E.g., *Hague v. C.I.O.*, 307 U.S. 496 (1939); *Bridges v. California*, 314 U.S. 252 (1941); *Jones v. Opelika*, 319 U.S. 103 (1943); *West Virginia State Board of Education v. Barnette*, 319 U.S. 624 (1943); *Thomas v. Collins, loc. cit.; Saia v. New York;* 334 U.S. 558 (1948); *Kovacs v. Cooper, loc. cit.;* and *Terminiello v. Chicago*, 337 U.S. 1 (1949).

[51]E.g., Stone in *Jones v. Opelika*, 316 U.S. 584 (1942), at 608; Douglas in *Murdock v. Pennsylvania*, 319 U.S. 105 (1943), at 115; Rutledge in *Thomas v. Collins, op. cit.*, at 530; and Reed in *Kovacs v. Cooper, op. cit.*, at 88. See also *Prince v. Massachusetts*, 321 U.S. 158 (1944); *Follett v. McCormick*, 321 U.S. 573 (1944); *Marsh v. Alabama*, 326 U.S. 501 (1946), at 509; and *Saia v. New York, op. cit.*, at 562.

[52]*Kovacs v. Cooper, op. cit.*, at 90. For example, Black did in his dissenting opinion in *Morey v. Doud*, 354 U.S. 457 (1957), at 471.

[53]313 U.S. 299 (1941).

[54]*Newberry v. United States*, 256 U.S. 232 (1921).

latter. The second case, *Smith v. Allwright*,[55] logically resulted from the first. Here, the Court, again overruling precedent,[56] outlawed, as an unconstitutional violation of the Fifteenth Amendment, the so-called white primary, a device to bar blacks from the effective exercise of the ballot in several states of the deep South. Rejecting the contention that the Democratic Party of Texas was "a voluntary association" and thus free to discriminate in its membership, the 8 : 1 majority held that the Party acted as an agent of the State of Texas because of the character of its duties—such as providing election machinery and candidates. Of equal, if not greater, importance in the judicial assault on legislation restricting basic political processes is the matter of equitable representation. In March 1962 the Supreme Court finally found sufficient votes to declare that the age-old practice of deliberate mal-, mis-, or non-apportionment of representative legislative districts in the several states was a controversy that it had the power, the right, and the duty to adjudicate. This decision in the case of *Baker v. Carr*[57]—which Chief Justice Warren[58] regarded as "the most important case we decided in my time"[59]—sharply departed from the erstwhile Court practice of regarding this kind of controversy as a "political question"[60] to be "handled" by the political rather than the judiciary branch. *Baker* broke with that precedent. Justice Frankfurter—"the Emily Post of the Supreme Court," in Fred Rodell's nastily memorable phrase—joined by his disciple on the bench, John Marshall Harlan II, wrote an impassioned sixty-eight-page dissenting opinion reiterating his life-long judicial philosophy that the courts must stay out of what he termed the "political thicket." Warning that the Court would find itself immersed in a

[55]321 U.S. 649 (1944). (Justice Roberts was the sole dissenter here.)

[56]*Grovey v. Townsend*, 295 U.S. 45 (1935).

[57]369 U.S. 186 (1962).

[58]Ironically, fifteen years earlier, as Governor of California, he had successfully opposed reapportionment. It matters what post one holds.

[59]Interview with author, Washington, D.C., May 24, 1969. Warren's view of the case's significance—whether or not one accepts his ranking—was amply vindicated, and quickly so: after but eight years following the extensions of *Baker*-opened principles *cum* yardsticks to congressional districts, the Bureau of the Census reported that the average deviation from the ideal district-size in the 93d (January 1973) Congress was but half of 1 percent, as contrasted with 17 percent in the 88th (January 1965)!

[60]E.g., *Colegrove v. Green*, 328 U.S. 549 (1946), and *South v. Peters*, 339 U.S. 276 (1950).

"mathematical quagmire," he admonished the majority of six: "There is not under our Constitution a judicial remedy for every political mischief. In a democratic society like ours, relief must come through an aroused popular conscience that sears the conscience of the people's representatives."[61] But the majority of the general public had seen one attempt after another to "sear the conscience" frustrated for generations. Indeed, in many of the transgressing states the very imbalance of representative districts rendered "an aroused public conscience" impossible. The Court, prodded by a swelling chorus of citizens who were discriminated against, notably the urban masses, had had enough, and the commands of Article One and Amendment Fourteen provided the necessary interpretative authority to bring about the "more exacting judicial scrutiny" called for in the second paragraph of Justice Stone's Footnote Four.

The decision in *Baker v. Carr*[62] that the federal courts do have jurisdiction in cases involving state legislative apportionment became a vehicle for logical substantive extensions. In 1963, in the *Georgia County Unit* case,[63] the Court, agreeing with the lower federal district court that the notorious "county unit" scheme[64] violated the equal protection of the laws clause of the Fourteenth Amendment, enunciated the principle of "one person, one vote"[65]—the equality of every voter with every other voter in the state when he or she casts a vote in a statewide election. One year later, the Court extended the principle to *Congressional* districts.[66] Then, perhaps most dramatically, in a group of six cases in June of 1964, it required that representation for *both*

[61]369 U.S. 186, dissenting opinion, at 270. For almost three decades after *Baker* the Court managed to avoid the ancient political hanky-panky of the *gerrymander*. When it finally "handled" it in 1986, it did so in a disturbingly split 4 : 3 : 2 holding in *Davis v. Bandemer*, 54 LW 4898. In effect, the holding seemed to say that gerrymandering *may* be illegal or unconstitutional as a violation of the equal protection clause. *But* it will be very hard to prove it—and here it was *not proved*. What we are seeing, of course, is additional judicial involvement.

[62]The vote was 6 : 2. Justice Charles E. Whitaker did not participate.

[63]*Gray v. Sanders*, 372 U.S. 368.

[64]Under it each of Georgia's counties received a minimum of two and a maximum of six electoral votes (for the eight most populous counties), with each county's vote going to the candidate receiving the largest popular vote therein—resulting in rank discrimination that saw the small counties receiving from 11 to 120 times as much representative weight as the largest.

[65]Justice Douglas spoke for the 8 : 1 Court here.

[66]*Wesberry v. Sanders*, 376 U.S. 1 (1964).

houses of state legislatures must be apportioned to reflect "approximate equality" (a decision not only extended subsequently to reach *local* elections of varied character,[67] but one that would ultimately result in the further extension to a Court-call for "absolute equality"!).[68] Wrote Chief Justice Warren for a majority of six: "Legislatures represent people, not trees or acres. Legislators are elected by voters, not farms or cities or economic interests. . . . To the extent that a citizen's right to vote is debased, he is that much less a citizen. The weight of a citizen's right to vote cannot be made to depend on where he lives."[69] Stone would have been pleased; Frankfurter was not.

In paragraph 3 Stone so explicitly spells out the "double standard" as to be appropriately credited with its parenthood. It is self-evident that the special judicial protection he suggests for frequently unpopular

[67]E.g., *Avery v. Midland County,* 390 U.S. 474 (1968); and *Hadley v. Junior College Dist. of Metro. Kansas City, Mo.,* 397 U.S. 50 (1970).

[68]*Kirkpatrick v. Preisler,* 394 U.S. 526 (1969); and *Wells v. Rockefeller,* 394 U.S. 542 (1969). But the Court, 6:3, refused in 1973 to extend the principle to *elected judges* (*Wells v. Edwards,* 409 U.S. 1095) and to such special purpose governing agencies as a Board of Directors of a Water District (*Salyer Land Co. v. Tulare Lake Basic Water Storage District,* 410 U.S. 719). And, 5:3, during the same term of Court it permitted a Virginia deviation of 16.4 percent, holding (via Justice Rehnquist) that its one-person-one-vote doctrine, which it did emphatically reaffirm here, need not be applied so strictly to *state* as to *congressional* apportionment. Rehnquist reasoned that a state legislative apportionment plan could therefore include "a certain amount of arithmetical discrepancy if it was deliberately drawn to conform to the boundaries of political subdivisions." (*Mahan v. Howell,* 410 U.S. 315.) The rationale of the latter decision was subsequently confirmed in a series of cases involving 7.8 and 9.9 percent variances in other states. (*Gaffney v. Cummings,* 412 U.S. 735, and *White v. Regester,* 412 U.S. 755, both in 1973, too. On the other hand, the latter case sustained, for the first time, an attack on multi-member districts as tending "unconstitutionally to minimize the voting strength of racial groups.") But a mere 4.4 percent deviation in congressional districting was vetoed by the Court at the same time (*White v. Weiser,* 413 U.S. 783); and an attempt by North Dakota to deviate by 20 percent was unanimously declared unconstitutional in 1975. (*Chapman v. Meier,* 420 U.S. 1.) See also *Ball v. James,* 451 U.S. 355 (1981), which upheld, 5:4, voting for directors of a public water district *restricted* to property owners. The dichtomy in the Court's now rigid one-person-one-vote approach between federal and state redistricting/reapportionment was reemphasized in two controversial 1983 holdings, both 5:4, but in opposite divisions, due to Justice O'Connor's posture: *Karcher v. Daggett,* 462 U.S. 725, where the population differential in a congressional district was *less than* seven-tenths of 1 percent and *Brown v. Thomson,* 462 U.S. 835, where the state legislative district differential was a major 89 percent (one seat to Wyoming's least populous county).

[69]*Reynolds v. Sims,* 377 U.S. 533, at 562. Five other cases were decided simultaneously, all based on the same general principle, with the votes ranging from 8:1 to 6:3. (See pp. 633–713.)

racial, religious, and political minorities and other often helpless and small groups is preeminently designed for and directed to their political-cultural activities. Underlying his call for special scrutiny is the fact that these groups demonstrably needed or need special aid and protection to attain and maintain their full measure of constitutionally guaranteed citizenship. The current struggle of political, religious, gender, and particularly racial minority groups bears witness to the case for the "preferred freedom" doctrine suggested by Stone on that Opinion Monday in 1938.

But is the implicit "double standard" justifiable at all? Do particular Justices of the Supreme Court of the United States have a moral as well as a constitutional mandate to create and apply such a standard, to guard against what has been called the "mistaken self-abnegation" that would allow the basic freedoms to be "eroded to the point where their restoration becomes impossible"?[70] There is considerable room for disagreement, both in legal contemplation and in political philosophy,[71] some of which is outlined below.

A TRIO OF SUGGESTED JUSTIFICATIONS FOR THE DOUBLE STANDARD

Of the numerous reasons which have been advanced in support of the double standard, three in particular have commanded potent, although not unanimous, backing:

1. *The Crucial Nature of Basic Freedoms.* As Justices Holmes, Brandeis, Cardozo, and Stone, among others, so ably demonstrated, those freedoms which can be considered basic are those upon which all other freedoms in democratic society rest. For example, when the principles of freedom of speech and press are contingent upon prior cen-

[70]Loren P. Beth, "The Case for Judicial Protection of Civil Liberties," 17 *The Journal of Politics* 112 (February 1955).

[71]See, for example, the divergent points of view presented by Richard Funston and Henry J. Abraham in 90 *Political Science Quarterly* 2 (Summer 1975), entitled respectively "The Double Standard of Constitutional Protection in the Era of the Welfare State" and " 'Human' Rights vs. 'Property' Rights: A Comment on the 'Double Standard.' " See also the profoundly thoughtful analytical essay by Rogert G. McCloskey, "Economic Due Process and the Supreme Court: An Exhumation and Reburial," in Philip B. Kurland, ed., *The Supreme Court Review* (Chicago: University of Chicago Press, 1962). Also noteworthy is the clarion call for a restoration of the erstwhile judicial protection of economic-proprietarian liberties by Bernard H. Siegan in his *Economic Liberties and the Constitution* (Chicago: University of Chicago Press, 1980). He fully supports the erstwhile *Lochner* doctrine and decision on property/liberty grounds.

sorship, they become a mockery. When the right to worship depends upon majoritarian whims or police ordinances, it becomes meaningless. When the rights to register and vote are dependent upon the race of the applicant or the amount of his property, they become travesties of the democratic political process. To paraphrase Justice Jackson in the *West Virginia Flag Salute* case,[72] the very purpose of the Bill of Rights was to withdraw those freedoms which can be considered basic from the "vicissitudes" of political controversy, from the grasps of majorities and public officials, and to hold them aloft as legal principles to be applied by the judiciary. Thus, such fundamental rights as freedom of expression and religion simply are not delegatable to the majority will; such economic-proprietarian problems as the rate of income tax assuredly are. As Justice Stone put it in a memorable dissenting opinion less than three years following his Footnote Four in *Carolene:*

> The very fact that we have constitutional guarantees of civil liberties and the specificity of their command where freedom of speech and religion are concerned require some accommodation of the powers which government normally exercises, when no question of civil liberty is involved, to the constitutional demand that these liberties be protected against the action of government itself. . . . The Constitution expresses more than the conviction of the people that democratic processes must be preserved at all costs. It also is an expression of faith and a command that freedom of mind and spirit must be preserved, which government must obey, if it is to adhere to that justice and moderation without which no free government can exist.[73]

Thus embracing a demonstrable change in its own scale of jurisprudential values, it fell to the post-1937 Court to recognize and attempt to preserve those freedoms which are deemed basic or crucial to the democratic process. And to achieve this, the Court has moved to apply the "double standard" to them when the other branches of government have either consciously or unconsciously failed to heed or comprehend the essence of Stone's admonition—as perceived by a majority of its membership.

A sophisticated, complex, and original defense *cum* contribution for the partial justification under this first rubric of *a,* but not necessarily *the,* double standard assessed herein is John Hart Ely's influential

[72]*West Virginia State Board of Education v. Barnette,* 319 U.S. 624 (1943).
[73]*Minersville School District v. Gobitis,* 310 U.S. 586 (940), at 602–603, 606–607.

Democracy and Distrust: A Theory of Judicial Review.[74] Seminal to his theory is his exhortation for a *process*-oriented jurisprudence (which he saw in much of what the Warren Court did, e.g., in the legislative apportionment "one-person-one-vote" cases) but against a value-imposing one, such as that manifested by an earlier Court in *Lochner v. New York*[75] and by the Burger Court in the contentious abortion cases of *Roe v. Wade* and *Doe v. Bolton*.[76] He sternly rejects judicial intervention for both. Thus, while applauding as the essence of judicial review the Warren Court's safeguarding of the basic processes of democracy and its preservation of minority rights as part of that process, he is critical of what he perceived as the Court's, as well as others', notion that its Justices had a better understanding of or handle on attitudes commonly held by the body politic.

2. *The Explicit Language of the Bill of Rights.* An excellent case can be made for the viability of the double standard simply based upon the very language of the Bill of Rights (most of which, as we shall see,[77] has been made applicable to the several states by way of the "due process of law" clause of the Fourteenth Amendment). The economic-proprietarian safeguards of the Bill are couched in the most general of terms: the command of the Fifth and Fourteenth Amendments that no person "be deprived of life, liberty, or *property, without due process of law*" raises more questions than it settles. Certainly the Founding Fathers did not specify what they meant by "property" except that one should not be "deprived" of it without "due process of law." As already noted, during the fifty years prior to 1937 the Court interpreted the clause so stringently that legislative efforts in the economic-proprietarian sphere were all but futile. To do so the Court had to read into the language of the "due process" clauses concepts that *may* have been implicit but were certainly not explicit. On the other hand, the language governing what we commonly regard as our basic human freedoms is not only explicit, it is categorical. Madison's terminology for the First Amendment is precise:

> Congress shall make no law respecting an establishment of religion, or prohibiting the free exercise thereof; or abridging the freedom of speech, or

[74](Cambridge: Harvard University Press, 1980.)
[75]418 U.S. 445 (1905).
[76]410 U.S. 113 and 410 U. 479, respectively (1973).
[77]Chapter III, *infra*.

of the press; or the right of the people peaceably to assemble, and to petition the government for redress of grievances.

Succeeding amendments in the Bill, such as those embodied in Amendments Four, Five, and Six, refer specifically to a host of other basic rights as well, be they substantive or procedural. That their interpretation has proved difficult and troublesome over the years does not, however, invalidate their explicitness, and it is their explicitness that makes a strong case for invocation of the double standard.[78]

Yet an acceptance of the double standard does not necessarily mean embracing the "literalism" of Justice Black, whose support of the doctrine was grounded on the Constitution's *verbiage.* If he found it spelled out, it became an *absolute,* which, by definition, places him in the camp of those who see a double standard, although he steadfastly refused to accept the slogan. To him it was the explicitness of the language, its categoricalness, that is decisive. Thus, his firm contention, reiterated throughout his long career on the high bench,[79] that when the First Amendment says "Congress *shall make no law . . . abridging* the freedom of speech, or of the press," it means just that: NO LAW! It most emphatically does not mean, for example, "no law except such as may be necessary to prevent the viewing of obscene movies," or "no law except what may be needed to curb seditious utterances," or "no law except one to punish libel and slander." As he put it in a famous article:

> Some people regard the prohibitions of the Constitution, even its most unequivocal commands, as mere admonitions which Congress [and by

---

[78]In Justice Black's always eminently quotable exhortation: "I think that state regulations [of economic affairs] should be viewed quite differently than where it [*sic*] touches or involves freedom of speech, press, religion, assembly, or other *specific safeguards of the Bill of Rights.* It is the duty of this Court to be alert to see that these *constitutionally preferred rights* are not abridged." (Dissenting opinion in *Morey v. Doud,* 354 U.S. 457 [1957]), at 471. (Italics supplied.) See Archibald Cox, *The Role of the Supreme Court in American Government* (New York: Oxford University Press, 1976), p. 51, for another illustration for support of the dichotomy.

[79]Hugo L. Black, "The Bill of Rights," 35 *New York University Law Review* 866 (April 1960). See also his "follow-up" article in 37 *New York University Law Review* 569 two years later; his March 1968 Carpentier Lee Lectures; his famed TV interview with reporters Eric Sevareid and Martin Agronsky in December 1968; and his definitive book, based on the Carpentier Lee Lectures, *A Constitutional Faith* (New York: Alfred A. Knopf, 1968). "Thus it is *language and history,*" he wrote in the latter, "that are the crucial factors that influence me in the interpretation of the Constitution—not reason-

implication, the states] need not always observe . . . formulations [which] rest, at least in part, on the premise that there are no "absolute" prohibitions in the Constitution, and that all constitutional problems are questions of reasonableness, proximity, and degree. . . .

I cannot accept this approach to the Bill of Rights. It is my belief that there *are* "absolutes" in our Bill of Rights, and they were put there on purpose by men who knew what words meant, and meant their prohibitions to be "absolutes." . . . I am primarily discussing here whether liberties *admittedly* covered by the Bill of Rights can nevertheless be abridged on the ground that a superior public interest justifies the abridgement. I think the Bill of Rights made its safeguard superior.[80]

And later, discussing the First Amendment, which was to him "the heart of our Bill of Rights, our Constitution, and our nation,"[81] Black wrote: "The phrase 'Congress shall make no law' is composed of plain words, easily understood. . . . Neither as offered nor as adopted is the language of this Amendment anything less than absolute. . . ."[82] Whether or not one agrees with Black's "absolutist" thesis—and a good many observers, of course, do not[83]—it nonetheless lends strong support to the argument for the existence of a hierarchy of values and the priority within that hierarchy of those liberties specifically listed in the Bill of Rights. Even Justice Frankfurter, who rejected absolutism as well as any formula such as the double standard, declared in a significant opinion that matters like press censorship and separation of Church and State are different from economic policy matters because "history, through the Constitution, speaks so decisively as to forbid legislative experimentation" with them.[84]

---

ableness or desirability as determined by the Justices of the Supreme Court." (At p. 8. Italics added.) He died on September 25, 1971, having served more than thirty-four years.

[80]"The Bill of Rights," *op. cit.,* at 866–67.

[81]See especially his *A Constitutional Faith, op. cit.,* particularly Chapter III, "The First Amendment," pp. 43 ff.

[82]"The Bill of Rights," *op. cit.,* at 874. For a superb study of Black's absolutism, see James J. Magee, *Mr. Justice Black: Absolutist on the Court* (Charlottesville: University Press of Virginia, 1980).

[83]E.g., Leonard W. Levy, *Freedom of Speech and Press in Early American History: Legacy of Suppression* (New York: Harper & Row, 1963), p. xxi; Harry M. Clor, *Obscenity and Public Morality: Censorship in a Liberal Society* (Chicago: University of Chicago Press, 1969), p. 89; and Walter F. Berns, *The First Amendment and the Future of American Democracy* (New York: Basic Books, 1977), *passim.*

[84]*American Federation of Labor v. American Sash and Door Co.,* 335 U.S. 538

3. *The Appropriate Expertise of the Judiciary.* If one accepts the first two reasons in support of the double standard, a third follows quite logically: no other agency or institution of the United States government has proved itself either so capable of performing, or so willing to undertake, the necessary role of guardian of our basic rights as the judicial branch. Since the legislative and executive branches, for reasons inherent in our political system, have failed to fulfill this role adequately, it has fallen to the judiciary. And it is a role procedurally enhanced by the Supreme Court's all but absolute prerogative of determining the kind of cases that will reach its docket—which thus enables it to concentrate on articulating the libertarian realm. As Robert H. Jackson, who came to the Supreme Court from prominent service in the executive branch, observed: "The people have seemed to feel that the Supreme Court, whatever its defects, is still the most detached, dispassionate, and trustworthy custodian that our system affords for the translation of abstract into concrete constitutional commands."[85] With these words he echoed James Madison, who, in presenting the original Bill of Rights to Congress in 1789, remarked:

> If they are incorporated into the Constitution, independent tribunals of justice will consider themselves in a peculiar manner the guardians of those rights; they will be an impenetrable bulwark against every assumption of power in the legislative or executive; they will be naturally led to resist every encroachment upon rights expressly stipulated for in the Constitution by the declaration of rights.[86]

Yet, if the Supreme Court is indeed the appropriate governmental agency to buttress and safeguard our fundamental rights, few would seriously contend that, in equal measure, its province is to rule on the

---

(1949), at 550. For a fine, perceptive, evaluative biographical essay on Felix Frankfurter, see Joseph P. Lash, *From the Diaries of Felix Frankfurther* (New York: W. W. Norton & Co., 1975). See also Michael E. Parrish, *Felix Frankfurter and His Times* (New York: The Free Press, 1982).

[85]*The Supreme Court in the American System of Government* (Cambridge: Harvard University Press, 1955), p. 23. Designed as the Godkin Lectures at Harvard University, the book was edited and published with the aid of Jackson's son after his father's death of a heart attack shortly before he was to deliver the lectures—a task then assumed by the son.

[86]*Annals of Congress,* 1st Cong., 1st Sess., June 8, 1789 (Washington, D.C., 1834), Vol. I, p. 457.

validity of economic legislation and administration. Because of its insufficient expertise and its crowded docket, the Court is not prepared to make the kind of economic judgments that would veto legislative actions and intent. It is the people's representatives who are best qualified to give expression to the requirements of economic life, to the experimentation and resolution that go into public planning. "We refuse to sit as a 'superlegislature,'" as Justice Black once noted, "to weigh the wisdom of legislation. . . . Whether the legislature takes for its textbook Adam Smith, Herbert Spencer, Lord Keynes, or some other is no concern of ours."[87] Or, in the words of then Associate Justice Abe Fortas: "The courts may be the principal guardians of the liberties of our people. They are not the chief administrators of its economic destiny."[88] Or, as Justice Stewart suggested in a later case, in which the Court refused to extend the "strict scrutiny" of the "new" equal protection concepts to state welfare programs, "the intractable economic, social, and even philosophical problems presented by public welfare assistance programs are not the business of this Court."[89]

Here, then, judicial self-restraint and the assumption of legislative know-how and representativeness are in philosophical accord—and it is here that the double standard thus finds perhaps its clearest justification. Few have stated this distinction as well as Justice Oliver Wendell Holmes, Jr., who was no personal friend, indeed, of legislative "fooling around" with "economic do-gooding." But he was a jurist who believed resolutely—although he was often alone and practically never carried the Court with him on that issue—that under a democratic government the people have every right to experiment legislatively with their economic fate, even if he personally were to consider their action ignorant. As he said to his colleague Stone, after more than a half-century on the Supreme Courts of Massachusetts and the United States, and at the age of ninety:

Young man [Stone was then sixty], about seventy-five years ago I learned that I was not God. And so, when the people want to do something [in the realm of economic legislation] I can't find anything in the Constitution

[87]*Ferguson v. Skrupa*, 372 U.S. 726 (1963), at 732.
[88]*Baltimore and Ohio Railroad Co. v. United States*, 386 U.S. 372 (1967), at 478.
[89]Opinion for the Court in *Dandridge v. Williams*, 397 U.S. 471 (1970), at 487.

expressly forbidding them to do, I say, whether I like it or not, "Goddamit, let 'em do it."[90]

Holmes expressed the same judicial posture more specifically to John W. Davis, the unsuccessful Democratic nominee for the Presidency in 1924, sometime U.S. Solicitor-General, and famed corporate attorney: "Of course, I know, and every other sensible man knows, that the Sherman Law [Anti-Trust Act of 1890] is damned nonsense, but if my country wants to go to hell, I am here to help it."[91] Yet, for the First Amendment liberties, Holmes rejected this "pure democracy" approach. He was convinced that the Constitution neither provided nor intended the luxury of such risk in that sphere. Whereas property, to him, was "social" in origin, civil liberties were "human." In full concord with such post-1916 allies as Justices John H. Clarke, Brandeis, Stone, and, on occasion, Hughes,[92] he simply did not consider the average American citizen "very enlightened"—to employ Justice Jackson's phrase—on the subject of civil rights and liberties. Hence Holmes suggested that judges "should not be too rigidly bound to the tenets of judicial self-restraint in cases involving civil liberties."[93] Or, as New York State Supreme Court Justice Samuel Hofstadter put the general issue: "If a judge loses his capacity for indignation in the presence of injustice, he may not be less of a judge, but he is less of a man."[94]

The above suggested trio[95] of justifications, considered separately

---

[90]As quoted by Charles P. Curtis in *Lions Under the Throne* (Boston: Houghton Mifflin Co., 1947), p. 281.

[91]As told by Francis Biddle in *Justice Holmes, Natural Law, and the Supreme Court* (New York: The Macmillan Co., 1961), p. 9.

[92]Holmes served on the Court from 1902 to 1932; Clarke, 1916–22; Brandeis, 1916–39; Stone, 1925–46 (the last five years as Chief Justice); and Hughes, 1910–16 (Associate Justice) and again 1930–41 (as Chief Justice). See Appendix A.

[93]As asserted by Chief Justice Stone in a letter to Clinton Rossiter, April 12, 1941, and noted by Alpheus T. Mason in his *Harlan Fiske Stone: Pillar of Law* (New York: Viking Press, 1956), p. 516.

[94]Obituary, *The New York Times*, July 12, 1970, p. 65L.

[95]The earlier editions of this book (1967, 1972, 1977, and 1982) all argued—albeit in terms of decreasing conviction—for the existence of a *fourth* justification for the application by the judiciary of the described double standard, namely the discrepancy in readily available and effective *access* to the judicial process, especially to the appellate levels, between economic-proprietarian and civil rights–civil liberties interests, be they on an

and together, suggests a *prima facie* case for the existence of the judicial "double standard." In purely academic terms, the "double standard" may neither be morally nor logically convincing—and it raises very serious, indeed fundamental, questions about the nature of judicial power and that of the judicial process under the American system. Thus the veteran constitutional law expert, Gerald Gunther, wisely asks, can the different standards of review really "be justified because of an inherent difference in the 'fundamentalness' of economic rights and other personal rights?" And, furthermore, "are the 'social' and even 'philosophical' problems truly less intractable in the modern areas of intervention?" Is it really true that "protection of property and economic interest have less textual and historical basis than protection of other interests?"[96] Yet, *pace* these fundamental and haunting doubts, the double standard, as it is now in place, does stand as a practical recognition of one of that system's crucial and realistic facets of government and politics under law. Within often ill-defined limits, the case for the special protection of civil rights and liberties is strong.

Granting the strength of the case, however, does by no means vitiate the presence of some troubling questions, among which the following quintet are both typical and sensitive: (1) Given the existence of the double standard, and the Court's evident continuing commitment to it, how will additional lines be drawn? (2) What are the factors that influence further line-drawing and what issues will be considered likely targets? (3) What compels line-drawing in each instance—is it judicial philosophy, the quest for justice, the democratic ethos, personality,

---

individual or group level. If, as is patently demonstrable, that was indeed the case throughout the history of our judicial process, it is assuredly no longer. The post–World War II receptiveness by the judiciary to the docketing of allegations of denial of civil rights and liberties—which began to see its day in court under the chief justiceship of Fred. M. Vinson (1946–53), came into full bloom during that of Earl Warren (1953–69), and has become a widely presumed quasi-entitlement—is proof positive of the now well-established ability of once-encumbered individuals and groups to be heard at the bar of the courts. This does not, of course, mean that a du Pont firm might not have more financial and personnel clout in fielding legal talent facilely than, say, a member of the Jehovah's Witnesses. But if help is needed, it is now clearly available: the plethora of libertarian activist interest groups; public interest attorneys; public defenders; congressionally funded legal aid; and a generally more sympathetic and receptive judiciary have all combined to render unrealistic, indeed inaccurate, a continuing claim for the existence of that fourth factor—although it may command resuscitation.

[96]*Cases and Materials on Individual Rights in Constitutional Law,* 3d ed. (Mineola, N.Y.: The Foundation Press, Inc., 1981), pp. 161–62.

political or social pressures? (4) Has the Court favored certain civil liberties more than others, and why, thereby further defining or confusing the double standard present as it draws further lines, and what determines how finely these lines will be drawn? And (5), what are the current motivations behind contemporary line-drawing, and have they changed since the double standard was created? The chapters to follow will endeavor to deal with some of these fundamental, haunting questions.

chapter III

The Bill of Rights and Its

Applicability to the States

Historical Background

The applicability of the Bill of Rights to the several states is an intriguing question laced with some fascinating constitutional and political history. The English common law, colonial charters, legislative enactments, and a variety of events in the thirteen colonies were the chief elements contributing to the basic rationale for a Bill of Rights. But to create the latter was far from the presumably facile task viewed by some rather naively as all but unanimously preordained. Much opposition abounded, largely based on the belief by a good many that a Bill of Rights was simply unnecessary, that the states, after all, had their own Bill of Rights, and that the body of the Constitution, as it finally surfaced at the September 17, 1787, conclusion of the Constitutional Convention's deliberations, contained ample safeguards against national (federal) mischief. Yet, ultimately persuaded by that trio of noble Virginians, Messrs. Jefferson, Madison, and Mason—who had first to convince themselves of its wisdom—what we know today as our 462-word Bill of Rights, comprising the first 8 articles of amendment to the basic document (or 10, to some who prefer to include Amendments Nine and Ten), was born and submitted to the First Congress for its approval in April of 1789, with the young but politically savvy Madison as its floor manager.[1] Congress eventually sent twelve amendments to the states for ratification as the Bill of Rights, but two failed to be adopted (one calling for apportionment of legislators, the other dealing with the pay of members of Congress).

Fully alive now to the need for its approval, Mr. Jefferson had written

[1] See the vivid study by Robert A. Rutland, *The Birth of the Bill of Rights, 1776–1791.* (Boston: Northeastern University Press, 1983).

to Mr. Madison on March 15, 1789, that ''The Bill of Rights is necessary because of the legal check which it puts into the hands of the judiciary.'' What he meant was a legal check against the *national* government—he was not worried greatly about the states since they had their own Bill of Rights, restrictions that the framers considered comfortably satisfactory. The central government, however, was a different matter, and there is simply no doubt whatever that the overriding reason for the Virginians' authorship and sponsorship of the federal Bill of Rights was to place demonstrably far-reaching restraints on the fledgling central government. Indeed, the very first phrase of Article One of the approximately twenty-five assorted rights to be found in the Bill of Rights reads: ''*Congress* shall make no law . . .'' Although the noun ''Congress'' reappears nowhere in the remainder of the eight articles that constitute the document at issue, the latter was unquestionably intended to be applicable against the national government only. Certainly that was the understanding with which the eleven states ratified the Bill of Rights—although Madison would soon come to believe that, once having become the law of the land, it ought to be applied against the states as well as against the national government. James Madison would quickly be joined by elements of the propertied community who advanced similar contentions. But, and one might well say appropriately, it would fall to our fourth Chief Justice, another renowned Virginian, John Marshall,[2] to be the first to adjudicate the question when, in 1833, in his 33rd year on the Court, he authored the Court's landmark opinion in *Barron v. Baltimore*.[3] As was the case with the vast majority of the great nationalist's plethora of opinions, he spoke for a unanimous tribunal.

Mr. Chief Justice Marshall and Barron's Wharf. The basis for the litigation in *Barron v. Baltimore* was laid when the City of Baltimore, Maryland, began to pave some of its streets. In so doing its engineers found it necessary to divert several streams from their natural courses; near one, Barron's Wharf, this resulted in deposits of gravel and sand which filled up the channel and prevented the approach of vessels. John Barron's fine wharf, previously the one with the deepest water in the

[2]For an excellent biography of Marshall as Chief Justice, see Albert J. Beveridge, *The Life of John Marshall,* 4 vols. (Boston: Houghton Mifflin Co., 1919).
[3]7 Peters 243 (1833).

harbor, was thus turned into little more than a useless inlet. Not amused, Mr. Barron obtained eminent legal counsel and went to court. He alleged that Baltimore's actions had violated that clause of the Fifth Amendment of the United States Constitution which expressly proscribes the taking of private property "for public use without just compensation." Although Barron won his argument at the level of the trial court, which awarded him $4,500 in damages, his joy was short-lived. Baltimore appealed the verdict to the Maryland State Court of Appeals, which reversed the decision. The unhappy Barron then appealed his case to the United States Supreme Court on a writ of error.[4]

Marshall announced that "the question thus presented is, we think, of great importance, but not of much difficulty."[5] In a handful of pages he demolished Barron's fundamental contention that whatever is forbidden by the terms of the Fifth Amendment to the national government is also forbidden to the states and that the Court therefore has an obligation to construe the Fifth's "guarantee in behalf of individual liberty" as a restraint upon *both* state and national governments. The Chief Justice's response was phrased in historical and constitutional terms:

> The Constitution was ordained and established by the people of the United States for themselves, for their own government, and not for the Government of the individual States. Each State established a Constitution for itself, and, in that Constitution, provided such limitations and restrictions on the powers of its particular government as its judgment indicated. The people of the United States framed such a government for the United States as they supposed best adapted to their situation, and best calculated to promote their interests. The powers they conferred on the government were to be exercised by itself; and the limitations on power, if expressed in general terms, are naturally, and, we think, necessarily applicable to the government created by the instrument. They are limitations of power granted in the instrument itself; not of distinct governments, framed by different persons and for different purposes.
>
> If these propositions be correct, the fifth amendment must be understood as restraining the power of the general government, not as applicable to the

---

[4]A discontinued writ. It served to bring the entire record of a case proceeding in a lower court before the Supreme Court for its consideration for alleged "errors of law" committed below.

[5]*Barron v. Baltimore, op. cit.*, (1833), at 247. It was the last constitutional law decision in which the great chief justice participated.

States. In their several constitutions they have imposed such restrictions on their respective governments as their own wisdom suggested, such as they deemed most proper for themselves. It is a subject on which they judge exclusively, and with which others interfere no further than they are supposed to have a common interest.

. . . These statements [the Bill of Rights] contain no expression indicating an intention to apply them to the state governments. This court cannot so apply them.

. . . This court . . . has no jurisdiction of the cause; and [it] is dismissed.[6]

Marshall had spoken, Barron had lost, and the Court's unanimous opinion that there was "no repugnancy between the several acts of the general assembly of Maryland . . . and the Constitution of the United States"[7] became the law of the land. Citizens like Barron were destined to have no further recourse until the ratification in 1868 of the Fourteenth Amendment, probably the most controversial and certainly the most litigated of all amendments adopted since the birth of the Republic.

The Fourteenth Amendment

The Fourteenth Amendment[8] did not in and of itself overturn the *Barron* precedent: Lively disagreement continues over the purpose of the framers of the Amendment and the extent of its intended application, if any, to the several states. But certain evidence does exist and merits close examination.

Some Historical Facts. The *facts* surrounding the proposal and passage of the Fourteenth Amendment in the 39th Congress (1865–67)— led by the Radical Republicans and their Committee of Fifteen[9]—are

[6]*Ibid.,* at 247–48, 250, 251.

[7]*Ibid.,* at 251.

[8]For a collection of fine essays, including one by Chief Justice Warren, commemorating the Amendment's Centennial in 1968, see Bernard Schwartz, ed., *The Fourteenth Amendment: Centennial Volume* (New York: New York University Press, 1970).

[9]Composed of twelve Republicans and three Democrats, it consisted of nine U.S. Representatives and six U.S. Senators, under the chairmanship of Republican Senator William Fessenden of Maine. It was essentially the congressional "policy committee," whose real leaders comprised four Radical Republicans: Representatives Thaddeus Stevens of Pennsylvania and John A. Bingham of Ohio and Senators Jacob Howard of Michigan and Lyman Trumbull of Illinois.

fewer than the resultant conjectures and analyses. We do know, however, that: (a) the 52 United States Senators (42 Republicans and 10 Democrats) and 191 Representatives (145 Republicans and 46 Democrats) wanted to do something to ameliorate the lot of blacks; (b) *de minimis*, they intended to embody the provisions of the Civil Rights Act of 1866, forbidding "discrimination in civil rights or immunities . . . on account of race" in the Amendment—although *political* rights—including jury service, for example—were excluded from that understanding; (c) at least to some extent, they were concerned with civil rights generally; and (d) they were interested in extending increased protection to personal property and personal security as well as to human rights.[10] We also know that (e) the Amendment was intended to remedy the lack of a "citizenship" clause in the original Constitution—and the initial sentence of the first of its five sections makes this clear: "All persons born or naturalized in the United States, and subject to the jurisdiction thereof, are citizens of the United States and of the State wherein they reside." This, of course, would include blacks. We further know (f) from the language of the last section, number 5, that there was some intention to provide Congress with the necessary power, if not the tools, to enforce the provisions of the Amendment: "The Congress shall have power to enforce, by *appropriate legislation,* the provisions of this article."[11] We also know (g) that,

[10]Historians now generally agree that the word "person" instead of "citizen" was adopted by the Drafting Committee in the "due process" and "equal protection" clauses to extend protection to *corporations* as well as human beings. The Supreme Court officially adopted this point of view in 1886 in *Santa Clara County v. Southern Pacific Railroad,* 118 U.S. 394.

[11]In part thanks to this provision (italics supplied) and, by implication, to the almost identically worded Section 2 of Amendment Fifteen, Congress found authority to enact certain sections of the landmark Civil Rights Act of 1964. One of its most significant sections, that dealing with discrimination in public accommodations, was passed under the congressional power over interstate commerce, and was specifically upheld by the U.S. Supreme Court in December 1964. (See *Heart of Atlanta Motel v. United States,* 379 U.S. 241, and *Katzenbach v. McClung,* 379 U.S. 294.)

Congress also utilized the "appropriate legislation" section of the Fifteenth Amendment to enact portions of the Voting Rights Act of 1965, which met and withstood two constitutional challenges in 1966 on the strength of the section's wording and intent. (See *South Carolina v. Katzenbach,* 383 U.S. 301, and *Katzenbach v. Morgan,* 384 U.S. 641). The 1970 amendment lowering the voting age to eighteen was upheld as to *federal* elections, but struck down as to *state and local* elections in a five-opinion, 184-page decision in *Oregon v. Mitchell,* 400 U.S. 112 (1970). The Twenty-sixth Amendment resulted as a direct consequence.

unlike the "privileges or immunities" and "due process of law" clauses, the "equal protection of the laws" clause of the Amendment had no antecedent meaning but originated in the committee that drafted it—which could hardly have foreseen its subsequent controversial history and judicial application. And, finally, we know (h) that with respect to the matter of the reach of the Bill of Rights, both the heart and the greatest source of confusion and controversy of the famed Amendment is the well-known phrasing of the second, lengthy sentence of Section 1, which was briefly composed by Republican Representative John A. Bingham of Ohio:

> No State shall make or enforce any law which shall abridge the privileges or immunities of citizens of the United States; *nor shall any State deprive any person of life, liberty, or property, without due process of law;* nor deny to any person within its jurisdiction the equal protection of the laws.[12]

There is no disagreement that the italicized portion of the Fourteenth, which was lifted verbatim from the language of the Fifth Amendment, thus was intended to provide guarantees against *state* infringement supplemental to the Fifth's mandate against federal infringement. What does cause major disagreement, however, can be illustrated by two questions: first, *did* the framers of the Amendment intend to "incorporate" or "nationalize" or "carry over" the *entire* Bill of Rights through the wording of its "due process of law" clause, thereby making it applicable to the several states;[13] and second, regardless of their intention, *should*

---

[12]Italics supplied.

[13]I realize that to use the terms "incorporation," "nationalization," "application," "carrying over," and "absorption," more or less synonymously and interchangeably is heresy to a good many members of the legal and academic community, if indeed it is not regarded as simply wrong. With all due respect and deference to those who do distinguish between these terms both literally and substantively (see, for example, Justice Frankfurter's important "Memorandum" described on pages thirty-four and thirty-five, *infra*), the basic issue involved clearly comes down to the answer to the following crucial question: is a certain provision in the federal Constitution, is a specific right enumerated in the federal Bill of Rights, *applicable to the states* via the "due process" clause of the Fourteenth Amendment or is it *not* applicable? If it is held to be so applicable by the judiciary, then it is "incorporated," "nationalized," "carried over," "applied," or "absorbed." To the affected litigants it does not matter what the process is called—what matters is whether or not it signifies state acquiescence with federal standards. This is not to say, of course, that I do not recognize basic historical and linguistic distinctions between the concepts of "incorporation" and "absorption," for example; and I have

the Bill of Rights be applied to the states, given the nature of the rights involved and the demands of the democratic society in which we live?

The Intention of the Framers. The Fourteenth Amendment was passed by Congress on June 16, 1866, ratified by the required three-fourths of the states—ten of these then being Southern Reconstruction governments under duress[14]—and was proclaimed in effect on July 28, 1868. The Amendment had significant political overtones, for it was the key plank of the first Reconstruction platform drafted by the Radical Republicans, led by Thaddeus Stevens of Pennsylvania, Roscoe Conkling of New York, and George Boutwell of Massachusetts. Indeed, the Amendment's passage by Congress in June 1866 provided the Radical Republicans with a welcome, ready-made campaign issue for the November 1866 election campaigns. Attention directed to the Amendment was almost wholly concerned with the political implications of bestowing full citizenship upon blacks. But there is no record of any campaign discussion or analysis of the matter of the application of the Bill of Rights to the states via its "due process of law" or any other clause. There was much talk of the Amendment giving teeth to the

---

been fascinated and intrigued by the long-standing controversies that have engulfed them. But, given the judicio-legal developments of the past two or three decades, e.g., the 1965 decision in the *Connecticut Birth Control* case (*Griswold v. Connecticut*, 381 U.S. 479, discussed at length on pp. 92–98, *infra*), the distinctions are blurred. What matters constitutionally, to repeat, is whether a federal provision or standard, as interpreted and declared by the Court, does or does not apply to the states.

[14]By March 1, 1867, there were thirty-seven states in the Union, including those of the old Confederacy. This meant that twenty-eight would have to ratify the Amendment to bring it into effect. But by that time only twenty states had ratified, among them Tennessee as the sole Southern state. Consequently, the congressional Radicals passed a law which in fact put the Southern states on notice that they would not be readmitted to the Union "officially" unless they: (1) ratified the Fourteenth Amendment and (2) extended the vote to adult males "of whatever race, color, or previous condition." This resulted in action by a sufficient number of Southern states, where federal troops still attested to the Reconstruction era. President Johnson vetoed the act, but Congress passed it over his veto. The law accomplished its purpose: between April and July 1868 the legislatures of Arkansas, Florida, North Carolina, Louisiana, South Carolina, Alabama, and Georgia acquiesced and the necessary figure (twenty-eight) had been attained. (Actually, in the interim New Jersey and Ohio had withdrawn their earlier ratifications—something they might no longer be able to do today, given the implications of the Supreme Court's 1939 decision in *Coleman v. Miller*, 307 U.S. 433—but Massachusetts, Nebraska, and Iowa had come aboard. Moreover, the Secretary of State *disregarded* the former two states' withdrawal votes and proclaimed the Amendment in effect, with Congress supporting his action by adopting a concurrent resolution to that effect.)

Thirteenth Amendment and securing the "fundamental rights and fundamental freedoms of all men."[15]

In the face of the many disagreements on the "intent" of the framers, some argue that their intent no longer matters, for the "felt necessities of the time" (Justice Holmes's celebrated phrase) and the inevitable growth of the Constitution, may *a fortiori* dictate the application of the Bill of Rights to the several states regardless of the framers' intention. However, since it is preferable to have historical data to back one's contentions, both the proponents and opponents of total or even partial incorporation continue to invoke history. A great deal of published research on historical justification is available, yet there is no conclusive answer, for the evidence is not persuasive. Originally, those opposing the incorporation interpretation enjoyed a slight edge. Briefly, they contended that had the framers of the Fourteenth Amendment intended to "incorporate" or "carry over" or "nationalize" the Bill of Rights to the states, they would have spelled it out specifically rather than employ the general language of the "due process of law" clause. The proponents, on the other hand, argued, and continue to argue, that the famous clause was adopted as "shorthand" for the Bill of Rights, and that the framers utilized it both to broaden and to strengthen fundamental guarantees of rights and liberties. It is still possible to emerge with diverse conclusions, particularly in the light of the lengthy and heated congressional debates on the subject. What is certain is that since the Supreme Court first "incorporated" aspects of the Bill of Rights in 1925,[16] the process has been sporadic; but it proved to be increasingly embracing as well as continuous over the next four decades—although it may well now have run its course.

Some Protagonists. The earliest spokesman for total incorporation of the Bill of Rights was Justice John Marshall Harlan (1877–1911), but his was a lonely voice. In his thirty-four-year career on the highest bench,[17] time and again Harlan unsuccessfully championed that inter-

---

[15]The quotation is from a speech by Representative Lyman Trumbull of Pennsylvania.

[16]See text on p. 46 and fn. 20, *infra,* relative to the one earlier (1897) incorporation, i.e., of *eminent domain* guarantees.

[17]Harlan served longer than any other except Justice William O. Douglas (1939–75), Justice Stephen J. Field (1863–97), Chief Justice Marshall (1801–35), and Justice Black (1937–71).

pretation.[18] He was not even partially vindicated until 1925, when Justice Edward T. Sanford delivered his dictum in *Gitlow v. New York*[19] albeit a case could arguably be made for the contention that the concept of *eminent domain* was applied formally to the states via Amendment Fourteen in a Harlan opinion in 1897.[20] And as late as 1947 in the famous *Adamson* case,[21] Justice Frankfurter rejected the concept of incorporation as one manufactured out of whole cloth. Both the concept itself and the term ''incorporation'' were anathema to him. Indeed, his last publication before his death in 1965 was an attack on ''incorporation'' and a defense of ''absorption.''[22] As he put it in a well-known passage:

> Of all these [43] judges [of the Supreme Court who passed on the question of incorporating the Bill of Rights via the ''due process of law'' clause of Amendment Fourteen] only one, *who may respectfully be called an eccentric exception*, ever indicated the belief that the Fourteenth Amendment was a shorthand summary of the first eight Amendments, theretofore limiting only the Federal Government, and that due process incorporated those eight Amendments as restrictions upon the powers of the States.[23]

The ''eccentric exception'' was, of course Harlan—whose grandson by the same name became a Frankfurter ally on the incorporation question

[18]See, for example, his solo dissenting opinions in *Hurtado v. California*, 110 U.S. 516 (1884); *Maxwell v. Dow*, 176 U.S. 581 (1900); and *Twining v. New Jersey*, 211 U.S. 78 (1908). There were several others—he was a consistent advocate. See my ''John Marshall Harlan: The Justice and the Man,'' 46 *Kentucky Law Journal* 448 (Spring 1958), especially pp. 469–70.

[19]268 U.S. 652. Gitlow lost, but the carry-over principle was given its first public judicial notice. See pp. 63 ff., *infra*.

[20]*Chicago, Burlington & Quincy RR v. Chicago*, 166 U.S. 226. Yet in footnote four in his landmark *Palko* decision (see pp. 72 ff., *infra*) Justice Cardozo suggested that its inclusion—like that of others—was due *not* to its enumeration in the Bill of Rights, but because it is ''included in the conception of 'due process of law.' '' However that may be, some observers, including Justice Tom Clark, concluded that, in effect, the Harlan opinion in *Chicago, Burlington* ''completely undermined'' *Hurtado v. California*, 110 U.S. 516 (1884)—see pp. 64 ff., *infra*—although clearly not overruling it, and thus ''laid the basis for *Gitlow v. New York*.'' Yet while that was important, it was not the gravamen of the Court's intention: its overarching concern lay with the strengthening of the constitutional protection of property rights.

[21]*Adamson v. California*, 332 U.S. 46 (1947).

[22]''Memorandum on 'Incorporation' of the Bill of Rights into the Due Process Clause of the Fourteenth Amendment,'' 78 *Harvard Law Review* 746–83 (1965).

[23]*Adamson v. California, op. cit.*, at 62 (Italics supplied.)

when he joined the Court as President Eisenhower's second appointee in 1955.[24]

Adamson v. California. It was Justice Black who became the leading proponent of incorporation—and he seized upon the aforementioned case of *Adamson v. California* to expound his views. At issue, briefly, was a provision of California law that permitted court and counsel to comment upon the failure of a defendant to explain or deny evidence against him, thus allowing the court and the jury to consider it in reaching a verdict. Admiral Dewey Adamson, under sentence of death for first degree and burglary murder and with past convictions for burglary, larceny, and robbery,[25] not only called no witnesses in his behalf but chose not to take the stand during his trial, a decision on which both the trial judge and the prosecuting attorney commented adversely. (Such comments have been statutorily proscribed on the *federal* level since 1878.) In his appeals, Adamson argued that the California law put him into an impossible situation: if he testified, the previous convictions would thus be revealed to the jury; and if he did not, comments by the judge and prosecutor would, in effect, convert his silence into a confession of guilt. (Only a few other states permitted the California procedure at the time.) In short, he claimed that the adverse comments by the two officials violated his constitutional privilege against compulsory self-incrimination under the Fifth Amendment of the federal Constitution, which he deemed incorporated and hence applicable to the states under the "due process of law" clause of the Fourteenth. He ultimately lost 5:4 at the bar of the Supreme Court. In an opinion written by Justice Stanley F. Reed, and joined by Chief Justice Vinson, and Associate Justices Robert H. Jackson and Harold H. Burton, the high tribunal held that the self-incrimination clause of the Fifth was *not* incorporated or applicable and that the State of California "may control such a situation in accordance with its own ideas of the most efficient administration of criminal justice."[26] Justice Frankfurter provided the decisive fifth vote

[24]Eisenhower's first appointee was Earl Warren to succeed the deceased Chief Justice Fred M. Vinson in 1953.

[25]Adamson had a highly prolific and interesting prison record, involving hobbies that included collecting the tops of women's stockings.

[26]*Adamson v. California,* 332 U.S. 46, at 57. (But see pp. 87–88, *infra,* for its overruling in 1964.) Adamson was executed in St. Quentin's gas chamber at the end of 1949, following several additional unsuccessful appeals.

in a long concurring opinion in which, as noted above, he took specific issue with the heart of Justice Black's dissenting opinion.

In his dissent, supported by a 33-page appendix that quoted extensively from the congressional debates involving Amendment Fourteen, Black was joined wholly by Justice Douglas and in part by Justices Murphy and Rutledge (who both, as we shall see later, wanted to go even beyond the Black position on incorporation—as indeed Douglas utlimately did, too). Black's opinion remains the most celebrated analysis of the intention of the framers of Section 1. Elaborately researched, it insisted that one of the chief objects to be accomplished by the first section of the Fourteenth Amendment, "separately, and as a whole,"[27] was to apply the *entire* Bill of Rights to the states. In his own words:

> My study of the historical events that culminated in the Fourteenth Amendment, and the expressions of those who opposed its submission and passage, persuades me that one of the chief objects that the provisions of the Amendment's first section, separately, and as a whole, were intended to accomplish was to make the Bill of Rights applicable to the states. With full knowledge of the *Barron* decision, the framers and backers of the Fourteenth Amendment proclaimed its purpose to be to overturn the constitutional rule that case had announced. This historical purpose had never received full consideration or expression in any opinion of this Court interpreting the Amendment. . . .[28]

Responding to Justice Frankfurter's contrary views and call for more demonstrable proof (where Frankfurther believed none existed), Black observed: "I cannot consider the Bill of Rights to be an outworn Eighteenth Century 'straight jacket'. . ." and concluded:

> I believe [that] the original purpose of the Fourteenth Amendment [was] to extend to all the people of the nation the complete protection of the Bill of Rights. To hold that this Court can determine what, if any, provisions of the

---

[27]*Ibid.*, at 71. Periodically Black made it clear that, notwithstanding his emphasis on certain occasions on one or the other of the specific sentences and phrases composing Section 1 of the Fourteenth Amendment, that Amendment "*as a whole* makes the Bill of Rights applicable to the States. This would certainly include the language of the Privileges or Immunities Clause as well as the Due Process Clause." (From his 1968 concurring opinion in *Duncan v. Louisiana,* 391 U.S. 145, at 166, n.1.)

[28]*Adamson v. California, op. cit.,* at 71–72.

Bill of Rights will be enforced, and if so to what degree, is to frustrate the great design of a written Constitution.[29]

Justice Black, in his almost three and a half decades on the Supreme Court, never wavered from these basic convictions—convictions buttressed by the expansive support extended to them by Professor W. W. Crosskey of the University of Chicago in a major essay a few years after *Adamson*.[30] His staunchest historical-constitutional ally has been Professor Horace Flack. After a careful study of the debates of the 39th Congress, their newspaper coverage, and the election speeches of members of Congress in the fall of 1866, Flack concluded that Congress

> had the following objects and motives in view for submitting the First Section of the Fourteenth to the states for ratification. First, to make the National Bill of Rights applicable to the states; secondly, to give constitutional validity to the Civil Rights Act [of 1866]; and thirdly, to declare who were the citizens of the United States.[31]

Black's opinion was soon challenged in almost every detail by Professor Charles Fairman of the Harvard Law School, a leading expert on constitutional law, in an article in the *Stanford Law Review*.[32] Fairman accused Black of deliberate distortion of the verities of the debates in the 39th Congress to prove his point. In a companion article in the same issue,[33] Professor Stanley Morrison, of the Stanford University School of Law, seconded Fairman's rejection of Black's thesis. But Morrison did so with considerably less vehemence, and not so much on the basis of what was said during the congressional debates as on the strength of the judicial history of the clause following the Amendment's adoption. Noting that only the elder Harlan had consistently supported Black's incorporation interpretation, Morrison sided

---

[29]*Ibid.*, at 89.

[30]Charles Fairman, " 'Legislative History,' and the Constitutional Limits on State Authority," 22 *University of Chicago Law Review* 1 (1954).

[31]Horace Flack, *The Adoption of the Fourteenth Amendment* (Baltimore: The Johns Hopkins University Press, 1908), p. 94.

[32]"Does the Fourteenth Amendment Incorporate the Bill of Rights? The Original Understanding," 2 *Stanford Law Review* 5 (December 1949).

[33]"Does the Fourteenth Amendment Incorporate the Bill of Rights? The Judicial Interpretation," *ibid.*, p. 140.

with Frankfurter's analysis and statistics in his concurring opinion in the *Adamson* case.[34] He refers to the refusal of such "libertarian activist" justices as Holmes, Brandeis, Stone, Hughes [*sic*], and Cardozo to incorporate the Bill of Rights *per se* and *seems* to score a telling point by recalling that Black himself did not dissent from, or write a separate concurring opinion to, Cardozo's famous majority opinion in the 1937 *Palko* case[35] (see pp. 72 ff., *infra*): that Cardozo opinion established a hierarchy of basic human rights which would henceforth be considered applicable to the states via Amendment Fourteen—namely, those "implicit in the concept of ordered liberty"—while at the same time establishing a *non-applicable* group.[36]

It is only fair to note at once here in Black's defense, however, that: (a) he had just joined the Court a few weeks earlier; (b) thus he might well have believed that it would be ungracious as well as foolhardy to proclaim a new jurisprudential posture; (c) the Cardozo majority opinion did, after all, announce the incorporation of the most precious of all basic human freedoms, notably First Amendment rights; and (d), as Black himself had explained in his *Adamson* dissent: "[I]f the choice must be between the selective process of the *Palko* decision applying some of the Bill of Rights to the States, or the *Twining* rule applying none of them, I would choose the *Palko* selective process."[37] He reiterated in a footnote to his dissent in *Griswold v. Connecticut* twenty-eight years after *Palko,* that he "agreed to follow" the Palko rule as a second-best method to "make [at least some of the] Bill of Rights safeguards applicable to the States."[38] Although not as dramatically critical as Fairman, Morrison does suggest that Black clearly had an ulterior motive in his interpretation of the events surrounding the framing of the Fourteenth Amendment: the establishing of a rule of law for civil rights and liberties that would be both drastic and simple and that would guarantee certainty for all future litigation, the carrying-over *in*

---

[34]*Adamson v. California, op cit.*

[35]*Palko v. Connecticut,* 302 U.S. 319.

[36]Among the latter were the Fifth Amendment's safeguards against double jeopardy (at issue in *Palko*) and compulsory self-incrimination (at issue in *Adamson*).

[37]*Adamson v. California, op. cit.,* at 89. He restated this position two decades later, one of the last times he spoke on "incorporation." (*Duncan v. Louisiana,* 391 U.S. 145 [1968], at 171.)

[38]381 U.S. 479, at 526, n. 21.

toto of the Bill of Rights via Amendement Fourteen, through either its "due process" or its "privileges or immunities" clause.

A sixth protagonist, Professor J. B. James of Georgia Wesleyan College, in his 1956 book *The Framing of the Fourteenth Amendment*,[39] agrees with Fairman and Morrison that Black's facile and sweeping interpretation of the congressional debates of 1866 is erroneous—but only *because* it is so sweeping and facile. With some reservations, James nonetheless does share Black and Flack's conclusion that, on balance, the Amendment's framers did intend to incorporate the Bill of Rights. Although such a thought may have been entirely foreign to the collective majority who supported its passage, James, as did Flack—and Professor Jacobus ten Broek, who shares most of James's views on the entire matter[40]—presents strong evidence that the Amendment's floor managers indeed intended its incorporation.[41] This is particularly true of Representative Bingham, the author of the pertinent provisions of Section 1, whom Black called "without extravagance . . . the Madison of [that section] of the Fourteenth Amendment."[42] Contrary to James's and other earlier belief, we now know that, significantly, Bingham *was* fully aware of the Supreme Court's decision in *Barron v. Baltimore*[43] when he led the debates on Amendment Fourteen in the House.[44] As a matter of fact, it was this ruling, he said, which made necessary "the adopting of the [Fourteenth] Amendment."[45] Certain in his belief that the Bill of Rights was designed to be

[39](Urbana: University of Illinois Press.)

[40]See Jacobus ten Broek, *The Antislavery Origins of the Fourteenth Amendment* (Berkeley: University of California Press, 1951): "The rights sought to be protected," he asserted severally, "were men's natural rights, some of which are mentioned in the first eight amendments and some of which are not" (e.g., at 223).

[41]E.g., James *op. cit.*, pp. 85, 130 ff.

[42]*Adamson v. California, op. cit.*, at 74.

[43]7 Peters 243 (1833).

[44]See *Congressional Globe*, 39th Cong., 1st Sess. (Washington, D.C.: Blair and Rives, 1866), pp. 1088–90.

[45]*Ibid.*, p. 1089. In 1871, during a debate on the now ratified Amendment Bingham observed that in 1865–66 he had closely "re-examined" Marshall's decision in *Barron*, wherein the Chief Justice had stated that "had the framers of these Amendments [I–VIII] intended them to be limitations on the power of state governments, they would have imitated the framers of the Original Constitution and have expressed their intention." Bingham then significantly added, "acting upon this suggestion I did imitate the framers of the Original Constitution." *The Globe*, 42nd Cong., 1st Sess., 1871, Appendix, p. 150.

national in scope, Bingham argued on the floor that had the 39th Congress meant the Bill of Rights to be solely applicable to the *federal* government, the wording of the Amendment's Section 1 would have so stated. James demonstrates quite convincingly that when Bingham and Republican Senator Jacob M. Howard of Michigan, the Amendment's floor manager in the upper house, spoke of the "fundamental rights of free men," they specifically meant the Bill of Rights. They wanted the proposed Amendment to overrule *Barron v. Baltimore*.

Senator Howard, in fact, clearly insisted that the national Bill of Rights *in its entirety* was incorporated into Section 1, a section that in his judgment embodied not only the "privileges and immunities" of Article Four, Paragraph 2, of the Constitution, but also all those rights guaranteed by the first eight amendments to the Constitution. Thus, in explaining the contents of the Amendment, he stated: "To these privileges and immunities [Art. Four, ¶2], whatever they may be for they are not and cannot be fully defined . . . to these should be added the personal rights guaranteed and secured by the first eight amendments to the Constitution." Enumerating these, he continued:

[T]hese are secured to citizens solely as citizens of the United States, . . . they do not operate in the slightest degree as restraints or prohibitions upon state legislation. . . . *The great object of the first section of this amendment is, therefore, to restrain the power of the states and compel them at all times to respect these fundamental guarantees.*[46]

Nonetheless, Professor Fairman, with some support from Professor Morrison, still insists that the use of the phrase "fundamental rights" or "fundamental guarantees" was specifically intended to *exclude* the Bill of Rights. Fairman does admit that Senator Howard expressly stated that the "privileges or immunities" clause of Section 1 of the Fourteenth should be construed as embracing what Howard termed "the personal rights" of the first eight amendments of the Bill of Rights. But Fairman insists that Bingham merely "talked around the point." Fairman's position received highly vocal support in 1977 with the publication of Professor Raoul Berger's fascinatingly controversial *Government by*

[46]*The Globe, op. cit.*, 39th Cong., p. 2765. (Italics supplied.)

Judiciary: The Transformation of the Fourteenth Amendment.[47] Berger concludes that his study of the "debates of the history of the period leads [him] fully to concur with Fairman," quoting approvingly Fairman's statement that the "freedom that states traditionally have exercised to develop their own systems of administering justice repels any thought that . . . Congress would . . . have attempted [to incorporate] . . . the country would not have stood for it, the legislatures would not have ratified."[48] The historians Kelly and Harbison, on the other hand, side with James's, Crosskey's, and Black's historical (and, incidentally, Black's constitutional) interpretation, and state flatly that Bingham and Howard agreed not only that the "privileges or immunities" clause "incorporated the entire federal Bill of Rights as a limitation upon the states," but that the "due process" clause was lifted from the Fifth Amendment and thus "became a guarantee against state action."[49] And independent scholarly investigations by such knowledgeable legal commentators as Louis Henkin, Frank Walker, and Michael Kent Curtis[50] agree that there remains no genuine doubt that the framers of Amendment Fourteen intended it as a lever for the application of the Bill of Rights to the several states of the Union, with Curtis penning a learned point-by-

[47](Cambridge: Harvard University Press), Chapter 8, "Incorporation of the Bill of Rights in the Fourteenth Amendment," pp. 134–156.

[48]*Ibid.*, p. 156. See also Berger's "Incorporation of the Bill of Rights in the Fourteenth Amendment: A Nine Lived Cat," 42 *Ohio State Law Journal* 435 (1982), and his *Death Penalties: The Supreme Court's Obstacle Course* (Cambridge: Harvard University Press, 1982), especially Chapter 2, "Incorporation of the Bill of Rights."

[49]Alfred H. Kelly and Winfred A. Harbison. *The American Constitution: Its Origin and Development*, 4th ed. (New York: W. W. Norton and Co., 1970), p. 463.

[50]Louis Henkin, "Selective Incorporation in the Fourteenth Amendment," 73 *Yale Law Journal* 74 (1963); Frank H. Walker, Jr., "Constitutional Law—Was it Intended that the Fourteenth Amendment Incorporates the Bill of Rights?", 42 *North Carolina Law Review* 925 (1964); Michael Kent Curtis, "The Bill of Rights as a Limitation on State Authority: A Reply to Professor Berger," 16 *Wake Forest Law Review* 1 (1980); his "The Fourteenth Amendment and the Bill of Rights," 14 *Connecticut Law Review* 2 (1982), and "Further Adventures of the Nine Lived Cat: A Response to Mr. Berger on Incorporation of the Bill of Rights," 43 *Ohio State Law Journal* 89 (1982); Berger's response in 44 *Ohio State Law Journal* (1983), "Incorporation of the Bill of Rights: A Reply to Michael Curtis"; and the latter's "Still Further Adventures of the Nine Lived Cat: A Rebuttal to Raoul Berger's Reply on Application of the Bill of Rights to the States," 62 *North Carolina Law Review* 3 (1984). John Hart Ely concludes, "this is an argument no one can win," *Democracy and Distrust: A Study of Judicial Review* (Cambridge: Harvard University Press, 1980), p. 25.

point rebuttal of Raoul Berger's historical arguments. Curtis returned to the fray in a recent full-length book treatment of the issue,[51] strongly arguing the case for full incorporation. Although his evidence may be neither new nor definitive, Curtis demonstrates persuasively that, given the antislavery movement's role in the genesis of the Fourteenth Amendment, its framers did indeed appear to intend to apply the provisions of the entire Bill of Rights to the several states. Moreover, he offers an intriguing analysis of, and a convincing exhortation to resurrect, the long-emasculated "privileges or immunities" ("P or I") clause of the Amendment's Section 1. And, in his meticulously researched and lucidly presented work, he presents an up-to-date retort to contemporary attacks on the incorporation doctrine, in particular Attorney-General Edwin Meese III's controversial July 1985 statement to the American Bar Association, in which Meese questioned that doctrine's "intellectually shaky" foundation and declared it to be utterly lacking any constitutional justification.

A Verdict? Regardless of personal intellectual and emotional commitments on the basic question of incorporation, the various positions indicate how speculative history can be and may become. The German historian Leopold von Ranke's exhortation that it is essential to determine *"wie es eigentlich gewesen"* ("how it actually was") is noble and human, but at times futile. However, such evidence as the history of the debates provides seems to substantiate Professor James's basic point that we need not accept Justice Black's expansive evaluation of the events of the 39th Congress to side with his basic conclusion: there seems little doubt that the Amendment's principal framers and managers, Representative Bingham and Senator Howard, if not every member of the majority in the two houses of Congress, did believe the Bill of Rights to be made generally applicable to the several states via Section 1. And *no* member of that Congress, before he voted on the Amendment, contradicted Bingham's and Howard's final statements to that extent.[52]

---

[51]*No State Shall Abridge: The Fourteenth Amendment and the Bill of Rights* (Duke University Press, 1986).

[52]Flack, *op. cit.*, pp. 81, 87. On the entire controversy, see also Chapter 3, "The Nationalization of the Bill of Rights," of Arthur A. North, S. J., *The Supreme Court: Judicial Process and Judicial Politics* (New York: Appleton-Century-Crofts, 1966). For its specific relevance to the desegregation-segregation issues of the 1950s and 1960s, see

This conclusion does not, however, necessitate concurrence with the matter of the *wisdom* of such an incorporation, nor with the judicial formulae devised therefore.[53] Nor does it gainsay the fact that when Senator Howard's "privileges or immunities" clause (and his and Representative Bingham's incorporation contentions for it) had its first judicial test in the *Slaughterhouse Cases*[54] a mere five years after the adoption of the Fourteenth Amendment, it sustained a crushing and lasting defeat.

The Slaughterhouse Cases of 1873. These remarkable cases, also referred to as the "Dual Citizenship" cases, delivered the second of the one-two knockout punches to the theory of a national applicability of the Bill of Rights, the first such punch having been *Barron v. Baltimore* forty years earlier. It will be recalled that in *Barron* the unanimous Court had ruled that the Bill was *not* applicable to the several states, either by expressed or implied language. The *Slaughterhouse Cases* not only reconfirmed the *Barron* holding but went considerably further by ruling that the "privileges or immunities" clause of the Fourteenth Amendment did not, and was not intended to, protect the rights of *state* citizenship, but solely those of *federal* citizenship. In the words of this never-to-date overruled decision written for the narrow 5 : 4 majority[55] by Justice Samuel F. Miller of Iowa by way of Kentucky: "It is quite clear, then, that *there is a citizenship of the United States, and a cit-*

the lengthy and learned essay "The Original Understanding and the Segregation Decision" by Alexander M. Bickel in his *Politics and the Warren Court* (New York: Harper & Row, 1965), pp. 221–61. Bickel's conclusion is that the authors of the Fourteenth Amendment ultimately chose language which would be capable of growth. It follows that "the record of history, properly understood, left the way open to, in fact invited, a decision based on the moral and material state of the Union in 1954, not 1877" (p. 261). For an intriguing complementary—and wholly different—analysis of the intentions of Bingham (and Senator Roscoe Conkling), namely, that the due process of law clause was drafted to "take in the whole range of national economy," making *corporations* among the intended beneficiaries of the draft, see Howard Jay Graham, "The Conspiracy Theory of the Fourteenth Amendment," 47 *Yale Law Journal* 371 (1938), and Charles A. and Mary R. Beard, *The Rise of American Civilization* (New York: The Macmillan Co., 1927). See also Wallace Mendelson, "A Note on the Cause and Cure of the Fourteenth Amendment," 43 *The Journal of Politics* 152 (February 1981).

[53]See pp. 107 ff., *infra.*

[54]*The Butchers' Benevolent Association of New Orleans v. Crescent City Live-Stock Landing and Slaughter-House Co.*, 16 Wallace 36 (1873).

[55]With Miller were Associate Justices Nathan Clifford (Maine), David Davis (Illinois), William Strong (Pennsylvania), and Ward Hunt (New York).

izenship of a state, which are distinct from each other, and which depend upon different characteristics or circumstances in the individual.''[56] Thus the ''citizens'' protected by the ''P or I'' clause of Amendment Fourteen are such ''citizens'' only in their capacity as ''citizens of the United States,'' *not* in their capacity or role as ''*state* citizens.''

. The cases had arisen as a result of a statute regulating the livestock slaughtering business, which had been enacted by the Louisiana Reconstruction government in 1867. In the law, its ''carpetbag''[57] legislature (unquestionably under corrupt influence) had conferred upon a single firm what, to all intents and purposes, constituted a monopoly of the New Orleans slaughterhouse business, preventing some one thousand firms and persons already established in the city from continuing in that activity. A number of the adversely affected parties filed suit in the courts of Louisiana, basing their complaint largely on alleged violation of their rights under the Fourteenth Amendment. Losing in the lower courts, they ultimately reached the State Supreme Court, which was equally unsympathetic to their claim and held that the contested Louisiana law was a valid and legal exercise of the state police power.[58] The aggrieved litigants then appealed to the United States Supreme Court.

Although four main constitutional issues were raised by the opponents of the Louisiana monopoly statute, the chief concern of the Court in its majority opinion was with the appellants' crucial contention that the law constituted a *prima facie* violation of that portion of Section 1 of Amendment Fourteen which states that ''No State shall make or enforce any law which shall abridge the privileges or immunities of citizens of the United States. . . .''[59] In other words, the basic claim of the aggrieved businessmen was that the quoted clause clearly implied,

[56]*Op. cit.,* at 74. (Italics supplied.)

[57]''Carpetbagger'' denotes a Northerner who went South after the Civil War to obtain office or employment by morally questionable and often corrupt methods.

[58]Accruing to the states under Article Ten of the Bill of Rights, the ''police power'' is generally regarded as embracing and extending to these concepts of state authority: (1) health, (2) welfare, (3) morals, (4) safety, (5) regulation of business (and labor and agricultural) activities.

[59]The other three were that the statute (1) created an ''involuntary servitude'' forbidden by Amendment Thirteen, (2) denied the appellants the ''equal protection of the laws'' under Amendment Fourteen, and (3) deprived them of their property ''without due process of law,'' also safeguarded by Fourteen.

indeed commanded, the protection of all civil rights and liberties *by the federal government* and that the several states could not, on pain of violating the Fourteenth Amendment, deny or abridge any rights accruing to citizens of the United States residing within their borders.

But the majority of five justices rejected this contention out of hand. They would have no part of this, or any related, notion of incorporating, of "carrying over," the prerogatives of the Bill of Rights so as to make them applicable to the states. Moreover, the Miller decision absolved the federal government from any obligation to protect "privileges or immunities" against state violation, a logical induction from the Court majority's basic premise that the *states* had the obligation to protect not only the rights guaranteed by their own bills of rights but the entire body of rights and liberties under the common law.

In short, the majority's decision meant that the "privileges or immunities" clause of the newly enacted Amendment really *meant nothing at all* insofar as the states were concerned. As has been well pointed out by one close student of the *Slaughterhouse Cases,* the Court's distinction between state and national citizenship made of the P or I clause a mere tautology since the rights of "citizens in the several states" could never have been *constitutionally* abridged by any state anyway. Thus, "the labors of the framers of the Fourteenth Amendment were nullified by a few strokes of Justice Miller's busy pen."[60] But *why?* The question is a natural one, given the history of the adoption of the Amendment (no matter which version) and the general acquaintance of all the justices with the activities and debates in the 39th Congress. In the opinion of most competent observers, the Court majority was simply unwilling to permit such a far-reaching alteration in the turbulent, beleaguered antebellum federal system—the relation of state and federal governments—by an "ambiguous" amendment to the Constitution.[61] Consequently, the majority of five expounded the at least plausible conception of dual citizenship, by which practically all common private rights were removed from the federal sphere of control. The majority also believed (and this idea was widely held at the time, as already noted) that the overriding, if not the sole, purpose of Amendment Fourteen was the

[60]Loren P. Beth, "The Slaughterhouse Cases—Revisited," 23 *Louisiana Law Review* 487 (April 1963), at 492.

[61]See *ibid.,* at 493. This is also C. Vann Woodward's view in his *Reunion and Reaction* (New York: Doubleday Anchor, 1956).

protection of blacks in exercising their *civil,* although not their political, rights.

But what, then, about existing "privileges or immunities" of *national* citizenship, which, by its own admission and by its creation of a "dual citizenship," the majority held to be protected against action by state governments, too? The Miller opinion avoided precise definitions and limits, but, quoting from one of his own 1868 opinions,[62] it suggested the appropriateness of the following "rights" of the national citizen as *bona fide* "privileges or immunities":

> To come to the seat of government to assert any claim he may have upon that government, to transact any business he may have with it, to seek its protection, to share its offices, to engage in administering its functions . . . of free access to its seaports . . . to the subtreasuries, land offices, and courts of justice in the several states . . . to demand the care and protection of the Federal government over his life, liberty, and property when on the high seas or within the jurisdiction of a foreign government . . . the writ of habeas corpus . . . to use the navigable waters of the United States, however they may penetrate the territory of the several States. . . .[63]

Also on Miller's list, significantly reemphasized as "rights of the citizen guaranteed by the *Federal* Constitution," were the "right[s] to peaceable assembly and petition for redress of grievances. . . ."[64] This represents, of course, a line of reasoning typical of the non-incorporation argument, then and today: that the Fourteenth Amendment extended no "rights" to citizens of the United States; that most of their rights had the same status as before, existing under *state* protection rather than national protection; that the "citizens" presumably protected by the P or I clause are "citizens" only in the sense that they are "citizens" of

---

[62]*Crandall v. Nevada,* 6 Wallace 36.

[63]*The Slaughterhouse Cases,* 16 Wallace 36 (1873), at 73–75. These rights had been originally identified as "privileges or immunities" in Justice Bushrod Washington's opinion in *Corfield v. Coryell,* 6 F. Cas. 546.

[64]*Ibid.* Depending upon one's interpretation, "the right peaceably to assemble" was one of the "privileges or immunities" of United States citizenship reconfirmed three years later in *United States v. Cruikshank,* 92 U.S. 542. But in the key aspect of its holding by Chief Justice Waite, *Cruikshank* declared that Fourteen "adds nothing to the rights of one citizen as against another. It simply furnishes a federal guarantee against any encroachment by the States upon the fundamental rights which belong to every citizen as a member of society." (At 554.)

the United States—emphatically not in their capacity as *state* citizens.[65] As pointed out before, this kind of reasoning renders the Fourteenth Amendment useless as a legal tool, for no state could ever *constitutionally* abridge or deny the rights of "citizens in the several states." Thus, all that seemed to remain of the Amendment, given the majority's reasoning in the *Slaughterhouse Cases* a mere handful of years after its birth, was a vague, generally accepted understanding that it was intended to bring about citizenship for the Negro. In one participant's views, the Court's construction of the P or I clause had reduced it to "a vain and idle enactment."[66]

Of the three dissenting opinions by Associate Justices Noah H. Swayne—who pointedly accused the Court majority of having turned "what was meant for bread into a stone"[67]—Stephen J. Field, and Joseph P. Bradley, the most important was Field's, in which Chief Justice Salmon P. Chase concurred. But it should be noted that it is to Bradley to whom goes the credit for being "first" to advocate "incorporation" via the P or I clause of all rights "specified in the original Constitution or in the early Amendments of it."[68] Although Field had begun his long judicial career with a general inclination in favor of individual rights, this bias ultimately resolved itself into a "special emphasis on the sanctity of economic freedom."[69] Field's *Slaughterhouse* dissent is therefore deceptive in its overall implications, for it does argue angrily for an interpretation of the Fourteenth Amendment and its P or I clause that would insist upon man's "fundamental rights, privileges, and immunities which belong to him as a free man

[65]James Wilson, one of Pennsylvania's delegates to the Constitutional Convention of 1787, had made a point of calling the attention of his fellow delegates to the fact that the Constitution, if ratified, would create a dual citizenship—but the significance of this was both overlooked and misunderstood.

[66]Justice Field's categorization, dissenting in the *Slaughterhouse cases, op. cit.,* at 96.

[67]*The Slaughterhouse Cases, op. cit.,* at 129.

[68]*Ibid.,* at 118. Field, whose longevity in service on the Court—almost thirty-five years—stood as a record until Douglas—who would serve thirty-six and a half—overtook him in 1975—will be remembered in the annals of constitutional law and development primarily as the "spokesman of rugged American individualism and laissez faire." (Rocco J. Tresolini, *American Constitutional Law,* 2nd ed. [New York: The Macmillan Co., 1965], p. 742.) Field had served on the California Supreme Court for six and a half years before his promotion by President Lincoln in 1863 to the U.S. Supreme Court.

[69]Robert G. McCloskey, *American Conservatism in the Age of Enterprise* (Cambridge: Harvard University Press, 1951), pp. 122–23.

and a free citizen.''[70] To Field, the citizenship clause made state citizenship both subordinate to and derivative of national citizenship. As a result of Section 1 of Amendment Fourteen, he argued, ''a citizen of a state is now only a citizen of the United States *residing* in that state.''[71] But Field's cardinal argument against the majority decision was based not so much on the cause of basic human freedoms as it was on the doctrine of vested property rights—a cause he was to espouse throughout his long tenure with consistency, self-assurance, and emotion. For Field, *the* ''privilege'' and/or ''immunity'' that was at issue here was the absolute right to engage in business of butchering. Louisiana's statutory interference with that right was to Field the crime *par excellence* of a governmental roadblock in the path of Darwinian-Spencerian economics.[72] For him, as McCloskey observed, ''the property right is the transcendent value; political ambition ranks next when it is relevant; and the cause of human or civil rights is subordinate to these higher considerations.''[73] Field's dissenting opinion was thus of but limited comfort to those who looked toward a ''nationalization'' of basic human rights and liberties. When he spoke of the ''equality of right'' to labor freely, he looked toward that period of half a century when the Supreme Court would strike hard at any legislative (and administrative) action it deemed violative of the sanctity of property, and of the ''freedom of contract'' concept it was soon to read into the ''due process of law'' clause of both the Fifth and the Fourteenth Amendments.[74]

[70]*The Slaughterhouse Cases, op. cit.,* at 95.

[71]*Ibid.* (Italics supplied.)

[72]Oversimplified, perhaps, this was Field's philosophy of the survival of the fittest in terms of classical nineteenth-century capitalism.

[73]McCloskey, *op. cit.,* pp. 122–23. A considerably more charitable view of Field's stance is taken by Arthur A. North, S. J., in *The Supreme Court: Judicial Process and Judicial Politics* (New York: Appleton-Century-Crofts, 1966), pp. 91–96. He flatly states that not only Harlan but Field and Brewer ''accepted the theory'' of incorporation (North, p. 96). North appears to have arrived at that conclusion chiefly because of Field's posture in the 1892 case of *O'Neil v. Vermont* (see footnotes 74–76 and text, pp. 60–62). But Field resigned from the Court five years later and his nephew Brewer, a fellow dissenter in *O'Neil*—as was Harlan, of course—changed his views on the matter, with only Harlan thus remaining as an ''incorporationist.''

[74]To Field's great satisfaction, the word ''person'' in the latter clause was extended to corporations in 1886, via an announcement from the bench by Chief Justice Waite, in *Santa Clara County v. Southern Pacific Railroad Co.,* 118 U.S. 394—in no small measure due to the interpretative efforts of Roscoe Conkling, who had been a member of the Joint Congressional Committee that had drafted the Fourteenth Amendment.

Except for a handful of instances,[75] and particularly when they involved a charge against a state of "cruel and unusual" punishment,[76] Field found no such justification for protection of the basic freedoms of the Bill of Rights, however—and he was clearly disdainful of his long-time colleague John Marshall Harlan's advocacy of total incorporation. Indeed, when the Court, seven years after *Slaughterhouse*, held unconstitutional racially based discrimination in jury impaneling by Virginia and West Virginia, Field entered a vigorous dissent, contending that the "equal protection of the laws" clause "did not prevent the outright exclusion of blacks" by states acting under their elective authority.[77]

Nonetheless, the Field dissent dramatized both the interest in the meaning of the most important of the Civil War Amendments and its possible role as a catalyst in a "nationalization" of basic rights and liberties. The *Slaughterhouse* holding of "dual citizenship" has never been overruled,[78] and the P or I clause of Amendment Fourteen has become "practically a dead letter"; it has been more or less outflanked ever since,[79] but emphatically not so the "due process of law" and the "equal protection of the laws" clauses, however—which in fact have become a "second" Bill of Rights. And, of course, Congress has begun to make use of the potentially far-reaching provisions of Section 5 of the Amendment, which gives it "power to enforce, by appropriate legisla-

---

[75]*Neal v. Delaware*, 103 U.S. 379 (1880); *Bush v. Connecticut*, 107 U.S. 110 (1882); *In re Kemmler*, 136 U.S. 436 (1890); *McElvaine v. Brush*, 142 U.S. 155 (1891); and *O'Neil v. Vermont*, 144 U.S. 323 (1892).

[76]In the last-named case he did thus note the following in his dissent:

> While, therefore, the ten Amendments, as limitations on power, and, so far as they accomplish their purpose and find their fruition in such limitations, are applicable to the Federal Government and not to the States, yet, so far as they declare or recognize the rights of persons, they are rights belonging to them as citizens of the United States under the Constitution; and the Fourteenth Amendment, as to all such rights, places a limit upon state power by ordaining that no State shall make or enforce any law which shall abridge them. If I am right in this view, then every citizen of the United States is protected from punishments which are cruel and unusual. [At 363.]

[77]See *ex parte Virginia* and *Strauder v. West Virginia*, 100 U.S. 339 and 100 U.S. 303 (1980), respectively.

[78]After the Reconstruction government was turned out of office in Louisiana, the *Slaughterhouse* statute was promptly repealed. Then the *monopoly* went to court, claiming violation of *its* due process of law under Amendment Fourteen. But, with Justice Miller again writing the opinion, the due process claim here lost 9 : 0. (*Butcher's Union Slaughter-House v. Crescent City Live-Stock Landing Co.*, 111 U.S. 746 [1884].)

[79]Morrison, *op. cit.*, fn. 34, at 144.

tion,'' the Amendment's aforegone provisions.[80] *Ergo,* the P or I clause is in effect no longer needed.

To the ''due process of law'' clause of the former and the incorporation problem we can now return, noting en route the criticism of *Slaughterhouse* by one of the earliest American political scientists, John W. Burgess, who pronounced the decision ''entirely erroneous'' from whatever view he regarded it, be that ''historical, political, or juristic.''[81] As he wrote in 1890 in his classic two-volume work, *Political Science and Comparative Constitutional Law:*

> I say that if history has taught us anything in political science, it is that *civil liberty is national in its origin, content and sanction* . . . if there is but a single lesson to be learned from the history of the United States, it is this: Seventy years of debate and four years of terrible war turn substantially upon this issue, in some part or other; and when the Nation triumphed in the great appeal to arms, and addressed itself to the work of readjusting the forms of law to the now undoubted condition of fact, it gave its first attention to the nationalization in constitutional law of the domain of civil liberty. *There is no doubt that those who framed the thirteenth and fourteenth amendments intended to occupy the whole ground and thought that they had done so.* The opposition charged that these amendments would nationalize the whole sphere of civil liberty; the majority accepted the view; and the legislation of Congress for their elaboration and enforcement proceeded upon that view. In the face of all these well known facts it was hardly to be doubted that . . . [the Supreme Court] *would unanimously declare the whole domain of civil liberty to be under its protection against both the general government and the commonwealths.* Great, therefore, was the surprise . . . when the decision in the *Slaughterhouse Cases* was announced. . . .[82]

Whatever one's conclusions regarding the intent of the framers of the Fourteenth Amendment, and its role as a vehicle for the applicability of the Bill of Rights to the several states, we know that there has been piecemeal ''incorporation'' or ''nationalization'' or ''absorption'' of the Bill of Rights by judicial interpretation and, as we shall see later, it

---

[80]For example, sections of the Civil Rights Act of 1964. Congress has also resorted to the almost identically worded provision of Section 2 of the Fifteenth Amendment—as in the Voting Rights Acts of 1965, 1970, and 1975.

[81]*Political Science and Comparative Constitutional Law* (Boston: Ginn & Co., 1890), Vol. I, p. 226.

[82]*Ibid.,* pp. 225–26. (Italics supplied.)

came about at a steadily accelerating rate following Justice Sanford's limited initial acceptance of the concept in 1925. Thus, we now turn to the historical evolution of the incorporation issue, followed by a consideration of the various judicial "positions" on, and the wisdom of, incorporation itself.

The Evolution of "Incorporation"

PRE-1937 DEVELOPMENTS

The 1833 *Barron v. Baltimore*[83] decision firmly shut the judicial and constitutional door on any notions of incorporation until the passage of the Fourteenth Amendment appears to have opened it in 1868; the *Slaughterhouse Cases*[84] relocked it in 1873; and matters seemed to be settled, *res judicata*[85]—reconfirmed in 1899, with the Court reiterating that "the first ten Amendments to the Federal Constitution contain no restrictions on the powers of the state, but were intended to operate solely on the Federal government."[86]

Justice Harlan. Only Harlan, the one-time Kentucky slaveholder,[87] continued to raise the incorporation problem with both conviction and consistency. He would never fail in appropriate cases—of which there really were not very many—to write impassioned opinions in dissent, urging his associates to accept the principle of the nationalization of the Bill of Rights.

Harlan's solitary dissenting opinions from three well-known decisions demonstrated his unshakable belief that the Fourteenth Amendment was intended to incorporate the *entire* Bill of Rights—if for no other reason than that he regarded *all* of the rights in the Bill of Rights as "fundamental" and therefore applicable to the states via the "due

[83] 7 Peters 243.

[84] 16 Wallace 36.

[85] *Res judicata* connotes authoritative, settled law. In other words, it represents *the* essential law involved.

[86] *Brown v. New Jersey*, 175 U.S. 172, at 174. The Court, speaking through Justice Brewer, was unanimous, Harlan, perhaps somewhat surprisingly, concurring separately without opinion.

[87] See the Harlan symposium in the spring 1958 issue of the *Kentucky Law Journal;* my "John Marshall Harlan: A Justice Neglected," 41 *Virginia Law Review* 871 (November 1955); and the excellent essay by Jacob Landynski, "John Marshall Harlan and the Bill of Rights: A Centennial View," 49 *Social Research* (Winter 1982), pp. 899–926.

process of law" clause of Amendment Fourteen. The first of these, *Hurtado v. California* (1884),[88] turned on the question of whether California's 1879 substitution of the practice of "information"[89] for indictment by a grand jury constituted a violation of the "due process" guarantees of the Fourteenth Amendment because of the requirements of the Fifth Amendment. Joseph Hurtado was tried on the basis of "information," convicted of the murder of one José Antonio Estuardo, and sentenced to be hanged. His appeal to the United States Supreme Court accordingly alleged deficient procedural due process. But the Court, in an elaborate 7:1 decision, delivered by Justice Stanley Matthews, rejected that contention, ruling that the substitution of "information" for a grand jury indictment did not violate due process of law because it was merely a "preliminary proceeding" and thus not essential to due process; that, in any event, the Fourteenth's language simply did not contain, and did not mandate, a grand jury provision— had that been the intention, contended Matthews, it would have stated so specifically. Harlan's scholarly dissent not only disagreed with the majority's analysis, but argued at length his belief that the Bill of Rights *is* incorporated via the due process clause of Amendment Fourteen. It meant, he insisted, that "there are principles of liberty and justice lying at the foundation of our civil and political institutions which no state can violate consistently with that due process of law required by the 14th Amendment in proceedings involving life, liberty or property."[90]

The second case, *Maxwell v. Dow*,[91] came sixteen years later. Not only was the matter of the substitution of "information" for a grand jury indictment—this time by Utah—again present, but a far more important collateral issue was at stake: Charles Maxwell's trial by a Utah jury of eight instead of twelve. Convicted of the crime of armed robbery, Maxwell argued that he had been deprived of both "due process of law" and, especially, his "privileges and immunities" as a United States citizen; that the Bill of Rights' Fifth and Sixth Amend-

---

[88]110 U.S. 516.

[89]"Information" is a common law practice whereby the prosecuting officer merely submits his charges in the form of an affidavit of evidence, supported by sworn statements, to a trial court. It is still used widely by the states and, to a much lesser degree, by the federal government, in civil and non-capital criminal cases at the district court level.

[90]*Hurtado v. California, op. cit.*, at 546. Hurtado died in his jail cell of a pulmonary embolism one month after the Supreme Court's decision.

[91]176 U.S. 581 (1900).

ments, guaranteeing grand jury indictment and trial by jury in criminal cases, respectively, were incorporated via Amendment Fourteen. "No, not at all," said the Supreme Court, with Justice Rufus W. Peckham writing for the 8 : 1 majority. Peckham, heavily relying on the *Slaughterhouse* precedent, admonished his colleagues to look to the Amendment's language rather than its proponents' speeches. Not only did he see no violation of due process by the procedures employed by Utah, but neither the "due process" nor the "P or I" clause comprehended the rights listed in the federal Bill of Rights. In short, any thoughts of incorporation were to be rejected logically:

> . . . [W]hen the Fourteenth Amendment prohibits abridgment by the states of those privileges and [*sic*] immunities which [the individual] enjoys as such citizen, it is not correct or reasonable to say that it covers and extends to certain rights which he does not enjoy by reason of his citizenship, but simply because those rights exist in favor of all individuals as against Federal government powers.[92]

Harlan, the sole dissenter, was not impressed by this reasoning; scoffing at what he regarded as deliberate blindness and verbal gynmastics, he reiterated his *Hurtado* view that, indeed, the Fourteenth Amendment intended to incorporate the entire Bill of Rights. Pointing to the Court's firm 8 : 1 decision in favor of property rights pronounced just three years earlier,[93] he warned that "no judicial tribunal has authority to say that some of [the Bill of Rights] may be abridged by the States while others may not be abridged."[94] To him, each one of the rights was fundamental and *ergo* applicable to the states, for he regarded *all* federal rights possessed by citizens *prior* to the adoption of Fourteen as being among the "privileges or immunities" which were secured against encroachment by the states.

The last pertinent example of Harlan's lone stand on the issue was the 1908 case of *Twining v. New Jersey*,[95] which involved the controversial constitutional guarantee against compulsory self-incrimination. The

[92]*Ibid.*, at 595–96.

[93]*Chicago, Burlington and Quincy Railroad v. Chicago*, 166 U.S. 226 (1897).

[94]176 U.S. 581, *op. cit.*, at 616. Maxwell's sentence was commuted in 1903, but he was killed in a gunfight not long thereafter.

[95]211 U.S. 78.

president of the Monmouth Safe & Trust Co., Albert C. Twining, and its treasurer, David C. Cornell, had been indicted by a New Jersey grand jury for having deliberately and knowingly displayed a false paper to a bank examiner with full intent to deceive him as to the actual condition of their firm. At the trial the two defendants neither called witnesses nor took the stand in their own defense. Very much in the fashion of the trial judge in *Adamson v. California*[96] four decades later, the *Twining* trial judge, Wilbur A. Heisley, commented adversely and extensively from the bench on the defendants' failure to take the stand. His charge to the jury contained the following statements: "Because a man does not go upon the stand you are not necessarily justified in drawing an inference of guilt. But you have a right to consider the fact that he does not go upon the stand where a direct accusation is made against him." The jury returned a verdict of guilty as charged against both defendants, who ultimately appealed to the United States Supreme Court, contending first, that the exemption from self-incrimination is one of the privileges or immunities of citizens of the United States which the Fourteenth Amendment forbids the states to abridge, and second, that the alleged compulsory self-incrimination constituted a denial of due process of law. This time Justice William H. Moody spoke for another 8 : 1 majority that rejected, again, not only the specific contentions but the larger issue of the Bill of Rights' incorporation. However, citing *Chicago, Burlington & Quincy RR. v. Chicago*,[97] he significantly now granted the "possibility" that due process meant that "some of the personal rights safeguarded by the first eight Amendments against national action may also be safeguarded against state action."[98]— yet only if an affirmative response to the following question is called for: "Is it a fundamental principle in liberty and justice which inheres in the very idea of free government and is the inalienable right of a citizen of such a government?"[99] Moody answered his rhetorical question by declaring it inapplicable in the instant *Twining* case because he regarded the privilege against self-incrimination as "not fundamental in due process of law, nor an essential part of it."[100] John Marshall Harlan predictably repeated his plea for incorporation, based on

[96]332 U.S. 46 (1947).
[97]166 U.S. 226 (1897).
[98]*Twining v. New Jersey, op. cit.*, at 99.
[99]*Ibid.*, at 106.
[100]*Ibid.*, at 110.

what he continued to regard as the commands of the Constitution. Until he died in 1911, he endeavored to convince at least a bare majority of his colleagues of the correctness of his position. But he was not to see the victory that was to come only from future judicial interpretations—one that was all but total by the late 1960s. Well might one of his biographers write that Harlan had always "maintained an unswerving faith in the role of the Supreme Court as defender of the citizen's liberties and guardian of American constitutional ideals. . . ."[101] So he had indeed, and not only in the realm of incorporation (as we shall have occasion to see later).[102]

The Gitlow Case. Despite the rising concern expressed for civil rights and liberties by Justice Holmes and Brandeis, who joined the Court in 1902 and 1916, respectively, incorporation of the Bill of Rights seemed a lost cause until June 8, 1925, when it received its first official judicial recognition, on an at least *partial* basis, in the famous case of *Gitlow v. New York.*[103]

Benjamin Gitlow, an active exponent of extreme left-wing causes and a member of the most radical wing of the Socialist Party, had run afoul of New York State's Criminal Anarchy Act of 1902—which was passed in the wake of President William McKinley's assassination in late 1901. He was tried and convicted—after forty-five minutes of jury deliberations—for having "advocated, advised, and taught the duty, necessity, and propriety of overthrowing and overturning organized government by force, violence, and unlawful means by certain writings" (the "Left Wing Manifesto" and "The Revolutionary Age"). Appealing his conviction through the appropriate tiers of the New York State courts to the United States Supreme Court, he alleged that the New York statute violated both the Fourteenth Amendment's due process clause and the freedom of speech guarantees of the First. Gitlow lost on his basic claims, the Court ruling 6 : 2—Justice Stone not participating—that the

---

[101]Alan F. Westin, "John Marshall Harlan and the Constitutional Rights of Negroes: The Transformation of a Southerner," 66 *Yale Law Journal* 710 (1957).

[102]See, for example, the most famous of all his dissents, in *Plessy v. Ferguson*, 163 U.S. 537 (1896).

[103]268 U.S. 652. A case can be made for the contention that a number of earlier 1920s cases had "moved" the Court to its *Gitlow* position—e.g., *Gilbert v. Minnesota*, 254 U.S. 325 (1921), but by *dictum* only; *Prudential Insurance Co. v. Cheeks*, 259 U.S. 530 (1922); *Meyer v. Nebraska*, 262 U.S. 390 (1923); and *Pierce v. Society of Sisters*, 268 U.S. 510 (1925). See Klaus H. Heberle, "From Gitlow to Near: Judicial 'Amendment' by Absent-Minded Incrementalism," 34 *The Journal of Politics*, 458–83 (1972).

statute violated neither due process in general nor free speech in particular. However, while clearing Mr. Gitlow's path to a New York jail by ruling that the latter's writings did not constitute the advocacy of abstract doctrine but embodied "the language of direct incitement,"[104] the author of the Court's majority opinion, Justice Sanford, made judicial history by the first formal embrace of incorporation of provisions of the Bill of Rights, speech and press:

> For present purposes we may and do assume that freedom of speech and of the press—which are protected by the First Amendment from abridgement by Congress—*are among the fundamental personal rights and "liberties" protected by the due process clause of the Fourteenth Amendment from impairment by the States.*[105]

This renowned Sanford dictum[106] was fully subscribed to by all of his colleagues, including, of course, Justices Holmes and Brandeis. That the two dissented here in one of Holmes's most celebrated opinions was not because of the incorporation announcement, but, as we shall have occasion to assess later in connection with freedom of expression in Chapter V, because they simply did not believe that Gitlow's action presented any "clear and present" danger[107] to the State of New York. Drawing the kind of line discussed in Chapters I and II, Justice Holmes pointed out that "every idea is an incitement," that "eloquence may set fire to reason. . . ." But regardless of Benjamin Gitlow's defeat—in later days he became a well-paid informant for the government in subversive-activities matters[108]—the "carry-over" doctrine concerning the Fourteenth Amendment had been officially enunciated.

The Doctrine Confirmed and Expanded. That the Gitlow incorporation development was neither a fluke nor a passing pronouncement in

---

[104]*Gitlow v. New York, op. cit.,* at 665.

[105]*Ibid.,* at 666. (Italics supplied.) Many had long treated it as such.

[106]Properly known as *obiter dictum,* it is a statement of opinion by a judge that is not necessary to the conclusion on the merits of the case.

[107]That famous doctrine, first enunciated in *Schenck v. United States,* 249 U.S. 47 (1919), by Holmes and Brandeis, will be fully treated in Chapter V.

[108]Especially in the 1940s and 1950s (usually at $50 a day). He had served three years of a five- to ten-year sentence, being pardoned by Governor Al Smith, who opined that Gitlow had been "sufficiently punished for a political crime" (*The New York Times,* December 12, 1925, p. 1). Gitlow died in 1965, aged seventy-three, having become a confirmed anti-Communist.

dictum soon became apparent. Only two years later, the Supreme Court, again speaking through Justice Sanford, confirmed unanimously the nationalization of *freedom of speech* in the case of *Fiske v. Kansas.*[109] Here, for the first time, it upheld a personal liberty claim under the Fourteenth Amendment, ruling specifically that a Kansas criminal syndicalism statute—very similar to the New York one in *Gitlow* (although Sanford did not discuss *Gitlow*'s issues and decision at all)—did indeed violate the due process clause of the Fourteenth Amendment, as applied to Harold Fiske, because of the free speech strictures of the First Amendment. It has long been argued,[110] with considerable persuasiveness, that a more elaborate and more definitive, and hence more clearly precedent-setting case for the incorporation of speech, is the 1931 Hughes opinion in *Stromberg v. California.*[111] There, nineteen-year-old Yetta Stromberg, a member of the Young Communist League, had led 40 ten- to fiften-year-old children in a summer camp pledge of allegiance to a red flag, and found herself in multiple violation of a California statute prohibiting the display of such flags. The Chief Justice, speaking for a 7 : 2 majority (Justices Butler and McReynolds in dissent), admonished: "It has been determined that the concentration of liberty under the due process clause of the Fourteenth Amendment embraces the right of free speech (citing, among others, the *Gitlow* and *Fiske* cases)."[112] In any event, incorporation of *freedom of the press* followed not long thereafter in the well-known 1931 prior-censorship case of *Near v. Minnesota.*[113]

In *Near,* this time speaking for a majority of five, Hughes declared unconstitutional, as "an infringement of the liberty of the press guaranteed by the Fourteenth Amendment," the so-called Minnesota Gag Law, which permitted prior restraint from publishing under certain circumstances. He wrote: "It is no longer open to doubt that the liberty of the press and of speech is safeguarded by the due process clause of the Fourteenth Amendment from invasion by state action. It was found

[109]274 U.S. 380 (1927). *Fiske* was sponsored by the I.W.W. Indeed, all cases involving the incorporation of the First Amendment were group-sponsored.

[110]See Herberle, *op. cit.* He insists that "the question of incorporation was not settled until the decisions in *Stromberg* and *Near*," with the Court there relying "on *Gitlow, Whitney* [*v. California,* 274 U.S. 357, (1927)] and *Fiske.*" (At 477.)

[111]283 U.S. 359.

[112]*Ibid.,* at 368.

[113]283 U.S. 697, at 723.

impossible to conclude that this essential personal liberty of the citizen was left unprotected by the general guarantee of fundamental rights of person and property."[114]

Less than a year later, the incorporation doctrine moved out of the realm of the First Amendment and, for the first time, into the area of the guarantee of a fair trial, in general, and *counsel in capital criminal cases*, in particular. The vehicle was the first of the notorious "*Scottsboro Cases*," *Powell v. Alabama*,[115] which was destined to become a *cause célèbre* in the records of applications of due process of law to black defendants. Writing for a majority of seven, Justice George Sutherland overturned the conviction in the Alabama courts of seven indigent, ignorant, minor blacks who had been falsely charged with the rape of two white girls, and convicted in a one-day trial in a mob-dominated atmosphere without the benefit of proper defense counsel. Reversing and remanding their conviction to the trial court with a stern call for a fair trial, the Court held that

> . . . the right to counsel . . . provided in the Sixth Amendment [as applied to this case] is of such a character that it cannot be denied without violating those "fundamental principles of liberty and justice which lie at the base of all our civil and political institutions."[116] . . . [It] is obviously one of those compelling considerations which must prevail in determining *whether it is embraced within the due process clause of the Fourteenth Amendment, although it is specifically dealt with in another part of the federal Constitution*. . . . [T]he necessity of counsel was so vital and imperative that the failure of the trial court to make an effective appointment of counsel was likewise a denial of due process of law within the meaning of the Fourteenth Amendment. . . .[117]

Sutherland hinted of the applicability of the new role of law to *noncapital* criminal cases as well, but chose to state that it was not necessary to determine that question "now."[118] In any event, new ground

---

[114]*Ibid.*, at 707.

[115]287 U.S. 45 (1932). So termed because the accused were all apprehended near the Alabama town of Scottsboro.

[116]Quoting from *Hebert v. Louisiana*, 272 U.S. 312 (1926), at 316.

[117]*Ibid.*, at 71. Sutherland also took the occasion to reaffirm the incorporation of "freedom of speech and of the press," at 67.

[118]The Court's ruling in *Betts v. Brady*, 316 U.S. 455 (1942), restricted its application

had been broken, with Justices Pierce Butler and James C. McReynolds as the sole dissenters from the incorporation phase of the case.

The fourth aspect of the Bill of Rights to be thus nationalized was the First Amendment's guarantee of *free exercise of religion* in 1934. This was determined in 1934 in the interesting and important case of *Hamilton v. Regents of the University of California.*[119] All students at the University of California, a public state institution, were then required to take military drill on pain of expulsion. But one among them, Albert Hamilton, holding religious convictions against the bearing of arms, refused to participate in the program and was consequently expelled. He filed suit, contending that his religious beliefs entitled him to exemption by virtue of both Amendments One and Fourteen. When his case reached the United States Supreme Court, Justice Butler, speaking for his unanimous colleagues, ruled that Hamilton's religious convictions were indeed safeguarded by the Bill of Rights, and that freedom of religion was henceforth to be regarded as incorporated via the "due process of law" clause of Amendment Fourteen.[120] However, the Court went on to rule that, despite its holding on incorporation, Hamilton was *not* entitled to an exemption from the state requirement of military training because, after all, he was not *compelled to attend* the University of California. Since he had readily chosen to attend that institution of his own free will, his due process of law was in no sense being violated by a requirement to comply with the University's, i.e., the State of California's, rules and regulations while in attendance.

In 1937, a few months earlier than the landmark incorporation case of *Palko v. Connecticut,*[121] the First Amendment's *freedom of assembly* and, by implication, its freedom "to *petition* the Government for a redress of grievances" became the fifth and sixth segments of the Bill of

---

to *capital* criminal cases, yet *Gideon v. Wainwright,* 372 U.S. 335 (1963), extended it to all criminal cases, save certain misdemeanors. But that holding was later interpreted as comprehending all non-traffic misdemeanors involving *any* imprisonment. (*Argersinger v. Hamlin,* 407 U.S. 25 [1972], and *Scott v. Illinois,* 440 U.S. 367 [1979]).

[119]293 U.S. 245.

[120]Some observers, including North, *op. cit.,* regard this statement of incorporation as well as a similar one made in the case by Justice Cardozo's concurring opinion (*ibid.,* at 265) as *dicta.* They prefer to point to *Cantwell v. Connecticut,* decided six years later, as the "incorporator" by rule of law rather than *dictum* of the free exercise clause (310 U.S. 296, at 303).

[121]302 U.S. 319.

Rights to be "carried over." *De Jonge v. Oregon*[122] again involved a state criminal syndicalism law: Dirk De Jonge had been convicted in Oregon's Multnomah County under such a statute, which made it a criminal offense to advocate "crime, physical violence, sabotage, or any unlawful acts or methods as a means of accomplishing industrial change or political revolution." There was no record that De Jonge had advocated what the statute proscribed, nor did the indictment charge him specifically with having done so. The sole charge against him was that he had participated in an advertised political meeting of the Communist Party, of which he was an admitted member. The meeting, concededly peaceful, had been held by the Portland section of the Party to protest alleged brutality and unlawful activity by the Portland police and conditions at the county jail. Speaking for his unanimous Court, Chief Justice Hughes pointed out that "peaceable assembly for lawful discussion, however unpopular the sponsorship, cannot be made a crime," and that "the holding of meetings for peaceable political action cannot be proscribed." Further declaring that the right of peaceable assembly "is a right cognate to those of free speech and free press and is equally fundamental," he proceeded to hold that assembly, too, is thus one of "those fundamental principles of liberty and justice" that are made applicable to the states via the due process clause of the Fourteenth Amendment.[123]

Hence, when the *Palko* case appeared on the Court's calendar for decision, the entire First Amendment and the right to counsel provision of the Sixth (at least in capital criminal cases) had been firmly incorporated. But what was needed was a more thorough discussion that would deal with the theoretical as well as the practical issues involved in "nationalizing" the Bill of Rights. Appropriately, it fell to the eloquent Justice Benjamin N. Cardozo to perform that task. His all-too-brief, six-year tenure on the Court culminated in *Palko v. Connecticut*.

THE DOCTRINE SPELLED OUT: CARDOZO AND PALKO

Frank U. Palko had been indicted by the State of Connecticut for murder in the *first* degree for the fatal shooting of two policemen. The trial jury—as juries have been known to do with predictable unpredict-

---

[122]299 U.S. 353 (1937).
[123]*Ibid.*, at 364.

ability—found him guilty of *second-degree* murder, however, and he was accordingly sentenced to life imprisonment with a recommendation that he never be paroled. Pursuant to a statute of 1866, however, and with the permission of the trial judge in the case, the State of Connecticut then appealed the conviction on the lesser count to the highest state court, the Court of Errors. In its petition Connecticut charged that the action in the trial court constituted an "error of law to the prejudice of the state"; the Court of Errors agreed, reversing the judgment below, and ordered a new trial. Although Palko objected that the second trial would place him twice in jeopardy for the same offense——an action forbidden by the terms of the Fifth Amendment, and, as he urged, consequently forbidden also by those of the due process clause of the Fourteenth—his retrial took place soon thereafter.

This time the trial jury returned a verdict of murder in the *first* degree, and the judge sentenced Palko to death. Having exhausted his judicial remedies at the state level, Palko then appealed to the United States Supreme Court; again he contended that "whatever is forbidden by the Fifth Amendment is forbidden by the Fourteenth also."[124] For reasons to be outlined presently, the Supreme Court, speaking through Justice Cardozo, ruled against Palko's claims on all counts; Justice Butler dissented without opinion (an intriguing but not very helpful practice).[125] Frank Palko was subsequently executed by electrocution. Macabre though it may be, a cynic could comment that, given the importance of his case for the future of civil rights and liberties, he did not die in vain.

The "Honor Roll" of Superior Rights. Justice Cardozo's opinion was recognized at once as a judicial landmark for several reasons: (1) It established a yardstick by which to measure the incorporation problem, and thus govern judicial action. (2) It provided official judicial recognition for the formerly unpredictable claim that, under certain conditions, and in certain areas—based upon a hierarchy of values—the several

[124]*Ibid.*, at 322.

[125]Robert Lewis Shayon told me in November 1966 that he had discussed the *Palko* case in considerable detail with Frank Palko's court-appointed attorney, David Goldstein, a distinguished Bridgeport, Connecticut, lawyer. According to Goldstein, Butler's reason for dissenting—even without opinion—was based on his conviction that the State of Connecticut had in effect denied Palko's due process of law. During oral argument, Butler was "very tough" on the state's attorney, at one point shouting, "What do you want? Blood?"

states are beholden to the commands of the federal Bill of Rights via the Fourteenth Amendment. (3) It laid the groundwork for the support of both the theory and the practice of a judicial double standard in the interpretation of basic human rights.[126] Practically speaking, what the Cardozo opinion accomplished was to deny or reject any *general* rule of overall incorporation, while acknowledging that there are, and indeed must be, some rights in the Bill that are fundamental enough to require "incorporation" or "absorption."

Justice Cardozo's *Palko* opinion thus established the "Honor Roll of Superior Rights," to which his life-long admirer and ultimate successor on the Supreme Court, Felix Frankfurter, so irreverently referred as the "slot machine theory . . . some are in and some are out." Although he refused to regard the "due process of law" clause of the Fourteenth Amendment as "shorthand" for the Bill of Rights, Cardozo nonetheless set himself the task of distinguishing those basic rights that he and his supporters viewed as "of the very essence of a scheme of ordered liberty" from those without which "justice would not perish" and which were not therefore "implicit in the concept of ordered liberty." Explaining his rationale further, he wrote movingly of "those fundamental principles of liberty and justice which lie at the base of all our civil and political institutions," and of principles of justice "so rooted in the traditions and conscience of our people as to be ranked as fundamental."[127] (It is significant to note the recurrent use of the concept of "fundamental" rights in juxtaposition to what, as we shall see below, are termed "formal" rights on the scale of basic rights and liberties.)[128] Recognizing the difficulties of evaluation and interpretation inherent in his dichotomy, and anticipating both the criticism and some of the problems that would follow, Cardozo resorted to the "freedom of thought and speech" as his cardinal illustration: "Of that freedom one may say that it is the matrix, the indispensable condition, of nearly

---

[126]See the discussion in Chapter II, *supra*.

[127]302 U.S. 319 (1937), at 325.

[128]The Court had established a dichotomy between "formal" and "fundamental" rights at the turn of the century in answering the question of how many, and which, of the rights in the Constitution were to be applicable automatically to possessions and territories. The "fundamental" ones only, held the Court in the series of *Insular* cases from 1901 to 1905. See especially *Hawaii v. Mankichi*, 190 U.S. 197 (1903), and *Rasmussen v. United States*, 197 U.S. 516 (1905). What is "fundamental" is of course a value judgment.

every other form of freedom. With rare aberrations, a pervasive recognition of that truth can be traced in our history, political and legal. . . ."[129]

For the other group, these "formal" rights in the Bill without which "justice would not perish," Cardozo cited the right to trial by jury and the immunity from prosecution "for a capital or otherwise infamous crime" except as a result of an indictment, explaining that, indeed, they may have "value and importance," but

> even so, they are not of the essence of a scheme of ordered liberty. To abolish them is not to violate a "principle of justice so rooted in the traditions and conscience of our people as to be ranked as fundamental." . . . Few would be so narrow as to maintain that a fair and enlightened system of justice would be impossible without them. . . .[130]

Then, turning specifically to another right, the immunity from compulsory self-incrimination, he noted that "[T]his too might be lost, and justice still be done. . . . Justice . . . would not perish if the accused were subject to a duty to respond to orderly inquiry."[131] Cardozo thus insisted that in the realm of chiefly *procedural* rights, in general, and the protection against double jeopardy at issue in the *Palko* ruling, in particular, the question to be posed by the appellate tribunal must be, as Justice Harlan had phrased it decades earlier, all embracing: "Does it violate those 'fundamental principles of liberty and justice which lie at the base of all our civil and political institutions?'" "The answer," judged Cardozo, "surely must be 'no,'" for, he explained: "[Connecticut] is not attempting to wear the accused out by a multitude of cases with accumulated trials. It asks no more than this, that the case against him shall go on until there shall be a trial free from the corrosion of substantial legal error."[132] In his view, Connecticut had sought no more than parity with the defendant in the right to continue a case "until there shall be a trial free from the corrosion of substantial legal error." A defendant was given the right to appeal errors adverse to him. "A reciprocal privilege . . . has now been granted to the state. . . ." And

---

[129]*Palko v. Connecticut, op. cit.*, at 327.
[130]*Ibid.*, at 325.
[131]*Ibid.*, at 326.
[132]*Ibid.*, at 328.

he concluded on a note of assurance: "There is here no seismic innovation. The edifice of justice stands, in its symmetry, to many, greater than before."[133]

A Caveat. It is essential to recognize at once that, despite the *Palko* dichotomy between the components of the Bill of Rights that are and those that are not "implicit in the concept of ordered liberty,"[134] Justice Cardozo made it clear that the several states would still be subject to the judicial test of whether or not a duly challenged law or action constituted a violation of the "due process of law" concept of the Fourteenth Amendment *per se*. In other words, simply because only some of the rights are *ipso facto* applicable to the states via the Fourteenth Amendment, it does not mean that the states are free to violate the basic concepts of due process of law to which all persons in their jurisdictions are entitled. In such claims the judicial test then becomes the one so faithfully and ardently embraced by Justice Frankfurter during his career on the Supreme Court: does the alleged state violation constitute conduct that "shocks the conscience," or, in the less inhibited language of Justice Holmes, "does it make you vomit?" Given the divergent status of consciences, and the different physiological responses to shock, it is obvious that the answer in individual cases is difficult and often unpredictable. We shall have occasion to return to this particular problem of drawing lines when we consider the various choices or "positions" on the incorporation question offered by justices of the Supreme Court and other knowledgeable participants in the search for justice.

POST-PALKO DEVELOPMENTS

The test devised by Justice Cardozo in *Palko* presumably permitted, if it did not indeed invite, subsequent alteration of the newly created incorporation "line." That line, *as of the famous Opinion Monday in 1937,* had created the dichotomy shown in the following table (3.1).

As the limited number of *a*-marked items in the table indicates, Cardozo did not specifically cover each and every aspect of the Bill of

---

[133]*Ibid.*
[134]Louis Lusky protests that "ordered liberty is too vague to describe a national objective. . . . It is a vehicle for whatever meaning the Court gives it, and thus enables the Court to apply its own conceptions of public policy." *By What Right?* (Charlottesville: The Michie Co., 1975), pp. 105, 107.

Table 3.1

THE STATUS OF "INCORPORATION" AS OF *PALKO* (1937)

AMENDMENT	"INCORPORATED" (AND YEAR)	VOTE	NOT "INCORPORATED"
One	Speech.[a] (1925 and 1927) Press.[a] (1925 and 1931) Free Exercise of Religion[a] (1934 and 1940) Peaceable Assembly.[a] (1937) Right of Petition. (1937)	9:0 and 7:2 9:0 and 5:4 9:0 and 9:0 8:0 8:0	Separation of Church and State.
Two			Keep and Bear Arms.
Three			No Quartering of Soldiers.
Four			Evidence Admitted as Result of Unreasonable Search and Seizure.[a]
Five	Due Process of Law (as per Fourteenth). Eminent Domain Safeguards.[b] (1937 and 1897, resp.)		Grand Jury Indictment[a] or Presentment. Double Jeopardy.[a] Compulsory Self-Incrimination.[a]
Six	Counsel in Criminal Cases[a] (later judicially abridged to read "in capital" criminal cases only—but then reinterpreted to read "all criminal cases"). Fair Trial. (1932 and 1937, resp.)	9:0 and 8:1	Speedy and Public Trial. Impartial Jury Trial in Criminal Cases.[a] Nature and Cause of Accusation. Compulsory Process for Appearance of Witness. Confrontation of Accusers.
Seven	Fair Trial. (1937)	7:2 and 9:0	Jury Trial in Civil Cases.[a]
Eight	Fair Trial. (1937)	9:0	Excessive Bail and Fines. Cruel and Unusual Punishments.

[a] Specifically mentioned in the *Palko* opinion by Justice Cardozo.
[b] Alluded to in his Footnote Four. (See also footnote 20, p. 16, and footnote 20, page 46, *supra*.)

Rights. But his language made quite clear that the underlying principles of our federal government structure demand that the states be permitted to follow their own practices and discretion in the realm of procedural due process so long as they provide a full measure of ''due process of law'' in each and every instance.

1947 and 1948: Two Additions. The Cardozo ''Honor Roll'' stood for almost a quarter of a century. During that period it was extended only twice: to include the concept of *''separation of Church and State''* in the already incorporated exercise of freedom of religion and to require *public* trials. The vehicle for the former was the 1947 *New Jersey Bus* case[135] (which we shall have occasion to discuss in considerable detail in Chapter VI). Pertinent here is the entire Court's acknowledgment (despite its 5 : 4 split on the specific merits of the case) that a *bona fide* violation of the principle of the separation of Church and State is constitutionally proscribed by *both* the terms of the First Amendment and the ''due process of law'' clause of the Fourteenth Amendment. The ''public'' trial requirement came with a 7 : 2 opinion by Justice Black (Justices Frankfurter and Jackson dissenting) in 1948 as a result of the secret sentencing of a Michigan citizen, William D. Oliver, by a judge serving as a one-man grand jury, a practice statutorily sanctioned in his home state's Oakland County.[136]

1961: The Cleveland Search and Seizure Case. The year 1961 heralded a new burst of judicial activity (some would say ''activism''). It was the Fourth Amendment's guarantee against *unreasonable searches and seizures* that was next to be incorporated. The fruit of such seizures

[135]*Everson v. Board of Education of Ewing Township*, 330 U.S. 1. Justice Black preferred to think of *Murdock v. Pennsylvania*, 319 U.S. 105 (1943), as the vehicle of incorporation of separation of Church and State.

[136]*In re Oliver*, 333 U.S. 257 (1948). At first blush the case seemed to turn on simple due process considerations. But in later opinions the Supreme Court specifically (e.g., *Duncan v. Louisiana*, 391 U.S. 145 [1968]) referred to *Oliver* as having incorporated ''public'' trials. However, a 5 : 4 Court ruled in a hotly criticized 1979 decision that ''members of the public have no constitutional right under the Sixth and Fourteenth Amendments to attend criminal trials'' *if* the defendant, the prosecutor, and the presiding judge agree to close the courtroom to press and public. (*Gannett v. De Pasquale*, 443 U.S. 368.) But see the more or less contrary 7:0 holding in 1980 (*Richmond Newspapers v. Virginia*, 448 U.S. 555), confining *Gannett* to *pre*-trials; see also the 1982 follow-up holding in *Globe Newspaper Co. v. Superior Court*, 457 U.S. 596, and subsequent cases (pp. 228 ff., *infra*).

had long before ceased to be admissible as evidence in *federal* court.[137] States, too, had been judicially forbidden to engage in *unreasonable* searches and seizures as of 1949 in the 6 : 3 *Wolf* decision,[138] but the traditions of common law—namely, that if the evidence is trustworthy, i.e., if it is "material, relevant, and probative," it *is* admissible regardless of how it was acquired[139]—nonetheless were held to permit their "fruit," i.e., their results, as admissible evidence in *state* court proceedings. The judicial rationale for this rather astonishing dichotomy was that the victim of such evidence could trigger "the remedies of private action"—namely, *sue* the procurer of the illegally obtained, but admitted, evidence for civil damages, or call for criminal proceedings against officials engaged in unlawful searches. Demonstrably, the Court thus chose to regard the *exclusionary rule as an evidentiary rule—not as a constitutional provision.*[140] *Wolf* was reaffirmed narrowly (5:4) in a controversial 1954 California case in which Justice Tom C. Clark, the future author of *Mapp,* cast the decisive vote.[141]

Because of her 1961 case, Ms. Dolree (Dolly) Mapp, a Cleveland woman of questionable reputation, catalyzed the carry-over of the federal principle to the states. Acting on alleged information that Ms. Mapp, and possibly her daughter by an erstwhile marriage, were hiding (a) a fugitive and (b) "a large amount of policy paraphernalia" on the

[137]*Weeks v. United States,* 232 U.S. 383 (1914). The *judicially created* rule thus prohibits the admissibility in criminal trials of evidence seized in violation of Amendment Four.

[138]*Wolf v. Colorado,* 339 U.S. 25 (1949). Here, the Court in effect announced the "incorporation" of the Fourth Amendment's pertinent guarantees but, as explained, at once neutralized or negated it by continuing to sanction admissibility of evidence so obtained by the *states*—in this state case, the confiscation of Dr. Wolf's appointment books. Thus, the *Weeks* rule (*loc. cit.*) did not—yet—apply to the states.

[139]The courts of England and almost all of those of the world's other lands still maintain that particular common law approach to the acquisition of evidence, relying instead on civil, criminal, and disciplinary remedies against offending police officers. See J. David Hirschel, "What Can We Learn from the English Approach to the Problem of Illegally Seized Evidence?", 67 *Judicature* 9 (April 1984).

[140]In rejecting the application of the exclusionary rule in the State of New York in 1926, Cardozo, then a judge on its Court of Appeals, had asked the celebrated question whether "the criminal is to go free because the constable had blundered?" (*People v. Defore,* 242 N.Y. 13, at 19–25.)

[141]*Irvine v. California,* 347 U.S. 128. The others, like Clark, who joined Justice Jackson's reluctant majority opinion, were Chief Justice Warren and Justices Reed and Minton. Dissenters were Black, Douglas, Frankfurter, and Burton.

top floor of their two-story family dwelling, police forced their way into the house without a warrant of any kind—they feigned one by brandishing a blank white sheet of stationery—and found, after an unedifying struggle and a widespread search, some "obscene materials." On the strength of these, Ms. Mapp was convicted of the illegal possession of obscene materials in violation of an Ohio statute. The Ohio judiciary upheld her conviction, but the Supreme Court, on appeal, reversed it in *Mapp v. Ohio,* [142] in what *The New York Times* appropriately termed "an historic step," and Harvard Law School Dean—soon to be Solicitor-General of the United States—Erwin Griswold saw as requiring "a complete change in the outlook and practices of state and local police." [143] Speaking for the 6:3 majority—Justices Frankfurter, Harlan, and Whittaker dissenting—Justice Clark overruled the long-standing precedents, especially *Wolf,* and, now fully incorporating the Fourth Amendment's applicable guarantee, ruled that "all evidence obtained by searches and seizures in violation of the Constitution is, by that same authority [Amendment Four], inadmissible in a state court . . ."; and: "since the Fourth Amendment's right of privacy has been declared enforceable against the States through the Due Process Clause of the Fourteenth [although not, as it held in 1984, to those in prison cells[144]] it is enforceable against them by the same sanction of exclusion as is used against the Federal Government." [145] Thus, in the words of a leading student of search and seizure problems, the *Mapp* decision "clearly catapulted the exclusionary rule into a position at the core" of the Fourteenth Amendment. [146] Yet 1974 witnessed a distinct

[142]367 U.S. 643 (1961). Actually, albeit upholding her *conviction,* the Ohio Supreme Court declared the pertinent Ohio statute unconstitutional by a majority vote of 5:2. However, since the Ohio State Constitution permits only *one* dissenting vote on the seven-man Ohio Supreme Court in cases of declarations of unconstitutionality, the law survived. (170 Ohio St. 427–28, 166 NE 2d 387, 398.) Ms. Mapp managed to run afoul of the law in subsequent years and, ironically, filed an appeal from a conviction for narcotics trafficking in New York in 1975 on the strength of the 1961 decision. (*The New York Times,* December 15, 1975, p. 35c.)

[143]June 20, 1961, p. 1, and as quoted in *ibid.,* December 15, 1975, p. 35c.

[144]*Hudson v. Palmer,* 468 U.S. 517.

[145]*Mapp v. Ohio, op. cit.,* at 655. Federal standards of "reasonableness" were specifically confirmed as applicable to the conduct of state police officers in *Ker v. California,* 374 U.S. 23 (1963).

[146]Jacob W. Landynski, "Search and Seizure," Chapter 2 in Stuart S. Nagel, ed., *The Rights of the Accused,* Vol. I (New York: Sage Publications, Inc., 1972), p. 47. For an

dilution of its safeguards at the level of grand juries,[147] and considerable agitation for the rule's abridgement, if not its outright abolition, was manifest in Congress, segments of the judicial branch (encouraged by the Chief Justice of the United States), and the organized bar. Indeed, 1976 would see two 6 : 3 rulings sharply reducing the power of *lower* federal courts in *habeas corpus* proceedings to set aside *state* convictions that relied on illegally obtained evidence, and another 6 : 3 one refusing to apply the rule to *civil* cases.[148] In 1982 the Court, emphasizing a changed tenor vis-à-vis the states' power over the administration of justice, ruled 6:3 that objections to state trial procedures must be raised at the time of the trial,[149] and that there must be total exhaustion of the claim, below.[150] And 1984 would see a potentially far-reaching limitation of the exclusionary rule in two key decisions.[151]

1962: The California Narcotics Addiction Proof Case. The next incorporation came scarcely a·year after *Mapp.* California, a source of considerable litigation on constitutional questions, provided the vehicle that would bring about the nationalization of the Eighth Amendment's guarantees against the *infliction of "cruel and unusual punishments"* (a judicial action for which Justice Field had called seventy years earlier).[152] Because that issue itself was but fleetingly discussed and briefed, some doubt existed as to whether the Supreme Court actually intended to incorporate the provision; but the general assumption now is that Justice Stewart's language did, in effect, apply to the states those

---

enlightening analysis of Justice Clark's seminal role in *Mapp*, and his role perceptions as a member of the Court, see Dennis D. Doran, ''Seize the Time: Justice Tom Clark's Role in *Mapp v. Ohio*,'' in Victoria L. Swigent, ed. *Law and the Legal Process* (Beverly Hills, Calif.: Sage Publications, 1982).

[147]*United States v. Calandra,* 414 U.S. 338, in which the Court, by a 6 : 3 vote, wrote a significant exception into the rule by holding that grand juries *may* use illegally obtained evidence as a basis for questioning witnesses without violating their constitutional rights.

[148]*Stone v. Powell* and *Wolff v. Rice,* 428 U.S. 465, and *United States v. Janis,* 428 U.S. 433, respectively. (On the other hand, in 1979 the Court reconfirmed—albeit by a mere 5 : 4 margin—the federal courts' *habeas corpus* authority in cases of alleged racial discrimination [*Rose v. Mitchell,* 443 U.S. 545].)

[149]*Engle v. Isaac,* 456 U.S. 107. See also *United States v. Frady,* 456 U.S. 152 (1982).

[150]*Rose v. Lundy,* 255 U.S. 509 (1982).

[151]*United States v. Leon,* 468 U.S. 897, and *Massachusetts v. Sheppard,* 468 U.S. 981.

[152]See pp. 60 ff., *supra.*

basic strictures of the last article of amendment in the Bill of Rights.[153] His allies in that interpretation were the Chief Justice and Justices Black, Douglas, and Brennan; Justice Harlan concurred, but on the narrower ground of violation of due process of law. Justice Byron R. White, joined by Justice Clark, wrote his first dissenting opinion on the bench in the case, accusing the Court of meddling unjustifiably with the state's criminal justice jurisdiction and discretion. At issue was a California statute making it a crime "to be under the influence of, or be addicted to narcotics, or to make unprescribed use of them"; "status" violations were punishable by a mandatory ninety-day jail sentence.

Walter Lawrence Robinson—who died a year before he won his case—had been arrested on a Los Angeles street by police, whom he told that he used narcotics; his arms bore what appeared to be hypodermic needle marks. (The case had nothing to do with the *sale* of narcotics.) He had been charged with violation of the statute and sentenced to jail. On appeal, Robinson's counsel successfully raised the "cruel and unusual punishment" issue on the ground that the law did not require *proof* of purchase or use of the drugs. Accepting this argument for the Court majority, Justice Stewart declared the statute unconstitutional as a violation of the Eighth and Fourteenth Amendments. As he viewed it, the law fell into the same category as one purporting to make it a criminal offense "for a person to be mentally ill, or a leper, or to be afflicted with venereal disease." Carrying over the pertinent provision of Amendment Eight, he held: ". . . a state which imprisons a person thus afflicted as a criminal, even though he had never touched any narcotic drug within the state or been guilty of any irregular behavior there, inflicts a cruel and unusual punishment in violation of the Fourteenth Amendment."[154] In a significant concurring opinion, Justice

---

[153]*Robinson v. California,* 370 U.S. 660 (1962). In the bizarre 1947 Louisiana "double electrocution" case, Justice Reed had voiced "the assumption, but without so deciding, that violation of the principles of the *Fifth* and *Eighth* Amendments, as a double jeopardy and *cruel and unusual punishment,* would be violative of the due process clause of the Fourteenth Amendment." (*Louisiana ex rel. Francis v. Resweber,* 329 U.S. 459, at 462. Italics supplied.) For accounts of that grisly case see the series of essays by Barrett E. Prettyman, Jr., *Death and the Supreme Court* (New York: Harcourt, Brace, 1961), and the informatively detailed more recent study of Arthur S. Miller and Jeffery H. Bowman, "Slow Dance in the Killing Ground: The Willie Francis Case Revisited," 32 *De Paul Law Review* (Fall 1982), pp. 1–75.

[154]*Ibid.,* at 666–67. But in 1968 the Court refused to extend the *Robinson* principle to chronic alcoholics, in a case involving one of Leroy Powell's 100 (!) prior convictions for

Douglas regarded Robinson's conviction of being an addict as *the* specific "cruel and unusual punishment," not his confinement. Addicts, suggested Douglas, should be cured, not jailed.

---

public intoxication. The Court held 5:4 that a Texas statute making it a crime to be "found in a state of intoxication in any public place" could not be *ipso facto* held to be "irrational" in line with the *Robinson* reasoning. For, wrote Justice Thurgood Marshall, Powell was not "convicted for being a chronic alcoholic, but for being in public while drunk on a particular occasion." (*Powell v. Texas,* 392 U.S. 514, at 532.) Nor, held the Court *per curiam* (6:3), is a forty-year sentence for trafficking in marijuana "cruel and unusual punishment." (*Hutto v. Davis,* 454 U.S. 370 [1982].) On the other hand, the "cruel and unusual punishment" concept became the constitutional hook on which the Court, in a nine-opinion *per curiam* decision running to 243 pages, hung the 5:4 ruling on the last day of its 1971–72 term, that capital punishment, as it was then administered under certain state laws, was unconstitutional. (*Furman v. Georgia,* 408 U.S. 238 [1972].) When Congress and thirty-five states subsequently responded by enacting new laws, designed to meet the Court's objections but to retain capital punishment, a new judicial test on the latter's constitutionality loomed as a certainty. It came on July 2, 1976, in a series of twenty-four (!) opinions in five cases covering various capital punishment laws from five states. By a vote of 7:2 the high tribunal ruled in an opinion, announced by Justice Stewart, that the death penalty is *not* inherently cruel or unusual, at least not in murder cases, *provided* that judges and juries have been given "adequate information and guidance" for determining whether the sentence is appropriate in a particular case. (*Gregg v. Georgia,* 428 U.S. 513.) But the Court held 5:4 in 1976 that "mandatory" capital punishment laws that require the death penalty for every defendant convicted of one or more of five categories of murder may not be imposed (*Roberts v. Louisiana,* 428 U.S. 335), and it also disallowed a similar North Carolina law (*Woodson v. North Carolina,* 428 U.S. 280). Louisiana tried to rescue the law by applying it only to anyone convicted of murdering a fireman or a policeman, but it, too, fell 5:4 (*Roberts v. Louisiana II,* 431 U.S. 633 [1977]). Georgia's attempt to render rape a capital crime was struck down, also in 1977, by the Court 7:2, assuming it was applied to an "adult woman," as constituting an impermissible cruel and unusual punishment. (*Coker v. Georgia,* 433 U.S. 584.) As the Court put it 7:1 in 1978, "every conceivable mitigating factor" must be considered. (*Lockett v. Ohio,* 438 U.S. 586.) Thus, it overruled a conviction in 1982 involving the brutal, unprovoked murder of a traffic policeman by a sixteen-year old using a sawed-off shotgun, holding 5:4 via Justice Powell that the accused's "uniqueness as an individual" had not been properly taken into account. (*Eddings v. Oklahoma,* 455 U.S. 104.) See also the Court's proscription of execution of insane prisoners, again 5:4, in *Ford v. Wainwright,* 54 LW 4799 (1986). But it allowed 5:4 the imposition of the death penalty for *accomplices,* even if the latter neither killed nor intended to kill. (*Tison v. Arizona,* 55 LW 4496 [1987]). And in a dramatic 5:4 decision, written by Justice Powell in 1987, the Justices ruled that a state's capital punishment system was constitutional despite the fact that killers of white people have been more frequently sentenced to die than killers of blacks. (*McCleskey v. Kemp,* 55 LW 4537). Obviously the Court, although granting the constitutionality of the death penalty, has rendered its application extremely difficult, lacking a specific request by the accused to be put to death (as had occurred nine times at this writing, March 1988). The number of executions since the 1976 decision stood at 98 at that time, with some 1,900 individuals on death row.

1963: Clarence Earl Gideon's Right to Counsel Case. Of far greater significance, because of the large numbers of individuals affected, is the celebrated case of *Gideon v. Wainwright.*[155] It is probably the most famous "incorporation decision" since *Palko.* In effect, it nationalized the right to counsel in *all*—save certain misdemeanor—criminal cases, *be they capital or non-capital.* As indicated earlier, a good many observers had quietly assumed that Justice Sutherland's language in the *Scottsboro Case*[156] had fully intended to incorporate the right to counsel in criminal cases generally. This understanding seemed to be confirmed by Justice Cardozo's choice of words in *Palko*—"the right of one accused of crime to the benefit of counsel"[157]—but the Court held to the contrary in the case of *Betts v. Brady*[158] in 1942. There, Justice Owen J. Roberts, speaking for a 6 : 3 majority, had ruled that the due process clause of the Fourteenth Amendment did *not* require counsel to be furnished by a state (here Maryland) in *non-capital* criminal cases unless "special" or "exceptional" circumstances, such as "mental illness," "youth," or "lack of education," were present. It was the *Betts* ruling that was specifically overturned by a unanimous Supreme Court, some twenty-one years later, with the opinion delivered with great conviction and satisfaction by the same man who had dissented in *Betts*—Justice Black.

The *Gideon* case, about which so much has been written,[159] and for good cause, reached the highest tribunal on a writ of *certiorari* as a result of a penciled petition *in forma pauperis,*[160] composed with painstaking precision on lined prison-regulation paper by Clarence Earl Gideon. Without a lawyer and penniless, he had been committed to a Florida jail as a result of a criminal conviction for "having broken and entered a poolroom with intent to commit a misdemeanor"[161] on the

---

[155]372 U.S. 335 (1963).

[156]*Powell v. Alabama,* 287 U.S. 45 (1932).

[157]*Palko v. Connecticut,* 302 U.S. 319 (1937), at 324.

[158]316 U.S. 455.

[159]The best full-length book—a superb account—is Anthony Lewis, *Gideon's Trumpet* (New York: Random House, 1964). Gideon died in 1972; his name now a household word in the annals of justice. A gravesite service in Hannibal, Missouri, in 1984 honored him as "the catalyst for the U.S. Public Defender system."

[160]"In the form of a pauper; as a poor man."

[161]A misdemeanor is an indictable offense, not usually serious enough to be classified as a crime—but it is so in Florida and increasingly so elsewhere. In 1972, however, all imprisonable misdemeanors, beyond mere fine cases, were accorded full *Gideon* rights

strength of testimony by a man who later turned out to have been the culprit himself! Gideon's request for counsel to represent him at his trial had been refused because of Florida's then valid requirement under the *Betts* precedent, that court-appointed counsel be reserved for capital criminal cases. To Gideon's warm plea in the courtroom, "Your Honor, the United States Constitution says I am entitled to be represented by Counsel," Trial Judge Robert L. McCreary, Jr., could only say, in accordance with his Florida mandate, "I am sorry, but I cannot appoint Counsel to represent you in this case."[162] Gideon thereupon acted as his own lawyer—but not too successfully: found guilty, he was sentenced to five years' imprisonment.

No knowledgeable observer of the judicial process and the Supreme Court was surprised that the Court overturned the *Betts* decision so decisively and unanimously[163] when Gideon managed to get his case "up"—his appeal before the Supreme Court briefed and argued by the Court-appointed, crack Washington attorney and future Associate Justice of the highest tribunal, Abe Fortas. Briefs *amicii curiae*[164] from only two states—Alabama and North Carolina—supported Florida's plea to the Court that it leave *Betts v. Brady*[165] intact; yet twenty-three states argued, in Justice Black's words, "that *Betts* was an anachronism when handed down and that it should now be overruled." "We agree," concluded Black triumphantly, noting that in its *Betts* decision the Court had "departed from the sound wisdom upon which its holding in *Powell v. Alabama*[166] rested." Ruling squarely that a state's failure to appoint counsel in a non-capital case—whether requested to do so or not— deprived the indigent defendant in a criminal proceeding of due process of law under the Fourteenth Amendment, as comprehended by the right

---

(*Argersinger v. Hamlin*, 407 U.S. 25), and they were unanimously made retroactive one year thereafter (*Berry v. Cincinnati*, 414 U.S. 29), as *Gideon* had also been in 1963 in *Pickelseimer v. Wainwright*, 375 U.S. 2. However, the Court ruled 5:4 in 1979 that *Argersinger* and *Berry* extend only to those instances in which there is a "likelihood" of actual imprisonment, as contrasted with a mere "possibility." Thus, a *fine* in a petty case would *not* trigger the *Gideon* or *Argersinger* right to assigned counsel. (*Scott v. Illinois*, 440 U.S. 367.)

[162]*Gideon v. Wainwright, op. cit.*, at 335–36.

[163]Justices Douglas and Harlan wrote separate concurring opinions.

[164]A brief *amicus curiae*, i.e., "friend of the Court," enables an interested third party to enter the case, with the consent of the other litigants and/or the Court.

[165]316 U.S. 455 (1942).

[166]287 U.S. 45 (1932).

to counsel requirements of the Sixth, Black remarked that it was "an obvious truth" that "in our adversary system of criminal justice any person hailed into court who is too poor to hire a lawyer cannot be assured a fair trial unless counsel is provided for him."[167] Another long-overdue aspect of incorporation had thus been accomplished, one which, as will be determined in the next chapter, was to be significantly broadened in succeeding years.[168]

Moreover, for once Congress responded promptly and affirmatively by enacting the Criminal Justice Act (C.J.A.) of 1964, designed to provide more adequate representation of defendants in federal courts in all non-petty cases. Not only that, but within two years the legislatures and courts of twenty-three states took specific actions to implement the spirit as well as the letter of *Gideon*. As amended in 1970, the 1964 C.J.A. authorizes both the creation of federal or community public defender organizations in "high volume districts" and the necessary compensation for legal assistance at *every* step and stage of the criminal process, from the arrest to appeals, *including* post-conviction and ancillary proceedings relative to the criminal trial. No wonder the *Gideon* case stands as a landmark! However, to limit cascading claims of "poor representation," the Court, in an interesting and important 8 : 1 decision in 1984—written by Justice O'Connor, with Justice Marshall in lone dissent—ruled that to prevail in such a claim a defendant must demonstrate that the lawyer's work fell "below prevailing professional norms" and that without counsel's professional errors the outcome would have been different.[169] Yet, perhaps believing a more broadly gauged standard to be apposite, the Court, just a few months later, ruled 7 : 2, in a Brennan opinion one year later, over dissents by Burger and Rehnquist, and for the first time, that a criminal defendant has a "constitutional right to *effective* assistance by counsel on [the first]

---

[167]*Gideon v. Wainwright, op. cit.*, at 355. On remand to the Florida trial court, Gideon was quickly retried and acquitted with the aid of a local attorney.

[168]See, for example, these decisions liberalizing even further the right to counsel: *Massiah v. United States*, 377 U.S. 201 (1964); *Escobedo v. Illinois*, 387 U.S. 478 (1964); the series of June 1966 cases expanding the *Escobedo* decision, headed by *Miranda v. Arizona*, 384 U.S. 436; *Orozco v. Texas*, 394 U.S. 324 (1969); *Coleman v. Alabama*, 399 U.S. 1 (1970); *Argersinger v. Hamlin*, 407 U.S. 25 (1972); and *United States v. Henry*, 447 U.S. 264 (1980).

[169]*Strickland v. Washington*, 467 U.S. 1267.

appeal.''[170] And it also held, 8 : 1, that a state must provide an *indigent criminal* defendant with free psychiatric assistance in preparing an insanity defense if the defendant's sanity "at the time of the crime is seriously in question.''[171] Obviously, the issue of "effectiveness" of counsel remains far from settled; it is a veritable hornets' nest. And just around the corner waited another contentious sector of the Bill of Rights: the Fifth Amendment's stricture against compulsory self-incrimination.

1964: The Self-Incrimination Cases. The frequently predicted and much publicized *self-incrimination safeguards* were incorporated in a significant dual decision in the last days of the 1963–64 term. In two cases[172] the Court dramatically overruled its 1908 decision in the *Twining* case,[173] thus adopting Justice Harlan's lone dissent therein to render another signal contribution to the broadening concept of criminal jurisprudence.

The first case was from Connecticut and concerned one William Malloy, who had been arrested during a gambling raid in 1959 by Hartford police. Pleading guilty to the crime of "pool-selling," he was sentenced to one year in jail and fined $500. Some sixteen months thereafter Malloy was ordered to testify in an official, court-sanctioned inquiry into alleged gambling and other criminal activities in the county. Asked a number of questions about events surrounding his own arrest and conviction, Malloy refused to answer any of them "on the grounds it may tend to incriminate me." He was held in contempt and incarcerated "until he was willing to answer the questions." His appeal via a writ of *habeas corpus* was rejected all along the judicial hierarchy in Connecticut, its highest tribunal ultimately ruling, *inter alia,* that the Fifth Amendment's privilege against self-incrimination was not available to a witness in a state proceeding and that the Fourteenth Amendment "extended no privilege to him." The Connecticut courts relied, of course, on past Supreme Court rulings to that effect. But they were not

---

[170]*Evitts v. Lucy,* 469 U.S. 387 (1985). However, one year later, the U.S. Court of Appeals for the District of Columbia interpreted *Evitts* to apply solely to "grossly inadequate" representation. (*Watson v. United States,* 54 LW 2559.)

[171]*Ake v. Oklahoma,* 470 U.S. 68.

[172]*Malloy v. Hogan,* 378 U.S. 1 (1964), and *Murphy v. Waterfront Commission of New York Harbor,* 378 U.S. 52 (1964).

[173]*Twining v. New Jersey,* 211 U.S. 78 (see p. 65, *supra*).

to fall. Over vigorous dissenting opinions by Justices Harlan and Clark, who firmly rejected nationalization of the Fifth, and by Justices White and Stewart, who questioned the propriety of the privilege's invocation in the instant case, a majority of five members of the Court extended the "incorporated" side of the Cardozo table. Speaking for the Chief Justice, Justices Black, Douglas, Goldberg (who had replaced the retired Frankfurter two years earlier), and himself, Justice Brennan held that the Fourteenth Amendment, which assures all citizens due process of law, guaranteed the petitioner the protection of the Fifth Amendment's privilege against compulsory self-incrimination. In language redolent with appeals for a system of "nationalized" criminal justice, Brennan pronounced the *Twining*[174] and *Adamson*[175] decisions wrong constitutional law and announced that, "*a fortiorari*,"

> [t]he Fourteenth Amendment secures against state invasion the same privilege that the Fifth Amendment guarantees against federal infringement—the right of a person to remain silent unless he chooses to speak in the unfettered exercise of his own free will, and to suffer no penalty . . . for such silence.[176]

The New York companion case turned on the refusal of William Murphy to give testimony to the New York Waterfront Commission, which was then investigating a work stoppage at certain New Jersey piers. Murphy had been promised immunity from prosecution in return for his testimony; but he refused this offer, fearing that his answers might incriminate him under *federal* law to which the grant of immunity did not purport to extend. Overruling its own precedents,[177] the Supreme Court, without dissent this time, categorically rejected "the established rule that one jurisdiction within our federal structure may

[174]*Ibid.*

[175]*Adamson v. California*, 332 U.S. 46 (1947). The specifics of *Adamson*, i.e., comments upon failure by the accused to take the stand, were overruled in *Griffin v. California* 381 U.S. 957 (1965), Griffin's victorious counsel being the same attorney, Morris Lavine, who had lost in *Adamson* eighteen years earlier! In an elaborate "follow-up" 1981 decision the Court held 8 : 1 that, upon a defendant's request, the presiding judge *must* instruct the jury not to draw an adverse inference from the invocation of the Fifth Amendment by someone on trial. (*Carter v. Kentucky*, 450 U.S. 288.)

[176]*Malloy v. Hogan, op. cit.*, at 8.

[177]*United States v. Murdock*, 284 U.S. 141 (1931); *Feldman v. United States*, 322 U.S. 487 (1944); *Knapp v. Schweitzer*, 357 U.S. 371 (1958).

compel a witness to give testimony which could be used to convict him of a crime in another."[178] Although two of the justices, in a concurring opinion by Harlan, joined by Clark, objected to the "mixing together" of the Fifth and the Fourteenth Amendments, the Court unanimously agreed with its spokesman, Justice Arthur J. Goldberg: "We hold that the Constitutional privilege against self-incrimination protects a state witness against incrimination under Federal as well as state law and a Federal witness against incrimination under state as well as Federal law."[179] While the case featured three separate opinions[179a]—two of these concurring on different grounds—and the individual justices may have accepted the Goldberg conclusion for varying reasons, it nevertheless represented another broadening of the application of the Bill of Rights to the states.

1965 and 1967: The Texas Confrontation of Witnesses Cases. Next in line was the clause of the Sixth Amendment that provides: "In all criminal prosecutions, the accused shall enjoy the right . . . to be confronted with the witnesses against him. . . ." Did it, too, apply with equal effect to proceedings in state courts by virtue of the due process clause of Amendment Fourteen? Yes, held a unanimous Supreme Court, although the four opinions in the case were based on different grounds.

Granville Pointer (and a cohort, Earl Dillard) had been charged with robbing Kenneth W. Phillips of $375 "by assault, or violence, or by putting in fear of life or bodily injury."[180] At the preliminary hearing before a state judge, called the "examining trial" in Texas, Phillips gave detailed testimony including an identification of Pointer, who, although present throughout the hearing, had no attorney and made no effort to cross-examine Phillips. At Pointer's trial the State submitted evidence that Phillips had recently moved to California and had no intention whatever of returning to Texas. The trial judge permitted the prosecution to introduce the transcript of Phillip's testimony at the preliminary hearing, over the repeated objections of Pointer's counsel. In each instance the trial judge overruled the defense objections on the

[178]*Murphy v. Waterfront Commission of New York Harbor, op. cit.,* at 77.
[179]*Ibid.,* at 77–78. The holding was extended (7:2) in 1979 to apply to testimony before a grand jury. (*New Jersey v. Portash,* 440 U.S. 450.)
[179a]Those by Justices Goldberg, White, and Harlan.
[180]*Pointer v. Texas,* 380 U.S. 400 (1965).

ground that Pointer had had ample opportunity to cross-examine Phillips at the preliminary hearing stage. The Texas Court of Criminal Appeals affirmed Pointer's conviction—but the Supreme Court of the United States reversed it 9 : 0, though it was divided on the bases for its action.

Justice Black, speaking for the Court, referred to the spate of recent decisions holding applicable to the states various guarantees in the Bill of Rights, including the Sixth Amendment's right to counsel and the Fifth's guarantee against compulsory self-incrimination. He ruled: "We hold today that the Sixth Amendment's right of an accused to confront the witnesses against him is likewise a fundamental right and is made obligatory on the States by the Fourteenth Amendment."[181] Black then observed that the inclusion in the Sixth Amendment of *the right of confrontation* "reflects the belief of the Framers . . . that confrontation was a fundamental right essential to a fair trial in a criminal prosecution."[182] And he concluded that since the right of confrontation comprehended the right to cross-examine, reversal was mandatory. Henceforth, the same standards that protect litigants against federal encroachment of this right would be applicable and enforceable against the states. A precedent of more than six decades thus stood overruled.[183]

Three concurring opinions were filed, each dealing with the "incorporation doctrine." Justice Goldberg, evidently eager to go on record with *his* approach to the problem—for he had not been on the Court when the issue was joined in the *Adamson* case[184] in 1947—acknowledged that, on the record, the "incorporation doctrine" had never really commanded a majority of the Court. However, he sternly rejected both the Frankfurter case-by-case "was it due process?" approach and the *Palko* "is it implicit in the concept of ordered liberty?" test. In effect, he embraced the applicability to the states of the *fundamental* guarantees of the Bill of Rights, and he clearly did not particularly care *how* this was done by the Court or by what name the process would be

[181]*Ibid.*, at 403.
[182]*Ibid.*, at 404.
[183]*West v. Louisiana*, 194 U.S. 258 (1904). Unlike Clarence Earl Gideon, however, Granville Pointer, when retried below, was convicted again (Phillips now appearing as the prosecution's star witness) and was sentenced to prison for five years to life.
[184]332 U.S. 46.

known—just so long as those guarantees were indeed made obligatory for the states via the Fourteenth Amendment.[185]

Justice Harlan, while concurring in the result of *Pointer*, nevertheless re-expressed his conviction that the majority's holding constituted "another step in the onward march of the long-since discredited 'incorporation' doctrine."[186] Exhorting the Court to return to a policy of "leaving room for differences among states," he wrote that *he* would have reversed Pointer's conviction on the basis that the procedure followed by Texas had deprived Pointer of due process of law guaranteed by the Fourteenth Amendment, "independently of the Sixth."[187] Harlan freely acknowledged that the right of confrontation is indeed "implicit in the concept of ordered liberty," which mandated its observance by Texas. But he lashed out at "incorporation" as being "incompatible with our constitutionally ordained federal system" as well as "unsound doctrine."[188] Once again he pointed to what he saw as the value of the states as "laboratories" that must not be "subordinated to federal power." Taking issue with that contention, Justice Goldberg wrote in his concurring opinion that while it was good that the states should be able to try social and economic experiments, he did not believe that this "includes the power to experiment with the fundamental liberties of citizens safeguarded by the Bill of Rights."[189]

In his brief concurring opinion, Justice Stewart took to task the Black opinion for the Court as a "questionable tour de force . . . entirely unnecessary to the decision of this case. . . ."[190] He said that *he* would have reversed Pointer's conviction on the simple ground that Pointer had been clearly deprived of liberty without due process of law in express violation of the Fourteenth Amendment—which, of course, constitutes the case-by-case approach to the applicability question. But on the same day the Court proceeded to apply the new ruling in reversing a conviction in a similar case.[191] And in 1967 it logically, and

---

[185]*Pointer v. Texas, op. cit.*, at 414.
[186]*Ibid.*, at 408.
[187]*Ibid.*
[188]*Ibid.*, at 409.
[189]*Ibid.*, at 413.
[190]*Ibid.*, at 410.
[191]*Douglas v. Alabama*, 380 U.S. 415 (1965), with the same Court "line-up," although Justice Brennan wrote the opinion here.

unanimously, extended the *Pointer* holding to cover compulsory process to obtain and thus to confront *favorable* witnesses, too (*Pointer* having dealt with *adverse* witnesses), in another Texas controversy.[192] Again, the Court was unanimous, its decision written by Chief Justice Warren—and again Justice Harlan's concurring opinion represented an important lecture on the basic incorporation controversy.

1965: "Incorporation" Reargued: The Connecticut Birth Control Case. As if to continue the "argument" among themselves on incorporation, which they had once again raised in the first *Texas Confrontation* case[193] in 1965, the Supreme Court justices addressed themselves to it with gusto in their controversial six-opinion decision in *Griswold v. Connecticut,* now generally referred to as the *Birth Control* case.[194] Our concern here is less with the merits of the decision than with the reasoning employed by the six opinion writers on the incorporation problem (which, depending upon one's analysis, either did or did not have something to do with the holding in the case itself). It suffices to note that the Court, by a 7 : 2 vote, invalidated an old and generally unenforced Connecticut statute that made it a crime for any person, married or single, to *use* any drug or other article or device for the purpose of preventing conception or to give information or instruction in their use. The Court's opinion was delivered by Justice Douglas and its judgment of reversal of the defendants'[195] convictions was agreed to by the Chief Justice and Associate Justices Clark, Harlan, Brennan, White, and Goldberg. But only Clark fully accepted Douglas's reasoning (at least he wrote no opinion); Harlan, White, and Goldberg wrote separate concurring opinions, with the Chief Justice and Brennan joining in Goldberg's. Justices Black and Stewart wrote separate dissenting opinions, each specifically also joining the other's. There is now some

[192]*Washington v. Texas,* 388 U.S. 14. Jackie Washington's Sixth and Fourteenth Amendment rights were held fatally encumbered because, under an applied Texas rule, a co-defendant was barred from appearing as a witness in his favor.

[193]*Pointer v. Texas,* 380 U.S. 400.

[194]381 U.S. 479.

[195]They were Estelle T. Griswold, Executive Director of the Planned Parenthood League of Connecticut, and Dr. C. Lee Buxton, a licensed physician teaching at Yale University's School of Medicine, who served as medical director for the League's New Haven Center. They gave information and medical advice to married persons on means of preventing conception, were found guilty of violating the Connecticut statute at issue, and were fined $100 each. Their appeal was on Fourteenth Amendment grounds.

fairly strong evidence that the godfather of the Douglas opinion was Brennan.

Douglas noted at the outset that the Court was here confronted with a *bona fide* controversy that it could properly decide, one involving "the constitutional rights of married people with whom [the defendants, leaders of the Planned Parenthood League] had a professional relationship."[196] He reviewed several Court decisions that, in his judgment, established "that specific guarantees in the Bill of Rights have *penumbras*, formed by emanations from those guarantees that help give them life and substance,"[197] penumbras that reached areas not specifically mentioned in the Bill. He thereupon cited five different amendments the "penumbras" of which "create zones of privacy," among them the First Amendment's protection of the right of association, the Third's prohibition of quartering of soldiers in homes, the Fourth's guarantee against unreasonable searches and seizures, the Fifth's against compulsory self-incrimination. He added, in a coup of potential trail-blazing, the *Ninth Amendment*, justifying its inclusion as a beacon to illuminate "the zone of privacy created by [the] several fundamental constitutional guarantees."[198] The 1973 *Abortion Cases* were just around the jurisprudential corner.

Predictably, the concurring opinions raised the issue of "incorporation," and, specifically, whether—in the light of the expansive Douglas opinion—it was indeed limited to the Bill of Rights. Justice

[196]*Griswold v. Connecticut, op. cit.,* at 481.

[197]*Ibid.,* at 484 (Italics supplied.)

[198]*Ibid.,* at 485. Six years later, and this time squarely based on the equal protection clause as well as on considerations of "privacy," the Court, speaking through Justice Brennan—with only Chief Justice Burger in dissent—held 6:1 that Massachusetts could not outlaw the distribution of contraceptives to *single* persons when these are legally available to married ones. (*Eisenstadt v. Baird,* 405 U.S. 438 [1972].) The vote declaring the ninety-three-year-old law unconstitutional was only 4:3, however. And five years thereafter (1977), a seriously divided Court struck down 7:2, 6:3, and 5:4 New York State's broad anti-contraception advertising and distribution law on the following grounds: (1) violation of Amendment One (the State's proscription of the advertising or display of contraceptives); (2) violation of due process of law because of the rights of privacy inherent in Amendments Fourteen and Nine (the State's limitations of sales to physicians, pharmacies, and drugstores); and, (3) again invoking the recently found prerogatives of privacy emanating from due process considerations (the State's forbidding of the dispensing of contraceptives to those aged sixteen or younger). (*Carey v. Population Services International,* 431 U.S. 678.)

Harlan, in his separate concurring opinion, saw the issue in terms of the requirement of basic values that are "implicit in the concept of ordered liberty"—the *Palko* and case-by-case approach to the scope of the due process clause of the Fourteenth Amendment rather than "incorporation." He was persuaded that the Connecticut statute did unconstitutionally infringe the due process clause, which "stands . . . on its own bottom," and which is not dependent on "one or more provisions of the Bill of Rights . . . or any of their radiations. . . ."[199]

Justice Goldberg, whom the Chief Justice and Justice Brennan joined in his concurring opinion, made clear his conviction that the due process clause was neither limited to, nor necessarily so broad as, the Bill of Rights, but rather that it "protects those personal rights that are fundamental." In sweeping language, he emphasized the relevance of the Ninth Amendment to the Court's holding, contending that its language and history reveal that "the Framers of the Constitution believed that *there are additional fundamental rights, protected from government infringement, which exist alongside those fundamental rights specifically mentioned in the first eight constitutional amendments.*"[200] In other words, he viewed the Ninth Amendment—which Madison had proposed as a concession to Alexander Hamilton and James Wilson's opposition to a Bill of Rights, opposition based on the fear that non-enumerated rights would be jeopardized—as a lever for the protection of all those "fundamental rights" not specifically protected by the first eight via the "liberty" safeguard in the due process clauses of both the Fifth and the Fourteenth Amendments. The Ninth, he reiterated several times in his opinion, "is surely relevant in showing the existence of other fundamental personal rights now protected from state as well as federal infringement."[201]

Goldberg thus rejected the Black approach to incorporation because it would *limit the rights eligible for incorporation to those specifically*

[199]*Ibid.*, at 500.

[200]*Ibid.*, at 488. (Italics supplied.)

[201]E.g., *ibid.*, at 493. Many scholars support this view: e.g., Bennett B. Patterson, the author of one of the very few works on the Ninth Amendment, *The Forgotten Ninth Amendment* (Indianapolis: Bobbs-Merrill, 1955)—although Patterson acknowledges that the Ninth may well simply be viewed as a "basic statement of the inherent natural rights of the individual" (p. 4).

listed in the Bill of Rights. For to Black, the committed literalist, it had to be spelled out verbatim in the document to be applicable.

Justice White's relatively brief concurring opinion saw a clear-cut violation of substantive due process by the Connecticut statute because of its "too sweeping" provisions which entered "a realm of family life which the state cannot enter."[202] In short, incorporation or no incorporation, the crux of the matter to White was that the due process clause, which prohibits states from depriving any person of "liberty" without due process of law, was clearly violated by the restrictions of the Connecticut law.

In dissenting, Justice Black took pains to announce his complete agreement with all of the "graphic and eloquent strictures and criticisms" leveled at what his colleague Stewart, dissenting with him, termed "this uncommonly silly . . . asinine . . . law"—under which no one had ever been prosecuted—but he rejected the majority's collective reasoning. "[T]he law is every bit as [personally] offensive to me as . . . it is to my Brethren," he began his dissent.[203] Characteristically, he noted the absence of a *specific* constitutional provision that proscribed an invasion of privacy, which he styled "a broad, abstract, and ambiguous concept"—one he viewed merely as a "statement" of policy—and he warned that the Court's reliance on the Ninth Amendment together with the due process clause would give the "federal judiciary the power to invalidate any legislative act which the judges find irrational, unreasonable or offensive."[204] To accept such an approach, he believed, was to revive the "shocking" doctrine rejected

---

[202]*Ibid.*, at 502. Since *Griswold*, a spate of Ninth Amendment litigation has been spawned. Among the claims and/or decisions: the Ninth does *not* grant a right: to smoke marijuana (*People v. Glaser*, 238 C.A.2d 819, 48 Cal. Reptr. 427 [1965]); to refuse army induction (*U.S. v Uhl*, 436 F.2d 773, 9th Cir. [1970]); or to marry a person of the same sex (*Baker v. Nelson*, 489 U.S. 810 [1971]). The applicability of the Ninth to the long-hair syndrome remained guarded and clouded (cf. *Dawson v. School Board*, 322 F. Supp. 286 [1971], and *Davis v. Firment*, 269 F. Supp. 524), for a number of years; but a 7 : 2 decision in 1976 in favor of the application of state authority under duly guarded police powers seems to have settled the matter, at least for the time being. (*Kelley v. Johnson*, 425 U.S. 238.) *Griswold*, of course, was parent to the 1973 *Abortion* cases of *Roe v. Wade* and *Doe v. Bolton*, 410 U.S. 113 and 410 U.S. 479, respectively. (See the following pages.)

[203]*Loc. cit.*, at 507.

[204]*Ibid.*, at 509, 511.

by the Court three decades earlier under which it had for so long struck down—by virtue of a power "bestowed on the Court by the Court"[205]—federal and state statutes in the *economic* realm because of alleged violations of substantive due process of law based on such notions as the sanctity of contracts. "Privacy," he declared, "is a broad, abstract, and ambiguous concept" that can be readily expanded or shrunk by later decisions. This proved to be a prophetic statement, of course: in January 1973 down came the bombshell privacy-based, six-opinion *Abortion* cases, holding 7 : 2 that the right of "privacy," derived largely from the "liberty" concept of due process of law under the Fourteenth Amendment, and partly from the Ninth (*stare decisis Griswold*), rendered unconstitutional all state laws (46) that prohibited or restricted a woman's right to obtain an abortion during the first three months of pregnancy.[206] Lest he be misunderstood, Black reiterated his belief that the Court does have the power, "which it should exercise," to hold laws unconstitutional where they are forbidden by the Constitution, and that he fully believed, then as before, that the specifics of that document are incorporated and made applicable to the states via the due process clause of the Fourteenth Amendment. Yet, like Stewart in his dissenting opinion—who sarcastically commented that "to say that the Ninth Amendment has anything to do with this case is to turn somersaults with history"[207]—Black could find nothing in the Constitution

---

[205]*Ibid.*, at 520.

[206]*Roe v. Wade*, 410 U.S. 113, and *Doe v. Bolton*, 410 U.S. 179. The holding was made retroactive in a 9 : 0 *per curiam* decision in 1975 in *Louisiana State Bd. of Medical Examiners v. Rosen*, 419 U.S. 1098—and both reconfirmed and indeed extended in 1976 in a series of cases headed by *Planned Parenthood of Central Missouri v. Danforth*, 429 U.S. 52, and in 1979 in *Bellotti v. Baird*, 443 U.S. 622, although a mite equivocally. But, as Black had warned, it has also proved at least partly "shrinkable." Thus, a trio of 1977 cases held that neither the Constitution nor federal legislation *compels* states to fund non-therapeutic abortions for women in financial need. (*Beal v. Doe, Maher v. Doe,* and *Poelker v. Doe*, 432 U.S. 438, 526, and 519, respectively. See also *Colautti v. Franklin*, 439 U.S. 379 [1979].) And a six-opinion 5 : 4 decision in 1980 upheld the Hyde Amendment enacted by Congress, banning Medicaid financing by the federal government of abortions in all but a handful of cases (e.g., instances of promptly reported rape or incest or "where the life of the mother would be endangered if the fetus were carried to term"). (*Harris v. McRae*, 448 U.S. 297.) *Cf. H. L. v. Matheson*, 450 U.S. 398 (1981), backing 6 : 3 a Utah pre-aboration parental *notification*—but *not* interdiction—requirement for teen-agers living at home. See also the trio of 1983 abortion decisions, broadly affirming *Roe* and *Doe*, and the 1986 holding in *Thornburgh v. American College of Obstetricians and Gynecologists* (cited in Chapter I, *supra*, fn. 19).

[207]*Griswold, op. cit.*, at 527.

and its amendments to forbid the passage of the Connecticut law. Quoting from his dissenting opinion in *Adamson v. California*[208] almost two decades earlier, he cautioned that

> . . . to pass upon the constitutionality of statutes by looking to the particular standards enumerated in the Bill of Rights and other parts of the Constitution is one thing; to invalidate statutes because of application of "natural law" deemed to be above and undefined by the Constitution is another.[209]

Amplifying this position in his *A Constitutional Faith* three years later, Black observed that "even though I like my privacy as well as the next one, I am nevertheless compelled to admit that government has a right to invade it unless prohibited by some specific constitutional provision." For he could "find in the Constitution no language which either specifically or impliedly grants to all individuals a constitutional right of privacy."[210]

Black's formula always was that the First Amendment protects freeom of *expression,* and it does that absolutely. Yet it does not protect "conduct" ("physical activities")—be that conduct a racial "sit-in"[211] or the use of contraceptive devices.[212] And he quoted with full agreement a famous statement by Judge Learned Hand on the matter of judicial invalidation of legislation offensive to the jurists' personal preferences: "For myself it would be most irksome to be ruled by a bevy of Platonic Guardians, even if I knew how to choose them, which I assuredly do not."[213] But in the footnote giving the above statement's citation, Black had to acknowledge that although he agreed with Hand's

---

[208]U.S. 46 (1947), at 90–92.

[209]*Griswold v. Connecticut, op. cit.,* at 525.

[210](New York: Alfred A. Knopf, 1968), p. 9. How subjective the concept of "privacy" is, and how vexatious its judicial application, may be illustrated by pointing to two lower court decisions in 1970 which, *both* citing *Griswold,* struck down a Texas sodomy statute as an unconstitutional invasion of privacy while upholding a 1796 New Jersey statute proscribing fornication! (*Buchanan v. Bachelor,* 308 F. Supp. 729, and *State v. Lutz,* 57 N.J. 314.) But late in 1977 the New Jersey Supreme Court did rule the old statute unconstitutional, 5 : 2, as a violation of "the right to privacy." (*State v. Saunders,* 75 N.J. 200.) To compound the "privacy" issue, the U.S. Supreme Court in 1986 upheld 5 : 4 Georgia's anti-sodomy statute, even as applied to consensual adults in private. (*Bowers v. Hardwick,* 54 LW 5064.)

[211]See Chapter VII, *infra.*

[212]*Griswold v. Connecticut, op. cit.,* at 507–8.

[213]*Ibid.,* at 526.

"criticism of use of the due process formula, I do not agree with all the views he expressed about construing the specific guarantees of the Bill of Rights."[214] Of course, Black could not; for, ironically, in his 1958 book, *The Bill of Rights*[215]—which contains the "platonic guardians" statement so approvingly quoted by Black—Hand, rejecting any double-standard justifications between "economic" and "civil libertarian" rights, took considerable pains to contend that the Court, on which Black then served, had gone too far, in a number of cases, in holding legislation to be in violation of *specific* guarantees of the Bill of Rights.[216]

1966: Formally Incorporating the Right to Trial by an "Impartial" Jury. The first incorporation by the Court following its thorough *reprise* analysis and exposition of the basic issues in *Griswold* turned out to be something that had long been assumed to have been incorporated—the right to trial by an *impartial* jury. Indeed, the requirement of a *fair trial*, a cornerstone of the judicial process, would naturally assume trial by an *impartial* jury, provided a jury trial were granted in the first place, of course. (The right to a trial by jury *per se* was not incorporated until the *Duncan* case[217]—see below—and it reached only criminal cases above the petty level.) However, although disposing of the matter in a *per curiam* opinion,[218] the Court evidently deemed it necessary and/or politic to inform the states that the Sixth Amendment's requirement for an "impartial" jury was indeed applicable to them as well as to the federal government. The case concerned a bailiff named Gladden who made the following statements to the sequestered jury trying one Lee E. A. Parker: "Oh, that wicked fellow, he is guilty. . . . If there is anything wrong, the Supreme Court will correct it."[219] The Court did—although hardly along the lines Bailiff Gladden could have expected!

[214]*Ibid.*, n. 23.

[215](Cambridge: Harvard University Press, 1958.)

[216]*Ibid.*, pp. 35–45.

[217]*Duncan v. Louisiana*, 391 U.S. 145 (1968). See the discussion, pp. 81–84, *infra*.

[218]An unsigned, normally very brief, opinion for the Court, its authorship unknown to the outside world, applying *res judicata* (settled law).

[219]*Parker v. Gladden*, 385 U.S. 363 (1966), at 364. In his excellent full-length study, "The Supreme Court and the Second Bill of Rights" (Madison: University of Wisconsin, 1981), Professor Richard C. Cortner disagrees with the above conclusion that *Parker* incorporated the impartial requirement of Amendment Six. Instead, he views *Parker* as a confirmation of the Sixth's confrontation and cross-examination rights. Justice Brennan for one, however, expressed agreement with my position in response to an oral *quaere* (January 15, 1969). The vote in *Parker* was 8:1, Justice Harlan dissenting (at 366).

1967: The Right to a Speedy Trial. With the right to a *public* trial by jury incorporated in 1948, it was only a question of time until the collateral Sixth Amendment requirement of a *speedy* trial—which had received recognition as early as 1166 in the Assize of Clarendon— would also be rendered applicable by the Court. Its vehicle became the case of a professor of zoology at Duke University, Peter H. Klopfer, who had been indicted by the State of North Carolina for criminal trespass after he took part in a sit-in at the then segregated Watts Motel and Restaurant in Chapel Hill. The controversy arose in 1964, and Professor Klopfer was indeed tried soon thereafter; however, the jury failed to agree on a verdict and a mistrial was declared by Trial Judge Raymond B. Mallard, thus heralding a new trial. A year passed without a second trial, and when Professor Klopfer officially demanded either to be tried forthwith or have his case dismissed, the judge granted, instead, State Prosecutor (District Solicitor) Thomas Cooper's motion for a *nolle prosequi* (which permits a prosecutor to place an indictment in an inactive status, without bringing the case to trial, but "retaining it for use at any future time"—a procedure then permitted by thirty states). The exasperated Professor Klopfer appealed, arguing that this action denied his Sixth Amendment right to a speedy trial, which he regarded as applicable to the states. Denying his appeal, the North Carolina Supreme Court ruled in January of 1966 that a defendant's right to speedy trial—which the tribunal readily acknowledged—does not encompass "the right to compel the state to prosecute him." In Klopfer's instance this meant that he would continue to be subject to a retrial at any time, at the discretion of the state, on the basis of the "suspended" trespass indictment. He appealed to the Supreme Court of the United States.

In another milestone decision in constitutional development,[220] the Court unanimously sided with the appellant. Speaking for six justices as well as himself, Chief Justice Warren called the North Carolina practice at issue an "extraordinary criminal procedure," noting that the North Carolina Supreme Court's position "has been explicitly rejected by every other state court which has considered the question."[221] Clearly, he concluded, the procedure served to deny Professor Klopfer "the right to a speedy trial which we hold is guaranteed to him by the Sixth

---

[220]*Klopfer v. North Carolina*, 386 U.S. 213 (1967).
[221]*Ibid.*, at 219.

Amendment of the Constitution of the United States"[222]—thus incorporating the requirement. Not surprisingly on the basis of his record on the matter, Justice Harlan, while voting to reverse the North Carolina decision—noting that he "entirely agree[d] with the result reached in the Court"—wrote a separate concurring opinion in which he again voiced his rejection of what he viewed as the "rigid uniformity" in state procedures brought about by "incorporation" or "absorption," explaining that *he* would have struck down the state's procedure because it was violative of the "fundamental fairness" guaranteed by the due process of law clause of Amendment Fourteen.[223] Justice Stewart simply noted that he concurred, but did not elaborate. In 1974 Congress, led by the retiring Senator Sam J. Ervin, Jr. (D.-N.C.), enacted the Federal Speedy Trial Act,[224] setting up a schedule to be implemented over a five-year period of time limits—ultimately (June 30, 1980) reaching a low of a hundred days—during which criminal charges had to be either brought to trial or dropped. As to the precise nature of the time period to be considered, the Court ruled 7 : 1 in 1975 that it is the period between trial and *either* arrest or indictment, whichever comes first.[225]

---

[222]*Ibid.*, at 222. It was on denial-of-speedy trial grounds that, in 1980, Green Beret Doctor Jeffrey R. MacDonald found his conviction of the murder of his wife and two children overturned 2 : 1 by the United States Court of Appeals for the Fourth Circuit. (*United States v. MacDonald*, 632 F.2d 258.) But he was reconvicted in a subsequent trial.

[223]*Ibid.*, at 226–27. On remand to the trial court, the charges against Klopfer were dismissed. Had Harlan lived to witness them, he would very likely have approved the Court's actions in two 1971 cases, in which—without dissent—it declined to review two lower court holdings which, based on the facts at issue, held: (a) that an eighteen-month delay from arrest to trial did not necessarily deprive a defendant of his rights to a speedy trial (*Blevins v. U.S.*, 404 U.S. 823); and (b) that neither did a governmental delay for five years of an indictment after the alleged criminal offense took place (*Quinn v. U.S.*, 404 U.S. 850).

[224]18 U.S.C. §§ 3161 *et seq.*

[225]*Dillingham v. United States*, 423 U.S. 64. (The Chief Justice dissented.) In 1977, in a speedy-trial case ruling, a federal district court declared the statute unconstitutional as an "impermissible legislative encroachment on the judiciary." (*United States v. Howard*, 440 F. Supp. 1106.) On appeal, the U.S. Court of Appeals for the Fourth Circuit affirmed on *other* grounds, finding that "the issue of constitutionality was not raised and therefore not properly before it." (*Ibid.*, 590 F.2d 564, at 568 n.4.) The United States Supreme Court denied *certiorari* in 1979. (*Ibid.*, 440 U.S. 976.) Thus, notwithstanding the trial court's holding—which may be viewed as a declaratory judgment (see my *The Judicial Process, op. cit.*, pp. 375–76)—the Act remains the law of the land (Summer 1987), as amended and strengthened in 1979. Indeed, by 1980 some 96 percent of district criminal

1968 Gary Duncan's Right to a Trial by Jury in a Criminal Case. An appeal coming up from a decision by the Supreme Court of Louisiana afforded the United States Supreme Court the long-anticipated occasion to incorporate the *right to be tried by jury in criminal cases* (above the petty level).[226] With the right to a "fair," a "public," an "impartial," and a "speedy" trial already established as incumbent upon the states, it was only a question of time until the Court would similarly deal with the fundamental right of a trial by jury *per se,* at least in criminal cases. Yet it took until 1968 and Gary Duncan's appeal of a conviction for simple battery, which, under Louisiana law, was punishable by a maximum of two years' imprisonment and a a $300 fine. Duncan, a nineteen-year-old black convicted in Plaquemines parish[227] court of slapping a white boy on the elbow and sentenced to sixty days in jail and a $150 fine, had sought a trial by jury. But because the Louisiana Constitution granted jury trials only in cases in which capital punishment or imprisonment at hard labor might be imposed, the trial judge denied Duncan's request, and the latter appealed to the Supreme Court, contending that the Sixth and Fourteenth Amendments to the federal Constitution secured the right of jury trial in state criminal prosecutions, such as his, where a sentence as long as two years could be pronounced. The Court agreed, 7:2.

---

cases reached trial within 100 days. In 1981, however, a federal district court once again declared the act *ultra vires* as "an unconstitutional encroachment upon the Judiciary" (*United States v. Brainer,* 515 F. Supp. 627 [D.Md.], at 630—only to see itself reversed by the Fourth Circuit Court of Appeals one year later: *ibid.,* 691 F. 2d 691). It is fair to conclude that, in effect, the speedy trial issue, *pace* the 1974 statute, is now still demonstrably governed by the Supreme Court's unanimous holding—two years prior to the Speedy Trial Act's birth—that the Sixth Amendment's speedy trial guarantee, in conjunction with the Fifth Amendment's speedy trial guarantee, in conjunction with the Fifth and Fourteenth Amendments' due process of law mandates, must be treated on a case-by-case basis; that, according to the unanimous opinion's author, Justice Powell (White, with Brennan, concurring separately), an "admittedly difficult" balancing test for determining a defendant's constitutional right to a speedy trial must be applied. Such tests, carefully applied, concluded Powell, would meet constitutional obligations vis-à-vis the state, defendants, and judicial obligations under the separation of powers. (*Barker v. Wingo,* 407 U.S. 514.) Further such balancing occurred in 1986 when the Supreme Court ruled 5:4 that the speedy trial requirement does not bar the federal government from prosecuting Indian activist Dennis Banks and three others on ten-year-old firearms charges. (*United States v. Kenneth Moses Loud Hawk,* 54 LW 4083.)

[226]*Duncan v. Louisiana,* 391 U.S. 145 (1968).

[227]This oil-rich parish was long bossed by the powerful, skillful political leader Leander H. Perez—a virulent segregationist and anti-Semite.

Speaking for the majority, Justice White, in a relatively brief opinion, reviewed aspects of the history of the judicially mandated application of the several provisions of the Bill of Rights to the states, and concluded simply but firmly, after reviewing the specific nature of the controversy and the history of trial by jury:

> Because we believe that trial by jury in criminal cases is fundamental to the American scheme of justice, we hold that the Fourteenth Amendment guarantees a right of jury trial in all criminal cases which—were they to be tried in a federal court—would come within the Sixth Amendment's guarantee. Since we consider the appeal before us to be such a case, we hold that the Constitution was violated when appellant's demand for jury trial was refused.[228]

Justice White pointed out that so-called petty offenses have traditionally been tried without a jury, and said this would continue to be true under the *Duncan* ruling. He noted that, in federal cases, a "petty" offense is one carrying a maximum penalty of six months' imprisonment and a $50 fine. Beyond that, he left for future decisions the delineation of "serious" from "petty" cases because, in the Court's view, the conviction of Gary Duncan[229] was clearly a "serious" one.[230]

Three other opinions were featured in the milestone case. Justice Black, joined by Douglas, took the occasion to reiterate the convictions and beliefs concerning incorporation he had first set out so prominently in the *Adamson* case[231]—although he applauded the Court for reaching "almost" the same result via the "selective" incorporation approach (which he was thus "very happy to support" as a means to his desired end) and to dispute the stance again espoused in *Duncan* by his long-time opponent on incorporation, Justice Harlan. Black did so primarily because of Harlan's notable dissenting opinion, which may well have been the latter's most eloquent in the long incorporation debate. For, joined by Stewart, Harlan not only disputed the assertion that due process of law requires the application of federal jury trial standards, he

---

[228]*Duncan v. Louisiana, op. cit.,* at 149–50.

[229]Because Louisiana refused to comply in its lower court hierarchy, Duncan was not free from the threat of further prosecution until the federal courts effectively enjoined Plaquemines parish by late 1971. (*Perez v. Duncan,* 404 U.S. 1017, *certiorari* denied.)

[230]See the 1970 decision in *Baldwin v. New York,* 399 U.S. 66.

[231]See pp. 47 ff., *supra.*

also took pains to deliver another lecture against incorporation *per se;* against "selective" incorporation; and against the Court's reading of history, which, he charged, made "no sense"—thus once again opting for a case-by-case "fundamental fairness" approach. To Harlan, the 1833 holding of *Barron v. Baltimore*[232] was still good law: he never regarded it as having been overruled by the Fourteenth Amendment,[233] warmly pleading in conclusion for a return to Justice Brandeis's "celebrated dictum" of 1932 that it is "one of the happy incidents of the federal system that a single courageous state may, if its citizens choose, serve as a laboratory. . . ."[234] Until the day he left the Court in 1971, Harlan never failed to warn against "stifling flexibility in the States." He would have been pleased had he lived to see the Court's 5 : 4 ruling in 1976 which, seemingly narrowing the *Duncan* opinion, held that a state may indeed deny a defendant a jury in his initial trial on a criminal charge, *if* it allows that defendant, through an appeal, to get a completely new (*de novo*) second trial in which there *is* a jury.[235]

And in a separate concurring opinion, siding with the White holding, Justice Fortas went on record as voicing his concern lest the ruling be regarded as "automatically [to] import all the ancillary rules which have been or may hereafter be developed incidental to the right of jury trial in the federal courts." He saw "no reason whatever," for example, "to assume that [the *Duncan* decision] should require us to impose federal requirements such as unanimous verdicts or a jury of 12 [a figure with a 600-year history in Anglo-Saxon law] upon the States."[236] When the Court had an opportunity to rule in 1970 on Florida's six-man jury in non-capital cases, it upheld the practice 7 : 1.[237] Justice White again wrote the opinion; Justice Marshall dissented—contending that the Sixth Amendment requires a twelve-man jury.[238] Indeed it does,

[232]See pp. 39–41, *supra.*

[233]*Duncan v. Louisiana, op. cit.,* at 172.

[234]Quoting from Brandeis's opinion in *New State Ice Co. v. Liebmann,* 285 U.S. 262, at 280, 311.

[235]*Ludwig v. Massachusetts,* 427 U.S. 618.

[236]*Duncan v. Louisiana, op. cit.,* at 213.

[237]*Williams v. Florida,* 399 U.S. 78. The issue promised to arise again in future terms of Court.

[238]In a footnote, White pointed out that the Court was not determining the *minimum* number *permissible,* "but we do not doubt that six is above that minimum." (*Ibid.,* at 91.)

ruled a bare five-man majority two years later, *but* only in *federal* cases—Justice Powell providing the key vote in his concurring opinion, which, however, *upheld* 5 : 4 the right of Louisiana[239] to render 9 : 3 and that of Oregon[240] 10 : 2 and 11 : 1 verdicts in *criminal* cases. Powell insisted that the Sixth Amendment intended to require *federal* courts to employ the unanimous twelve-member jury of the English common law tradition; but he did not view the due process of law clause of the Fourteenth as requiring similar unanimous verdicts in *state* criminal trials. Justice Blackmun, also in the majority, noted that he would have "great difficulty" in upholding a 7 : 5 verdict, however. Dissenting in both cases were Justices Douglas, Brennan, Stewart, and Marshall, who insisted that the federal standards apposite under Amendment Six are *ipso facto* incorporated. In 1973 down came the anticipated ruling by the Court regarding federal *civil* trials: in a 5 : 4 opinion, interestingly authored by one of the dissenters in the two aforementioned cases, Justice Brennan, the Court ruled that resort to fewer than twelve-member juries—long practiced and authorized at the level of the states—is not unconstitutional under the Seventh Amendment's guarantee of a trial by jury in civil cases if the value of the suit exceeds $20, nor is it proscribed statutorily.[241] (Here a six-member federal civil jury was utilized.) Justice Powell joined his colleagues Douglas, Stewart, and Marshall in dissent. In 1978 the Court drew a line on the size of juries in *criminal* cases; however, scattering all over the legal landscape in five separate opinions, it held 9 : 0 that a jury of *fewer* than six could not stand—here striking down Georgia's use of a five-member panel, although the latter's vote in the case had been unanimous. (*Ballew v. Georgia,* 435 U.S. 223.) Nor, said the Court 9 : 0 in 1979, could a 5 : 1 jury verdict stand—evidently thus drawing a firm line at six-member unanimous juries as the minimum constitutionally acceptable in state non-petty offenses criminal cases. (*Burch v. Louisiana,* 441 U.S. 130.)

1969: Applying the Constitutional Prohibition Against Double Jeopardy. The *Duncan* decision had left the Fifth Amendment safeguard against being "twice put in jeopardy of life or limb" as the most

---

[239]*Johnson v. Louisiana,* 406 U.S. 356 (1972).
[240]*Apodaca v. Oregon,* 406 U.S. 404 (1972).
[241]*Colgrove v. Battin,* 413 U.S. 149.

fundamental among the few still not incorporated. The Court had had a number of opportunities to come to grips with the problem,[242] but it was not until the case of *Benton v. Maryland*[243] that it found an appropriate one. Granting *certiorari* in 1968, it limited itself to the following two crucial questions: (1) Is the "double jeopardy" clause of the Fifth Amendment applicable to the States? (2) If so, was the petitioner twice put in jeopardy? Its affirmative response to both questions made Court history by incorporating the contentious provision.

John Dalmer Benton had been indicted and tried in 1965 in Prince George's County for burglary, housebreaking, and larceny. He was convicted of burglary and found not guilty on the larceny charge, and the State did not press charges on the housebreaking count. He was sentenced to ten years in jail on the burglary conviction. Subsequently both his indictment and conviction were set aside by the Maryland Court of Appeals under a ruling that struck down a section of the Maryland Constitution requiring jurors to swear their belief in the existence of God as a condition of jury service.[244] Reindicted and retried for *both* burglary and larceny, he was now convicted on *both* charges and sentenced to fifteen years for burglary plus five years for larceny, the sentences to run concurrently. Benton's convictions were affirmed in the appropriate Maryland courts and he appealed to the highest court in the land *in forma pauperis,* arguing that the larceny conviction should be reversed on double jeopardy grounds since he had been found innocent on *that* charge in his first trial. He also argued that the burglary conviction could not stand, on the theory that the jury was influenced by testimony on the larceny count.

Speaking for a 6:2 Court majority,[245] Justice Marshall held the double jeopardy provision to represent "a fundamental ideal in our constitutional heritage . . . that . . . should apply to the States through the Fourteenth Amendment." Adding that "[i]nsofar as it is inconsis-

---

[242]E.g., *Cichos v. Indiana,* 383 U.S. 966 (1966), when it granted *certiorari* only to dismiss the writ as having been "improvidentially granted," 385 U.S. 76 (1967).

[243]392 U.S. 925 (1968), *certiorari* granted.

[244]*Schowgurow v. State,* 240 Md. 121 (1965).

[245]*Benton v. Maryland,* 395 U.S. 784 (1969). (Justice Fortas had resigned from the Court two months prior to this June 23, 1969, decision, which came on the very last day of Earl Warren's sixteen-year service as Chief Justice of the United States.)

tent with this holding, *Palko v. Connecticut* is overruled," he explained:

> Our recent cases have thoroughly rejected the *Palko* notion that basic con-
> stitutional rights can be denied by the States as long as the totality of the
> circumstances does not disclose a denial of "fundamental fairness." Once it
> is decided that a particular Bill of Rights guarantee is "fundamental to the
> American scheme of justice," *Duncan v. Louisiana*, the same constitutional
> standards apply against both the State and Federal Governments. *Palko's*
> roots had thus been cut away years ago. We today only recognize the
> inevitable. . . . The validity of [Benton's] larceny conviction must be
> judged, not by the watered-down standard enunciated in *Palko,* but under the
> Court's interpretations of the Fifth Amendment double jeopardy
> provision.[246]

Needless to relate, Justice Harlan was hardly prepared to "recognize the inevitable" so recognized by Marshall for the Court's majority! Joined by his frequent sympathizer in the incorporation cases, Stewart, he dissented sharply from the reversal of Benton's conviction because he did not think that the Court should have "reached out" to decide the merits of the case. However, if those were to be reached, he made resolutely clear that he, too, would have been prepared to reverse the larceny conviction on constitutional grounds—*but,* naturally, via the "traditional due process approach" of *Palko v. Connecticut*[247] (as he always viewed that)—rather than the majority's route of "incorporating" all of the details of the federal double-jeopardy guarantee.[248] Once more he

---

[246]*Ibid.,* at 795–96. The Court apparently left undisturbed its long-standing policy of upholding separate state and federal prosecutions of the same offense, although a 6 : 3 ruling in 1977 seemed to open the door for its reconsideration. (*Rinaldi v. United States,* 434 U.S. 22, based on *Petite v. United States,* 361 U.S. 529 [1960].) *Res judicata* reposes in two 1959 decisions: *Bartkus v. Illinois,* 359 U.S. 121, and *Abbate v. United States,* 359 U.S. 187. For an apparent narrowing of the protection against double jeopardy in the instance of the length (or brevity) of *sentences,* see Justice Blackmun's late 1980 opinion for a 5 : 4 Court in *United States v. DiFrancesco,* 449 U.S. 117; the Court's 9 : 0 reaffirmation in 1981 of the constitutionality of imposing consecutive sentences for a single federal offense that violates two laws (*Albernaz v. United States,* 450 U.S. 333); and the 1982 holding (5 : 4 in *Tibbs v. Florida,* 457 U.S. 31) that the double jeopardy clause does not bar a retrial after a defendant's conviction because the verdict had been reversed as being against the weight of the evidence. But *cf. Bullington v. Missouri,* 451 U.S. 430 (1981).

[247]See pp. 72 ff., *supra.*

[248]*Benton v. Maryland, op. cit.,* at 808.

warned against the Court's "march" toward incorporation, expressing his "protest against a doctrine which so subtly, yet profoundly, is eroding many of the basics of our federal system."[249]

As the Supreme Court of the United States prepared to return to its labors in the fall of 1987—for its second term under Chief Justice William H. Rehnquist—no further provisions of the Bill of Rights had been incorporated since *Benton* did so for the double jeopardy clause in 1969. But, in effect, only a few provisions still remained "out": grand jury indictment; trial by a jury in *civil* cases; excessive bail[250] and fines prohibitions; the right to bear arms; and the Third Amendment safeguards against involuntary quartering of troops in private homes. The close attention given during the sixteen years of the Warren Court's existence to problems of criminal justice, against the backdrop of fundamental concepts and concerns of due process of law, plus mounting legislative concern with such safeguards as bail,[251] may well leave those few that are indeed still "out" out. What is crucial is the increasing recognition and acceptance, both on and off the bench, that if there is anything at all "national" in scope and application under the United States Constitution, it is our fundamental civil rights and liberties.

Leading Positions on Incorporation

It may be useful to summarize the major judicial positions taken on the question of incorporation of the Bill of Rights by representative past and present members of the Supreme Court. Although close students of the problem can determine as many as eight or nine such positions, one may eschew fine distinctions and point to four chief ones:

[249]*Ibid.* Actually, the terms of the remand of the *Benton* case to the Maryland courts could not have completely displeased Harlan. For what the Supreme Court did was to send Benton's conviction back down for "re-examination," stating that it was "not obvious on the face of the record that the *burglary* conviction was affected by the double jeopardy violation." (*Ibid.*, at 809. Italics supplied.) In other words, although the provision was now incorporated, each case would still have to be examined to determine whether or not there was double jeopardy *qua* double jeopardy. And as a matter of fact, Benton's ten-year conviction for burglary in his first trial in 1965 did stand up.

[250]The intriguing *quaere* as to whether the Constitution does, in fact, guarantee a "right to bail" (as contrasted with the acknowledged guarantee against its excessiveness when granted) was before the Court in 1982, but it "ducked" the issue by mooting the case. (*Murphy v. Hunt*, 455 U.S. 478 [1982].

[251]See the important Federal Bail Reform Act of 1966.

The *first* position is probably, although arguably, still the current doctrine of a majority of the Court: Selective incorporation, or the concept of the "Honor Roll of Superior Rights."[252] Since the *Palko* case in 1937,[253] this position has been adhered to by a majority of the members of the Court—a shifting majority, but a majority nonetheless. Among those who thus labored to "incorporate" the gradually increasing string of rights from the Bill of Rights without advocating *total* incorporation *per se* have been Chief Justices Hughes, Stone, and Warren (although it is possible to make a good, if inconclusive, case for the acceptance of not only total incorporation by the latter two but of total incorporation "plus"); Associate Justices Brandeis, Cardozo, Reed, Jackson, Burton, Clark, White, Blackmun, and Stevens (but almost all with some reservations in the area of criminal procedural safeguards). This majority position—now entering its sixth decade— possesses both the virtues of flexibility and compromise and the vices of selectivity and uncertainty. These properties would be applicable even if one were to view the Court's majority position as one more adequately described as "selective incorporation plus," given its recent repeatedly demonstrated willingness to broaden "due process" and "equal protection" understandings.

The *second* position on incorporation is the "fair trial" or "case-by-case" rule. This position was consistently and prominently advocated by Justice Frankfurter, and faithfully continued, with some bows toward the Cardozo reasoning in *Palko,* but not toward the *Palko* doctrine itself, by "F.F." 's jurisprudential student and companion, the younger John Marshall Harlan—although Harlan's may well be viewed as a separate "fundamental rights" posture—and, after some initial uncertainty, by Stewart. To a lesser degree it was favored by Chief Justice Vinson and Justices Sherman Minton and Charles E. Whittaker. That also was the position of Chief Justice Warren Earl Burger, and is that of his successor, William H. Rehnquist, and probably of Justice Sandra Day O'Connor. Its most articulate enunciator on the "Burger Court," however, soon became Justice Lewis F. Powell, Jr., whose jurisprudence was closely akin to, and represented a blend of, that of

---

[252]For a scholarly view that the notion of "selective" incorporation is a misnomer and/or represents a "widespread misconception," see Jacob W. Landynski, "Due Process and the Concept of Ordered Liberty: 'A Screen of Words Expressing Will in the Service of Desire'?", 2 *Hofstra University Law Review* 1 (Winter 1974).

[253]*Palko v. Connecticut,* 302 U.S. 319.

Justices Frankfurter and Harlan. It is essentially a "case-by-case" approach which closely examines on its own merits each individual claim of violation of due process of law, determines whether or not the common law as well as statutory law principles of "a fair trial" were accorded to the petitioner, and tests his claim against the requirement of "due process of law"—as that elusive concept may be viewed by a majority of the Court. It is here that the famous Frankfurter *quaere,* whether the governmental action does in effect "shock the conscience"[254] or violate "common standards of civilized conduct," is asked. If the answer is yes, the partisans of the case-by-case approach will then hold due process of law to have been violated. For the adherents to this group of justices, however, such a decision will be without any reference to incorporation of the Bill of Rights, wholly or partly. In short, the "fair trial" test adherents reject both the *selective* incorporation approach of the Cardozo test and the *total* incorporation approach of the elder John Marshall Harlan. They reject the total incorporation (and certainly total incorporation "plus") as an example of "judicial legislating," and as a clear-cut violation of the principles of federalism and the commands of the Constitution. They reject selective incorporation as an unwise and unworkable resort to the vague tenets of "natural law," as the "slot machine approach," whereby, in Justice Frankfurter's words, "some are in and some are out," and as the creation of a hopeless, artificial, and unfair distinction among our basic rights and liberties. Yet to Justice Black the "due process" approach was itself plainly a "natural-law due process" formula.[255]

Pertinent illustrations of the Frankfurter "fair trial" approach are the *Adamson* case,[256] discussed earlier in this chapter, and the *Rochin* case.[257] Reed's majority[258] simply had not been violated and their consciences had not been shocked by California's statute that permitted

[254]That test was one of Justice Black's particular *bêtes noires.* "I do not wish," as he once said to Edmond Cahn, "to have to pass on the laws of this country according to the degree of shock I receive! Some people get shocked more readily than others." ("Justice Black and First Amendment 'Absolutes': A Public Interview," 37 *New York University Law Review* 549 [1962], at 562.)

[255]E.g., *Harper v. Virginia Board of Elections,* 383 U.S. 663 (1966), at 677–79; and *Griswold v. Connecticut,* 381 U.S. 479 (1965), at 525.

[256]*Adamson v. California,* 332 U.S. 46 (1947).

[257]*Rochin v. California,* 342 U.S. 165 (1952). See Chapter IV, *infra.*

[258]They were joined by Chief Justice Vinson and Associate Justices Jackson and Burton.

official courtroom comment on the fact that the accused, Adamson, refused to take the stand in his defense. In *Rochin,* the conduct of certain Los Angeles County police officers so outraged their standards and so shocked their consciences that the accused's conviction was unanimously reversed by the Court—although two justices, Black and Douglas, concurred on separate grounds: "incorporation" of the Bill of Rights safeguards involved in *Rochin.* Also, in the 1964 self-incrimination cases, Justice Harlan II and his supporters' consciences were *not* "shocked" by Connecticut's procedures denying Malloy's self-incrimination claims,[259] but they *were* shocked by the New York Harbor Waterfront Commission's treatment of Murphy's compulsory testimony claims.[260] In *Malloy,* Harlan's case-by-case approach—one always exhortative of his consistently reiterated warning that the states should not be put into "a consitutional straitjacket"—thus enabled him to see due process accorded to the petitioner—while his five colleagues who constituted the Court majority here not only disagreed with his conclusions on the presence of due process but, going further, incorporated the Fifth Amendment's self-incrimination issue. In *Murphy,* on the other hand, Harlan did see a violation of the petitioner's due process, and he thus joined his unanimous brethren to reverse Murphy's contempt conviction. In *Argersinger,*[261] which applied the *Gideon*[262] incorporation of the right to counsel to incarceratable misdemeanors as well, Justice Powell concurred in the reversal of Argersinger's conviction, but wrote an important, thoughtfully developed concurring opinion opting for the case-by-case approach. In 1978 he rearticulated his objection to "jot-for-jot" incorporation—this time in dissenting in a double jeopardy case, in which he was joined by Chief Justice Burger and Justice Rehnquist.[263] This Frankfurter-Harlan-Powell position has the virtues of extensive judicial discretion and minute individual examination and the vices of potential unpredictability and subjectivity.[264]

---

[259]*Malloy v. Hogan,* 378 U.S. 1 (1964).

[260]*Murphy v. Waterfront Commission of New York Harbor,* 378 U.S. 52 (1964).

[261]*Argersinger v. Hamlin,* 407 U.S. 25 (1972).

[262]*Gideon v. Wainwright,* 372 U.S. 335 (1963).

[263]*Crist v. Bretz,* 437 U.S. 28.

[264]For an articulate and warm endorsement of the Frankfurter approach to the problem, see "The Bill of Rights as a Code of Criminal Procedure," Chapter 11 in Henry J. Friendly, *Benchmarks* (Chicago: University of Chicago Press, 1967). For Harlan's reiterated support, see especially his *Duncan* dissenting opinion, *op. cit.,* 391 U.S. 145 (1968),

Given the facts of all-but-total incorporation, the Court's approach may now, in effect, if not in theory, constitute the Court's practical position with regard to any future extension of incorporation.

The *third* judicial posture, total incorporation of the Bill of Rights, was, of course, ardently and faithfully advocated by Justice John Marshall Harlan, the elder—however he may have chosen to express it linguistically. It is a doctrine espoused after *Palko* most notably by Justice Black, with early support from Douglas, Murphy, and Rutledge, and later from Goldberg (all four of whom, however, wanted to go even beyond Black's incorporation to achieve maximum application of the federal Constitution to the states and eventually did so). Simply stated, the Black formula asserts not only that the due process of law and the privileges or immunities clauses of the Fourteenth Amendment mandate the total incorporation of the *specific* commands of the Bill of Rights,[265] but that even if history does not provide a foolproof guide, the logic of life in democratic society in our times dictates such a position as a matter of minimum fairness and necessity. Yet it should be remembered that the Black position on nationalization *in toto* extends only to those guarantees *specifically spelled out in the Constitution and its amendments.* To Black, for whom any kind of "natural law" formula was anathema, the first section of the Fourteenth Amendment absolutely incorporated the specifics of the first eight amendments, but *it was also confined to them.* Time and again he made it clear that natural law may *not* be employed by the judiciary either to expand or to limit legislative powers beyond the commands of the Bill of Rights—to do so he regarded as an "incongruous excrescence on our Constitution."[266] This approach possesses the undeniable virtues of both simplicity and predictability and the vices of dogmatism and questionable interpretation of the Fourteenth Amendment in particular and the United States Constitution in general.

---

at 171. The Frankfurter-Powell approach, with particular reference to the Burger Court period (1969–86), is ably chronicled and evaluated by Raold Y. Mykkeltvedt in his *The Nationalization of the Bill of Rights: Fourteenth Amendment Due Process and the Procedural Rights* (Port Washington, N.Y.: National University Publications, 1983).

[265]See his concurring opinion in *Duncan, op. cit.,* at 166, n. 1, for a firm reiteration of his credo just two years prior to his death.

[266]*Adamson v. California,* 332 U.S. 46 (1947), at 75. See also *Griswold v. Connecticut, 381 U.S. 479 (1965), at 511–13;* and *Harper v. Virginia Board of Elections,* 383 U.S. 663 (1966), at 675–76.

The *fourth,* and for our purposes last, position is really an extension of the third: namely, that the Bill of Rights in all its majestic guarantees may not suffice to ascertain full "due process of law," and that therefore it may be necessary to draw on a kind of total incorporation *plus* approach in order to do full justice to the allegedly aggrieved. Known as the "total incorporation plus theory," it was initially most notably expounded in the immediate post-*Palko* era by Justices Murphy and Rutledge. In their dissenting opinion in the famed *Adamson* case,[267] written by Murphy, the words and intent are clear—although they stopped well short of concise explication:

> We agree that the specific guarantees of the Bill of Rights should be carried over intact into the first section of the Fourteenth Amendment. But [we are] not prepared to say that the latter is entirely and necessarily limited by the Bill of Rights. *Occasions may arise where a proceeding falls so far short of conforming to fundamental standards of procedure as to warrant constitutional condemnation in terms of a lack of due process despite the absence of specific provision in the Bill of Rights. . . .*[268]

Justices Black and Douglas, who had also dissented in *Adamson,* did not then address themselves to the issue raised by their two junior colleagues; they were simply content to advocate total incorporation. However, while Black would always resolutely reject the "incorporation plus" philosophy on the grounds that concepts of intrinsic justice may *be used neither to limit nor to expand* individual rights *beyond what is spelled out in the Bill of Rights,* Douglas rapidly drew closer to the Murphy-Rutledge position. In effect, not long after Murphy's and Rutledge's untimely deaths in 1949, he wholly embraced the "incorporation plus" doctrine. "The Bill of Rights Is Not Enough" was the title of one of his essays,[269] symptomatic of this intriguing position, which might be called a "super-fair-trial" rule. Justice Goldberg demonstrated his sympathy toward that constitutional posture with his important concurring opinion in the *Connecticut Birth Control* case[270] in which he was significantly joined by Chief Justice Warren and also

[267]*Adamson v. California, op. cit.*
[268]*Ibid.,* at 124. (Italics supplied.)
[269]38 *New York University Law Review* 207 (April 1963).
[270]*Griswold v. Connecticut,* 381 U.S. 479 (1965).

Justice Brennan. Goldberg, it will be recalled, made a point of stating that the due process clause was "neither limited to nor necessarily as broad as" the Bill of Rights, but rather that it "protects those personal rights that are fundamental."[271] Despite the theoretical loophole for a contraction of incorporation in view of the "nor as broad as" phrase of the statement just quoted, the Goldberg position, embraced also by Warren, and somewhat later, but then both enthusiastically and expansively, by Brennan and Marshall, constitutes the acceptance of "incorporation plus"—with the possibility of a retrenchment when deemed necessary (an unlikely assumption). Moreover, it accepts the spirit and letter of the Douglas position on the Ninth Amendment announced in the *Birth Control* case, which is patently the most advanced of all positions on the basic issue[272]—one that would, of course, readily lend itself to a "selective incorporation *plus*" conceptualization for those unwilling to accept the "total incorporation *plus*" approach.

Some Guesses and a Judgment. Those very few federally ascertained rights that are still "out" of the mandatory due process of law concept of Amendment Fourteen are all likely to remain out, at least formally. Essentially, there are but five: one is the Fifth Amendment's provision for indictment by grand jury in a "capital, or otherwise infamous crime." Evidently deeming it neither vital nor fundamental as a necessary prerequisite for due process in all state cases, the Court again in 1968 denied *certiorari* in a case challenging its non-applicability in certain criminal cases in Connecticut. There, one Edward R. Gyuro, convicted of breaking into a store and attempting to abscond with five fur coats, appealed his sentence of three to seven years in prison.[273] Like many other states, Connecticut utilizes "information" rather than grand jury indictment, under which the public prosecutor merely submits his charges against an accused in the form of an affidavit of evidence, supported by sworn statements, to a court of original jurisdiction for trial-docketing.

A second provision not likely to be incorporated is the Seventh Amendment right to a jury trial in *civil* cases in controversies valued at more than $20. This is obviously even less of an essential due process

---

[271]*Ibid.*, at 493.
[272]*Ibid.*, at 485.
[273]*Gyuro v. Connecticut*, 393 U.S. 937.

guarantee than grand jury indictment—and, in fact, there has been little formal demand for its "nationalization." After having denied the application of the Amendment to the states in 1916,[274] the Court had an opportunity to adjudicate the issue in 1968, but it denied *certiorari* in a case concerning a 1964 car-train collision in Grand Prairie, Texas, in which a seventeen-year-old University of Texas student was severely injured.[275] The student, Roger McBeth, had unsuccessfully asked for a jury trial rather than the summary judgment proceeding obtained in the Texas courts by the Texas and Pacific Railway. In 1973 the Court made it clear that it would not overturn its 1968 holding.[276] The issue rearose in 1987 in a case raising the question whether the Constitution guarantees jury trial in a lawsuit brought by the federal government under the Clean Water Act.[277]

Third is the matter of the Eighth Amendment exhortation against a requirement of "excessive bail . . . and fines." There is, of course, no *constitutional* guarantee of bail as such—only one against "excessive" bail, if bail is granted in the first place, and what is excessive necessarily rests upon a judicial determination[278] which also pertains to "excessive" fines.[279] However, the entire problem of bail has become a very visible issue, given the late 1960s and 1970s preoccupation with the "law and order" syndrome, and it has received considerable attention in both the legislative and the administration-of-justice arenas. Demands for bail reform were largely responsible for the Bail Reform Acts of 1966 and 1984. The latter, a response to considerable public clamor, provided for a measure of "preventive detention" legislation

[274]*Minneapolis & St. Louis R.R. v. Bombolis*, 241 U.S. 211, at 217.

[275]*McBeth v. Texas & Pacific Railway*, 390 U.S. 387 (1968).

[276]*Colgrove v. Battin*, 413 U.S. 149 (1973).

[277]*Tull v. United States*, 55 LW 3054.

[278]The leading decision here is *Stack v. Boyle*, 342 U.S. 1 (1951). The yardstick laid down by the Court is that fixing of bail must be based "upon standards relevant to the purpose"—i.e., the "punishment" must fit the "crime."

[279]In one of the very few Supreme Court cases on record involving fines, the high tribunal held in 1971 that it constitutes a violation of the equal protection clause of Amendment Fourteen to limit punishment to payment of a fine for those who are *able* to pay it, yet to convert a fine to imprisonment for those who are *unable* to pay it. (*Tate v. Short*, 401 U.S. 395.) But Justice Brennan's opinion emphasized that there are a number of ways to enforce judgments against those unable to pay—e.g., seven states (and England and Wales, for example) allow installment payments. (England and Wales also permit the garnishing of wages.)

by enabling the denial of bail at the pretrial level to any defendant who seems to endanger public safety, although the statute levels a heavy burden on detention-oriented prosecution. By a 6:3 vote the Court upheld the controversial provision in 1987.[280] Whatever the ultimate fate of bail legislation and litigation, it does not seem likely that the Court will "incorporate" the anti-excessiveness proviso; when it does get cases relating to the problem, it is far more likely to adjudicate them on the basis of the broad and time-honored due process–fair trial requirements, as indeed it has done.[281]

Fourth is the often purposely (by opponents of gun control legislation) incompletely quoted Second Amendment proviso: "A well-regulated militia being necessary to the security of a free State, the right of the people to keep and bear arms, shall not be infringed." If any provision of the Bill of Rights seems to need no judicial protection, Amendment Two is it, so powerful have been the forces opposed to effective regulatory legislation. In the one fairly recent case on record that did reach the Supreme Court, the high tribunal denied review for want of a substantial federal question, the tribunal below having held categorically that Amendment Two does not apply to the states[282]— that, indeed, "as the language of the Amendment itself indicates, it was not framed with individual rights in mind";[283] and that "[e]nough has been said to differentiate the second amendment from those which protect individual rights and, as such, have been carried over into the fourteenth amendment."[284]

Fifth, and last, is the seldom-perceived Third Amendment, which proscribes involuntary peacetime and illegal wartime quartering of sol-

---

[280]*United States v. Talemo*, 55 LW 4063. The record pre-trial detention to date (1988) is 31 months.

[281]*Ibid.* One federal court would, however, apply the provision to the states. (*Pilkington v. Circuit Court*, 324 F.2d 45–46 [1963].) See *Murphy v. Hunt, op. cit.*, p. 86, fn. 250.

[282]*Burton v. Sills*, 394 U.S. 812 (1969), appeal dismissed. A ban on the sale *and* possession of handguns by the town of Morton Grove, Illinois, was upheld by a U.S. District Court in 1981, over objections of alleged violations of Amendments Two and Fourteen. (*Quilici v. Village of Morton Grove*, 532 F.Supp. 1169.) In a 2:1 vote the U.S. Seventh Circuit Court of Appeals affirmed at the end of 1982. (*Ibid.*, 695 F 2d 261.) And the U.S. Supreme Court denied review one year later. (*Ibid.*, 464 U.S. 863.)

[283]*Ibid.*, 248 F 2d 521 (1968), at 526.

[284]*Ibid.*, at 528. See also *Presser v. Illinois*, 116 U.S. 52 (1886), and *United States v. Miller*, 307 U.S. 174 (1939).

diers in private homes. No record of any violations exists; no challenge under the Amendment has ever reached the Supreme Court; and the lower federal courts have seen just one, which was dismissed as being without merit.[285]

Reflecting upon these considerations involving the five "outs," perhaps it is just as well that they remain unincorporated. The "selective incorporation" concept—which, as suggested, should perhaps now be labelled as "selective incorporation *plus*"; the Court's increasingly "open-ended" omnipresent concern for "equal protection" and "due process of law," and their extension to heretofore only marginally covered groups;[286] the obvious presence of a "double standard" in favor of basic human rights;[287] and the Court's embrace of "suspect" and "almost suspect" fundamental rights categories, in which legislation must show a "compelling" state interest rather than mere legislative "rationality" in order to pass "close scrutiny" constitutional muster,[288] are now facts of constitutional law and interpretation. They all combine to render plausible the argument and plea that the federal principle might well continue to permit the states to pursue their own procedural standards in the remaining non-incorporated areas. If so, however, these standards obviously must scrupulously meet, reflect,

[285]*United States v. Valenzuela*, 95 F. Supp. 363 (1951).

[286]Thus note the significant 1967 decision, *In the Matter of Gault*, 387 U.S. 1, which in effect extended most of the Bill of Rights to juvenile offenders (a notable exception being the right to a trial by jury—see *McKeiver v. Pennsylvania*, 403 U.S. 528 [1971]). An intriguing extension of far-reaching implications came with the Supreme Court's contentious 5 : 4 decision in 1975 in *Goss v. Lopez*, holding for the first time that young people are entitled by the Constitution's due process concepts to the same sort of protection against unfair interference with their education (here summary ten-day or less suspension from public schools) that adults enjoy when the Government tries to deprive them of their rights. (419 U.S. 565.) And the same majority held shortly thereafter that school officials who unfairly discipline students cannot defend themselves against civil rights suits by claiming ignorance of the students' basic constitutional rights (*Wood v. Strickland*, 420 U.S. 308 [1975]. On the other hand, the Court, in a 5 : 4 opinion written by Justice Powell, held in 1977 that the spanking of school children by teachers or other school officials does not violate the Constitution's Eighth Amendment ban against cruel and unusual punishment, stressing the broad public acceptance of the practice. (*Ingraham v. Wright*, 430 U.S. 651.) And in 1984 it ruled 6 : 3 that laws (present then in all fifty states) under which juveniles charged with delinquency may be held in pretrial detention to prevent them from committing additional crimes are constitutional. (*Schall v. Martin*, 467 U.S. 253.)

[287]See Chapter II, *supra*, pp. 11 ff.

[288]*Ibid.*

and adhere to, the demands of due process of law. In the words of the wise counsel of Justice Goldberg in his concurring opinion in *Pointer v. Texas*,[289]

> to deny to the States the power to impair a fundamental constitutional right is not to increase federal power, but, rather, to limit the power of both federal and state governments in favor of safeguarding the fundamental liberties of the individual. In my view this promotes rather than undermines the basic policy of avoiding excess concentration of power in government, federal or state, which underlies our concepts of federalism.[290]

[289]380 U.S. 400 (1964).
[290]*Ibid.*, at 414.

chapter *IV* *The Fascinating World of "Due*

Process of Law"

The concept "due process of law" has been an integral part of much of what we have been discussing. It is both subordinate and coordinate to any consideration of "values and lines" in the realm of civil rights and liberties. The presence or absence of no concept is mentioned more frequently in our judicio-legal process than "due process of law"; today its banner is raised in a host of appellate cases at the level of the United States Supreme Court, whereas that high tribunal decided but *one* case on "D.P." grounds between 1789 and 1866! Its terminology, if not its clear meaning, is found in Amendments Five and Fourteen of the Constitution, both of which issue clarion calls to national and state governments, respectively, for the presence and maintenance of "due process of law." In the words of Amendment Five, ratified on December 15, 1791: "No person shall . . . be deprived of life, liberty, or property, *without due process of law . . .*";[1] and in the words of Amendment Fourteen, ratified on July 23, 1868: "No State shall . . . deprive any person of life, liberty, or property, *without due process of law. . . .*"[2] Towering disagreements as to the meaning of that command have plagued us and will undoubtedly continue to do so, thus complicating seriously attempts at line-drawing—as the aforegone analysis of the question of the incorporation of the Bill of Rights has demonstrated. Yet basic guidelines do exist, and, no matter how vexatious and hazardous the task at hand may well be, they do enable us to come to grips with the central meaning of "due process of law."

[1]Italics supplied.
[2]Italics supplied.

Some Basic Guidelines

Although it may well be futile to attempt definitive interpretations of "due process of law," it is possible to delineate certain fundamentals. One basic requirement of the concept "due process of law" is that government may not act in an "arbitrary," "capricious," or "unreasonable" manner in performing its task vis-à-vis the body politic. The judicial branch as the ultimate guardian of our Constitution-guaranteed civil rights and liberties has the delicate and difficult task of ascertaining the constitutional appropriateness of governmental action by weighing it against what amount to common-law notions of "arbitrariness," "capriciousness," or "unreasonableness"—although this adjectival test has been vehemently and consistently rejected as a usable measure by some prominent jurists, such as Justice Black, a dedicated Constitutional *literalist*. [3]

Suffice it to say that opinions differ widely on the meaning of these concepts. What may be "arbitrary" to some legislators and executives may seem "reasonable" to others; what may be "capricious" police behavior in the eyes of a prisoner may be "fair" in the eyes of the apprehending and prosecuting authorities; and what may well seem to be an "unreasonable" interpretation by an administrative agency in the view of an affected business concern or educational institution may appear "reasonable" to the agency's commissioners. Does the matter, then, become merely one of opinion, or are there ascertainable standards? The answer cannot be conclusive: there *are* standards, of course, but until they have been judicially tested and pronounced, they remain general standards based as much on civilized notions of fairness and decency—not infrequently widely personalized divergent ones—as on any written commands, whether statutes, ordinances, or even constitu-

---

[3]See, among others, his scathing lecture on the subject in his *A Constitutional Faith* (New York: Alfred A. Knopf, 1968), Chapter II, "Due Process of Law," pp. 23 ff. It probably represents the fullest statement of his due process philosophy. In essence, he hinged it to Lord Coke's understanding of *per legem terrae*, the "law of the land" provision of the Magna Carta, Chapter 29, which to Black represented *already existing constitutional provisions; the Bill of Rights; plus all laws that had been passed pursuant to constitutional power at the time the alleged offense was committed*. To Coke, however, "by the due course and process of law" was almost certainly confined to *judicial proceedings*—not to substantive or contextual aspects of a statute.

tions, federal or state. At the federal level, because of the specific exhortations of the Constitution and the centralizing tendency of having only one final arbiter, "due process" standards are generally both more predictable and more ascertainable than at the *state* level. Fifty separate units of government, despite the mandates and implications of the Fourteenth Amendment *and of their own bills of rights,* bring normally a more fluid, less predictable, and, in the main, less "generous" interpretation of "due process of law" to the individual than is customarily true at the federal level. However, given the post-1937 stance of the United States Supreme Court, the states, too, consequently have had to pay far more attention to the fundamental concepts of "fairness and decency," which are so vital to the presence of "due process of law"— and it is fair to say that they are "coming around" increasingly.

A General Definition. Any general definition of "due process of law" must take into account the genesis of the concept. It was originally derived from English common law—probably during the reigns of Henry I (1100–1135) and Henry II (1154–89). Its more obvious antecedent is the Magna Carta of 1215, Chapter 29 (Chapter 39 in a later version), which declares: "No free man shall be taken, outlawed, banished, or in any way destroyed, nor will we proceed against or prosecute him, except by the lawfull judgment of his peers and by the law of the land." As Professor A. E. Dick Howard of the University of Virginia School of Law has pointed out in his commentary on the Magna Carta, as early as 1354 the words "due process" were used in an English statute interpreting the Magna Carta, and by the end of the fourteenth century "due process of law" and "law of the land" were interchangeable. The English colonists who established our courts brought the expression "due process of law" with them.[4] As it developed, "due process of law" restrained a head of government from arbitrarily depriving a member of his realm of life, liberty, or property. In due course this notion was embraced by all other departments of govern-

[4]A. E. Dick Howard, *Magna Carta: Text and Commentary* (Charlottesville: University of Virginia Press, 1964). See also Justice Black's commentary on the subject in his *A Constitutional Faith, op. cit.,* especially pp. 30–38. But for a much more restrictive interpretation—which sees "due process" as wholly *procedural*—see Keith Jurow, "Untimely Thoughts: A Reconsideration of the Origins of the Process of Law," 19 *The American Journal of Legal History* 265 (1975). Jurow thus sides with both Alexander Hamilton's interpretation of "due process of law" (see fn. 11, p. 95, *infra*) and Justice Frankfurter's (see pp. 98 ff. *infra*).

ment as well; it has been an essential fact of governmental life on this side of the ocean since the Constitution's adoption in 1789.

Perhaps the best brief definition of due process of law was contained in the first Justice John Marshall Harlan's dissenting opinion in 1884, in *Hurtado v. California.*[5] Governments, he wrote, should be confined within the limits of those fundamental *"principles of liberty and justice,* lying at the foundation of our civil and political institutions, which no State can violate consistently with that due process of law required by the Fourteenth Amendment in proceedings involving life, liberty, or property."[6] This noble phrase, then advanced on the losing side of the judicial ledger, became firmly implanted on the majority side with its acceptance, clarification, and refinement by Justice Cardozo, more than half a century later, in *Palko v. Connecticut.*[7]

But what are those "fundamental principles of liberty and justice" that constitute the irreducible minimum of due process of law? We may discover them from a variety of sources:

the body of constitutions,
bills of rights,
customs, conventions, and traditions,
legislative enactments,
executive ordinances, decrees, and practices,
judicial interpretations and precedents;

and significantly, from what one commentator aptly termed "current views of right and wrong which collectively have come to be accepted as a part of the established law of the land."[8] The concept of due process of law and its application to our federal and state governments is based on an extensive reservoir of *constitutionally expressed and implied limitations upon governmental authority,* ultimately determined by the judicial process, and upon those basic notions of fairness and decency which govern, or ought to govern, the relationships between rulers and ruled. Although Justice Frankfurter's record is, of course,

---

[5]110 U.S. 516.
[6]*Ibid.,* at 546. (Italics supplied.)
[7]302 U.S. 319 (1937). See Chapter III, *supra,* pp. 72 ff.
[8]Professor Jesse T. Carpenter in Edward C. Smith and Arnold J. Zurcher, eds., *Dictionary of American Politics* (New York: Barnes & Noble, 1955), p. 128.

based on the subjective case-by-case approach described earlier, rather than a clearly delineated one, he viewed this flexible concept of due process of law as ". . . compounded by history, reason, the past course of decisions, and stout confidence in the democratic faith which we profess. . . ."[9] Yet in 1924, while Professor of Constitutional Law at Harvard, he had written that "[t]he due process clauses ought to go,"[10] a philosophical commitment he reiterated frequently from the bench.

Substantive and Procedural Due Process of Law

Any explanation of due process of law must consider its two "types" or aspects—*substantive* and *procedural*—for judicial disposition of due process litigation necessarily turns on the *kind* of violation that is alleged by a petitioner. Although neither is as readily definable nor as clearly separable from the other as is sometimes claimed, it is essential to understand at least a general distinction between the two. We may view *substantive* due process as referring to the *content or subject matter* of a law or an ordinance; i.e., whether what it deals with, what it is trying to accomplish, *contextually* conforms to due process of law. On the other hand, *procedural due process*—the more litigated of the two—refers to the manner in which a law, ordinance, administrative practice, or judicial task is carried out, i.e., whether the procedures employed by those who are charged with the application of the law or ordinance violate *procedural* due process, regardless of the substance of the former. For nearly a century procedural due process was viewed in American jurisprudence as the *only* "due process" extant.[11] Substantive due process was not "discovered" formally by the judiciary as a

[9]*Joint Anti-Fascist Refugee Committee v. McGrath*, 341 U.S. 123 (1951), concurring opinion.

[10]"The Red Terror of Judicial Reform," 40 *New Republic* 10, at 113.

[11]Thus Alexander Hamilton: "The words 'due process' have a precise technical import, and are *only* applicable to the process and proceedings of the courts of justice; *they can never be referred to an act of the legislature." The Papers of Alexander Hamilton* (New York: Columbia University Press, 1962), p. 35. (Italics supplied.) Justice Frankfurter, deeply troubled by the increasing judicial resort to substantive due process rulings at home, was instrumental, upon being asked for his advice, in having India's Constitution of 1950 adopt in its Article 21 a concept of "due process of law" that reads that no one shall be deprived of due process of law "except in accordance with the *procedure* established by law." (Italics supplied.)

viable "tool" until the now famed *Wynehamer* case in 1856,[12] in which New York's courts struck down a New York State liquor prohibition law. Here, then, for the first time, a court read "due process" to "prohibit, *regardless* of the matter of procedure, a certain kind or degree of exertion of legislative power altogether": due process, rather than merely protecting the "mode of procedure," was made to reach "the substantive content of legislation."[13] In both the substantive and procedural due process concepts the judicial test of constitutionality or legality has become more or less the same: is the governmental action "arbitrary," "capricious," "unreasonable," "invidious," "irrelevant," or "irrational" either in content or in procedure?[14] If it is, the action by government and/or its agent will then fall—and on occasion *both* substantive and procedural violations have been present. To Justice Black, however, courts had *no* power, whatsoever, to pass on the "reasonableness" of state or federal legislation.

SUBSTANTIVE DUE PROCESS

As the discussion of the post-1937 "double standard" has demonstrated,[15] the Supreme Court has largely abandoned substantive due process of law as a check on legislative *economic-proprietarian* regulation. This does not mean, of course, that legislatures are free to disregard the basic standards of substantive due process when legislating in the realm of the economy—indeed, the Court will permit no obvious violation.[16] But it does mean that in line with its latter-day double-

[12]*Wynehamer v. People,* 13 N.Y. 358 (1856). Raoul Berger refers to *Wynehamer* as the *locus classicus* of substantive due process: *Government by Judiciary: The Transformation of the Fourteenth Amendment* (Cambridge: Harvard University Press, 1977), pp. 254–55. Wallace Mendelson finds it in an earlier New York case, however: *Taylor v. Sorter,* 4 Hill 140 (N.Y. 1843).

[13]See Gerald Gunther, quoting Edward S. Corwin, in the former's *Individual Rights in Constitutional Law,* 4th ed. (Mineola, N.Y.: Foundation Press, Inc., 1986), p. 111, fn. 3.

[14]These six adjectives were listed by Justice Black in his *dissenting* opinion in *Harper v. Virginia Board of Elections,* 383 U.S. 673 (1966), at 673, as the governing tests for claims of violations of the Fourteenth Amendment's "equal protection of the laws" clause.

[15]See Chapter II, *supra.*

[16]E.g., *Shapiro v. Thompson,* 394 U.S. 618 (1969)—alluding to the "very means to exist," i.e., food, clothing, and shelter—and similar late 1960s and mid- and early 1970s judicial checks in the general area of welfare and poverty (when viewed as bearing upon individual constitutional rights). *Shapiro* has been heavily attacked, however.

standard canons of judicial self-restraint, the Court will generally bend over backward to uphold such legislation. In the area of civil liberties, however, judicial action in the substantive due process area is now frequent, and while the Court is called upon to pass judgment less often in that sphere than in the procedural one, no term passes without some challenges to governmental enactments on substantive due process grounds. Many of these fall into the area of the First Amendment freedoms,[17] in particular the freedom of expression[18] and religion, and, with steadily mounting frequency since the 1950s, Fourteenth Amendment egalitarian aspects (discussed in subsequent chapters). A pertinent illustration is sterilization legislation.

Carrie Buck Loses. Carrie Buck, an eighteen-year-old, purportedly feeble-minded white woman from Charlottesville, Virginia, allegedly the illegitimate daughter of a state-proclaimed "maritally unworthy . . . shiftless, ignorant, and worthless . . ." feeble-minded mother, and herself the mother of a supposedly mentally defective, concededly feeble-minded, illegitimate baby, was committed in 1924 to the Virginia State Colony for Epileptics and the Feeble-Minded—where her mother, Emma, probably the mother of two other illegitimate children, had also once been committed. A Virginia statute, enacted earlier in 1924, provided that the health of the patient and the welfare of society may be promoted in certain cases by the sterilization of mental defectives, under careful safeguard; that the sterilization may be effected in males by vasectomy and in females by salpingectomy, without serious pain or substantial danger to life; that the Commonwealth of

[17]Space does not here permit a discussion of the following three basic substantive due-process safeguards found in the body of the Constitution (Article One): the writ of *habeas corpus, ex post facto laws,* and bills of attainder.

[18]Thus, ready candidates for declarations of unconstitutionality—usually unanimously—are such patently vague enactments as "vagrancy," "loitering," and "public nuisance" laws. (E.g., *Papachristou v. City of Jacksonville,* 405 U.S. 156 [1972].) A "vague" statute, according to a classic 1926 definition by Justice Sutherland, is one which "either forbids or requires the doing of an act in terms so vague that men of common intelligence must necessarily guess at its meaning and differ as to its application, [and thus] violates the first essential of due process of law." (*Connally v. General Construction Co.,* 269 U.S. 385, at 391.) See also Cincinnati's abortive law making it a crime for three or more persons to assemble on city sidewalks "and there conduct themselves in a manner annoying to persons passing by." (*Coates v. Cincinnati,* 402 U.S. 611 [1971].) Ditto Houston's statute making it a crime to oppose or "interrupt any policeman in the execution of his duty", the Court ruling 8:1 that the law was "unconstitutionally overbroad." (*Houston v. Hill,* 55 LW 4823 [1987].)

Virginia "is supporting in various institutions many defective persons who if now discharged would become a menace but if incapable of procreating might be discharged with safety and become self-supporting with benefit to themselves and to society"; and that experience has shown that heredity plays an important part in the transmission of insanity, imbecility, idiocy, feeble-mindedness, and epilepsy. The law went on to state that whenever the superintendent of certain institutions, including the State Colony at Lynchburg, where Carrie and her mother were committed, shall be of the opinion that it is for the best interests of the patient and of society, he may have the operation "performed upon any patient afflicted with hereditary forms of insanity, imbecility," etc., if he complies with the careful provisions by which the law protects the patient from possible abuse.[19]

Dr. J. H. Bell, the Superintendent of the State Colony for Epileptics and the Feeble Minded—prodded by the statute's author, Democratic Senator Aubrey Strode, and its leading philosophical proponent, Dr. Albert S. Priddy—recommended to his Board of Directors that Carrie Buck be sterilized. The Board, in compliance with the apparently succinctly drawn law, ultimately so ordered. Carrie may have been feeble-minded, but she understood what was about to happen to her. On her request for a lawyer, her guardian, Robert S. Shelton, chose a former Colony director, and Strode's close friend, Irving Whitehead. He set in motion the elaborate appellate procedure provided under the act and applied to the County Circuit Court for reversal of the order; but it affirmed the sterilization decree. Carrie's less than enthusiastic petitioners then appealed to the Virginia Supreme Court of Appeals, which agreed with the conclusion reached below that the application of the sterilization law in the case would be a "blessing" for feeble-minded patients like Carrie. The next legal step was an appeal to the Supreme Court of the United States, the constitutional issues raised by Whitehead being alleged denial of *substantive* due process and the "equal protection of the laws," both under the Fourteenth Amendment. The lawyer for the Colony in the case was none other than Albert Strode! Carrie's attorney had no quarrel with the *procedural* aspects of the Virginia law,

[19]Act of March 20, 1924, ch. 394, 1924 Va. Acts 569. Specifically, the statute provided for sexual sterilization of any state hospital inmate who was "insane, idiotic, imbecile, feeble-minded or epileptic, and by the laws of heredity . . . the probable potential parent of socially inadequate offspring likewise afflicted."

readily granting that they provide full due process of law; the attack was upon the *substance* of the legislation. In brief, Whitehead contended in a rather skimpy brief of eight pages (Strode's ran to forty-five) that not only was the sterilization order unauthorized on the existing grounds but that "in no circumstances could such an order be justified" under substantive due process of law; that it was on its face arbitrary, capricious, and unreasonable. Moreover, argued the attorney, Virginia had violated Carrie's, and similarly afflicted candidates', substantive due process and equal protection of the laws because the law reached only the "small number who are in the institutions named and is not applied to the multitude outside."[20]

Over Justice Butler's dissent[21] without a written opinion (an annoying idiosyncrasy), Justice Holmes upheld Virginia's statute and action, joined by Chief Justice Taft[22] and Associate Justices Van Devanter, McReynolds, Brandeis, Sutherland, Sanford, and Stone. Holmes reasoned that since the public welfare has more than once called, and may at almost any time call, upon the best citizens for their lives, it would be "strange if it could not call upon those who already sap the strength of the State for these lesser sacrifices often not felt to be such by those concerned, in order to prevent our being swamped with incompetence." Having established that premise the eighty-six-year-old Holmes—a confirmed Malthusian since boyhood—continued with an oft-quoted passage:

> It is better for all the world, if instead of waiting to execute degenerate offspring for crime, or to let them starve for their imbecility, society can prevent those who are manifestly unfit from continuing their kind. The principle that sustains compulsory vaccination is broad enough to cover cutting the Fallopian tubes. . . . Three generations of imbeciles are enough.[23]

[20]*Buck v. Bell*, 274 U.S. 200 (1927).

[21]Attributed by one close student of the case to Butler's Roman Catholic–based religious opposition to sterilization. See Paul A. Lombardo, "Three Generations of Imbeciles: New Light on *Buck v. Bell*," 60 *New York University Law Review* 1 (April 1985), pp. 30–62, at 57. See also Stephen J. Gould, "Carrie Buck's Daughter," *Natural History* (July 1984), pp. 14–18, whose findings support Lombardo's.

[22]In a letter to Helen Heron (May 6, 1927) he applauded: "[Holmes's] quickness and his powers of catching and stating the point succinctly are marvelous. His brilliance does not seem to abate at all." (Lombardo, *loc. cit.*, at 57.)

[23]*Buck v. Bell*, *op. cit.*, at 207 (1927).

As to the allegations of denial of the equal protection of the laws—i.e., that the Virginia statute did not reach "the multitude outside" state institutions—Holmes commented that "it is the usual last resort of constitutional arguments to point out shortcomings of this sort." The answer to *that* argument, said the dedicated exponent of judicial self-restraint, is that

> the law does all that is needed when it does all that it can, indicates a policy, applies it to all within the lines, and seeks to bring within the lines all similarly situated so far and so fast as its means allow. Of course so far as the operations enable those who otherwise must be kept confined to be returned to the world, and thus open the asylum to others, the equality aimed at will be more nearly reached. Judgment affirmed.[24]

Almost sixty years after the 1927 decision in *Buck v. Bell*, painstaking research by Dr. Paul A. Lombardo of the Institute of Law, Psychiatry, and Public Policy of the University of Virginia[25] demonstrated with considerable conviction that the *Buck v. Bell* suit in fact "originated as a means of vindicating the moralism and private prejudices of three professional and political colleagues: the state-legislator (Strode) who drafted the law and defended it in court; the physician (Priddy) whose fervent belief that sterilization could rid society of undesirables spurred the statute's enactment; and the attorney (Whitehead) who represented Carrie Buck." It is Dr. Lombardo's conclusion that Carrie, her mother, and her daughter were not imbeciles, but rather the unfortunate victims of an elaborate legislative and judicial compaign that resulted in the legally sanctioned sterilization of Carrie and thousands of other Americans—not only in Virginia but throughout much of the nation.

Although the underlying philosophy of *Buck v. Bell* has thus been subjected to heavy and trenchant criticism—arguably partly with the hindsight of socio-medical developments since the 1920s—it still serves to illustrate well some of the problems inherent in the concept of substantive due process of law: the *lawmakers'* prerogative to determine public policy, but presumably one permissible under the Constitution; the *judges'* responsibility ultimately to determine the legality and/or constitutionality of that public policy once the issue reaches them—

[24]*Ibid.*, at 208.
[25]Lombardo, *op. cit.*, fn. 21 and accompanying text.

without, however, substituting their own notions of wisdom and desirability for that of the lawmakers, to whom judicial deference is due under the so crucial institution of the separation of powers. Obviously, the line between "judicial judging" and "judicial lawmaking" is a thin and indeed a vexatious one. The courts had no problem with Virginia's sterilization law in *Buck v. Bell*—they upheld it all but unanimously. It is a valid question, however, whether they *should* have found constitutional barriers in the case. Almost certainly, they would have today. On the other hand, was the Supreme Court justified in striking down, on the basis of violations of substantive due process, legislation as that at issue in the aforediscussed case of *Griswold v. Connecticut,*[26] legislation that was as silly as it was unenforceable—but was there warrant to throw it out rather than have the people cause their legislators to alter it? Similar questions attend a veritable host of judicial decisions in a broad spectrum of legislative and executive actions—alluded to or analyzed throughout these pages—thus giving life to the omnipresent difficulties of delineating the appropriate parameters of judicial power.

Carrie Buck, her appeal to the United States Supreme Court for a rehearing having been denied,[27] was ultimately sterilized[28]—one of 8,300 Virginians between 1922 and 1972, when Virginia decided to discontinue such sterilizations. Although its most stringent features were repealed in 1974 and 1981—especially those relating to *involuntary* sterilization—a sterilization law remains on the statute books.[29] But fifteen years after her future chance of motherhood had thus been surgically terminated, one man *won* his battle against sterilization on both "substantive due process" and "equal protection" grounds, in a case often regarded as a sequel to *Buck v. Bell*. His name was Arthur Skinner—and he was not precisely a pillar of the community.

Arthur Skinner Wins. An Oklahoman habitually in trouble with the law, Arthur Skinner was convicted in 1926 of the crime of stealing three

[26]See the detailed discussion, *supra,* pp. 74–78.

[27]*Buck v. Bell, op. cit.* Carrie died in 1983; her daughter, Vivian, had died at age eight, 51 years earlier.

[28]A challenge to a Nebraska statute similar to, but not identical with, Virginia's, was dismissed by the Court well over four decades later. (*Cavitt v. Nebraska,* 396 U.S. 996 [1970].) And in the 1973 *Abortion* cases the Court reaffirmed its initial decision in *Buck.* (*Roe v. Wade,* 410 U.S. 113, at 154)

[29]Virginia began to conduct a massive media campaign in 1984 in an effort to reach those 1922–72 sterilizees who might still not know *why* they could not have children.

chickens and was sentenced to the Oklahoma State Reformatory. Three years later he was convicted of the crime of robbery with firearms and was again sentenced to the Reformatory. In 1934 he was once more convicted of robbery with firearms, and was sent to the penitentiary, where he was when, in 1935, Oklahoma enacted a new statute, known as the Habitual Criminal Sterilization Act. It was legislated in a burst of moralistic enthusiasm, with assurances not only of its wisdom but of its constitutionality. The law defined a "habitual criminal" as a person who, having been convicted two or more times for crimes "amounting to felonies involving moral turpitude" either in Oklahoma or in any other state court, is *thereafter* convicted of a *third* such felony in Oklahoma and duly sentenced to a term of imprisonment in an Oklahoma penal institution. The statute then provided that the Oklahoma attorney-general could institute "a proceeding against such a person in the Oklahoma courts for a judgment that such person be rendered sexually sterile," and continued:

> If the court or jury finds that the defendant is an "habitual criminal" and that he "may be rendered sexually sterile without detriment to his or her general health," then the court "shall render judgment to the effect that said defendant be rendered sexually sterile" by the operation of a vasectomy in case of a male and of a salpingectomy in case of a female.[30]

The Act went on to state that offenses arising out of the violation of "the prohibitory laws, revenue acts, embezzlement, or political offenses, shall *not* come or be considered within" its terms. In other words, one might commit a crime in these areas and *not* have them count as one of the three crimes that led to the knife for those who committed felonies[31] involving "moral turpitude."

Arthur Skinner was not so fortunate. He had already committed his three felonies involving "moral turpitude." Thus he was a perfect candidate when the sterilization statute became law. For a year he seemed to have escaped, but in 1936 the attorney-general of Oklahoma began proceedings against him. Properly following every prescribed aspect of procedural due process of law under the statute, the state

---

[30]*Skinner v. Oklahoma*, 316 U.S. 535 (1942). Did he mean a "salpingotomy"?

[31]A felony is a crime graver in general, or more serious in nature and penal consequence, than a misdemeanor.

prosecutor steered the case through the various stages, challenged at each by Skinner's attorneys. But by a 5 : 4 decision, a judgment directing that the vasectomy be performed on Skinner was ultimately affirmed by the Oklahoma Supreme Court.[32] Now thoroughly frightened, Arthur Skinner appealed the statute's constitutionality to the United States Supreme Court.

Of the members of the Court that had sealed Carrie Buck's fate fifteen years earlier, all except Chief Justice Stone—who was then an Associate Justice—had died, resigned, or retired. Stone, who had sided with the 8 : 1 majority in that earlier case, now joined the unanimous 1942 Court, although he disagreed with certain aspects of the expansive opinion written by Justice Douglas.[33] Be it said at once that the Supreme Court did not *reconsider* its *Buck v. Bell*[34] decision—which still stands.[35] While, in a concurring opinion, Justice Jackson pointedly warned that there are "limits to the extent to which a legislatively represented majority may conduct biological experiments at the expense of the dignity and personality and natural powers of a minority,"[36] Stone, in his own concurring opinion, made it quite clear (he used the term "undoubtedly") that he still considered *Buck v. Bell* to have been properly decided.[37]

The Douglas opinion for the Court, joined by Justices Roberts, Black, Reed, Frankfurter, Murphy, and Byrnes, was actually less concerned with "due process of law" than with what it viewed as Skinner's denial by Oklahoma of the "equal protection of the laws." Still, the absence of substantive due process was clearly implied, since Douglas, by continuous implication if not by language, demonstrated that, in fact, the law deprived Skinner of "a basic liberty" by its "inequality," one here involving "one of the basic civil rights of man."[38] And it was

[32]*Skinner v. Oklahoma*, 198 Okl. 235, 115 P. 2d 123.
[33]*Skinner v. Oklahoma*, 316 U.S. 535.
[34]274 U.S. 200 (1927).
[35]See p. 128, footnote 28, supra.
[36]*Skinner v. Oklahoma*, 316 U.S. 535, at 546.
[37]*Ibid.*, at 544.
[38]*Ibid.*, at 541. "Marriage and procreation," added Douglas, "are fundamental to the very existence and survival of the race." But see p. 128, footnote 28, *supra* and Justice Marshall's dissenting opinion, *joined by his colleague Douglas*, referring to *Buck* and *Skinner*, in *San Antonio Independent School District v. Rodriguez*, 411 U.S. 1 (1973), at pp. 70 ff.

not difficult for him to find the manifold aspects of inequality that were indeed inherent in the Act. Directing his attention to the provision that *included larceny* but *excluded embezzlement* as a crime leading toward sterilization, he wrote with indignation:

> A person who enters a chicken coop and steals chickens commits a felony . . . and he may be sterilized if he is thrice convicted. If, however, he is the bailee of the property and fraudulently appropriates it, he is an embezzler. . . . Hence no matter how habitual his proclivities for embezzlement are and no matter how often his conviction, he may not be sterilized.[39]

Douglas reminded Oklahoma and the nation that when the law "lays an unequal hand" on those who have committed intrinsically the same quality of offense and sterilizes one and not the other, it has made "as invidious a discrimination as if it had selected a particular race or nationality for oppressive treatment."[40] And he concluded that while there had been "saving features" in the *Buck v. Bell* circumstances, none were present in the *Skinner* case:

> Sterilization of those who have thrice committed grand larceny with immunity for those who are embezzlers is a clear, pointed, unmistakable discrimination. Oklahoma makes no attempt to say that he who commits larceny by trespass or trick or fraud has biologically inheritable traits which he who commits embezzlement lacks. . . . The equal protection [of the laws] clause would indeed be a formula of empty words if such conspicuously artificial lines could be drawn. . . .[41]

To Stone, however, the most significant question of line-drawing involved was not one of "equal protection," but "of whether the wholesale condemnation of a class to such an invasion of personal liberty . . . satisfies the demands for due process."[42] To him and to the entire Court, it clearly did not,[43] and Arthur Skinner escaped the sur-

[39]*Ibid.*, at 539.
[40]*Ibid.*, at 541.
[41]*Ibid.*, at 541, 542.
[42]*Ibid.*, at 544.
[43]In 1965 the Supreme Court refused to rule whether sterilization of a California man violated the Eighth Amendment's ban on "cruel and unusual punishment." (*In re Miguel Vega Andrada*, 380 U.S. 953.) He had agreed to the vasectomy, but he later charged it

gical reaches of the statute, which was thus declared unconstitutional. Of course, there is a limit on the kind of laws regulating life, liberty, and property that a legislature can make.[44] Notwithstanding the high judicial regard for self-restraint vis-à-vis legislative activities, the demands of due process of law (here substantive due process) will continue to require delineation.[45]

PROCEDURAL DUE PROCESS

Despite the recent cascading of litigation designed to achieve egalitarianism, the number of cases reaching the Supreme Court of the United States on grounds of alleged abridgment or denial of *procedural* due process of law still far outweigh those concerned with alleged *substantive* infringements. This is entirely natural, for it is in the execution, administration, and interpretation of the meaning of statutes and executive ordinances that actions of the agents of the governmental process are likely to be challenged on due process grounds, and courts

---

was coerced and "inflicted" as punishment in a misdemeanor case in which he was charged with failure to provide for his four children by his first wife. Having later resumed payments to his ex-wife, and having married his common-law wife (by whom he had had a child out of wedlock), he subsequently sought to have the vasectomy "undone," a feat successful in only 50 percent of such cases. On the other hand, in 1975 a Minnesota jury awarded $19,500 in damages to a couple whose eighth child was conceived six months after the husband underwent a vasectomy. (The defendants in the case, brought by Mr. and Mrs. Eugene Sherlock, were the Stillwater, Minnesota, Clinic and Dr. John Stratte, a member of the Clinic, who had performed the vasectomy.) (*The New York Times,* June 11, 1975, p. 39c.)

[44]As of 1980, sterilization laws were present on the books of twenty-seven states—all of these *eugenic* in kind (and largely unenforced).

[45]A twist to the sterilization problem is illustrated by the case of one Nancy Hernandez, a twenty-one-year-old mother of two, who faced jail in California in 1966 because she refused to submit to sterilization as a condition of probation on a misdemeanor offense. She had pleaded guilty to a minor narcotics charge, and was given a suspended sentence and freed on probation by Municipal Court Judge Frank P. Kearney provided she agreed to sterilization. At first she agreed, but then she changed her mind, and her court-appointed lawyer obtained a writ of *habeas corpus.* Judge Kearney's order was subsequently overruled as "arbitrary and outside the law" by Superior Court Judge C. Douglas Smith. (See *The New York Times,* June 9, 1966, p. 51*l*; and *Time,* June 3, 1966, p. 32.) On the other hand, a twenty-four-year-old unwed mother agreed to be sterilized in order to reduce her sentence for killing her four-day-old son (who was her fourth child born out of wedlock). The mother, who had an I.Q. of 62 and a mental age of twelve, was asked by Philadelphia Common Pleas Judge Raymond Pace Alexander if she understood the meaning of sterilization. "Yes, sir," Miss Francine Rutledge replied, "I don't want no more babies." (*The Philadelphia Evening Bulletin,* June 1, 1966.)

are both better equipped and more role-justified in addressing situations involving *procedural* than substantive due process of law. "The history of liberty," once wrote Justice Frankfurter persuasively in a federal case, "has largely been the history of observance of procedural safeguards."[46] Indeed, due process of law, as already explained, was originally, and for nearly 100 years after the birth of the Republic, interpreted as a *procedural* restriction upon government. It concerned itself, more or less, not with *what* government was doing but *how* it was doing it. Much is involved, of course, in the concept of procedural due process of law: it all but defies definition. It embraces a general standard of *fairness*. As a minimum, it denies to "governments the power to filch away private rights by hole-and-corner methods."[47] A host of practices fall into that category: for example, deliberately "stacked" juries; coerced confessions; lack of adequate notice; compulsory self-incrimination; denial of counsel at various stages in criminal justice; denial of counsel in criminal cases; and *unreasonable* searches and seizures. The difficulty arises, of course, in a consideration of the question when, for instance, a confession *is* coerced, or when a search and/or seizure *is* or becomes "unreasonable." The incorporation of federal standards in criminal justice cases has tended increasingly to narrow the scope of state violations of the standard of fairness, but lines must still be drawn. Among the mass of complex and contentious cases in the realms of search, seizure, counsel, notice, confession, and compulsory self-incrimination, the three to follow will illuminate both the difficulties involved and the differences of opinion on the meaning and requirements of procedural due process of law.

The Case of Antonio Richard Rochin. Rochin, habitually in trouble with the Los Angeles police—more often than not because of drugs—lived in a modest two-story house with his mother, common-law wife, and several brothers and sisters. For some time the County had tried to "get the goods," literally and figuratively, on Rochin. In June of 1949 the County received what its agents had reasonable ground to believe was reliable information that Rochin was selling narcotics. Hence, early on the morning of July 1, 1949, three deputy sheriffs appeared at the

---

[46]*McNabb v. United States,* 318 U.S. 332 (1943), at 347.

[47]J. A. Corry and Henry J. Abraham, *Elements of Democratic Government,* 4th ed. (New York: Oxford University Press, 1964), p. 267.

Rochin homestead. Finding the door open, they entered, called a soft "hello," walked to the second floor, and forced open the door of Rochin's room. The deputy sheriffs had neither search nor arrest warrants. Inside his room Rochin was sitting partly dressed on the side of the bed, on which his spouse was lying. On the night table the deputies spied two morphine capsules. When they shouted "Whose stuff is this?" Rochin quickly grabbed them and put them in his mouth. The agents of the law thereupon "jumped upon him," kicking and pummeling him, in the mistaken expectation that he would relinquish the pills. He swallowed them. The officers then administered a thorough beating to the by then prostrate Rochin, hoping that he would vomit the desired evidence. Ultimately, the deputies tied and gagged Rochin and took him to Angelus Emergency Hospital, where they ordered a resident physician to administer to the immobile yet irate Rochin an emetic through a stomach tube that had been inserted forcibly. The procedure did have the desired effect: Rochin vomited the two morphine capsules, which the police agents presented as the necessary evidence at his trial. Over the defendant's objections that the police methods of obtaining evidence were not precisely in accordance with procedural due process of law, and despite the frank acknowledgment of the above-described facts by one of the participating deputies, Rochin was convicted and sentenced to a sixty-day prison stint.

He immediately appealed this conviction to the proper appellate tribunal, the California District Court of Appeal. To his chagrin and surprise, that tribunal *affirmed* the trial court's holding, despite its judicial finding that the officers "were guilty of unlawfully breaking into and entering defendant's room and were guilty of unlawfully assaulting and battering defendant while in the room . . . [and] were guilty of unlawfully assaulting, battering, torturing and falsely imprisoning defendant at the alleged hospital. . . ."[48] What more is necessary to establish rank violation of procedural due process of law and a reversal of the conviction? On the *federal* level, the recovered morphine capsules would indubitably have been regarded as the fruit of an *unreasonable* search and seizure, forbidden by the Fourth Amendment and as a violation of the Fifth's guarantees against compulsory self-incrimina-

[48]*People v. Rochin,* 101 Cal. App. 2d 140 (1950).

tion. But it was not until the dramatic and traumatic *Mapp* case[49] in 1961 that the United States Supreme Court ruled that all evidence obtained by searches and seizures in violation of the Fourth Amendment is inadmissible in *state* as well as federal courts in criminal trials.[50]

Since *Rochin* came almost a decade prior to *Mapp,* unless the defendant could demonstrate a violation of the due process of law clause of the Fourteenth Amendment he would have no case, for in 1952 neither the exclusionary rule of the Fourth Amendment nor the compulsory self-incrimination safeguards of the Fifth was held applicable to the states. And California, in line with standing traditions of common law then in use by roughly one-half of the states, did *not* bar the admission at the trial stage of evidence obtained illegally. It did enable the aggrieved party to *sue* the offending officers, with scant hope of success, needless to add, yet such an action in no manner affected his obligation to pay fines and go to jail. This accounts for the reasoning of the District Court of Appeal. Rochin next appealed to the California Supreme Court, which denied his petition for a hearing without opinion. But two of the seven justices dissented from this denial and, in doing so, expressed themselves in significant language. They contended that:

> . . . a conviction which rests upon evidence of incriminating objects obtained from the body of the accused by physical abuse is as invalid as a conviction which rests upon a verbal confession extracted from him by such abuse. . . . Had the evidence forced from the defendant's lips consisted of an oral confession that he illegally possessed a drug . . . he would have the protection of the rule of law which excludes coerced confessions from evidence. But because the evidence forced from his lips consisted of real objects the People of this state are permitted to base a conviction upon it. [We two] find no valid ground of distinction between a verbal confession extracted by physical abuse and a confession wrested from defendant's body by *physical abuse.*[51]

[49]*Mapp v. Ohio,* 367 U.S. 643. See pp. 78–81, *supra.*

[50]But note its amendatory rulings in 1976, sharply reducing the power of *lower federal courts* in *habeas corpus* proceedings to set aside *state court* convictions that relied on illegally obtained evidence. (*Stone v. Powell* and *Wolff v. Rice,* 429 U.S. 465.) Chief Justice Burger, the chief opponent of the exclusionary rule, commented in a concurring opinion that the rule's "function is simple—the exclusion of truth from the factfinding process." (At 496.)

[51]*People v. Rochin,* 101 Cal. App. 2d 140, at 149, 150. (Italics supplied.)

When the unhappy Rochin then appealed to the Supreme Court of the United States, he was granted *certiorari* and, in due course, his conviction was unanimously reversed on grounds of rank violations of the very rudiments of procedural due process of law. In what would soon be regarded as one of his most important and colorful opinions, Justice Frankfurter spoke for the Court. He not only outlined the "responsibilities" of both the state and federal courts and wrote a significant essay on the meaning of due process of law, but he restated his own case-by-case approach to the question of the applicability of the commands of the Constitution.[52]

"The vague contours of the Due Process Clause do not leave judges at large,"[53] Frankfurter explained; rather, they place upon the Supreme Court the duty of exercising a judgment "within the narrow confines of judicial power in reviewing State convictions, upon interests of society pushing in opposite directions . . . duly mindful of reconciling the needs both of continuity and of change. . . ."[54] He sternly lectured California that the proceedings by which its agents had obtained Rochin's conviction "do more than offend some fastidious squeamishness about combatting crime too energetically." Then came the sentence that represented his test, his creed, in determining the presence or absence of due process of law: *"This is conduct that shocks the conscience."*[55] And he continued to prove why it did:

Illegally breaking into the privacy of the petitioner, the struggle to open his mouth and remove what was there, the forcible extraction of his stomach's contents—this course of proceeding by agents of government to obtain evidence is bound to offend even hardened sensibilities. They are methods too close to the rack and the screw to permit of constitutional differentiation.[56]

[52]See Chapter III, *supra.*

[53]Perhaps not; but there are more than a few observers who agree with Justice Douglas's frank avowal that "[d]ue process, to use the vernacular, is the wild card that can be put to use as the judges choose." (As quoted by Ray Forrester, "Are We Ready for Truth in Judging?", 63 *American Bar Association Journal* 213 [September 1977].) Douglas, of course, was a prime practitioner of that "wild card"!

[54]*Rochin v. California,* 342 U.S. 165 (1952), at 172, 173.

[55]*Ibid.,* at 172. (Italics supplied.)

[56]*Ibid.*

Although Frankfurter went out of his way to assure the states that they had considerable leeway in their administration and enforcement of justice, he reminded them that it is, and must always be, axiomatic that "States in their prosecution respect certain decencies of civilized conduct." Reversing Rochin's conviction for the unanimous Court, Frankfurter terminated his opinion in words symptomatic of his judicial posture on the entire incorporation problem:

> Due process of law, as a historic and generative principle, precludes defining, and thereby confining, these standards of conduct more precisely than to say that convictions cannot be brought about by methods that offend a "sense of justice."[57]

Precisely because of the vagueness of that "sense of justice" and, of course, because of their deep commitment to the underdog, Justices Black and Douglas, although naturally voting for the reversal of Rochin's conviction, wrote separate concurring opinions, contending that, while the case was rightly decided, it was decided on wrong grounds. In a judgment which has been since confirmed in the history of incorporation, the two justices held that the basic constitutional issue involved in *Rochin v. California* was not at all the one Frankfurter expressed, that is, a violation of the procedural due process guarantees of the Fourteenth Amendment. Rather, held Black and Douglas, it was that California's agents had, in fact, clearly and unmistakably violated the *specific* command of the Fifth Amendment that "No person . . . shall be compelled in any criminal case to be a witness against himself," a command which, in their view, extended to the states via the due process of law clause of the Fourteenth Amendment. To base the reversal of Rochin's conviction on a violation of procedural due process was constitutionally a Pyrrhic victory in the eyes of these two advocates of total incorporation of the Bill of Rights. The "Does it shock the conscience?" test, based on a case-by-case approach to the presence or absence of due process of law, seemed a travesty of justice to Black and Douglas. As Black put it: "I long ago concluded that the accordion-like qualities of this philosophy must inevitably imperil all

[57]*Ibid.*, at 173.

the individual liberty safeguards specifically enumerated in the Bill of Rights."[58] To him, the Frankfurter opinion was a testimonial to "what I object to most in what I consider to be an unwarranted interpretation of the Due Process Clause [for] the elaborate verbal standards offered- . . . are to me merely high-sounding rhetoric[59] void of any substantive guidance as to how a judge should apply the Due Process Clause."[60]

Nonetheless, the case was decided, and Rochin owed the reversal of his conviction to considerations of procedural due process. Two related cases, decided five and fourteen years later, will illustrate both the assets and liabilities of that due process test approach.

The Case of Paul H. Breithaupt. While driving a pickup truck on a New Mexico highway, one Paul H. Breithaupt collided with a passenger car. Three occupants in the car lost their lives; Breithaupt was seriously injured but eventually recovered. When the police arrived on the scene of the collision they detected unmistakable alcoholic odors and, on investigating, not only found an almost empty pint bottle of liquor in the glove compartment of his truck but also thought they detected telling vapors on his breath. The three bodies were taken to the morgue; Breithaupt was taken to the nearest hospital.

As he lay in the emergency room of the hospital, the smell of liquor on the unconscious man's breath was unmistakable, and one of the state patrolmen who had been at the scene of the accident requested that a sample of the patient's blood be taken. An attending physician, using a hypodermic needle, withdrew approximately 20 cubic centimeters of blood from the unconscious Breithaupt and turned the sample over to the patrolman in charge, who submitted it for the customary laboratory analysis. The analysis proved to contain 0.17 percent alcohol.

When Breithaupt was well enough to stand trial, the state charged him with involuntary manslaughter. The clincher proved to be the damaging sample analysis, which was submitted as New Mexico's chief

---

[58]*Rochin v. California*, 342 U.S. 165, at 177.

[59]"What in the world is that," he observed to his son, "but testing a law on the judges' notion of right and wrong?" (Hugo Black, Jr., *My Father: A Remembrance* [New York: Random House, 1975], p. 104.)

[60]*A Constitutional Faith, op. cit.*, pp. 29–30. Black felt similarly about the equal protection of the laws clause—as he demonstrated again in one of his last opinions prior to his retirement in 1971, when, writing in dissent, he warned: "The Equal Protection Clause is no more appropriate a vehicle for the 'shock the conscience' test than is the Due Process Clause." (*Bodde v. Connecticut*, 401 U.S. 371, at 394.)

evidence of the accused's culpability. An expert in toxicology and hematology testified that a person with 0.17 percent[61] alcohol in his blood was decidedly under its influence. Over Breithaupt's objection on procedural due process grounds, the trial judge admitted the blood test results into evidence, and Breithaupt was duly convicted. He accepted his conviction and sentence of imprisonment without appealing.

Later he had second thoughts, and sought release by petitioning the Supreme Court of New Mexico for a writ of *habeas corpus*.[62] That tribunal did hear argument on his petition, but denied the desired writ as being groundless. Breithaupt then petitioned the United States Supreme Court for a writ of *certiorari,* which the Court granted. In essence, Breithaupt contended that his conviction was a *prima facie* violation of procedural due process of law, because it was based on an involuntary blood test taken while he was unconscious. No one had asked him for his consent, and he could not have responded in his "senseless condition" even if he had wanted to. Thus he pleaded violation of his liberty without the procedural due process of law guaranteed him by the Fourteenth Amendment. Relying on the Court's unanimous opinion in the *Rochin* case, he argued that the conduct of the state officers of New Mexico involved in his conviction offended that "sense of justice" of which the justices spoke in *Rochin;* that New Mexico's conduct here, just as much as California's there, represented, in Justice Frankfurter's test phrase, "conduct that shocks the conscience."

But two-thirds of the members of the Court disagreed. Seeing an important distinction between the procedures utilized by agents of government in *Rochin* and *Breithaupt,* they were quite prepared to draw a line between the two cases. Speaking for the majority of six, Justice Clark began his explanation of the distinction by holding that there is nothing "brutal" or "offensive" in the taking of a sample of blood when done, as it was in this case, under the protective eye of a physician. He acknowledged that the driver of the death truck was unconscious when the blood was taken, but that "the absence of conscious consent, without more, does not necessarily render the taking a violation of a constitutional right; and certainly the test as administered

---

[61]In the vast majority of states, the "legally drunk" level is at a much lower percentage, usually between 0.08 and 0.15—in Virginia, for example, 0.10.

[62]The "Great Writ"—the "highest remedy for anyone imprisoned"—is applicable

here would not be considered offensive by even the most delicate.'' Furthermore, Clark went on, endeavoring to explain the labyrinth of the due process test,

> due process is not measured by the yardstick of personal reaction . . . of the most sensitive person, but by that whole community sense of ''decency and fairness'' that has been woven by common experience into the fabric of acceptable conduct. *It is on this bedrock that this Court has established the concept of due process.* The blood test procedure has become routine in our everyday life.[63]

He proceeded to point out that

> as *against the right of an individual* that his person be held inviolable, even against so slight an intrusion as is involved in applying a blood test of the kind to which nearly millions of Americans submit as a matter of course nearly every day, *must be set the interests of society* in the scientific determination, one of the great causes of the mortal hazards of the road. And the more so since the test likewise may establish innocence, thus affording protection against the treachery of judgment based on one or more of the senses.[64]

Here again, we see the quest for the just line between the rights of an individual citizen and those of society at large—a line particularly difficult to draw when it comes to due process in general and *procedural* due process in particular. But three justices objected vigorously to the reasoning of the majority of six. Speaking for himself and Associate Justices Black and Douglas—the latter also wrote a separate dissent—Chief Justice Warren dissented on the ground that *Rochin* was not distinguishable at all but should, in fact, be controlling. He observed that the majority's opinion suggests that an invasion of private rights—

''in all cases of a wrongful deprivation of personal liberty. Where the detention of an individual is under process for criminal or supposed criminal causes, the jurisdiction of the court and the regularity of the commitment may be inquired into.'' It is, to put it somewhat differently, ''a writ directed to the person detaining another, and commanding him to produce the body of the person or persons detained. . . . [Its] purpose . . . is to test the legality of the detention or imprisonment, not whether he is guilty or innocent.'' (*Black's Law Dictionary*, 5th ed., 1979, p. 638.)

[63]*Breithaupt v. Abram*, 352 U.S. 432 (1957), at 436. (Italics supplied.)

[64]*Ibid.*, at 439. (Italics supplied.)

i.e., Breithaupt's body—is "brutal" or "offensive" only if the police use force to overcome a suspect's resistance. With deep feeling, the Chief Justice contended that he could not accept "an analysis that would make physical resistance by a prisoner [as in *Rochin*] a prerequisite to the existence of his constitutional righis."[65] Urging that Breithaupt's conviction be reversed, he asked rhetorically whether the taking of spinal fluid from an unconscious person would be condoned because such tests are commonly made and might be made as a scientific aid to law enforcement, and concluded that

> only personal reaction to the stomach pump and the blood test can distinguish them. To base the restriction which the Due Process Clause imposes on state criminal procedures upon such reactions is to build on shifting sands. We should, in my opinion, hold that due process means at least that law enforcement officers in their efforts to obtain evidence from persons suspected of crime must stop short of bruising the body, breaking skin, puncturing tissue or extracting body fluids, whether they contemplate doing it by force or by stealth.[66]

In his separate dissenting opinion, joined by his colleague Black, Justice Douglas stated as the crux of the whole matter his firm belief that, under our system of government, "police cannot compel people to furnish the evidence necessary to send them to prison."[67] To Black and Douglas a case such as *Breithaupt* merely confirmed the fears and reservations they expressed in *Rochin:* that the test of whether the conscience is shocked was so uncertain and so subjective that to render justice with an equal eye and an even hand was all but impossible. Their solution, of course, was to incorporate the entire Bill of Rights via the Fourteenth Amendment and thus make the former's specific provisions applicable to the states.

Yet *Breithaupt* was confirmed by a 5:4 majority in 1966 in *Schmerber v. California*[68] even in the face of the incorporation of the self-incrimination clause that had taken place two years earlier[69]—

[65]*Ibid.*, at 441.
[66]*Ibid.*, at 442.
[67]*Ibid.*, at 443.
[68]384 U.S. 757 (1966).
[69]*Malloy v. Hogan*, 378 U.S. 1.

demonstrating the vital fact of constitutional life that incorporation does not obviate the need for line-drawing but necessitates line-drawing of a different genre. This has been particularly characteristic of the problems of searches and seizures,[70] and compulsory self-incrimination. In the *Schmerber* majority opinion, written by Justice Brennan and joined by Justices Clark, Harlan, Stewart, and White, the Court held that the privilege against self-incrimination does not permit a driver to balk at giving a sample of his blood, taken by medical personnel in a medical environment, for a test to determine if he is drunk. (Schmerber's blood sample showed a blood-alcohol level of 0.18 per cent; California and most other states consider 0.15 per cent as presumptive proof of drunkenness.) The Brennan opinion, relying in part on a 1910 opinion written by Justice Holmes,[71] declared that the Fifth Amendment protected an accused person from "the use of physical or moral compulsion" to extort "testimonial or communicative" evidence that could be used against him; *but* that "compulsion which makes the body of a suspect or accused the source of 'real or physical' evidence" that, like a blood sample, *did not involve personal communication or testimony,* did not violate the self-incrimination rule. He made it clear that arrested persons might be required by the police to submit to "fingerprinting,[72] photographing or measurements, to write[73] or speak[74] for identification, to

---

[70]See, e.g., the "stop-and-frisk" and other "limited intrusion" cases: *Terry v. Ohio,* 392 U.S. 1 (1968); *Peters v. New York* and *Sibron v. New York,* 392 U.S. 40 (1968); *Davis v. Mississippi,* 394 U.S. 721 (1969); *Adams v. Williams,* 407 U.S. 143 (1972)— which held that the police may "stop-and-frisk" a suspect on any anonymous tipster's word that the suspect is carrying a loaded pistol; *Terry*'s extension to property in the 1983 automobile search case of *Michigan v. Long,* 463 U.S. 1032; the expansive 1973 decisions of *United States v. Robinson,* 414 U.S. 218, and *Gustafson v. Florida,* 414 U.S. 260; and the "anti-rigid-time-limit" 1985 decisions in *United States v. Sharpe* and *United States v. Johns,* 470 U.S. 675 and 469 U.S. 478, resp. See also the Airport "Profile" security cases of *United States v. Mendenhall,* 446 U.S. 544 (1980); *Florida v. Royer,* 460 U.S. 491 (1983); and the discussion on pp. 175 ff., *infra.*

[71]Brennan paraphrased Holmes's point on obtaining evidence from the actual person of an accused, discussed in *Holt v. United States,* 219 U.S. 245, at 252–53: "The prohibition of compelling a man in a criminal court to be a witness against himself is a prohibition of the use of physical or moral compulsion *to extort communications from him,* not an exclusion of his body as evidence when it may be material." (Italics supplied.)

[72]This includes the taking of samples from beneath the fingernails of a murder suspect. (*Cupp v. Murphy,* 412 U.S. 291 [1973].)

[73]Confirmed 6:3 (with Brennan in partial dissent) with regard to a grand jury witness who refused to furnish a specimen of his handwriting. (*United States v. Mara,* 410 U.S. 19 [1973].)

[74]Confirmed 6:3 (with Brennan again in partial dissent) with regard to a grand jury

appear in court, to stand, to assume a stance, to walk or to make a particular gesture."[75] In the majority's view the extraction of blood "performed in a reasonable manner," as here, thus did not offend that "sense of justice" of which the Court's majority spoke in *Rochin;* nor did it violate the protection now binding upon the states against unreasonable searches and seizures because (a) there was "plainly probable cause" to arrest and charge Schmerber; (b) the arresting officer "might reasonably have believed" that he was confronted with an emergency, in which the delay necessary to obtain a warrant, under the circumstances, threatened "the destruction of evidence"; and (c) the test chosen to measure Schmerber's blood-alcohol level was "reasonable." The Constitution of the United States, Brennan concluded, "does not forbid the States minor intrusions into an individual's body under stringently limited conditions [such as these at issue in *Schmerber*]." (But in 1973, the Court, while affirming two California decisions, added the due process requirement that a suspect motorist *must be arrested* before a blood sample may be taken—else any subsequent conviction would fail to meet the basic strictures of the *Miranda* tests.)[76] And eighteen years after *Schmerber* its author would speak for a 9 : 0 Court in ruling that the forced removal of a bullet from the chest of an armed robbery suspect was *not* "reasonable," that it patently violated the Amendment's intended safeguards.[77]

Dissenting opinions in *Schmerber* were written by the Chief Justice and Justices Black and Fortas, with Douglas joining Black's. (Warren, Black, and Douglas had been the three *Breithaupt* dissenters." "To reach the conclusion," wrote Black, "that compelling a person to give

---

request to record a witness's voice for identification purposes. (*United States v. Dionisio,* 410 U.S. [1973].)

[75]*Schmerber v. California, op. cit.,* at 764. (Many states employ other methods of detecting inebriation, such as the drunkometer or breathing apparatus. Twenty-one [1988] have "implied consent laws," meaning that anyone who drives there agrees to submit to a test of some sort or lose his road privileges. Some give drivers a choice between blood, breath, and urine tests.)

[76]*California v. Hills* and *California v. Foreman,* 410 U.S. 908. *Miranda,* of course refers to *Miranda v. Arizona,* 384 U.S. 436 (1966), discussed at length, *infra.* In a related 1983 development, the Court, 7 : 2, upheld a South Dakota law that gives the driver the right to refuse to take a blood alcohol test, but explicitly provides that such a refusal can be introduced as evidence. Justice O'Connor's opinion for the majority rejected the defendant's Fifth Amendment claim by pointing to the inherent "free choice" he exercised. (*South Dakota v. Neville,* 51 LW 4148.)

[77]*Winston v. Lee,* 470 U.S. 753 (1985).

his blood to help the state convict him is not equivalent to compelling him to be a witness against himself strikes me as quite an extraordinary feat."[78] With obvious feeling he concluded that he deeply regretted the Court's holding and that he would continue to believe "with the Framers that these constitutional safeguards broadly construed by independent tribunals of justice provide our best hope for keeping our people free from governmental oppression."[79]

THE DILEMMA

We know now, of course, that during the 1960s a majority of the Court gradually moved toward incorporation in a process that has come very close to totality. Thus, since *Breithaupt* in 1957, the following pertinent prohibitions and provisions of the Bill of Rights have been ruled applicable to the several states by way of the "due process of law" clause of the Fourteenth Amendment:

1961: unreasonable searches and seizures (Fourth Amendment):[80]
1962: cruel and unusual punishment (Eighth Amendment);[81]
1963: counsel in *all* criminal cases (Sixth Amendment),[82] (save certain non-imprisonable misdemeanors);[83]
1964: compulsory self-incrimination (Fifth Amendment);[84]
1965: confrontation by adverse witness (Sixth Amendment),[85] extended in 1967 to embrace favorable witnesses;[86]
1967: a speedy trial (Sixth Amendment);[87]
1968: trial by jury in non-petty criminal cases (Sixth Amendment);[88]
1969: double jeopardy (Fifth Amendment).[89]

[78]*Ibid.*, at 773.
[79]*Ibid.*, at 778.
[80]*Mapp v. Ohio*, 367 U.S. 643. (See pp. 78–81, *supra*, for necessary elaboration.)
[81]*Robinson v. California*, 370 U.S. 660.
[82]*Gideon v. Wainwright*, 372 U.S. 355.
[83]*Argersinger v. Hamlin*, 407 U.S. 25 (1972). But the holding accorded full *Gideon* rights to all likely imprisonables. *Not*, however, ruled the Court 8 : 1 in 1984, to prison inmates held in a special detention unit while under investigation for a crime *committed in prison*. (*United States v. Gouveia*, 467 U.S. 180.)
[84]*Malloy v. Hogan*, 378 U.S. 1, and *Murphy v. Waterfront Commission of New York Harbor*, 378 U.S. 52.
[85]*Pointer v. Texas*, 380 U.S. 400.
[86]*Washington v. Texas*, 388 U.S. 14.
[87]*Klopfer v. North Carolina*, 386 U.S. 213.
[88]*Duncan v. Louisiana*, 391 U.S. 145.
[89]*Benton v. Maryland*, 395 U.S. 784.

"stacked" juries, from "quickie" trials, are as national in scope, at least in theory, as they would be if they had been derived from just one basic document rather than from fifty-one documents. In the words of Justice Black in his landmark 1940 opinion in *Chambers v. Florida:* "The requirement—of conforming to fundamental standards of procedure in criminal trials—was made operative against the States on [*sic*] the Fourteenth Amendment. . . ."[94] And, as Chief Justice Warren wrote at Christmas time of 1967: "The methods we employ in the enforcement of our criminal law have aptly been called the measures by which the quality of our civilization may be judged."[95]

Critical Reactions. Yet, precisely because our federal system is a multiple system of justice, particularly in the realm of criminal procedure, the United States Supreme Court has been increasingly called upon to adjudicate conflicting claims between individuals and society; and many public officials in most states have felt that, in so doing, the Court has made it increasingly difficult for them to bring accused violators of the law to bay. The federal judiciary, in particular the Supreme Court, has been bitterly assailed—often in intemperate language. Law enforcement officers, from long-time F.B.I. head J. Edgar Hoover to the lowliest deputy sheriff, raising their voices in protest against what they have viewed as "undue sentimentality toward lawbreakers," have charged the judiciary with making the job of the police authorities not only difficult but well-nigh impossible.

Nor have these charges and complaints been confined to the executive-administrative and legislative segments of the government; members of the judiciary itself have gone on record as viewing with alarm the tough due process standards imposed by the Warren Court, particularly in the realm of procedure in criminal cases. In the Brune Report[96]

---

[94]309 U.S. 227, at 241. The *Chambers* opinion contains one of *the* great Black exhortations: "Under our constitutional system courts stand against any winds that blow as havens of refuge for those who might otherwise suffer because they are helpless, weak, outnumbered, or because they are nonconforming victims of prejudice and public excitement." (*Ibid.*, at 241.)

[95]"Discriminating Against the Poor and the Fourteenth Amendment," 81 *Harvard Law Review* 435 (December 1967).

[96]Named after the Chief Judge of Maryland, who headed the "Committee on Federal-State Relationships as Affected by Judicial Decisions" of the 1958 Conference of Chief Justices. The Brune Report is reprinted in full in numerous legal journals, among others, the *Harvard Law Record* of October 23, 1958.

thirty-six state chief justices protested what they considered "a dangerous development in Supreme Court adjudication." The report expressed general alarm over what the majority regarded as the "erosion of the federal system," and, exhorting the Court to return to the "greatest of all judicial powers—the power of judicial self-restraint," addressed itself censoriously to most of the controversies that have embroiled the Court in the recent past. The report particularly criticized the steady evolution by Court mandate of the due process and equal protection clauses of the Fourteenth Amendment as criteria with which the states must comply in exercising their authority; it concluded that, by assuming legislative authority and acting without judicial restraint, the Court had expanded national power and contracted the power of the states. This is not the place to discuss and attempt to rebut the specific charges thus flung—it has been well done by others[97]—but there is much to be said for Paul A. Freund's contention that all the Court has really demanded of the states under the due process concepts of Amendment Fourteen is that in order to "turn square corners" in dealing with sensitive areas of human liberty, they should follow procedures that are consistent with due process of law.[98] In his study of the Brune Report, Eugene V. Rostow concluded that its findings represent "not so much a protest against the Court as against the tide of social change reflected in the Court's opinions."[99]

Most vocal of all critics has been Congress. It came within a hair's breadth of drastically and dramatically restricting the appellate jurisdiction of the Supreme Court in a series of 1957–58 measures, generally known as the Jenner-Butler Bill(s).[100] And the Omnibus Crime statutes of 1968 and 1970 were clearly designed to limit, if not necessarily roll back, some of the Court's most contentious holdings in the realm of criminal justice. In fact, three sections of the 1968 bill specifically

[97]For example, E. V. Rostow's biting attack on the report in Chapter 3, "The Court and Its Critics," in his fine book, *The Sovereign Prerogative: The Supreme Court and the Quest for Law* (New Haven: Yale University Press, 1962).

[98]*The Supreme Court of the United States: Its Justices, Purposes, and Performance* (Cleveland: The World Publishing Co., 1961), p. 87.

[99]*Ibid.*, p. 111.

[100]For an excellent account and analysis of the fascinating background of the fate of the Jenner-Butler measures, see Walter F. Murphy, *Congress and the Court* (Chicago: University of Chicago Press, 1962); also C. Herman Pritchett, *Congress versus the Supreme Court* (Minneapolis: University of Minnesota Press, 1961).

endeavored to "overrule" the Court's decisions in the *Mallory* (arraignment), *Miranda* (confessions), and *Wade* (eyewitness/lineup) cases.[101]

Still, as we have seen, even some members of the Supreme Court itself have expressed serious alarm about the standards and requirements set by a majority of their fellow justices in certain instances, particularly in regard to procedural due process—e.g., the angry dissenting opinion by Justice Byron White, joined by Justices Harlan and Clark, in *Massiah v. United States*.[102] It involved questions of the Fifth Amendment's protection against compulsory self-incrimination, the Sixth Amendment's right to counsel and, by implication, the Fourth Amendment's safeguards against unreasonable search and seizure.

Winston Massiah and the Law. Massiah, a merchant seaman on the crew of the S.S. *Santa Maria* in 1958, was engaged in a narcotics traffic conspiracy, and about to transport a quantity of narcotics aboard the *Santa Maria* from South America to New York City. As a result of tips received by federal customs officers, the ship was searched on its arrival in New York. Parcels containing three and a half pounds of cocaine were found in the afterpeak of the vessel, and Massiah was connected with their presence. He was arrested, promptly arraigned, and then indicted for violating the federal narcotics laws; he retained a lawyer, pleaded not guilty, and was released on bail. All of these various steps[103] fully met the requirements of due process of law. Also indicted three months after Massiah as a co-conspirator, and charged with the same substantive offense, was one Jesse Colson.

In November 1959, while free on bail, Massiah met Colson, who was also out on bail. The two men went for a ride in the latter's automobile and soon parked on a New York street. There, Massiah began a lengthy discussion regarding his part in the narcotics transportation conspiracy,

---

[101]Their citations, respectively, are: *Mallory v. United States*, 354 U.S. 499 (1957); *Miranda v. Arizona*, 384 U.S. 436 (1966); and *United States v. Wade*, 388 U.S. 218 (1967). In 1972, the Court did in fact itself overrule *Wade* insofar as it applied to pre-grand jury indictments. (*Kirby v. Illinois*, 405 U.S. 951.) Nor does *Wade* apply to the technique of photo-identifications in the absence of the suspect. (*United States v. Ash*, 413 U.S. 300 [1973].) See also the 7:2 further widening of the eyewitness rule in 1977. (*Manson v. Brathwaite*, 432 U.S. 98.)

[102]377 U.S. 201 (1964).

[103]For a brief description of these "steps," from apprehension to trial and beyond, see my *The Judicial Process: An Introductory Analysis of the Courts of the United States, England, and France*, 5th ed. (New York: Oxford University Press, 1986), pp. 137–41.

making innumerable incriminating statements—incriminating, that is, if they had been made in the presence of public officials. But, or so Massiah had every reason to believe, Colson was a co-conspirator—hardly a government agent!

However, his "buddy" Colson, a few days after his indictment and subsequent bailing, had decided to cooperate with government agents in their continuing investigation of the kind of activities in which the two had allegedly been engaged. Hence Colson permitted a federal agent named Finbarr Murphy to install a radio transmitter under the front seat of the Colson car. By this means, Murphy, equipped with an appropriate receiving device, could overhear from some distance away conversations carried on in Colson's vehicle. And by prearrangement with Colson, Murphy was parked near the spot, but out of sight, of the Colson automobile. Murphy was an eager and accurate listener to Massiah's talkathon.

At the subsequent trial, agent Murphy was permitted by the United States District Court judge to testify regarding the Massiah statements he had overheard. Massiah's defense counsel vigorously objected on two distinct and independent grounds: the alleged violation of the Fourth Amendment's proscription against the admission of evidence obtained as a result of unreasonable searches and seizures, and the alleged violation of Massiah's rights established under the Fifth *and* Sixth Amendments because of the admission in evidence of the *incriminating statements* he had made in the car *after he had been indicted* and *in the absence of his retained counsel.* The jury convicted Massiah and he was sentenced to nine years in prison. His conviction was affirmed by the U.S. Circuit Court of Appeals; he appealed to the U.S. Supreme Court, which granted *certiorari.*[104]

Addressing himself to the second argument and concentrating upon the italicized portions of the defendant's claims, Justice Stewart's majority opinion for six members of the Court did not reach the *Fourth* Amendment question at all, although it was implicit in the litigation, of course. Stewart, hardly a "bleeding heart," very simply pointed out for himself, the Chief Justice, and Associate Justices Black, Douglas, Brennan, and Goldberg that Massiah had been denied the basic protections of the Sixth and Fifth Amendments' guarantees of the right of

---

[104]*Massiah v. United States,* 374 U.S. 805 (1963).

counsel and against compulsory self-incrimination, respectively; the information that convicted him had been "deliberately elicited from him" by federal agents "*after* he had been indicted and in the absence of his counsel." Winston Massiah "did not even know that he was under interrogation by a government agent." Concluded Stewart: "*Fourth* Amendment problems aside . . . all that we hold is that a defendant's own incriminating statements, obtained by federal agents under the circumstances here disclosed, could not constitutionally be used by the prosecution as evidence against *him* at his trial."[105] And Massiah's conviction was thus reversed—which, since it had been based on what was now held to have been illegally obtained and illegally admitted evidence, meant that he went scot-free.

The majority's reasoning infuriated Justice White. His lengthy dissenting opinion for himself and Justices Clark and Harlan asked precisely the sort of question a concerned observer of criminal justice might ask:

> Undoubtedly, the evidence excluded in this case would not have been available but for the conduct of Colson in cooperation with agent Murphy, but *is it this kind of conduct which should be forbidden to those charged with law enforcement?* It is one thing to establish safeguards against procedures fraught with the potentiality of coercion and to outlaw "easy but self-defeating ways in which brutality is substituted for brains as an instrument of crime detection."[106]

But in the *Massiah* case, he continued, there was no "substitution of brutality for brains, no inherent danger of police coercion justifying the prophylactic effect of another exclusionary rule." The petitioner, White went on, had not been interrogated in a police station, had not been surrounded by numerous officers, questioned in relays, or been forbidden access to others. "Law enforcement," he commented, "may have the elements of a contest about it, but it is not a game."[107]

The White dissent warned repeatedly against drawing the line in criminal justice between the rights of society and those of the accused

---

[105]*Massiah v. United States,* 377 U.S. 201 (1964), at 207. (Italics supplied for "Fourth" only.) See *Massiah*'s extension to a prison setting in 1980. (*United States v. Henry,* 447 U.S. 264.)

[106]*Ibid.*, at 213. (Italics supplied.)

[107]*Ibid.*

too much in favor of the accused. It was a pungent attack on the whole approach of the Court's majority, not just in *Massiah* but in numerous other cases in this field of adjudication, in the judicial quest for a balance of interests in our federal system between fairness for the criminal suspect and adequate protection for the public at large. White expressed concern lest the *Massiah* decision discourage both the ordinary citizen and the confessed criminal "from reporting what he knows to the authorities and from lending his aid to secure evidence of crime. . . . Certainly after this case the Colsons will be few and far between, and the Massiahs can breathe much easier, secure in the knowledge that the Constitution furnishes an important measure of protection against faithless compatriots. . . ."[108] And, seconding a contention so frequently voiced by law enforcement officers, White warned that "meanwhile, of course, the public will again be the loser and law enforcement presented with another serious dilemma."[109] Less than five weeks later Justice White was to have occasion to become even more alarmed, although this time he gained the vote of Justice Stewart while retaining the support of Justices Clark and Harlan.

Danny Escobedo's Right to Counsel.[110] On the night of January 19, 1960, Manuel Valtierra, the brother-in-law of a twenty-two-year-old Chicago laborer named Danny Escobedo, was fatally shot in the back. At 2:30 A.M. on the following morning Danny, his now-widowed sister Grace, and two of Danny's friends, Bobby Chan, seventeen, and Benni DiGerlando, eighteen, were arrested by Chicago police *without* warrants and questioned intensively at headquarters. Danny refused to make any statement whatever to his questioners. At 5:00 P.M. on that afternoon, after a full fourteen and a half hours of interrogation, he was released together with the others pursuant to an Illinois state court writ of *habeas corpus* obtained for him by attorney Warren Wolfson, who had once represented Escobedo in a personal injury case and had been called into the present case by Chan's mother. But on January 30, DiGerlando allegedly voluntarily confessed to his part in the crime and informed the police authorities that Danny was the one who had fired the fatal shots. Between 8:00 and 9:00 P.M. on the day of DiGerlando's assertions, Danny Escobedo was rearrested and, his hands manacled

---

[108]*Ibid.*, at 212.
[109]*Ibid.*
[110]*Escobedo v. Illinois*, 378 U.S. 478 (1964).

behind his back, taken to police headquarters together with the also rearrested Grace and Chan.

En route to the police station, one of the officers told Danny that DiGerlando had named him as the slayer of his brother-in-law. At his trial, Danny swore—without any contradiction from the officers involved—that "the detectives said they had us pretty well, up pretty tight, and we might as well admit to this crime," to which, Danny testified, he replied, "I am sorry but I would like to have advice from my lawyer." On arrival at the police station around 9:00 P.M. Danny had been taken to the Homicide Bureau for questioning, after having been in the "lockup" for a while. In vain he asked to see his lawyer, Wolfson. The latter, having been told of the rearrest by Chan's mother, had immediately gone to the police station, where he arrived moments after Danny. Wolfson at once asked to see Danny, but the police told him, "Danny doesn't know you." Wolfson unsuccessfully repeated the request to see his client on some five or six separate occasions throughout the evening, but each was denied politely by the authorities, although he quoted to Homicide Bureau Chief Flynn the pertinent section of the Illinois Criminal Code which allows an attorney to see his client "except in cases of imminent escape." Wolfson and Danny did chance to catch a glimpse of each other "for a second or two" when the lawyer spotted Danny through a half-open door, waved to him, and was greeted by a similar wave by Danny—whereupon the door was quickly closed. At 1:00 A.M., realizing that he was not going to get anywhere, Wolfson signed an official complaint with Commissioner Phelan of the Chicago Police Department and left.

The interrogation of Danny Escobedo went on apace, despite his repeated unsuccessful pleas to see his attorney. At the trial the defendant and his interrogators disagreed on Danny's assertion that a Spanish-speaking interrogator, Officer Montejano, had offered to let his sister, Chan, and him "go home" if Danny "pinned it on DiGerlando." But the record showed that when DiGerlando and Danny were confronted with each other during the course of the night, Danny called DiGerlando a liar and said, "I didn't shoot Manuel, you did." In this manner, of course, Danny for the first time admitted to some knowledge of the crime, at least indirectly. Then, in the face of Montejano's alleged promise that a full statement would free him, Grace, and Chan, Danny further implicated himself as well as the other three accused in the murder plot. At this point, an assistant state's attorney, Theodore J. Cooper, was summoned by the interrogating officers "to take" a full statement. Mr. Cooper, an experienced lawyer, not only failed to advise Danny of his constitutional rights before, during, or after "taking" the statement, but his questions were obviously carefully framed so as to assure admissibility into evidence at the trial. In any event, the record stands undisputed that no one during the interrogation advised Danny of his rights and that at no time during the long evening, despite repeated requests by Danny and Wolfson, was he allowed legal counsel. Danny, Grace, and Chan were all indicted for murder, but Grace was later acquitted for lack of evidence, and the charges against Chan were dropped. DiGerlando, who charged subsequently that his confession was beaten out of him, received a life sentence. As for Danny, his defense moved, both before and during his trial, that the incriminating statement he had given to Cooper be suppressed; but the trial judge ruled the confession to have been voluntary. Danny Escobedo, thus convicted of murder and sentenced to a twenty-year term in prison—he had a record of sundry previous arrests—appealed his sentence to the Supreme Court of Illinois on several grounds of due process of law.

On February 1, 1963, that tribunal reversed Danny's conviction, holding that the defendant understood that "he would be permitted to go home if he gave the statement and would be granted an immunity from prosecution."[111] But the State successfully petitioned for a rehearing—resulting in a reversal and the sustaining of the conviction below. The court ruled: "[T]he officer [Montejano] denied making the promise and the trier of fact believed him. We find no reason for disturbing the trial court's finding that the confession was voluntary."[112] Danny Escobedo's counsel then appealed to the United States Supreme Court for review—his last hope—and won the first round when the Court granted a writ of *certiorari* in order to consider whether the petitioner's statement to Cooper was in fact constitutionally admissible at his trial.[113] On June 22, 1964, in the narrowest possible division, 5:4, the Court responded "no," reversed Danny's conviction, and remanded it to the Illinois trial court "for proceedings not inconsistent

[111]*Ibid.*, at 483.
[112]*Ibid.*, at 484.
[113]*Escobedo v. Illinois*, 375 U.S. 902 (1964).

with this opinion."[114] But the State of Illinois decided that it could not obtain a conviction without the now inadmissible statement and dropped the charges, and Danny was released from jail, where had had spent almost four and a half years.

To understand the Supreme Court's majority opinion by Justice Goldberg for himself, the Chief Justice, and Associate Justices Black, Douglas, and Brennan, it is necessary to recognize not only the "toughening and tightening" of due process standards demanded of the states by the Warren Court, but also what it had done concerning both the right to counsel and the use of confessions between the day of Danny's arrest in 1960 and his appeal to the court of last resort in 1964. Regarding the right to counsel, the Supreme Court in 1961 had overruled the capital criminal conviction of Charles Clarence Hamilton on the *sole* ground, and for the first time, that the defendant had not been represented by counsel at the *arraignment,*[115] a "critical stage."[116] Two years later the *Gideon* case[117] was decided, which extended the absolute right of indigents to have counsel assigned in *all* criminal cases— save those involving certain misdemeanors[118]—by making the Sixth Amendment's requirements of "the Assistance of Counsel" obligatory upon the states via the due process of law clause of the Fourteenth Amendment. (On the same day, the Court extended the right to counsel to appeals.)[119] And two weeks after *Gideon,* the Court reversed the capital conviction of one Robert Galloway White *solely* because the defendant had not been represented by counsel at an even earlier stage than arraignment, namely, the "preliminary examination."[120] The

[114]*Escobedo v. Illinois,* 378 U.S. 478 (1964).

[115]That stage of the proceedings in criminal justice when a prisoner is called to the bar of the court of jurisdiction to be identified, to hear the formal charges against him, and to make an appropriate plea.

[116]*Hamilton v. Alabama,* 368 U.S. 52 (1961).

[117]*Gideon v. Wainwright,* 372 U.S. 335 (1963). See Chapter III, *supra,* pp. 84 ff.

[118]And these, except for non-imprisonable mere fine and traffic cases, were covered in a 1972 ruling. (*Argersinger v. Hamlin,* 407 U.S. 25.) But there must be a "likelihood" of imprisonment, as per the 1979 holding in *Scott v. Illinois,* 440 U.S. 367.

[119]*Douglas v. California,* 372 U.S. 535, *But* the Court in 1974 held (6 : 3) that does not necessarily entitle anyone to *free* legal counsel to pursue a "discretionary" *state* appeal, or a similar appeal to the U.S. Supreme Court beyond the initial "as a matter of right" appeal from a conviction. (*Ross v. Moffit,* 417 U.S. 600.)

[120]*White v. Maryland,* 373 U.S. 59 (1963). In the "preliminary examination" stage, following arrest, the apprehended is brought before a magistrate or a commissioner to determine whether he shall be released or *be held to answer* for the alleged offense.

White decision was based on the "critical stage logic" of the *Hamilton* case.[121] Regarding the problem of "voluntary confessions," which was so crucial in the *Escobedo* ruling, the Court had for some time shown increasing concern about their use as the basis for convictions in criminal cases. Until the late 1950s, the failure to bring an accused in promptly for a preliminary examination, the number of hours of interrogation, the refusal to allow communication with counsel, and long incommunicado detention had not in and of themselves been considered enough to violate due process of law on the *state* level.[122] However, by the beginning of the 1960s, the stringent new judicial approach had become readily apparent; one well-known instance of the reversal of a conviction based on a "voluntary confession" occurred in the case of Raymond L. Haynes because the State of Washington authorities had refused to permit him to telephone his wife, who would then have called an attorney.[123] Then came the decision in *Massiah*.[124]

In overturning Danny Escobedo's conviction, the five-man Supreme Court majority stated the requirements for *early* implementation of the now "nationalized" right to counsel in all criminal cases *and* a confirmed, fundamental, judicially established distrust of confessions. The basic effect of Justice Goldberg's opinion for the slender majority was to cause "the adversary system, traditionally restricted to the trial stage, [to be] hauled back slowly into the earlier stages of criminal proceedings."[125] Goldberg's specific point in *Escobedo* was quite simply and unequivocally that a person can consult with a lawyer *as soon as* a police investigation makes him a prime suspect. Anticipating the heavy professional and lay criticism that was to come as a result of the decision, and combating the four dissenters, Goldberg concluded that the *Escobedo* decision did not affect the powers of the police to investigate "an unsolved crime," but *when*, as in Danny's case, "*the process shifts from investigatory to accusatory*—when its focus is on the accused *and its purpose is to elicit a confession*—our adversary system

[121]*Hamilton v. Alabama*, op. cit.
[122]E.g., *Lisenba v. California*, 314 U.S. 219 (1941); *Crooker v. California*, 357 U.S. 433 (1958); *Cicenia v. Lagay*, 357 U.S. 504 (1958).
[123]*Haynes v. Washington*, 373 U.S. 503 (1963).
[124]*Massiah v. United States*, 377 U.S. 201 (1964).
[125]*The Defender Newsletter*, November 2, 1964, p. 2.

begins to operate, and, under the circumstances here, the accused must be permitted to consult with his lawyer."[126] Earlier, Goldberg had spelled out the majority's specific holding as follows:

> We hold, therefore, that where, as here, the investigation is no longer a general inquiry into an unsolved crime but has begun to focus on a particular suspect, the suspect has been taken into police custody, the police carry out a process of interrogations that lends itself to eliciting incriminating statements, the suspect has requested and been denied an opportunity to consult with his lawyer, and the police have not effectively warned him of his absolute constitutional right to remain silent, the accused has been denied "the Assistance of Counsel" in violation of the Sixth Amendment to the Constitution as "made obligatory upon the States by the Fourteenth Amendment" . . . and that no statement elicited by the police during the interrogation may be used against him at a criminal trial.[127]

The four dissenting Justices, however, were not convinced, as they made clear in three separate opinions: one by Harlan, one by Stewart—who had not only been on the other side in *Massiah*,[128] but had written its majority opinion—and one by White, who was joined by Clark and, again, by Stewart. The over-all tenor of the dissenting opinions was one of genuine concern, indeed conviction, that the decision would hamper criminal law enforcement. Harlan wrote that he regarded the new rule formulated by the majority as "most ill-conceived and that it seriously and unjustifiably fetters perfectly legitimate methods of criminal law enforcement."[129] Stewart reasoned that the decision would have an extremely "unfortunate impact" on the fair and adequate administration of criminal justice. He explained his *Massiah* stand on the basis of what he deemed the overriding fact that Massiah had already been arraigned and indicted, after which the incriminating evidence was elicited from him by trickery while he was free on bail.[130] The longest dissent was White's, who argued that the new ruling would cripple law enforcement and would render its tasks "a great deal more difficult."

---

[126]*Escobedo v. Illinois*, 378 U.S. 478 (1964), at 492. (Italics supplied.)
[127]*Ibid.*, at 490–91.
[128]*Massiah v. United States*, 377 U.S. 201 (1964).
[129]*Escobedo v. Illinois*, 378 U.S. 478 (1964), at 493.
[130]*Ibid.*

Bitterly, he asserted that from now on an accused's right to counsel would require "a rule wholly unworkable and impossible to administer unless police cars are equipped with public defenders and undercover agents and police informants have counsel at their side."[131] After pleading for more "reasonableness" and a more balanced approach that would eschew such a stringent and "nebulous" rule, the one-time Deputy Attorney-General of the United States (under President John F. Kennedy) concluded wistfully:

> I do not suggest for a moment that law enforcement will be destroyed by the rule announced today. The need for peace and order is too insistent for that. But it will be crippled and its task made a great deal more difficult, all in my opinion, for unsound, unstated reasons, which can find no home in any of the provisions of the Constitution.[132]

Across the country the police and prosecuting authorities alike echoed the four dissenting jurists. Yet two years later many, although not most, of the nation's top prosecutors would concede that law enforcement had not suffered from *Escobedo.*

There is no question, however, that the *Escobedo* decision, far more than *Massiah,* presented both the legal profession and the police author- ities with an enormous challenge. To interrogate a suspect behind closed doors in order to secure a confession not only was a concept based on the custom and usage of centuries, but it had become a deeply entrenched police practice, strongly supported by both "traditional" and "reform" elements in the ranks of those charged with the admin- istration of criminal justice. Fully aware of this apprehensiveness and the general unpopularity of the decision, Justice Goldberg endeavored to put matters in their proper focus by appealing for a return to the obligations and commands of law enforcement by a government in democratic society:

> We have . . . learned the . . . lesson of history that no system of criminal justice can, or should, survive if it comes to depend for its continued effec- tiveness on the citizens' abdication through unawareness of their constitu- tional rights. No system worth preserving should have to *fear* that if an

[131]*Ibid.,* at 496.
[132]*Ibid.,* at 499.

accused is permitted to consult with a lawyer, he will become aware of, and exercise these rights. *If the exercise of constitutional rights will thwart the effectiveness of a system of law enforcement, then there is something very wrong with that system.*[133]

The Miranda Bombshell. By January 1966 two United States Courts of Appeals had interpreted *Escobedo* in diametrically opposite ways. Duty-bound to referee such a conflict, the Supreme Court fully sifted 170 confession appeals and accepted for review four cases involving four individuals.[134] Known by its leading case, *Miranda v. Arizona,* the package decision consolidated the appeals of persons convicted on the basis of confessions made after extended questioning by officers of the law in which they were not informed of their rights to remain silent. The crimes of which they were found guilty included kidnapping, rape, robbery, and murder—all major felonies. Although *Miranda* is essentially a Fifth Amendment coerced confession case, it links naturally to the Sixth Amendment (and Fourth Amendment) problems raised by *Massiah* and, particularly, *Escobedo.*

Ernesto A. Miranda, 21, a Phoenix, Arizona, truck driver, had been convicted in the Arizona courts and sentenced to twenty to thirty years in prison for the kidnapping and rape of an eighteen-year-old girl. He was taken into custody, identified by the girl in a lineup, and questioned by two police officers. Two hours later the officers—following Miranda's oral confession admitting and describing the crime—also produced a handwritten one by him, on which was superimposed a typed statement that the confession was made voluntarily, without threats or promises of immunity, "and with full knowledge of my legal rights, understanding any statement I may make will be used against me." Over the objections of his defense counsel, Miranda's written confession was admitted into evidence and served as the basis for his conviction—and his appeal (plus the appeals of the similarly affected principals in the other three cases) to the highest tribunal in the land.

On June 13, 1966, in what must rank as the most bitterly criticized, most contentious, and most diversely analyzed criminal procedure decision by the Warren Court, came its 5 : 4 answer: the *Escobedo* rule was

[133]*Escobedo v. Illinois, op. cit.,* at 490. (Italics supplied except for "fear.")
[134]*Miranda v. Arizona, Vignera v. New York, Westover v. United States, California v. Stewart*—all 384 U.S. 436 (1966).

extended significantly to prohibit police interrogation of any *suspect in custody,* without his consent, unless a defense attorney is present at the arrest stage. In effect, the Supreme Court thus answered two years of bitter criticism over its *Escobedo* ruling with a sweeping libertarian opinion that mandated important changes in police interrogation as practiced in most of the states. While the Court did not outlaw voluntary confession, and stopped short of an *absolute* requirement that a lawyer be present before a suspect can be questioned, there is no doubt that the majority opinion intended to extend *Escobedo.* Written by the Chief Justice himself, who was joined by Justices Black, Douglas, Brennan, and Fortas, it was introduced with the dry and cautious comment, "The cases before us raise questions which go to the very root of our concepts of American criminal jurisprudence."[135] But its holding was dramatic, and it took Warren more than one hour to read the entire sixty-one-page opinion to a packed and hushed Court audience. Over the bitter dissents by Justices Clark, Harlan, Stewart, and White (Harlan, his face flushed and his voice occasionally faltering with emotion, denounced the decision orally from the bench on that Opinion Monday, terming it "dangerous experimentation" at a time of a "high crime rate that is a matter of growing concern," a "new doctrine" without substantial precedent, reflecting "a balance in favor of the accused"[136]), the Court, through the Chief Justice's opinion, in effect laid down the following rules which police (see also Figs. 4.1 and 4.2) must follow before attempting to question an *arrested* criminal suspect:

1. He must be told that he has the right to stay silent.
2. He must be told that anything he says may be used against him in court.
3. He must be told that he has the right to have an attorney with him before any questioning begins.
4. He must be told that, if he wants an attorney but cannot afford one, an attorney will be provided for him free.[137]

[135]*Miranda v. Arizona, op. cit.,* at 437.
[136]*The New York Times,* June 14, 1966, p. 1, as reported by Fred P. Graham.
[137]A warning in the language of the Court's opinion would thus read: "The law requires that you be advised that you have the right to remain silent, that anything you say can be used against you in a court of law, that you have the right to the presence of an attorney, and that if you cannot afford an attorney one will be appointed for you prior to any questioning if you so desire." (*Miranda v. Arizona, op. cit.,* at 479.) But "no talismanic incantation" is required. (*California v. Prysock,* 453 U.S. 355, 1981.)

PHILADELPHIA POLICE DEPARTMENT

Standard Police Interrogation Card

WARNINGS TO BE GIVEN ACCUSED

We have a duty to explain to you and to warn you that you have the following legal rights:

A. You have a right to remain silent and do not have to say anything at all.

B. Anything you say can and will be used against you in Court.

C. You have a right to talk to a lawyer of your own choice before we ask you any questions, and also to have a lawyer here with you while we ask questions.

D. If you cannot afford to hire a lawyer, and you want one, we will see that you have a lawyer provided to you, before we ask you any questions.

E. If you are willing to give us a statement, you have a right to stop any time you wish.

75-Misc.-3
(10-9-67)

FIGURE 4.1

5. If, after being told this, an arrested suspect says he does not want a lawyer and is willing to be questioned, he may be, provided that he reached his decision "knowingly and intelligently."

6. If, after being told all his rights, a suspect agrees to be questioned, he can shut off the questions any time after they have started, whether or not he has an attorney with him.

Apprised of the Court's decision, Danny Escobedo commented, "I think it was very nice of them. Something good."[138]

In February 1967 Miranda was tried and convicted again—for the

---

[138]*The New York Times*, June 19, 1966, Sec. 4, p. 1e.

PHILADELPHIA POLICE DEPARTMENT

Reverse Side of Standard Police Interrogation Card

QUESTIONS TO BE ANSWERED BY ACCUSED

1. Do you understand that you have a right to keep quiet, and do not have to say anything at all?

2. Do you understand that anything you say can and will be used against you?

3. Do you want to remain silent?

4. Do you understand that you have a right to talk with a lawyer before we ask you any questions?

5. Do you understand that if you cannot afford to hire a lawyer, and you want one, we will not ask you any questions until a lawyer is appointed for you?

6. Do you want either to talk with a lawyer at this time, or to have a lawyer with you while we ask you questions?

7. Are you willing to answer questions of your own free will, without force or fear, and without any threats or promises having been made to you?

FIGURE 4.2

Supreme Court had only reversed his first conviction, not quashed his indictment—this time on the basis of properly admitted testimony by his common-law wife, Twila Hoffman. She told the Arizona Superior Court Trial Judge Lawrence T. Wren in open court that Miranda had admitted committing the crime when she talked with him in jail—where he was serving a twenty- to twenty-five-year sentence for robbery. Their conversation occurred[139] *after* the Supreme Court had handed down its original decision. Subsequently, having been found guilty by a jury deliberating eighty-three minutes, he was thus sentenced to the

---

[139]"When I visited him in jail," testified Mrs. Hoffman, "he admitted to me that he had kidnapped the girl and roped her up, then took her into the desert and raped her." (*Time Magazine,* March 3, 1967, p. 49.)

same twenty- to thirty-year term in state prison. He appealed *that* case, too, but the Court refused to grant him a second hearing,[140] ditto a third one in which three Phoenix lawyers had filed a new appeal contending that a *voluntary* confession, given to police during an interrogation,[141] was no more valid as evidence than an *involuntary* one under such circumstances. Miranda was paroled in 1972, having served a total of nine years; but he again ran afoul of the law in 1974 (illegal gun possession and drug charges—subsequently dismissed because of Fourth Amendment violations); he was paroled later that year. Yet, all but magnet-like, he was returned to the Arizona State Prison for violations of his parole in early 1975—and once again released later that year. In early 1976, now thirty-four, he was slain in a Phoenix, Arizona, skid row bar in a quarrel over a card game. When the police arrested the prime suspect they used a "Miranda Card" to read him his constitutional rights.

Reverting to the original 1966 decision,[142] despite public and private outcries that rivaled, if they did not exceed, those following such hotly opposed Warren Court decisions as the 1954 and 1955 *Public School Segregation* cases,[143] and the 1962 and 1963 *Public Prayer and Bible Reading* cases,[144] *Miranda v. Arizona* was now the law of the land! Indeed, the remaining three years of the Warren Court were to see a number of extensions.[145] Guidance cards such as those advocated by the Philadelphia Police Department (reproduced above) were introduced

[140]*Miranda v. Arizona*, 396 U.S. 868 (1969).

[141]*Ibid.*

[142]*Miranda v. Arizona*, 384 U.S. 436 (1966). For a reflective, engagingly written look back twenty years later, see Liva Baker, *Miranda: Crime, Law and Politics* (New York: Atheneum, 1983).

[143]*Brown v. Board of Education of Topeka, Kansas*, 347 U.S. 483 (1954), and the implementation decision, *ibid.*, 349 U.S. 294 (1955).

[144]*Engel v. Vitale*, 370 U.S. 421 (1963), and *Abington School District v. Schempp* and *Murray v. Curlett*, 374 U.S. 203 (1963).

[145]For example, to juveniles in most although not all of its aspects, *In the Matter of Gault*, 387 U.S. 1 (1967); to the questioning of prison inmates when unconnected with the incarceration offense itself, *Mathis v. United States*, 391 U.S. 1 (1967); to questioning of a subject at home rather than elsewhere, *Orozco v. Texas*, 394 U.S. 324 (1969). The Burger Court would extend it to the "preliminary hearing stage," *Coleman v. Alabama*, 399 U.S. 1 (1970), and to post-arrest questioning by psychiatrists in capital punishment cases, *Estelle v. Smith*, 451 U.S. 454 (1981). But it refused to extend it to the traffic court level, *David v. Strelecki*, 393 U.S. 933 (1968), or to indigent parents in *civil* proceedings involving the termination of their legal relationship with their children, *Lassiter v. Department of Social Services*, 452 U.S. 18 (1981).

in many a jurisdiction even while the nationwide assault on the *Miranda* decision continued. It was capped, in a very real sense, by an (afore-mentioned) congressional response: Title II of the Omnibus Crime Control and Safe Streets Act of 1968. That heatedly debated Title added a new section to the pertinent provision of the United States Code,[146] stating that in *federal* prosecutions a confession "shall be admitted in evidence if it is voluntarily given." Paraphrasing the five most pertinent subsections of the measure, Title II stated that judges need only consider "the totality of circumstances" in which a confession was obtained before they rule whether it was voluntary. Since that was, in effect, more or less the formula *before* Miranda, it was a foregone conclusion that the Court would find itself confronted with a test of the constitutionality of that aspect of Title II. It fell to the Burger Court to reach the specific issue of the failure of police to give the required *Miranda* warnings in the 1971 *Harris* case.[147] There, in a 5:4 decision, the Chief Justice—joined by his fellow Nixon appointee Blackmun, and Justices Harlan, Stewart, and White (who had all been in dissent in *Miranda*)—stated that although an unwarned suspect's confession (such as Harris's) could not be admitted as *evidence,* it could henceforth be introduced in the courtroom by the prosecution in an endeavor to impeach an accused's testimony, on the central ground of the latter's *credibility, if* the accused had chosen to take the stand to testify in his behalf. In a sharp dissent, Justice Brennan, joined by his colleagues Black, Douglas, and Marshall, warned that the majority's decision in effect meant that police may now "freely interrogate an accused incommunicado," despite *Miranda*. A good many Court observers concluded that with the *Harris* decision—which, based upon what Justice White characterized as the need to "testify truthfully or suffer the consequences," was reconfirmed and perhaps even expanded in a 5:4 ruling in 1980—[148] the Court had clearly "sounded a retreat" from *Miranda*.[149]

[146]Section 3501, Ch. 18 U.S.C. Note especially 3501 (b).

[147]*Harris v. New York,* 401 U.S. 222.

[148]*United States v. Havens,* 446 U.S. 620. The case dealt with an Indiana lawyer who had smuggled cocaine into the country; it was seized without a warrant, and the defendant moved to exclude the evidence from the trial. His co-defendant had pleaded guilty, and lawyer Havens's seemingly false answers to the prosecution's questions on cross-examination were, the Court ruled, "reasonably suggested" by the defendant's own direct testimony.

[149]E.g., Abraham S. Goldstein, Dean of the Yale Law School, in *The New York Times,* May 3, 1971, p. 35*l*. But for a view that *Miranda,* though possessing significant educa-

Further evidence had come with the Court's 1973 upholding of a guilty plea even though the defendant had not known that the confession he had—admittedly voluntarily—given would have been inadmissible at his trial under *Miranda*.[150] Then, in 1974, in a surprisingly lopsided 8 : 1 ruling—with only Justice Douglas in dissent—the Court held that the *Miranda* rules would not bar damaging evidence from a witness who, the defendant had told police questioners, would *corroborate* his alibi.[151] What defendant Tucker was entitled to, wrote Justice Rehnquist for the majority, was the barring of *his* own statements at the trial; but the testimony of his presumed friend could properly be used because it served the legitimate trial purpose of discovering the pertinent facts. Added proof that the Court no longer considered the prescribed *Miranda* warnings as a fundamental rock of criminal justice came in mid-1975: it held 6 : 2 that a defendant, who, once having been duly informed of his rights under the *Miranda* rules and having acknowledged understanding them, then made incriminating statements to the arresting officer in abeyance of access to his lawyer, could have these statements used against him on trial—but only to raise doubts as to his credibility after he gave *Harris*-like contrary testimony on the stand.[152] And the end of 1974 brought a 6 : 2 decision continuing *Miranda's* reinterpretation: over bitter dissents by Justices Brennan and Marshall, who predicted "ultimate overruling of *Miranda's* enforcement of the privilege against self-incrimination," the Court ruled that after a suspect exercises his right to remain silent about one crime, police may still validly question him about *another* (here after a two-hour interval).[153] Moreover, as the Court held in a less-than-crystal-clear mid-1976 multiple—although unanimous—opinion, the *Miranda* warnings need not be given to suspects called to testify before *grand*

---

tional value, may have been, in terms of tangible effects upon interrogation practices, "an act of judicial futility," see Otis H. Stephens, Jr., *The Supreme Court and Confessions of Guilt* (Knoxville: The University of Tennessee Press, 1973).

[150]*Schneckloth v. Bustamonte*, 413 U.S. 218.

[151]*Michigan v. Tucker*, 417 U.S. 433.

[152]*Oregon v. Hass*, 420 U.S. 741.

[153]*Michigan v. Mosley*, 423 U.S. 96. But *cf. Edwards v. Arizona*, 451 U.S. 477 (1981), involving further questioning about the *same* crime in the absence of a lawyer, which went 9 : 0 the other way. The latter was extended 6 : 3 in 1986 by a ruling that barred the police, in the absence of a lawyer, from questioning a defendant who has made his request for counsel at an arraignment with a view primarily to representation in future court proceedings. (*Michigan v. Jackson*, 106 S.Ct. 1404.)

Table 4.1

RULINGS BY THE UNITED STATES SUPREME COURT (UNDER
AMENDMENTS SIX AND FOURTEEN) IN FAVOR OF THE GUARANTY OF
COUNSEL[a] IN CRIMINAL CASES: ARRANGED BY PROCEDURAL
AND CHRONOLOGICAL STAGES

VOTES OF JUSTICES (FOR:AGAINST)	PROCEDURAL STAGE IN CRIMINAL JUSTICE SYSTEM	PROCE-DURAL ORDER[b]	CHRONOLOGICAL STAGE BY CASES (CITATION & YEAR)	CHRONO-LOGICAL ORDER
9:0	Arraignment	7	*Hamilton v. Alabama,* 368 U.S. 52 (1961)	1
9:0	Trial	9	*Gideon v. Wainwright,* 372 U.S. 335 (1963)[c]	2
6:3	Appeal	10	*Douglas v. California,* 372 U.S. 535 (1963)	3
9:0	Preliminary Hearing	6	*White v. Maryland,* 373 U.S. 59 (1963)	4
6:3	Post-Indictment	5	*Massiah v. United States,* 377 U.S. 201 (1964)	5
5:4	Pre-Indictment Confession	4	*Escobedo v. Illinois,* 378 U.S. 478 (1964)	6
5:4	Arrest	2	*Miranda v. Arizona,* 384 U.S. 436 (1966)	7
6:3	Line-up	8	*United States v. Wade,* 388 U.S. 218 (1967)[d]	8
		8	*Gilbert v. California,* 388 U.S. 263 (1967)[d]	8
9:0	Probation Hearing	11	*Mempa v. Rhay,* 389 U.S. 128 (1967)	9
6:2	Quasi-Arrest	1	*Orozco v. Texas,* 394 U.S. 324 (1969)	10
6:2	Pre-Indictment Preliminary Hearing	3	*Coleman v. Alabama,* 399 U.S. 1 (1970)	11
8:1	Revocation of Probation or Parole	12	*Gagnon v. Scarpelli,* 411 U.S. 778 (1973)	12
7:2	Counsel Must be "Effective" on Appeal	10A	*Evitts v. Lucy,* 469 U.S. 387 (1985)	13

[a]In 1975, the Court ruled (6:3) that a defendant may move to *waive* the right to counsel in favor of self-representation, if recognized as "competent" to do so, and if the waiver is "voluntary and intelligent"—standards to be judge-decided. (*Faretta v. California,* 422 U.S. 806.)

[b]Number 1 represents the earliest and number 12 the latest stage in the criminal justice procedural process.

Table 4.1 *(Continued)*

^cExtended in 1972 (9:0) to cover *all* offenses involving possible imprisonment, whether they be classified as petty, misdemeanor, or felony, "absent a knowing and intelligent waiver." (*Argersinger v. Hamlin*, 407 U.S. 25.) Interpreted in 1979 (6:3) as extending only to those offenses in which a defendant *was in fact sentenced* to a term of imprisonment. (*Scott v. Illinois*, 440 U.S. 367 [1979].)

^dSignificantly narrowed in 1972 (5:4) so as to extend now only to post-Grand Jury indictment line-ups (*Kirby v. Illinois*, 405 U.S. 951); and in 1973 (6:3) as *not* to apply to the photo-identification stage in the accused's absence (*United States v. Ash*, 413 U.S. 300).

juries.[154] On the other hand, a 6:3 majority ruling later that year strengthened the *Miranda*-emphasized right to silence at the arrest stage by holding that a defendant's remaining silent, after being advised of his right to remain silent under questioning, could not be used against him in a trial.[155] And when the Court had a seemingly golden opportunity to overrule *Miranda* in the grisly Iowa child-murder *Williams* case in 1977, it demurred in an emotion-charged 5:4 decision that produced five opinions.[156] Obviously staking out a case-by-case course rather than attempting to draw a firm *Miranda*-application line, the high tribunal, three years later, distinguished its earlier Iowa decision in a not unsimilar Rhode Island case (6:3); but it now provided a definition of the meaning of "interrogation" to be used as a guide by police in criminal cases.[157] "Interrogation," explained Justice Stewart in his opinion for the majority, should be viewed neither to be limited to direct questioning of a suspect nor to be so expansive as to cover an offhand remark a police officer might make within the suspect's hearing. When the Iowa *Williams* case was remanded for a new trial, Williams was again found guilty of first-degree murder, carrying a mandatory life sentence in that state. He again appealed his conviction to the federal judiciary, and scored a victory at the bar of the United States Court of Appeals for the Eighth Circuit in 1983. But when the Supreme Court

[154]*United States v. Mandujano*, 425 U.S. 564.

[155]*Doyle v. Ohio* and *Wood v. Ohio*, 426 U.S. 610.

[156]*Brewer v. Williams*, 430 U.S. 387 (known as the *Christian Burial Speech* case). Attorneys-general from twenty-one states had filed briefs *amici curiae* unsuccessfully supporting Iowa.

[157]*Rhode Island v. Innis*, 446 U.S. 291 (1980). The Supreme Court's opinion was written by Chief Justice Burger, with Justices Brennan and Marshall dissenting. (Italics added.)

reviewed the case in 1984 it overruled the lower tribunal 7 : 2, holding: "If the prosecution [as it has here] can establish by a preponderance of the evidence that the information *ultimately or inevitably would have been discovered by lawful means,* then the deterrence rationale [of the exclusionary rule] has so little basis that the evidence should be received."[158]

On the overarching question of "voluntariness" in confession cases, an issue so central to the *Miranda* rules, especially in the light of the aforementioned 1968 congressional statute supportive of voluntariness, the Court may well be on the road to the British case-by-case approach on the issue. That conclusion was strengthened by a 1977 holding (6 : 3) which was supportive of precustodial behind-closed-doors questioning, although the suspect had admitted committing the crime, thus presumably requiring custody and the full panoply of the *Miranda* rules; but he had been permitted to leave after questioning.[159] Further proof of the all but unavoidable case-by-case approach is provided by a 1979 decision (6 : 3) that apparently expanded the right to questioning in the absence of an attorney,[160] while one in 1980 reversed (8 : 1) the armed-robbery conviction of a Louisiana man because there was no evidence that he had "knowingly and intelligently" waived his rights before making the inculpatory statement.[161] Yet in addition to the Court's new approach represented by the *Nix* case,[162] it also held in 1984 that "overriding considerations of public safety" *may* justify immediate questioning without giving a suspect first the *Miranda* warnings against self-incrimination.[163] On the other hand, it ruled 5 : 4 that the *Miranda* doctrine applies to a suspect for *any* crime, no matter how minor, *except* for "ordinary roadside traffic stops."[164] And in 1986 the Court ruled 6 : 3 that a suspect's post-arrest, post–*Miranda* warnings silence could

[158]*Williams v. Nix,* 700 F. 2d 1164 (1983), and *Nix v. Williams,* 467 U.S. 431 (1984), at 444. (Italics supplied.)

[159]*Oregon v. Mathiason,* 429 U.S. 492.

[160]*North Carolina v. Butler,* 441 U.S. 369.

[161]*Tague v. Louisiana,* 444 U.S. 469. For a perceptive, lucidly written summary article on aspects of the Fifth Amendment, see David M. O'Brien, "The Fifth Amendment: Fox Hunters, Old Women, Hermits, and the Burger Court," 54 *Notre Dame Lawyer* 26 (October 1978). See *Edwards v. Arizona* and *Estelle v. Smith, supra.*

[162]*Nix v. Williams, supra,* fn. 158.

[163]*New York v. Quarles,* 467 U.S. 649.

[164]*Berkemer v. McCarty,* 468 U.S. 420 (1984).

not be used by the prosecution as evidence of his sanity.[165] But, as if to reemphasize the all but necessary *ad hoc* nature of passing judgment on *Miranda*-type cases, while stipulating 6 : 3 that the right to be represented by an attorney was the *suspect's* right, not the attorney's,[166] the Court in 1986 also explicitly reaffirmed its holdings in *Miranda* that police must inform arrested suspects of their rights to remain silent and to have a lawyer present, and that police must stop questioning any suspect who asks to see a lawyer.

That, of course, brings us back to the basic dilemma of values and lines. The presence of lines and limits, and the need to draw them wisely and well, is at least as pressing and arguably more widely perceived in the realm of criminal justice than in any of the other areas under discussion in the civil libertarian spectrum.

Due Process of Law in Perspective

No one challenges the basic contention that both the individual and society are entitled to a full measure of "due process of law." In the opinion of a good many observers, however, the balance has shifted to the side of the potential or actual lawbreaker. Thus, the Supreme Court and the lower federal judiciary have come under fire because of their tightening of due process concepts in its decisions, particularly in the field of criminal justice. Has the judiciary, in particular the Supreme Court, gone too far—or not far enough? There is no answer that will please everyone, but it is possible to consider some fundamental points.

"THE CRIMINAL GETS THE BREAKS"

This caption in an article in *The New York Times Magazine,* written by Dean Daniel Gutman of the New York Law School[167] after *Escobedo,* but almost two years prior to *Miranda,* has lost neither its pertinency nor timeliness with the passage of years. Then, as Chief Justice Burger has endeavored to drive home at every opportunity both

[165]*Wainwright v. Greenfield,* 54 LW 4077.

[166]*Moran v. Burbine,* 54 LW 4265.

[167]November 29, 1964, p. 36 ff. (The New York Law School is not to be confused with the New York University School of Law.)

on and off the bench,[168] Dean Gutman, with unassailable statistics demonstrating a continued upward trend in crime—a trend that has not only persisted into the 1980s but has exacerbated—warned that "we do not solve the problem of dealing with those who make crime their business by providing procedural methods of escape for the guilty, to the detriment of the law-abiding who are victimized by the lawless." After reciting a number of the more controversial Supreme Court decisions "in favor of criminals"—among them the *Massiah* and *Escobedo* rulings—the author called for a series of steps to be taken "within the framework of the Constitution and the Bill of Rights" to remedy the situation. Among them were (a) legislation to permit wiretapping, pursuant to court order, for evidence of major crimes; (b) "recodification" of procedural requirements for search and seizure, "which are distinctive for ancient strictures no longer valid"; (c) extension of the right to detain and interrogate, with due safeguards against coercion or other violation of constitutional rights; (d) classification of the "extent and application" of the concept of right to counsel; and (e) "relaxation of the rule excluding all evidence improperly obtained, so as to vest discretion as to admission in the trial judge." Such a list prompts recognition of the paradox that the administration of justice poses to thoughtful and committed Americans like Dean Gutman, the members of the Supreme Court, and their respective supporters and detractors in the lay as well as the professional public. The basic issues are likely to continue to remain unresolved—notwithstanding the recurrent, variegated, earnest efforts of such qualified professional and lay, public and private groups as the American Bar Association; the President's National Commission on the Causes and Prevention of Violence; the Council of States; nationwide organizations of chiefs of police and district attorneys; Ralph Nader; Common Cause; local crime-fighting citizens' groups; educators; or, for that matter, the perpetual, if uneven, and not infrequently incomprehensibly self-defeating activity by Congress in the popular "law-and-order" realm.

Has the Court Been Too Lenient? It is entirely natural to ask whether the courts have not in fact tipped the balance of justice in favor of the criminal to the detriment of the public. Given a post-1938 rise in crime at a rate eight to ten times as fast as the growth of America's popula-

---

[168]E.g., his annual "State of the Judiciary Messages" and his opinions in such opposite cases as *Bivens v. Six Unknown Named Agents*, 403 U.S. 388 (1971), and *Stone v.*

tion—and still climbing in the 1980s—it is understandable that professionals and laymen alike should be fond of quoting Justice Cardozo's well-known observation that "[J]ustice is due the accused, but it is also due the accuser"; that the "concept of fairness must not be strained till it is narrowed to a filament," coupled with the memorable Cardozo *quaere* whether the "criminal is to go free because the constable has blundered."[169] In the words of Justice Stanley Reed, the "purpose of due process is not to protect an accused against a proper conviction, but against an *unfair* conviction."[170] Or, as Justice Robert H. Jackson pointed out in a case involving the question of due process in connection with the composition of a "blue ribbon"[171] jury: "Society also has a right to a fair trial. The defendant's right is a neutral jury. He has no constitutional right to friends on a jury."[172]

Yet in insisting upon strict standards of decency and fairness in governmental law-making, law-enforcing, and prosecuting, the courts simply perform the historic function of protecting the rights of the individual against the alleged unlawful acts of government. Justice Brennan once put the matter well in speaking for the 7:1 Supreme Court in a reversal of the conviction of union leader Clinton E. Jencks, a suspected perjurer of Communist persuasion, who had not been permitted to attempt to impeach testimony given to the F.B.I. on the basis of which he had been found guilty and convicted in the trial court below: ". . . the interest of the United States in a criminal prosecution . . .[and any of the several states] *is not that it shall win a case, but that justice shall be done.*"[173] There is no doubt that this philosophy is "hard to take" in specific instances—but can there really be any compromise with it under our form of government? The answer must be a firm "No!"

Powell, 428 U.S. 465 (1976). In his 1981 Message he pointed out that in 1980 Washington, D.C., with a population of 650,000, had more criminal homicides than Sweden and Denmark, with an aggregate population of more than 13,000,000!

[169]*People v. Defore*, 242 N.Y. 13 (1926), at 19–25.

[170]*Adamson v. California*, 330 U.S. 46 (1947), at 130. (Italics supplied.)

[171]A special jury which in some jurisdictions—e.g., Manhattan—could be selected by the jury commissioner from those qualified as trial jurors on the basis of special or superior qualifications. With the enactment of the Federal Jury Selection Act of 1968 it is no longer *legal* on the *federal* level (but it has never been held to be *unconstitutional*).

[172]*Fay v. New York*, 332 U.S. 261 (1947), at 288–89, upholding New York's "blue ribbon" jury.

[173]*Jencks v. New York*, 353 U.S. 657 (1957), at 668, quoting from Justice Sutherland's opinion in *Berger v. United States*, 295 U.S. 78 (1935), at 88. (Italics supplied.)

True, indeed, that men and women like Rochin, Jencks, Mapp, Mallory,[174] Massiah, Escobedo, Robinson, Malloy, Murphy, and Miranda are neither paragons of citizenship nor likely to "stay out of trouble," despite their "victories" at the bar of the Supreme Court. Indeed, almost all of them did run afoul of the law again. That, however, is not the main issue; what *is* the issue is the need to provide justice in accordance with the commands of our constitutional principles, in this case due process of law—which, on the other hand, knows and should know limits, too.

But to devote some thought to certain of the specific attacks upon Supreme Court rulings, *just which* of the more recent controversial issues would we have the Court or—failing its acquiescence to a hearing—the legislative branches alter, if not negate? The famed *Gideon* decision that guaranteed counsel in state criminal proceedings for indigent defendants in non-capital as well as capital criminal cases?[175] Or its subsequent extension to the preliminary hearing stage?[176] Or its further extension to the interrogation stage following arrest?[177] Can any member of a democratic society *honestly* argue the point that counsel in a criminal case is a luxury, that he who cannot afford it is not entitled to it? Or that, as in Danny Escobedo's situation, a request to consult with

---

[174]Of the famed "Mallory Rule," under which the Court held in 1957 (*Mallory v. United States*, 354 U.S. 449) that officers must take an arrested person "without unnecessary delay" before the nearest available commissioner (he had been held overnight and interrogated by the police for seven hours ere this was done)—thus reversing Mallory's conviction and death sentence in a rape case. Mallory later went on to assault another woman and to burglarize a house and rape the housewife. Convicted on the latter two counts, he was ultimately sentenced to twenty-two years in the Pennsylvania State Penitentiary. After having served eleven and one-half years, he was released late in 1971. Soon thereafter, in July 1972, he was caught in the acts of robbing a couple and raping the woman and was shot fatally by Philadelphia Fairmount Park police when he tried to flee and pulled a gun on two officers. The *Mallory* "without unnecessary delay" rule became a focal point of congressional attacks on the Court and the subject of one of the "repealer" provisions in Title II and III of the Omnibus Crime Control and Safe Streets Act of 1968 (discussed, pp. 164 ff. and 184 ff. *supra*). A confession is now admissible if a judge rules that it was indeed voluntary and that the delay before the confession's presentation to a magistrate was not "unreasonably longer than necessary." (The outer limit seems to be six hours.) *Mallory* remains judicially untested specifically, but the Court appears to have more or less accepted it.

[175]*Gideon v. Wainwright*, 372 U.S. 335 (1963).

[176]*White v. Maryland*, 373 U.S. 59 (1963).

[177]*Miranda v. Arizona*, 384 U.S. 436 (1966).

one's attorney prior to a police interrogation is somehow loading the dice against the government?

Or to consider an allied area of due process, are we really prepared to oppose or even reverse the Court's 1964 decision that the Fifth Amendment's tradition-heavy guarantee against compulsory self-incrimination is applicable to the states as well as the federal government?[178] Admittedly, there are matters of degree involved here—as there are in all of these areas—but there can hardly be any compromise with the elementary command that a suspect need not "sing" unless he so desires or unless he is given full statutory immunity.[179] The initial fears, and subsequent charges, that the *Miranda* decision would seriously interfere with the normal tendency to confess have not been borne out by resulting statistical evidence.[180]

[178]*Malloy v. Hogan,* 378 U.S. 1 (1964).

[179]See *Ullmann v. United States,* 350 U.S. 422 (1956), *Murphy v. Waterfront Commission of New York Harbor,* 378 U.S. 52 (1964), and *New Jersey v. Portash,* 440 U.S. 450 (1979). The sufficiency of the protection provided by the "immunity bath" section of the 1970 federal omnibus crime statute, and almost identical state legislation, came under simultaneous constitutional attack in 1971 in both a state (*Zicarelli v. New Jersey State Commissioner of Investigation,* 406 U.S. 472) and a federal case (*Kastigar v. United States,* 406 U.S. 441). Both pieces of legislation—which provided a more limited type of immunity, known as *"use"* immunity rather than the normal complete or *"transactional"* immunity—were upheld in 5 : 2 opinions, written by Justice Powell, with Justices Douglas and Marshall in dissent (Brennan and Rehnquist not participating). The essential difference between "use" and "transactional" immunity is that the latter covers *any and all aspects* of a matter for which a respondent is given immunity in return for waiving his rights against self-incrimination, whereas "use" immunity, while barring "investigatory leads" against an "immunized" respondent, does *not* prevent the prosecution from using evidence against him *if* such evidence is derived and developed from a source *wholly independent* of the "immunized" respondent's testimony—not an easy line to draw. (*Zicarelli v. New Jersey,* 401 U.S. 933.)

[180]Following the uproar caused by this and the other *Miranda* rules, the findings of a major statistical study were disclosed by Evelle E. Younger, then District Attorney of Los Angeles County (which has the largest case load in the country) and later Attorney-General of California. The survey, which covered 4,000 felony cases, and the results of which frankly "amazed" Mr. Younger, showed that confessions were needed for successful prosecution in fewer than 10 percent of the 4,000 cases, and that 50 percent of the suspects were confessing *despite* the warning by the police. "The most significant things about our findings," commented Younger (a former F.B.I. agent), "are that suspects will talk regardless of the warning and furthermore it isn't so all-fired important whether they talk or not." (*The New York Times,* August 21, 1966, Sec. 1, p. 52). The Younger study confirmed similar findings by Brooklyn Supreme Court Justice Nathan R. Sobel and by Detroit Chief of Detectives Vincent W. Piersante. (See Sidney Zion, "So They Don't Talk," *The New York Times, op. cit.,* Sec. 4, p. 13.) An eighteen-month study of the

Of course, it is revolting to find that obvious, confessed murderers go scotfree (indeed, the phrase "getting away with murder" applies here literally), as, for example, one Arthur Culombe did in a grisly, multiple murder case in Connecticut.[181] But the partially demented Culombe's confession had been *coerced* by Connecticut authorities in the most devious and patently illegal manner, involving the accused's family. True, one may well ask why the State was not justified in utilizing *any* methods that would bring such a criminal to justice. The answer is simple: because of our civilized standards of decency, fair play, and due process, our Constitution simply and resolutely proscribes such methods. In the words of Justice Clark in the 1961 *Mapp* case: "Nothing can destroy a government more quickly than its failure to observe its own laws, or worse, its disregard of the character of its own existence."[182] Which does not gainsay the frustrations of public officials such as Warren Earl Burger, who, just prior to his accession to the Chief Justiceship of the Supreme Court of the United States, wrote:

> The seeming anxiety of judges to protect every accused person from every consequence of his voluntary utterances is giving rise to myriad rules, subrules, variations and exceptions which even the most alert and most sophisti-

---

effects of *Miranda* in Pittsburgh, Pa., reconfirmed the above: while confessions had dropped slightly since the June 1966 decision, the number of suspects who pleaded guilty had increased slightly as well. (*The New York Times*, December 31, 1967, Sec. 1, p. 25.) An eleven-week Yale University study in 1967 yielded similar results. (*Ibid.*) So did a May 1968 Washington, D.C., study. (*Ibid.*, May 14, 1968, p. 60.) And so did a separate project observing custodial police interrogation in the District of Columbia. (66 *Michigan Law Review* 1347–1422, May 1968.) By 1970, after four years of close concern with the problem, Fred P. Graham concluded in a lengthy report that "despite evidence that crime has been steadily outstripping" the capacity of big-city law enforcement officers to control it, they "are becoming less disturbed by the Supreme Court's rein on their conduct towards suspects." (*The New York Times*, April 6, 1970, p. 1*l.*) See also the 1967 report of the International City Managers Association, *Public Management* (July), pp. 183–90, which confirms the above. The Yale and Washington, D.C., studies cited above, as well as similar compliance studies in Green Bay, Kenosha, Racine, and Madison, Wisconsin, showed that while implementation of *Miranda* was slow, grudging, and sometimes ineffective, overt flouting of the Court's norms by the police was a rarity. For the Wisconsin results, see Neal Milner, "Comparative Analysis of Patterns of Compliance with Supreme Court Decisions: *Miranda* and the Police in Four Communities," 5 *Law and Society Review* (August 1970), pp. 119–34.

[181]*Culombe v. Connecticut*, 367 U.S. 568 (1961).

[182]*Mapp v. Ohio*, 367 U.S. 643, at 659.

cated lawyers and judges are taxed to follow. . . . We are approaching the predicament of the centipede on the flypaper—each time one leg is placed to give support for relief of a leg already "stuck," another becomes captive and soon all are immobilized. . . . We are well on our way to forbidding any utterance of an accused to be used against him unless it is made in open court. Guilt or innocence becomes irrelevant in the criminal trial as we flounder in a morass of artificial rules—poorly conceived and often impossible of application.[183]

The Fourth Amendment Can of Worms. There is neither time nor space to survey each of the various contentious and difficult areas in which the lines of private and public rights converge. But one last illustration: the complex matter of permissible search and seizure—which may well be *the* most complex to analyze as well as to adjudicate. Under the Fourth Amendment, *unreasonable*[184] searches and seizures are forbidden; out of this mandate grew the so-called exclusionary rule applied to the federal government as of 1914[185] and, as we noted in the *Mapp* case,[186] to the states as of 1961. The exclusionary rule now forbids the use of *any* illegally obtained evidence to convict an accused in *court*, although the as yet (spring 1988) largely untested Organized Crime Control Act of 1970 contains a provision of questionable constitutionality, which sets a five-year statute of limitations on challenges by defendants of evidence from leads picked up by officers during *illegal* searches.[187] The basic exclusionary rule also means that an otherwise illegal search is not rendered legal simply by what it turns up; *ergo,* "fishing expeditions" on the part of police in search of evidence

[183]As quoted in Alpheus T. Mason and William M. Beaney, *American Constitutional Law,* 5th ed. (Englewood Cliffs, N.J.: Prentice-Hall, Inc., 1972), p. xv.

[184]An eternally controversial adjective!

[185]*Weeks v. United States,* 232 U.S. 383. See Yale Kamisar's extensive supportive discussion of the rule, "Is the Exclusionary Rule an 'Illogical' or 'Unnatural' Interpretation of the Fourth Amendment?," 62 *Judicature* (August 1978), pp. 67–84. For a contrary view, see Judge Malcolm Richard Wilkey, "The Exclusionary Rule: Why Suppress Valid Evidence?", *ibid.* (November 1978), pp. 215–32. The rule has spawned an enormous amount of passionate as well as dispassionate commentary in books, journals, the press, other media, and the *Congressional Record.* See the Court's 1983 embarrassment on the issue in *Gates v. Illinois,* 462 U.S. 213.

[186]*Mapp v. Ohio, op. cit.* See also pp. 132–44, supra.

[187]It *was* upheld as to the questioning of grand jury witnesses. (*United States v. Calandra,* 414 U.S. 338 [1975].)

are thus out. Before asking for an arrest warrant,[188] the police officer must convince the warrant-issuing magistrate of his "personal knowledge" of "probable cause." To obtain a search warrant, the place to be searched and the object(s) to be seized must be described "particularly." When, surprisingly, the Supreme Court ruled (5 : 3) in 1978 that police can get warrants to make *un*announced searches of places owned or occupied by persons believed to be innocent of criminal activities,[189] Congress responded two years later by enacting the Privacy Protection Act of 1980, severely limiting such searches. In any event, warrants are not issuable for "general" searches. Nor does a warrant to search a particular place *automatically* authorize the police to search anyone who happens to be there—as, for example, in a public bar.[190]

But there are, because there must be, situations in which the search of a person or the *immediate* surroundings is lawful *if* it is "incidental" to a legal arrest—i.e., one authorized by an arrest warrant or on the basis of probable cause—but such an "incidental" search, to be considered "reasonable," must *really* be "confined to the immediate vicinity of the arrest . . . to the area within the arrestee's reach at the time of his arrest, the area from which he might gain possession of a weapon or destructible evidence."[191] *Mere* "suspicion," without more, is never enough to meet the constitutional commands, yet the concept of "*reasonable* suspicion" has been judicially justified in, for example, upholding "profile"-triggered airport searches of drug traffic[192] and hijacking suspects. And, of course, there are instances, other than the narrowly drawn "incidental" search rule, in which it *is* possible to

[188]It may be either a daytime or nighttime warrant. (*Gooding v. United States*, 416 U.S. 430 [1974].)

[189]*Zurcher v. Stanford Daily*, 463 U.S. 547. "The critical element in a reasonable search," wrote Justice White in this highly controversial case, "is not that the owner of the property is suspected of crime, but that there is reasonable cause to believe that the specific things to be searched for and seized are located on the property." (At 556.) Because the case involved the press, sundry First Amendment issues were also raised and disposed of.

[190]*Ybarra v. Illinois*, 444 U.S. 85 (1979). But otherwise admissible evidence is not suppressible simply on the ground that it was unlawfully seized from a third party not before the court in a trial. (*United States v. Payner*, 447 U.S. 727 [1980].)

[191]*Chimel v. California*, 395 U.S. 752 (1969), at 763, which "toughened" the standards of *United States v. Rabinowitz*, 399 U.S. 56 (1950).

[192]*United States v. Mendenhall*, 446 U.S. 554 (1980). But cf. *Reid v. Georgia*, 448 U.S. 438 (1980), and *Florida v. Royer*, 460 U.S. 419 (1983).

search without a search warrant, *provided there is probable cause.*[193] Some examples would be: to discover weapons and/or prevent the destruction of evidence,[194] the common-law right of an arresting police agent to search when he has reasonable grounds to believe that a crime is being committed or that an individual on the scene is "armed and dangerous,"[195] and, again always assuming the presence of "probable cause," in the case of *moving* vehicles.[196] No such justifiable probable cause exists, however, the Supreme Court held (7 : 1) in 1979, in standard so-called police spot checks of automobile drivers' credentials on the public highways, *unless* the officer has some "articulable and reasonable suspicion that the motorist is unlicensed or [the auto] unregistered or [there is some other] violation of law."[197] Nonetheless, as the Court made clear unanimously in 1981, police may indeed stop vehicles when "the totality of circumstances" suggests its occupants may be involved in a crime (here the transportation of illegal aliens in Arizona).[198] Indeed, in 1982 a 6 : 3 ruling announced that henceforth, if probable cause justifies the search of a lawfully stopped vehicle, it justifies the search of *every* part of the vehicle and its contents that could conceal the object of the search.[199] Warrantless *aerial* searches of pri-

[193]"Probable cause" is, of course, enormously difficult to define—and to disprove. The Court's most frequently quoted definition is taken from Justice Douglas's opinion in *Henry v. United States,* 361 U.S. 98 (1959): "Probable cause exists if the facts and circumstances known to the officer warrant a prudent man in believing that the offense has been committed." (At 102.) See also the application of the "in plain view" doctrine, rejected in *Arizona v. Hicks,* 55 LW 4258 (1987).

[194]*Agnello v. United States,* 268 U.S. 20 (1925).

[195]See the several late 1960s and early 1970s "stop-and-frisk" cases cited in footnote 70, on p. 142, *supra.* See also *Pennsylvania v. Mimms,* 434 U.S. 106 (1977).

[196]*Carroll v. United States,* 267 U.S. 132 (1925). *Cf. New York v. Belton,* 453 U.S. 454 (1981), holding that no warrant is needed to search a car's passenger area post-arrest.

[197]*Delaware v. Prouse,* 440 U.S. 648. The decision still allows the police to set up roadblocks for license and registration checks, however—prompting the dissenting Justice Rehnquist to observe that motorists, "like sheep, are much less likely to be 'frightened' or 'annoyed' when stopped en masse"; that, therefore, police can now stop "*all* motorists," but not "*less* than all motorists." (At 664.) The "stop them all at a roadblock" practice of Charlottesville, VA., was upheld by the Court in 1986. (*Lowe v. Virginia,* 54 LW 3630.)

[198]*United States v. Cortez,* 455 U.S. 923, See also *Robbins v. California,* 453 U.S. 320 (1981).

[199]*United States v. Ross,* 456 U.S. 798. *Cf. United States v. Hensley,* holding that a warrant is needed for closed containers in a car's trunk. (453 U.S. 912).

vate areas were upheld 5 : 4 in 1986 in the instance of government investigators who used a plane to observe and photograph fenced off areas where "pot" was grown in one case and possible air pollution violations were suspected in the other.[200] Moreover, as it had ruled (6 : 3) in 1973, *if* there is "probable cause" to take a person into custody, "the fact of lawful arrest establishes the authority to search" the person "reasonably" (and not just in instances of suspected *serious* crimes;[201] nor does it have to be justified, like the *Terry* "stop-and-frisk" case,[202] which did *not* initiate an incident that led to an arrest but turned on the grounds of protecting the police officer from harm). And the Court added (6 : 2) in 1976 that the Constitution does *not* require law enforcement officials to obtain warrants before they make arrests in *public places*—even when there is adequate time to obtain a warrant—provided there is probable cause that a felony has been committed.[203] But as it held in 1980, a warrant *is* needed for routine felony arrests in *private* homes, absent "exigent circumstances,"[204] and not only must a confession thus obtained without a warrant be excluded, but the rule can be applied retroactively to 1980.[205] Frustrating as it may be, the constitutional rules must be observed—by the protagonists on both sides.

"Good Faith" and the Exclusionary Rule. Seventy years after *Weeks*,[206] thirty-five years after *Wolf*,[207] and twenty-three years after

[200]*California v. Ciraolo*, 54 LW 4464, and *Dow Chemical Co. v. United States*, 54 LW 4464. Also (6 : 2 in 1988) warrantless search of trash (*Calif. v. Greenwood*).

[201]*United States v. Robinson* and *Gustavson v. Florida*, 414 U.S. 218 and 414, respectively. U.S. 260, respectively, and a contraband search warrant provided police power for "temporary detention." (*Michigan v. Summers*, 452 U.S. 692 [1981].)

[202]*Terry v. Ohio*, 392 U.S. 1 (1968), an 8 : 1 decision written by Chief Justice Warren, Justice Douglas dissenting. See its extension to property, here the passenger area of a car in *Michigan v. Long*, 463 U.S. 1032 (1983).

[203]*United States v. Watson*, 423 U.S. 411. See *Donovan v. Dewey*, 452 U.S. 594 (1981).

[204]*Payton v. New York*, 445 U.S. 573. For an excellent analysis—as of 1966—of the entire search-and-seizure syndrome see J. W. Landynski, *Search and Seizure and the Supreme Court* (Baltimore: The Johns Hopkins Press, 1966). See also that author's work cited in footnote 146, p. 80, *supra*. For a more recent study see J. D. Hirschel, *Fourth Amendment Rights* (Lexington: D.C. Heath Co., 1979).

[205]*United States v. Johnson*, 457 U.S. 537 (1980). And, going further, the Court ruled 6 : 2 in 1984 that the police are almost never justified in entering a private home without a warrant to arrest someone for a minor *civil* offense (here drunken driving) on the first infraction. (*Welsh v. Wisconsin*, 466 U.S. 740.)

[206]*Weeks v. United States*, 232 U.S. 283 (1914).

[207]*Wolf v. Colorado*, 338 U.S. 25 (1949).

Mapp,[208] the heated and continuingly contentious controversy over the exclusionary rule came to a head in 1984. Dividing 7 : 2 and 6 : 3, the Supreme Court adopted the governmentally long-sought "good faith" exception to the rule. It held, speaking through Justice White, that the exclusionary rule should not apply when the police act in "objectively reasonable" reliance on a search warrant that at the time appears to be valid, even though it later proves defective. Over bitter dissents on Amendment Four grounds by Justice Brennan, who was joined by Justice Marshall in both cases and by Justice Stevens in the second,[209] White ruled that by suppressing "inherently trustworthy, tangible evidence," the exclusionary rule imposed "substantial social costs" that, at least in the context of a seemingly valid search warrant, outweighed the benefit achieved by deterring official misconduct. Legislation to accomplish the formal adoption of the good faith rule was introduced by Senator Strom Thurmond (R.-S.C.) in the spring of 1986, but it failed of adoption. Yet the Court itself expanded the "good faith" rule in 1987 by holding that evidence obtained in a search under an unconstitutional regulatory statute authorizing warrantless searches of certain businesses may be used if the police reasonably believed the law to be constitutional.[210] It is fair to conjecture that the Court will handle future exclusionary rules cases on an *ad hoc* basis and that the Justices will continue to be closely divided on the rule's range, extent, and application. It is, after all, a judge-made rule, not a constitutional requirement, and can be judge-altered, as indeed it has been with the adoption of the "good faith" concept.

That the Fourth Amendment line will continue to be a live, vexatious one is certain.[211] As Justice Brandeis mused six decades ago, the mind

---

[208]*Mapp v. Ohio*, 367 U.S. 643 (1961).

[209]*Massachusetts v. Sheppard*, 468 U.S. 981 (1984), and *United States v. Leon*, 468 U.S. 897, respectively.

[210]*Illinois v. Krull*, 55 LW 4291. See also its 1987 confirmation of the vitality of the "good faith" rule in *Maryland v. Garrison*, 55 LW 4190.

[211]Thus, the Court's 6 : 3 holding in *New Jersey v. T.L.O.*, 469 U.S. 325 (1985), established a "balancing approach" between individual and societal rights in the application of the Fourth Amendment to students in public schools. In the New Jersey case at issue, the Court approved warrantless searches of pupils on the school grounds during school hours on a case-by-case basis, with the test being the presence of "reasonable grounds" rather than the tougher one of "probable cause." Specifically, the case here involved the use and/or dissemination of controlled substances by students.

can hardly foresee what scientific developments may lie in store for us—and they are certain to affect Fourth Amendment mandates.

The Case Study of Wiretapping. To illustrate the aforegone further, wiretapping, one of the most vexatious of the due process problems, is *not* unconstitutional—or at least the Supreme Court has never so held it. The famous 5:4 *Olmstead* case of 1928 set the tone,[212] Chief Justice Taft holding it *not* to be a Fourth Amendment violation because the telephonic messages at issue did not involve a physical intrusion on the defendant's premises, nor was any "material thing" seized. Justice Holmes's vigorous dissent that it is "dirty business,"[213] and Justice Brandeis's prophetic warning about the "progress" of science, also rendered in a separate dissenting opinion—one of *the* great dissents in the Court's annals[214]—failed to command a majority. The response to *Olmstead* was the Federal Communications Act of 1934, which (like some state statutes) expressly forbade it; yet the F.B.I. successfully qualified it with the interpretation that mere "interception" is not a violation of the Act's famous Section 605 *unless there* is also *"divulgence"* —an interpretation that served as the agency's rationale for much of its wiretapping, despite the language of Section 605. Hence we had something that was proscribed yet went on constantly.

But does not wiretapping make the citizen prey to the very kind of "fishing expedition" which is theoretically forbidden under the Fourth Amendment? The modern scientific "advances" in the realm of detection, so perceptively predicted by Brandeis, are rapidly reducing privacy to a shibboleth. Thus, as was vividly demonstrated to a subcommittee of the United States Senate's Committee on the Judiciary,[215] we now have available such eavesdropping devices as tiny radio transmitters that can be concealed in a martini olive, with the toothpick serving as the antenna; in a woman's purse or her brassiere—even in the cavity

[212]*Olmstead v. United States,* 277 U.S. 438. (Italics supplied.)

[213]"We have to choose," he observed, "and for my part I think it a less evil that some criminals should escape than that the government would play an ignoble part." (*Ibid.,* at 470–471.)

[214]Among its memorable language: "The makers of our Constitution . . . conferred, as against the government, the right to be let alone—the most comprehensive of rights and the right most valued by civilized men. . . . Men born to freedom are naturally alert to repel invasions of their liberty by evil-minded rulers. The greatest dangers to liberty lurk in insidious encroachment by men of zeal, well-meaning but without understanding." (At 478.)

[215]See *Life,* May 20, 1966, pp. 38–47.

of a tooth of an intimate associate! Then there is the laser, a device which can transmit a concentrated beam of light to a room several blocks away so as to reflect back a television picture of everything happening in the room, including the sound! Perhaps it was specters such as these that caused Justice Nathan R. Sobel of the New York State Supreme Court (Brooklyn Division) to declare unconstitutional on March 1, 1965, the New York State law that had authorized court-approved electronic eavesdropping on a suspect's private premises. In his thirty-two page opinion, Justice Sobel held the law invalid because the eavesdropping orders it authorized could not, in his judgment, meet the standards required for the issuance of search warrants under the Fourth Amendment.[216] Just a year later, the Federal Communications Commission issued an order prohibiting private citizens from using radio devices to eavesdrop. Theoretically, the F.C.C. order made illegal such equipment as the tiny radio transmitters described above (unless everyone present knew the equipment was being used). Yet it did *not* affect the use of a miniature tape recorder directly connected to a small camouflaged microphone, since no radio transmission was involved—although the same kind of eavesdropping may take place. Nor did the ban affect law enforcement agencies, such as the F.B.I., the Internal Revenue Service, or state and local police and similar authorities. However, in July 1967 the then Attorney-General, Ramsey Clark, in a dramatic order going far beyond any previously issued governmental limitations in the wiretapping and eavesdropping field, issued sweeping new regulations forbidding all wiretapping and virtually all eavesdropping except in national security cases. The new rules generated considerable controversy and opposition among federal agents and prosecutors,[217] and they were relaxed by the Nixon Administration.

Indeed, by that time a number of legal experts had become convinced that the Supreme Court's *Griswold* ruling in 1965,[218] which, as noted in Chapter III, invalidated Connecticut's birth control statute by enunciat-

---

[216]*People v. Grossman*, 257 N.Y.S. 2d 266. He was reversed a year later by the Appellate Division, but he was more or less vindicated in 1967 when the United States Supreme Court declared the New York law unconstitutional in *Berger v. New York*, 388 U.S. 41.

[217]Thus, F.B.I. Director J. Edgar Hoover referred to Clark as the "worst Attorney-General" he had served under in fifty years in Washington, "even worse than Bobby Kennedy." (*Time*, November 30, 1970, p. 11.)

[218]*Griswold v. Connecticut*, 381 U.S. 479. See pp. 92 ff., *supra*.

ing a new "right of privacy," had laid the basis for an eventual judicial outlawing of wiretapping and other forms of electronic eavesdropping. It was argued that the new right of privacy could be held to override the technical distinction of a physical intrusion that the Court made both in the *Olmstead* case[219] and in subsequent decisions involving other electronic eavesdropping,[220] and thus render all such intrusions unconstitutional.[221] On the other hand, it might well be asked, could not and should not the kind of search and seizure represented by wiretapping be authorized under our Constitution? Although wiretapping and electronic eavesdropping are clearcut invasions of the basic rights of privacy, perhaps they *are* necessary in cases of subversive activities, seditious conduct, espionage, kidnapping, and certain other major crimes. Perhaps a good case *can* be made for eavesdropping in the fields just mentioned when the act is duly requested *and judicially authorized before the fact*, notwithstanding the reprehensible nature of the incursions of privacy involved. However, it would be much harder to make a viable case for such intrusions on privacy in crimes like fraud, racketeering, prostitution, and gambling, or for the "investigation" of public and private employees in anything but highly secret positions.[222] In the final analysis, our response must turn first on the constitutionality of any such proposed action and second on its wisdom. And even assuming the former, any thoughts on the wisdom of such action must confront the basic issues raised by Justice Brandeis in his memorable dissent in the *Olmstead* case, when he wrote:

The makers of our Constitution undertook to secure conditions favorable to the pursuit of happiness. They recognized the significance of man's spiritual

---

[219]*Olmstead v. United States*, 277 U.S. 438 (1928). The vote in that case, as noted earlier above, was 5:4; the majority opinion was written by Chief Justice Taft and joined by Associate Justices Van Devanter, McReynolds, Sutherland, and Sanford. The dissenters, in addition to Holmes and Brandeis, were Justices Butler and Stone—all of whom wrote dissenting opinions.

[220]E.g., *Goldman v. United States*, 316 U.S. 129 (1942), and *On Lee v. United States*, 343 U.S. 747 (1952). (*Lee* was reconfirmed, 5:4, in 1971, in *United States v. White*, 401 U.S. 745.) Cf. *Silverman v. United States*, 365 U.S. 505 (1961).

[221]Such a ruling would presumably reach the so-called distinction between "wiretapping" and "bugging," a distinction that sees the latter as not proscribed. It was embraced by sundry law-enforcement officials, apparently including the then ex–U.S. Attorney-General Robert F. Kennedy. (See David Lawrence, "Rightfully Bugging," the *New York Herald Tribune* [International Edition], July 9, 1966, p. 8.)

[222]An interesting case for such a balancing approach to the use of wiretapping and

nature, of his feelings and of his intellect. They knew that only a part of the pain, pleasure and satisfactions of life are to be found in material things. They sought to protect Americans in their beliefs, their thoughts, their emotions and their sensations. They conferred, as against the Government, *the right to be let alone—the most comprehensive of rights and the right most valued by civilized men.* To protect that right, every unjustifiable intrusion by the Government upon the privacy of the individual, whatever the means employed, must be deemed a violation of the Fourth Amendment. . . .[223]

The Court—the recipient of so many governmentally, especially legislatively, "passed bucks"—in its 1967 catalytic *Katz* case[224] seemed to take a long stride toward a possible solution of at least the eavesdropping ("bugging") aspect of the problem, and, by implication, of the entire privacy/instrusion dilemma. In that decision, with a solo dissent by Justice Black—who consistently rejected the contention that the specific safeguards of the Fourth Amendment, as spelled out therein, apply to eavesdropping because the Amendment speaks only of "persons, houses, papers, and effects"—the Court *eased curbs* on "bugging" *while adding safeguards* against it! Justice Stewart's majority opinion, noting that the Fourth Amendment should not "be translated into a general constitutional right of privacy,"[225] made it clear that the Constitution does not forbid electronic "bugging" by law enforcement officers *if* they first obtain warrants authorizing the eavesdropping— warrants being a basic requirement of the Fourth Amendment, of course. *But,* at the same time, with *Katz* the Court extended the reach of that Amendment by holding that the search warrant procedure must be followed by the police officers even when they plan to eavesdrop on persons in semi-public places, such as a phone booth. Moreover, and significantly, the Court threw out its old "physical trespass" test by ruling that the trespass *per se* was not the crucial point, that the Fourth

electronic eavesdropping was made by Alan Westin in his *Privacy and Freedom* (New York: Atheneum, 1967), *passim.*

[223]*Olmstead v. United States, op. cit.,* at 478. (Italics supplied.) Philippa Strum reports that one of Brandeis's working folders for *Olmstead* contains a 1928 clipping reporting on the development of "something called television." Brandeis, she comments, was a great believer in progress—"but not all progress was good." See her *Louis D. Brandeis: Justice for the People* (Cambridge: Harvard University Press, 1984), p. 325.

[224]*Katz v. United States,* 389 U.S. 347. The vote was 7:1, Justice Marshall not participating.

[225]*Ibid.,* at 350.

Amendment "protects people not places."[226] In effect, *Katz* thus overruled both the "material things seized" rationale of the *Olmstead* holding[227] and the "physical intrusion" distinction of the *Goldman* case[228] (which had come midway between the *Olmstead* and *Katz* decisions). The latter also lessened the effect of the Court's 5 : 4 decision in *Berger v. New York* a few months earlier in 1967,[229] when it had narrowly invalidated the aforementioned New York statute authorizing electronic eavesdropping because, as Justice Tom Clark—an ex-Attorney-General of the United States—wrote for the majority, the "statute is too broad in its sweep, resulting in a trespassory intrusion into a constitutionally protected area" and did not provide for "adequate judicial supervision or protective procedures."[230] What *Katz* did, then, was to enable the enactment of both wiretapping and eavesdropping ("bugging") statutes, *provided* the carefully delineated Fourth Amendment safeguards against unreasonable searches and seizures were scrupulously observed by *all* branches of the government, both statutorily and procedurally.[231]

Against the backdrop of the rising controversy of the "law and order" issue, Congress took the *Katz* cue and enacted Title III of the Omnibus Crime Control and Safe Streets Act of 1968, headed "Wiretapping and Electronic Surveillance." It permits *court-approved* interceptions by both federal and state law enforcement officials in the investigation of a large number of listed crimes[232]—there were 648 such court-authorized, although not necessarily applied, orders in 1983

[226]*Ibid.*, at 351. See the Court's 7 : 2 majority emphasis of that crucial point in its 1977 striking down of a conviction obtained in a federal case involving a 200-pound footlocker filled with marijuana. (*United States v. Chadwick*, 433 U.S. 1.) But the Court also pointed out three years later that the *legality* of a search is challengeable only if an accused can demonstrate "an expectation of privacy in the premises searched." *United States v. Salvucci*, 448 U.S. 83 (1980). See, too the aerial surveillance cases, *supra*, fn. 200.

[227]*Katz v. United States, op. cit.*, at 351.

[228]*Goldman v. United States*, 316 U.S. 129 (1942), as distinguished by *Silverman v. United States*, 365 U.S. 505 (1961), in which the use of a "spike mike" was held to be an actual physical intrusion.

[229]388 U.S. 41.

[230]*Ibid.*, at 44, 60. It was Clark's valedictory opinion.

[231]See the informative analysis of privacy by David M. O'Brien, "Reasonable Expectations of Privacy: Principles and Policies of Fourth Amendment–Protected Privacy," 13 *New England Law Review* 663–738 (1978), and the same author's *Privacy, Law, and Public Policy* (New York: Frederick A. Praeger, 1979).

[232]E.g., for the *state* level: murder, kidnapping, gambling, robbery, bribery, extortion,

(440 state, 208 federal); 816 in 1971; 864 in 1973; 871 in 1974; 626 in 1977 (549 of these state and 77 federal); and 578 in 1982 (130 of these federal). More than half involved alleged gambling offenses, which consistently lead the "tap" field, followed by those for drug-related crimes (that now cover *circa* one-fifth of the total) throughout the United States.[233] The sharp drop as of 1976 reflects a cutback in gambling investigations (in part because of mounting costs). Replete with procedural safeguards—with an eye toward *Katz*—the law has a contentious "exemption" section in the case of "an emergency situation exist[ing] with respect to conspiratorial activities threatening the national security interest or to conspiratorial activities characteristic of organized crime."[234] Under its terms, and if the action at issue is so classified by either the United States Attorney-General or the principal prosecuting attorney of any state or its subdivisions, interception may proceed *without* court order, provided an application for an order is obtained and entered "within forty-eight hours after the interception has occurred or begins to occur."[235] Here, then, is the loophole—which may or may not be justifiable and constitutional, and will assuredly be judicially tested.[236]

A different, and perhaps even more significant test, however, had come in 1971, when, breaking new ground in a surprisingly bold decision, United States District Judge Warren J. Ferguson ruled in Los Angeles that the federal government's "no-warrant-needed" national security wiretap policy, allegedly inherent in a perhaps even more contentious section of the 1968 statute than the one discussed above, which states that the law's provisions "do not restrict the constitutional powers of the President,"[237] was unconstitutional as applied to *domestic* cases (rather than foreign ones). As he put the issue:

---

or dealing in narcotics, marijuana, or other dangerous drugs, etc. (Section 2516–[2]). Some of these also apply in the federal sector.

[233]Based on annual reports by the United States Attorney-General and the Administrative Office of the United States Courts.

[234]Section 2518(7).

[235]Section 2518(7)(b).

[236]By mid-1987 lower federal courts had reached conflicting results; but no Supreme Court test had occurred. *United States v. Chavez,* 416 U.S. 562 (1974), in the eyes of at least some observers, seemed to approve the procedure tangentially in a 5 : 4 holding.

[237]Section 2511(3). Among other things, it states: "Nothing contained in this chapter . . . shall limit the constitutional power of the President to take such measures as he

National security cannot be invoked to abridge basic rights. . . . To guarantee political freedom, our forefathers agreed to take certain risks which are inherent in a free democracy. It is unthinkable that we should now be required to sacrifice those freedoms in order to defend them.[238]

Shortly thereafter, Judge Ferguson's ruling was echoed in an even more strongly worded decision against the government's interpretation of its asserted authority under the 1968 Wiretapping Act by United States District Judge Damon J. Keith in a Detroit case.[239] The government appealed; lost 2 : 1 at the bar of the United States Court of Appeals for the Sixth Circuit in April, which held, *inter alia*, that there was not "one written phrase" in the Constitution or statutes to support the Administration's view that federal agents might legally wiretap radical domestic groups without court order;[240] and took a further appeal to the Supreme Court.[241] In one of those decisions that render the study of the judicial process so fascinatingly unpredictable, down came the Burger Court's response in its next term: in an 8 : 0 opinion—Justice Rehnquist abstaining—written by Justice Powell, who, as a private citizen, not so long theretofore had *supported* publicly the Government's claim of constitutional authority for wiretapping of radical domestic groups *sans* warrant, the unanimous Justices declared the practice of doing so *without prior judicial approval* to be an unconstitutional invasion of Fourth Amendment guarantees, as well as being unauthorized under the 1968 statute![242] "The price of lawful public dissent," in Powell's words, "must not be a dread of subjection to an unchecked surveillance power. Nor must the fear of unauthorized official eavesdropping deter citizen

---

deems necessary to protect the nation against actual or potential attack or other hostile acts of a foreign power. . . ."

[238]*United States v. Smith*, 321 F. Supp. 424.

[239]*Plamondon v. Mitchell*, decided January 25, 1971. (See following footnote.)

[240]*United States v. United States District Court for the Eastern District of Michigan*, 444 F. 2d 651 (1971).

[241]A collateral issue had reached the Court in 1969, when it held that any criminal defendant had the right to see directly all transcriptions unexpurgated by a judge of his conversations picked up by an "illegal" police listening device. The purpose of the decision was to let defendants rest assured that no illegally obtained evidence was used against them—the government being forced either to turn the transcripts of the "illegal" tap over to defendants or to drop the case against them. (*Alderman v. United States*, 394 U.S. 165.)

[242]*United States v. United States District Court for the Eastern District of Michigan*, 407 U.S. 297 (1972).

dissent and discussion of government action in private conversation."[243]

The Court left open the statute's application to *foreign* groups suspected of subversive activity—a facet it refused 3:5 pointedly to explore when it had an opportunity to do so in 1974.[244] Four years thereafter, however, Congress—allowing for narrow exceptions—enacted legislation requiring federal court approval before the government can conduct electronic surveillance in *foreign* intelligence cases. Concurrently, Congress further narrowed the government's authority to obtain judicial warrants for *domestic* national security wiretaps and bugging. Chairman Birch Bayh (D.-Ind.) of the Senate Intelligence Committee hailed the measure as "a landmark in the development of effective legal safeguards for constitutional rights."[245] On a related matter involving the 1968 wiretapping law, it had administered another defeat to the Government's attempts to use tapping more facilely: in two devastating, unanimous decisions in mid-1974, the Court threw out the convictions of two accused criminals[246] because of "shortcuts" under the 1968 statute taken by Attorney-General John N. Mitchell some years earlier. While the Justices acknowledged that the law had indeed vastly expanded federal investigative authority to tap, that authority hinged expressly on the personal approval in advance by the Attorney-General or by an especially designated assistant. But dozens of authorizations, including those involved in the two cases before the Court, had simply been initialled "JNM" by a minor Mitchell aide, Sol Lindenbaum, or sometimes even just by the latter's secretary! That irregularity, held the normally decidedly "pro" law-and-order Justice White, was no mere technicality: Congress had clearly and carefully required that "the mature judgment of a particular, responsible official" would be involved in any decision to tap. As a result of the Court's ruling, nearly two years of determined hard work by federal investigators was wiped out, and at least sixty cases involving no fewer than 626 accused gamblers, narcotic dealers, and other racketeers were

---

[243]*Ibid.*, at 314.

[244]*Ivanov v. United States,* 419 U.S. 881 (1974).

[245]*The Washington Post,* October 26, 1978, p. A2. (The new legislation was in 18 USCS § 2511.) See the Foreign Intelligence Surveillance Act of 1978.

[246]*United States v. Giordano,* 416 U.S. 505, and *United States v. Chavez,* 416 U.S. 562.

imperiled.[247] Such, however, is the price of constitutional guarantees: shortcuts à la Mitchell's can simply not be condoned, nor, it is to be hoped, will they be, so long as we are governed by our Constitution's letter and spirit. In that spirit Congress enacted in 1986 a modernization of the wiretapping statutes designed to protect the privacy of modern high-tech communications. Henceforth, in the absence of a warrant it will thus also be just as illegal to eavesdrop on someone's electronic mail, video conference call, conversation on a cellular car phone, or computer-to-computer transmission as it continues to be to wiretap a telephone.

Law, Order, and Justice Reconsidered. Notwithstanding the great, and entirely understandable, public outcry to do something about the now so shockingly predictable annual, upward of 10 percent rise[248] in crime—which sees six million Americans set upon by violent criminals annually—there are no shortcuts in democratic society to regulation, prosecution, and conviction. But it would be sophistry to gainsay the genuine concern, both lay and professional, over the contemporary broadening of judicial "supervision" in the realm of criminal justice and the resultant stringent new rules of procedure that have evolved. Given the epidemically increasing rate of crime—of which less than 20 percent is officially reported[249]—are there alternatives to "easy" or "shortcut" apprehensions, prosecutions, and convictions that either circumvent, dilute, or disregard basic constitutional guarantees? Among them may well be such fundamental ones as deterrents and, arguably most significantly, the certainty of punishment—hardly a hallmark under our criminal justice system. And since, according to the most authentic and reliable recent statistics,[250] between 65 and 92 percent of

[247]See the account in *Time*, May 27, 1974, p. 57.

[248]*Annual Reports* of the Federal Bureau of Investigation, 1970 ff. Its report for 1979 showed a 9.1 percent overall increase, but an 11.0 percent one in violent crime—the sharpest rise in four years.

[249]See *the New York Times*, April 15, 1974, p. 1. See also the works by Wilson and Silberman, fn. 250, *infra,* and the F.B.I.'s annual *Uniform Crime Report*.

[250]See James Q. Wilson's estimate of 87 percent in his fine *Thinking About Crime* (New York: Random House, 1985); among others, the President's Crime Commission's conclusion that 85 percent of those arrested for crimes more serious than a traffic offense have been arrested before, and that the average man who has been arrested once will be arrested seven more times. (*The New York Times Magazine*, May 11, 1969, p. 136.) According to Chief Justice Burger, 65 percent of the 200,000 persons serving prison sentences in 1970 would be reconvicted. (*The Philadelphia Evening Bulletin*, February

those booked on criminal charges were recidivists ("repeaters"), it seems entirely reasonable to ask whether our courts have not been "too soft" on them and, instead, thus might well be more severe in the type and length of sentences meted out to recidivists. The public has the right to be protected from habitual criminality; and perhaps longer, less readily commutable, and less easily parolable sentences[251] may well be in order,[252] especially since only one out of fifty *reported* crimes results in conviction—and but one out of every five such crimes *is* reported![253] It does seem that trial judges and parole officers have often been guilty of the kind of leniency in criminal cases involving "repeaters" that may be appropriate only for an initial offense; that—and this is more troubling—the criminal is not infrequently regarded as the victim of society

---

23, 1970.) According to ex-Attorney-General Ramsey Clark, 87 percent of the major crimes committed in the United States are committed by youths who were previously convicted of an earlier offense. (Speech at Temple University, April 1970.) The F.B.I.'s *Uniform Crime Report* of 1967 reported that of 17,000 randomly selected prisoners released in 1963, a total of 92 percent had been rearrested by 1967 (p. 28). According to the same source, almost 90 percent of those who were arrested for major crimes during 1967 had been arrested previously; 70 percent had been convicted; and 50 percent had served jail sentences of over ninety days (p. 23). Although hardly without a considerable number of critics on grounds of reliability or accuracy, the F.B.I.'s annual *Uniform Crime Reports* are an important source of a host of pertinent statistics. "The public notion and the police idea of revolving door crime is thus borne out," reported Marvin E. Wolfgang, head of the Center for Studies in Criminology and Criminal Law at the University of Pennsylvania, in releasing a 1969 pilot study of 9,978 boys born in 1945. Six percent of those boys committed 5,305 crimes, nearly nine apiece. (Release to the press, September 28, 1969.) Of 14,214 adults arrested for major crimes in 1971, 69 percent had been arrested before and averaged 5.8 arrests each. (The *Philadelphia Inquirer*, April 1, 1972, p. 7.) For a recent, widely acclaimed study of crime in America and its attempted control, see Charles E. Silberman, *Criminal Violence, Criminal Justice* (New York: Random House, 1978; Vintage Books, 1980). The author's "Appendix: Notes on Crime Statistics" (pp. 606–17) represents an unique approach to an analysis of their gathering and utilization. The Bureau of Judicial Statistics reported a 75 percent recidivist rate for state prisoners in early 1985. (*The New York Times*, March 4, 1985, p. A4.)

[251]For a useful compendium on diverse criminal sentencing, see the special issue of 60 *Judicature* 5 (December 1976), "Criminal Sentencing: A Game of *Chance.*" And see 63 *Judicature* 4 (October 1979) for some fascinating, thought-provoking comparative data on the utilization of fines in lieu of imprisonment in sentencing in England and Wales.

[252]I am aware of the general opposition to that suggestion by most sociologists and psychologists. But there is also considerable support from experts on criminology and urbanology as, prominently, James Q. Wilson (see footnote 250, *supra*). Thus, in arguing for longer jail terms as a practical deterrent to the growing crime menace, Wilson is scornful of utopian-minded "intellectuals" who, in his view, refuse to acknowledge that "wicked people exist" and are loath to be critical of "humankind."

[253]58 *Judicature* 10 (May 1975), p. 466. See also 63 *Judicature* 4 (October 1979).

To the Editor:

I, along with a vast number of my fellow citizens, am in contempt of court. The reason? Typical articles in today's *Times,* to wit:

*Page 1: A story about the capture of Nathan Giles, convicted murderer who was out on parole when he allegedly committed the particularly horrible murder of a nurse.

*Page B1: Davreaux Wiggins, convicted of pushing a stewardess in front of a subway train, then kicking her in the face when she tried to escape. He told police this was his fourth recent such incident. Judge George Roberts gave him half the sentence that could have been imposed. Beware of subway platforms four years hence when Mr. Wiggins may be back at work.

*Page B3: Because of the technicality that a convicted rapist committed his crime in Queens rather than Brooklyn, the New York State Court of Appeals, in its infinite wisdom, ruled that he must be retried. Three members of the court expressed doubt that the defendant would be tried again. And, if he will be retried, imagine the anguish that his victim must suffer for the second time.

I once was under the impression that one of the functions of the courts was to see that justice was done so that the public would be protected. Until there is more evidence of this I will remain in contempt of court.

Max Kohn
Philadelphia, Dec. 1, 1978

[The writer was a consultant to the Citizens Crime Commission of Philadelphia.]
SOURCE: *The New York Times,* December 8, 1978, p. A28.

rather than society as the victim of the criminal; that, in the view of many onlookers, "there is more concern with the criminal than with the victim."[254] But there is another aspect to that suggestion.

Because "bigger and better" prison sentences will not solve the problem of crime, a plea for toughness in sentencing must join one for more effective efforts in prison rehabilitation; for more modern institutional facilities; and for more appropriately trained professional personnel. Revelations in 1969 and 1970 of conditions in prisons, styled "universities of crime" by President Nixon, gave shocking proof of the state of America's prisons—of which six that were still in use in 1971 were built in the eighteenth century, and four prior to George Washington's inauguration.[255] In the last three decades, at least eight presidential commissions, dozens of legislative reports, and more than a thousand books and articles have pleaded for prison reform. Although we have witnessed some *bona fide* groping for such reform,[256] the future still looked bleak in the late 1980s. Coordination and improvement of federal, state, and local systems is vital. Of course, there is a limit to the type of rehabilitation that a prison can provide, but much more can be done than is done at present—although some leading experts, James Q. Wilson for one, contend that hardened criminals are not rehabilitatable,[257] and Charles E. Silberman, while somewhat less pessimistic, perhaps, on overall solutions to crime prevention and control, concludes that "[n]o approach to rehabilitation seems to work."[258] The public, however, must be willing to foot the bill for such measures; insistence on more

[254]In 1984 Congress enacted the Federal Victims of Crime Act (P.L. 98-473, Title II, Ch. 14), which established a Crime Victim Fund in the Department of the Treasury to be supported by fines levied in connection with federal criminal cases.

[255]*The New York Times,* January 7, 1971, Sec. 1, p. 1. See also "U.S. Prisons: Schools for Crime," *Time,* January 18, 1971, p. 48.

[256]E.g., the imaginative new federal prison complex in Butner, North Carolina, which opened in mid-1976, designed and organized to try a new tack in penology. Another is the ultra-modern federal minimum security prison at Eglin Air Force Base in Florida (where Maryland's deposed Governor Marvin Mandel began to serve his three-year sentence in 1980). "The best and most advanced prison ever built" was opened in 1982 in Oak Park Heights, Minnesota. The 400-bed facility has a large gym, chapel, educational complex, and competent security control center. Each cell is a private room with a solid door, stainless-steel toilet, sink, mirror, desk, shelves, and a thickly mattressed bed.

[257]"I have not heard an intellectually respectable defense of criminal rehabilitation." (Quoted by *Time,* June 30, 1975, p. 22.) See also his book cited in fn. 250, *supra,* and Chief Justice Burger's imaginative May 1981 proposals.

[258]Silberman, *op. cit.,* p. 247.

protection has been accompanied, all too often and contradictorily, by opposition to paying for it.

Whether or not these suggestions might help us come to grips with important aspects of the problem and assuage the very real and justifiable[259] fears of the lay and professional public—or whether such statutes as the Organized Crime Control Act of 1970, with its drastic provisions, have some answers—when it comes to the fundamental standards of due process of law under our Constitution, there can be no compromises, no shortcuts. "The interest of . . . [the government]," to quote again Justice Brennan, ". . . is not that it shall win a case, but that justice shall be done."[260] There should be no reason whatsoever why, in our democratic society, well-trained, professional agents of the law cannot apprehend and convict alleged criminals without, in the process, becoming criminals themselves. As Arnold S. Trebach put it so well in his *The Rationing of Justice,* the argument against greater protection for the rights of the accused "reduces itself to an argument *for* violation of the law in order to enforce it. It is a crime to violate the rights of *any* person," whether he be a criminal or a saint. Under our system, in the words of Chief Justice Warren to *New York Times* correspondent Anthony Lewis, the prosecutor "is not paid to convict people. He is there to protect the rights of the people in our community and to see that when there is a violation of the law, it is vindicated by trial and prosecution under fair judicial standards."[261] A poignant Warren trademark thus was to interrupt a learned counsel's argument citing precedent and book with the simple, almost naïve-sounding *quaere:* "Yes, but was it fair?" Deeply concerned with social justice, that remarkable, if hardly uncontroversial, public servant once mused: "You sit there, and you see the whole gamut of human nature. Even if the case being argued involves only a little fellow and $50, it involves justice. That's what is important."[262]

---

[259]Thus, from 1961 to 1979 the rate of robberies increased 256 percent, forcible rape 174 percent, aggravated assault 176 percent, and murder 107 percent. And the rate for these violent crimes as well as property crimes like burglary is still rising sharply, averaging 10 percent per category. (See F.B.I. *Uniform Crime Report*, released September 29, 1980 and subsequent annual reports.),

[260]*Jencks v. United States,* 353 U.S. 657 (1957), at 668.

[261]"A Talk with Warren on Crime, the Court, the Country," *The New York Times Magazine,* October 19, 1969, p. 126.

[262]From *Time*'s obituary essay, July 22, 1974, p. 66.

As he did so frequently, Justice Brandeis went to the heart of the matter in his dissent in the *Olmstead* case in 1928:

Decency, security, and liberty alike demand that government officials shall be subjected to the same rules of conduct that are commands to the citizen. In a government of laws, existence of the government will be imperilled if it fails to observe the law scrupulously. Our government is the potent, the omnipresent teacher. For good or for ill, it teaches the whole people by example. Crime is contagious. If the government becomes a lawbreaker, it breeds contempt for law; it invites every man to become a law unto himself; it invites anarchy. To declare that in the administration of the criminal law the end justifies the means—to declare that the government may commit crimes in order to secure the conviction of a private criminal—would bring terrible retribution. Against that pernicious doctrine this court should resolutely set its face.[263]

In the main the Supreme Court has for some time now[264] been setting its face "against that pernicious doctrine," and it has done so regardless of criticism. Still, "courts should not blindly reach out and find merit in a constitutional claim where none exists."[265] And the Supreme Court of the United States is obliged ever to be alive to the admonition by one of its most thoughtful and literate members, Justice Robert H. Jackson, that it must not en route "convert the constitutional Bill of Rights into a suicide pact."[266]

[263]*Olmstead v. United States*, 277 U.S. 438 (1928), at 485. Chief Justice Warren would echo these haunting thoughts well in his opinion for the Court in *Spano v. New York*, 360 U.S. 315, three decades later: "The police must obey the law while enforcing the law; . . . in the end life and liberty can be as much endangered from illegal methods used to convict these thought to be criminals as from the actual criminals themselves." (At 320.)

[264]For an intelligent critique of aspects of that dénouement, see Henry J. Friendly, *Benchmarks* (Chicago: University of Chicago Press, 1967), especially Chapter 11, "The Bill of Rights as a Code of Criminal Procedure." See also the aforementioned somber, enlightening, critical Wilson and Silberman works, fns. 250, 257, and 258, *supra,* and *Time's* issues of June 30, 1975, and March 23, 1981, devoted to "The Crime Wave."

[265]Dissenting opinion by Justice Matthew J. Jasen of the New York Court of Appeals in *People v. Rogers*, 48 N.Y. 2d 167 (1979).

[266]Dissenting opinion, *Terminiello v. Chicago*, 337 U.S. 1 (1949), at 37. See text and fn. 170 on p. 238, *infra,* for a fuller discussion of that statement. For an echo see Chief Justice Burger's 1981 majority opinion in *Haig v. Agee*, 453 U.S. 280.

chapter *V* The Precious Freedom of Expression

If we Americans have, and practice, "ambivalence"[1] as our primary ideology, the realm of the precious freedom of expression is assuredly a case in point. The commonplace expression "It's a free country, isn't it—so I can darn well say what I please!" is in fact sincere, for its underlying philosophy is ingrained in the body politic's notion of what democratic America means. But its paradox is that throughout history we so often permit, wink at, even encourage, its violation in practice. Thus we have been quite willing to curb the "dangerous," the "seditious," the "subversive," the "prurient," the "obscene," the "libelous," and a host of other presumably undesirable modes and manners of expression that—at a particular time and place— seemed to justify repression. Yet, unless one accepts the absolutist approach advocated so consistently by Justice Black and his supporters (an approach that nonetheless still necessitates an answer to the basic question of just what "expression" *is*), the need to draw some line is primary, for, as Black observed in a famous 1941 dissenting opinion: "Freedom to speak and write about public questions is as important to the life of our government as is the heart of the human body. In fact, this privilege is the heart of our government! If that heart be weakened, the result is debilitation; if it be stilled, the result is death."[2] Justice Brandeis, whose last two years of service on the bench of the highest court coincided with Black's first two, tried to provide a memorable guideline when, in a concurring opinion joined by his colleague

[1]This was cogently suggested by Professor Robert G. McCloskey of Harvard University in "The American Ideology," an essay in Marian D. Irish, ed., *Continuing Crisis in American Politics* (Englewood Cliffs, N.J.: Prentice-Hall, 1963).
[2]*Milk Wagon Drivers Union v. Meadowmoor Dairies,* 312 U.S. 287, at 301–2.

Holmes, he defended the "chance-taking" aspects of freedom of expression in ringing terms:

> [Those who won our independence] believed that freedom to think as you will and to speak as you think are means indispensable to the discovery and spread of political truth; that without free speech and assembly, discussion would be futile; that with them, discussion affords ordinarily adequate protection against the dissemination of noxious doctrine; that the greatest menace to freedom is an inert people; that public discussion is a political duty; and that this should be a fundamental principle of the American government.[3]

Judicial Line Formulae

The difficulty of any attempt to establish viable standards in the realm of freedom of expression is apparent. Yet, as five key example areas to be discussed below will indicate, attempts at judicial tests, doctrines, or formulae have been of lasting concern to the Court. Much depends on the definition of terms which determine a particular judicial decision. But—in addition to the self-evident one of "balancing" competing interests—we can isolate at least two, perhaps three, major judicial "tests," all of them post–World War 1 phenomena.

THE "CLEAR AND PRESENT DANGER" TEST

Certainly the best-known is the "clear and present danger" test. Credit for its authorship has generally been given to Justice Holmes, actively supported by Justice Brandeis, although there are some observers who would grant United States Court of Appeals' Judge Learned Hand an important assist in the birth of the doctrine, if not with its central idea. It was first used in 1919 in the *Schenck* case.

Schenck v. United States.[4] In 1917 Charles T. Schenck, general secretary of the Socialist Party, and some of his associates sent out some 15,000 leaflets to potential and actual draftees under the Conscription Act, urging the young men—in impassioned language—to resist the draft. The leaflets' text intimated that conscription was despotism in its

---

[3]*Whitney v. California,* 274 U.S. 357 (1927), at 375.
[4]*Schenck v. United States,* 249 U.S. 47 (1919).

worst form and a "monstrous wrong against humanity, in the interest of Wall Street's chosen few." It urged them not to "submit to intimidation . . . from cunning politicians and a mercenary capitalist press" and referred to the Constitution as an "infamous conspiracy."

Under the Espionage Act of 1917, which had specifically proscribed the kind of activities in which Schenck and his colleagues had engaged, the federal government indicted them on three counts: (1) conspiracy to cause insubordination in the armed forces of the United States, and to obstruct the recruiting and enlisting services; (2) conspiracy to use the mails for the transmission of matter declared to be non-mailable under the Espionage Act; and (3) the unlawful use of the mails for the transmission of the matter under (2). Schenck and his co-defendants were convicted in a federal trial court over their objections that the pertinent provisions of the Espionage Act constituted a violation of the freedom of speech and press guaranteed by the First Amendment. Unanimously rejecting the petitioner's contentions, the Supreme Court, speaking through Justice Holmes, enunciated its new "clear and present danger" doctrine. As the then seventy-eight-year-old jurist explained in a memorable passage:

> We admit that in many places and in *ordinary times* the defendants in saying all that was said in the circular would have been within their constitutional rights. *But the character of every act depends upon the circumstances in which it is done.* . . . The most stringent protection of free speech would not protect a man in *falsely* shouting fire in a theatre and causing a panic. It does not even protect a man from an injunction against uttering words that have all the effects of force. . . . *The question in every case is whether the words used are used in such circumstances and are of such a nature as to create a clear and present danger that they will bring about the substantive evils that Congress has a right to prevent.* When a nation is at war many things that might be said in time of peace are such a hindrance to its effort that their utterance will not be endured so long as men fight and that no Court could regard them as being protected by any constitutional right.[5]

The doctrine was designed to draw a sensible and usable line between the rights of the individual and those of society at the point where the former's actions or activities tended to create a danger to organized

---

[5]*Ibid.*, at 52. (Italics supplied.)

society so "clear and present" that government, the servant of the people—here the representative legislative branch by way of a wartime emergency statute—had a right to attempt to prevent the individual's actions or activities in *advance*. Schenck and his associates deemed such a statute to be an unconstitutional invasion of their First Amendment rights. But the Court—here handing down its *first* ruling on a claim that an act of *Congress* violated freedom of expression *per se*— resorted to its new doctrine and concurred with the government that the exigencies of wartime provided sufficient justification for its passage; that, indeed, any government worthy of the name would protect itself against the danger "clear and present" of interference with the so basic element of conscription for military service. It would be difficult to quarrel with that contention. And just one Opinion Day after *Schenck,* Holmes again was the author of two unanimous opinions for the Court upholding the Act of 1917 anew, in which he again invoked the "clear and present danger" test, but without elaborating. One of the cases involved a pro-German newspaperman,[6] the other the famous Socialist leader Eugene V. Debs.[7] Not entirely happy with the nomenclature, Brandeis—as would Jackson in the *Dennis* case in 1951[8]—preferred to categorize the doctrine as a "rule of reason"[9]—which, of course, it has to be in order to be viable. As he saw the test, correctly applied it would preserve the right of free speech both from "suppression by tyrannous, well-meaning majorities, and from abuse by irresponsible, fanatical minorities."

Abrams v. United States.[10] As if to demonstrate almost immediately the difficulties inherent in the "clear and present danger" formula, its two leading champions found themselves in the minority in the cele-

---

[6]*Frohwerk v. United States,* 249 U.S. 204 (1919). Frohwerk had inserted several articles in a Missouri German-language newspaper, challenging the purposes of the War as well as the merits and constitutionality of the draft.

[7]*Debs v. United States,* 249 U.S. 211 (1919). Debs was charged with an attempt to cause insubordination in the Army and to obstruct recruiting.

[8]See Jackson's concurring opinion, discussed at p. 245, *infra*.

[9]See his dissenting opinion in *Schaefer v. United States,* 251 U.S. 466 (1920): "If the words were of such a nature and were used under such circumstances that men, judging in calmness, could not reasonably say that they created a clear and present danger that they would bring about the evil that Congress sought and had a right to prevent, then it is the duty of the trial judge to withdraw the case from the consideration of the jury; if he fails to do so, it is the duty of the appellate court to correct the error." (At 483.)

[10]250 U.S. 616 (1919).

brated *Abrams* case barely six months after the *Schenck* decision. This time the Sedition Act of 1918, which went considerably beyond its predecessor, the Espionage Act of 1917, was at issue. It made punishable what two subsequent observers justly called "speech that in World War II would have been deemed mere political comment."[11] It thus rendered punitive any "disloyal, profane, scurrilous, or abusive language about the form of government, the Constitution, soldiers and sailors, flag or uniform of the armed forces," and it also made unlawful any "word or act [favoring] the cause of the German Empire . . . or [opposing] the cause of the United States." Under the statute, Jacob Abrams, a twenty-nine-year-old self-styled "anarchist-Socialist," and four young associates (all aliens) were apprehended for distributing certain English and Yiddish-language leaflets from rooftops on New York City's Lower East Side late in August 1918. These leaflets—headed "AWAKE! AWAKE, YOU WORKERS OF THE WORLD! REVOLUTIONISTS"—urged the "workers of the world" to resist the Allied and American military intervention against the Bolsheviki in Russia's Murmansk and Valdivostok areas during the summer of 1918. They bitterly denounced President Woodrow Wilson for his decision to intervene and exhorted "the workers of the world" to a general strike in order to prevent future shipment of munitions and other war materials to the anti-Soviet forces. The English-language leaflet closed with the following observation: "P.S. It is absurd to call us pro-German. We hate and despise German militarism more than do your hypocritical tyrants. We have more reasons for denouncing German militarism than has the coward in the White House."[12]

Four of the five defendants were found guilty in the United States District Court for the Southern District of New York; the fifth was acquitted because of insufficient evidence. The judge[13] sentenced the three men, including Abrams, to the maximum of twenty years' imprisonment in a federal penitentiary and a $4,000 fine each; the lone woman, 4'9" Mollie Steiner, received fifteen years and a $500 fine. (Four

[11]Alpheus T. Mason and William M. Beaney, *American Constitutional Law*, 4th ed. (Englewood Cliffs, N.J.: Prentice-Hall, 1968), p. 495.

[12]As quoted by Zechariah Chafee, Jr., in his classic *Freedom of Speech in the United States* (Cambridge: Harvard University Press, 1954), p. 110. See also Richard Polenberg, *Fighting Faiths: The Abrams Case* (New York: Viking Press, 1988).

[13]Visiting Trial Judge Henry DeLamar Clayton of Alabama (as a member of Congress he was the author of the Clayton Anti-Trust Act of 1914).

years later President Harding commuted their sentences on the condition that they all embark at once for their native Russia, now the Soviet Union—which they did.) When their appeal reached the Supreme Court, Justice John H. Clarke, in a 7 : 2 opinion, agreed that the defendants had intended to "urge, incite, and advocate" curtailment of production deemed necessary to the conduct of the war effort, a crime under the Sedition Act and its predecessor statute. Clarke granted that the "primary purpose and intent" of the petitioners "was quite obviously to aid the cause of the Russian Revolution"—which was not forbidden *per se* under either of the statutes involved. But, he ruled,

> the plan of action which they adopted necessarily involved, before it could be realized, defeat of the war program of the United States, for the obvious effect of this appeal, if it should become effective, as they hoped it might, would be to persuade persons . . . not to aid government loans and not to work in ammunition factories.[14]

The question that arises at once, of course, is whether the advocacy of a general strike constituted the kind of direct threat to the war effort that the laws under which they were indicted and sentenced envisaged. A plausible case could certainly be made, as indeed it was made by Zechariah Chafee, that "interference with the war was at the most an incidental consequence of the strikes [they clamored for], entirely subordinate to the longed-for consequences of all this agitation, withdrawal from Russia . . ." and should certainly *not* be made the main basis for punishments restricting open discussion.[15]

And while the majority of seven saw a "clear and present" danger, the doctrine's authors *dissented* in an opinion written by Justice Holmes. With Brandeis concurring, Holmes penned the best that he (or anyone else, one may add) could say on the matter, to which the following impassioned excerpt testifies:

> . . . when men have realized that time has upset many fighting faiths, they may come to believe even more than they believe the very foundations of their own conduct that the ultimate good desired is better reached by *free trade in ideas*—that the best of truth is the power of the thought to get itself

---

[14]*Abrams v. United States,* 250 U.S. 616 (1919), at 621.
[15]*Freedom of Speech in the United States, op. cit.,* p. 134.

accepted in the competition of the market, and that *truth is the only ground upon which their wishes can be safely carried out.* That at any rate is the theory of our Constitution. *It is an experiment, as all life is an experiment.* Every year if not every day we have to wager our salvation upon some prophecy based upon imperfect knowledge. While that experiment is part of our system I think that we should be *eternally vigilant against attempts to check the expression of opinions that we loathe and believe to be fraught with death,*

—and here, of course, he draws the line— *"unless they so imminently threaten immediate interference with the lawful and pressing purposes of the law that an immediate check is required to save the country."*[16] Holmes and Brandeis saw no such interference in what Holmes called the "surreptitious publishing of a silly leaflet" by an unknown man. Assuredly, noted Holmes, this did in no sense constitute "a present danger of immediate evil," and he warned his fellow countrymen and their legislators that "[o]nly the emergency that makes it immediately dangerous to leave the correction of evil counsels to time warrants making any exception to the sweeping command, 'Congress shall make no law abridging freedom of speech.' "[17] Holmes was not speaking of *acts,* but of *"expressions of opinions and exhortations,* which were all that were uttered here." He concluded that beyond doubt they "were deprived of their rights under the Constitution of the United States."[18]

THE "BAD TENDENCY TEST"

If the *Abrams* majority did not theoretically modify the "clear and present danger" doctrine, it assuredly sidetracked it for all intents and purposes. The *official* modification came six years later in the *Gitlow* case.

Gitlow v. New York.[19] The facts and circumstances surrounding this

---

[16]*Abrams v. United States, op. cit.,* at 630. (Italics supplied.) Justice Frankfurter wrote of those deeply moving (and provocative) words: "It is not reckless prophecy to assume that his famous dissenting opinion in the *Abrams* case will live so long as English prose retains its power to move." (*Justice Holmes and the Supreme Court* [Cambridge: Harvard University Press, 1938], pp. 54–55.) And Max Lerner commented that Holmes's language "has economy, grace, finality, and is the greatest utterance on intellectual freedom" by an American, ranking in the English language with Milton and Mill." (*The Mind and Faith of Justice Holmes* [Boston: Little, Brown & Co., 1943], p. 50.)

[17]*Abrams v. United States, op. cit.,* at 630–31.

[18]*Ibid.,* at 631. (Italics supplied.)

[19]*Gitlow v. New York,* 268 U.S. 652 (1925).

famous decision have been amply outlined and discussed earlier.[20] However, we must examine here the Supreme Court majority's holding, over the dissenting opinion by Justice Holmes, in which once again Justice Brandeis concurred, that "certain writings" of Benjamin Gitlow constituted a *"bad tendency"* to "corrupt public morals, incite to crime, and disturb the public peace." The majority thus affirmed Gitlow's conviction under New York State's Criminal Anarchy Act of 1902, which prohibited the "advocacy, advising, or teaching the duty, necessity or propriety of overthrowing or overturning organized government [New York's] by force or violence" and the publication or distribution of such materials. Despite the fact that there was no evidence of any effect from the publication of Gitlow's "Left Wing Manifesto," Justice Sanford, speaking for the Court, contended that the "State cannot reasonably be required to measure the danger from every such utterance in the nice balance of a jeweler's scale"[21] and ruled that because a

> single revolutionary spark may kindle a fire that, smoldering for a time, may burst into a sweeping and destructive conflagration . . . [the State] may, in the exercise of its judgment, suppress the threatened danger in its incipiency.[22]

Obviously, this was no longer the "clear and present danger" test. When the State is empowered to suppress a mere *threat* in its very *incipiency*, the line is being drawn on the basis of a "bad tendency" rather than on that of a "clear and present" danger. There was hardly anything very "clear" or "present" in Gitlow's activities, confined as they were to the written exhortations of a rather pathetic individual. As Professor Chafee, America's leading expert on freedom of expression during the second quarter of the twentieth century, commented: "Any agitator who read these thirty-four pages to a mob would not stir them to violence, except possibly against himself. This Manifesto would disperse them faster than the Riot Act."[23]

In asking itself whether Gitlow's activities had created or constituted a *"bad tendency" to bring about a danger* (a phrase from the

[20]See Chapter III, *supra*, on "incorporation," especially pp. 67–68.
[21]*Ibid.*, at 669.
[22]*Ibid.*
[23]*Freedom of Speech in the United States, op. cit.*, p. 319.

Schaefer[24] decision five years earlier), the majority shifted the balance between the individual and the state toward the latter. Thundered Holmes:

> If what I think the correct test is applied it is manifest that there was no present danger of an attempt to overthrow the government by force. . . . It is said that this manifesto was more than a theory, that it was an incitement. *Every idea is an incitement.* It offers itself for belief and if believed it is acted on unless some other belief outweighs it or some failure of energy stifles the movement at its birth. The only difference between the expression of an opinion and an incitement in the narrower sense is the speaker's enthusiasm for the result. *Eloquence may set fire to reason.*[25]

Holmes pointed out, as he had in similar circumstances in his *Abrams* dissent, that the charges against the defendant alleged *publication,* and nothing more. And, calling a democratic spade a democratic spade, he commented:

> If in the long run the beliefs expressed in proletarian dictatorship are destined to be accepted by the dominant forces of the community, the only meaning of free speech is that they should be given their chance and have their way.[26]

He was naturally confident, as was Justice Douglas in his dissenting opinion in the *Dennis* case[27] a quarter of a century *later,* that "the American people want none of Communism [whose] doctrine is exposed in all its ugliness . . . its wares unsold."[28] In a very real sense the issue for both Holmes and Douglas came down to a matter of faith in the ability of the American people to choose their destiny in the absence of demonstrable, overt, illegal *actions* or conduct.

[24]*Schaefer v. United States,* 251 U.S. 466 (1920).

[25]*Gitlow v. New York, op. cit.,* at 673. (Italics supplied.)

[26]*Ibid.* In 1968 the Court would refuse to *review,* with Justice Douglas in a long dissenting opinion from that refusal, the conviction under the same statute of Marxist William Epton. (*Epton v. New York,* 390 U.S. 29, appeal dismissed.) In 1971, it also refused to review another New York case, which in 1969 had been construed below like *Gitlow* and *Epton* (*Samuels v. Mackell,* 401 U.S. 66); ditto a similar California case (*Younger v. Harris,* 401 U.S. 37 [1971]). But it had declared Ohio's criminal syndicalism law unconstitutional in 1969 in the significant *Brandenburg* case, discussed in connection with *Whitney,* pp. 203–6, *infra.* (*Brandenburg v. Ohio,* 395 U.S. 444.)

[27]*Dennis v. United States,* 341 U.S. 494 (1951).

[28]*Ibid.,* at 588–89.

EXPANDING "CLEAR AND PRESENT DANGER"

Holmes and Brandeis recognized that some amplification of their "clear and present danger" test was needed to prevent its demotion to the "bad tendency" level. Their opportunity came some two years following the *Gitlow* decision in *Whitney v. California.*[29]

Whitney v. California. Miss Charlotte Anita Whitney, a niece of one of the pillars of *laissez-faire* American capitalism, Justice Stephen J. Field, was one of the band of disenchanted adventurers who, in 1919, helped to organize the Communist Labor Party of California. Motivated largely by her passionate espousal of the cause of the poor, she readily permitted herself to be elected as a member of the C.L.P.C. during its 1919 convention held in Oakland. The Party's constitution was quite clear on its affiliation with both the Communist Labor Party of America and the Communist International of Moscow. Miss Whitney's activities brought her into conflict with California's Criminal Syndicalism Act of 1919. She soon found herself indicted on five counts, and subsequently convicted of one: that on November 28, 1919, she "did then and there unlawfully, willfully, wrongfully, deliberately and feloniously organize and assist in organizing, and was, is, and knowingly became a member of an organization, society, group and assemblage of persons organized and assembled to advocate, teach, aid and abet criminal syndicalism."[30]

On appeal, Miss Whitney protested, as she had during her trial, that at no time did she wish her Party to engage in any acts of violence or terror, but the intermediate appellate tribunal affirmed her conviction and the State Supreme Court refused to review her case, which then went on to the United States Supreme Court. At issue was the association between due process of law and First Amendment guarantees, against the basic charge of a criminal conspiracy—an activity that falls outside the protection of free speech. Again Miss Whitney lost. Justice Sanford, here writing the opinion for a unanimous Court that *included* Justices Holmes and Brandeis, agreed that the State of California had an inherent right to guard statutorily against the alleged conspiracy—and neither Holmes nor Brandeis disputed the Court's finding that there was sufficient evidence to point to the existence of such a conspiracy to

[29]274 U.S. 357 (1927).
[30]*Ibid.*, at 358.

violate the Criminal Syndicalism Act, that the group had transgressed the bounds of a political party, and had in fact become a conspiracy to commit serious crime. However, in a highly significant concurring opinion, joined by Holmes, Brandeis rejected the majority's interpretation of a section of the law that made it a crime not only to advocate or teach or practice criminal syndicalism, or conspire to do so, but also to be in "association with those who proposed to teach it." Here Brandeis and Holmes saw a lurking and grave threat to the concept of "clear and present danger" as they had conceived of it; thus, with the *Gitlow* "bad tendency" doctrine in mind, the two jurists endeavored not only to resurrect their original "clear and present danger" concept but to strengthen it. In a ringing admonition—which reportedly so moved the then Governor of California, C. C. Young, that he later pardoned Miss Whitney—Brandeis's concurrence—which, in effect, reads like a dissent[31]—attempted to clarify, expand, and liberalize the doctrine by joining to its basic test the requirement of *"imminence"*:

> Fear of serious injury cannot alone justify suppression of free speech and assembly . . . there must be reasonable ground to fear that serious evil will result if free speech is practiced. There must be reasonable ground to believe *that the danger apprehended is imminent.* There must be reasonable ground to believe that the evil to be prevented is a serious one. . . . In order to support a finding of clear and present danger *it must be shown either that immediate serious violence was to be expected or was advocated, or that the past conduct furnished reason to believe that such advocacy was then contemplated.*
>
> Those who won our independence by revolution were not cowards. They did not fear political change. They did not exalt order at the cost of liberty. To courageous, self-reliant men, with confidence in the power of free and fearless reasoning applied through the processes of popular government, *no danger flowing from speech can be deemed clear and present, unless the incidence of the evil apprehended is so imminent that it may befall before there is opportunity for full discussion.* If there be time to expose through

[31]And so it was! *But* it had been written originally for *Ruthenberg v. Michigan,* 273 U.S. 782 (1927), a case mooted by Ruthenberg's death and dismissed that March. Brandeis subsequently seized upon the opportunity of *Whitney* to incorporate the central points of that dissent into what is his concurring opinion for *Whitney.* (See Klaus H. Heberle, "From Gitlow to Near . . . ," 34 *Journal of Politics* 468 [1972].)

discussion the falsehood and fallacies, to avert the evil by the processes of education, *the remedy to be applied is more speech, not enforced silence.*[32]

In his and Holmes's opinion, "such . . . is the command of the Constitution."[33]

Specific vindication of the Brandeis-Holmes view in their *Whitney* concurrence did not really come until they were long dead. A United States District Court declared the California Criminal Syndicalism Law unconstitutional in 1968 in *Younger v. Harris,* although the Supreme Court set the verdict aside on technical grounds two years later.[34] But the Court did dispose of Ohio's similar statute in the key 1969 *Brandenburg* decision,[35] in which it *specifically* overruled its 1927 *Whitney* holding. Clarence Brandenburg, a Ku Klux Klan leader, was convicted, fined, and sentenced to jail under the law at issue,[36] and challenged the latter on First and Fourteenth Amendment grounds. Pointing to a spate of intervening decisions,[37] the Court's unsigned (*per curiam*) opinion reemphasized the

principle that the constitutional guarantees of free speech and free press do not permit a State to forbid or proscribe advocacy of the use of force or of law violation *except* where such advocacy is directed to inciting or producing *imminent* lawless action and is likely to incite or produce such action.[38]

[32]*Ibid.,* at 377. (Italics supplied.)

[33]*Ibid.*

[34]*Younger v. Harris,* 281 F. Supp. 507, and *Younger v. Harris,* 401 U.S. 37 (1971), respectively.

[35]*Brandenburg v. Ohio,* 395 U.S. 444 (1969).

[36]Brandenburg had invited a television cameraman to a cross-burning ceremony, where he was filmed vowing "revengeance" against the nation's leaders and making slurring and vile remarks about "niggers" and "kikes," e.g., that "the nigger should be returned to Africa, the Jew returned to Israel." During the "organizational meeting," some in the group of about twelve hooded Klansmen were seen brandishing firearms.

[37]E.g., *Dennis v. United States,* 341 U.S. 494 (1951); *Yates v. United States,* 354 U.S. 298 (1957); *Noto v. United States,* 367 U.S. 290 (1961); and *Bond v. Floyd,* 385 U.S. 116 (1966).

[38]*Brandenburg v. Ohio, op. cit.,* at 444. (Italics supplied.) Supported by Justice Black in separate concurring opinions, Justice Douglas restated the two libertarians' firm faith, namely, that there is "no place in the regime of the First Amendment for any 'clear and present danger' test, whether strict and tight as some would make it, or free-wheeling as the court in *Dennis* rephrased it." (At 454.) Judge Learned Hand's opinion in *Masses Publ. Co. v. Patten,* 244 Fed. 535 (1917), considered but rejected Holmes's future test as

Mere advocacy is thus no longer punishable on pain of violating Amendments One and Fourteen; but *direct incitement to imminent action* is.[39]

Thus, we again see the basic dilemma inherent in the two approaches to freedom of expression in democratic society. No matter what the language employed, no matter what the rationalization by individuals in specific situations, it comes down to a reading of the Constitution in its historical-evolutionary setting, against what Holmes called "the felt necessities of the time." And underlying the entire problem is, inevitably and necessarily, the faith one has in a free people's willingness and ability to experiment, to take chances, to govern itself in a democratic society.

"Preferred Freedoms" and Beyond. Chapter II noted that the Supreme Court in the late 1930s and much of the 1940s—in line with the Brandeis-Holmes philosophy expressed in *Whitney* and other cases—adopted the view that there should be "more exacting judicial scrutiny" of First Amendment freedoms. The Court thus identified a constitutionally protected area of "preferred freedom," based upon the famous footnote by Justice Stone in *United States v. Carolene Products Co.,*[40] where the future Chief Justice had called for a special niche for "legislation which restricts the political processes."[41] A concept enthusiastically embraced by Justices Black, Douglas, Murphy, and Rutledge when they served together with Stone from Rutledge's appointment in 1943 to the deaths of Stone, Rutledge, and Murphy, it was to be joined to the "clear and present danger plus imminence" doctrine.

But when Harlan Stone died in 1946, Fred Vinson replaced him as Chief Justice, foreshadowing trouble for the new "line" established by the civil libertarians. And when Murphy and Rutledge both died in the summer of 1949, their replacements, Justices Clark and Minton, together with the new Chief Justice and the "holdovers"—Justices Reed, Frankfurter, Jackson, and Burton—constituted a majority that almost

---

"too slippery, too dangerous to free expression." Instead he urged the adoption of a "strict," "hard," "objective" test, focusing on the speakers words: if the language used was solely that of a direct incitement to illegal action, speech could be proscribed; otherwise it was protected. However, Hand evidently abandoned this approach a few years later and embraced the "clear and present danger" test.

[39]For a pertinent later illustration, see *Hess v. Indiana,* 414 U.S. 105 (1973).

[40]304 U.S. 144 (1938).

[41]*Ibid.,* at 152. See the extended discussion of *Carolene, supra,* pp. 16–22.

at once departed from the philosophy of "preferred freedom." "McCarthyism" had cast its long shadow. Indeed, in the landmark *Dennis*[42] internal security case even the "clear and present danger" doctrine underwent a rather dramatic transformation into what some observers viewed as a "grave and probable" test patterned upon Judge Learned Hand's lower court opinion,[43] on which Chief Justice Vinson leaned very heavily in his *Dennis* majority opinion.[44] Others felt that in fact the Court had adopted as its new freedom of expression doctrine a "possible and remote danger" test.[45] Unquestionably, "bad tendency" had taken over from "clear and present danger." However, soon after Earl Warren became Chief Justice on Vinson's death in 1953, the Court returned to the "clear and present danger" test, even restoring its "imminence" appendage. Indeed, some even felt that the new Court adopted a "super-preferred" standard vis-à-vis claims of racial discrimination and due process standards of criminal justice. It did retain the "bad tendency" test in the national security field for a while longer but, by the *late* 1950s, in cases such as *Yates v. United States*,[46] the Court, after some wavering and broken-field strategy, returned to the "clear and present danger" plus imminence test for the national security field also. With the advent of the "Burger Court" in 1969, Warren Earl Burger having replaced Earl Warren in the center chair, a change of direction could not be ruled out. However, there was no return to the Vinson approach. Indeed, despite some narrowing in the realms of "obscenity" and, arguably, aspects of freedom of the press,[47] freedom of expression was given generous interpretations by the Burger Court, notwithstanding the departures from the Court of its great champions, Justices Black and Douglas, in 1971 and 1975, respectively. Thus, a 1978 opinion by the Chief Justice strongly reaffirmed a tough "clear and present" standard upon any legislative attempts to bridle freedom of speech.[48] The Burger Court in fact emphasized an additional type of

---

[42]341 U.S. 494 (1951).

[43]*Dennis v. United States,* 183 F. 2d 201 (1950), at 212.

[44]*Op. cit.,* fn. 42, *supra,* at 510 ff.

[45]Alfred H. Kelly and Winifred A. Harbison, *The American Constitution: Its Origins and Development,* 2nd ed. (New York: W. W. Norton & Co., 1955), p. 893.

[46]354 U.S. 298 (1957). See the discussion of the case, pp. 246 ff., *infra.*

[47]See pp. 252 ff. and pp. 218 ff., *infra,* respectively.

[48]*Landmark Communications, Inc. v. Virginia,* 435 U.S. 829 (1978). He quoted a passage from Justice Brandeis's concurrence in *Whitney v. California (op. cit.,* pp. 203

"preferred freedom," the so-called suspect categories of race, alienage and national origin, and—although not quite so clearly—sex, which were accorded special judicial protection alongside other fundamental rights regarded as entitled to "close scrutiny" by the courts. If any retrenchment was in evidence, it was in the field of criminal justice, but even there the Court's record was not one-sided.[49] The same philosophy or policy has characterized the Rehnquist Court (at least as of early 1988). On the other hand, as 1988 entered the annals, it was obvious that none of the Nixon-Ford-Reagan appointees to the high bench[50] would be committed to the *absolutist* reading of freedom of expression brought to the Court by Black and Douglas for almost four decades.

Some Basic Concepts

Since we cannot here attempt to cover all, or even most, aspects of "freedom of expression," we shall concentrate on those that illustrate the fundamental problem and are of enduring interest.

A Basic Definition. In its overall context, freedom of expression connotes the broad *freedom to communicate*—a concept that far transcends mere speech. It embraces the prerogative of the free citizen to express himself—verbally, visually, or on paper—without *prior* restraint, and if the expression meets the test of truth, the prerogative necessarily extends to the post-utterance period. It is vital to recognize at the outset that freedom of expression extends not only to speech and press but also to areas of *conduct* laced or tinged with expression such as those of press, assembly, petition, association, lawful picketing, and other demonstrative protests. To point to its diversity and range, freedom of expression now apparently extends also to independent individual or group *spending* by and for a candidate for federal elective

---

ff.) that began: "A legislative declaration does not preclude enquiry into the question whether, at the time and under the circumstances, the conditions existed which are essential to validity under the Federal Constitution." (At 843–44.)

[49]See Chapter IV, *supra*.

[50]In addition to the 1969 Burger for Warren switch, the following replacements had taken effect by mid-1988: Blackmun for Fortas (1970); Powell and Rehnquist for Black and Harlan (1971); Stevens for Douglas (1975); O'Connor for Stewart (1981); Rehnquist as Chief Justice for Burger (1986); Scalia for the Associate Justiceship vacated by Rehnquist's elevation (1986); and Kennedy for Powell (1988).

office, but *not* in the form of unlimited *contributions*,[51] to purely "commercial speech,"[52] including even the right of professionals to advertise their fees (on a "limited, factual basis");[53] to banks and business corporations making contributions or expenditures for the purpose of influencing votes on referendum proposals (even those not materially affecting their assets or property), of expressing their views on public issues, and of promoting their products (even by advertising or inserting them in customer utility bills);[54] to realtors posting "for sale" or "sold" signs in front of a home in a racially tense community and to door-to-door soliciting during reasonable hours;[55] to persons marching in Nazi uniforms replete with the hated swastika symbol in a community peopled largely by survivors of Nazi concentration camps;[56] and to the right of NAACP members to engage in a political and economic boycott without being liable for damages suffered by targeted businesses.[57] Astonishingly, freedom of expression even extends to the time-honored practice of dismissal of public employees because of their political beliefs, unless, as Justice Stevens explained ultimately, "party

[51]See the complex six-opinion decision by the Court in 1976, replete with partial dissents and partial concurrences, in which it tested the Federal Election Campaign Act of 1974 in *Buckley v. Valeo*, 424 U.S. 1, and the follow-up (7:2) in 1985 in *Federal Election Commission v. National Conservative Political Action Committee*, 470 U.S. 480, as well as the 1986 holding, 5:4, that struck down as unconstitutional a regulation that prohibited political expenditures by non-profit advocacy groups in *Federal Election Commission v. Massachusetts Citizens for Life*, 55 LW 4067. But note its 1981 ruling (8:1), striking down a Berkeley, California, law that had limited campaign *contributions* by committees in *referendum* campaigns. (*Citizens Against Rent Control v. City of Berkeley*, 454 U.S. 290.) See also the related 5:4 one in *California Medical Association v. Federal Election Commission*, 49 LW 4842 (1981).

[52]*Virginia State Board of Pharmacy v. Virginia Citizens Consumer Council*, 425 U.S. 748 (1976).

[53]*Bates v. Arizona State Bar*, 433 U.S. 350 (1977). It was significantly expanded in 1982 in *In re R.M.J.*, 455 U.S. 191.

[54]*First National Bank v. Bellotti* 435 U.S. 765 (1978), and *Consolidated Edison v. Public Service Commission* and *Central Hudson Gas Co. v. Public Service Commission*, 100 S. Ct. 2326 and 2343 (1980), respectively.

[55]*Linmark Associates v. Willingboro*, 431 U.S. 85 (1977) and *City of Watseka v. Illinois*, 55 LW 3492 (1987), respectively.

[56]*Smith v. Collin*, 436 U.S. 953 (1978), the controversial Skokie, Illinois, case that caused problems of consistency for some of the most devoted exponents of freedom of expression. See Donald A. Downs, *Nazis in Skokie: Community and the First Amendment* (Notre Dame, Ind.: Notre Dame University Press, 1985).

[57]*NAACP v. Claybourne Hardware Co.*, 458 U.S. 886 (1982).

affiliation is an appropriate requirement for the effective performance of the public office involved."[58] The Court's rulings here voided a "patronage" practice as old as the nation itself!

Yet since—*pace* Justice Black—none of these freedoms can be absolute, any basic definition must consider the inevitability of limits—limits that recognize the rights of the minority in a majoritarian system, without, however, subscribing to a philosophy of the "tyranny of the minority." Thus, the Court has repeatedly pointed out that the First Amendment does *not* "afford the same kind of freedom" to communicate *conduct* as to that which it extends to "pure speech."[59] There is no doubt that picketing, for example, is a vital prerogative of the freedom of expression; however, mass picketing; picketing that applies physical force to those who might wish to exercise their equal rights of freedom of expression by disregarding the picket line; or certain kinds of picketing violative of a picketee's property rights or picketing utterly unrelated to a picketee's "operations"; or picketing interrogation of secondary boycott statutes, is *not*.[60] Screaming "fire" in a crowded theater—to use the famed Holmesian illustration—upon discovery of a blaze is not only "freedom of speech" but a dutiful exercise of citizenship; but if there is *no* fire, the call is not freedom of expression but license. Nor does freedom of expression extend to the construction of buildings and sleeping in parks near the White House, as the Court held 7:2 in 1984.[61] *Actual, overt* incitement of the overthrow of the government of

---

[58]*Elrod v. Burns,* 427 U.S. 346 (1976), and *Branti v. Finkel,* 445 U.S. 507 (1980). The former decision had confined its application to "below public policy-making levels," but the latter one expunged any such distinction, exempting only posts in which the hiring authority can demonstrate that party affiliation is an appropriate requirement for the effective performance of the public office involved.

[59]E.g., see Justice Goldberg's opinion for the Court in *Cox v. Louisiana,* 379 U.S. 536 (1965), at 555, and the Court's striking down of a Los Angeles ordinance prohibiting *all* "First Amendment activities" in the city's main airport terminal. (*Board of Airport Commissioners v. Jews for Jesus,* 107 S.Ct. 2568 [1987].)

[60]Compare and contrast *Thornhill v. Alabama,* 310 U.S. 88 (1940) with *Giboney v. Empire Storage and Ice Co.,* 336 U.S. 490 (1949); *Amalgamated Food Employees Union v. Logan Valley, Inc.,* 391 U.S. 309 (1968) with *Lloyd Corp. Ltd. v. Tanner,* 407 U.S. 551 (1972), *Hudgens v. N.L.R.B.,* 424 U.S. 507 (1976); and *Pruneyard Shopping Center v. Robins,* 447 U.S. 74 (1980), *Carey v. Brown,* 447 U.S. 455 (1980), and *National Labor Relations Board v. Retail Store Employees Union,* 447 U.S. 607 (1980) with the last four aforementioned cases. There is patent need for more judicial clarifying of the problems created in picketing. *Cf.* the 1988 *De Bartolo* case (56 LW 4328).

[61]*Clarke v. Community for Creative Non-Violence,* 468 U.S. 288.

the United States by force and violence, accompanied by the language of direct and imminent incitement, is not freedom of expression but a violation of Court-upheld legislation proscriptions; yet the *theoretical* advocacy of such overthrow, on the other hand, has been a judicially recognized protected freedom since 1957.[62] If a written work has "literary, artistic, political or scientific value," it is not proscribable as being "pornographic";[63] but this safeguard may be vitiated by its publisher's "pandering."[64] Publicly addressing someone as "damned Fascist" and "Goddamned racketeer" can hardly be considered freedom of speech—in fact, those terms have been judicially held to be "fighting words" that are proscribable *if* (and it is a big "if") the proscribing statute is carefully and narrowly drawn[65]—but calling a duly convicted thief "thief" or "crook" presumably can be considered freedom of

[62]See *Yates v. United States*, 354 U.S. 298 (1957), particularly Justice Harlan's opinion for the 6 : 1 Court.

[63]*Jenkins v. Georgia*, 418 U.S. 153 (1974).

[64]*A Book Named "John Cleland's Woman of Pleasure" v. Massachusetts*, 383 U.S. 413 (1966).

[65]*Chaplinsky v. New Hampshire*, 315 U.S. 568 (1942)—opinion for the unanimous Court by Justice Frank Murphy, then its leading civil libertarian. The New Hampshire statute had enacted the common-law "fighting words" doctrine: "No person shall address any offensive, derisive or annoying word [directly] to any other person who is lawfully in any street or other public place, nor call him by any offensive or derisive name." The state court had interpreted it to ban "words likely to cause an average addressee to fight," and "face to face words" likely to produce an immediate violent breach of the peace by the addressee. Although the "fighting words" test has continued to be relied upon, it has presented major problems when applied to the "profane," the "obscene," and the "libelous," as noted *infra*, pp. 211–17. By and large the Court's posture has been *one of focusing on* the specific "circumstances" in which the contested speech is uttered and, increasingly, on proof that the "fighting words" were intentionally, directly, and specifically addressed to an *identifiable individual rather than to a group.* See, for example, its 5 : 2 distinction of *Chaplinsky* in the 1972 Georgia "bad language" case of *Gooding v. Wilson*, 405 U.S. 418, which disallowed (4 : 3) a Georgia statute as "on its face" unconstitutionally vague and overbroad. The law provided that any person "who shall without provocation use to or of [another person] opprobious words or abusive language tending to cause a breach of the peace" was guilty of a misdemeanor. On the other hand, the same Court *declined* (8 : 1) to review a lower-court decision that there is no "constitutional privilege to shout four-letter words on a public street" in a case in which a policeman arrested a man for disorderly conduct on the grounds that he had used obscene language. (*Von Schleichter v. United States*, 409 U.S. 1063). For proof that the Court continues to find the Chaplinsky test extremely vexatious in application, see Justice Powell's diverse, pained opinions in the 1972 "foul language trilogy" cases of *Rosenfeld v. New Jersey, Lewis v. New Orleans,* and *Brown v. Oklahoma,* reported as 408 U.S. 901, 913, and 914, respectively—all propounding definitional "overbreadth" and/or "vagueness" problems in the free-speech realm.

speech—at least until the epithet's target has paid his debt to society. Nor is there a constitutionally protected right to libel or slander, but what constitutes libel or slander, and what the exercise of First Amendment rights, has proved to be a veritable public-law snake pit. Broadly speaking, at least of this writing (early 1988), the law seems to be that a *public* official or even a public "figure" or public "person" is not entitled to damages unless he or she can prove "actual malice," i.e., proof that the defamatory statement was made "with knowledge that it was false or with reckless disregard of whether it was false or not"— which, rather than simple truth or falsehood, thus becomes the test.[66] Furthermore, only those false statements made with a "high degree of awareness of their probative falsity" may be the subject of either civil or criminal sanction[67]—which, however, does not mean that in *no* circumstances will a public official be judicially found to have been libeled.[68] Although the test is naturally less stringent in the instance of *private* or *quasi-private* persons,[69] who may win cases by proving carelessness, irresponsibility, or a similar "lapse," the line remains ambiguous.[70] Thus, while in 1971 the Court applied its free press

[66]*The New York Times v. Sullivan*, 376 U.S. 254 (1964). This important test, since referred to as the "*New York Times* Rule," was initially expanded in *Ocala Star Banner v. Damron*, 401 U.S. 295 (1971), but then narrowed in *Time, Inc. v. Firestone*, 424 U.S. 448, a narrowing that was patently continued in two 8:1 holdings in 1979, in which the Court made clear that it would no longer be very generous in protective characterizations of "public"; that, to qualify for the "public" label, there would have to be proof that an individual made a deliberate, affirmative injection-effort for the public limelight or be a policy-maker. In other words, it would now no longer neither be so difficult to recover for an alleged libel nor so easy to hide under the "public" characterization. (*Hutchinson v. Proxmire*, 443 U.S. 111 and *Wolston v. Reader's Digest Association*, 443 U.S. 157.) See also the implications of the interesting verdicts against novelist Gwen Davis and her publisher, Doubleday, one year later. (*Mitchell v. Bindrin* and *Doubleday v. Bindrin*, 444 U.S. 984; *certiorari* denied.) An early 1981 Court refusal to review appeared designed to continue the narrowing of "public" characterization. *London Times-Mirror v. Arctic Co.*, 449 U.S. 1102. But *cf.* the 1988 ruling (8:0) in *Hustler v. Falwell*, 56LW 4180.

[67]*Garrison v. Louisiana*, 379 U.S. 64 (1964).

[68]E.g., *Ginzburg v. Goldwater*, 396 U.S. 1049 (1970); *Indianapolis Newspapers, Inc. v. Fields*, 400 U.S. 930 (1970); and *Cape Public Co. v. Adams*, 434 U.S. 943 (1977).

[69]See *Curtis Publishing Co. v. Butts*, 338 U.S. 130 (1967), *Matus v. Triangle Publications*, 408 U.S. 930 (1972), and *Patrick v. Field Research Corp.*, 414 U.S. 933 (1973). See also the cases noted in fn. 66, *supra*.

[70]E.g., compare *Associated Press v. Walker*, 388 U.S. 130 (1967) with the three cases listed in footnote 68, *supra*, and *Greenbelt Coop. Pub. Assn. v. Bresler*, 298 U.S. 6 (1970). And compare them with *Time, Inc. v. Firestone, op. cit.*, in fn. 66, *supra*, and the three 1979 and 1980 cases also cited there.

doctrine to *news* "about private individuals involved in matters of public or general interest,"[71] rendering collection of damages extremely difficult, it distinguished that decision three years later when it held 5 : 4 that an ordinary citizen "elevated to sudden prominence by news events" can sue any newspaper or radio or television station that circulated a false and defamatory account of his role in those events; that a publisher or broadcaster of *defamatory falsehoods* about a *private* individual's involvement in a public issue may *not* assert the 1964 "*New York Times* Rule" as protection against liability for actual damages, at least where "the substance of the defamatory statement makes substantial danger to reputation apparent.[72] Nonetheless, by 1974 the Court had drawn a *seemingly* sharp distinction between an ordinary citizen libeled by a news account and "public officials and public figures [who] have voluntarily exposed themselves to incurring risk or injury from defamatory falsehoods."[73] The new doctrine raised doubts about such famed past (1967) decisions as *Time, Inc. v. Hill*[74] in which "newsworthiness" had narrowly triumphed over "privacy." However, in 1975 an 8 : 1 majority, striking down a Georgia law that made it a misdemeanor to print or broadcast the name of a rape victim, and barring the right of the victim or her parents to invoke "invasion of privacy" as a basis for a suit, held that the media cannot be subjected to either civil or criminal liability for disseminating *accurately* data that are available from public law enforcement records.[75] Moreover, the Court ruled (5 : 3) in 1976

---

[71]*Rosenbloom v. Metromedia*, 403 U.S. 29 (1971) at 44: "Voluntarily or not we are all public men to some degree," in Justice Brennan's words, at 48. See also *Edwards v. New York Times Co., certiorari* denied, 434 U.S. 1002 (1977).

[72]*Gertz v. Robert Welch, Inc.*, 418 U.S. 323, at 348. (But see text for fn. 73, *infra*.)

[73]*Gertz*, fn. at 345. That it was but a "seemingly" sharp one was demonstrated by its 5 : 3 narrowing of the "public *figure*" concept in 1976 when it upheld a $100,000 libel award won by a prominent Palm Beach, Fla., socialite, Mary Alice Firestone, whose notorious divorce proceedings had been publicized by *Time* magazine. (*Time, Inc. v. Firestone*, 424 U.S. 448.) The gravamen of Justice Rehnquist's opinion was that Mrs. Firestone was not a "public figure," since she had not assumed "any role of especial prominence in the affairs of society other than perhaps Palm Beach society," and because she had not thrust herself to the forefront of any particular public controversy in order to influence the resolutions of the issues involved in it. (*Ibid.*, at 453). Room for doubt about that analysis of the facts persists, however.

[74]385 U.S. 374. It involved *Life*'s review of the play *The Desperate Hours*, starring the young Paul Newman. Richard M. Nixon represented Hill (the loser); Harold Medina, *Time, Inc.* (the winner).

[75]*Cox Broadcasting Corp. v. Cohn*, 420 U.S. 469. The case involved the grisly rape and murder of a young woman whose grieving parents wanted privacy.

that "reputation" is neither "liberty" nor "property" for purposes of an alleged civil rights violation.[76] Justices Black and Douglas, of course, never had difficulty in the realm of libel (nor does Justice Brennan): they considered an "unconditional right to say what one pleases about public affairs to be the *minimum* guarantee" under Amendments One and Fourteen.[77] They would have been aghast had they been on the Court in 1979 when it ruled 6 : 3 that, given the "malice aforethought" test-requirement of *The New York Times* case, a public official had a right to request reporters to testify on their "state of mind" in connection with their leveling of charges against him or her.[78] Nor would they have been amused in the face of the Court's 5 : 4 narrowing of the libel shield in 1985, when it ruled that the First Amendment does not protect against punitive damage awards *unless* the libelous statements involve "matters of public concern."[79] On the other hand, in a major victory for the news media, it ruled 5 : 4 in 1986 that people suing news organizations for libel must overcome the difficult burden of proving that the published statements about them were false.[80] And just a bit later in 1986 the Court held 6 : 3, in what seemed to be a major weakening of *Herbert v. Lando*,[81] that when examining a motion for summary judgment of a libel suit, judges must determine "whether the evidence presented is such that a reasonable jury might find that actual malice had been shown with convincing clarity."[82]

As a further illustration of the elusiveness of drawing the line for freedom of expression: petitioning and demonstrating against the draft are both *bona fide* manifestations of freedom of expression, but the burning of draft cards is not. "We cannot accept the view," wrote

[76]*Paul v. Davis*, 424 U.S. 693.

[77]See *The New York Times v. Sullivan, op. cit.*, at 296, Justice Black's concurring opinion, for a comparative analysis of the right to denounce. (Italics supplied.)

[78]*Herbert v. Lando*, 441 U.S. 153. The majority opinion in this contentious decision was written by Justice White, the dissenters being Justices Brennan, Stewart, and Marshall.

[79]*Dun & Bradstreet v. Greenmoss*, 472 U.S. 749 (1985). See the two fascinating 1984 libel trials involving General William C. Westmoreland and Israeli General Ariel Sharon, both of whom were unsuccessful. Two excellent books dealing with them: *Vietnam on Trial: Westmoreland v. C.B.S.*, by Bob Brewin and Sydney Shaw (New York: Atheneum, 1987), and *Blood Libel: The Inside Story of General Ariel Sharon's History-Making Suit Against Time Magazine*, by Uri Dan (New York: Simon & Schuster, 1987).

[80]*Philadelphia Newspapers v. Hepps*, 54 LW 4373.

[81]See *supra*, fn. 31 and accompanying text.

[82]*Anderson v. Liberty Lobby*, 54 LW 4755.

Chief Justice Warren in the leading case for his 7 : 1 Court, with only Justice Douglas in dissent, "that an apparently limitless variety of conduct can be labelled 'speech.' "[83] Justice Black, who drew the line at "conduct" rather than "expression," was in the majority here. And he strongly dissented from the Court's 7 : 2 holding, just a year later, that the wearing of black armbands by high school students constituted constitutionally protected "symbolic" free speech.[84] Only Justice Harlan sided with him in what they viewed as a matter of proscribable *conduct*. Again Black, this time joined in dissent by Justices Fortas and White and Chief Justice Warren, saw as proscribable conduct rather than symbolic free speech the action of Sidney Street, a Brooklyn bus driver, who, while loudly cursing an American flag, burned it in outrage in 1966 after he had learned that James Meredith, the civil rights activist, had been shot and wounded in an ambush.[85] To compound the difficulties *and* unpredictabilities of this realm, the majority opinion was written by Justice Harlan, who had dissented in the black armband case![86] On the other hand, the Court found no difficulty at all in unanimously declaring unconstitutional a part of a federal law that barred theatrical performers from wearing a United States military uniform *if* their role was intended to discredit the armed forces;[87] the law had permitted performances that were laudatory! Appropriately, that classic symbolic freedom of expression opinion was written by Mr. Justice Black. But it was by a mere one-vote margin (5 : 4) that the Court ruled

[83]*United States v. O'Brien* and *O'Brien v. United States*, 391 U.S. 367 (1968), at 376.

[84]*Tinker v. Des Moines Independent Community School District*, 393 U.S. 503 (1969). The *Tinker* decision was confirmed in 1972 when the Court refused to review a lower tribunal's decision permitting a public school teacher of English to wear a black armband on Vietnam Moratorium Day—despite his subsequent suspension for continued political activity and educational disruption. (*Board of Education v. James*, 409 U.S. 1042.) But compare the 1986 "firm in your pants" case of *Bethel School District v. Fraser*, 54 LW 5054, in which a 7 : 2 Supreme Court upheld a school district's punitive action involving a student speaker and the 1987 ruling (5 : 3) in *Hazelwood School District v. Kuhlmeier*, 56 LW 4079; upholding the censoring of sexual explicitness in a student newspaper.

[85]*Street v. New York*, 394 U.S. 576 (1969). "We don't need no damn flag," Street had shouted. "I burned it! If they let this happen to Meredith, we don't need an American flag." So-called do-not-dishonor-the-flag statutes—e.g., *Smith v. Goguen*, 415 U.S. 566 (1974)—came before the court increasingly in the mid-1970s, most of them falling to challenges of "vagueness." Yet the Court has consistently supported *bona fide* flag-mutilation laws, e.g., *Kime v. United States*, 459 U.S. 949 (1982).

[86]He was joined by Justices Douglas, Brennan, Stewart, and Marshall.

[87]*Schacht v. United States*, 398 U.S. 58 (1970).

in 1971 that the display on a jacket of the epithetical phrase "Fuck the draft" in a corridor of the Los Angeles courthouse is constitutionally protected speech and may not be made a criminal offense[88]—with the Court for the first time spelling out that Anglo-Saxon term (Justice Harlan, of all people, writing for the Court). Yet his colleague Black was one of three dissenters who saw "mainly conduct," very little "expression." As he frequently did, Black here evidently drew the proverbial line based on his belief that, in words he employed elsewhere, "a law which primarily regulates conduct but which might also indirectly affect speech can be upheld if the effect on speech is minor in relation to the need for control of the conduct."[89]

Throughout our history, law-making and judicial authorities have had to wrestle with these and similar questions—including such, perhaps less than earthshaking, ones as to the right of public school boards and other public agencies to prescribe the length of the hair sported by those under their aegis.[90] Limitations, today almost entirely of a statutory nature, are thus present on both the national and state levels of government—a phenomenon almost unknown prior to World War I. Thus, there is scant doubt that Congress has the authority to guard against sedition and subversion;[91] it has asserted it rather widely, especially in periods of national emergency and throughout the Cold War, enacting three controversial pieces of legislation in less than fifteen years: the Smith Act of 1940, the Internal Security Act of 1950 (passed over President Truman's veto), and the Communist Control Act of 1954. The

[88]*Cohen v. California*, 403 U.S. 15. Relatedly, see *Papish v. Board of Curators of University of Missouri*, 410 U.S. 667 (1973), which 6 : 3 overturned a student's expulsion for circulating "offensive ideas" in print in a campus publication that used the "M_____ F_____" expletive with obvious relish in connection with the trial and acquittal of the member of an organization called "Up Against the Wall, Motherfucker." (A headline story was entitled "M_____ F_____ acquitted," and it printed a political cartoon depicting police raping the Statute of Liberty and the Goddess of Justice.)

[89]Dissenting opinion, *Barenblatt v. United States*, 360 U.S. 109 (1959), at 141.

[90]Although the Court has been on both sides of the issue in its decisions, and may well have to come down with a definitive one ultimately, by and large it has sided with duly constituted authorities, assuming reasonable rules are at stake. See, e.g., *Olff v. East Side Union High School District*. 404 U.S. 1042 (1972); *Jackson v. New York City Transit Authority*, 419 U.S. 831 (1974); and *Kelley v. Johnson*, 425 U.S. 238 (1976).

[91]*Sedition* consists of publications, utterances, or other activities, short of treason, which are deemed to encourage resistance to lawful authority. *Subversion* comprehends participation in or advocacy of any organized activity to overthrow an existing government by force.

cases and, moreover, were not even truthful. But justifying his drawing a generous line here, he argued that

> in the borderline instances where it is difficult to say upon which side of the line the offense falls, we think the specific freedom of public comment should weigh heavily against a possible tendency to influence pending cases. Freedom of discussion should be given the widest range compatible with the essential requirement of the fair and orderly administration of justice.[97]

Not long thereafter, the Court, although splitting 6 : 3, reaffirmed the aforegone cases in *Craig v. Harney*[98] which involved an intemperate and inaccurate attack on a lay judge who had directed a verdict in a civil suit. Reversing the resultant contempt citations by the judge against a Corpus Christi, Texas, publisher, editorial writer, and news reporter, the Court, although admitting that the "news articles were by any standard an unfair report of what had transpired," held through Justice Douglas:

> The vehemence of the language used is not alone the measure of the power to punish for contempt. The fires which it kindles must constitute an imminent, not merely a likely, threat to the administration of justice. The danger must not be remote or even probable; it must immediately imperil.[99]

And the Court sustained this general approach to the problem in a key case on the issue when it held, 5 : 2, in *Wood v. Georgia*[100] that an elected sheriff in Bibb County, Georgia, could not be cited for contempt of court because, in "An Open Letter to the Bibb County Grand Jury," he expressed his "personal ideas" when he criticized a judge of the Superior Court who had instructed the grand jury in racially charged, intemperate tones. Over dissents by Justices Harlan and Clark, Chief Justice Warren's opinion for the Court concluded that the majority's examination of Sheriff Wood's actions "did not present a danger to the

[97]*Pennekamp v. Florida, op. cit.*, at 347.
[98]331 U.S. 367 (1947).
[99]*Ibid.*, at 376.
[100]370 U.S. 375 (1962).

administration of justice that should vitiate his freedom to express his opinions in the manner chosen."[101]

Another facet of the vexatious issue is personified by the resolution of *Irvin v. Dowd*,[102] in which a unanimous Supreme Court struck down a state conviction *solely* on the ground of prejudicial pretrial publicity—a case that emphasizes the collateral question of the impact of broad press freedom on the individual on trial rather than its impact upon the tribunal itself. Nothing happened to the offending newspapers or their "roving reporters" in Gibson County, Indiana, nor to the Evansville radio and television stations that blanketed the county with the news of petitioner Irvin's alleged crime of six murders in the vicinity of Vandenburgh County. But the accused's detention and death sentence were vacated and remanded in an opinion by Justice Clark, replete with criticism of an irresponsible press. Justice Frankfurter, concurring, administered a lecture to the news media, reminding them warmly that freedom implies responsibility:

> . . . this is, unfortunately, not an isolated case that happens in Evansville, Indiana, nor an atypical miscarriage of justice due to anticipatory trial by newspaper instead of trial in court before a jury. . . . But, again and again, such disregard of fundamental fairness is so flagrant that the Court is compelled, as it was only a week ago, to reverse a conviction in which prejudicial newspaper intrusion has poisoned the outcome. . . . This Court has not yet decided that the fair administration of criminal justice must be subordinated to another safeguard of our constitutional system—freedom of the press, properly conceived. The Court has not yet decided that, while convictions must be reversed and miscarriages of justice result because the minds of jurors or potential jurors were poisoned, the poisoner is constitutionally protected in plying his trade.[103]

[101]*Ibid.*, at 395. On the other hand, as Justice Goldberg made clear in *Cox v. Louisiana*, 379 U.S. 559 (1965)—*op. cit.*, p. 210, fn. 59—a state has the right to enact a statue forbidding picketing or parades in or near a court house "with intent of interfering with [the] administration of justice or [of] influencing any judge, juror, witness, or court officer." (At 560, 567.)

[102]366 U.S. 717 (1961). During *voir dire* 370 of 430 admitted believing Irvin guilty.

[103]*Ibid.*, at 729, 730. We should note here that—perhaps as a precursor of the *Estes* decision (see pp. 180–83, *infra*)—the Court, in *Rideau v. Louisiana*, 373 U.S. 723 (1963), voided on due process grounds the murder conviction of a defendant whose confession to a sheriff had been televised and thrice beamed at potential jurors throughout the area. Three seated jurors admitted to having viewed it.

In other words, the Court's resolution here was—as it has often been the case—to effect a "compromise" under which both the press and the accused "win"—and society loses.

It is difficult enough to find the line when responsibility obtains, but how much more so when the press ignores its responsibility? Must we really continue to believe that there is an unlimited right to conduct *ex parte* public trials in the press, on the radio, and on television? The British have long since answered that fundamental question in the negative. There, any publication of information about a defendant in a criminal case *before* the trial starts leads to punishment for contempt of court. Nothing that might conceivably affect the attitude of a potential juror may be revealed unless and until it is formally disclosed in court. Large fines have been meted out to newspapers that have violated the so-called Judges Rules, some of which have been enacted into formal statutes. To cite some examples: a small weekly newspaper in Eastbourne (on England's south coast) was fined the equivalent of $500 for saying that a defendant wore a dark suit and glasses, had been married on New Year's Day, and was being held on a serious charge.[104] A Scottish newspaper, *The Daily Record* of Edinburgh, was fined $21,000 for using on its front page a picture of a soccer star charged with "indecent exposure." In addition, Chief Assistant Editor Robert Johnson—who was in charge when the issue went to press—was fined $1,400, and the only reason no individual was sent to jail for contempt was that the editor responsible had been at home sick that night. "How is a judge or jury to know," asked the presiding judge in the case, "that the witness is identifying the man seen on the occasion of the crime and not the man whose photograph has been blazoned on the front page of a newspaper?"[105] In general, it is British doctrine that from the moment the police announce that an individual will be charged to the final disposition of the case—including appeals—nothing may be published about a defendant that might in any way influence the proceedings

---

[104]*The New York Times,* March 22, 1974, p. 4.

[105]As reported by the Associated Press in the *New York Herald Tribune,* February 12, 1960, p. 6. See also "British Verdict on Trial-by-Press," by Anthony Lewis, in *The New York Times Magazine,* June 20, 1965, p. 31; the excellent comparative column by Richard Eder, "Curbs on Press Shield British Suspect," in *The New York Times,* March 22, 1974, p. 4; and "Press Freedom, Security Fight Waged in Britain," by Don Neuchterlein, *The* (Charlottesville, Va.) *Daily Progress,* January 29, 1984, p. E3.

against him. Usually the only exception made is for information that comes out in the courtroom.[106]

Two significant United States Supreme Court rulings in 1965 and 1966 well pinpoint the omnipresent fact that, under our system, fundamental fairness cries out for a "balance" between freedom of the press and the right of the public to be informed, on the one hand, and the press's responsibilities and the right of the accused. The first ruling involved the conviction for swindling of Texas financier and "wheeler dealer" Billie Sol Estes, who had been tried and convicted (among several other earlier convictions) in a Tyler, Texas, courtroom in 1962. During the pretrial hearing, extensive and obtrusive television coverage took place: "The courtroom," reported *The New York Times,* "was turned into a snake-pit by the multiplicity of cameras, wires, microphones and technicians milling about the chamber."[107] Estes' appeal to the United States Supreme Court alleged denial of his constitutional rights of "due process of law." In a six-opinion, 5:4 decision, the Court laid down a rule that televising of "notorious" criminal trials is indeed prohibited by the "due process of law" clause of Amendment Fourteen, and it reversed Estes's conviction.[108] But it was a far from clear decision insofar as the basic problem of freedom of the press and fair trial goes. Four justices,[109] through Justice Clark, said that "the time honored principles of a fair trial" are violated when television is allowed in any criminal trial. A fifth, Justice Harlan—supplying the winning vote—agreed, but only because the Estes trial was one of "great notoriety," and he made clear that he would reserve judgment on more routine cases. Four dissenting justices[110] objected on constitutional grounds to the blanket ban at this stage of television's development, holding that there was insufficient proof that Estes' rights had here been violated.[111]

[106]An average "allowable" report is this acount from *The Daily Telegraph* (August 8, 1970, p. 9): "A man was . . . charged with the attempted murder of . . . two women. He will appear at Exmouth magistrates' court today."

[107]June 9, 1965, p. 31c.

[108]*Estes v. Texas,* 381 U.S. 532 (1965).

[109]Clark, Warren, Douglas, and Goldberg.

[110]Stewart, Black, Brennan, and White.

[111]*Estes v. Texas* still provides the law. But the use of television in courtrooms had become much more frequent; by late 1987 thirty-nine states permitted at least some form of TV coverage; and the Supreme Court had almost eagerly confronted the issue in 1981 in what gave promise of becoming a seminal decision: *Chandler v. Florida* (1981). Its

The second case involved the Court's striking down of the 1954 second-degree-murder conviction of a Cleveland, Ohio, osteopath, Dr. Samuel H. Sheppard, for the bludgeon-murder of his pregnant wife.[112] Dr. Sheppard had been in jail until 1964, when a federal district judge in Dayton granted a writ of *habeas corpus* and released him from the Ohio penitentiary, ruling that prejudicial publicity had denied him a fair trial. Two years later the Supreme Court affirmed that action by a vote of 8 : 1, giving Ohio authorities a choice of retrying him or of dismissing the case against him. (Ohio decided to retry him on the murder charge; the jury acquitted him in November 1966 after a trial that was a model of courtroom decorum!) Justice Clark's majority opinion pointed to the circus atmosphere that attended Dr. Sheppard's sensationalized trial. For example, the trial judge, Edward Blythin, positioned the press inside the lawyer's rail so close to the bench that it was in effect impossible for defense attorneys to consult with either their client or the judge without being overheard. When the jurors viewed the scene of the murder at Dr. Sheppard's home, a representative of the press was included in the group, while other reporters hovered overhead in a press helicopter. Radio and television commentators, among them Bob Considine, Dorothy Kilgallen, and Walter Winchell, kept up drum-fire of accounts of alleged multiple illicit liaisons by the defendant. Television broadcasts spewed forth from the room adjacent to the jury deliberation chamber. Jurors were photographed and interviewed by the news media, as were witnesses. In setting aside Dr. Sheppard's conviction, Clark restated the Court's concern that had led it to void Billie Sol Estes's conviction just a year earlier, namely, that the presence of a large, ill-controlled news media contingent can deny a defendant that "judicial serenity and calm" which the "due process of law" guaran-

---

8 : 0 ruling, penned by Chief Justice Burger, with concurring opinions by Justices Stewart and White—Justice Stevens not participating—held that, notwithstanding objections by the defendant, states may permit the news media to televise, i.e., to photograph and broadcast, criminal trials; that controlled televising (in Florida one camera and one cameraman) did not necessarily jeopardize the constitutional guarantees to a fair trial. While *Chandler* dealt only with a *state* trial, the extension of its gravamen to the federal sphere was a distinct possibility. But, as Chief Justice Burger announced again in 1984 and 1985, "There will be no cameras in the Supreme Court of the United States while I sit there." E.g., *The Washington Post*, November 13, 1984, p. A-5. None had entered the Rehnquist Court by mid 1988. (*Chandler*'s citation: 449 U.S. 560.)

[112]*Sheppard v. Maxwell*, 384 U.S. 333 (1966).

tees of the Constitution mandate for a fair trial—even in the absence of proof that the jury was in fact prejudiced by the publicity. And Clark added significantly that although the various officials involved could probably stifle most sources of prejudicial trial publicity, he would not rule out the possibility that *a judge could take direct action* against a newspaper, for example, if it persisted in violating defendants' rights.[113] The lone dissenting vote was cast by Justice Black—but without a written opinion, the record merely noting ''Mr. Justice Black dissents.''[114]

The dilemma remains; but in *Estes* and *Sheppard* the Court probably gave a signal in the direction of considerably more concern for fairness to those on trial.[115] Such a trend was also indicated by the actions taken by bar associations and jurists in a number of states, among them New Jersey, New York, and Pennsylvania, and, perhaps most significantly, by a widely circulated 226-page report by the American Bar Association's Advisory Committee on Fair Trial and a Free Press. Known as the Reardon Report for its chairman, Massachusetts Supreme Judicial Court Justice Paul C. Reardon, it set out detailed rules aimed at drastically curtailing the flow of information about arrested persons that is made available to the press in most communities. Sharply tightening the canons of legal ethics, it also recommended that judges be given the power to punish newsmen for contempt.[116] The resultant uproar from the media was at least in part instrumental in the adoption of a new set of rules by the Judicial Conference of the United States, recommended by a special committee headed by Judge Irving Kaufman of the United States Court of Appeals for the Second Circuit. In part patterned upon the Reardon Report, the Judicial Conference rules attempt to discourage publicity that might influence a jury and result in an unfair trial but, unlike the Reardon-ABA code, do not attempt to define any standards for the news media or police working beyond the confines of the

[113]*Ibid.*, at 357–62.

[114]*Ibid.*, at 363.

[115]In October 1966 the Texas Court of Criminal Appeals reversed the murder conviction of Jack Ruby, who had been sentenced to death in 1964 for the slaying of Lee Harvey Oswald, the presumed assassin of President Kennedy. The Court cited the rampant publicity (as well as inadmissible evidence) and, for Ruby's new trial, ordered a change of venue from Dallas County where the shooting took place. But Ruby's fatal illness intervened.

[116]For its text see *The New York Times,* February 20, 1968, pp. 1, 35c.

courtroom.[117] In particular, the "Kaufman Rules" do not include the three most controversial Reardon provisions: (1) exclusion, under some circumstances, of newsmen from preliminary hearings and other hearings held out of the presence of the jury; (2) extension to policemen of the curbs covering lawyers; and (3) recommendation that judges bring contempt-of-court citations against newmen who publish material "wilfully designed" to influence a trial's outcome. Predictably, it was the Kaufman Committee's recommendations, not Reardon's, that seem to have become part of the rules, more or less, in every federal and many a state court in the nation. But, despite a helpful 1969 "Code of Professional Responsibility" for lawyers issued by the American Bar Association,[118] and some encouraging signs that judges are indeed committed to the Kaufman rules—with some prepared to go even beyond them toward those suggested by the Reardon Report[119]—the basic dilemma[120] of drawing lines between the right to a fair trial and that of freedom of the press remains. It was back before the highest court in 1976, involving a sensational Nebraska multiple-murder case, in which Hugh Stuart, the trial judge, had imposed a very broad "gag order" sharply restricting pretrial coverage.[121] The Supreme Court's answer came quickly, 9:0, and to the delight of the media—although the five different opinions delivered in the case[122] evinced considerable line-drawing difficulties: in general, judges may *not* impose such orders on the press that forbid publication of information about criminal cases—even if, in the judge's opinion, such an order would help to assure the defendant a fair trial by preventing prejudicial publicity.

The ABA entered the *Stuart* decision's spirit by adopting a new set of guidelines in late 1978, prohibiting a judge to seal off any portion of a

[117]For their text see *The New York Times,* September 20, 1968, p. 32c.

[118]See *The Philadelphia Evening Bulletin,* September 10, 1969, p. 26.

[119]Thus in 1973 the Supreme Court declined to review—Justice Douglas dissenting— the contempt of court convictions of two Louisiana reporters who had defied an order by a federal trial judge not to write articles about an open hearing in his court. The United States Court of Appeals for the Fifth Circuit had found the secrecy order unconstitutional, but ruled that the reporters were subject to contempt proceedings anyway. (*Dickinson v. United States,* 414 U.S. 979.)

[120]See the Alfred Friendly and Ronald L. Goldfarb proposals in their *Crime and Publicity: The Impact of News on the Administration of Justice* (New York: The Twentieth Century Fund, 1967).

[121]*Nebraska Press Association v. Stuart,* 427 U.S. 539.

[122]By Chief Justice Burger and Justices Brennan, White, Powell, and Stevens.

trial or pretrial proceedings and from limiting comments to the press by attorneys—unless it could be shown that publicity would "create a clear and present danger" to a criminal suspect's ability to obtain an impartial jury, and unless other less restrictive alternatives, such as changing the location of the trial, would be impossible.[123] If these developments seemed to have a settling effect, it was a short-lived one, for down came the Supreme Court with its contentious, momentous 5 : 4 decision in the 1979 case of *Gannett Co. v. DePasquale*.[124] Two defendants in a New York State prosecution for second-degree murder, robbery, and grand larceny, arguing that their Sixth Amendment right to a fair trial had already been seriously threatened by a redolent building up of pretrial publicity, moved at a *pretrial* hearing that the press and the public were to be excluded from the hearing during which the trial judge, Daniel DePasquale, was to hear arguments and rule on a defense motion to suppress certain physical evidence and alleged involuntary confessions. The New York District Attorney did not oppose the motion; a reporter present said nothing—and the trial judge, granting the defense motion, held a closed hearing. When, on the following day, the reporter objected and requested access to any and all pertinent records of the hearing, the judge declined, contending that, at least at this stage of the proceedings, the defendants' Sixth Amendment rights to a fair trial outweighed any First Amendment rights of the press or the public to disclose the contents of the suppression hearing. The Gannett newspaper organization sought a writ of prohibition and *mandamus* against Judge DePasquale, and the Appellate Division of the New York Supreme Court vacated the closure order as an impermissible *prior restraint* in violation of Amendments One and Fourteen and an invasion of the public's interest "in open judicial proceedings." On further appeal, however, the highest New York tribunal, its Court of Appeals, upheld Judge DePasquale—who, ironically, in the meantime had made the suppression hearing transcripts available—and the United States Supreme Court promptly granted *certiorari*.

Regrettably, the Court's multi-divided, five-opinion (four on the majority side) ruling, while upholding the suppression order, did little to clarify the gravamen of the basic controversy of the First versus the

[123]Published August 25, 1978.
[124]443 U.S. 368.

Sixth Amendment. Some among the five prevailing Justices (Stewart, who authored the controlling plurality opinion, Burger, Powell, Rehnquist, and Stevens) seemed to confine their holding of suppressibility to the *pre*-trial stage; others, e.g., Rehnquist, to both pretrial *and* trial; others, personified by the controlling plurality opinion by Stewart, seemed to leave the matter to another day by simply asserting that "members of the public have no constitutional right under the Sixth and Fourteenth Amendment to attend criminal trials."[125] All five on the prevailing side in effect thus agreed that these guarantees, hallmarked by the Sixth Amendment, mandated the right to a *public trial* only for the defendant—a right dating from eleventh-century England; that, however, it provides no such guarantee to the press or the public. Writing for his dissenting colleagues Brennan, White, and Marshall, Justice Blackmun, however, saw a clear-cut right of press access in the Sixth Amendment—except in "highly unusual circumstances . . . not present here"[126]—both at the pretrial *and* the trial stage of a criminal case, all events observed being publishable and reportable consistent with the First Amendment.

Given the multi-faceted, quasi-confusing opinions in the DePasquale case, that "another day" was not long in coming—especially since some 200 state and local judges had attempted to bar the press from their courts in the interim. At the very end of its 1979–80 term, the Court returned to the fray with its eagerly awaited decision in *Richmond Newspapers v. Virginia.*[127] With native Virginian Justice Powell abstaining, the high tribunal now ruled firmly 7 : 1—Justice Rehnquist in solitary dissent—that, "absent an overriding interest to the contrary," the *trial* of a criminal case must be open to the public. Six of the Justices agreed—in what was a constitutional "first"—that there is a First Amendment guarantee of *access* to open trials; a seventh preferred to see it as a Sixth Amendment right. The controlling opinion—among seven rendered—written in twenty-four pages of ringing tones of support for press access by the press's latter-day villain, Chief Justice Burger, emphasized that the public and the press have a constitutional right to witness criminal trials—a right that is "implicit in the guaran-

[125]*Ibid.*, at 379.
[126]*Ibid.*, at 448.
[127]448 U.S. 555 (1980).

tees of the First Amendment for freedom of speech, of the press and of
assembly'' and in the Ninth Amendment's grant to ''the people'' of
''certain rights'' not specifically enumerated elsewhere.[128] Acknowledging that a trial may be closed in ''rare circumstances'' (that were
unspecified), the Chief Justice held that, to have justice carried out, the
process must also ''satisfy the appearance of justice . . . that can best
be provided by allowing people [and, of course, the press] to observe
it.''[129] It was clearly a watershed decision—a signal victory for freedom of communication. It was one that indeed was broadened two years
later in a 6:3 holding, authored by Justice Brennan, that states (here
Massachusetts) may *not* pass sweeping laws requiring that the press and
public be barred from trials, even during testimony by juvenile (in this
case below eighteen) rape or other sexual assault victims.[130] The Chief
Justice plus Justices Rehnquist and Stevens dissented.

The post–*Richmond Newspapers* stance in favor of the press continued apace, notwithstanding an occasional ''no.'' Thus, on the same
opinion day in 1984, with Justice Powell writing for the 9:0 Court in
both cases, the high tribunal ruled (1) that a Georgia judge could not
keep press and public out of a hearing on the admissibility of wiretap
evidence in a state gambling case, even though the defendant wanted an
open hearing—for the judge's order was too broad and too vague by
failing specifically to justify the reasons for closing the hearing without
considering alternatives.[131] *But* (2) that a judge in Washington State
acted properly when he ordered newspapers—in a *civil* suit—not to
publish material they had obtained during pretrial ''discovery'' proceedings in a libel suit against them.[132] That the latter holding was
patently an exception to the *Richmond Newspapers* rule was underscored by a far-reaching decision at the end of the Court's term in 1986,
when a 7:2 vote, in an opinion written by the retiring Chief Justice
Burger, made crystal clear that the press and public do indeed have a
constitutional right to attend *pretrial* hearings as well as trials in criminal cases under most circumstances.[133] Burger, noting that ''the pre-

[128]*Ibid.*, at 559.
[129]*Ibid.*, at 560.
[130]*Globe Newspaper Co. v. Superior Court,* 457 U.S. 596 (1982).
[131]*Waller v. Georgia,* 467 U.S. 39.
[132]*Seattle Times Co. v. Rhinehart,* 467 U.S. 20.
[133]*Press-Enterprise Co. v. Superior Court of California,* 54 LW 4869.

liminary hearing is often the final and most important step in the criminal proceeding,'' ruled that the press and public may be excluded from such hearings only if there is a ''substantial probability'' that a criminal defendant's right to a fair trial would be prejudiced by publicity and if that right could not be adequately protected through other means. The decision represented an extension of the 1980 *Richmond Newspapers*[134] precedent by, in effect, opening the entire criminal justice system in America to public scrutiny. To all intents and purposes, the 1979 *DePasquale* holding[135] was thereby overruled.

The Pentagon Papers Case. Central to the embattled ''free press *versus* fair trial'' syndrome is, of course, the fundamental issue of *access by and to the media*—access without prior restraint, again involving that ubiquitous line between societal and individual rights. What had appeared at first glance to be a golden opportunity in 1971 for the Supreme Court to find and draw a significant portion of such a line, while concurrently enunciating a ringing defense of freedom of the press on First Amendment grounds, had in fact turned out little more than a qualified one, at best, on both counts. At issue was the now famous *Pentagon Papers*, the publication—initially by *The New York Times* and then by several other leading newspapers—of a massive 7,000-page series of secret governmental documents dealing with the origins of the United States' involvement in Vietnam. These classified documents, compiled some years earlier by order of Secretary of Defense Robert S. McNamara, had been written by a team of distinguished experts; they had fallen into the hands of *The Times* through the instance of one of their authors, Daniel Ellsberg. Their publication became an immediate *cause célèbre*.

A series of legal maneuvers commenced instantly, with the United States Government, through Attorney-General John N. Mitchell, asking for an injunction against *The Times* (and subsequently *The Washington Post*) to suppress any further publication of the ''Pentagon Papers'' on the grounds of national security. It represented the first time in the history of the Republic that such *prior* restraint had been requested by the federal government.[136] Without going into the details of the legal

[134]*Richmond Newspapers v. Virginia*, 448 U.S. 555.

[135]*Gannett Co. v. DePasquale*, 443 U.S. 368.

[136]The only time to date (early 1988) in which the federal government ever succeeded in obtaining a prior restraint order came in the 1979 ''Hydrogen Bomb Article'' case

maneuvers—all of which are carefully set forth in what became an instant all-time "best seller," *The Pentagon Papers*[137]—some federal courts granted, and some denied, injuctions in whole or in part. Inexorably, but with uncommon speed, what promised to be a major constitutional law case wound its way to the Supreme Court of the United States, which proceeded to delay its scheduled summer adjournment in order to hear oral arguments in the *Times* and *Washington Post* cases on June 27. The eagerly awaited decision was handed down three days later.[138]

The case had been expected to produce a landmark ruling on the circumstances under which prior restraint could be imposed upon the press, but because no opinion by a single justice commanded the support of a majority, only the unsigned *per curiam* opinion, read for his Court by Chief Justice Burger, will serve as a precedent. There was a judicial outpouring of *nine* opinions! Six of these[139] rejected the government's contention that the further publication of the "Papers" be enjoined on the grounds of national security because, as the justices held variously, to do so in the circumstances at issue would impose an *unconstitutional prior restraint* upon the freedom of the press guaranteed by the First Amendment. The three dissenters,[140] on the other

---

("The H-Bomb Secret: How We Got It, Why We're Telling It"), *United States v. Progressive, Inc.* (467 F. Supp. 990). There U.S. District Judge Robert W. Warren, painfully and with the utmost reluctance, became the first federal jurist in our history to issue an injunction imposing prior restraint on the press in a national security case. However, in July 1980 the federal government decided to drop the litigation as a result of an agreement with *The Progressive*, under which thirty-eight of seventy-two impounded documents would be released in their entirety, along with parts of most of the others. Judge Warren readily agreed to dismiss the case. *Snepp v. United States*, 444 U.S. 507 (1980), was another controversial press decision. There the Court ruled (6:3) that an agreement requiring employees of the Central Intelligence Agency not to publish "any information" about the agency without specific prior approval is a judicially enforceable contract that applies to both classified and non-classified information—and Frank W. Snepp, a former C.I.A. officer who published his account of the fall of Saigon, *Decent Interval*, without such permission, was compelled to turn over to the C.I.A. the entire earnings of the book ($142,090 by August 1980).

[137]*The New York Times,* based on investigative reporting by Neil Sheehan (New York: Bantam Books, Inc., 1971).

[138]*The New York Times v. United States,* 403 U.S. 713 (1971), and *United States v. The Washington Post,* 403 U.S. 713 (1971).

[139]By Justices Black, Douglas, Brennan, Stewart, White, and Marshall.

[140]The Chief Justice and Justices Harlan and Blackmun. See Floyd Abrams, "The Pentagon Papers, A Decade Later." *The New York Times Magazine,* June 7, 1981, pp. 22 ff.

hand, held that courts should not refuse to enforce the executive branch's conclusion that material be kept confidential on matters affecting foreign relations—so long as a Cabinet-level officer personally so decided.

In effect, however, with the exception of Justices Black and Douglas, who restated their long-held absolutist belief that the First Amendment forbids *any* judicial restraint on speech and press, the difference of opinion among the justices turned on whether the government had *proved* that publication of the "Pentagon Papers" would constitute "immediate and irreparable harm to the nation." Only Chief Justice Burger and Justices Harlan and Blackmun believed that the government had made such a case; Justices Brennan, Stewart, White, and Marshall did not, although on varying grounds and in varying degrees. In brief, then, the highest tribunal of the land held (6 : 3) that the government had failed to meet the heavy burden it must in any attempt to block news articles *prior* to publication: namely, the presumption *against* the constitutionality of such an interference with basic First Amendment rights. Yet, fascinating though the dénouement was, the Court's ruling was on narrow grounds—there was no "seismic innovation" here.

On a tangential question, however, the Court did rule (5 : 4) in 1972 that there was *no* First Amendment right to refuse to provide grand juries in *criminal* cases with the names of confidential sources and related information obtained by journalists in their line of duty[141]—a principle that was even extended to appropriate *civil* cases in 1977.[142] It was reconfirmed below in the much publicized 1978–79 litigation involving the refusal of *The New York Times'* ace reporter, Myron A. Farber, to turn over defense-requested notes in the sensational multiple-murder case of Dr. Mario E. Jascalevich. And to date (spring 1988) the Court has committedly adhered to its precedent.[143] The Court also held 5 : 4 that congressional immunity did not prevent a grand jury from

[141]*Branzburg v. Hayes*, 408 U.S. 665. Reconfirmed in *Pennington v. Kansas*, 440 U.S. 929 (1979).

[142]*Tribune Publishing Co. v. Caldero*, 434 U.S. 930.

[143]Farber went to jail for forty days for contempt of court. The controversy ended when a jury acquitted Dr. Jascalevich. Farber's contention that New Jersey's press "shield law" vitiated any obligation to turn over his notes was rejected by the state's Supreme Court. *In re Farber*, 78 N.J. 259, *certiorari* denied, *New York Times Co. v. New Jersey*, 439 U.S. 997 (1978). Yet two years later, in 1980, that same tribunal upheld, by a 6 : 1 vote, *Shrewsbury Daily Register* reporter Robin Goldstein's refusal to do likewise under the now amended law, which requires the utilization of "less intrusive" sources. (*In the Matter of the Application of Robin Goldstein re: Subpoena*, 82 N.J. 446.)

asking Senator Mike Gravel (D.-Alaska) or his aides certain questions about his version of the "Pentagon Papers"—including where he had obtained them.[144]

A further press-freedom-limiting decision by the same 5:4 majority[145] came in June 1973, when the Court sustained a Pennsylvania ordinance prohibiting newspapers from carrying sex-designated employment advertisements.[146] On the other hand, friends of freedom of the press rejoiced in June 1974, when, speaking through Chief Justice Burger, it unanimously struck down a Florida law requiring newspapers to print *replies*—as distinct from *retractions* from defamation—from political candidates attacked in their columns. "A responsible press is an undoubtedly desirable goal," wrote Burger, "but press responsibility is not mandated by the Constitution, and, like many other virtues, it cannot be legislated."[147] The aforegone *Tornillo* decision was not a surprise, of course: for while the Court's 1939 holding in *Red Lion Broadcasting Co. v. F.C.C.*[148] appeared to recognize a *limited* right of access to the broadcast media under the Commission's "fairness" doctrine, the Court concluded in its 1973 *C.B.S. v. Democratic National Committee* ruling that the F.C.C. act in the "public interest" required an F.C.C. ruling that broadcasters accept paid editorial advertisements.[149] Nor does that Amendment bar the F.C.C. from prohibiting radio broadcasting of "offensive—indecent but not obscene—words," to wit, what the Court in its 5:4 ruling characterized as the "seven dirty words," used by comedian George Carlin in a twelve-minute monologue over station WBAI-FM New York.[150] And the

[144]*Gravel v. United States*, 408 U.S. 697 (1972).

[145]Chief Justice Burger and Associate Justices White, Blackmun, Powell, and Rehnquist. Dissenters were Justices Brennan, Stewart, Marshall, and Stevens.

[146]*Pittsburgh Press Co. v. Pittsburgh Commission on Human Relations*, 413 U.S. 376—obviously because of the Court's "close scrutiny" test (see Chapter II, *supra*) applied to gender. See also a similarly intriguing line-drawing decision affecting competing interests, here race and religion, in *Norwood v. Harrison*, 413 U.S. 455 (1973). But *cf. Linmark Associates v. Willingboro*, fn. 8, *supra*, involving expression and race.

[147]*Miami Herald Publishing Co. v. Tornillo*, 418 U.S. 241, at 256.

[148]395 U.S. 367. Strengthened in *C.B.S. v. F.C.C.*, 453 U.S. 367 (1981).

[149]412 U.S. 94. But it *must* sell time in federal campaign races.

[150]*F.C.C. v. Pacifica Foundation*, 438 U.S. 726 (1978). The words, characterized by the majority as "patently, offensively, referring to excretory and sexual organs and activities," were "shit, piss, fuck, cunt, cocksucker, motherfucker, and tits." (At 751–55.) The Court's five-opinion line-up consisted of the Chief Justice and Justices Powell, Blackmun, Rehnquist, and Stevens in the majority, with Justices Brennan, White, Stewart, and Marshall dissenting.

above-outlined *Pittsburgh Press* case[151] was distinguished in 1975 when the Court held (7 : 2) that Virginia had violated the First Amendment when it tried to punish a newspaper editor for publishing an advertisement telling of New York abortion services because abortions were illegal in Virginia.[152]

2. *Free Speech and Freedom from Noise.* In a different although related form of the dilemma, during the 1948 presidential elections, two interesting cases involving sound trucks caused the Court to draw two different lines between "freedom and order"—lines that are illustrative of the inherent complexities.

In the first case, *Saia v. New York,*[153] the petitioner was a minister of the Jehovah's Witnesses. Wishing to broadcast his gospel in Lockport, New York, Samuel Saia had run afoul of a city ordinance forbidding the use of sound-amplification devices except for "public dissemination of items of news and matters of public concern provided that the same be done under permission obtained from the Chief of Police." Refused a new permit on the grounds that complaints had been made about his prior sound-amplified speeches on religious (and not exactly very popular) subjects, Saia nevertheless decided to proceed to lecture, by means of loudspeakers, in a small city recreational park. He was convicted, fined, and sentenced to jail. Speaking for a closely divided Court (5 : 4), Justice Douglas held the ordinance "unconstitutional on its face, for it establishes a *previous restraint* on the right of free speech."[154] The right to be heard, concluded Douglas, was here placed impermissibly at the "uncontrolled discretion of the Chief of Police." However, to the four dissenting justices—Frankfurter, Reed, Jackson, and Burton—this was not a free speech issue at all since no one, they contended, had stopped Saia from using his voice; rather, it was a question of the protection of society's unwilling listeners by a non-arbitrary, non-capricious, non-discriminatory ordinance. But they lost.

They *won*, however, only eight months later in *Kovacs v. Cooper,*[155] with a ruling concerning the validity of a Trenton, New Jersey, ordinance. This time Henry Wallace's Progressive Party was involved. The

[151]See fn. 146, *supra.*

[152]*Bigelow v. Virginia,* 421 U.S. 809. Justices Rehnquist and White dissented.

[153]334 U.S. 558 (1948).

[154]*Saia v. New York, op. cit.,* at 559–60. (Italics supplied.) Douglas was joined by Chief Justice Vinson and Associate Justices Black, Murphy, and Rutledge.

[155]336 U.S. 77 (1949).

case went 5:4 *contra*, Chief Justice Vinson switching sides and thus providing the key vote for the upholding of Trenton's law, which prohibited the use on the city's "public streets, alleys or thoroughfares" of any "device known as a sound truck, loud speaker or sound amplifier . . . [that] emits therefrom loud and raucous noises. . . ." Speaking for the new majority, Justice Reed, while emphasizing the "preferred position of free speech in a society that cherishes liberty for all," distinguished *Kovacs v. Cooper* from the *Saia* case on the grounds that the Trenton ordinance was carefully drawn and that the kind of discretionary power that the Court had found fatal to the Lockport ordinance was not present in Trenton's. The four dissenters (Black, Douglas, Murphy, and Rutledge, who, with the Chief Justice, had made up the majority in the *Saia* case) saw a rank violation of Charles Kovacs's right to freedom of expression under Amendments One and Fourteen.[156]

3. *Freedom of Street Corner Exhortation.* Two famous decisions, illustrating the importance of specific facts in particular court cases, were announced by the Supreme Court on the same day in 1951. The first favored free-speech claimant Carl Jacob Kunz, an ordained Baptist minister of rather unsavory reputation and long a thorn in the side of New York City police authorities because of his penchant for inflammatory addresses against Jews and Catholics in areas abounding with these two groups (minorities in most areas of the country, but certainly not in New York City). Preaching under the auspices of what he called the "Outdoor Gospel Work," of which he was the self-appointed director, Kunz had in 1946 asked for and received a permit under a New York City ordinance that made it unlawful to hold public worship meetings on the streets without first obtaining a permit from the City Commissioner of Police. Aware of what Kunz had done with his 1946 permit—that was revoked after a hearing—the Commissioner several

[156]The issue has a habit of recurring. Thus, in 1966 U.S. District Court Judge Alfred L. Luongo ruled that the city of Chester, Pa., was entitled to establish certain controls over operation of a sound truck, but could not charge a $25 fee for its operation. His decision came in a suit brought by the NAACP. (*The Philadelphia Evening Bulletin,* April 28, 1966.) And in 1970 the Maryland Supreme Court struck down a Baltimore ordinance banning the use of loudspeakers without a permit. The law allowed the mayor and police commissioner to issue permits for "events of public interest"; it exempted newspapers, which were allowed to broadcast important news and sports items throughout the city. In effect, this accorded authorities the right to decide who would be permitted to exercise free speech! (For an account see 270 *Civil Liberties* 7 [July 1970].)

times refused a new one to Kunz, each time pointing to the fact that the 1946 revocation was based on clear evidence that Kunz had publicly ridiculed and denounced other religious beliefs in his meetings. In 1948 Kunz, having decided to hold one of his meetings *without* a permit, was arrested for speaking at Columbus Circle, and fined $10 for violating the New York City ordinance in question. In an 8 : 1 opinion for the Court, Chief Justice Vinson addressed himself exclusively to the matter of prior suppression of free speech, concluding that "it is sufficient to say that New York cannot vest restraining control over the right to speak on religious subjects in an administrative official where there are no appropriate standards to guide his action."[157] There was a solitary, but lengthy and vigorous, dissenting opinion by Justice Jackson. He pointed to the kind of "preachings" Kunz made, which, on his arrest in 1948, included the following observations:

> The Catholic Church makes merchandise out of souls . . . [Catholicism] is a religion of the devil . . . [the Pope] is the anti-Christ. . . . The Jews . . . are Christ-killers. . . . All the garbage [the Jews] that didn't believe in Christ should have been burnt in the incinerators. It's a shame they all weren't.[158]

To Jackson, the Chief American Prosecutor at the Nuremberg War Crimes Trials, this public speech was too "intrinsically incendiary and divisive," given the delicate and emotional nature of the two subjects of "race and religion," to permit the type of constitutional protection claimed by Kunz and confirmed by Jackson's eight fellow judges. "The consecrated hatreds of sect," concluded the lone dissenter, "account for more than a few of the world's bloody disorders. These are the explosives which the Court says Kunz may play with in the public streets, and the community must not only tolerate but aid him. I find no such doctrine in the Constitution."[159]

Yet, on the same day of Court, just a few pages along in the same *United States Reports*,[160] the majority seemed to adopt the very ideas that Jackson alone expressed in the *Kunz* case! Involved here was the

---

[157]*Kunz v. New York*, 340 U.S. 290 (1951), at 295.

[158]*Ibid.*, at 296.

[159]*Ibid.*, at 314.

[160]The official volumes reporting all Supreme Court decisions.

free speech claim of one Irving Feiner, an adolescent sidewalk orator who, using derogatory language about public officials and certain interest groups, had harangued a crowd of some seventy-five to eighty white and black persons in a predominantly black residential area of Syracuse, New York. He was publicizing a "Young Progressives" meeting to be held that evening in a local hotel rather than in the public school auditorium originally scheduled, because the permit granted for the latter had been revoked as a result of local pressure-group activities. In the course of his speech Feiner referred to President Truman as a "bum"; to Mayor Costello of Syracuse as a "champagne-sipping bum" who "does not speak for the Negro people"; to Mayor O'Dwyer of New York City as a "bum"; to the American Legion as "a Nazi Gestapo"; and, in what the record described as "an excited manner," yelled: "The Negroes don't have equal rights; they should rise up in arms and fight for them."[161]

Feiner's statements "stirred up a little excitement," and one of the bystanders called out that if police did not get that "son of a bitch" off the stand, he would do so himself. (The police later admitted that there was "not yet a disturbance," but that there did occur "angry muttering and pushing.") At this point one of the two police officers detailed to the area stepped forward and arrested Feiner to "prevent [the events] from resulting in a fight," since Feiner—who had been holding forth for over thirty minutes—had disregarded two earlier requests by the policeman to stop speaking. The New York State trial judge concluded that the police officers were justified in taking the action "to prevent a breach of the peace," and the intermediate appellate tribunal concurred. New York State's highest court, the Court of Appeals, then affirmed the findings below, stating that Feiner, "with intent to provoke a breach of the peace and with knowledge of the consequences, so inflamed and agitated a mixed audience of sympathizers and opponents that, in the judgment of the police officers present, a *clear danger* of disorder and violence was threatened."[162] Speaking for himself and five of his colleagues—Associate Justices Reed, Frankfurter, Jackson, Burton, and Clark—Chief Justice Vinson agreed with the findings of "three New York courts" that Feiner's free speech claims were spurious: that, while

161*Feiner v. New York*, 340 U.S. 315 (1951), at 330.
162*Ibid.*, at 318, n. 2. (Italics supplied.)

his right to hold his meeting and utter the derogatory remarks was uncontested and uncontestable, the police officers were justified in making the arrest because they

> were motivated solely by a proper concern for the preservation of order and protection of the general welfare, and that there was no evidence which could lend color to a claim that the acts of the police were a cover for suppression of [Feiner's] views and opinions. Petitioner was thus neither arrested nor convicted for the making or the content of his speech. Rather, *it was the reaction which it actually engendered.*[163]

It was precisely from this last sentence that Justices Black, Douglas, and Minton dissented strongly in two separate opinions, Minton joining Douglas's and Black writing his own. In brief, the dissenters rejected the majority's two key points, namely, that danger of a riot existed and that Feiner had perpetrated a breach of the peace. They denied that the facts demonstrated "any imminent threat of riot or uncontrollable disorder,"[164] and declared that the record merely showed "an unsympathetic audience and the threat of one man to haul the speaker from the stage. *It is against that kind of threat that speakers need police protection,*" concluded Justice Douglas,[165] pointing to what he and the other dissenting jurists viewed as the duty of the police: to, as Black put it, protect Feiner's "constitutional right to talk" rather than to arrest him.

And there, of course, lies the dilemma: at what point should speech be prohibitable? When it stirs to anger? When it creates opposition? When it creates disorder? But who is to say that the latter cannot be artificially stimulated, even created? Could not, as Black, Douglas, and Minton tried to plead in *Feiner,* a strong point be made that the police have an obligation to protect the *maker* of the speech *against* a hostile audience? To raise these fundamental questions is to recognize the difficulty of any all-embracing response. Does it depend not only upon the *content* of a speech but *how* it is *delivered?* And with what identifiable purpose and direction?[166] What of such emotion-charged issues as those that informed the wrenching 1978 Skokie, Illinois, Nazi Party

[163]*Ibid.,* at 319–20. (Italics supplied.)
[164]*Ibid.,* Black, dissenting opinion, at 325.
[165]*Ibid.,* dissenting opinion, at 331.
[166]See *Chaplinsky v. New Hampshire,* fn. 65, *supra,* and its subsequent interpretation.

activities?[167] What of the nature of the mass protests and demonstrations in the context of the contemporary youth and race "evangelism"? "Incitement," too, is a double-edged sword. After all, as Justice Holmes put it so perceptively in his memorable dissenting opinion in the *Gitlow* case,[168] "[E]very idea is an incitement. . . . The only difference between the expression of an opinion and an incitement in the narrower sense is the speaker's enthusiasm for the result. Eloquence may set fire to reason."[169] Whatever the elusive answer, democratic society demands that it be a generous one. If that means taking chances, so be it—but, as Justice Jackson put it so eloquently in his already alluded-to dissent in the *Terminiello* case, we are assuredly not obliged to be so doctrinaire and so devoid of practical wisdom as to "convert the constitutional Bill of Rights into a suicide pact."[170]

4. *Free Expression and Association and Subversive Activity: The National Security Syndrome.* The fact and concept of subversive activity and how to meet it have concerned the nation sporadically since its birth. From the hated Alien and Sedition Acts of 1798 through the trying eras of the Civil War, World War I, the "red scare" of the 1920s, post–World War II, McCarthyism, and the Cold War, the legislative and administrative remedies adopted to deal with the problem of national security have often been dominant concerns. And the resultant statutes, executive orders, and legislative investigations have almost all,

[167]See *Village of Skokie v. National Socialist Party,* 69 Ill. 2d 605; 373 N.E. 2d 21 (1978). See also *Smith v. Collin,* fn. 56, *supra,* on the same case.

[168]*Gitlow v. New York,* 268 U.S. 652 (1925).

[169]*Ibid.,* at 673.

[170]*Terminiello v. Chicago,* 337 U.S. 1 (1949), at 37, an interesting and troublesome case, demonstrating that very problem. In *Terminiello,* the Court, dividing 5 : 4, reversed the breach-of-peace conviction of a professional rabble-rouser (a suspended Catholic priest) who had *really* caused a riot. But the year was 1949—with Justices Murphy and Rutledge still on the bench (they both died later that year). And Douglas's majority opinion was based on a dubious procedural analysis: that the oral charge of the jury by the trial judge was ambiguous and imprecise in its explanation of the municipal ordinance defining "disorderly conduct" under which Terminiello had been tried and convicted. In fact, Douglas had initially voted to *sustain* the conviction—but then changed his mind and was assigned the writing of the opinion for the Court by Black (the senior justice on that side of the issue, Chief Justice Vinson being in dissent). Reed provided the decisive fifth vote, persuaded by Douglas's reasoning. (The other three dissenters were Frankfurter, Jackson, and Burton, with Jackson there penning his celebrated warning. Jackson's full statement was: "There is danger that, if the Court does not temper its doctrinaire logic with a little practical wisdom, it will convert the constitutional Bill of Rights into a suicide pact.")

sooner or later, found themselves in judicial hot water, agitated by the friction between freedom of expression and association and national security and how to draw viable and allowable lines. Answers given by the judicial branch in this area—if answers they be—have understandably been perhaps more cautious and more circumspect than for any other aspect of the freedom at issue. Nonetheless, as the McCarthy-tinged 1950s turned into the 1960s, the courts became increasingly generous toward the individual's constitutional claims as against those of majoritarian society. Hence, for example, while necessarily recognizing the right and duty of the legislative branch to keep itself informed in order to legislate more wisely, both to "oversee" the executive branch and to inform the public, the Supreme Court has also recognized that there are, and must be, limits on the range and extent of the power to investigate. Among these are the witness's right to decline to respond by invoking the Fifth Amendment's privilege against compulsory self-incrimination, though in many areas he or she may be compelled to testify in return for immunity from prosecution;[171] to refuse to reply if the question is beyond the investigating committee's mandate;[172] and to have "explicit and clear" knowledge of the subject to which the interrogation is deemed pertinent.[173] Yet as other decisions of the Court have shown, great difficulties here are the matters of "pertinency"[174] and just what constitutes "exposure for the sake of exposure."[175]

Similarly troublesome has been the matter of "loyalty and security." The Court has been called upon repeatedly to draw lines between the rights of the individual under the Bill of Rights, which one assuredly does not surrender simply because he or she works for the government, and the rights of the state, which has a basic obligation to protect its

[171]E.g., *Ullmann v. United States*, 350 U.S. 422 (1955), and *Murphy v. Waterfront Commission of New Jersey Harbor*, 378 U.S. 52 (1964).
[172]E.g., *United States v. Rumely*, 345 U.S. 41 (1953).
[173]E.g., *Watkins v. United States*, 354 U.S. 178 (1957).
[174]E.g., *Barenblatt v. United States*, 360 U.S. 109 (1959).
[175]E.g., *Braden v. United States*, 365 U.S. 431 (1961). *Cf. DeGregory v. Attorney-General of New Hampshire*, 383 U.S. 825 (1966). Most notoriously prominent in these investigations was "HUAC" (the House Committee on Un-American Activities). Restyled the Internal Securities Committee—its constitutionality upheld in 1968 in *Stamler v. Willis*, 393 U.S. 212—it was abolished in 1975 and its functions transferred to the House Committee on the Judiciary. The Senate's counterpart, the Judiciary Committee's Internal Security Subcommittee, was disbanded in 1977; but a Subcommittee on Security and Terrorism was constituted in 1981.

citizenry from subversion by disloyal elements. Grave problems have surrounded the nature and meaning of the terms "loyalty" and "security," as well as the compatibility of appropriate security legislation and ordinances with the prerogatives of free citizens. Avoiding the constitutional issues whenever possible, the Court handed down several significant guidelines, chiefly by statutory interpretation. Thus, federal employee loyalty-security regulations, which initially seemed to have a rather free rein, found themselves increasingly confined in coverage and held to ever more strict requirements of procedural due process as of the mid-1950s.[176] At least one key aspect of the issue was more or less settled when a special three-judge federal court ruled in 1969 that the statute on which the then twenty-five-year-old *loyalty oath* requirement for federal employees was based was "unconstitutionally vague" not only as a violation of the Fifth Amendment's due process of law clause but also, in the ruling of the 2 : 1 majority opinion by Judges J. Skelly Wright and Harold Leventhal of the United States Court of Appeals for the District of Columbia, as a violation of the strictures against "odious test oaths" inherent in Article Six of the Constitution.[177] When the U.S. Department of Justice decided not to appeal the decision to the Supreme Court, the Civil Service Commission quietly informed all federal departments and agencies that prospective employees would henceforth no longer have to sign the controversial affidavit stating that the applicant was neither a Communist nor a Fascist nor sought to overthrow the United States Government by force and violence.[178]

The Warren Court did squarely face the constitutional issue in a related matter—namely, the government's policy of barring employment to otherwise qualified individuals *merely* because of their beliefs and/or associations. While never having wavered from basic erstwhile,

---

[176]*Peters v. Hobby*, 349 U.S. 341 (1955); *Cole v. Young*, 351 U.S. 356 (1956); *Service v. Dulles*, 354 U.S. 363 (1957); *Vitarelli v. Seaton*, 359 U.S. (1959); *Greene v. McElroy*, 361 U.S. 374 (1959).

[177]*Stewart v. Washington*, 301 F. Supp. 610. Judge John Lewis Smith, the third member of the tribunal, agreed that the oath was invalid, but he did not agree that the wording of the law itself was unconstitutional.

[178]*The New York Times*, January 7, 1970, p. 1. And in late 1976 it ordered the elimination of *all* political loyalty questions on federal job application forms. (*Ibid.*, September 9, 1976, p. 1.) Four years later, the Carter Administration forbade government officials from inquiring into the sexual habits of employees or individuals seeking most federal jobs—an order that represented a major boost for the rights of homosexuals. (*The Washington Post*, May 14, 1980, p. C2.)

and entirely logical, holdings that there is no *ipso facto* constitutional *right* to work for the *government*,[179] the Court nonetheless made clear in a series of cases in the late 1960s that the First Amendment is not vitiated simply because someone happens to be, or aspires to be, a governmental employee. Thus, speaking through Chief Justice Warren in the 1967 *Robel* case, it declared unconstitutional (6 : 2)—as a violation of First Amendment rights of freedom of association—a provision of the Subversive Activities Control (McCarran) Act of 1950 that made it a crime for members of the Communist Party to work in defense plants, regardless of the "quality and degree" of that membership.[180] And the Court extended the aforegone ruling to the maritime industry early in 1968, holding unanimously that Herbert Schneider, a Seattle marine engineer and former Communist Party member who had applied for clearance in 1964, could not be barred from employment simply because of his beliefs or associations.[181] The government, wrote Justice Douglas for the Court, has every right to enact legislation to safeguard American shipping from subversive activity, but Congress had not, under the applicable statute—the Magnuson Act of 1950—given the executive branch the power "to ferret out the ideological strays."[182]

A host of state "loyalty" statutes and allied requirements have fallen on grounds of both substantive and procedural due process, often in concord with freedom of expression guarantees. Thus, while some practices have been upheld as valid exercises of the state police power—particularly *affirmative* rather than *disclaimer* loyalty oaths[183]—others have fallen, more often than not because of the "vice of vagueness": the sweeping implications of such terms as "subversive organizations," "subversive persons," or "sympathetic association with."[184] In fact, state loyalty oaths began to fall like veritable flies as of 1966,

---

[179]*United Public Workers v. Mitchell,* 330 U.S. 75 (1947).

[180]*United States v. Robel,* 389 U.S. 258. (See discussion, *infra.*)

[181]*Schneider v. Smith,* 390 U.S. 17. In that case, however, the Court applied statutory construction to the Magnuson Act of 1950 rather than hold it unconstitutional.

[182]*Ibid.,* at 26. Congress threatened to overturn the two decisions, but never did.

[183]*Garner v. Board of Public Works of Los Angeles,* 341 U.S. 716 (1951); *Gerende v. Board of Supervisors,* 341 U.S. 56 (1951); *Adler v. Board of Education of New York,* 342 U.S. 485 (1952), but overruled by *Keyishian,* see fn. 185, *infra; Knight v. Board of Regents of New York,* 390 U.S. 36 (1968); *Hosack v. Smiley,* 390 U.S. 744 (1968); *Lisker v. Kelly,* 410 U.S. 928 (1971).

[184]*Wieman v. Updegraff,* 344 U.S. 183 (1952); *Shelton v. Tucker,* 364 U.S. 479 (1960); *Baggett v. Bullitt,* 377 U.S. 360 (1964).

and by 1969 the vast majority of the disclaimer-type state oaths as well as "mixed" disclaimer-affirmative types[185] were a thing of the past.[186] And attacks, albeit unsuccessful,[187] were also launched against even the simple "positive" type.

Here, again, the advocates of maximum security and those who believe that democratic society must take risks for the sake of freedom are at loggerheads. It is far easier to criticize than to solve. And it has been understandably rare for the Court to be unanimous in any such cases unless the restrictions involved were clearly and patently unconstitutional.[188]

In the three major federal statutes that have been enacted since 1940 to combat subversion and increase national security, heavy judicial involvement was inevitable, given the nature of the controversy and the delicacy and difficulty of producing legislation that would achieve the desired goal without impinging upon fundamental individual liberties. The triumvirate of laws, in the order of their enactment, are the Smith Act of 1940, the Subversive Activities Control (McCarran) Act of 1950, and the Communist Control Act of 1954. We need not here be concerned with this last, hastily enacted, largely floor-legislated statute, since it has been more or less ignored by the Department of Justice as a basis for possible prosecution. Although it did figure tangentially in

---

[185]*Elfbrandt v. Russell*, 384 U.S. 11 (1966); *Keyishian v. Board of Regents of New York*, 385 U.S. 589 (1967), overruling *Adler*, fn. 183, *supra; Whitehill v. Elkins*, 389 U.S. 54 (1967).

[186]E.g., *Rafferty v. McKay*, 400 U.S. 954 (1970), in which the Court affirmed a lower-court holding that struck down California's loyalty oath for teachers by relying on *Baggett v. Bullitt, op. cit.* The oath at issue was the "mixed" type, reading: "I solemnly swear (or affirm) that I will support the Constitution of the United States of America, the Constitution of the State of California, and the laws of the United States and the State of California, and will . . . promote respect for the flag and . . . respect for law and order and . . . allegiance to the government of the United States." Had the oath stopped with "California" and before "and will" it would undoubtedly have been upheld as a simple affirmative oath (like those enumerated in fn. 183, *supra*). However, narrowly dividing 4 : 3, the Court in 1972 upheld a two-part Massachusetts loyalty oath which, in addition to the standard "uphold and defend" clause, requires public employees to pledge that they will "oppose" the overthrow of the federal and state governments by force, violence, "or by any illegal or unconstitutional methods." (*Cole v. Richardson*, 405 U.S. 676.)

[187]E.g., *Fields v. Askew*, 414 U.S. 1148 (1974).

[188]E.g., *Wieman v. Updegraff, op. cit.*, in which the Court unanimously struck down an Oklahoma loyalty oath law that made even *innocent* membership in a proscribed organization an offense.

three cases in 1956, 1961, and 1970,[189] it had not been frontally adjudicated by the Court as of early 1988, and it is not likely to be.

The first major test of anti-Communist legislation involved the Smith Act: the 1951 case of *Dennis v. United States*.[190] Here, in a 6:2 decision, featuring five separate opinions (the opinion for the Court by Chief Justice Vinson, two separate concurring opinions by Justices Frankfurter and Jackson, and two separate dissenting opinions by Justices Black and Douglas), the Supreme Court upheld the Smith Act's constitutionality. It did so against the contentions by Eugene Dennis and his ten co-leaders of the American Communist Party that the statute infringed on First Amendment guarantees of freedom of expression, in addition to violating substantive due process guarantees under the Fifth Amendment because of vagueness. The eleven top leaders had been indicted and tried in United States District Court Judge Harold Medina's tribunal, and after a sensational nine-month trial were found guilty of conspiracy[191] to teach and advocate the overthrow of the United States Government by force and violence, and a conspiracy to organize the American Communist Party to teach and advocate the same offenses proscribed and rendered criminal by the terms of the Smith Act. Their appeal to the United States Court of Appeals for the Second Circuit had been unanimously rebuffed. In upholding the challenged segments of the Act, the Chief Justice, speaking for himself and Associate Justices Reed, Burton, and Minton,[192] focused on what the majority regarded as the conspiratorial nature of the defendants' activities. Calling upon the "clear and present danger" formula—a judicial doctrine utilized in freedom of expression cases, to be discussed below—Vinson ruled that these activities transgressed the permissible line between the exercise of individual rights of peaceful advocacy of change and the right of society to ascertain national security as viewed by the Smith Act. But in invok-

---

[189]*Pennsylvania v. Nelson*, 350 U.S. 497, *Communist Party v. Catherwood*, 367 U.S. 389, and *Mitchell v. Donavan*, 398 U.S. 427, respectively. In the 1961 case it ruled 9:0 (via Harlan) that the Communist Party could not be banned from state unemployment systems; and in the 1970 case it pointedly declined to rule on the Act's constitutionality.

[190]341 U.S. 494.

[191]A conspiracy is commonly regarded as any combination of two or more persons to commit an unlawful act or accomplish some unlawful purpose by illegal means.

[192]Justice Clark, who, as President Truman's Attorney-General, had brought the indictments in the case, did not participate.

ing the concept that the activities of the eleven did indeed constitute a clear and present danger which Congress had a right and duty to prevent, he added an important qualification originally expressed by Chief Judge Learned Hand in the case of the Court of Appeals below: "In each case [courts] must ask whether the gravity of the 'evil,' discounted by its improbability, justifies such invasion of free speech as is necessary to avoid the danger."[193] "We adopt this statement of the rule," the Chief Justice went on, because it is "as succinct and inclusive as any other we might devise at this time. It takes into consideration those factors which we deem relevant, and relates their significance. More we cannot expect from words."[194] Explaining the community's justification for its national security policy, he continued:

> The formation by [the convicted Communist Party leaders] of such a highly organized conspiracy, with rigidly disciplined members subject to call when the leaders, these petitioners, felt that the time had come for action, coupled with the inflammable nature of world conditions, similar uprisings in other countries, and the touch-and-go nature of our relations with countries with whom the petitioners were in the very least ideologically attuned, convince us that their convictions were justified on this score.[195]

"And this analysis," wrote the Chief Justice determinedly, "disposes of the contention that a conspiracy to advocate, as distinguished from the advocacy itself, cannot be constitutionally restrained, because it comprises only the preparation. *It is the existence of the conspiracy which creates the danger.*"[196] Earlier, he had anticipated one objection by commenting that "clear and present danger" cannot mean that before the "Government may act, it must wait until the *putsch* is about to be executed, the plans have been laid and the signal is awaited."[197] And he rejected success or probability of success as a criterion.

Justice Frankfurter's concurring opinion was characteristic of his jurisprudential philosophy: to him, the decisive consideration was the Court's obligation to exercise judicial self-restraint by recognizing that the legislative assumption in passing the Smith Act was a reasonable one, consummated by reasonable representatives of the body politic. He

---

[193]*Dennis v. United States*, 183 F. 2d 201 (1950), at 212.
[194]*Dennis v. United States*, 341 U.S. 494 (1951), at 510.
[195]*Ibid.*, at 510–11.
[196]*Ibid.*, at 511. (Italics supplied.)
[197]*Ibid.*, at 509.

was troubled by the law, however, and warned that "it is a sobering fact that in sustaining the conviction . . . we can hardly escape restriction on the interchange of ideas"; that without "open minds there can be no open society."[198] Yet he emphatically held to his creed that even "free-speech cases are not an exception to the principle that we are not legislators, that direct policy-making is not our province."[199] Only if the legislative determination on how competing interests might best be reconciled is clearly "outside the pale of fair judgment" would the Court be justified in exercising its veto. The obvious difficulty, of course, remains: how and when to judge what is "outside." On the other hand, Justice Jackson, in his concurring opinion, pursued a different tack; waving aside the intricate free-speech problem line *per se*—he rejected application of the clear and present danger doctrine "to a case like this"—he concentrated almost exclusively on what he chose to see as *the* crux of the case—a conviction of and for *conspiracy*—"as that is the case before us." Eleven times in two paragraphs of his opinion he used the noun "conspiracy," commenting that the "Constitution does not make conspiracy a civil right."[200]

Justices Black and Douglas dissented vehemently. In separate opinions they *denied* the existence of a danger either clear or present enough to justify what they regarded as a rank invasion of the prerogatives of freedom of expression (although Douglas, unlike Black, granted that "freedom to speak is not absolute"); charged that the Court's majority had, in effect, introduced a formula far less "tough" for the government to cope with than the "clear and present danger" concept Chief Justice Vinson ostensibly employed; and fervently argued for "full and free discussion even of ideas we hate." Justice Douglas belittled the alleged internal strength and threat of the Communist movement, pointing out that in America "they are miserable merchants of unwanted ideas: their wares remain unsold."[201] Justice Black closed his opinion with the observation that

> Public opinion being what it now is, few will protest the conviction of these Communist petitioners. There is hope, however, that in calmer times, when

[198]*Ibid.*, at 556.
[199]*Ibid.*, at 539.
[200]*Ibid.*, at 572.
[201]*Ibid.*, at 589.

present pressures, passions and fears subside, this or some later Court will restore the First Amendment liberties to the high preferred place where they belong in a free society.[202]

Whatever the substantive merits of the Black position, this statement proved to be correct both as an analysis and as a prophecy. By June 1957, the federal authorities had obtained 145 indictments and 89 convictions under the Smith Act. But then, a six-member majority of the Supreme Court[203]—with only Justice Clark in dissent—drastically and dramatically limited the application of the Act by handing down a series of significant amendatory interpretations in the difficult case of *Yates v. United States.*[204] Writing an intricate opinion for the Court, Justice Harlan narrowed the meaning of the term "to organize"—one that Congress, clearly in retaliation, again broadened in 1962—and endeavored to establish an important legal distinction under the Smith Act between the *statement of a philosophical belief and the advocacy of an illegal action.* The Court took pains to make clear that the Smith Act still stood and there was no attempt to overrule the *Dennis* case. But it was obvious that the federal government would now no longer be statutorily able to punish members of the American Communist Party, such as Oleta O'Connor Yates and her co-defendant "second-string Communists," *for expressing a mere belief in the "abstract idea"* of the violent overthrow of the government. It would now have to prove that individuals on trial for alleged violations of the Smith Act had *actually intended,* now or in the future, to overthrow the government by force and violence, or to persuade others to do so. Moreover, the government would still have to demonstrate that the language employed by the advocates of actual overthrow was in fact "calculated to incite to action . . . to *do* something, now or in the future, rather than merely *believe* in something."[205] This, of course, it should be observed, was no longer the Vinson Court of 1951; the Chief Justice had died in 1953 and had been replaced by Earl Warren; Robert Jackson, who died a year

[202]*Ibid.,* at 581.

[203]Justices Brennan and Whittaker did not participate in the case.

[204]354 U.S. 298 (1957).

[205]*Ibid.,* at 325. The Court did distinguish the cases of the fourteen petitioners in *Yates,* however, ordering the acquittal of five, and remanding the case of the remaining nine for a new trial—based on the newly created *Yates* line.

later, was succeeded by John Marshall Harlan; and although they took no part in the consideration or decision of *Yates*, William Brennan and Charles Whittaker had supplanted the resigned Sherman Minton and the retired Stanley Reed. Remaining were Tom Clark, who had not participated in *Dennis* and now dissented in *Yates;* Felix Frankfurter and Harold Burton, who made up part of the *Yates* majority; and the *Dennis* dissenters, Hugo Black and William Douglas—who concurred in the decision in part, but also dissented in part because of their insistence that Amendment One renders any such legislation unconstitutional on its face.

The public reaction to *Yates* was adverse; the line created by the Court between "theoretical" and "actual" advocacy did not assuage the uneasy feelings of both the opponents and proponents that it would prove to be a vexatious distinction indeed. Hence it came as less than a total surprise that four years later the Court, in *Scales v. United States*,[206] the first test involving the so-called membership clause[207] of the Smith Act, upheld that clause in the face of stringent constitutional challenges on the grounds of First and Fifth Amendment infringements. Justice Harlan, speaking for the 5:4 majority, ruled that a person who was a "knowing, active" member of a subversive group, and who personally had a "specific intent to bring about violent overthrow of the government," could be convicted under the statute—and Junius Irving Scales, whose membership in the Party the Harlan opinion categorized as "indisputably active," went to jail.[208] Yet in a companion case decided on the very same day, also testing the validity of a conviction under the "membership clause," Harlan, adhering to his *Yates* dichotomy between a philosophical belief and advocating an illegal action, *switched* sides, together with his four *Scales* supporters, to bring about a 9:0 vote *against* the culpability of one John Francis Noto.[209] Noto, held Harlan for the Court, including the Chief Justice and Justices Black, Douglas, and Brennan—who had all dissented from the *Scales*

---

[206]*Scales v. United States*, 367 U.S. 203 (1961).

[207]The Act, among other things, made a felony the acquisition or holding of knowing membership in any organization which advocates the overthrow of the Government of the United States by force or violence. (18 U.S.C. #2385, 18 U.S.C.A. #2385.)

[208]After having served fifteen months of his six-year sentence, he was pardoned by President Kennedy on Christmas Day 1962. Ironically, he had broken with the Communist Party four years before he went to jail.

[209]*Noto v. United States*, 367 U.S. 290 (1961).

decision[210]—did not meet the "knowing, active" membership test necessary for conviction. Again we see the difficult and delicate case-by-case balancing problem in freedom of expression.

As if to demonstrate that fact of governmental and societal life, on the very day of the two decisions in *Scales* and *Noto*, a 5:4 verdict upheld the registration requirements of the second national security statute, the McCarran or Subversive Activities Control Act of 1950,[211] the Court's line-up being the same as in *Scales*. Under that statute, the Subversive Activities Control Board (S.A.C.B.) could, after a due hearing, order any Communist "action" or "front" group to register—and it had so ordered the American Communist Party. But for more than a decade the Party had refused to register, and it challenged the order as a violation of freedom of expression and association and (in view of the Smith Act's criminal sanction) as compulsory self-incrimination under the Fifth. In one of the longest opinions in the Court's history, Justice Frankfurter, speaking also for his colleagues Clark, Harlan, Whittaker, and Stewart, upheld the forced disclosure of Communist Party members' names. With characteristic caution, and deference to the legislative branch, the Frankfurter opinion failed to consider the basic issue of compulsory self-incrimination under Amendment Five (or any of several other constitutional questions raised by the defense). Rather, he based his ruling strictly upon a judgment that the "registration requirement of #7 [of the McCarran Act], on its face and as here applied, does not violate the First Amendment."[212] Dissenting, Warren, Black, Douglas, and Brennan, in three separate opinions, not only flayed the Court majority for ducking the crucial self-incrimination issue, but also exhorted it to recognize, in Justice Douglas's words, that "our Constitution protects all minorities, no matter how despised they are."[213]

Yet the Court's hand was forced on the compulsory self-incrimina-

[210]These four now *concurred;* they would have preferred to dismiss the indictment, not merely to reverse the conviction. Speaking for the four, Black wrote: "I cannot join in an opinion which implies that the existence of liberty is dependent upon the efficiency of the Government's informers" (at 302). He viewed the majority opinion as a clarion call to the government to maintain a permanent staff of informers who are prepared to give up-to-date information with respect to the Communist Party's present policies.

[211]*Communist Party v. Subversive Activities Control Board,* 367 U.S. 1 (1961).

[212]*Ibid.*, at 105.

[213]*Ibid.*, at 190.

tion issue just two years later, when the United States Court of Appeals for the District of Columbia *did* squarely meet that aspect of the registration issue by *reversing* the Communist Party's conviction in a federal trial court for its failure to register under the McCarran Act's commands. The reversal[214] was on narrow grounds and did not necessarily settle the self-incrimination matter,[215] but it did uphold the Communist Party's constitutional argument that since the Smith Act treats it as a criminal conspiracy, compelled registration would *ipso facto* be self-incriminating. Since "mere association with the party incriminates," ruled the unanimous intermediate appellate tribunal in its opinion by Chief Judge Bazelon, statutory registration would indeed force self-incrimination in the face of Fifth Amendment guarantees to the contrary. When the United States Government appealed that holding to the Supreme Court, the latter eschewed the opportunity to expound on the problem and, by refusing without comment to review the decision, maintained the Government's defeat.[216]

Two weeks later, however, the Court did come to constitutional terms with another section of the McCarran Act, which it had also purposely ignored in the 1961 decision: the denial of passports to members of the American Communist Party and its "fronts." In a 6:3 decision, written for the Court by its most junior member in point of service, Justice Goldberg, the majority ruled the provision "unconstitutional on its face" as a deprivation of liberty guaranteed by the "due process of law" concept of the Fifth Amendment because it "too broadly and indiscriminately restricts the right to travel."[217] The three dissenters, Justices Clark, Harlan, and White, contended with feeling that that right was not absolute, and that its denial on national security grounds was entirely reasonable under the circumstances at issue. Sub-

[214]*Communist Party v. United States,* 331 F. 2d 807 (1963).

[215]"We hold only that the availability of someone to sign the forms was an element of the offense; that the officers, who should otherwise have signed, were unavailable by reason of their valid claim of the privilege against self-incrimination; that the government had the burden of showing that a volunteer was available; and that its failure to discharge this burden requires reversal of this conviction." (*Ibid.,* at 815.)

[216]*United States v. Communist Party,* 377 U.S. 968 (1964).

[217]*Aptheker v. Secretary of State,* 378 U.S. 500 (1964), at 514. The Act's controversial Title II, its detention provision, was repealed by the Senate by unanimous vote in 1969, the House followed suit (356:49) in 1971. But *cf. Haig v. Agee,* 453 U.S. 280 (1981).

sequently the Court granted *certiorari* in two cases again challenging the McCarran Act requirement that *individual members* of the Communist Party, rather than the Party itself, register with the government.[218]

It took until 1965, but when the Court's decision was announced, it was unanimous. Speaking through Justice Brennan, it held *unenforceable* the Justice Department orders requiring two alleged subversives, William Albertson and Roscoe Quincy Proctor, to register under the McCarran Act, ruling that such registration would expose them to prosecution under other federal laws "in an area permeated with criminal statutes."[219] The opinion stopped short of declaring the "individual membership registration" provision of the Act *unconstitutional*, because a Party member could waive his self-incrimination privilege and register. But the obvious effect of the Court's holding was to make the registration requirement governmentally unenforceable and thus unusable. In an area of freedom of expression in which unanimity is so demonstrably hard to attain, the Court thus stood as one with Brennan's holding that "the requirement to accomplish registration by completing and filing [the required form] is inconsistent with the protection of the self-incrimination clause [of the Fifth Amendment to the Constitution of the United States]."[220]

In 1968, faced with a now practically toothless Subversive Activities Control Board, Congress enacted a compromise measure designed to keep the S.A.C.B. in business, notwithstanding the several damaging Supreme Court and lower-court rulings affecting its functions. It provided that the S.A.C.B. could hold hearings to determine whether individuals were Communists and whether organizations were either Communist "front" or Communist "action" groups. If it so determined, the S.A.C.B. could then *itself* register them. The dubious constitutional provisions of the 1968 statute were tailor-made for a judicial test, and Simon Boorda, a Utah teacher ordered by the S.A.C.B. to register, and

[218]*Albertson v. Subversive Activities Control Board,* 381 U.S. 910, and *Proctor v. Subversive Activities Control Board,* 381 U.S. 910 (1965). Earlier, the Court had vacated two orders requiring Communist "fronts" to register, ruling that the record in the cases was "too stale" for a serious constitutional adjudication. *American Committee for Protection of Foreign Born v. Subversive Activities Control Board,* 380 U.S. 503; and *Veterans of the Abraham Lincoln Brigade v. Subversive Activities Control Board,* 380 U.S. 513 (1963).

[219]*Albertson v. Subversive Activities Control Board,* 382 U.S. 70 (1965).

[220]*Ibid.,* at 76.

then registered as "Communist" by the Board itself upon his refusal to do so, brought suit in 1969. The United States Court of Appeals for the District of Columbia declared the registration procedures authorized under the 1968 law unconstitutional as a rank violation of the First Amendment's guarantee of freedom of association.[221] The Justice Department appealed, but the Supreme Court denied review, thus upholding the lower tribunal's decision.[222] President Nixon revitalized the S.A.C.B. by executive order in 1971, indeed expanding its scope. Although Congress approved that move in 1972, it slashed the S.A.C.B.'s budget by 50 percent later, and the President's budget message for 1973 omitted all funds for it. It died a quiet death on June 30, 1973.

Foreshadowing its increasing strictness vis-à-vis legislative experimentations in the internal security realm, the Court had entered virgin territory in 1965 in the battleground between freedom of expression and national security by declaring unconstitutional for the very first time a *congressional* statute on grounds of First Amendment freedom of speech. While federal statutes had heretofore fallen on other grounds, frequently because of due process violation, for one, and many a state law had been struck down on the freedom of expression issue by its incorporation via Amendment Fourteen, this was a novel development. Unanimously, the Court now threw out a 1962 federal law that had required persons to whom "Communist political propaganda" from abroad was addressed to make a special request to the Post Office to deliver it. Under the statute—which did not cover sealed letters—the Customs Bureau gave the Post Office Department a list of countries from which printed Communist propaganda emanated. At the eleven entry points postal officials examined the material and, if they decided that it was "Communist political propaganda," intercepted it. The Department then notified the persons to whom it was addressed that they could receive it only if they returned an attached reply card within twenty days; if they did not respond, the mail was destroyed! Justice Douglas's stern opinion concluded that:

> [T]he act as construed and applied is unconstitutional because it requires an official act [returning the reply card] as a limitation on the unfettered exer-

[221]*Boorda v. Subversive Activities Control Board*, 421 F. 2d 1142 (1969).
[222]*Subversive Activities Control Board v. Boorda*, 397 U.S. 1042 (1970).

cise of the addressee's First Amendment rights. . . . The addressee carries an affirmative obligation which we do not think the Government may impose on him. . . . The regime of this *act is at war with the "uninhibited, robust, and wide-open" debate and discussion that are contemplated by the First Amendment.*[223]

Perhaps more than any of the other examples of "line-drawing," that of the riddle of national security in the days of the Cold War may serve to demonstrate that there are no easy answers to the problem of the balance between freedom of expression and the security requirements of the land. It is a demonstrable fact of life that dedicated democrats may well find themselves on opposite sides of the question.[224] A rather less vital but intriguing, titillating, and vexatious question concerns the line between freedom of expression and "obscenity."

5. *What is Obscene and When Is It?* The temptation to wallow a bit here is strong, but space demands confinement to some fundamental considerations. The obvious difficulty is again the problem of definition—Chief Justice Warren regarded it, in retrospect, as the Court's "most difficult" area of adjudication.[225] What is "obscenity" to some is mere "realism" to others; what is "lascivious" in the eyes of one reader is merely "colorful" in those of another; what is "lewd" to one parent may well be "instructive" to another. In one Southern city, the censorship board thus ruled "obscene" a movie which showed black and white children playing together in a school yard.[226] In cosmopolitan Chicago, the Police Board of Censorship held "obscene" Walt Disney's film on a vanishing prairie, which showed a buffalo giving birth in a snowstorm.[227] New York's Board of Regents—that state's

[223]*Lamont v. Postmaster-General* and *Fixa v. Heilberg*, 381 U.S. 301 (1965). (Italics supplied.)

[224]Carl Friedrich, a close student of the problem and convinced that it defies satisfactory solution by the judiciary—let alone the legislature—suggested that a *constitutional* amendment be passed specifically to deal with the security issue. (See his "Rights, Liberties, Freedoms: A Reappraisal," 57 *American Political Science Review* 857 [December 1963].)

[225]Interview, Sacramento, California, June 26, 1969, as quoted in *The New York Times*, June 27, 1969, p. 1*l*. It did not take the Court's then newest and youngest member, Justice John Paul Stevens, long to observe in 1977 that its "thinking on obscenity is intolerably vague and makes evenhanded enforcement virtually impossible." (*The Daily Progress*, March 2, 1977, p. A-8.)

[226]*The New York Times*, June 27, 1969, p. 1*l*.

[227]*Ibid.*

official censor of movies—was never troubled by the charming little movie *The Moon Is Blue,* in which its actors used such commonplace terms as "pregnant" and "virginity"; but Maryland and the United States Navy deemed it "lewd" and "lascivious," and accordingly banned the showing of the film—lest it have dire effects on the viewers. On the other hand, New York banned the distribution of *Lady Chatterley's Lover,* charging that "the whole theme of this motion picture is immoral [under the applicable New York statute], for that theme is the presentation of adultery as a desirable, acceptable and proper pattern of behavior."[228] In unanimously reversing the New York action, the Supreme Court issued a number of opinions,[229] but they turned, more or less specifically, on the vagueness of the concept "immorality" and the problem of censorship generally. In this concurring opinion, Justice Frankfurter stated the crux of the matter—differences of opinion as to the meaning of terms and differences of taste:

> As one whose taste in art and literature hardly qualifies him for the *avant-garde,* I am more than surprised, after viewing the picture, that the New York authorities should have banned "Lady Chatterley's Lover." To assume that this motion picture would have offended Victorian moral sensibilities is to rely on the stuffiest of Victorian conventions. Whatever one's personal preferences may be about such matters, the refusal to license the exhibition of this picture . . . can only mean that [the portion of the New York statute in question] forbids the public showing of any film that deals with adultery except by way of sermonizing condemnation or depicts any physical manifestation of an illicit amorous relation.[230]

In general, the trend has been to throw out, on constitutional or statutory grounds, most state visual *prior* censorship laws, or, if not the laws themselves, the *procedures* involved. And in 1975 *live theatrical productions*—here the musical *Hair*—were judicially recognized for the first time as enjoying the same kind of constitutional safeguards against prior restraints as do the press, books, and the movies.[231] Only a

---

[228]*Kingsley International Pictures v. Regents,* 4 N.Y. 2d 349 (1957).

[229]*Kingsley International Pictures v. Regents,* 360 U.S. 684 (1959). Opinions were by Justices Stewart, Black, Frankfurter, Douglas, Clark, and Harlan—the last five all concurring in the result, but on varying grounds.

[230]*Ibid.,* at 691–92.

[231]*Southeastern Promotions, Ltd., v. Conrad,* 419 U.S. 892.

handful of states now have such statewide laws, and the *procedures* used by several have been declared unconstitutional.[232] A good many cities still do have censorship ordinances, but where the requirement is for licensing *in advance* of exhibition, only three were still enforced in 1980, Chicago's, for one, having been declared unconstitutional in 1968.[233] These statistics do not, however, cover state criminal statutes against the showing of obscene films *not subject to prior censorship;* these are still widespread and, of course, raise a different, no less difficult, issue. Moreover, when it comes to *general* antiobscenity laws, the federal government as well as all states except New Mexico had such laws on their books in the late 1980s.[234] Thus, while there is now fairly general consensus about the illegality of *prior* censorship, whatever the medium of expression, there still exists broadly general agreement that obscenity, at least in public, is at best of no redeeming social value and at worst actively corruptive of morals and must be both interdictable *and* punishable. The increase in printed smut throughout the country that seems to have accompanied judicial reversals of state obscenity convictions has thus given rise to fairly widespread outcries and demands for curbs—both genuine and hypocritical—from citizens and citizen groups. If only we could agree on just what is obscene! How can ideas and morality be protected concurrently? In 1968 President Johnson, in response to statutory authority, appointed a blue-ribbon eighteen-member Federal Commission on Obscenity and Pornography. Its report, two years later, *inter alia* recommending the elimination of all restrictions on *adults* wishing to obtain sexually explicit books,

[232]E.g., *Freedman v. Maryland,* 380 U.S. 51 (1965), where the law had provided *no* judicial participation in barring of a film, nor a time limit for the required administrative hearing. The Ohio obscenity statute fell unanimously in 1973 because it failed to provide a prior adversary hearing for an "obscenity" determination. (*Huffman v. United States District Court for Northern District of Ohio,* 414 U.S. 1021.) And a Louisiana law, under which *Last Tango in Paris, The Stewardesses,* and several magazines had been banned as "lewd, lascivious, filthy or sexually indecent," was declared unconstitutional in 1974 on both substantive ("vague") *and* procedural (no "probable cause" had to be shown) grounds. (*Louisiana v. Gulf State Theatres,* 417 U.S. 911.)

[233]*Teitel Film Corp. v. Cusac,* 390 U.S. 139. Here the *prescribed* administrative process stretched from fifty to fifty-seven days, and it lacked a provision for judicial review.

[234]In 1971 the Supreme Court, by 7:2 and 6:3 votes respectively, upheld the constitutionality of the federal statute that prohibits the knowing use of the mails for delivery of obscene matter and the right of customs agents to seize obscene "photographs, books, and advertisements coming into the country from abroad." (*United States v. Reidel* and *United States v. Thirty-Seven Photographs,* 402 U.S. 363.)

pictures, and films, not only caused a storm of righteous controversy, but was officially denounced and formally rejected by the pure United States Senate by a roll call vote of 60 : 5[235]—an action warmly endorsed by President Nixon, who agreed with the Reverend Dr. Billy Graham that the report was "one of the worst, most diabolical reports ever made by a Presidential Commission. . . . [that] no Christian or believing Jew could possibly support. . . ."[236] Almost two decades later, on the other hand, another Presidential Commission on Pornography, formed for President Reagan by Attorney-General Meese, concluded in a lengthy public report that offered a twenty-six-page list of recommendations, that most pornography sold in the United States is potentially harmful and can lead to violence. It strongly urged action against the "porno" industry.[237] The fundamental issue involved, whether certain forms of pornography are indeed harmful to the public and thus might be legitimately restricted by the government without violating the First Amendment, is unlikely to be settled by this—or any other—report. Ultimately, the Court will be called upon to do so—and it is not precisely anxious to comply.[238]

Other democracies throughout the world have also wrestled with this problem, admittedly under different national and cultural traditions, and their solution has been far from easy. For example, the Chambre de Droit Publique of Switzerland's highest tribunal, the Tribunal Fédéral Suisse, had to deal with "indecency" charges against one Werner Kunz, a Zürich producer of three "naturalist" films, who found himself censored because he had shown "nudism" on the beaches and on snow-covered mountains. Now, did this showing of nudity constitute "naturalist beauty" or "indecent character"? The seven jurists rendered a split decision on each count: yes, 5 : 2, it was indecent to exhibit nudity publicly in the white snow; but no, 4 : 3, it was not indecent to show it publicly on the beach.[239]

---

[235]The five courageous libertines who bucked the Puritan tide were Clifford Case (R.-N.J.), Jacob K. Javits (R.-N.Y.), George S. McGovern (D.-S.D.), Walter F. Mondale (D.-Minn.), and Stephen M. Young (D.-Ohio). Evidently neither political party had a corner on purity!

[236]*The New York Times*, October 14, 1970, p. 30.

[237]*The New York Times*, May 16, 1986, p. B-13.

[238]*Ibid.*, May 18, 1986, p. B-13, and *Time* magazine, July 21, 1986, pp. 26 ff.

[239]*Chambre de Droit Publique*, P110/CG, Séance du 7 décembre 1960, at 7–8. See Francis William O'Brien's perceptive account, "Movie Censorship: A Swiss Comparison," 1966 *Duke Law Journal* 3 (Summer), pp. 634–68.

On the other hand, small and homogeneous Denmark—and the two preceding adjectives, particularly the second, are crucial to the *modus operandus*—decided to pioneer in 1967, when its *folketing* (the uni-cameral legislature) abolished all sanctions against the "production," import, export, and distribution of *written* pornography. The Danish Commission on Criminal Law, which had initially recommended both laws, had done so because it had been fully convinced by psychologists and sociologists that there was no *provable* nexus between pornography and corruption of sexual mores. The results were such that exactly two years later Denmark became the first state formally to abolish *every* legal sanction against pornography for *adults*. Its 1969 statute does continue to provide prison terms of up to six months for purveying pornography to children (defined as being under age sixteen), and the police do act against the "related" realms of brothels and narcotics.[240]

Turning back to the large and heterogeneous United States of America—and those two appropriate adjectives assuredly make a major difference in any attempted resolution of the problem, as all public and private sectors that have been brave enough to resolve it have repeatedly found out—most attempts to censor *written publications* have turned on the use of certain famous or infamous Anglo-Saxon four-letter words. Generally, books and allied media have enjoyed at least as much judicial protection against unbridled censorship as have movies. Obviously, obscenity, or, more precisely, "hard-core pornography"—as it has been increasingly classified by the Court—may be forbidden, but the problems of classifications, sanctions, and punishment are indeed vexatious. Justice Stewart, for one, who backed censorship *solely* if the material represented "hard-core pornography," threw up his judicial hands when specifically asked its meaning in 1964, responding "[all I can say is that] I know it when I see it."[241] And he stuck to this

---

[240]See the account by Bernard Weintraub in *The New York Times*, January 26, 1976, p. 5.

[241]*Jacobellis v. Ohio*, 378 U.S. 184, concurring opinion, at 197. "Don't you mean, my Brother," rejoined a pixyish Justice Douglas from the bench, "you know it when you feel it—given the definition of 'prurient,' i.e. to itch, long, lecher, lust?" In a post-retirement 1981 news conference, Justice Stewart had definite second thoughts about his now legendary 1964 observation: "In a way I regret having said what I said about obscenity—that's going to be on my tombstone. When I remember all the other solid words I've written, I regret a little bit that if I'll be remembered at all, I'll be remembered for that particular phrase." (As quoted in the *Washington Post*'s obituary, written by Al Kamen, December 8, 1985, p. A18.)

position. Justice Harlan tried to be more precise when he explained that, to him, ''hard core'' signifies ''that prurient material that is patently offensive or whose indecency is self-demonstrating''[242]—which is not crystal clear either, as definitions go.

One person's smut may well be another one's Chaucer! Or, as Harlan put it once, ''One man's vulgarity is another man's lyric.''[243] But, logically, as the Supreme Court held 8½ : ½ (Justice Harlan concurred in part and dissented in part) in *Smith v. California,*[244] the proprietor of a bookstore cannot constitutionally be punished for offering an ''obscene'' book, here *Sweeter than Life,* for sale—an act banned by the terms of a Los Angeles city ordinance—if he was *unaware* that the book was in fact obscene. And Eleazar Smith was thus absolved of the charges against him. Yet, it may be asked, if the book had already been adjudged ''obscene'' in another jurisdiction, could Mr. Smith really plead ignorance, or lack of *scienter,*[245] regarding continued sales of the volume? At least one student of the field observed that he certainly could not,[246] and fourteen years later the Supreme Court seemed to agree.[247] Actually, the Court ruled on the *scienter* matter in the *Smith* case only tangentially: the controlling point there was that the burden of proof of criminal violation was held to rest upon the state. To shift that burden to the individual constitutes an impermissible requirement, which the Court underscored again in 1971 when it declared two *federal* ''mail block'' laws unconstitutional because they had placed the burden of proof on the individual rather than on the government—the latter not being required to obtain a prompt judicial determination whether, in fact, the material was obscene.[248] The highest tribunal has gone further to condemn on constitutional grounds the kind of ''informal cen-

[242]*A Book Named ''John Cleland's Woman of Pleasure'' v. Massachusetts,* 383 U.S. 413 (1966), dissenting opinion.

[243]*Cohen v. California,* 403 U.S. 15 (1971), at 25, majority opinion.

[244]361 U.S. 147 (1959).

[245]*Scienter* means having such knowledge as charges a person with the consequences of his or her actions.

[246]Paul G. Kauper, *Civil Liberties and the Constitution* (Ann Arbor: University of Michigan Press, 1962), p. 71.

[247]In 1973 it thus dismissed 5 : 4 a challenge to a New York statute that created a presumption that the seller of obscene materials knows the character of its contents. (*Kirkpatrick v. New York,* 414 U.S. 948.) The four dissenters argued that the word ''obscene'' was impermissibly vague.

[248]*Blount v. Rizzi* and *United States v. The Book Bin,* 400 U.S. 410.

sorship'' practiced by the ''Rhode Island Commission to Encourage Morality in Youth,'' a unit statutorily created and empowered to educate the public ''concerning any book, picture, pamphlet, ballad, printed paper or other things containing obscene, indecent or impure language, or manifestly tending to the corruption of the youth . . . and to investigate and recommend the prosecution of all violations of [the statute involved.]''[249] Such action, held Justice Brennan for the 8 : 1 Court, constituted ''in fact a scheme of state censorship effectuated by extra-legal sanctions; they acted as an agency not to advise but to suppress.''[250]

That the Court's search for a viable standard has been extremely difficult[251] is illustrated by some additional examples. In a well-known 1957 case, *Butler v. Michigan,* it held unconstitutional a Michigan law that forbade ''any person'' to sell or give away anything ''containing obscene, immoral, lewd or lascivious language . . . tending to incite minors to violent or depraved or immoral acts, *manifestly tending to the corruption of the morals of youth.*''[252] Speaking for the unanimous Court, Justice Frankfurter set aside the conviction of Alfred E. Butler, who had sold such a book (*The Devil Rides Outside*) to another adult, here a policeman. (The book is a story of a young American's visit to a Benedictine monastery in France to study Gregorian chants. As a result of his observations of the monks he aspires to resemble them, particularly in the virtue of chastity, although he is obsessed by sex and indulges in several sordid amours.) The Court's ruling was on the ground that the state could not, under its police power, quarantine ''the general reading public against books not too rugged for grown men and

[249]*Bantam Books, Inc. v. Sullivan,* 372 U.S. 58 (1963), at 59–60.

[250]*Ibid.,* at 72. The lone dissenter was Harlan.

[251]In the eleven-year period between the 1957 *Roth* and *Alberts* decisions and that of *Ginsberg v. New York* in 1968 (see below for discussion and citation), the Court undertook a full-scale review of obscenity law in thirteen major cases. In those thirteen cases, members of the Court turned out fifty-five separate opinions. ''The subject of obscenity . . . that intractable problem,'' as Justice Harlan observed laconically in 1968, ''has produced a variety of views among the members of the Court unmatched in other courses of constitutional adjudication.'' (*Interstate Circuit v. Dallas,* 390 U.S. 676, at 704–5.) It is no wonder, then, that Chief Justice Warren would regard *it* as the most vexatious of all lines to draw in the eternal contest between individual and societal rights. His successor found the going equally rough—the Burger Court dividing 5 : 4 in a bloc of eleven cases decided on a single 1973 Opinion Day, for example! Does smut perhaps lie ''in the groin of the beholder''? (Clor, quoting Charles Rembar, *infra,* fn. 268.)

[252]352 U.S. 380 (1957). (Italics supplied.)

women in order to shield juvenile innocence. . . . Surely, *this is to burn the house to roast the pig.*"[253] Frankfurter, hardly a foe of reasonably drafted, tightly drawn[254] police-power legislation, continued:

> We have before us legislation not reasonably restricted to the evil with which it is said to deal. The incidence of this [law] is to reduce the adult population of Michigan to reading only what is fit for children. It thereby arbitrarily curtails one of those liberties of the individual, now enshrined in the due process clause of the Fourteenth Amendment, that history has attested as the indispensable conditions for the maintenance and progress of a free society.[255]

A few weeks later, a divided Court attempted to provide a viable yardstick, which has since proved to be but partly successful. In the combined *Roth* and *Alberts* cases,[256] featuring five opinions, the justices who joined in the majority's holding[257] did their best to "balance" the rights involved by establishing the "prurient interest" test[258]—and thereby at last abandoned the nineteenth-century standard, based upon an English case, *Regina v. Hicklin:*[259] its test was "whether the *tendency* of the matter charged as obscenity is to *deprave and corrupt* those whose *minds are open* to such immoral influences and into whose hands a publication of this sort may fall." Here, speaking through Justice Brennan—frequently called upon to write opinions in this sphere—the Court upheld both a federal statute forbidding the transportation through the mails of "obscene, lewd, lascivious, indecent, filthy or vile" materials *and* a state statute forbidding the sale or advertisement of "obscene or indecent matter" on the strength of the new "prurient interest" concept. This test, as elucidated by Brennan,

[253]*Ibid.*, at 383. (Italics supplied.)
[254]E.g., see his opinion for the Court in *Kingsley Books, Inc. v. Brown*, 354 U.S. 436 (1957).
[255]*Butler v. Michigan, op. cit.*, fn. 252, *supra*, at 383–84. (Italics supplied.)
[256]*Roth v. United States* and *Alberts v. California*, 354 U.S. 476 (1957).
[257]Justices Brennan, Frankfurter, Burton, Clark, and Whittaker. The Chief Justice concurred separately; Justice Harlan concurred in *Alberts* but dissented in *Roth;* Justices Black and Douglas dissented in both.
[258]"Prurient," according to *Webster's*, signifies "itching; longing; of persons, having lascivious longings; of desire, curiosity, or propensity, lewd." (7th ed., Springfield, Mass.: 1969, p. 688.)
[259]L.R.3Q.B.360 (1868). (Italics supplied.)

was to determine "*[w]hether to the average person, applying contemporary community standards, the dominant theme of the material, taken as a whole, appeals to prurient interests,*"[260] and whether, in addition, the material "goes substantially beyond the customary limits of candor." That Brennan cited "impure sexual thoughts" as one example of "prurient interests" ought to demonstrate the intriguingly difficult nature of the test. On the other hand, he made clear that by "obscenity" the Court had in mind only material that was "*utterly without redeeming social importance*"[261] (a concept *cum* test which, Justice Black would write later is "as uncertain, if not more uncertain, than is the unknown substance of the Milky Way").[262]

What Brennan himself regarded as the "difficult, recurring and unpleasant task" of setting a national moral criterion for a heterogeneous people such as the citizenry of the United States was accentuated by the wistful dissenting opinion of Justice Douglas, joined by his colleague Black. He questioned "prurience" as a viable standard, commenting that "the arousing of sexual thoughts and desires happens every day in normal life in dozens of ways."[263] He cited a questionnaire sent to female college and normal school graduates in the late 1920s which asked "what things were most stimulating sexually?" Of 409 replies, 218 responded "man."[264] After a lengthy lecture on the First Amendment guarantees of free expression, Douglas concluded that he, for one, "would give the broad sweep of the First Amendment full support. I have the same confidence in the ability of our people to reject noxious literature as I have in their capacity to sort out the true from the false in theology, economics, politics, or any other field."[265]

---

[260]*Roth v. United States* and *Alberts v. California,* 354 U.S. 476 (1957), at 489. (Italics supplied.)

[261]On this point see his fine article, based on the 1965 Meiklejohn Lecture at Harvard University, "The Supreme Court and the Meiklejohn Interpretation of the First Amendment," 79 *Harvard Law Review* 1–20 (November 1965). (Italics supplied.)

[262]Dissenting in *Ginzburg v. United States,* 383 U.S. 463 (1966), at 480. Seven years later the Court would abandon that test—but substitute a new one which would have been equally unacceptable to the now deceased champion of absolutist freedom of expression. (*Miller v. California,* 413 U.S. 15, and *Paris Adult Theater v. Slaton,* 413 U.S. 49, discussed on pp. 266–67, *infra.*)

[263]*Roth v. United States* and *Alberts v. California, op. cit.,* fn. 256, *supra,* at 509.

[264]Douglas quoted from Leo M. Alpert, "Judicial Censorship of Obscene Literature," 52 *Harvard Law Review* 40 (1938), at 73. Ninety-five young women said "books," forty "drama," twenty-nine "dancing," eighteen "pictures," nine "music;" others were scattered over a variety of subjects.

[265]*Roth v. United States* and *Alberts v. California, op. cit.,* fn. 256, *supra,* at 514.

Yet the Court seemed to have created a line with its "prurient interest" test, which it further refined, perhaps liberalized, in 1962 in *Manuel Enterprises, Inc. v. Day.*[266] There, Justice Harlan, writing for the 6 : 1 Court majority—which was badly split, however, on just what was being decided—held not only that the matter challenged must be "so offensive as to affront current community standards of decency," but that the indecency must be "self-demonstrating." In other words, Harlan joined "patently offensive" to "prurient interest" in an attempt to find a more precise line.[267] Another explanation and refinement came in a multiple 1964 decision, in which it was Justice Brennan who, speaking for a majority of six, made it clear that the *Roth-Alberts* test reference to "contemporary community standards" was intended to establish a *national* standard rather than a "particular local community standard"[268]—an interpretation that would hold for a decade.[269]

Thus the Court by 1964 had established a basic constitutional requirement that material attacked on grounds of "obscenity," or any other similar concepts, *must be judged not by its isolated parts, but by the dominant theme of the material as a whole.* The Court had made clear that freedom of expression carries with it the inherent privilege of "unconventional," "controversial," even "immoral" advocacy, *provided* the manner in which this is done is not "obscene" under the established guidelines. Moreover, the Court would obviously not permit loosely drawn administrative and/or legislative procedures, nor would it assume automatic *scienter* of possession of obscene matter on the part of the vendors.

However, in March of 1966 along came the rather surprising *Ginzburg* decision.[270] There, in a welter of fourteen opinions by seven justices in three cases decided together,[271] the Court, narrowly dividing 5 : 4 in the lead case (*Ginzburg*). demonstrated that, notwithstanding its

[266]370 U.S. 478.

[267]*Ibid.,* at 483.

[268]*Jacobellis v. Ohio,* 378 U.S. 184, at 193. For an interesting study, which comprises a major appeal for reliance on the good sense of the *local* community, see Harry M. Clor, *Obscenity and Public Morality: Censorship in a Liberal Society* (Chicago: University of Chicago Press, 1968).

[269]It fell—at least temporarily—in favor of *"local"* in *Miller* and *Paris Adult Theatre* in 1973. (See fn. 288, *infra;* the discussion of the two cases, *infra,* pp. 266 ff.; and fn. 295 with accompanying text, p. 268, *infra.*)

[270]*Ginzburg v. United States,* 383 U.S. 463.

[271]*Ibid.* (decided 5 : 4); *Mishkin v. New York,* 383 U.S. 502 (6 : 3); and *A Book Named "John Cleland's Woman of Pleasure" v. Massachusetts,* 383 U.S. 413 (6 : 3).

recent "liberalizing" decisions in the obscenity field, it was also by no means necessarily averse to "toughening" its *Roth-Alberts* test. Ralph Ginzburg, publisher of the magazine *Eros* and other erotic literature,[272] stood convicted on twenty-eight counts of violating the federal obscenity statute at issue in the *Roth* case, not because the material in itself was obscene, but *because of the manner in which it was "exploited," i.e., advertised*—advertisement permeated "with the leer of the sensualist."[273] As Justice Brennan, the Court's "obscenity expert," put the matter for himself, the Chief Justice, and Associate Justices Clark, White, and Fortas (with Justices Black, Douglas, Stewart, and Harlan dissenting in four separate opinions):

> Where an exploitation of interests in *titillation by pornography* is shown with respect to material lending itself to such exploitation through pervasive treatment or description of sexual matters, such evidence may support the determination that the material is obscene even though in *other contexts* the material would escape such condemnation.[274]

In other words, in "close cases," evidence of pandering may be "probative with respect to the nature of the material."[275] But to Justice Black, the majority's stance fatally misinterpreted the First Amendment, for, as he put it: "I believe that the Federal Government is without power whatever under the Constitution to put any type of burden on speech and expression of ideas of any kind (as distinguished from conduct). . . . I would reverse this case and announce that neither Congress nor the states shall pass laws which in any manner abridge freedom of speech and press—whatever the subjects discussed."[276]

The quest for a viable line continued apace after *Ginzburg*, and while

---

[272]*Eros*, a hard-cover magazine of expensive format; *Liaison*, a biweekly newsletter; and *The Housewife's Handbook on Selective Promiscuity*, a short book. (He also published the controversial magazine *Fact*, which figured in the *Ginzburg v. Goldwater* libel case. See p. 212, *supra*.)

[273]*Ginzburg v. United States, op. cit.*, fn. 270, *supra*, at 468. After unsuccessfully seeking mailing privileges from the postmasters of Intercourse, Pa., and Blue Ball, Pa., Ginzberg finally obtained them from Middlesex, N.J.

[274]*Ibid.*, at 475. (Italics supplied.) Ginzburg's five-year sentence was eventually reduced to three. He did not begin to serve it until February 1972, and was paroled and released that October.

[275]*Ibid.*, at 474. (Reconfirmed in 1977 in *Splawn v. California*, 431 U.S. 595.)

[276]*Ginzburg, op. cit.*, fn. 270, *supra*, at 476. (Parentheses in original.)

no new rule emerged readily, there were definite signs that one would—sooner or later—and that it woud attempt to distinguish between minors and adults, between private and public exposure, and between "captive" and "escapable audiences." It began to take shape with three decisions, known as the Redrup group,[277] that were rendered *per curiam* in 1967. As usual, the justices remained divided on the meaning of "obscenity," and sidestepped a great many issues. However, in this group of three cases involving ten "girlie" magazines and two paperbacks which had all been ruled "obscene" by state courts in Arkansas, Kentucky, and New York, the Warren Court, in joining the three cases and reversing the convictions in each, pronounced three identifiable "rules of thumb" (although still ducking such ticklish issues as just what is a "girlie magazine"). Rule 1 noted that in none of the three cases did the state law in question reflect a "specific and limited state concern for juveniles." Rule 2 explained that in none of the cases was there any effort of "pandering" *à la Ginzburg.* And Rule 3 pointed out that none of the materials in question was "forced" on an unwilling public.[278] These rules or guidelines now began to be present in whole or in part, expressly or impliedly, in most of the important subsequent cases. Thus, in 1968, the Court in a very real sense seemed

[277]*Redrup v. New York, Gent v. Arkansas,* and *Austin v. Kentucky,* 386 U.S. 767. Shortly after these decisions, the Court upheld a conviction based on a public display of allegedly obscene sculpture in its owner's backyard since it was "positioned" in a manner so obtrusive as to be unavoidable. (*Fort v. City of Miami,* 389 U.S. 918, [1967].)

[278]What of an outdoor movie screening of conceivably obscene movies visible from twelve to fifteen homes and passing motorists? Unless the obscenity statute involved explicitly gives fair and due notice concerning "context" or "location," its application, ruled an unanimous Court in 1972, is "impermissibly vague" under Due Process considerations. (*Rabe v. Washington,* 405 U.S. 313.) It affirmed this stance in 1975 when it struck down 6:3 as an unconstitutional interference with free speech a Jacksonville, Florida, ordinance making drive-in theatres criminally liable for showing films including nudity that are visible outside the theatre grounds. Speaking for the majority, Justice Powell held that "the privacy interest of persons on the public streets cannot justify this censorship of otherwise protected speech on the basis of its contents." (*Erznoznik v. Jacksonville,* 419 U.S. 822.) But zoning either concentrating or dispersing "adult" movies is constitutional. (*Young v. American Mini Theatres,* 427 U.S. 50 [1976].) On the other hand, note *Schad v. Mount Ephraim,* 452 U.S. 61 (1981), in which the Court ruled 7:2 that communities which permit commercial activity may not use their zoning power to exclude live entertainment (here a nude dancer in a glass booth in a so-called adult bookstore). But in two 1986 decisions the Court, by lopsided 7:2 and 6:3 votes, *upheld* the power of communities to "zone in" certain "adult entertainment." (*Renton v. Playtime Theatres,* 106 S.Ct. 925, and *Arcara v. Cloud Books,* 106 S.Ct. 3172, resp.)

to "codify" its majoritarian conviction—with Black and Douglas always, and Stewart often, in dissent—that it would *not* strike down carefully drawn statutes aimed at the protection of juveniles. In the leading case of *Ginsberg v. New York* (no relation to *Ginzburg v. United States*) the Court ruled 6 : 3 that New York could indeed make it a crime knowingly to sell "to minors under 17 years of age material defined to be obscene to them whether or not it would be obscene to adults." Hence Sam Ginsberg, who in 1965 had sold two "girlie magazines" to a sixteen-year-old boy in Ginsberg's Bellmore, Long Island, "Sam's Stationary and Luncheonette," found himself in trouble with New York State's law on the subject, and appealed his resultant conviction on First Amendment grounds. Speaking for the Court majority, Justice Brennan made it clear that New York's "prohibition does not bar parents who so desire from purchasing the magazines for their children," and, of course, they were free to buy them for themselves—for they were *not obscene for adults*. Dissenting Justices Black, Douglas, and Fortas mocked this distinction, with Douglas angrily writing: "As I read the First Amendment, it was designed to keep the state and the hands of all state officials off the printing presses of America and off the distribution systems for all printed literature."[279] Yet the double standard of obscene-for-child-not-obscene-for-adult had been firmly embraced. And not only has it stood to date (early 1988), it was reaffirmed by a 9 : 0 decision, authored by Justice White, upholding New York State's broad authority to combat *child* pornography by banning the production, sale, and distribution of such material, whether or not it is legally obscene.[280]

An additional principle was established, firmly and unanimously (although there were three separate opinions), in 1969 in the case of *Stanley v. Georgia*.[281] Federal and state agents had entered the Atlanta home of Robert Eli Stanley in 1967 to search for proof of suspected bookmaking. They failed to unearth any evidence of gambling, but they did find three reels of film that, as they later testified in court, depicted "successive orgies of seduction, sodomy, and sexual intercourse." Stanley was jury-convicted under a Georgia law that forbids *possession*

[279]390 U.S. 629, at 655. In a concurring opinion, Justice Harlan criticized the Court for avoiding a definition *cum* explanation of "girlie magazines."

[280]*New York v. Ferber*, 458 U.S. 747 (1982).

[281]394 U.S. 557.

of obscene material and was sentenced to a year in prison. Delivering the opinion for the Court, its then junior member, Justice Thurgood Marshall, agreed with Stanley's contention that his First and Fourteenth Amendment rights had been violated, for the mere *private* possession of obscene matter cannot constitutionally be made a crime. The Court took pains to note that its holding in no way infringes upon the right of states or the federal government to make possession of other items, such as narcotics, firearms, or stolen goods, a crime. But, in Marshall's words:

> Whatever may be the justifications for other statutes regulating obscenity, we do not think they reach into the privacy of one's own home. If the First Amendment means anything, it means that a State has no business telling a man, sitting alone in his own house, what books he may read or what films he may watch. Our whole constitutional heritage rebels at the thought of giving government the power to control men's minds.[282]

Hence it was entirely within that spirit that the Court, a year later, would uphold the right of individuals privately to show "stag" movies—even of women masturbating.[283] On the other hand, as the Court ruled ingeniously 6 : 3 in 1972, states, acting under their authority derived from the Twenty-First (!) Amendment, may—without doing violence to the First—shut down state liquor-licensed bars that, in the words of Justice Rehnquist's majority opinion, feature nude dancers and other "bacchanalian revelries."[284] Then in 1976 it upheld a Virginia law that provided criminal penalties for committing adult, consensual, private homosexual acts,[285] and a decade later it validated Georgia's ban on sodomy, at least as applied to homosexual conduct.[286]

But while these several landmark decisions settled, or at least seemed

---

[282]*Ibid.*, at 565.

[283]*California v. Pincus*, 400 U.S. 922 (1970).

[284]*California v. La Rue*, 409 U.S. 109. As Rehnquist delicately described the night club's activities: "Customers were found engaging in oral copulation with women entertainers; customers engaged in public masturbation; and customers placed rolled currency either directly into the vagina of a female entertainer, or on the bar in order that she might pick it up herself." (At 111.) See also *New York State Liquor Authority v. Bellanca*, 452 U.S. 714 (1982), which distinguished *La Rue* (this fn.) and affirmed the New York State Court of Appeal's declaration of unconstitutionality of the State's ban on topless entertainment.

[285]*Doe v. Commonwealth Attorney for the City of Richmond*, 425 U.S. 901 (1976). (See p. 271, *infra*.) But compare *Baker v. Wade*, 456 U.S. 1006 (1982).

[286]*Bowers v. Hardwick*, 54 LW 5064 (1986). But *cf. Watkins v. U.S. Army* (1988).

to settle, some of the major problems involved on the obscenity front, they did not—for they really could not—settle the basic problem of just what "obscene" means.[287] *Roth-Alberts, Ginzburg, Redrup, Ginsberg,* and *Stanley* had indeed provided some guidelines, but the very nature of the subject, and the public's understandable schizophrenic approach toward it, rendered additional litigation a certainty. And it was not long until the Court handed down a new—or perhaps another or additional— set of guidelines, intended to bring a degree of order into the vexatious subject.

Those new guidelines were announced in two 1973 cases.[288] Decided by the narrowest of margins (5 : 4), they were hardly conducive to future stability; yet they represented a significant development. Chief Justice Burger, speaking for himself and the three other Nixon appointees— Associate Justices Blackmun, Powell, and Rehnquist—plus Justice White, triumphantly noted that it was for "the first time" in sixteen years (referring to *Roth-Alberts*) that "a majority of this court has agreed on concrete guidelines to isolate 'hard core' pornography from expression protected by the First Amendment."[289] Designed to enable states and municipalities to ban books, magazines, plays, and motion pictures that are offensive to *local* standards, rather than the heretofore presumed prevalent single *national* standard, the five-man majority identified and promulgated the following trifold requirements as hence- forth applicable guidelines for the obscenity-law-of-the-land: In order to substantiate a charge of proscribable pornography: (1) "the *average* person applying contemporary [*local,* or, as later expanded, *state*] com- munity standards" must convincingly demonstrate that the allegedly obscene work in question, *taken as a whole* (not by its isolated parts), appeals to prurient interests; (2) that the material depicts or describes, "*in a patently offensive way,* sexual conduct *specifically defined* by applicable state law"; and (3) that, taken as a whole, the work "*lacks serious literary, artistic, political, or scientific value*" (which quickly

---

[287]For an excellent analysis and definition of the concept and application of "hard-core pornography," see William B. Lockhart and Robert C. McClure, "Obscenity Cen- sorship: The Core Constitutional Issue—What Is Obscene?", 7 *Utah Law Review,* 289 (1961). Their suggestion is that obscenity, in the constitutional sense, be limited to material *treated* like hard-core pornography by the *primary* audience to which it is addressed.

[288]*Miller v. California,* 413 U.S. 15, and *Paris Adult Theatre v. Slaton,* 413 U.S. 49.

[289]*Miller v. California, op. cit.,* at 29.

became known as "The LAPS Value Test").[290] In bitter, often sarcastic dissent, Justices Douglas, Brennan, Stewart, and Marshall predicted "raids on libraries"; contended that the new guidelines impinged seriously on free speech and free press; and warned that the necessary vagueness of any definition based on "local community" was redolent with censorship postures. Brennan, the author of *Roth* and *Alberts, Jacobellis, Ginzburg, Ginsberg, Mishkin,* and *Memoirs,* clearly abandoning his "compromise" or "balancing" position in those decisions, now concluded with deep feeling that "the time has come to make a significant departure from that approach," and offered the following formula as *the* viable, sensible approach to the obscenity problem:

> [W]hile I cannot say that the interests of the State—apart from the question of juveniles[291] and unconsenting adults—are trivial or nonexistent, I am compelled to conclude that these interests cannot justify the substantial damage to constitutional rights and to this Nation's judicial machinery that inevitably results from state efforts to bar the distribution even of unprotected materials to consenting adults. . . . I would hold, therefore, that at least *in the absence of distribution to juveniles or obtrusive exposure to unconsenting adults,* the First and Fourteenth Amendments prohibit the state and Federal governments from attempting wholly to suppress sexually oriented materials on the basis of their allegedly "obscene" content.[292]

But he spoke for the minority. The Burger majority had indeed fashioned new interpretative guidelines that embraced two major changes in the heretofore applicable obscenity law: (1) the substitution of *local* or, at most, *state* for *national* standards; and (2) the adoption of the LAPS value test for the erstwhile one of "utterly without redeeming social value."

Those observers who were skeptical as to the clarity and finality of the now pronounced—though not retroactive[293]—*Miller* and *Paris Adult Theatre* guideline triad did not have to wait long for confirmation of their analysis. Thus, notwithstanding its "old" (1971) guidelines vote (4 : 4), which upheld Maryland's highest court's 4 : 3 ruling that the

[290]*Miller v. California, op. cit.,* at 24. (Italics supplied.)

[291]Brennan joined the unanimous Court in 1982 when it upheld the "double standard" in instances involving juveniles. (See fn. 279, *supra.*)

[292]*Paris Adult Theatre v. Slaton, op. cit.,* fn. 288, *supra,* at 112–13.

[293]*Marks v. United States,* 430 U.S. 188 (1977).

controversial Swedish film *I Am Curious, Yellow* was obscene,[294] the "new" guidelines court ruled unanimously in 1974 that *Carnal Knowledge* was *not* obscene and could thus not be banned by Georgia.[295] Speaking through Justice Rehnquist, it emphasized that only material showing "patently offensive hard core sexual conduct" may be banned under the now applicable rules.[296] On the other hand, on the very same Opinion Day, an advertisement for an illustrated version of the report of the Presidential Commission on Obscenity and Pornography was held to be hard-core pornography, with Rehnquist now speaking for a 5:4 majority![297] To muddy the waters a mite further, the Court ruled 5:4 three years later that individuals are subject to the federal Comstock Act of 1873 ban on sending obscenity through the mail even if the state of their activity (here Iowa) has more permissive standards *and* despite the fact that the material's dissemination was wholly in-state.[298] Of course, it was not at all astonishing that the Court would run into a host of difficulty as to jury determinations of lines and limits governing the concepts of "average person" and "community standards"; and the Justices compounded the problem by adding a "reasonable person" test to their "community standard" yardstick.[299]

In the visual media, such as movies, the problem is, of course, considerably less complicated than in the realm of the printed word. For one thing, the movie-maker is usually acutely conscious of what he or she perceives as the public consensus and the reaction of the public's pocketbook. Moreover, the American movie industry has tried to bestow its own formal or prerelease seal of approval.[300] Self-policing is not, of course, a guarantee of good taste, but it does lodge responsibility

[294]*Grove Press, Inc. v. Maryland State Board of Censors*, 401 U.S. 480.

[295]*Jenkins v. Georgia*, 418 U.S. 153. (The four *Miller* and *Paris Adult Theatre* dissenters concurred only in the judgment, in effect saying "we told you so," while reiterating their previous objections to the majority's doctrine.)

[296]*Ibid.*, at 160 (quoting *Miller*, at 27).

[297]*Hamling v. United States*, 418 U.S. 87 (1974). Similarly, see the White-written 5:4 deicsion in *Ward v. Illinois* in 1977 (431 U.S. 767.)

[298]*Smith v. United States*, 434 U.S. 830 (1977).

[299]*Pinkus v. United States*, 436 U.S. 293 (1977), and *Pope v. Illinois*, 55 LW 4595 (1987).

[300]*The Man with the Golden Arm*, produced in 1955, dealing with the narcotics problem (producer Otto Preminger, United Artists Release), was the *first* movie released without that OK.

and judgment where it ought to lie: with the industry itself.[301] (The same may be said for the press.) The adult public, of course, should be free to patronize or to refuse to patronize the visual as well as the written media without governmental interference, or injunction by administrative or legislative fiat, or the censorial tactics of a powerful or vocal pressure group. If a movie is offensive to the sensibilities of a minority or majority group, that group is entirely free to advise and campaign against its patronization. But it is emphatically not free to prevent those who desire to patronize it from so doing. Freedom of expression is a two-edged sword. So is democracy.

Given the sizable number of federal and state statutes on the books, the obscenity question remains both current and vexatious in the absence of some such unlikely action as that taken by the Danes or that recommended by the abortive Presidential Commission on Obscenity and Pornography. This means, in effect, that we may expect continued, close, independent, case-by-case judicial scrutiny of findings of "obscenity," but with the aid of the new *Miller* and *Paris Adult Theatre* rules and guidelines, which were fashioned out of the experience of such earlier endeavors to determine lines and limits as those of *Roth-Alberts, Ginzburg, Redrup, Ginsberg, Ferber,* and *Stanley.* Censors will continue to find it difficult indeed to obtain judicial confirmation or support. On the other hand, it must not be assumed that the government has been, or is being, denied the authority to ban the sale and/or "pandering" of "hard-core pornography"—genuine smut—which, by self-demonstration, is patently offensive to current local or state community standards of decency, and thereby clearly appeals to prurient interests, particularly if advertised in "titillating" or "pandering" fashion. Pre-

---

[301]Perhaps partly copying the practices extent in, for example, the Scandinavian countries and in the United Kingdom, the movie industry published a much-heralded, simple Motion Picture Code of Self-Regulation late in 1968 which—amended early in 1970 and again in 1984—did provide the public with the following (and for harried parents rather helpful) rating symbols:

G = All ages admitted.

PG = All ages admitted. Parental guidance suggested.

PG 13 = Special Parental Guidance for children under thirteen urged. (Adopted in 1984.)

R = Restricted. Children under seventeen require accompanying parent or adult guardian.

X = No one under seventeen admitted.

sumably that type of filth and its method of dissemination would be classified as "hard-core pornography." Sex, which Justice Brennan— in his majority opinion in the key *Roth* and *Alberts* cases[302]—dubbed "a great and mysterious motive force in human life," has indeed, "indisputably been a subject of absorbing interest to mankind through the ages; it is one of the vital problems of human interest and public concern."[303] And, as he went on to point out, "sex and obscenity are not synonymous. On the other hand, obscene material is material which deals with sex in a manner appealing to prurient interests."[304] More-over, to reiterate, since *Ginzburg* something need *not* have a "prurient appeal" to the public at large to be declared obscene. It can now be so judged even if it panders merely to a "clearly defined deviant sexual group," such as homosexuals or masochists.[305] A book is not obscene because of "isolated parts"; the work must be viewed "as a whole," based on its "LAPS" (literary, artistic, political, or scientific) val-ues.[306] But this anticensorship rule may be vitiated by evidence of a publisher's pandering.[307] Thus the post–*Roth-Alberts* history, without settling the entire matter, has brought us closer to the possibility of drawing some lines, however serpentine they may well be. The lines inevitably deal with sex, a subject that, in Justice Black's dissenting words in the *Ginzburg* case, is "pleasantly interwoven in all human activities and involves the very substance of life itself."[308] As the 1970s turned into the 1980s, four aspects of the obscenity puzzle seemed to be *res judicata*—not withstanding the *Miller* and *Paris Adult Theatre* "retrenchment"—namely, that: (1) just about everything goes in the privacy of one's home—although the Court raised serious ques-tions about that verity in 1976 when, by simply affirming 6:3 a 2:1 Three-Judge U.S. District Court decision below, it upheld a Virginia

[302]*Roth v. United States* and *Alberts v. California*, 354 U.S. 476 (1957).

[303]*Ibid.*, at 487.

[304]*Ibid.*

[305]*Mishkin v. New York*, 383 U.S. 502 (1966).

[306]*Miller v. California*, 413 U.S. 15 (1973), at 24.

[307]*A Book Named "John Cleland's Woman of Pleasure" v. Massachusetts*, 383 U.S. 413 (1966).

[308]*Ginzburg v. United States, op cit.*, at 481. For an anthology dealing with diverse viewpoints on sexuality and the law, see Note, School of Law, Duke University, "Sex Offenses," 25 *Law and Contemporary Problems* 214 (1960).

law that provides felony penitentiary sentences of one to three years[309] for committing consensual, adult homosexual acts *in private*[310]; and when it confirmed that stance in 1986 by ruling 5 : 4, in a much-praised and much-condemned decision, that Georgia's statute, making it a crime for anyone to engage in oral or anal sex, was constitutional even when applied to consenting adults in private—here homosexuals;[311] (2) *public* hard-core pornography is not constitutionally protected;[312] (3) there now exists a judicially sanctioned "double standard" vis-à-vis obscenity legislation directed at minors and adults; and (4) while there is no judicially recognized *national* community standard, *local* (or *state*)

[309]Va. Code §18.1-212 (Cum. Supp. 1974): "Crimes against nature.—If any person shall carnally know in any manner any brute animal, or carnally know any male or female person by the anus or by or with the mouth, or voluntarily submit to such carnal knowledge, he or she shall be guilty of a felony and shall be confined in the penitentiary not less than one year nor more than three years."

[310]*Doe v. Commonwealth Attorney for the City of Richmond*, 425 U.S. 901 (1976), reconfirmed in *Enslin v. Bean*, 436 U.S. 912 (1978). The Court came under heavy criticism for deciding so privately crucial a matter without hearing oral argument and without issuing a formal opinion. (Four votes to hear the case were needed, but only Justices Brennan, Marshall, and Stevens voted in favor of oral argument on the merits.) *Cf.* the case of the dismissal of an admitted homosexual high school teacher in Washington State, *Gaylord v. Tacoma School District*, 434 U.S. 879 (1977). But see the supportive freedom-of-speech-and-assembly decision in the "campus recognition" of "Gay Lib" at the University of Missouri, *Ratchford v. Gay Lib*, 434 U.S. 1060 (1978). See also *People v. Onofre*, 451 U.S. 987 (1981), *certiorari* denied, and *Baker v. Wade*, 456 U.S. 1006 (1982).

[311]*Bowers v. Hardwick*, 54 LW 5064. Justice White penned the majority opinion, joined by Justices Rehnquist, O'Connor and the Chief Justice, plus Justice Powell, who concurred separately. Justices Brennan, Marshall, Blackmun, and Stevens dissented.

[312]Space does not permit a discussion of the fascinating clash between the competing constitutional values of freedom of expression and *privacy* that faced the Burger Court early in 1970. At issue was a 1967 federal anti-pandering law (enacted post-*Ginzburg*) which empowers any citizen to cut off the flow of mailed ads that he personally considers "erotically arousing or sexually provocative." The recipient simply notifies the Post Office, which then orders his name removed from the mailing lists. Unanimously, the Supreme Court upheld the law, Chief Justice Burger affirming ever citizen's right "to be let alone." He added: "A mailer's right to communicate must stop at the mailbox of an unreceptive addressee." (*Rowan v. United States Post Office Department*, 397 U.S. 728.) See also *U.S. Postal Service v. Council of Greenburgh Civic Assns.*, 49 LW 4813 (1981).

[313]A flurry of activity by various communities, led by Cleveland, Ohio, commenced in 1977 to "determine" such obscenity standards and lines (often by way of questionnaires distributed by trash collectors!). Note, for example, the accounts in *The New York Times*, June 11, 1977, and June 26, 1977, p. 8E. The head of the Cleveland branch of the American Civil Liberties Union, doubting that the poll, if incorporated in a projected anti-

standards *are* relevant[313] in obscenity litigation[314]—absent *federal* precedence.[315]

Some Concluding Thoughts

No other branch of our government is as qualified to draw lines between the rights of individuals and those of society as the Supreme Court of the United States. The legislative and executive branches yield all too easily to the politically expedient and the popular. Admittedly, the "clear and present danger" approach to freedom of expression, however amended and augmented by the "imminence" requirement, is far from perfect. But the sole alternative to it would be an almost total absence of immunity in the face of legislative actions. Freedom of expression cannot be absolute; but it can be protected to the greatest degree humanly feasible under the Constitution. And there are giants of liberal democracy who bridle at *any* restraint on free expression. Thus we had Justice Black in his absolutist approach to the problem[316] and, almost as absolute, the late educator-philosopher Alexander Meiklejohn, who held that while the First Amendment "does not forbid the abridging of *speech* . . . it does forbid the abridging of *freedom of speech*."[317]

For Alexander Meiklejohn, who, like Hugo Black, rejected the "clear and present danger" approach in favor of a more liberal standard, there is thus *never*, under the *First* Amendment, any right or reason to curb or abridge *freedom* of speech—at least not *public* speech (see below); dangers, even in wartime, are irrelevant; and the time of

smut law, would survive a serious court challenge, commented: "In our opinion it will probably wind up where it started—with the garbage men." (As quoted, June 26, *ibid.*)

[314]For a view warmly praising the Burger Court for adding "clarity to the constitutional law of obscenity by drawing lines which are in most respects clearer than those of earlier cases," see Lane V. Sunderland, *Obscenity: The Court, the Congress and the President's Commission* (Washington, D.C.: American Enterprise Institute for Public Policy Research, 1974), pp. 114–15.

[315]See *Smith v. United States, supra*, p. 268, where the federal standard was ruled to govern (5:4).

[316]E.g., his "The Bill of Rights," 35 *New York University Law Review* 865–81 (April 1960); and his *A Constitutional Faith* (New York: Alfred A. Knopf, 1968), especially Chapter II, "The First Amendment," pp. 43 ff. (See also, generally, Chapter II, *supra*.)

[317]*Free Speech and Its Relation to Self-Government* (New York: Harper & Brothers, 1948), p. 19. (Italics supplied.)

danger is precisely the time to show people that one means what one says and has the right to say it:

> If, then, on any occasion in the United States it is allowable to say that the Constitution is a good document it is equally allowable, in that situation, to say that the Constitution is a bad document. If a public building may be used in which to say, in time of war, that the war is justified, then the same building may be used in which to say that it is not justified. If it be publicly argued that conscription for armed service is moral and necessary, it may likewise be publicly argued that it is immoral and unnecessary. If it may be said that American political institutions are superior to those of England or Russia or Germany, it may, with equal freedom, be said that those of England or Russia or Germany are superior to ours. . . . When a question of policy is "before the house," free men choose it not with their eyes shut, but with their eyes open. To be afraid of ideas, any idea, is to be unfit for self-government.[318]

This stirring language should serve as a beacon to us all; but the fact remains that there *are* limits to the precious freedom and that we do need some such doctrine as "clear and present danger." Meiklejohn, however, proposed a different solution: he created a dichotomy of *public speech* and *private speech*, "public" speech pertaining to any matter that concerns politics—i.e., public policy and public officials. This type of speech, Meiklejohn held, is given *absolute* protection, in the interests of a self-governing free and democratic society, by the First Amendment and the "privileges or immunities" clause of the Fourteenth, and cannot be abridged at all. "*Private*" speech, he contended, pertains to speech that concerns only private individuals in their personal, private concerns, and can therefore be regulated or restricted—but *only* in accordance with the "due process of law" safeguards under the Fifth and Fourteenth Amendments. Noble as the Meiklejohn dichotomy may be,[319] it is burdened with what is clearly an unresolvable dilemma

---

[318]*Ibid.*, p. 27.

[319]For a similar dichotomy see George Anastaplo, *The Constitutionalist: Notes on the First Amendment* (Dallas: Southern Methodist University Press, 1970). He accepts "the First" as *absolute* in the "political" ("public business") area, *but* denies it in the "private" sector, specifically "artistic expression" and "problems of obscenity." He confines his reading to the *First* Amendment, not reaching the states via the Fourteenth. Meiklejohn, of course, does not exempt the states. The two also differ somewhat on the meaning of "public."

of its own: how to draw the line pragmatically between "public" and "private" speech. Much speech is private but has definite public ramifications—a viable line seems impossible to attain. Yet shortly before he died in 1965 Meiklejohn voiced the belief that the Supreme Court had, in effect, adopted his "public speech" approach because of its developing stance on litigation concerning libel, slander, and defamation of character, highlighted by the 1964 decision in *New York Times Co. v. Sullivan*.[320] There the Court held that a *public* official cannot recover libel damages for criticism of his official performance *unless he proves that the statement was made with deliberate malice*.[321] "It is an occasion for dancing in the streets," exclaimed Meiklejohn, according to Justice Brennan—who, however, preferred to leave to his readers "to say how nearly Dr. Meiklejohn's hope has been realized."[322]

Yet a staunch supporter of the Holmes-Brandeis "clear and present danger plus imminence" doctrine, Zechariah Chafee, Jr., the aforementioned towering advocate of free expression, had publicly disagreed with his revered teacher and friend Meiklejohn in 1949. Reviewing Meiklejohn's *Free Speech and Its Relation to Self-Government*,[323] Chafee charged that Meiklejohn, in his repeated challenge to Holmes and the "clear and present danger" doctrine, simply showed no realization of the long uphill fight that Holmes had to wage in order to secure free speech. After all, as Chafee explained appropriately in his review, it *was* Holmes who

> worked out a formula which would invalidate a great deal of suppression, and won for [free speech] the solid authority of a unanimous Court. After-

[320]376 U.S. 254.

[321]See discussion on pp. 212 ff., *supra*. Note that the Court has wavered on the *degree* of extending the "public" concept to "persons" and/or "figures" as well as "officials."

[322]See William J. Brennan, Jr., "The Supreme Court and the Meiklejohn Interpretation of the First Amendment," 79 *Harvard Law Review* (November 1965). Actually, the first to report Meiklejohn's "dancing in the streets" statement was Harry Kalven, Jr., in "A New Look at the Central Meaning of the First Amendment," *The Supreme Court Review* (1964).

[323]62 *Harvard Law Review* 891 (1949). See also Meiklejohn's "charges which I would bring against the 'clear and present danger' theory," in another among his important works on the freedom of speech problem, *Political Freedom: The Constitutional Powers of the People* (New York: Harper and Bros., 1948 and 1960), Oxford University Press edition (New York: 1965), pp. 75–76.

wards, again and again, when the test was misapplied by the majority, Holmes restated his position in ringing words which, with the help of Brandeis and [later, after he had become Chief Justice] Hughes, eventually inspired the whole Court.[324]

Of course, to support the "clear and present danger" doctrine, or that of "clear and present danger plus imminence," is not to ignore *its* inherent dilemmas—as the preceding discussion demonstrates. The very adjectives "clear" and "present" raise problems of great magnitude. Still, in both its basic philosophy and its application, the doctrine's overriding tenets are realistic in approach and reflect an attitude which is both liberal *and* conservative in the classic connotations of those two misunderstood adjectives. It is simply not possible to get away from the concept of "balancing"—a contentious term in some quarters[325]—liberty and authority, freedom and responsibility.[326] But

[324]*Op. cit.*, p. 901.

[325]See, for example, the intriguing law review debate between Professors Laurent Frantz and Wallace Mendelson over the validity of "balancing" as a technique in free speech cases: Frantz, "The First Amendment in the Balance," 71 *Yale Law Journal* 1424 (1962); Mendelson, "On the Meaning of the First Amendment: Absolutes in the Balance," 50 *California Law Review* 821 (1962); Frantz, "Is the First Amendment Law? A Reply to Professor Mendelson," 51 *California Law Review* 729 (1963); and Mendelson, "The First Amendment and the Judicial Process: A Reply to Mr. Frantz," 17 *Vanderbilt Law Review* 479 (1964). Speaking broadly, Professor Frantz was anti-, Professor Mendelson pro-"balancing"—but the reader is cautioned against oversimplification. See also the challenging article by Dean Alfange, Jr., "The Balancing of Interests in Free Speech Cases: In Defense of an Abused Doctrine," 2 *Law in Transition Quarterly* 1 (1965). Note, too, Justice Black's scathing denunciation of "balancing" in his *A Constitutional Faith, op. cit.,* and my pp. 23–25, *supra.* To him, of course, the "clear and present danger" doctrine—be it with or without the "imminence" requirement—was just another form of "balancing" and hence unacceptable under his reading of the absolutist commands of the First (and Fourteenth) Amendment. "[I]t has no place in [their] interpretation," as he admonished again shortly prior to the end of his long and distinguished career on the Court, in his concurring opinion in *Brandenburg v. Ohio,* 395 U.S. 444 (1968), at 449–50.

[326]In his interesting position essay on the overall question, *Freedom of Speech: The Supreme Court and Judicial Review* (Englewood Cliffs, N.J.: Prentice-Hall, 1966), Professor Martin Shapiro contends that although balancing "may still occasionally be useful in particular instances, it cannot be maintained as a general formula for a Court bent on fulfilling its First Amendment responsibilities" (p. 105). Issuing a clarion call for judicial activism, he sees the "preferred freedom" position as the only viable formula, one that he insists must "again become the dominant First Amendment doctrine of the Supreme Court" (p. 172). Again and again calling for judicial activism, judicial policy-making, in the freedom of speech sphere, he argues that American democracy "not only permits but invites and requires a strong measure of judicial activism here."

when "balancing" is called for, and in the absence of a danger clear, present, and imminent, we must presume the scale to be weighted on the side of the individual.

The philosophical test[327] to be applied is clear: will the forbidding of freedom of expression further or hamper the realization of liberal democratic ideals? The sole manner in which to moderate, remedy, or remove rankling discontent is to get at its causes by education, remedial laws, or other community action. Repression of expression will only serve to sharpen the sense of injustice and provide added arguments and rationalizations for desperate, perhaps reckless measures. Surely the loyalty of the mass of men to liberal democracy has been immensely strengthened by the right to free expression and the consequent feeling of a genuine stake in society, a society that allows the expression of our deepest and most rankling grievances. Hence repressive laws will fail to maintain "loyalty." While they may give a false sense of temporary security, since we would be excused from arguing the case for our ideals and for the carefully developed procedures for pursuing them, we must also recognize that freedom of utterance, even though it be rebellious, constitutes a safety valve that gives timely warning of dangerous pressures in our society. Committed to the principles of Western liberal democracy, we have a lasting obligation to leave open the political channels by which a governing majority can be replaced when it is no longer able to command popular support. However, to plead for a generous approach to freedom of expression is not to say that it is absolute. It is not; it cannot be. In the final analysis we must confidently look to the Court to draw a line based on constitutional common sense. No other agency of government is equally well qualified to do so.

[327]See J. A. Corry and Henry J. Abraham, *Elements of Democratic Government*, 4th ed. (New York: Oxford University Press, 1964), pp. 262 ff.

chapter *VI* Religion

If line-drawing in the realm of due process is difficult because of the ambiguity of the concept, and if it is elusive in determining the parameters of freedom of expression, it is preeminently delicate and emotional in the matter of religion. Religion, like love, is so personal and irrational that no one has either the capacity or justification to sit in judgment.[1] Any attempt by society to find and draw a line here is bound to be frustrating. Our own society is certainly no exception—although it is to America's credit that in probably no other area of civil rights and liberties have our agencies and agents of government maintained such a consistently good record. Even more than the freedom of the press has the freedom of religion been safeguarded from governmental interference. This is not to say, of course, that we have a perfect record; our early history is replete with both public and private discrimination against religious creeds, particularly Catholics, Quakers, and Jews. However, as we grew and developed as a nation, discrimination *by government* declined perceptibly and fairly rapidly. *Private* religious discrimination—which does still exist, and presumably always will to some degree—is no longer, if it ever was, sanctioned by government, and when it occurs it is preeminently of a "social" rather than a "religious" nature. The problems arise when attempts are made to commingle matters of religious belief with matters of state and to conduct policy in line with spiritual commitments.

The election of the first Roman Catholic president of the United

---

[1]Still, I am tempted to profess a modicum of "expertise": a product of secular secondary schools, I spent one year at a Roman Catholic university; was graduated from an Episcopal college; and married a Christian Scientist; our children went to Quaker schools (and to the same college as their father); and I was a long-time member of the Board of Trustees of an old Reform Jewish congregation.

277

States in 1960; the rise to public prominence and power of a host of members of religious minority groups; and the steadily increasing official proscription of public or quasi-public discrimination because of race, sex, religion, color, and national origin—brought to a dramatic climax in the Civil Rights Act of 1964, as amended—all augur well for a continuing increase in understanding and a continuing decline of the barriers built of religious discrimination. Nevertheless, problems of religious freedom still do arise and lines must be drawn. Our concern here lies predominantly in the *public* sector, and in how and where lines are drawn between the prerogatives of the free exercise of religion, and all the concept entails, and the right of society to guard against activity that would infringe upon the rights of other members of that society. The distinction is compounded by the unique collateral problem of the constitutional command against the "establishment" of religion; *it* has proved to be a hornet's nest indeed!

Some Basic Considerations

Basic to our understanding of the problem are three constitutional facts.

1. *The Proscription of Religious Tests in Article Six of the Constitution*. It is often forgotten that there exists in the body of our Constitution an important provision dealing directly with a crucial religious right, the forbidding of religious tests as qualifications for public office. The third section of Article Six, following the famed supremacy clause[2]—which constitutes all of Section 2—reflects the concern for religious liberty of four Virginians to whom, although they were not all participants in the Constitutional Convention, is due chief credit for our constitutional theory of freedom of religion: Thomas Jefferson,[3] James Madison,

[2] "This Constitution, and the Laws of the United States which shall be made in Pursuance thereof; and all Treaties made, or which shall be made, under the Authority of the United States, shall be the supreme Law of the Land; *and the Judges in every State shall be bound thereby, any Thing in the Constitution of Laws of any State to the Contrary notwithstanding.*" (Italics supplied.)

[3] Symptomatic of Jefferson's strong feelings about religious freedom is the following excerpt from a letter he wrote to Mrs. M. Harrison Smith on August 6, 1816: "I never told my own religion, nor scrutinized that of another. I never attempted to make a convert, nor wished to change another's creed. I have never judged the religion of others, and by this test, my dear Madame, I have been satisfied yours must be an excellent one to have produced a life of such exemplary virtue and correctness. For it is in our lives and not from our words that our religion must be read."

George Mason—who refused to sign the final draft of the Constitution because of the absence of a Bill of Rights—and, perhaps with an occasional aberration, Patrick Henry.[4] The Journal of the Convention for August 30, 1787, bears the following entry: "It was moved and seconded to add . . .—'but no religious test shall *ever* be required as a qualification to *any* office or public trust under the authority of the United States'; which passed unanimously in the affirmative."[5] Only North Carolina voted against the adoption of this clause.[6] Later, referring to the clause's significance, Justice Joseph Story commented: "The Catholic and the Protestant, the Calvinist and the Armenian [*sic*], the infidel and the Jew, may sit down to the Communion-table of the National Council, without any inquisition into their faith or mode of worship."[7]

Although this ban against religious test oaths settled matters at once insofar as public office under the federal government was concerned, it did become an issue in state and municipal public employment, and remained so for a good many years. Most states removed their mandated disqualifications against Jews and members of other theistic religions, but others, such as Arkansas, Maryland, Pennsylvania, and Tennessee, retained constitutional provisions compelling all would-be public office-holders to take an oath or make an affirmation of their belief in God. Inevitably, however, judicial nationalization of civil rights and liberties via the "due process of law" clause of the Fourteenth Amendment ultimately reached the area of religion.[8] And in 1961 the Supreme Court addressed itself specifically to the religious oath clause in *Torcaso v. Watkins*.[9]

In that case Roy Torcaso, an aspirant for the minor state office of notary public in Maryland, refused to abide by his state's requirement, imbedded in a clause of its Constitution, that all office-holders declare

---

[4]Anson Phelps Stokes and Leo Pfeffer, *Church and State in the United States,* rev. one-vol. ed. (New York: Harper & Row, 1964), pp. 65 ff.

[5]Jonathan Elliot, *The Debates in the Several State Conventions,* 2nd ed. (Philadelphia: Lippincott & Co., 1854), Vol. I, pp. 277. (Italics supplied.)

[6]With the substitution of a semicolon for the dash before "but" and of a period for the semicolon after "States," it became the last phrase of Article Six, Section 3.

[7]As quoted in Phelps and Pfeffer, *op. cit.,* p. 91.

[8]See Chapter III, *supra,* and, *inter alia, Hamilton v. Board of Regents of California,* 293 U.S. 245 (1934); *Cantwell v. Connecticut,* 310 U.S. 296 (1940); and *Everson v. Board of Education of Ewing Township,* 330 U.S. 1 (1947).

[9]367 U.S. 488.

their belief in the existence of God as a part of their oath of office. On Torcaso's refusal to take the oath his application was denied, and he appealed to the Maryland courts for a reversal of that ruling, alleging violation of the religious liberty guaranteed to him by the United States Constitution. When the state courts sided with Maryland, Torcaso took his case to the United States Supreme Court, which not only agreed with Torcaso's contentions, but declared the oath requirement unconstitutional as a violation of the "free exercise of religion" clause of the First Amendment of the federal Constitution. Unanimously, the Court, without any inquiry into what belief, if any, Roy Torcaso held—he was an atheist—declared that the state test oath constituted a clear invasion of "freedom of belief and religion." Moreover, wrote Justice Black for the Court, in placing Maryland on the side of "one particular sort of believer," namely, theists—those who believe in the existence of God—the constitutional requirement imposed a burden on the free exercise of the faiths on *non-believers* in violation of the free exercise clause.[10] To emphasize this point, Black appended what has become a well-known footnote in constitutional law: "Among religions in this country which do not teach what would generally be considered a belief in the existence of God are Buddhism, Taoism, Ethical Culture, Secular Humanism and others."[11] In other words, the Court made categorically clear that not only were religious test oaths barred, but theistic belief could not be a requirement for religious belief.[12] Put somewhat differently, the Court affirmed what has been, or should have been, apparent all along: that the Constitution of the United States, in guaranteeing freedom of religion, by implication also guarantees freedom of *irreligion*. Four years later, the Maryland Court of Appeals specifically extended that guarantee to invalidate a requirement that all Maryland jurors declare a belief in God.[13]

2. *The "Nationalization" of the Religion Clauses.* As we already know from Chapter III, the wording of the First Amendment, of which the religion phrases constitute the opening statements, confined the

---

[10]*Ibid.*, at 495.

[11]*Ibid.*, n. 11. See the developing argument on "Secular Humanism," which reached the federal judiciary in 1987.

[12]In this connection see the problem of the draft and conscientious objectors, discussed on pp. 285 ff., *infra.*

[13]*Schowgurow v. State*, 240 Md. 121 (1965).

inherent prohibitions against governmental action to the *federal* government. This made particular sense in the case of religion, for at the time
of the adoption of the Constitution of the United States many of the
original thirteen *states* had specific religious establishments or other
restrictive provisos. In fact, in the earliest days of the fledgling nation
only Virginia, led by Jefferson, Madison, and Mason, and Rhode Island
conceded full, unqualified freedom; New York *almost* did.[14] Two
states, Delaware and Maryland, demanded Christianity, Delaware also
insisting on assent to the doctrine of the Trinity; four, Delaware, North
Carolina, Pennsylvania, and South Carolina, called for assent to the
divine inspiration of the Bible, with Pennsylvania and South Carolina
further requiring a belief in heaven and hell, and South Carolina—the
only one among the thirteen—still speaking of religious ":toleration";
three, Maryland, New York, and South Carolina, excluded all ministers, even Protestants, from any civil office; five, Connecticut, Maryland, Massachusetts, New Hampshire, and South Carolina, insisted on
"Protestantism," or "Christian Protestantism"; and six, Connecticut,
Georgia, New Hampshire, New Jersey, North Carolina, and South Carolina, specifically adhered to religious establishments (Protestant).[15]
Hence it is not surprising that the First Amendment was widely regarded
as a protection of state establishments *against* congressional action. By
1833, however, following the capitulation of the Congregationalists in
Massachusetts, the fundamental concepts of freedom of religion had, to
all intents and purposes, become a recognized fact and facet of public
law, with only minor aberrations, throughout the young United States of
America.

It was thus but a matter of time for religious freedom and its attendant
safeguards for the separation between Church and State to become
binding under our Constitution *de jure* as well as *de facto*. As the
"incorporation," "absorption," or "nationalization" of the Bill of
Rights guarantees achieved judicial recognition, beginning with the
Sanford opinion in *Gitlow v. New York*[16] in 1925, it was but a question
of time until the Court would address itself to religion. And so it did,

---

[14]In addition to barring ministers from public office, New York required naturalized
citizens to abjure allegiance in all foreign ecclesiastical as well as civil matters.

[15]See Stokes and Pfeffer, *op. cit.*, Chapter 3, for a full account.

[16]268 U.S. 252. See Chapter III, *supra*.

first to the free exercise of religion in 1934 and 1940,[17] then to the
separation of Church and State in 1947.[18]

3. *The Two Aspects of the Religion Clause.* One of the difficulties in
the interpretation of the religion clause is that its language speaks of
both the "establishment" *and* the "free exercise" of religion. Certainly the two clauses are interrelated, but they are also separable.[19] The
author of the First Amendment, usually—although not always[20]—
regarded as Madison, even separated the two by a comma: "Congress
shall make no law respecting an establishment of religion, or prohibiting the free exercise thereof. . . ." When the Supreme Court first
undertook to "nationalize" the religion clauses in the *Hamilton* case[21]
in 1934, Justice Butler's opinion confined itself to Albert Hamilton's
claim of free exercise; the matter of "establishment" or separation of
Church and State was not properly at issue. Nor did it play a meaningful
role in the next great freedom of religion case to be decided by the
Supreme Court, six years later, *Cantwell v. Connecticut,*[22] which elaborated upon the *Hamilton* rationale. It was not until the *New Jersey Bus*
case,[23] seven years after *Cantwell,* that the Court, speaking through
Justice Black, held that the First Amendment's prohibition against legislation respecting an establishment of religion is also applicable to the
several states by virtue of the language and obligations of the Fourteenth
Amendment. Thus, by 1947, *both* aspects of the religion guarantee had
been judicially interpreted to apply to *both* the federal government and

[17]*Hamilton v. Regents of University of California,* 293 U.S. 245 (1934); and *Cantwell
v. Connecticut,* 310 U.S. 296 (1940).

[18]*Everson v. Board of Education,* 310 U.S. 1.

[19] This is not to say that commentators and students have not at times been puzzled both
as to the choice determined by the judiciary in specific cases and as to the viability of a
distinction in others. Illustrative of the problem is the challenge brought in 1974 by four
Roman Catholic students and priests against the University of Delaware's ban against
religious services on its property. The University argued—ultimately unsuccessfully—
that the establishment clause compelled it to ban such services; the students and priests
argued that the free exercise clause entitled them to hold such services. The Delaware
courts upheld the latter's claim and the U.S. Supreme Court declined to review the case,
thereby leaving the state's judgment in force. (*University of Delaware v. Keegan,* 424
U.S. 934).

[20]See Donald L. Drakeman, "Religion and the Republic: James Madison and the First
Amendment," 25 *Journal of Church and State* 427 (Autumn 1983), for one who does not
believe that Madison "drafted the language of the religion clauses" (at 431).

[21]*Hamilton v. Regents of California, op. cit.*

[22]310 U.S. 296 (1940).

[23]*Everson v. Board of Education of Ewing Township,* 330 U.S. 1 (1947).

the several states of the Union. Far more complicated, however, was the determination of the meaning, range, and extent of the two famous clauses.

Attempting To Define "Religion"

To state the problem is to see its complications. Yet in a government under law, whatever an individual's personal idea of religion might be, formal definitions have to be ventured. Each individual does, of course, possess the basic right, now one universally guaranteed and protected under our Constitution, to believe what he or she chooses, to worship whom and how he or she pleases, always provided that it does not impermissibly interfere with the right of others. Hence, we have those who believe in nothing; those who believe but doubt; those who believe without questioning; those who worship the Judeo-Christian God in innumerably different ways; those who adhere to Mohammed's creed; those who worship themselves; those who worship a cow or other animals; those who worship several gods—to mention just a few of the remarkable variety of expressions of belief that obtain.

Webster's New Collegiate Dictionary provides the following choices under the heading "religion":

> 1(a): the service or worship of God or the supernatural; (b): commitment or devotion to religious faith or observance; 2: a personal faith or institutionalized system of religious attitudes, beliefs, and practices; 3 (*archaic*): scrupulous conformity; 4: a cause, principle, or system of beliefs held to with ardor and faith.[24]

At best such a definition can offer a broad guideline of a non-binding nature. The same is more or less true of the kind of psychological guideline furnished by such thoughtful commentators as Professor Gordon W. Allport, who wrote that religion encompasses a value that every democrat "must hold: the right of each individual to work out his own philosophy of life, to find his personal niche in creation as best he can."[25] He further elaborated:

> A man's religion is the audacious bid he makes to bind himself to creation and to the Creator. It is his ultimate attempt to enlarge and to complete his

---

[24]8th ed. (Springfield, Mass.: G. & C. Merriam Co., 1975), p. 724, col. 1.
[25]Gordon W. Allport, *The Individual and his Religion*, 2d ed. (New York: The Macmillan Co., 1962), p. vii.

own personality by finding the supreme context in which he rightly belongs.[26]

One may agree with Allport's approach to a definition or interpretation—or Alfred North Whitehead's that it is "what each individual does with his own solitariness"[27]—but the authoritative definition *cum* constitutional interpretation had to come from the Supreme Court, acting either upon a congressional definition or within the confines of its common-law responsibilities.

The Supreme Court Defines Religion. The classic Court definition was authored by Justice Stephen J. Field in an 1890 case in which the Court unanimously upheld a lower court judgment that one Samuel Davis, a Mormon residing in the then Territory of Idaho, should be disqualified as a voter for falsifying his voter's oath "abjuring bigamy or polygamy as a condition to vote" since, as a Mormon, he believed in polygamy. Polygamy, then as now a criminal offense,[28] constituted a disqualification under territorial voting and other statutes. Field wrote for the court:

> [T]he term "religion" has reference to one's view of his relations to his Creator, and to the obligations they impose of reverence for his being and character, and of obedience to his will. It is often confounded with the cultus or form of worship of a particular sect, but is distinguishable from the latter. . . . With man's relations to his Maker and the obligations he may think they impose, and the manner in which an expression shall be made by him of his belief on those subjects, no interference can be permitted, provided always the laws of society, designed to secure its peace and prosperity, and the morals of its people are not interfered with.[29]

Thus, although giving religion the widest feasible interpretation in terms of individual commitment, Field found that Davis had violated the reservation of the last qualifying clause.[30]

[26]*Ibid.*, p. 142.

[27]"Religion in the Making," in F. C. S. Northrop and Mason W. Gross, eds., *Alfred North Whitehead: An Anthology* (New York: The Macmillan Co., 1953), p. 472.

[28]Utah's ban on polygamy, adopted in 1896 as a condition for attaining statehood, was reaffirmed in U.S. District Court in 1984.

[29]*Davis v. Beason*, 133 U.S. 333 (1890), at 342.

[30]See Jesse H. Choper, "Defining 'Religion' in the First Amendment," 1982 *University of Illinois Law Review* 3 (1982), in which the author suggests that the "seemingly intractable abstract question of what constitutes a religion need be answered in only a very

The "C.O." Problem. This Supreme Court definition of religion was most often tested in cases dealing with military exemptions and conscientious objectors. Exemption from the draft and/or combat service for those who oppose war on religious grounds is deeply rooted in American tradition and history—although it was not really formalized until post–Civil War days. Much litigation has attended this problem, frequently involving the Jehovah's Witnesses, who contend that every believing Witness is a "minister" and as such ought to be exempt from military service. Both the Society of Friends (the Quakers) and the Mennonites have made pacifism a dogma. And, of course, there has been a continuous stream of individual conscientious objectors, coming chiefly from small Protestant sects but from other faiths as well—a stream that in the 1960s became a formidable river with our lengthy Southeast Asia involvement.[31] Congress has been generous in recognizing *bona fide* conscientious objectors and in exempting these from military service,[32] although it is not at all clear that there exists a *constitutional* rather than a *moral obligation* to exempt conscientious objectors. It is quite possible to argue either—or both—sides of the issue. The two major draft statutes of this century, those of 1917 and 1940, both included exemption provisions. The former exempted from combat only members affiliated with some "well-recognized religious sect or organizations," such as "peace churches" or a "pacifist religious sect" like the Quakers. In 1940, however, Congress discarded *all* sectarian restrictions, so that conscientious objectors no longer had to belong to a church or other religious organization, provided their opposition to war was based upon "religious training and belief." Subsequent amendments to the 1940 statute, enacted in 1948 and 1951, expanded the prerogatives; but 1967 saw a distinct retrenchment.[33]

---

limited way for constitutional purposes." He looks to other provisions of the First Amendment as disposing of "almost all other problems fairly considered," such as "freedom of expression and freedom of association."

[31]In June 1970 alone, for example, 14,440 C.O. claims were officially filed. (*The New York Times,* July 25, 1970, p. 6*l.*)

[32]A C.O. who first claimed conscientious objector status *after* he received an induction notice, when, he asserted, his C.O. views "matured," appealed unsuccessfully for Supreme Court review of his problem in 1967. (*Gearey v. United States,* 389 U.S. 959, *certiorari* denied.)

[33]For an excellent treatment of the subject, although now dated, see Mulford Q. Sibley and Philip E. Jacobs, *Conscription of Conscience: The American State and the Conscientious Objector, 1940–1947* (Ithaca, N.Y.: Cornell University Press, 1952).

The problem in granting these exemptions has been, and is, the distinction between *bona fide* and not so *bona fide* claims. It is axiomatic in democratic society that men and women of abiding religious conviction who, either as individuals or as members of pacifist sects, hold creeds and beliefs that proscribe participation in war or related strife should neither be compelled to participate nor be jailed for refusing to do so. Yet what of those whose objections are not of a clearly identifiable, *bona fide* religious nature, but are probably preeminently moral and/or sociological, philosophical, or even political? Where does personal "policy-making" begin? Can it ever be given preference over duly enacted public policy, one that recognizes C.O. status in law, but chooses to establish definite, limiting, guidelines? And, to compound the inherent complexities, what of those whose conscientious objection is limited to a *particular* war, e.g., that in Vietnam?[34]

In 1965 the Supreme Court handed down a momentous decision in three cases involving the most recent provisions in the draft law exempting religious objectors from combat training and service. At issue was the restriction established by Congress in 1951 of exemption to "persons who by reason of religious training and belief are conscientiously

[34]This issue faced the Court repeatedly as of the late 1960s, often coupled with a challenge to the *legality* of the undeclared Indochina involvement. On several occasions, the Court denied review of the "legality" question involving individuals, e.g., twice in 1967, Justice Douglas dissenting from the denial in *both* cases, Justice Stewart in the second (*Mitchell v. United States*, 386 U.S. 972, and *Mora v. McNamara*, 389 U.S. 934); and, late in 1970, with the two dissenters joined by Harlan, it refused to entertain a lawsuit by the Commonwealth of Massachusetts which, based on a law it had passed, challenged the President's power to carry on the Vietnam war without a formal declaration of war (*Massachusetts v. Laird*, 400 U.S. 886). One year and one and one-half years later, with only Douglas and Brennan dissenting in both cases, it refused again (*Orlando v. Laird*, 404 U.S. [1971], and *Da Costa v. Laird*, 405 U.S. 979 [1972]). A different effort, basing the appeal on the question of congressional power to appropriate funds for an undeclared war, also failed in 1972, Douglas and Brennan dissenting. (*Sarnoff v. Schultz*, 409 U.S. 929.) And so did a similar one in 1973. (*Attlee v. Richardson*, 411 U.S. 94.) On the matter of conscientious objection to a *particular* war—or, as it may also be styled, *selective* conscientious objection—the Court had a test case before it in 1970, but (a) the issue came up tangentially in connection with the more pressing one of "non-religious conscientious objection" and (b) a majority of 5 : 3 held that the case had been improperly appealed to it from the District Court below (*United States v. Sisson*, 399 U.S. 267, an 83-page decision). To make clear that it was not engaging in an artful evasion—something of which it is eminently capable, and often for excellent reasons—the Court granted two appeals by selective conscientious objectors, of which it disposed in March 1971 (*Gillette v. United States* and *Negre v. Larson*, 401 U.S. 437). See pp. 241 ff., *infra*.

opposed to any participation in war." The definition spelled out "religious training and belief" as follows:

> Religious training and belief in this connection means an individual belief in a relation to a Supreme Being involving duties superior to those arising from any human relation, but does not include essentially political, sociological or philosophical views, or a merely personal moral code.[35]

Three men were involved in these 1965 *Draft Act* cases,[36] Daniel A. Seeger, Arno S. Jakobson, and Forest B. Peter. Seeger and Jakobson had been convicted by the United States District Court in New York, and Peter by the United States District Court in San Francisco, of refusing to submit to induction. Both New York convictions were reversed by the United States Court of Appeals for the Second Circuit, but the Appeals Court for the Ninth Circuit upheld the Peter conviction. Seeger had told the Selective Service authorities that he was conscientiously opposed to participation in war in any form because of his "religious" belief, but that he preferred to leave open the question of his belief in a Supreme Being rather than answer "yes" or "no." Jakobson asserted that he believed in a Supreme Being who was "Creator of Man," in the sense of being "ultimately responsible for the existence of" man, and who was the "Supreme Reality" of which "the existence of man is the result." Peter said the source of his conviction was "our democratic American culture, with its values derived from the Western religious and philosophical tradition." As to his belief in a Supreme Being, Peter added that he supposed "you could call that a belief in the Supreme Being or God. These just do not happen to be the words I use."[37]

In affirming the reversals by the Second Circuit Court of Appeals and in reversing the decision of that of the Ninth Circuit, the United States Supreme Court, while sidestepping constitutional questions, clearly broadened construction of the statutory provision quoted above. The

[35]50 App. U.S.C.A., §456 (j) (1951).

[36]*United States v. Seeger,* 380 U.S. 163 (1965). For a complete case study of *Seeger* (from start to conclusion), see Clyde E. Jacobs and John F. Gallagher, *The Selective Service Act: A Case Study of the Governmental Process* (New York: Dodd, Mead & Co., 1967), pp. 138–89.

[37]*United States v. Seeger, op. cit.,* at 165.

test of belief "in a relation to a Supreme Being," the Court held, is whether a sincere and meaningful belief which occupies in the life of its possessor a place *parallel* to that filled by the God of those admittedly qualifying for the exemption comes within the statutory definition. Applying this liberalizing test, the Court ruled that the beliefs expressed by the three men involved in the cases before it consequently entitled them to the exemption. Thus they created a new definition of the concept of religion under the Constitution, at least for pertinent statutory purposes. However, the Court, in a unanimous opinion written by its foremost religious layman, Justice Clark, added:

> We also pause to take note of what is not involved in this litigation. No party claims to be an atheist or attacks the statute on this ground. The question is not, therefore, one between theistic and atheistic beliefs. We do not deal with or intimate any decision on the situation in this case.[38]

Indeed, the Clark opinion and a concurring one by Justice Douglas read like a short course in theology, as *The New York Times* commented on the morning after.[39] The majority opinion quoted Paul Tillich, the Bishop of Woolwich, John A. T. Robinson, and the schema of the most recent Ecumenical Council at the Vatican to prove, as Clark put it, the "broad spectrum of religious beliefs found among us." These quotations, the opinion went on,

> demonstrate very clearly the diverse manners in which beliefs equally paramount in the lives of their possessors may be articulated. They further reveal the difficulties inherent in placing too narrow a construction on the provisions [of the particular sections of the Draft Act here at issue] and thereby lend conclusive support to the [broad] construction which we today find that Congress intended.[40]

Other than from Congress and the executive branch, there was astonishingly little criticism of this dramatic decision that recognized "a sincere and meaningful belief" as occupying a place "parallel to a belief in God." This abstemiousness differed markedly from the reac-

---

[38]*Ibid.,* at 173, 176.
[39]March 9, 1965, p. 43*l.*
[40]*United States v. Seeger, op. cit.,* at 183.

tion which had greeted (if that is the word!) the Court's memorable decision in the *New York Prayer* case[41] and the *Bible Reading* cases[42] a few years before. What the 1965 *Draft Act* cases proved conclusively is that there is less certainty in, and less emphasis on, a strictly construed traditional definition of religion. Instead, and without getting into the matter of distinctions between theistic and atheistic creeds and dogmas, a unanimous Supreme Court adopted broadened concepts of religious liberty and conscience by declaring that a conscientious objector need not believe in the orthodox concept of a Supreme Being. A "religious motivation," however vague or existential, was apparently still required, nonetheless.

On the other hand, neither the Administration nor Congress was happy with the *Seeger* decision, especially not the House of Representatives, where the powerful, hawkish L. Mendel Rivers (D.-S.C.), then the chairman of the House Armed Services Committee, was livid with rage and threatened immediate revenge. At first, he attempted to push through Congress a revised version of the 1951 C.O. provisions, which would have mandated the presence of a belief in an "organized" (and presumably "recognized") religion before an individual could qualify as "a *bona fide* C.O." When his move failed, he proposed a new version of the 1951 language, which became law in 1967. Rivers was aided by his Senate counterpart, Chairman John Stennis (D.-Miss.) as well as a general wave of resentment against eligible draftees because of the spate of draft-card burnings. The 1967 provision—coded as Section 6(j)—reads: *"Religious training and belief does not include essentially political, sociological or philosophical views, or a merely personal moral code."* A quick comparison with the 1951 language of the provision (cf. p. 236, *supra*) will show that the term "Supreme Being" was deleted from the 1967 draft law amendment, and with it the Supreme Court's generous interpretation of the term in the *Seeger* case. Or at least so Representative Rivers and his supporters thought. But it was a short-lived triumph. The warnings voiced by a sizable number of Mr. Rivers's colleagues, that Congress was about to create a troublesome constitutional *cul de sac*,[43] proved to be prophetic. In 1969 and 1970

[41]*Engel v. Vitale,* 370 U.S. 421 (1962).

[42]*Abington School District v. Schempp* and *Murray v. Curlett,* 374 U.S. 203 (1963).

[43]Fred P. Graham, "Again the Tough Issue of the C.O.," *The New York Times,* April 6, 1969, Sec. 4, p. 10.

three different United States District Courts ruled the new provision unconstitutional, on a veritable smorgasbord of grounds, as violative of the establishment clause of the First Amendment and of its free-exercise clause; of the due-process-of-law clause of the Fifth Amendment; even of the equal-protection-of-the-laws clause of the Fourteenth Amendment, which is not applicable to the federal government.[44] The lead case came from Judge Charles E. Wyzanski's tribunal in Boston: *United States v. Sisson,*[45] alluded to earlier, concerned the refusal of one John H. Sisson, a "selective" Vietnam war objector, to be inducted into the armed forces. The colorful trial judge ruled that Sisson could not "constitutionally be subjected to military orders which may require him to kill in the Vietnam conflict." A jury had found him duly guilty of refusing to submit to induction, but Judge Wyzanski sustained two of Sisson's contentions: (1) a "broad," primarily "free exercise" claim "that no statute can require combat service of a conscientious objector whose principles are either religious *or akin thereto*"; and (2) a "narrower" assertion concerning separation of Church and State, that "the 1967 draft act [section 6 (j)] invalidly discriminates in favor of certain types of religious objectors to the prejudice of *Sisson,*"[46] Heavily relying on the Clark opinion in *Seeger,* Wyzanski concluded:

> In short, in the draft act Congress unconstitutionally discriminated against atheists, agnostics, and men, like Sisson, who, whether they be religious or not, are motivated in their objection to the draft by profound moral beliefs which constitute central convictions of their beings.[47]

The Supreme Court, for technical and procedural reasons, would not then deal with the key *Sisson* issue on its merits, but it docketed two cases on the "selective" conscientious objection problem,[48] *and* it did come to grips with at least some of the aspects of the basic "religious" problem in its 1970 decision in the case of *Welsh v. United States.*[49]

---

[44]*United States v. Sisson,* 297 F. Supp. 902 (D. Mass. 1969); *Koster v. Sharp,* 303 F. Supp. 836 (E.D. Pa. 1969); and *United States v. McFadden,* 309 F. Supp. 502 N.D. Cal. 1970).

[45] See *United States v. Sisson, loc. cit.*

[46]*Ibid.,* at 906. (Italics supplied.)

[47]*Ibid.,* at 911.

[48]See pp. 241–43, *infra.*

[49]398 U.S. 333.

Elliott A. Welsh II, a twenty-eight-year-old Los Angeles com-
modities broker, had applied for draft exemption on C.O. grounds in
1964. In filling out the special form he took pains to cross out the words
"religious training"—partly to demonstrate that he was opposed to war
on broader historical, philosophical, and sociological grounds. His
application was denied all along the line for want of proof of a "religious basis" for his beliefs; he refused induction; and he was sentenced
to a three-year prison term. By a vote of 5 : 3, with Justice Black (a
captain in the Army in World War I) writing for four of the five justices
on the majority side, the Court reversed his conviction. Justice White (a
lieutenant commander in the Navy in World War II) dissented sharply,
joined by Chief Justice Burger and Justice Stewart (another naval officer in World War II). The Black opinion, which was joined by Justices
Douglas (a private in the Army in World War I), Brennan (an Army
colonel in World War II), and Marshall, was based on a broad and
generous construction of the *Seeger* rationale of five years earlier.
Welsh's conviction, wrote Black, was inconsistent with the *Seeger*
holding. He admitted that the draft law bars exemption based on
"essentially political, sociological or philosophical views, or a merely
personal moral code"—but he suggested that such views can readily be
held so firmly as to be "religious" within the meaning of the law.
According to Black's interpretation, then, the draft law actually
exempts "all those whose consciences, spurred by deeply held moral,
ethical or religious beliefs, *would give them no rest or peace* if they
allowed themselves to become a part of an instrument of war."[50] In
view of the explicit religious terminology in the crucial section 6(j) of
the statute, one might be pardoned for blinking a bit—and the three
dissenters did more than blink. "Saving #6(j) by extending it to include
Welsh cannot be done in the name of a presumed congressional will but
only by the Court's taking upon itself the power to make draft-exemp-
tion policy,"[51] wrote Justice White.

To the majority, however, the key element had become Welsh's
documented assertion that he believed "the taking of life—anyone's
life—to be morally wrong." Because he held this belief "with the

[50]*Ibid.*, at 344. (Italics supplied.) In 1973, with Justice Douglas and Stewart dissenting, the Court declined to consider applying the decision retroactively. (*Avery v. United
States*, 414 U.S. 922.)

[51]*Ibid.*, at 369.

strength of more traditional religious convictions," he was, in the considered judgment of the four members joining in the Court's majority opinion, entitled to exemption under the statute. Justice Harlan (an Air Force colonel during World War II) wrote his own concurrence, agreeing that Welsh was entitled to exemption, but for a dramatically different reason. In retrospect unhappy with the *Seeger* construction—although he had concurred in that decision, too—Harlan was even more unhappy with its expanded construction here. He now wanted to reach the constitutional question and, addressing it, urged that to deny Welsh an exemption *would show favoritism to religion* as opposed to non-religion, and thus violate the First Amendment's ban against governmental "establishment of religion."[52] This, of course, raises again the fascinating *quaere* of whether Congress could be *compelled* to grant C.O. exemptions under the "free exercise" (conscience?) clause of the First Amendment in the face of the Harlan assumption—one held by many others—that to do so would constitute a violation of its "establishment" clause. White, in his dissent, while acknowledging that Congress could not be *compelled* to grant exemption on religious grounds, contended that it certainly could legislate to recognize free exercise values—thus rejecting the Harlan posture on establishment. Given *that* dilemma, the Black solution may well be the most viable suggestion for a usable line, after all. Yet to apply that line equitably throughout the land presented a dilemma—as the Selective Service Director, Dr. Curtis Tarr, made clear, while valiantly attempting to issue guidelines to his 4,101 local draft boards.[53] There was much sympathy with his, and Congress's, unhappiness with the *Welsh* decision; but there was also much agreement with James Reston's poignant observation that, while recognizing the existence of what amounts to a "privileged sanctuary of conscience," there is

> something reassuring philosophically about the Supreme Court's support of
> ethical as distinguished from religious opposition to the war, something even

[52]*Ibid.*, at 357.

[53]The primary criterion for a C.O. henceforth, he told the boards, would be whether his beliefs were "sincere and deeply held," and not whether they were "comprehensible" to board members. A man must hold his "beliefs with the strength of traditional religious conviction," he wrote, and he must "demonstrate that his ethical or moral convictions were gained through training, study, contemplation or other activity, comparable in rigor and dedication to the processes by which traditional religious convictions are formulated." (*The New York Times,* July 6, 1970, p. 1*l.*)

exciting and ennobling about the American system that struggles with life's great imponderables.[54]

Those who were unhappy with *Welsh* would soon find themselves somewhat, if not totally, mollified, and those who were happy with *Welsh* would soon be somewhat, if not totally, disappointed in the face of the Court's momentous early 1971 decision in two cases that clearly raised the issue of "selective" conscientious objection. In other words, did the congressional, and judicially interpreted, provision for conscientious objection permit objection to only *some* wars, to "unjust" rather than "just" wars, to the Vietnam rather than some other past, present, or future wars? The Court responded "No!" without equivocation, in a joint 8 : 1 decision in *Gillette v. United States* and *Negre v. Larsen*.[55] Speaking for all members of the Court except the dissenting Justice Douglas, Justice Marshall held that Congress acted constitutionally when it ruled out "selective" conscientious objection by authorizing exemptions only for those men who were "conscientiously opposed to participation in war in *any* form," that the statutory provisions at issue did not unconstitutionally favor religious denominations that teach total pacifism and did not infringe upon the freedom of religion of those who believe that only "unjust" wars must be opposed. Declaring that the "affirmative purposes underlying §6(j) are neutral and secular"; that the rule against "selective" conscientious objection was "essentially neutral" in its treatment of various religious faiths—that there were ample "neutral, secular reasons to justify the line that Congress has drawn"—and that any "incidental burdens" felt by particular draftees were justified by "the Government's interest in procuring the manpower necessary for military purposes,"[56] Marshall thus rejected both the free exercise of religion and the separation of state and church claims lodged by the appellants. Douglas, on the other hand, saw a violation of both, especially of the former, and observed wistfully: "I had assumed that the welfare of a single human soul was the ultimate test of the vitality of the First Amendment."[57]

The government had readily conceded that Guy Porter Gillette and Louis A. Negre were sincere in their conscientious objection to the

[54]*Ibid.*, June 21, 1970, p. 16e.
[55]401 U.S. 437 (1971).
[56]*Ibid.*, at 462.
[57]*Ibid.*, at 469.

Vietnam war; but it insisted that they did not qualify for the C.O. exemption created by Congress because *they said that they did not oppose all wars.* Gillette, a rock musician, had told his draft board in Yonkers, New York, that his belief in the religion of humanism prevented him from serving in the military during the Vietnam war, which he considered unjust. The board denied him C.O. status because he frankly conceded that he would fight in defense of the United States or in a peace-keeping effort by the United Nations; he was convicted and given a two-year jail sentence for refusing to report for induction. Negre, a Bakersfield, California, gardener, a devout French-born Roman Catholic, who had studied the writings of St. Thomas Aquinas and other Catholic theologians who taught that "unjust" but not "just" wars should be opposed, had been drafted and had not reported for duty. However, when he was subsequently compelled to do so, he applied for a C.O. discharge; he was turned down, although the Army granted that his objections to the Vietnam conflict were indeed sincere. The lower courts concurred and Negre found himself transferred to Vietnam, where he began his quest for release.

Here, then—unlike the widespread protests that accompanied the successful draft-evasion-conviction-appeal by Cassius Clay, *alias* World Heavyweight Boxing Champion Muhammed Ali[58]—no one deemed questionable or "phony" the allegations or motivations of the two men involved, for they were obviously sincere in their opposition to the Vietnam conflict *per se.* But could they claim C.O. status under Section 6(j) of the Military Selective Service Act of 1967? In its firmly negative response, the eight-man majority dwelt at length on the government's assertions that its military capacity might be paralyzed if selective conscientious objection were recognized as a constitutional right. Justice Marshall pointed out that, among other touchy tasks connected with any such recognition, draft boards would be saddled with that of divining which draftees were sincere and which were having convenient attacks of selective conscience, inviting the very "real danger of erratic or even discriminatory decision-making in administrative practice."[59] Moreover, he opined, the nature of an unpopular war might change so that those who once considered it unjust would—or

[58]*Clay v. United States,* 403 U.S. 698 (1971). That opinion, rendered *per curiam* (probably authored by Justice Stewart), relied heavily on a procedural aberration by the Department of Justice in its prosecution.

[59]*Op. cit.,* at 462–63.

should—change their minds. It would be difficult to fault the logic of these basic contentions. Policy making by individual draftees would create a chaotic situation: the Court-defined C.O. line, which Congress reluctantly accepted but soon made the law of the land, seems to be the most generous and most liberal obtainable in the light of our democratic society's constitutional fundamentals.[60]

The Free Exercise of Religion

"Free exercise" brackets freedom of religious belief *and* freedom of religious action; it is linked closely with those other bastions of the First Amendment, freedom of speech, of the press, of assembly, and of petition. Indeed, any reading of the religion clause guarantee of the First Amendment that does not consider its dependence upon the other four guarantees spelled out in that provision of the Bill of Rights, and now carried over to the states via the Fourteenth Amendment, does a disservice to constitutional analysis and interpretation. The interrelationship is as real as it is significant.

A BASIC DILEMMA

The very language of the "free exercise" segment of the religion phrase poses a dilemma. It clearly militates against any governmental action "prohibiting the free exercise thereof." Unquestionably, the phrase is designed to mean what it says: Congress—and by interpretation the states—may not interfere with the sacred rights of freedom of religious "belief" and "exercise." Or, to put it somewhat differently, at a minimum the free exercise clause was intended to protect a wide range of religious observances from governmental interference. But as

[60]That line *has* other limits, of course. Thus, in an 8:1 opinion, written by Justice Brennan in 1976, the Court rejected free exercise and due process appeals by an "alternate service" C.O. seeking "G.I. Bill" educational benefits, despite congressional statutory exclusion therefrom. (*Johnson v. Robison*, 415 U.S. 361, with Douglas in lone dissent.) Nor, again 8:1—Douglas once more the only dissenter—can an employer withhold a lower rate from the income taxes due from C.O.s who object to supporting the defense budget. (*United States v. American Friends Service Committee*, 419 U.S. 7 [1974].) For a generally sympathetic analysis of selective conscientious objection, see Martin S. Sheffer, "The Free Exercise of Religion and Selective Conscientious Objection: A Judicial Response to a Moral Problem," 9 *Capital University Law Review* 6–29 (1979). For an even more supportive one, see Walter S. Griggs, Jr., "The Selective Conscientious Objector: A Vietnam Legacy," 21 *Journal of Church and State* 1 (Winter 1979).

Justice Roberts pointed out in his opinion for a unanimous Court in the 1940 *Cantwell* case, while "freedom of exercise" embraces both the freedom to *believe* and the freedom to *act,* "the first is absolute but, in the nature of things, the second cannot be. *Conduct* remains subject to [governmental] regulation for the protection of society. The freedom to act must have appropriate definition to preserve the enforcement of that protection."[61]

In every case, Roberts continued, "the power to regulate must be so exercised as not, in attaining a permissible end, unduly to infringe the protected freedom."[62] This, of course, raises as many *practical* questions as it settles. But the general line is at least perceivable in *Cantwell,* and it remains a landmark chiefly for three reasons: it embraces the dual aspects of "belief" and "action"; it reaffirms the absorption or incorporation of the freedom of religion guarantees into the Fourteenth Amendment; and it emphasizes the close link of the free exercise of religion with the other freedoms spelled out in the First Amendment.

The Jehovah's Witnesses. The *Cantwell* case was the first freedom of religion case involving the Jehovah's Witnesses to be decided by the United States Supreme Court. Actually, the initial litigation concerning that fundamentalist sect had come two years earlier, but it was decided in reference to the freedom of speech and press rather than those of the freedom of religion.[63] Not only have other so-called marginal religious groups increasingly proved victorious in free exercise claims, there has been a dramatic increase of late in the number of such cases filed.[64] The Jehovah's Witnesses have won over 90 percent of the host of significant First and Fourteenth Amendment cases which have come before the Court since the mid-1930s—their success due in considerable measure to the talents of their long-time chief legal counsel, Hayden C. Covington.[65] A dedicated sect of approximately 1,250,000 members

[61]*Cantwell v. Connecticut,* 310 U.S. 296 (1940), at 303. (Italics supplied.)

[62]*Ibid.,* at 304.

[63]*Lovell v. Griffin,* 303 U.S. 444 (1938). The next Jehovah's Witnesses case, also decided under the freedom of speech and press guarantees, was *Schneider v. Irvington, New Jersey,* 308 U.S. 137 (1939)—one year prior to *Cantwell,* which was thus the third Supreme Court case involving the Witnesses.

[64]From 56 cases in the decade ending in 1960 to 350 in that ending in 1980! See Frank Way and Barbara J. Burt, "The Free Exercise Clause and Marginal Religious Groups," paper prepared for delivery at the Western Political Science Association Meetings, San Diego, California, March 26, 1982.

[65]He was also Cassius Clay's (Muhammad Ali's) attorney in his aforementioned, eventually successful, battle to attain ministerial exemption as a Muslim. When apprised

throughout the world who believe that Armageddon is imminent, they base their creed on what they regard as utter obedience to the Bible. They accept the Biblical prophecy that Satan will be defeated in the cataclysm of Armageddon, followed by eternal life for the righteous. Their movement began in 1872, largely as the result of the efforts of Charles Taze Russell, a Pittsburgh merchant, who had become disenchanted with his Congregationalist Church. Russell began to preach the Adventist doctrine that the imminent second coming of Christ will trigger Armageddon, which he finally pegged at 1914. With a rapidly increasing following, Russell incorporated in 1884 the Watch Tower Bible and Tract Society, now generally known as the Jehovah's Witnesses ("Ye are my Witnesses, saith Jehovah," Isaiah 43:10). They deem Abel the first Witness, Christ the Chief Witness, and themselves direct descendants—3.5 million world-wide, 750,000 in the United States (1988)—from whose ranks Jehovah will select 144,000 members who will reign in heaven after Armageddon.

An impressively organized hierarchy with totalitarian overtones, the Witnesses—who shun all political activity, even voting—are fiercely evangelistic, and publicly so. Although inevitably polite, they persistently solicit and proselytize, push their two journals, *Awake!* and the *Watchtower,* and, if given permission, play their gramophone or tape recordings. To the Witnesses, the chief villains on earth are the leaders of organized religion in general, and the Roman Catholic Church in particular: the Witnesses' notorious gramophone record "Enemies" characterizes the Roman Catholic Church as "a great racket." It is no wonder, then, that they often find themselves in considerable litigation involving such matters as leaflet distribution, local and state censorship ordinances, parade permits, flag salutes, license taxes, conscientious objection to the draft (indeed, they insist that, as "ministers," they are *all* entitled to military deferments so that they may go about their primary task of proclaiming the impending Kingdom), public meetings, and blood transfusion requirements.[66] The *United States Reports* for the

---

of his 8 : 0 *per curiam* victory in the Supreme Court, Ali told reporters that he "thanked Allah." (*The Philadelphia Evening Bulletin,* June 28, 1971, p. 1.)

[66]See, *inter alia, Minersville, School District v. Gobitis,* 310 U.S. 596 (1940); *Cox v. New Hampshire,* 312 U.S. 569 (1941); *Martin v. Struthers,* 319 U.S. 141 (1943); *Jones v. Opelika,* 316 U.S. 584 (1942); *Prince v. Massachusetts,* 321 U.S. 158 (1944); *Marsh v. Alabama,* 326 U.S. 501 (1946); *Niemotko v. Maryland,* 340 U.S. 268 (1951); *Jehovah's Witnesses in the State of Washington v. King County Hospital,* 390 U.S. 598

past five decades list some fifty cases involving the Witnesses in one or more of the above problems. *Cantwell v. Conecticut*[67] was *not* one of the very few they lost.

Cantwell v. Connecticut. Newton Cantwell and his two teen-aged sons, Jesse and Russell, approached three pedestrians on Cassius Street in New Haven, an area whose inhabitants were 90 percent Roman Catholic, and asked their permission to play them a record on their portable phonograph. Obtaining that permission, the Cantwells put on "Enemies." One portion of the record stated in particular that the Roman Catholic Church was an instrument of Satan that had for fifteen hundred years brought untold sorrow and sufferings upon mankind by means of deception and fraud. The three listeners were, according to their own testimony, "rather tempted to strike the Cantwells," but confined themselves to an exhortation to "shut the damn thing off and get moving"—which the Cantwells did forthwith. No violence of any kind occurred, nor was it alleged. Nonetheless, the Cantwells were arrested, indicted, charged with, and convicted of two separate violations of Connecticut law.

One count of a five-count indictment charged them with soliciting funds and subscriptions for the Witnesses' cause without obtaining in advance—as required by a 1917 statute—a "certificate of approval" from the Secretary of the Connecticut Public Welfare Council, who was specifically empowered to determine, again in advance, whether the cause was either a "religious" one or one of a "*bona fide* object of charity." The second charge against the Cantwells was a breach of the peace, based on their stopping pedestrians on New Haven's public streets and asking them for permission to play the described phonograph record. The Cantwells appealed their convictions to the United States Supreme Court on both substantive and procedural grounds, alleging infringement of freedom of religion rights under both the First and Fourteenth Amendments on the first (substantive) count and violations of the Fourteenth Amendment alone on the second (procedural) ground. Agreeing, the Court reversed the convictions unanimously as constituting unconstitutional violations of the free exercise of religion, Justice

---

(1968); *Wooley v. Maynard*, 430 U.S. 705 (1977); *Palmer v. Board*, 444 U.S. 1026 (1980); and many others. The listing here is representative, not exhaustive.

[67]310 U.S. 296 (1940).

Roberts authoring the opinion. It provided the Court with the opportunity to comment upon and endeavor to explain the difficulties of drawing the line between freedom of religious belief and proscribable action in the realm of the free exercise of religion.

Roberts emphasized that there can be no doubt that a state has the right to guard against breaches of the peace and thus punish those who would incite, or be guilty of, such breaches—even as a result of religious motivations or considerations. Yet just because an individual, in his religious fervor, resorts to exaggeration and even vilification, thereby arousing public anger and ill will, does not *per se* render him liable to punishment unless there is a demonstrably clear and present danger to public peace. In the instance of the Cantwells there was no such danger or menace: no assault took place; there was no intentional discourtesy, no threatening bearing, no personal abuse—their arrest was patently unconstitutional. The Connecticut statute, which gave such broad prior censorship powers to an official of Connecticut's government, was held to constitute on its face an impermissible infraction of free exercise of religion guaranteed by the First Amendment, as absorbed by the Fourteenth. The Court ruled that for religious groups such as the Jehovah's Witnesses, Connecticut's requirement, as applied here, represented a "censorship of religion as a means of determining its right to survive"—a clear violation of the basic guarantee. Roberts took pains to acknowledge that nothing he had said for the Court was "intended even remotely to imply that, under the cloak of religion, persons may, with impunity, commit frauds upon the public." Endeavoring to establish a viable line, he observed that, certainly, penal laws are properly available to punish such proscribed conduct, and emphasized that even the exercise of religion may be at some slight inconvenience in order that the State may protect its citizens from injury:

> Without doubt a State may protect its citizens from fraudulent solicitation by requiring a stranger in the community, before permitting him to solicit funds for any purpose, to establish his identity and his authority for the cause which he purports to represent. The State is likewise free to regulate the time and manner of solicitation generally, in the interest of public safety, peace, comfort or convenience. But to condition the solicitation of aid for the perpetuation of religious views or systems upon a license, the grant of which rests in the exercise of a determination by state authority as to what is a

religious cause, is to lay a forbidden burden upon the exercise of liberty protected by the Constitution.[68]

The Cantwells had thus won an important victory not only for themselves but for the cause of religious liberty.

The Flag Salute Cases. But two weeks later, the next case to involve the Jehovah's Witnesses did not augur well in its decision for a continuing generous interpretation of the religious liberty clause. As a condition of attending the public schools of Minersville, Pennsylvania (population 10,000), *all* children were required to salute the national flag as part of a daily school exercise. Twelve-year-old Lillian Gobitis and her brother William, aged ten, children of Walter Gobitis, a member of the Jehovah's Witnesses, were expelled from the public schools for refusing to do so. To them, any compliance with such a requirement would have been tantamount to paying homage to a graven image—a mortal sin under the precepts of the Witnesses.[69] For a while Walter Gobitis bore the burden of sending them to private schools that did not mandate the flag salute. Unable to sustain that expense, however, and seeing three more of his children expelled from public school, Gobitis sued to enjoin the public authorities from continuing to exact participation of Lillian and William in the daily flag salute ceremony as a condition of their public school attendance. To his surprise and gratification, the United States District Court in Philadelphia granted his plea on the grounds that the expulsions violated the First, and through it the Fourteenth, Amendment's guarantees of religious liberty. Now it was the Minersville School District's turn to appeal, and it did so, first to the Circuit Court of Appeals, which sustained the District Court, and then

[68]*Ibid.*, at 306.

[69]The daily ceremony, in which all teachers as well as students participated, was a familiar one, with the following pledge recited in unison: "I pledge allegiance to my flag, and to the Republic for which it stands; one nation indivisible, with liberty and justice for all." While the words were spoken, teachers and pupils extended their right hands chest high in salute to the flag. In a letter to Superintendent of Schools Charles E. Rondabush, Lillian explained her three reasons for not saluting the flag: "1. The Lord clearly says in Exodus 20:3, 5 that you should have no gods besides Him and that we should serve Him. 2. The Constitution of [the] United States is based upon religious freedom. According to the dictates of my conscience, based on the Bible, I must give full allegiance to Jehovah God. 3. Jehovah my God and the Bible is my creed. I try my best to obey the Creator." William wrote a similar letter. (*Minersville School District v. Gobitis,* 310 U.S. 586 [1940], at 592.)

to the Supreme Court, which granted *certiorari*. The nation awaited its decision with considerable interest; both the Committee on the Bill of Rights of the American Bar Association and the American Civil Liberties Union had sought, and been granted, permission to enter the case in behalf of the Witnesses as *amici curiae*.

But to the astonishment of many—including some of those who consider themselves experts on the Court and its personnel—the Court *reversed* the judgment below and upheld the Minersville flag salute requirements by a resounding 8 : 1 vote.[70] Delivering the Court's opinion, Justice Frankfurter contended that religious liberty does not exempt citizens from obedience to general laws applicable to all and not designed to restrict religious beliefs as such. Explaining that "we live by symbols," Frankfurter—Vienna-born, who came to the United States at the age of twelve—exhorted the country that the "flag is the symbol of our national unity, transcending all internal differences, however large, within the framework of the Constitution."[71] He rejected the plea that the Gobitis children should be excused from "conduct required of all other children in the promotion of national cohesion," adding that "we are dealing with an interest inferior to none in the hierarchy of legal values. National unity is the basis of national security. . . ."[72] Frankfurter acknowledged that many might well doubt the effectiveness of the compulsory flag salute in the promotion of national unity and loyalty, but he insisted—characteristically for one so committed to the doctrine of judicial self-restraint—that, lest the Supreme Court become "the school board of the country," this was a decision to be made by the elected school officials against the backdrop of the basic "legislative judgment." He continued: "But to the legislature no less than to the courts is committed the guardianship of deeply-cherished liberties."[73] Joining the Frankfurter opinion were Chief Justice Hughes, Associate Justices McReynolds, Roberts, Reed, and—amazingly—Associate Justices Black, Douglas, and Murphy, whom prognosticators confidently expected to side with the sole dissenter, Justice Stone.

---

[70]*Minersville School District v. Gobitis*, 310 U.S. 586 (1940). The requirement was administrative, not legislative.

[71]*Ibid.*, at 596.

[72]*Ibid.*, at 595.

[73]*Ibid.*, at 598, 600.

Conceding that the personal liberty guarantees under the Constitution are by no means "always absolutes," and that "Government has a right to survive," Stone's dissent nonetheless bitterly assailed the majority's opinion as doing violence to "the very essence of liberty . . . the right of the individual to hold such opinions as he will and to give them reasonably free expression, and his freedom, and that of the state as well, to teach and persuade others by the communication of ideas."[74] He contended that the very essence of the liberty, which the freedom of the human mind and spirit and the freedom of reasonable opportunity to express them guarantee, is

> the freedom of the individual from compulsion as to what he shall think and what he shall say, at least where the compulsion is to bear false witness to his religion. If these guarantees are to have any meaning they must . . . be deemed to withhold from the state any authority to compel belief or the expression of it where that expression violates religious convictions, whatever may be the legislative view of the desirability of such compulsion.[75]

His noble spirit simply could not see how any inconveniences that might attend what he called "some sensible adjustment of school discipline" would present a problem "so momentous or pressing as to outweigh the freedom from compulsory violation of religious faith which has been thought worthy of constitutional protection."[76] He did not have to wait long, however, to see his reasoning become the majority opinion of the Court and thereby the law of the land.

To attain that constitutional turnabout, some crucial developments took place—all significant elements in the judicial process. One was the retirement of Chief Justice Hughes in 1941 and his replacement by Attorney-General Robert H. Jackson—although as an Associate Justice, President Roosevelt having seen fit to elevate Justice Stone to the Chief Justiceship. A closely related denouement was the resignation of Justice Byrnes late in 1942[77] and his replacement by the one-time dean of the University of Iowa School of Law, Wiley B. Rutledge. On paper, at least, the two new appointees could be expected to be more sym-

---

[74]*Ibid.*, at 604.
[75]*Ibid.*
[76]*bid.*, at 607.
[77]He had replaced Justice McReynolds, who had retired in 1941.

Table 6.1 *(Continued)*

DATE	CASE	VOTE	CONSTITUTIONAL ISSUES RAISED	DECISION AND COMMENTARY
1945	*In re Summers,* 325 U.S. 561.	5:4	Validity of Illinois's denial of admission to the bar of an otherwise qualified applicant who was a conscientious objector to war and who would therefore not serve in the state militia if called upon to do so under the state's constitutional provisions.	State's regulatory power upheld. Black, Douglas, Murphy and Rutledge dissented, contending unsuccessfully that a state has no right to "bar from a semi-public position, a well-qualified man of good character solely because" of his religious conviction.
1949	*State v. Bunn,* 336 U.S. 942.	No vote	Validity of North Carolina prohibition of handling of poisonous snakes in a "religious ceremony."	One of several such state laws upheld as valid exercise of police power via denial of writ of *certiorari*—most recently again in 1976. *(State ex rel. Swann v. Pack,* 424 U.S. 954.)
1951	*Breard v. City of Alexandria,* 341 U.S. 622.	7:2	Validity of ordinance banning the practice of summoning occupants of a residence to the door *without prior consent* for the purpose of soliciting orders for the sale of goods.	Upheld. Distinguished from other solicitation cases because of the presence of the commercial element here. Similarly, *Heffron v. Krishna Consciousness,* 452 U.S. 640 (1981), by involving state-fair soliciting.
1961	The Four Sunday Law cases; a. *McGowan v. Maryland,* 366 U.S. 420.	8:1	Validity of a series of so-called state Blue Laws, variously forbidding sales on Sundays. Challenges were brought on several grounds, including "due process of law," and "equal protection" of the laws, and the individual facts and circumstances of the cases varied. However-	Laws upheld. Discussed in detail in text below, pp. 319 ff.
	b. *Two Guys from Harrison-Allentown, Inc. v. McGinley,* 366 U.S. 582.	8:1		
	c. *Braunfeld v. Brown,* 366 U.S. 599.	7:2		
	d. *Gallagher v. Crown Kosher Market,* 366 U.S. 617.	6:3		

A Catalogue of Line Decisions. So manifold have been the Supreme Court's decisions concerning the free exercise of religion that it is impossible to detail them in the limited space available. But the tables below will at least serve to indicate a pattern—a pattern of demonstrable liberality on the part of the highest tribunal, a liberality based, in large measure, on the kind of basic convictions about individual freedom of conscience so well expressed by Justice Jackson in his *Barnette* opinion. Table 6.1 illustrates those instances in which the Court held *against* constitutional claims of freedom of religion and thus *in favor* of society's constitutional prerogative to promulgate and enforce the official statutes, ordinances, or practices involved. Table 6.2, in turn, demonstrates those instances in which the highest tribunal held in favor of the individual's contentions *versus* those of the state. Neither table is intended to be, nor could it be, exhaustive; rather, each will simply indicate the kind of values that America has embraced through the instrumentalities of the legislative and judicial processes.

THE DILEMMA COMPOUNDED

Before considering the far more intricate concept of the "establishment" of religion, its close relationship with the "free exercise" aspect may be demonstrated—following the tabular analysis—by pointing to at least one complex example,[96] namely, the Court's handling of the

---

[96]Space does not permit an examination of the tragic problem of drawing lines between the rights of parents and the right of the state, in *loco parentis,* when the parents' faith precludes or qualifies submittal to medical treatment. Since Christian Science practice, for example, *is* legal in every state of the Union such parents have the statutory right to determine the nature of the medical care, if any, their children who are minors are to receive. What, then, if a Christian Science child dies as a result of the parents' deliberate decision not to submit the child to orthodox medical treatment? For a pertinent illustration, see the case of *Commonwealth of Pennsylvania v. Cornelius, Philadelphia County (Pennsylvania)* Quarter Sessions, April Term, #105 (1956), which was *nolle prossed* at the request of the then district attorney, Victor H. Blanc. Numerous other examples could be readily cited, of course, involving particularly Jehovah's Witnesses and Seventh Day Adventists who have frequently refused—with varying degrees of success—to submit to such standard medical practices and/or legal requirements as blood transfusions or compulsory smallpox vaccinations. For a case involving the latter, see *Jacobson v. Massachusetts,* 197 U.S. 11 (1905). For one dealing with a Christian Scientist's successful refusal to take tranquilizers, see *Winter v. Miller,* 404 U.S. 985 (1971), *certiorari* denied. See also the fascinating case of *Karen Ann Quinlan,* in which the New Jersey Supreme Court ultimately ruled unanimously that the mechanical respirator that had kept her alive artificially for a year, could be disconnected if her father so decided, subject to medical and hospital concurrence. (*In the Matter of Karen Ann Quinlan,* decided March 31, 1976.) The United States Supreme Court denied review. (*Garger v. New Jersey,* 429 U.S.

Table 6.1

"Free Exercise" Cases Decided Against the Individual or Group

DATE	CASE	VOTE	CONSTITUTIONAL ISSUES RAISED	DECISION AND COMMENTARY
1878	Reynolds v. United States, 98 U.S. 145.	9:0	Validity of Congressional statute proscribing practice or advocacy of polygamy against claim of freedom of religious practice.	The first of the Mormon cases, holding religious beliefs not to justify polygamy.
1890	Davis v. Beason, 133 U.S. 333.	9:0	Validity of Idaho Territorial statute requiring an "oath abjuring bigamy or polygamy as a condition to vote."	Bigamy and polygamy regarded as crimes, not religious exercise. (Utah's subsequent ban of polygamy was again specifically upheld by the Court in 1984, in Potter v. Murray, 585 F. Supp. 1126.)
1890	The Late Corp. of the Church of Jesus Christ of Latter-Day Saints v. United States, 136 U.S. 1.	9:0	Validity of 1877 Congressional statute annulling charter of the Mormon Church and declaring all its property forfeited save for a small portion used exclusively for worship.	Law came as a result of the continued defiance of the Mormon Church regarding the practice of polygamy. Court saw no constitutional infirmities.
1929	United States v. Schwimmer, 279 U.S. 644.	6:3	Denial of naturalization application to 50-year-old Hungarian Quaker woman for refusing to pledge to "take up arms" on behalf of U.S.	First of the naturalization cases. Holmes, Brandeis, and Sanford dissented from the Butler opinion upholding denial, asserting "we are a Christian people . . . acknowledging with reverence the duty of obedience to the will of God." (At 625.) (Overruled in 1946.)
1931	United States v. Macintosh, 283 U.S. 605.	5:4	Denial of naturalization application to Canadian Baptist minister, a professor of theology and chaplain at Yale, for refusal to agree to defend U.S. by arms unless he were convinced of "moral justification."	Second of the naturalization denial cases. Hughes, Holmes, Brandeis, and Stone dissented from the Sutherland opinion. (Overruled in 1946.)
1934	Hamilton v. Regents of the University of California, 293 U.S. 245.	9:0	Refusal of Hamilton (and others) on grounds of conscience to take state-required courses in military science and tactics at state university.	Concurring opinion by Cardozo, joined by Brandeis and Stone, warned against carrying compulsion too far, but joined in Court's decision in favor of California.
1940	Minersville v. Gobitis, 310 U.S. 586.	8:1	Validity of compulsory flag salute contested by Jehovah's Witnesses.	Discussed in detail in text above, pp. 247 ff. (Overruled in 1943.)
1941	Cox v. New Hampshire, 312 U.S. 569.	9:0	Validity of N.H. statute requiring a permit to hold a procession or parade on a public street, but considering only time, manner, and place of the parade.	Jehovah's Witnesses failed to apply for a permit; engaged in a parade. Court upheld the "exercise of local control over the use of streets for parades and processions."
1942	Chaplinsky v. New Hampshire, 315 U.S. 568.	9:0	Validity of narrowly drawn N.H. law proscribing the "address [of] any offensive, derisive or annoying word to any other person who is lawfully in any street or other public place or call[ing] him by any offensive or derisive names."	Law upheld unanimously. A Jehovah's Witness called city marshal "God-damned racketeer" and "damned Fascist." Murphy wrote opinion. (See discussion in Ch. V, "The Precious Freedom of Expression," supra, pp. 210–13.)
1942	Jones v. Opelika [I], 316 U.S. 584.	5:4	Validity of Opelika ordinance imposing license taxes on bookselling—here by Jehovah's Witnesses.	Stone, Black, Douglas, and Murphy dissented from upholding of law. (Reversed in 1943.)
1944	Prince v. Massachusetts, 321 U.S. 158.	8:1	Validity of Mass. statute forbidding boys of under 12 and girls of under 18 to sell newspapers or periodicals on streets or in other publi...	Freedom of religious exercise here must give way to state's interest and righ...

Year	Case	Vote	Question/Issue	Decision
			ever, in all cases both the religious liberty *and* the establishment of religious claims were raised, particularly the former, in the attacks on the statutes' constitutionality.	
1967	*Garber v. Kansas*, 389 U.S. 51.	6:3	Alleged constitutional right of the Amish to refuse to send their children to *any* state-accredited schools.	*Per curiam* opinion upheld Kansas's requirement, because Amish may have own schools and own teachers—simple *accreditation* being the sole state requirement. Warren, Douglas, and Fortas dissented.
1971	*Gillette v. United States* and *Negre v. Larsen*, 401 U.S. 437.	8:1	Does the "free exercise" concept extend C.O. status to those whose opposition to war is confined to only "certain" or "just" wars rather than *all* wars?	Rejection of "selective" conscientious objection claim is discussed in detail in text above, pp. 293–95.
1974	*Johnson v. Robinson*, 415 U.S. 361 (1974).	8:1	Does the performance of "alternate" instead of regular military service entitle a "C.O." to educational benefits under the "G.I. Bill of Rights"?	With but Douglas dissenting, the Court, through Brennan, ruled that the statutorily authorized withholding of educational benefits to those who do not perform regular military service "involves only an incidental burden upon appellee's free exercise of religion—if indeed any burden exists at all."
1982	*United States v. Lee*, 455 U.S. 252.	8:0	Although Congress exempted *self-employed* Amish from paying Social Security taxes, must Amish *employers* pay them and Unemployment Compensation for their *employees* (even if they consider paying such taxes a sin).	Yes, for "the state may justify a limitation on religious liberty in cases [such as this] by showing that it is essential to accomplish an overriding governmental interest."

(*continued*)

Table 6.1 (Continued)

DATE	CASE	VOTE	CONSTITUTIONAL ISSUES RAISED	DECISION AND COMMENTARY
1983	Bob Jones University and Goldsboro Christian School v. United States, 461 U.S. 574.	8 : 1	Validity of the I.R.S.'s decision to withdraw tax-exempt status from educational institutions that discriminate racially on grounds of their religious dogma.	Upheld because of the government's "fundamental overriding interest in eradicating racial discrimination in education," an interest that "substantially outweighs whatever burden denial of tax benefits places on petitioners' exercise of their religious beliefs."
1985	Tony and Susan Alamo Foundation v. Secretary of Labor, 471 U.S. 290.	9 : 0	Does the First Amendment's free exercise component exempt an Arkansas-based religious group from complying with federal minimum wage laws?	"No," wrote Justice White, "it does not . . . unless, at a minimum, inclusion in the program actually burdens [the] freedom to exercise religious rights."
1986	Goldman v. Weinberger, 475 U.S. 503.	5 : 4	May an Orthodox Jewish rabbi and Air Force captain wear his yarmulke (skullcap) in the face of military dress codes to the contrary?	Notwithstanding petitioner's sincerely held religious beliefs, the military must be given a free hand to "foster instinctive obedience, unity, commitment, and esprit de corps," in Justice Rehnquist's majority opinion." (But note Congress's 1987 counteraction in effect reversing the Court.)
1986	Bowen v. Roy, 54 LW 4603.	8 : 1	May the Government use Social Security numbers for citizens in its administrative procedures even if it conflicts with their religious beliefs?	Chief Justice Burger held that the Constitution's protection of freedom of religion "does not afford an individual a right to dictate the conduct of the government's internal procedures." (White dissented.)

Table 6.2

"Free Exercise" Cases Decided in Favor of the Individual or Group

DATE	CASE	VOTE	CONSTITUTIONAL ISSUES RAISED	DECISION AND COMMENTARY
1892	*Church of the Holy Trinity v. United States*, 143 U.S. 226.	9:0	Can a Congressional statute prohibiting the importation of foreigners "under contract or agreement to perform labor in the United States" forbid, without violating "free exercise," of religion, a New York Church from contracting with an English clergyman to migrate to the U.S. and act as its rector and pastor?	Marshaling much evidence that "we are a religious people," the Court held that such a restrictive intent as claimed could not be validly imputed to the statute by the Government. Has overtones of Church-State "separationist" problem in addition to "free exercise."
1940	*Cantwell v. Connecticut*, 310 U.S. 296.	9:0	(a) Validity of Conn. statute requiring certificate from State Secretary of Welfare before soliciting funds, to let him determine whether the "cause is a religious one." (b) Cantwell's conviction for breach of the peace.	Both aspects discussed in body of text above. First case under the "freedom of religion guarantees" clause decided by Court to be applicable to states as well as federal government. Jehovah's Witness Cantwell won on both counts (a) and (b).
1943	*Jones v. Opelika [II]*, 319 U.S. 103.	5:4	Court's reconsideration of the *Jones v. Opelika* decision (see Table 6.1) of 1942, questioning validity of Opelika's ordinance imposing license tax on book-selling here by Jehovah's Witnesses.	Switch in favor of "J.W.s" was made possible largely by the new stance of Black, Douglas, and Murphy, the constancy of Stone, plus the replacement of the resigned Byrnes by Rutledge.
1943	*Murdock v. Commonwealth of Pennsylvania*, 319 U.S. 105. (See also *Follet v. McCormick*, 321 U.S. 573 [1944]).	5:4	Validity of statute requiring payment of a tax ranging from $1.50 to $20.00 a day for three weeks for the privilege of canvassing or soliciting orders for	Douglas opinion, joined by Stone, Black, Murphy, and Rutledge, held statute inapplicable to Witnesses, for "a person cannot be compelled to

(continued)

313

Table 6.2 (*Continued*)

DATE	CASE	VOTE	CONSTITUTIONAL ISSUES RAISED	DECISION AND COMMENTARY
			articles, as here applied to Jehovah's Witnesses.	purchase, through a license fee or a license tax, a privilege freely granted in the Constitution."
1943	*Martin v. Struthers*, 319 U.S. 141.	5:4	Validity of Struthers, Ohio, ordinance forbidding knocking on door or ringing of doorbell of a residence in order to deliver a handbill to occupant without his invitation.	Ordinance declared an unconstitutional abridgment of freedom of religion as applied to Jehovah's Witnesses who distribute their literature in this way.
1943	*Douglas v. City of Jeanette*, 319 U.S. 157.	9:0	Can public evangelism and proselytizing be stopped by police on Sundays, acting on numerous citizens' complaints?	Douglas's opinion held "no,"—that Jehovah's Witnesses had right to do so; that since these activities have the same claim to protection as the more orthodox and conventional exercises of religion. Angry Jackson concurrence exhorted community rights.
1943	*West Virginia State Board of Education v. Barnette*, 319 U.S. 624.	6:3	Validity of W. Va. compulsory flag salute—upheld in *Minersville* case (see above)—again contested on free exercise grounds.	Famed overruling of the *Minersville* decision. (Discussed in detail in body of text above, pp. 247 ff.)
1943	*Taylor v. Mississippi*, 319 U.S. 583.	6:3	Validity of Mississippi statute making it unlawful to urge people, on religious grounds, not to salute the flag.	If the Constitution bans enforcement of a regulation to salute the flag, it also prohibits the imposing of punishment for advising and urging, on religious grounds, that citizens refrain from saluting the flag.
1943	*Jamison v. Texas*, 318 U.S. 413.	8:0	Validity of Dallas ordinance prohibiting distribution of handbills in city streets.	A state may not prohibit distribution of handbills in city streets in the pursuit of a clearly religious activity merely

1944	*United States v. Ballard*, 322 U.S. 78.	5 : 4	May secular authority—in connection with alleged mail fraud—determine the truth of religious claims and beliefs, here the "I Am" movement?	because the handbills invite purchase of books or promote raising of funds for religious purposes. No matter how "preposterous" or "incredible" they may be, religious beliefs are not subject to findings of "truth" by fact-finding bodies. (Seriously fractured Court.)
1946	*Girouard v. United States*, 328 U.S. 61. (See also *Cohnstaedt v. Immigration and Naturalization Service*, 339 U.S. 901.	5 : 3	Re-examination of the *Schwimmer* and *Macintosh* question (see Table 6.1, *supra*) regarding denial of naturalization to conscientious objectors.	Court overruled its 1929 and 1931 decisions, adopting the then dissenting opinions of Justices Holmes and Hughes that religiously motivated refusal to bear arms does not manifest a lack of attachment to the U.S. Constitution.
1946	*Marsh v. Alabama*, 326 U.S. 501. (See also companion case of *Tucker v. Texas*, 326 U.S. 517 [1946]).	5 : 3	Validity of Alabama statute making it a crime to enter or remain on private premises—here the privately owned ship-building wharf of Chickasaw—after having been duly warned by the owner not to do so.	Distribution of religious literature by Jehovah's Witnesses cannot be banned even on the privately owned streets of a company town. First and Fourteenth Amendments guarantees apply here.
1951	*Niemotko v. Maryland*, 340 U.S. 268.	9 : 0	Validity of city of Havre de Grace ordinance allowing use of public parks for public meetings, including religious groups, by custom requiring an advance permit to be issued by City Council.	Denial of permit by City Council to Jehovah's Witnesses, evidently based on "unsatisfactory responses" to questions concerning their views of flag salutes, military service, Roman Catholicism, etc., held to be prior censorship, violative of First and Fourteenth Amendments.
1953	*Fowler v. Rhode Island*, 345 U.S. 67.	9 : 0	Application of Pawtucket public park meetings ordinance that, by in-	By treating the religious services of the Witnesses differently from those of

(continued)

Table 6.2 *(Continued)*

DATE	CASE	VOTE	CONSTITUTIONAL ISSUES RAISED	DECISION AND COMMENTARY
			terpretation, did not forbid church service in public parks to Catholics and Protestants, but did ban the Jehovah's Witnesses.	other faiths, Pawtucket had unconstitutionally abridged the religious freedom commands of the First and Fourteenth Amendments.
1961	*Torcaso v. Watkins,* 367 U.S. 488.	9:0	Validity of Maryland Constitution's provision of test oath of belief in the existence of God as prerequisite to holding public office.	Held a fatal invasion of freedom of belief and religion, violative of both the free exercise and establishment concepts. (See discussion *supra* in body of text, pp. 279–80.)
1963	*Sherbert v. Verner,* 374 U.S. 398.	7:2	Legality of South Carolina State's ruling that Seventh Day Adventist Sherbert's refusal to work on Saturdays (her Sabbath Day), a refusal for which she was discharged by her employers, did not constitute "good cause" under the law, and therefore did not entitle her to unemployment compensation benefit payments.	Despite its 1961 precedents in the *Blue Law Cases* (see Table 6.1 *supra* and discussion *infra,* pp. 319 ff.), the Court held that the denial of benefits to Sherbert constituted infringement of her constitutional rights under the First Amendment because her disqualification imposed a burden on the free exercise clause by forcing her to choose between adhering to her religious precepts and forfeiting benefits for abandoning these precepts and accepting employment. (See text, *infra,* pp. 322 ff.) But see *Thornton v. Caldor* (text, *infra,* p. 325) for a different interpretation, finding a *mandatory and absolute* statutory deference to a Sabbatarian an impermissible "establishment of

Year	Case	Vote	Question	Comment
1965	*United States v. Seeger, et al.*, 380 U.S. 163.	9:0	Validity of claim by Seeger and two others, alleging their exemptability under Draft Act provison governing conscientious objection "by reason of religious training and belief."	religion . . . by advancing a particular religious practice." Delicate question of meaning of "an individual's belief in a relation to a Supreme Being" interpreted broadly and liberally by unanimous Court. (See discussion *supra* in text, pp. 236 ff.)
1970	*Welsh v. United States*, 398 U.S. 333.	5:3	Does the Seeger decision and the Draft Act permit draft exemption as C.O. for purely moral and ethical reasons of conscience?	Broadening the "parallelism" of *Seeger* to extend to "strong beliefs about our domestic and foreign policy." (See text, *supra*, pp. 291–93.)
1971	*Winter v. Miller, et al.*, 404 U.S. 985.	9:0	May a Christian Scientist, involuntarily interred in a mental institution, be compelled to take tranquilizers in violation of her religion?	Court denied *certiorari* without comment. Court of Appeals below was divided, but upheld Ms. Miller's free exercise claim.
1972	*Wisconsin v. Yoder*, 406 U.S. 205.	6:1	May the Amish, given their well-established belief that education beyond the 8th grade teaches worldly values at odds with their religious creed, be thus compelled to attend school nonetheless?	In what was the first Supreme Court holding that ruled a religious group immune from compulsory attendance requirements, Chief Justice Burger found a violation of the Amish's free exercise of religion but made clear that this holding would *not* apply to "faddish new sects or communes."
1977	*Wooley v. Maynard*, 430 U.S. 705.	7:2	May N.H. require passenger automobiles to bear license plates with the motto "Live Free or Die" if contrary to J.W.'s religious creed?	Free exercise of religion (joined to freedom of expression), ruled the Chief Justice, includes "both the right to speak freely and the right to refrain from speaking at all." The N.H. law here compelled the J.W.s to be a

(*continued*)

Table 6.2 (*Continued*)

DATE	CASE	VOTE	CONSTITUTIONAL ISSUES RAISED	DECISION AND COMMENTARY
				"mobile billboard," objectionable to their beliefs. Rehnquist and Blackmun dissent.
1978	*McDaniel v. Paty*, 435 U.S. 618.	8 : 0	May Tennessee disqualify members of the clergy from being legislators or constitutional convention delegates?	A welter of opinions seemed to agree that the answer was clearly "no", but the reasoning saw both free exercise *and* separation of Church and State mandates for striking the statute down.
1979	*International Assn. of Machinists v. Anderson*, 440 U.S. 960.	7 : 2	Given the non-discrimination provisions of the Civil Rights Act of 1964, may a Seventh Day Adventist, on free exercise grounds, refuse to pay union dues?	With but Justices Brennan and White wishing to review the case, the Court upheld lower court's holding that, absent the union's ability to demonstrate "undue hardship," religious freedom had preference over payment of union dues.

1961 *Blue Laws Cases*[97] as seen against its decision, just two years later, in *Sherbert v. Verner*,[98] a case involving South Carolina unemployment compensation claims.

The Sunday Law Cases; Sherbert v. Verner and Beyond. The underlying principle of the manifold "Sunday" or "Blue Laws"—which still exist in several states in various forms and contain manifold inconsistencies and incongruities—is the right of a state, under its police power, to enact legislation providing for the Sunday closing of certain business enterprises, while permitting others to remain open. Undoubtedly there must be some logic to such intriguing provisions as those that—under the very same state laws—ban the sale of hosiery in hosiery shops on Sundays yet do not forbid it in drugstores; or those that permit the sale of "antiques" but not "reproductions"; or those that require candy stores to be closed but permit roadside candy counters to be open; or those that allow clam-digging but forbid oyster-dredging![99] Such logic, if any, is difficult to detect and certainly subject to some question. It was just such questioning and reasoning that brought a spate of Sunday law litigation to the bar of the Supreme Court in the 1960s. In addressing itself to the basic constitutional question, the Court combined four cases, some of them reaching it with diametrically opposed judgments from lower federal tribunals. Two of them[100] involved owners of highway discount department stores that were open for business seven days a week; the other two concerned smaller stores, owned and operated by Orthodox Jews who, given their religious convictions, closed their establishments on Saturdays but wanted them open on

---

922 [1976].) Similar actions followed elsewhere in the United States. Miss Quinlan lived for almost ten more years. Death, a friend, came at last on June 11, 1985. But other cases, e.g., those of Celia Cain and Rodney Poindexter, resulted in instantaneous death. (Duval County, Florida, December 4, 1976, and Los Angeles, California, October 8, 1980, respectively.) See my "Religion, Medicine, and the State," 22 *Journal of Church and State* 3 (1980).

[97]*McGowan v. Maryland,* 366 U.S. 420; *Two Guys from Harrison-Allentown, Inc. v. McGinley,* 366 U.S. 582; *Gallagher v. Crown Kosher Super Market of Massachusetts,* 366 U.S. 617; and *Braunfeld v. Brown,* 366 U.S. 599.

[98]374 U.S. 398 (1963).

[99]For an illuminating analysis of this—now declining—crazy-quilt pattern of exemptions and exceptions, see Richard Cohen, *Sunday in the Sixties* (New York: Public Affairs Committee, 1962).

[100]*McGowan v. Maryland* and *Two Guys from Harrison-Allentown, Inc. v. McGinley, op. cit.*

Sundays.[101] The four cases came from three different "Blue Law states," Maryland, Massachusetts, and Pennsylvania, and in all of them the constitutionality of the several statutes involved was under attack on the grounds that they infringed upon religious liberty in violation of the First Amendment; that they contravened the First's constitutional proscription against the establishment of religion; and that they constituted an unreasonable, arbitrary, and capricious classification, thus denying to the merchant involved the equal protection of the laws guaranteed under the Fourteenth Amendment.

Depending upon how one wishes to count or number opinions that are listed as "concurring and dissenting in part," at least eight and perhaps a dozen separate opinions were handed down in these four cases by an obviously uncomfortable and unhappy Court. It suffices to point to the fact that the prevailing opinion in each one of the four cases was written by Chief Justice Warren, whereas Justice Douglas dissented in each. The other justices ranged across an opinion spectrum that varied from 8 : 1 to 6 : 3. It is clear that the Court did not believe that a demonstrable case for the laws' unconstitutionality had been made; nor did it wish to strike down legislation that, to such a large degree, was based upon either legislative discretion or popular demand, legislation that not only varied widely in character and substance but that also was enforced only sporadically for the simple reason that so many consumers evidently did not wish it enforced—legislation that moreover, was in some cases at least based upon popular referenda.[102] Hence, although avowedly recognizing the "religious origin" of Sunday laws, the Chief Justice, in his four opinions, hit hard upon the general theme that, in effect, their religious purposes were no longer present; that the present-day purpose of a legislature in enacting such laws was to set aside a day not for religious observance but for "rest, relaxation, and family togetherness," with the motivation thus being "secular rather than religious"; that—with an eye toward the Orthodox Jewish merchants—although the freedom to hold religious beliefs and opinions is absolute, what was involved in the cases at issue was not freedom to hold religious beliefs or opinions *but freedom to act;* and that such freedom, even when

[101]*Gallagher v. Crown Kosher Super Market of Massachusetts* and *Braunfeld v. Brown, op. cit.*

[102]See the discussion by Murray S. Stedman, Jr., in his *Religion and Politics in America* (New York: Harcourt, Brace & World, 1964), especially pp. 71–74.

motivated by *bona fide* religious convictions, is not wholly free from legislative restrictions, duly enacted under the state police power. The Chief Justice indicated strongly that, although the Court would have wished that the states had passed so-called "Sabbatarian" laws designating Sunday as a day of rest while providing an exemption, or the choice of another day (as some states have done), it obviously could not compel the states to adopt such legislation in their sovereign discretion. Wisdom could not be the issue; constitutionality was—and it was deemed to have been met in view of what the Court regarded as the overridingly secular nature of the various laws. To Justice Douglas and his supporters in dissent, however, there was a patent violation of both the free exercise and the establishment clauses. Rejecting the majority's finding of predominating "temporal considerations," Douglas contended with feeling that when the laws are applied to Orthodox Jews or to "Sabbatarians," their absence of justice is accentuated. As he put it:

> If the Sunday laws are constitutional, Kosher markets are on a five-day week. Thus those laws put an economic penalty on those who observe Saturday rather than Sunday as the Sabbath. For the economic pressures on these minorities, created by the fact that our communities are predominantly Sunday-minded, there is no recourse. When, however, the State uses its coercive powers—here the criminal law—to compel minorities to observe a second Sabbath, not their own, the State undertakes to aid and "prefer one religion over another"—contrary to the command of the Constitution.[103]

Whatever the realities of the Sunday Closing Laws, and their degree of enforcement, there can be little doubt that, as Justice Stewart wrote in dissent in the pertinent Pennsylvania case,[104] the Orthodox Jew is forced into "a cruel choice . . . between his religious faith and his economic survival . . . a choice which . . . no State can constitutionally demand. . . . [T]his is not something that can be swept under the rug and forgotten in the interest of enforced Sunday togetherness."[105] To Justices Stewart, Brennan, and Douglas this was a gross violation of the constitutional right to the free exercise of religion. In a sense, Pennsylvania responded by enacting a "Sabbatarian" law in

[103]*McGowan v. Maryland,* 366 U.S. 420 (1961), dissenting opinion, at 577.
[104]*Braunfeld v. Brown,* 366 U.S. 599 (1961), dissenting opinion, at 616.
[105]*Ibid.,* at 616.

1967: it permits *bona fide* other-than-Sunday observers to remain open on Sunday, assuming they keep another Sabbath.

If the majority's reasoning in the *Sunday Closing Law* cases raised professional and lay eyebrows, they were *really* raised by the Court's opinion and decision in *Sherbert v. Verner*[106] two years later. As indicated in Table 6.2 above, this free exercise of religion case was brought by Mrs. Adell H. Sherbert, a member of the Seventh Day Adventist Church. For thirty-five years a loyal employee of the Spartan Mills, a textile mill in Spartanburg, South Carolina, she was on a five-day week when she formally joined the Church in 1957, thus enabling her to have her Sabbath on Saturdays, in accordance with the Church's precepts. In 1959 the firm changed the work week to six days for all three shifts that operated in the mill. When she refused to work on Saturdays, she was fired. Finding herself unable to obtain similar work because she would not labor on Saturdays, she filed a claim for unemployment compensation under the South Carolina Unemployment Compensation Act. But the State Employment Security Commission ruled that Mrs. Sherbert's restriction upon her availability for Saturday work disqualified her for benefits under the Act, which denies these to any insured workers who fail, "without good cause, to accept suitable work when offered by the employment office or the employer." The South Carolina Supreme Court sustained the Commission's finding 4 : 1, for in its judgment no restriction was placed upon Mrs. Sherbert's freedom of religion, since she remained free to observe her religious beliefs in accordance with the dictates of her conscience.

In language that could have been applied in the *Sunday Closing Law* cases to obtain results *opposite* from those reached here, the majority of seven, speaking through Justice Brennan—who had been unhappy about at least two of the *Sunday Closing Law* cases[107]—now *reversed* the South Carolina authorities. It did so on the grounds that the denial of benefits to Mrs. Sherbert constituted a clear infringement of, and burden upon, her constitutional rights of free exercise of religion under the First Amendment:

> *The ruling forces her to choose between following the precepts of her religion and forfeiting benefits, on the one hand, and abandoning one of the*

[106]374 U.S. 398 (1963).
[107]*Braunfeld v. Brown*, 366 U.S. 599, and *Gallagher v. Crown Kosher Market of Massachusetts*, 366 U.S. 617 (1961).

precepts of her religion in order to accept work, on the other hand. Government imposition of such a choice puts the same kind of burden upon the free exercise of religion as would a fine imposed against appellant for her Saturday worship.[108]

Justice Stewart wrote a separate concurring opinion, and Justice Harlan dissented in an opinion joined by his colleague White.

The disappointed owners of the Braunfeld and Crown stores had much cause to wonder why the Brennan language—particularly the portions italicized here—did not also fit *their* cases. Yet although Justices Stewart, Harlan, and White did indeed believe that the *Sherbert* decision had the effect of overruling the *Braunfeld* and *Crown* judgments, Brennan's majority opinion *distinguished* the former on the ground that the same practical difficulties and considerations arising from the granting of exemptions in Sunday Closing Laws did not apply and were not present in the South Carolina unemployment insurance problem. It is quite obvious that what the Court did here was to try to draw a line: to balance considerations of public policy against infringement on religious liberty. In the 1961 *Sunday Closing Law* cases the Court was *not* willing to make exemptions in laws of general application on grounds of claims of religious liberty *versus* economic hardship—in the 1963 *Sherbert* case it was. And this distinction was emphatically not due to changes in personnel, since Justices White and Goldberg, the successors to retired Justices Whittaker and Frankfurter, did not numerically or substantively affect the different results in the latter decision. Although the facts in the settings of the two cases differed, the difference was surely one of rationalization rather than of substance. The conclusion is inevitable that the distinction made in the *Sherbert* case is neither very logical nor very convincing.[109] The distinction advanced by Brennan that in the applicable *Blue Law* cases there was a "less direct burden upon religious practices" is highly questionable—or, as Justice Stewart put it in his concurring opinion, in which he strongly criticized the Brennan rationale, "[W]ith all respect, I think the Court is mistaken, simply as a matter of fact."[110] If anything, the secular pur-

[108]*Sherbert v. Verner, op. cit.,* at 404. (Italics supplied.)

[109]See the interesting analysis of this general problem in Paul G. Kauper, *Religion and the Constitution* (Baton Rouge: Louisiana State University Press, 1964), Chapter 2, "Religious Liberty: Some Basic Considerations."

[110]*Sherbert v. Verner, op. cit.,* at 477.

pose of the South Carolina statute was clearer than that of Pennsylvania's and Massachusetts's. The line the Court endeavored to establish here is simply not viable as a basic rule of law.[111] The Court's 1970 denial of *certiorari* in the case of a California Seventh Day Adventist construction worker, who unsuccessfully attempted to invoke *Sherbert* below, may represent some second thoughts—although the facts were rather different and his case did not involve similar hardship.[112] A 1981 case, however, relied on *Sherbert,* as did one in 1987, both by 8 : 1 votes in favor of the claimant.[113]

In a sense, the Court was given "a hand" by virtue of a provision of the Title VI of the Civil Rights Act of 1964, as amended, that—since the mid-1970s—requires employers "to make reasonable accommodations to the religious needs of employees [where] such accommodation can be made without undue hardship on the conduct of the employer's business." In the face of that provision's obvious judgmental flexibility, a 7 : 2 majority thus found in 1977 that Larry S. Hardison, a clerk at a large TWA maintenance base who had joined the Worldwide Church of God—a sect that proscribed work on Saturday—had not been deprived of his free exercise of religion since TWA had made every good faith effort to accommodate him. Hardison did not have enough seniority to select a non-Sabbath shift as a matter of right under the union agreement, and the union steward, at TWA's urging, had tried, but failed, to find someone who would exchange shifts.[114] That the

---

[111]For an interesting, perceptive analysis of the *Sherbert* decision, see Warren L. Johns, "The Rights to Rest," 66 *Liberty* 1 (January–February 1971), pp. 7 ff. See also his *Dateline Sunday, U.S.A.* (Mountain View, Calif.: Pacific Press Publishing Association, 1967).

[112]*Stimpel v. California State Personnel Board,* 400 U.S. 952 (1970). A somewhat related subject matter was addressed by the Court in 1972 to the same result when it declined to review a lower-court decision that required a member of the Seventh Day Adventist Church to join a union, despite his religious belief in freedom of choice, since he was employed in a plant with a duly adopted union shop contract. (*Hammond v. United Papermakers,* 409 U.S. 1028.)

[113]*Thomas v. Indiana Employment Security Review Board,* 450 U.S. 707 (1981), and *Hobbie v. Unemployment Appeals Commission,* 55 LW 4208 (1987).

[114]*Trans World Airlines, Inc. v. Hardison,* 432 U.S. 63. The dissenters were Justices Marshall and Brennan, who joined in an opinion by the former that was described by Justice White's majority opinion as including "hyperbole and rhetoric." Intriguingly, the provision at issue had been declared unconstitutional in 1977 by United States District Court Judge Manuel Real as a violation of the First Amendment's guarantee of separation of Church and State, (*Yott v. North American Rockwell Corporation,* 428 F. Supp. 763.) But the United States Court of Appeals for the Ninth Circuit reversed Judge Real in 1979. (*Ibid.,* 602 F. 2d 904.)

1964 provision's elasticity will afford considerable leeway was demonstrated in 1985, when the Court declared unconstitutional 8 : 1 a Connecticut law that had mandated an *absolute* right for employees *not* to work on their chosen Sabbath.[115]

Yet if the results in *Sherbert* and some of its offspring signify a more generous interpretation of the "free exercise" phrase, it may be welcomed in the light of the fundamental question of whether more harm is done to the democratic process by permitting an eccentricity of personal code or behavior, so long as no valid law is broken, than by trampling upon the non-conformist in the interest of the power of majoritarianism.[116] Because lines must be drawn along the way, and the drawing usually seems to fall to the Court, it is not surprising, then, that it would be guided on occasion, as it evidently was there, by certain judgments based on considerations of realistic subjectivity that inevitably characterize the political process. After all, the Supreme Court of the United States is a body at once legal, governmental, and political. With this thought we now turn to the Pandora's box of "establishment."

"Establishment": The Separation of Church and State

If the clause "Congress shall make no law respecting an establishment of religion" is commanding in tone and clear in syntax, it is utterly unclear in its intention. What does it mean? What does it forbid? References to history only intensify the riddle. And because the "establishment" and "free exercise" clauses are closely related, the complexities of establishment simply cannot be understood if they are treated or considered in isolation from the central problem of religious liberty itself.

A GLANCE AT HISTORY

Among America's revolutionary and post-revolutionary leaders, the persons who were initially responsible for the concept of non-establish-

---

[115]*Thornton v. Caldor,* 53 LW 4853.

[116]But, needless to say, there are limits: thus, in 1973 the Supreme Court dismissed the appeal of defendants in a marijuana case who contended that the use of the drug was part of their religious beliefs, protected by the free exercise clause. (*Gaskin v. Tennessee,* 414 U.S. 886). Dr. Timothy Leary, the stormy petrel of the 1960s and 1970s, had unsuccessfully endeavored to peddle a similar argument earlier. (*Leary v. United States,* 383 F. 2d 851 [1967].) See my "The Status of the First Amendment's Religion Clauses: Some Reflections on Lines and Limits," *Church and State* (Spring 1980).

ment and its incorporation into the Bill of Rights were Thomas Jefferson, James Madison, George Mason, Patrick Henry (on a somewhat different plane), and the Reverends Samuel Davies and John Leland.[117] Virginians all, they led and fought the good fight in the struggle that took place during Virginia's last days as a colony and early days as a state, a struggle similar to that which had taken place almost a century and a half earlier in Rhode Island and neighboring areas under Roger Williams. Williams, who has been appropriately called "the most advanced and effective advocate of religious freedom in colonial times,"[118] and his supporters fought less on the specific matter of "establishment" than on the general one of "freedom." Hence it is the Virginians who must receive chief credit for the notion and coinage of American theories of the separation of Church and State. Their influence was decisive, and their debates and writings on establishment are indeed still valuable sources of reference, even though they can be differently interpreted. A matter on which there is agreement, however, is that they strived, above all, for separation of Church and State in the sense that there should not be an Established Church—as the Episcopal (Anglican) Church was in Virginia at the time—and that there should never be "the preferred position of a favored Church." To achieve those minimum aims, Jefferson, Madison, Mason, and their allies struggled for more than a decade until they succeeded in bringing about the "disestablishment" of the Episcopal Church as the State Church of Virginia. This they accomplished with the enactment, after a nine-year battle, of Mr. Jefferson's great Bill for Establishing Religious Freedom on December 15, 1785, by a 74:20 vote of the House of Delegates.[119] It became law on January 19, 1786. The effect of this legislation—hereafter commonly referred to as the Disestablishment Bill—was far-reaching: Virginia's victory over establishment decisively influenced

[117]Of course, others who labored long before the Virginians (such as Roger Williams and the Reverend John Clarke) carved their niche in the history of religious liberty, but at a different moment in history, under different circumstances, and with different impact.

[118]Stokes and Pfeffer, *op. cit.,* p. 65.

[119]Its heart read: "Be it enacted by the General Assembly that no man shall be compelled to frequent or support any religious worship, place or ministry, whatsoever, nor shall be enforced, restrained, molested, or burthened in his body or goods, nor shall otherwise suffer on account of his religious opinions or belief; but that all men shall be free to profess, and by argument to maintain, their opinions in matters of religion, and that the same shall in no wise diminish, enlarge, or affect their civil capacities."

not only the ultimate course of action of her sister states but also that of the federal government. No wonder that Jefferson requested notation of his role in the epic struggle for religious freedom on his tombstone at Monticello, along with the other two achievements he considered of greater significance than his eight-year Presidency.[120]

Moreover, Madison's widely circulated and highly influential "Memorial and Remonstrance" of 1784–85, against the proposal of Virginia's House of Delegates to provide, through assessments, for teachers of the Christian religion, is as classic a statement as may be found in support of the separation of Church and State. Supported by Jefferson, the eloquent and lengthy fifteen-point document—the center-piece of Madison's works on the separation of Church and State— argued persuasively that the State as the secular authority must have jurisdiction over *temporal* matters; that such authority does not extend over *spiritual* matters, which lie in the domain of private belief and the churches (note: "churches," not "Church"). He warned persuasively that once they look to government for the achievement of their various purposes, the churches invite the sacrifice of their spiritual indepen-dence; and that when government enters upon the religious scene, it, in turn, enters into competition with the churches in seeking favors— thereby incurring the risk of ecclesiastical domination, with the atten-dant dangers of coercion of belief and persecution of dissenters.

Thus, to Jefferson and Madison, "children of the Enlightenment [who] represented the secular and humanistic view that supported reli-gious liberty and the separation of church and state,"[121] the principle of separation was absolutely indispensable to the basic freedoms of belief, conscience, and dissent. They were in no sense hostile to religion—far from it; they simply regarded it as an entirely private matter. Over-ridingly determined to keep religion out of the domain of public af-fairs,[122] they were as much concerned with freedom *from* religion as with

---

[120]"And not a word more" were his instructions for the epitaph he composed: "Here was buried Thomas Jefferson. . . ." First he listed his authorship of the Declaration of Independence, next that of the "Statute of Virginia for Religious Freedom," next "Father of the University of Virginia."

[121]Paul G. Kauper, *op. cit.*, p. 48.

[122]As President, Madison successfully vetoed a congressional "Act incorporating the Protestant Episcopal Church in the town of Alexandria, the District of Columbia." (February 21, 1811.) See 22 *Annals of Congress* 982–83.

freedom *of* religion—a concern still reflected in Virginia's Constitution today (the 1971 revision retaining it in full).[123]

Difficulties of Historical Application to Contemporary Problems. Following the obvious intent of Jefferson and Madison, it is clear that there can be neither an *official* Church nor even an especially *favored* Church in the United States or in any of its constituent subdivisions. Or, to put it somewhat differently, at a minimum the Establishment Clause prohibited the national government *both* from founding or perpetuating a state religion *and* from favoring any one religion or religions. What is far less clear, however, is the matter of state *aid* to religious activities, and state *cooperation.* If government treats *all* religions with an equal eye and an even hand, may it not, wholly in conformity with the Jefferson-Madison injunction, aid in furthering the spiritual development of Americans, whom the Supreme Court has repeatedly styled "a religious people"?[124] Is the government, in the words of an experienced student of philosophy and politics, "furthering a legitimate purpose when it acts to encourage, support, or aid the institutions of religious life," or is it "precisely the point of the 'no establishment' clause that it precludes government action to this end"?[125] How authoritative and decisive can the intent of men who wrote and lived almost two centuries ago be regarded when applied to the current scene (though we do know that Madison, for one, opposed tax exemption for churches, and even publicly opposed chaplaincies other than military ones)? The principle of "separation" *is* demonstrably present in both the spirit and the letter of the Constitution. Once again, then, we are faced with the line-drawing problem; once again we must look to the Court, even if its role has evolved as much by default as by affirmation.

A Solution That Is No Solution. Striving for a solution, the Court seized upon Jefferson's concept of the "wall of separation between Church and State," which he expressed in a letter to the Danbury Baptist Association in 1802. The idea that the clause against establish-

[123]The tough prohibitory language of its Bill of Rights bars "any appropriation of public funds, or personal property, or any real estate to any church, or sectarian society, association, or institution of *any kind whatever,* which is *entirely or partly, directly or indirectly,* controlled by any church or sectarian society." (Italics supplied.) (Article I, Section 16.)

[124]E.g., Justice Douglas's majority opinion in *Zorach v. Clauson,* 343 U.S. 306 (1952), at 313.

[125]Joseph Tussman, *The Supreme Court on Church and State* (New York: Oxford University Press, 1962), p. xv.

ment of religion by law was intended to erect "a wall of separation between Church and State" was initially expounded in the *First Mormon Polygamy* case[126] in 1879 by Chief Justice Waite, who wrote for a unanimous Court. The "wall of separation" clause reappeared in a far more significant, highly contentious, opinion by Justice Black for a 5 : 4 Court in the *New Jersey Bus* case[127] in 1947, when the narrow majority found that "wall" had *not* been breached by granting state subventions of $354.74 for bus fares to parents of twenty-one children in Ewing Township's four non-public, if non-profit (which here meant Roman Catholic), parochial schools as well as to public school children. As we shall have occasion to note again, Black reaffirmed the "wall" principle but ruled that it had *not* been breached here. His colleague Frankfurter, however, was not so sure and saw the "wall" "not as a fine line easily overstepped"; Justice Jackson quipped that that "wall" may become as winding as Jefferson's celebrated "serpentine wall" of single bricks on the grounds of his beloved University of Virginia at Charlottesville; and Justice Reed objected to drawing a rule of law from what he viewed as "a figure of speech." Fifteen years later, Reed's point was echoed by Robert M. Hutchins: "The wall has done what walls usually do: it has obscured the view. It has lent simplistic air to the discussion of a very complicated matter. Hence it has caused confusion wherever it has been invoked. . . . The wall has been offered as a reason. It is not a reason: it is a figure of speech."[128] And, to compound the basic problem for generations yet unborn, one of the five "wall" upholders in that *New Jersey Bus* case, Justice Douglas, seized upon the opportunity of the *New York Bible* case[129] to announce from

[126]*Reynolds v. United States*, 98 U.S. 145 (1879), at 164. Actually, that case rested essentially on the "free exercise" question.

[127]*Everson v. Board of Education of Ewing Township*, 330 U.S. 1 (1947). The case was brought as a taxpayer's suit by Arch R. Everson, executive vice-president of the New Jersey Taxpayers' Association, an economy-in-government group. The litigation was in fact sponsored and paid for by the Junior Order of United American Mechanics, a Protestant fraternal organization active in New Jersey. (Letter to me from Professor Daryl R. Fair of Trenton State College, December 13, 1974. Professor Fair has authored a fascinating background study of the statute and the several court cases involved. *"Everson v. Board of Education:* A Case Study of the Judicial Process," delivered as an address to the 1975 Meeting of the New Jersey Political Science Association, held at Rider College, Trenton, N.J., April 12, 1975.)

[128]*Christian Century,* December 4, 1963, p. 1512. See also "The Future of the Wall," in Dallin Oaks (ed.), *The Wall Between Church and State* (Chicago: University of Chicago Press, 1963), p. 19.

[129]*Engel v. Vitale*, 370 U.S. 421 (1962), at 443.

the bench that he *now* (1962) believed the *Bus* case to have been wrongly decided by him and his four colleagues who then (1947) constituted the majority.[130]

Obviously, then, that famous "wall of separation" seems to be made of different stuff and be of rather different height depending on its viewers, be they Supreme Court justices, other jurists, or subjective or objective commentators, lay or professional. As Harold Hammett put it intriguingly in his "The Homogenized Wall," for the wall to function properly "one must not be able to climb over, dig under, break through or sneak around to the other side."[131] Accordingly, he suggested not one wall between Church and State but two: with Church on one side, State on the other, and joint functions permitted by the First Amendment in the middle. Justice Black had firmly insisted that in the instance of the New Jersey bus subsidies to children attending the Township's non-profit parochial schools, the "wall" stood high and unbreached:

> The "establishment of religion" clause of the First Amendment means at least this: Neither a state nor the Federal Government can set up a church. Neither can pass laws which aid one religion, aid all religions, or prefer one religion over another. Neither can force or influence a person to go or remain away from church against his will or force him to profess a belief or disbelief in any religion. No person can be punished for entertaining or professing religious beliefs or disbeliefs, for church attendance or nonattendance. No tax in any amount, large or small, can be levied to support any religious activities or institutions, whatever they may be called, or whatever form they may adopt to teach or practice religion. Neither a state nor the Federal Government can, openly or secretly, participate in the affairs of any religious organizations or groups and vice versa. In the words of Jefferson, the clause against establishment of religion by law was intended to erect a "wall of separation between Church and State."[132]

In the light of the above manifesto, Black's concluding passage in his opinion must have come as a bit of a surprise to some of his readers as well as some of his colleagues: "The First Amendment has erected a

[130]Writing in 1967, Professor William A. Carroll, in a lengthy article, called the *Everson* definition "untenable . . . a sham" and urged that it be discarded for the sake of "ordered coherence." (See "The Constitution, the Supreme Court, and Religion," 51 *American Political Science Review* 663 [September 1967].)

[131]53 *American Bar Association Journal* 929 (October 1967).

[132]*Everson v. Board of Education of Ewing Township, op. cit.,* at 15–16.

wall between church and state. The wall must be kept high and impregnable. *We could not approve the slightest breach. New Jersey has not breached it here.*"[133] Had it not? In a lengthy, troubled dissent (in which his colleagues Frankfurter, Jackson, and Burton joined), and to which he appended Madison's "Memorial and Remonstrance Against Religious Assessment,"[134] Justice Rutledge found, on the contrary, that the "wall" *had* been breached, flagrantly and inexcusably. According to Justice Murphy's notes, Rutledge had already stated bluntly in the Justices' Conference on the case: "First it has been books, now buses, next churches and teachers. Every religious institution in [the] country will be reaching into [the] hopper for help if you sustain this. We ought to stop this thing at [the] threshold of [the] public school."[135] Now, writing his dissenting opinion, and rejecting the majority's so-called child benefit and/or public purpose theory—namely, that New Jersey's subsidy was meant for, and went to, the *child* rather than to the Church—Rutledge warned the majority that separation must be strictly construed. It is only by rigidly observing the prohibition against establishment, he contended, that

> the state can maintain its neutrality and avoid partisanship in the dissensions inevitable when sect opposes sect over demands for public moneys to further religious education, teaching or training in any form or degree, *directly or indirectly.*[136]

And in response to the many who have argued long and persistently that such aid would be no more than simple equity to atone for the fact that people whose children go to non-public schools must pay public taxes and often tuition too, Rutledge observed:

> Like St. Paul's freedom, religious liberty with a great price must be bought. And for those who exercise it most fully, by insisting upon religious educa-

[133]*Ibid.*, at 16. (Italics supplied.) The Court thus *affirmed* the judgment of the tribunal whence the case had come, the New Jersey Court of Errors and Appeals, which in turn had reversed a lower New Jersey court.

[134]Rutledge called it "at once the most concise and the most accurate statement of the views of the First Amendment's author concerning what is an 'establishment of Religion.'" (At 37.)

[135]Murphy Papers (located at the Michigan Historical Collections, University of Michigan, Ann Arbor), Docket Notes and Conference Notes, No. 52, Box 138. See also J. Woodford Howard, Jr.'s illuminating biography of Murphy, *Mr. Justice Murphy: A Political Biography* (Princeton: Princeton University Press, 1968), p. 448.

[136]*Everson v. Board of Education of Ewing Township, op. cit.*, at 59. (Italics supplied.)

tion for their children mixed with secular, *by the terms of our Constitution the price is greater than for others.*[137]

In another well-known dissent, Justice Jackson argued—quite plausibly—that the Black opinion was inconsistent with the Black decision, and that he (Jackson) was reminded of "Julia who, according to Byron's reports, whispering, 'I will ne'er consent,' consented."[138] And, referring to the Rutledge warnings, Jackson noted that "Catholic education is the rock on which the whole structure [of the Church] rests."[139] The divergent views of such devotees to the Constitution and the basic freedoms of mankind as Justices Black and Douglas and Rutledge and Jackson are proof positive that the doctrine of the "wall" is no solution *per se.*[140] It fails because the necessary line depends overridingly on public policy considerations—and on the interests of contending groups[141]—even if one believes, with Senator Sam J. Ervin (D.-N.C.), "in a wall between Church and State so high that no one can climb over it."[142]

SOME PRINCIPAL THEORIES OF SEPARATION

Since the "wall" approach is hardly definitive, let us analyze those principal theories of separation that have made themselves felt in the interpretation of the First Amendment. Again, in considering them we ought to keep in mind that a strict segregation between the "establishment" and "exercise" clauses of the First Amendment is not only an oversimplification, but misleading and a disservice to the discussion of the basic problem. A close reading of the major Supreme Court opinions specifically governing the issue of "establishment" or separation of Church and State,[143] rather than the specific issue of "free exer-

[137]*Ibid.* (Italics supplied.)

[138]*Ibid.*, at 19.

[139]*Ibid.*, at 24.

[140]For some interesting data concerning the justices' maneuverings and misgivings on *Everson,* see J. Woodford Howard, Jr., "On the Fluidity of Judicial Choice," 52 *American Political Science Review* 43 (March 1968).

[141]Withal, *Everson* continues to be reaffirmed, e.g., in late 1971 the Court refused to disturb a New Jersey law providing for free school transport for many private and parochial school students. (*West Morris Regional Board of Education v. Sills,* 404 U.S. 986.)

[142]As quoted in *Time* magazine, March 8, 1971, p. 30.

[143]These major opinions are indicated in Tables 6.3 and 6.4, *infra.* Probably the most significant ones for our present purposes are the *Everson, Zorach, Allen, Walz,*

cise''—assuming that dichotomy can ever be thus clearly delimited—presents three more or less identifiable Court theories[144]—depending upon one's count. (One can find more.)

1. *The Strict Separation or "No Aid" Theory.* Presumably incorporating the "wall" approach to the problem, this theory holds that there must be a strict separation of Church and State, and that government may not constitutionally provide support to religion or religious interests. The theory was demonstrably applied in the "released time" case of *McCollum v. Board of Education,*[145] where the Supreme Court ruled 8 : 1—the majority opinion written by Justice Black, the dissenting one by Justice Reed—that the "no aid" concept had been violated. At issue was Mrs. Vashti Cromwell McCollum's challenge[146] to the constitutional validity of a practice by the Board of Education of Champaign, Illinois, which enabled the interfaith Champaign Council on Religious Education to offer classes in religious instruction to public school children on public school premises. The religious classes were attended from thirty to forty-five minutes on Wednesdays by those public school students whose parents submitted written authorizations. Teachers were provided by the Council at no charge to the Board, but they were subject to the approval of Champaign's Superintendent of Schools. The classes were conducted in the regular school classrooms during school hours; those students who did not wish to stay for the religious sessions were required to go elsewhere in the building to pursue "meaningful secular studies." Evidently, these were not very meaningful in the case of those few students—such as young James Terry McCollum, whose family were professed agnostics—who did not stay for the Protestant, Catholic, or Jewish classes. Attendance at both the religious and lay classes was enforced strictly by secular teachers.

Strongly reiterating the "wall" principle that he had pronounced as

---

McCollum, Earley, Lemon, Tilton, Myquist, Engel, Schempp, Roemer, Wolman, Regan, Mueller, Marsh, Lynch, Jaffree, Thornton, Grand Rapids, and *Aguilar* cases. (See tables for citations.)

[144]These are discussed in detail in Kauper, *op. cit.,* Chapter 3. See also Richard E. Morgan, *The Supreme Court and Religion* (New York: The Free Press, 1972), Chapter 3 ff., and J. C. Choper, "The Religion Clauses," 41 *University of Pittsburgh Law Review* 4 (Summer 1980). The latter two present other theories.

[145]*Illinois ex rel. McCollum v. Board of Education,* 333 U.S. 203 (1948).

[146]See her interesting book on the case, *One Woman's Fight* (Boston: Beacon Press, 1961).

the author of the majority opinion in the *Everson Bus* case, Justice Black here found clear violations of the First and Fourteenth Amendments. He rejected the Board of Education's argument that, if the Court were to hold that a state cannot consistently, under these two Amendments, utilize its public school system to aid any or all religious faiths or sects in the dissemination of their doctrines and ideals, then the Court would "manifest a governmental hostility to religion or religious teachings." Black pointed to *Everson*, repeating its—his—language: ". . . the First Amendment has erected a wall between Church and State which must be kept high and impregnable." Because there was much lingering doubt as to just what had really happened to that "wall" in *Everson*, Black evidently felt constrained to spell out his conclusions on the violation of separation of Church and State again, and he closed his opinion with this admonition:

> Here [in *McCollum*] not only are the State's tax-supported public school buildings used for the dissemination of religious doctrines. The State also affords sectarian groups an invaluable aid in that it helps to provide pupils for their religious classes *through use of the State's compulsory public school machinery*. This is not separation of Church and State.[147]

On the other hand, Justice Reed, in solitary dissent, believed that the principle of *Everson* could accommodate the facts in *McCollum*. Sounding the frequently voiced argument that "devotion to the great principle of religious liberty should not lead us into a rigid interpretation of the constitutional guarantee that conflicts with accepted habits of our people," he observed sadly that here was "an instance where, for me, the history of past practices is determinative of the meaning of a constitutional clause not a decorous introduction to the study of its text."[148] Justices Reed and Black had been on the same side in the *Everson* case, although it will be recalled that Reed, perhaps sensing the expansiveness and uncertainty of the "wall" doctrine, and reflecting the fear

---

[147]*Illinois ex rel. McCollum v. Board of Education*, 333 U.S. 203 (1948), at 212. The supplied italics point to Black's key objection (as he would have cause to point out five years later in the *Zorach* decision, discussed *infra*, pp. 275–79).

[148]*Ibid.*, dissenting opinion, at 256. In an interview with Francis W. O'Brien (December 2, 1955), Reed confided that no opinion had ever won for him such a number of favorable letters as his *McCollum* dissent—"ten times more than any other."

of those who well recognized that it could "give" in either direction, had there objected to "drawing a rule of law from a figure of speech."

In the light of his position in the separation cases that were yet to follow,[149] and which would be consistent with his *McCollum* reasoning, Black's position in the *New Jersey Bus* case can best be explained in terms of a distinction he was willing to make under the strict separation theory between "incidental" aid to religion and "direct" aid. The situation in the *Bus* case was for him an entirely viable example of *incidental* aid—which, to him, constituted "*no* aid." He reasoned that since the purpose of the New Jersey ordinance was to provide nothing more than the *general public purpose* one of safe transportation of school children who were attending school under compulsory education laws, the fact that they happened to attend Roman Catholic parochial schools was not constitutionally fatal. For Black and his (then) supporters, the purpose of that aid was "secular" and "incidental" to the requirements of the compulsory school attendance statute, *hence appropriately directed to secular objectives*. In other words, the financial assistance given to the parochial school students was not the kind of "aid" forbidden under the "wall" doctrine of the *Everson* decision itself.

2. *The Governmental Neutrality Theory.* Under this theory, the establishment clause is viewed as requiring government to be resolutely "neutral" regarding religious matters. So neutral, in fact, that, in the interesting interpretation and application of the theory advanced by Professor Philip B. Kurland of the University of Chicago Law School, government cannot do anything which *either aids or hampers religion*[150]—that there must be, in other words, *a secular legislative purpose and primary effect that neither advances nor inhibits religion*. Professor Kurland reads the freedom and separation segments of the religion phrases as "a single precept that government cannot utilize religion as a standard for action or inaction because these clauses prohibit classification in terms of religion *either to confer a benefit or to impose a burden.*[151] This, of course, leaves us with the delicate and

[149]See discussion and Tables 6.3 and 6.4, *infra*.

[150]He has expressed this thesis frequently and in various media. See, for example, his essay "The School Prayer Cases," in Dallin H. Oaks, ed., *The Wall Between Church and State* (Chicago: University of Chicago Press, 1963), p. 160.

[151]*Ibid.*, n. 83. (Italics supplied.)

intriguing question as to the meaning not only of "benefit" and "burden" but of "neutral"—and, in the final analysis, of *religion* itself. It also leaves us with the suspicion that the suggested doctrine might well be rather hard on individual religious dissenters, which is something Kurland seems to acknowledge but does not quite concede.[152]

It was Justice Black who spoke for the Court's invocation of the neutrality theory most obviously, when he authored—fifteen years after the *Everson* and *McCollum* cases—what quickly became one of the most contentious and most misunderstood opinions of our time, the *New York Prayer* case.[153] Here, writing for a 6 : 1 majority, Black endeavored to make clear that the principle of the separation of Church and State could not permit the recitation in the public schools of a rather innocuous, twenty-two-word, non-denominational daily prayer that had been drafted by the New York State Board of Regents, a state agency composed of state officials. The prayer read as follows: "Almighty God, we acknowledge our dependence upon Thee, and we beg Thy blessings upon us, our parents, our teachers, and our country." It was recommended, although not required, for *viva voce* reading by teachers and students in the classrooms of the New York State public schools at the beginning of each school day. Numerous school boards adopted the recommendation, among them that of New Hyde Park, Long Island, which did so in 1958. Five parents[154] of ten children attending the school involved brought suit on the ground that the use of the official state-composed prayer in the public schools violated both separation of Church and State and freedom of religion. In his neither very lengthy nor very complex opinion for the Court, Justice Black agreed with the contentions of the parents and held the practice unconstitutional as a violation of the First and Fourteenth Amendments' ban on establishment of religion. "We think," he wrote,

> that by using its public school system to encourage recitation of the Regents' prayer, the State of New York has adopted a practice wholly inconsistent

[152]See his *Religion and the Law* (Chicago: Aldine Publishing Co., 1962), especially pp. 40 ff.

[153]*Engel v. Vitale,* 370 U.S. 421 (1962). Justices Frankfurter and White did not participate in the case.

[154]One Unitarian, one non-believer, one a member of the Ethical Culture Society, and two Jews.

with the Establishment Clause. *There can, of course, be no doubt* that New York's program of daily classroom invocation of God's blessing as prescribed in the Regents' prayer is a religious activity. It is a solemn avowal of divine faith and supplication for the blessings of the Almighty.[155]

Anticipating the public outcry that was to follow the ruling—and it proved to be quite an outcry, one that has hardly subsided, giving rise to a host of proposed constitutional amendments designed to overturn the decision (some 300 in the ensuing twenty-five years!)—he tried hard to put into words that the public might accept, and perhaps even appreciate, the manifold problems of personal commitments and drawing lines in case of majority-minority religion that continue to bedevil these controversies. Thus, he explained,

> [T]he constitutional prohibition against laws respecting an establishment of religion must at least mean that in this country it is no part of the business of government to compose official prayers for any group of the American people to recite as part of a religious program carried on by government.[156]

And over the objections of the one dissenter, Justice Stewart, who contended that the Court "has misspelled a great constitutional principle" by ruling that "an 'official religion' is established by letting those who want to say a prayer say it,"[157] Black concluded on a frank, terse, and hardly illogical note:

> It is neither sacrilegious nor antireligious to say that each separate government in this country should stay out of the business of writing or sanctioning official prayers and *leave that purely religious function to the people themselves and to those the people look to for religious guidance.*[158]

In an important footnote (#21), unfortunately largely ignored by the news media, Black tried to make clear—as he also did in two additional remarks he made orally from the bench on that Opinion Monday in June

---

[155]*Engel v. Vitale, op, cit.*, at 424. (Italics supplied.)

[156]*Ibid.*, at 425.

[157]*Ibid.*, dissenting opinion, at 445. (Bills, designed to strip the federal courts of jurisdiction over state-authorized voluntary prayers in public schools, passed the Senate 61 : 30 and 51 : 40 in 1979 but died in the House.)

[158]*Ibid.*, at 435. (Italics supplied.)

1962—that, contrary to his colleague Douglas's concurring opinion, he in no sense of the term intended his opinion for the Court to extend to ceremonial functions and observations with religious mottoes or religious characteristics.

Just one year after the controversial *Engel* decision, the Supreme Court reemphasized its resort to the neutrality theory in two "follow-up" cases, the *Bible Reading* cases of 1963, *Abington School District v. Schempp* and *Murray v. Curlett*.[159] Briefly, the *Schempp* portion of the two cases—which were decided together in a 144-page, five-opinion compendium—challenged the validity of a Pennsylvania law requiring the reading without comment of ten verses from the King James version of the Bible[160] on the opening of public school each day, although provision was made for a child to be excused from the exercises on the written request of a parent or guardian. The Schempps were faithful

[159]374 U.S. 203. A later (1968) prominent example of resort to the neutrality doctrine is the Court's unanimous declaration of unconstitutionality of Arkansas's "monkey law," which prohibited the teaching in its public schools and universities of the theory of evolution. (*Epperson v. Arkansas*, 393 U.S. 97.) But note that its new 1982 law, which—like Louisiana's of the same year—required public schools to balance the teaching of "evolution" with the theory of the "creation by a supreme power," was promptly declared unconstitutional by a federal court in *McLean v. Arkansas Board of Education*, 723 F.2d 45 (1982)—even as at least eleven other states were planning to enact similar legislation. In December 1986 the U.S. Supreme Court bit the proverbial bullet in the issue by hearing oral argument in *Edwards v. Aguillard*, 54 LW 3632. A packed courtroom witnessed spirited debate between opposing counsel, closely questioned by the Justices, sprinkled with references to the Bible, Aristotle, St. Thomas Aquinas, and Spinoza, and with echoes of the Scopes "monkey trial" of the 1920s. The eagerly anticipated decision, handed down in June 1987, evoked inevitably strong feelings pro and con. In a lengthy opinion penned by Justice Brennan, the Court ruled 7 : 2 that the Louisiana statute was unconstitutional because "the pre-eminent purpose of the Louisiana Legislature was clearly to advance the religious viewpoint that a supernatural being created humankind," and thus violated the First Amendment's ban against any law "respecting an establishment of religion." Justice Scalia's dissent, which was joined by Chief Justice Rehnquist, denounced the decision as a "repressive" and "illiberal" action that prevented the people of Louisiana from having "whatever scientific evidence there may be against evolution presented in their schools." (*Ibid.*, 55 LW 4860.)

[160]Bible reading has always engendered emotional reaction. One of the most tragic on record came in 1842 after Francis Kenrick, the Roman Catholic Bishop of Philadelphia, asked that either the Catholic (Douay) as well as the Protestant (King James) Bible be read in the public schools or Catholic public school children be excused from Bible reading. Rumors began to sweep the city that "Catholics were trying to drive the Bible from the schools." In May and July 1844 the worst riots in the city's history erupted over the Bible issue, leaving a dozen persons dead and two Catholic churches, a seminary, and fifty houses in Kensington in ruins. (*The Philadelphia Sunday Bulletin*, April 21, 1968.) A direct result was the development of a strong, separate Catholic school system.

Unitarians; Mrs. Madalyn E. Murray and her son, William J. Murray III, on the other hand,[161] were avowed atheists, contesting rulings of the Baltimore School Board that required reading of a Bible chapter "and-or the Lord's Prayer" at daily opening exercises in the public schools of that state. William had apparently been subjected to taunts and even physical assault in school because of his consistent opposition to these morning exercises.[162] (An interesting, although not uncommon, by-product of the two cases involved was that the two different lower courts, through which the cases passed to the United States Supreme Court, had reached opposite conclusions on the same constitutional issues.)

The Chief Justice assigned the writing of the decision to Justice Clark, a devout Presbyterian active in his church, who delivered an opinion redolent with diplomacy and acknowledgment of the significant place religion is presumed to hold in American society. He clearly endeavored to avoid the hostile, however uninformed, outcries that followed the Black opinion in the *Engel* decision. In the 8 : 1 ruling—from which only Justice Stewart dissented but, unlike his *Engel* dissent, now rather heavily on *procedural* grounds—Clark chose to rest both the decision and the burden of the opinion on a different plane, that of

[161]In 1970 the now Mrs. M. M. O'Hair unsuccessfully sought Supreme Court review of her contention that the reading of the Bible from outer space (by astronauts) violated the establishment clause. (*O'Hair v. Paine*, 397 U.S. 531, appeal dismissed.) Another attempt by the tenacious Mrs. O'Hair failed in 1971. (*Ibid.*, 401 U.S. 955.) But she did win her claim to tax-exempt status of an Atheist Library she set up in 1972—the I.R.S. agreeing to her demands rather than do battle in a lawsuit she was about to bring. (*The New York Times*, June 12, 1972, p. 19c.) In 1976 she announced her "resignation" as leader of "the American atheist community." (*Ibid.*, March 26, 1976, p. 28.) But, denounced as a "demon-directed damsel," she returned to the fray in 1978, filing suits to have the motto "In God We Trust" removed from the coin on which the image of suffragist Susan B. Anthony—alleged by Mrs. O'Hair to have been an atheist—appears, and indeed to have that motto expunged from all United States currency. She and her supporters also established a "Dial-an-Atheist" telephone message service in English and Spanish in New York and Chicago, designed to counter the "Dial-a-Prayer" inspirational message service long available in cities across the country. And in 1981 she filed an unsuccessful suit to stop the United States Court of Appeals for the Fifth Circuit from using its standard opening prayer, "Oyez, oyez, God save our nation and this honorable court."

[162]Two decades later, Bill Murray found God, quit his job, and set about making friends, embraced as a prodigal son. Surrounded by fundamentalist ministers and right-wing congressmen, he publicly broke with, and indeed scathingly condemned, his mother in a dramatic, well-advertised appearance before a large "In God We Trust" sign at the United States Capitol. (*The Washington Post*, May 21, 1980, p. C-1.)

governmental neutrality. How well he succeeded is perhaps tellingly illustrated by the fact that dozens of newspapers selected as the decisive segment of opinion the following explanation and exhortation by Clark:

> The place of religion in our society is an exalted one, achieved through a long tradition of reliance on the home, the church and the inviolable citadel of the individual heart and mind. We have come to recognize through bitter experience that *it is not within the power of government to invade that citadel, whether its purpose or effect be to aid or oppose, to advance or retard. In the relationship between man and religion, the state is firmly committed to a position of neutrality.*[163]

Not only was the opinion written by a devout Protestant, but among the five lengthy, separate concurring opinions was one delivered by that Court's Roman Catholic, Justice Brennan (whose comments embraced seventy-seven pages), and one by its Jewish member, Justice Goldberg. All five authors took great care to acknowledge the hallowed place of religion, yet all five firmly, and indeed repeatedly, referred to governmental neutrality as the *sine qua non* of the problem. Thus, the Court's emphasis was clearly on the theory of neutrality, a requirement based— as Justice Clark put it—on the possibility that "powerful sects or groups might bring about a fusion of governmental and religious functions or a concert or dependency of one upon the other."[164] The language, although evidently not the full intent, of the application of the principle of neutrality thus becomes that advanced by Professor Kurland, which asks whether the "purpose or primary effect" of an enactment is "either the enhancement or inhibition of religion":

> [T]o withstand the strictures of the Establishment Clause there must be a *secular legislative purpose and a primary effect that neither advances nor inhibits religion*. . . . [And] the fact [advanced by Pennsylvania and Maryland] that individual students may absent themselves upon parental request-

---

[163]E.g. (from the conclusion of the opinion), "Quotation of the Day," in *The New York Times*, June 18, 1963, p. 39*l*. (Italics supplied.) The citation is from 374 U.S. 203, *op. cit.*, at 226.

[164]*Abington School District v. Schempp* and *Murray v. Curlett*, 374 U.S. 203 (1963), at 222. Clark acknowledged that "the state may not establish a 'religion of secularism' in the public schools," but he insisted that the kind of neutrality required by the Court here would not bring about the establishment of such a "religion." (*Ibid.*, at 225.)

. . . furnishes no defense to a claim of constitutionality under the Establishment Clause.[165]

The religious practices authorized by Pennsylvania and Maryland, and challenged by the Schempps and Murrays, thus failed to meet the demands of the "neutrality" test, a test under which *both* religion clauses of the First Amendment place the government in a "neutral position" with regard to religion. As for the allegation that a logical concomitant of that "neutrality" policy would be, in effect, to render government hostile to religion, Justice Clark explained that the Court— and through it the country's constitutional framework—

> cannot accept that the concept of neutrality, which does not permit a State to *require* a religious exercise even with the consent of the majority of those affected, collides with the majority's right to free exercise of religion. While the Free Exercise Clause clearly prohibits the use of state action to deny the right of free exercise to *anyone*, it has never meant that a majority could use the machinery of the State to practice its beliefs.[166]

What Clark says here is surely a basic premise of our government under law: that majorities, even near-unanimous ones, cannot violate the Constitution! Thus, when Florida attempted to continue required prayers and Bible-reading in its public schools, a practice approved by its state supreme court, the United States Supreme Court, without even hearing argument, promptly reversed the tribunal by an 8:1 vote one year later.[167] When in 1965 the principle of P.S. 184 in Queens, New York, ruled that not even a "voluntary" recitation of a nursery school prayer in public schools could be said, the Supreme Court upheld him by refusing to review an appeal from his ruling.[168] The Court even let stand a 1968 lower-court ruling that a verse recited by *public* kindergarten children in De Kalb, Illinois, represented a violation of the separation principle, notwithstanding the deletion of the word

[165]*Ibid.*, at 222, 224. (Italics supplied.)

[166]*Ibid.*, at 225–26. (Italics supplied.)

[167]*Chamberlin v. Dade County Board of Instruction,* 377 U.S. 402 (1964). Justice Stewart dissented.

[168]*Stein v. Oshinsky,* 382 U.S. 957. The prayer, said before eating cookies and drinking milk: "God is great, God is good, and we thank him for our food, Amen."

"God,"[169] Justice Stewart dissenting. In 1971 the Court, 7:2, agreed with the New Jersey courts that to use the prayers in the *Congressional Record* as "voluntary devotional exercises" in the public schools constituted an impermissible "subterfuge."[170] Late in 1975 it declined an opportunity to consider whether public school children have a right to "pray aloud voluntarily" while in school, as the mother of a Massachusetts girl had sought unsuccessfully in the courts below.[171] Undaunted—and in concert with the actions by numerous other states, e.g., New Jersey and New Hampshire—Massachusetts enacted a law in 1980 that permitted ritual prayer, with provisions for abstention, in its public schools, only to see it struck down as "an unconstitutional sponsorship of religion," the twelve-page opinion citing the United States Supreme Court precedents.[172] In 1982 the Supreme Court unanimously affirmed the declaration of unconstitutionality by a lower federal court of Louisiana's daily voluntary school prayer in its public schools,[173] and in 1984 down went a similar statute by New Mexico.[174]

But a good many of the states—encouraged by supportive congressional manifestations—refused to give up and now increasingly commenced to concentrate on "silent prayer" rules for their public schools. The bellwether was Alabama, whose U.S. District Court Judge William Brevard Hand proved to be an important ally with a string of "pro-religion," "pro-accommodation" holdings—including one in 1987 that banned forty-four textbooks from Alabama public schools because, he ruled, they promoted the "religion" of "secular humanism." He was overturned unanimously by the U.S. Court of Appeals for the 11th

---

[169]The prayer: "We thank you for the flowers so sweet; We thank you for the food we eat; We thank you for the birds that sing; We thank you for everything." A principle, alas, is a principle. (*De Kalb v. De Spain*, 390 U.S. 906 [1968].)

[170]*Board of Education of Netcong, N.J. v. State Board of Education*, 401 U.S. 1013.

[171]*Warren v. Killory*, 423 U.S. 929 (1975). An attempt by an Albany, New York, student group, Students for Voluntary Prayer, to hold prayer meetings in a public school came to naught on separation grounds in a late-1980 unanimous twenty-three-page opinion by the United States Court of Appeals for the Second Circuit. (*Brandon v. Board of Education of Guilderland Central School District*, 487 F. Supp. 1219.) The U.S. Supreme Court subsequently denied *certiorari*. (454 U.S. 1123 [1981].)

[172]Massachusetts Supreme Judicial Court, March 13 and 27, 1980, opinions by Justices Herbert P. Wilkins and Benjamin Kaplan. (*Kent v. Commissioner of Education*, 402 N.E. 2d 1340, 1980 Mass. Adv. Sh. 803, 1980.)

[173]*Treen v. Karen B.*, 455 U.S. 913.

[174]*New Mexico v. Burciaga*, 464 U.S. 982.

Circuit.[175] In 1984 Judge Hand had upheld Alabama's statute authorizing a one-minute period of silence in all public schools "for meditation or prayer," ruling, *inter alia,* that "the establishment clause of the First Amendment to the United States Constitution does not prohibit the state from establishing a religion"[176]—a conclusion the Supreme Court later termed "remarkable." Not astonishingly, the U.S. Court of Appeals reversed Hand, and the Supreme Court affirmed that decision 6:3 in *Wallace v. Jaffree* in 1985.[177] However, the Court left open the possibility—arguably even the likelihood—that it would *uphold* the constitutionality of a statute that authorized a minute of *silence* but made no mention of *prayer.*[178] The issue reached the high tribunal in a New Jersey case late in 1987. But it managed to duck the explosive problem by ruling unanimously that state lawmakers favoring the law had no legal authority to present their case—i.e., that they lacked proper standing to sue.[179]

That the volatile, emotion-charged issue of public school prayer does not subside is manifested not only by the continuing efforts of states to come up with legislation that will pass judicial muster, and by the demonstrable fact that a plethora of communities still defy or ignore the now established law of the land, but also by repeated efforts in and by Congress to "overrule" the highest court in the land. Thus, both constitutional amendments and statutes have been introduced en masse with predictable regularity. Although none had passed both houses of Congress as of mid-1987, the United States Senate, trying a new approach, in 1979 had voted 49:37 and 51:40 to *deny appellate jurisdiction* to the Supreme Court of the United States in *Engel*-type and *Schempp*-type cases—obviously realizing that the Court would not reverse itself on the merits. The House failed to concur on both occasions; yet the 1980 and

---

[175]*Smith v. Bd. of School Commissioners of Mobile County,* 827 F.2d 684. The 600 Christian fundamentalist parents who had brought the suit decided not to appeal. And in another defeat for fundamentalists, the Court let stand a lower court ruling that parents do not have the right to insist that their children be excused from classes whose textbooks offend their religious beliefs. (*Mozert v. Hawkins County Board of Education,* 56 LW 2142 [1988].)

[176]*Jaffree v. Wallace,* 554 F. Supp. 1004.

[177]472 U.S. 38.

[178]*Ibid.* See especially the opinions by Justices Powell and O'Connor.

[179]*Karcher v. May,* 107 S. Ct. 946 (1987).

1984 presidential election campaigns rang with clarion calls to "put God back into the lives of our school children." Indeed, the Senate, late in 1981, had voted 70 : 12 to endorse "programs of voluntary prayer" in public schools. Four years later it approved a constitutional amendment to permit organized silent prayer in the public schools, but it failed to pass in the House. And in the election atmosphere of 1984 Congress not only endorsed a silent prayer bill (as an amendment to one extending a variety of educational programs), it also passed the Equal Access Act of 1984, which makes it unlawful for any public *secondary* school receiving federal financial assistance "and which has a limited open forum to deny equal access or a fair opportunity to, or discriminate against, any students who wish to conduct a meeting within that limited open forum on the basis of religious, political, philosophical, or other content of the speech at such meetings."[180] It is highly likely that the Court will be asked to pass on that legislation's constitutionality as well.

The concept of governmental neutrality can be interpreted in various ways, depending upon the interpreter and his philosophy. Thus, to Professor Wilbur G. Katz, it means that in order to be truly neutral, the government is in some instances *obliged* to give aid to religion in order to avoid restricting the complete enjoyment of religious liberty.[181] To some, anything but total neutrality is anathema;[182] to others, a neutrality that prevents a "just measure of governmental aid" is a violation of "the old American principles" of freedom of religion;[183] and to still others, it signifies that since government and religion both have roles to play in public life and the public order, and since they share some overlapping concerns and functions, neutrality can only mean that government policy must place religion neither at a *special advantage* nor a *special disadvantage*.[184] Professor Robert L. Cord has long maintained that genuine neutrality would encompass a restoration of the "no preference" doctrine of the First Amendment; i.e., that aid to religious institutions is entirely acceptable as long as no preference is accorded to

---

[180]For a conveniently analyzed text of the key provisions of the Equal Access Act, see *The New York Times*, July 26, 1984, p. A16.

[181]*Religion and American Constitutions* (Evanston, Ill.: Northwestern University Press, 1964), *passim*.

[182]E.g., Professor Leo Pfeffer, a distinguished student of the field.

[183]Father John Courtney Murray, S.J., "Law and Prepossessions?", 14 *Law and Contemporary Problems* 23 (1949).

[184]Professor Paul G. Kauper, *op. cit.*, Chapter 3, *passim*.

any one religion.[185] Professor William A. Carroll suggests that the "neutrality" definition and test assume a *complementary* interpretation of the religion clauses to the end that religion be defined "neutrally" so as to include "both belief and non-belief in God in regard to both the free exercise and the establishment clauses."[186] That the principle be applied with "benevolence" when applied to religious liberty in the public schools is urged warmly by Professor Ellis M. West.[187]

How, then, does the "no aid" theory expounded in the *Everson Bus* case[188] differ from the "neutrality" theory expounded in the *Public School Prayer* cases?[189] Although the response depends upon interpretation, one *can* with some assurance say that the "no aid" test inquires whether government is acting *in aid of religion* (in *Everson* the Court found that New Jersey's subsidy aided the *child* rather than the *Church*), whereas the "neutrality" test inquires whether government is placing religion at a patent advantage or disadvantage (which the Court answered in the former in the *Public School Prayer* cases).[190] There remains the third theory, which frankly recognizes governmental "accommodation"—to which an interesting "bridge" might be Richard E. Morgan's controversial proposition that "there is no anomaly in banning even modest prayers in the common public schools, while financially aiding specialized independent parochial schools where sectarian prayer is routine."[191]

[185]See, for example, his "Church-State Separation: Restoring the 'No Preference' Doctrine of the First Amendment," 9 *Harvard Journal of Law & Public Policy* 1 (Winter 1986).

[186]Carroll, *op. cit.*, pp. 664 ff., see especially pp. 664–66 and 673–74.

[187]"The Supreme Court and Religious Liberty in the Public Schools," 25 *Journal of Church and State* 87 (Winter 1983).

[188]*Everson v. Board of Education of Ewing Township*, 330 U.S. 1 (1947).

[189]*Engel v. Vitale*, 370 U.S. 421 (1962); and *Abington School District v. Schempp* and *Murray v. Curlett*, 374 U.S. 203 (1963).

[190]An interesting aspect of the problem of the Bible in the public schools was presented in New Jersey in 1953, in *Tudor v. Board of Education of Rutherford*, 14 N.J. 31, where the New Jersey Supreme Court held unconstitutional the state law sanctioning free distribution of Gideon Bibles (the King James version) at a group of public schools.

[191]Morgan, *op. cit.*, p. 207. See also Choper, *op. cit.*, fn. 144, for a different approach that propounds a line that would forbid governmental action *only* if its religious purpose "is highly likely to result in coercing compliance or influencing religious beliefs." See also Paul J. Weber and Dennis A. Gilbert, who in their *Private Churches and Public Money: Church-Government Fiscal Relations* (Westport: Greenwood Press, 1979) propose a doctrine of "fiscal neutrality." It would be based on an equal protection doctrine that protects free exercise without supporting establishment by taxing religious groups like

3. *The Governmental Accommodation Theory.* In his very lengthy concurring opinion in the *Public School Prayer* (Pennsylvania/ Maryland)[192] decisions, Justice Brennan, while acknowledging that the accommodation theory had no place in the particular cases at issue, was moved to explain that only a concept such as that of "accommodation" could effectively reconcile the natural clash between the free exercise and separation clauses; that *some* accommodation between government and religion and between Church and State could and should be accepted.[193] Readily granting that Pennsylvania and Maryland had gone beyond "accommodation" with their Bible-reading and public prayer legislation, thereby violating the basic concept of governmental neutrality required by the Constitution, he catalogued activities that could *not,* in his opinion, be held to be constitutional violations,[194] activities that, although religious in origin, have ceased to have religious meaning—such as the motto "In God We Trust" on currency and the belief expressed in the Pledge of Allegiance that the nation was founded "under God";[195] provisions for churches and chaplains in the armed forces and in penal institutions; draft exemptions for ministers and divinity students; the recital of invocational prayers in legislative assemblies; the appointment of legislative chaplains; inclusion of prayers in public school commencement programs;[196] teaching *about* religion in the public schools, i.e., the *study* of the Bible and other religious literature; *uniform* tax exemptions incidentally available to religious institutions;[197] other public welfare benefits which government makes

---

all other groups (unless exempt under the eleemosynary umbrella) while permitting them freely to participate in the political process. Thus, "fiscal neutrality" would treat religious and non-religious groups equally. Professor George Anastoplo's essential "line" test (see also p. 296, *infra*) is the answer to what he views as a simple yet logical *quaere:* does the *community* benefit?

[192]374 U.S. 203 (1963), commencing at 230.

[193]In 1971 there were still sixteen states that provided no "accommodation." By mid-1982 that number had shrunk to three (Florida, Georgia, and Oklahoma). See Albert R. Papa, *Auxiliary Services to Religious Elementary and Secondary Schools: The State of State Aid* (Washington, D.C.: Americans United for the Separation of Church and State, 1982).

[194]*Ibid.,* at 296–303.

[195]Indeed, in 1964 the Court refused to review—and thereby let stand—a ruling by the Appellate Division of the New York Supreme Court that upheld the use of the words "under God" in the Pledge of Allegiance (*Lewis v. Allen,* 379 U.S. 923).

[196]*Wood v. Mt. Lebanon Township School District,* 342 F. Supp. 1293 (W.D. Penn., 1972), affirmed 412 U.S. 967 (1974).

[197]In 1966 the Supreme Court seemed to reaffirm that sensitive issue by declining to

available to educational, charitable, and eleemosynary groups that *incidentally* aid individual worshippers; excuse of children from required school attendance on their respective religious holidays; the temporary use of public buildings by religious organizations when their own facilities have become unavailable because of disaster or emergency.

As if to indicate the difficulty of drawing such lines, Justice Douglas in *his* concurring opinion in the *Pennsylvania/Maryland* decisions essentially reiterated his strong stand in the *New York Prayer* case, where he had said that the "First Amendment . . . prevented secular sanctions to *any* religious ceremony, dogma, or rite."[198] But lest he be misunderstood, he emphasized his now firm conviction that the concept of the "wall" brooked no infraction or circumvention, whatever the circumstances, whatever the rationale:

the First Amendment does not say that some forms of establishment are allowed; it says that "no law respecting an establishment of religion" shall

---

review a unanimous decision by the Maryland Court of Appeals that the time-honored state tax exemptions for church buildings were *not* an unconstitutional "establishment of religion." (*Cree v. Goldstein,* 385 U.S. 816, and *Murray v. Goldstein, ibid.*) And in 1970, in the *Walz* case, with Justice Douglas in lone dissent, the Court specifically upheld the tax exemption of property used exclusively for religious purposes. Chief Justice Burger, contending that "there is room for play in the joints productive of a benevolent neutrality which will permit religious exercise to exist without sponsorship and without interference"—provided there results no "excessive entanglement" with religion—held for his 7 : 1 Court that there was no relation between tax exemption and establishment, and explained: "The grant of a tax exemption is not sponsorship since the government does not transfer part of its revenue to churches but simply abstains from demanding that the church support the state." (*Walz v. Tax Commission of the City of New York,* 397 U.S. 664, at 669–70.) To Douglas—and many another observer—however, "a tax exemption is a subsidy" pure and simple (at 704) and assuredly a far cry from the "wall of separation." It was the *Walz* case, and the Burger opinion therein, that in effect spelled out in detail the now widely accepted "three-pronged" test of constitutionality under any "accommodation" scheme, namely: (1) there must be a *primary secular* legislative purpose; (2) its effect must neither inhibit nor advance religion; and (3) its result must not foster an "*excessive* entanglement" of government and religion. (At 674, 675.)

The question of whether tax exemption could also be granted to church-owned *property* that is used for *business* purposes was answered by the Court in the *negative* in 1972 (6 : 1). See *Diffenderfer v. Central Baptist Church of Miami,* 401 U.S. 412.

The tax exemption issue was back before the Supreme Court in 1988 in a case raising the intriguing matter of the use of tax-exempt funds in political campaigns, here involving the abortion problem. (*United States Catholic Conference v. Abortion Rights Mobilization,* Docket No. 87-416.) But it appeared doubtful that the Court was eager to reach the merits of the case amidst indications that it might decide it on "standing" questions.

[198]*Engel v. Vitale,* 370 U.S. 421 (1962), at 442 n. 7.

be made. What may not be done directly may not be done indirectly lest the Establishment Clause become a mockery.[199]

This stand, of course, rejects *any* "theory of accommodation." Ironically, Justice Douglas had not only provided the necessary fifth vote that upheld New Jersey's public funds subsidy to students attending Catholic parochial schools, a position he then publicly repudiated in *Engel v. Vitale*[200] and would again attack in the *New York Text Book* case in 1968;[201] it was he who had written (a decade prior to the *Public School Prayer* cases) the majority opinion in *Zorach v. Clauson,* the *New York Released Time* case,[202] which well illustrates the accommodation theory that he now in effect rejected.

Zorach v. Clauson presented a situation ostensibly different from the one that had faced the Court in the *Champaign, Illinois, Released Time* case[203] four years earlier, in 1948. It will be recalled that the Court's 8 : 1 decision in that Illinois case struck down as a clear-cut violation of the separation of Church and State the Champaign School Board's practice of permitting the use of its public school facilities for weekly "released time" religious classes. The New York released-time arrangement differed on its face principally in that those public school students whose parents requested their attendance at religious instruction classes were in face *released* from classes at school to journey outside to the site of the religious classes. Those who did not participate in the released time program were required to remain in the public school buildings for instructional or study hall purposes. Theoretically, the public school teachers took neither public notice nor attendance of the student releases, but under the regulations promulgated by the Board of Education, the religious teachers did have to take attendance and file it with the individual's home-room teacher or the principal, who was required to keep a card attendance record.

The Supreme Court's six-man majority,[204] per the Douglas opinion,

---

[199]*Abington School District v. Schempp, op. cit.,* at 230, concurring opinion. He took pains publicly to reiterate that posture in 1964 in the *Chamberlin* case, cited on p. 280, footnote 167, *supra.*

[200]370 U.S. 421 (1962).

[201]*Board of Education v. Allen,* 392 U.S. 236.

[202]343 U.S. 307 (1952).

[203]*McCollum v. Board of Education,* 333 U.S. 203 (1948).

[204]Douglas, with Chief Justice Vinson and Justices Reed, Burton, Minton, and Clark.

found critical differences between *McCollum* and *Zorach*. Douglas, while acknowledging that the public school teachers "cooperated" with the program to the extent of enabling voluntary attendance of the religious classes, held that the New York program, unlike that struck down in Illinois, involved neither religious instruction in the public school classrooms nor the expenditure of public funds *per se*. He insisted that the Court was indeed following the *McCollum* case, but he added that this did not mean that the Court had to read into the Bill of Rights a "philosophy of hostility to religion." Musing that the constitutional standard of the separation of Church and State, like many problems in Constitutional Law, "is one of degree," he declared that Church and State need not be hostile to each other. Although granting that "[g]overnment may not finance religious groups nor undertake religious instruction or blend secular and sectarian education nor use secular institutions to force one or some religion on any person,"[205] he added in language that ultimately came to haunt him in light of his concurring opinions in the *Public Prayer* cases of 1962 and 1963: "But we find no constitutional requirement which makes it necessary for government to be hostile to religion and to throw its weight against efforts to widen the effective scope of religious influence."[206] The First Amendment, he had said earlier in his opinion, "does not say that in every and all respects there shall be separation of Church and State";[207] and he elaborated later in a phrase much quoted by those opposed to later decisions by the Court, in general, and Douglas opinions, in particular, that "we are a religious people whose institutions presuppose a Supreme Being."[208]

But three dissenters, Justices Black, Frankfurter, and Jackson, not only regarded the majority's findings as going far beyond any constitutionally permissible "accommodation," they also saw no difference "even worthy of mention" (in the words of Justice Black, the author of the *McCollum* opinion) between the Illinois and New York programs, except for the use of public school buildings. Black especially objected to what he regarded as the compulsory process aspects of the New York practice: "New York," he wrote angrily, "is manipulating its com-

[205]*Zorach v. Clauson,* 343 U.S. 306 (1952), at 314.
[206]*Ibid.*
[207]*Ibid.,* at 312.
[208]*Ibid.,* at 313.

pulsory education laws to help religious sects get pupils. *This is not separation but combination of Church and State.*"[209] As for the different use of the school buildings, Black noted: "As we attempted to make categorically clear, the *McCollum* decision would have been the same if the religious classes had *not* been held in the school buildings."[210] He concluded his opinion with an impassioned warning:

> State help to religion injects political and party prejudices into a holy field. It too often substitutes force for prayer, hate for love, and persecution for persuasion. Government should not be allowed, under cover of the soft euphemism of "co-operation," to steal into the sacred area of religious choice.[211]

To Justice Frankfurter, "the pith of the case" was that under New York's program, formalized religious instruction is instituted for other school activity which those who do not participate in the released time program are *compelled* to attend. He suggested that this coercion might well be met, and met constitutionally, if the public schools were to close their doors completely for an hour or two. leaving the pupils to go where they will, "to God or Mammon." This practice, known as "dismissed time," was then in vogue in three states, and had been readily upheld by the courts. Caustically, Justice Jackson, the third dissenter, commented that "my evangelistic brethren confuse an objection to compulsion with an objection to religion."[212] In his view the New York program operated to make religious sects beneficiaries of the power to compel children to attend secular schools, holding that the public school thereby "serves as a temporary jail for a pupil who will not go to Church."[213] He cautioned that "the day this country ceases to be free for irreligion it will cease to be free for religion—except for the sect that can win political power."[214] He ended his dissent on a note of combined alarm and sarcasm:

> . . . the *McCollum* case has passed like a storm in a teacup. The wall which the Court was professing to erect between Church and State has become even

[209]*Ibid.*, at 318. (Italics supplied.)
[210]*Ibid.*, at 316. (Italics supplied.)
[211]*Ibid.*, at 320.
[212]*Ibid.*, at 324.
[213]*Ibid.*
[214]*Ibid.*, at 325.

more warped and twisted than I expected. Today's judgment will be more interesting to students of psychology and of the judicial processes than to students of constitutional law.[215]

The *Zorach* decision, however, has not only *not* been overruled[216]—none of the above have, no matter which theory they might reflect—but the "accommodation" approach received further impetus when the Court in 1968 upheld New York's controversial 1965 law that *requires* public school systems to *lend* textbooks to students in private and parochial schools.[217]

In that *New York Textbook* case the Court ruled 6:3—in a case that appeared to open ever wider the door of accommodation—that the law directing school districts to lend $15 worth of textbooks each year to each pupil in grades 7 through 12 in non-public schools, which then cost the state *circa* $25,000,000 annually, was an entirely permissible "student benefit" rather than an impermissible "school benefit" program, and hence not violative of the First Amendment's strictures against establishment. In the majority opinion, Justice White—joined by Chief Justice Warren and Justices Brennan, Harlan, Stewart, and Marshall—thus clearly adopted the "child benefit" rationale of the *Everson* decision of two decades earlier.[218] He agreed that it would be unconstitutional for the state to purchase the books and *give* them *gratis* to parochial school students, but he noted that the law forbids that and merely requires the state to *lend* them. Underlying the legislature's action and the rationale of the earlier "child benefit" cases, contended White,

> has been a recognition that private education has played and is playing a significant and valuable role in raising national levels of knowledge, competence, and experience.[219]

But three opinions by three dissenters, Justices Black, Douglas, and Fortas, saw matters quite differently. Douglas pointed out that, in fact, the "statutory system provides that the parochial school will ask for the

[215]*Ibid.*

[216]Presented with a golden opportunity to reconsider it in 1976, the Court pointedly refused to do so. (*Smith v. Smith*, 429 U.S. 806, *certiorari* denied.)

[217]*The New York Textbook* case (*Board of Education v. Allen*, 392 U.S. 236).

[218]*Everson v. Board of Education of Ewing Township, N.J.*, 330 U.S. 1 (1947).

[219]*Board of Education v. Allen*, 392 U.S. 236 (1968), at 247.

books that *it wants*,"[220] with the local public school board then simply (or not so simply) having to decide whether to veto the selection made by the parochial school. And, he asked, with rather difficult-to-refute logic: "Can there be the slightest doubt that the head of the parochial school will ask for the book or books that best promote its sectarian creed?"[221] Black, passionately contending that his *Everson* line had been not only overstepped but utterly misinterpreted—for he saw all the difference in the world between *bus* aid and *book* aid, the first being "incidental" or "ancillary" to the educational process, the latter being crucial to and an integral part of that process—warned (with a wary eye toward the Federal Aid to Education Act of 1965, discussed below, and its presumed impending judicial tests):

> It requires no prophet to foresee that on the argument used to support this law others could be upheld providing for state or federal government funds to buy property on which to erect religious school buildings or to erect the buildings themselves, to pay the salaries of the religious school teachers, and finally to have the sectarian religious group cease to rely on voluntary contributions of members of their sects while waiting for the Government to pick up all the bills for the religious schools.[222]

Fortas, in what would be one of his last decisions prior to his resignation from the bench in 1969, categorically stated that *Allen* was simply and patently *not* within the principles of *Everson,* for:

> Apart from the differences between textbooks and bus rides, the present statute does not call for extending to children attending sectarian schools the same service or facility extended to children in public schools. *This statute calls for furnishing special, separate, and particular books, specially, separately, and particularly chosen by religious sects or their representatives for use in their sectarian schools. This is the infirmity.*[223]

But there were six votes on the majority side—cast by justices who evidently believed the New York Textbook Law to fit into the now widely accepted "child benefit" syndrome, who were willing, in

[220]*Ibid.*, at 256. (Italics supplied.)
[221]*Ibid.*
[222]*Ibid.*, at 253.
[223]*Ibid.*, at 271 (Italics supplied.)

White's words, to stipulate "evidence that parochial schools are performing, in addition to their sectarian function, the task of secular education."[224]

While the thrust of the times, the evolving nature of governmental aid to education, seemed then clearly to be on the side of the majority's reasoning in *Allen,* and while the latter's principle of the constitutionality of textbook *loans* was reaffirmed in 1973, 1975, and 1977 (in cases that, however, disallowed certain other state-devised attempts to "accommodate"),[225] there are obvious limits: thus, as the Court ruled unanimously in 1973—in a not necessarily overly convincing Burger opinion that professed to distinguish *Allen*—such free textbook aid may *not* constitutionally be extended to private academies (here under the terms of a 1940 Mississippi law) that have racially discriminatory admission policies.[226] Nor, 6:3, does *Allen* by any means sanction state forays that would provide *funds* for the purchase of textbooks to *parents* of non-public school students.[227]

That there are constitutional limits to "accommodation," even when the 1968 *Allen* textbook case decision appeared to have made these academic, had been made crystal clear by two 8:0 and 8:1 decisions handed down in 1971 that dealt with attempted aid going well beyond textbook loans or bus subventions. With only Justice White dissenting in the second, the Supreme Court, speaking through Chief Justice Burger—hardly a doctrinaire opponent of "accommodation"—declared unconstitutional as *"excessive entanglement* between Government and religion"—and therefore violative of the separation of Church and State mandated by the First Amendment—programs enacted by Pennsylvania in 1968 and Rhode Island in 1969 that provided *public funds* for *direct* aid for instruction in "non-religious subjects" to Roman Catholic and other church-related primary and secondary schools. The aid involved in the Pennsylvania statute included the partial payment of salaries of parochial school teachers by professing to

[224]*Ibid.,* at 248.

[225]*Committee for Public Education and Religious Liberty v. Nyquist,* 413 U.S. 476; *Meek v. Pittenger,* 421 U.S. 349; and *Wolman v. Walter,* 433 U.S. 229, respectively.

[226]*Norwood v. Harrison,* 413 U.S. 455. "The leeway for indirect aid to sectarian schools has no place in defining the permissible scope of state aid to private racially discriminatory schools." (At 464.) The *Norwood* case was reaffirmed in 1974 in *Evangeline Parrish School Board v. United States,* 416 U.S. 970.

[227]*Marburger and Griggs v. Public Funds for Public Schools,* 417 U.S. 961 (1974).

"purchase secular services" for their teaching of such "secular" subjects as mathematics, physical education, physical science, and modern
foreign languages (Latin, Hebrew, and Classical Greek were expressly
excluded) and also for the purchase of textbooks and instructional materials. Lower federal courts had subsequently declared the Rhode Island
law, which provided for a 15 percent supplement to private school
teachers of secular subjects using the same instructional materials as
those in the public schools, unconstitutional as violative of the establishment clause; but Pennsylvania's statute had been upheld.

In agreeing with the Rhode Island and disagreeing with the Pennsylvania decisions below, the Supreme Court gave renewed firm notice
that while it did not retreat from its earlier "accommodation" holdings—such as its bus and textbook decisions—there were definite limits to "accommodation" lest it violate the separation of Church and
State, that "excessive entanglement" would and could not be tolerated.
Explaining that the Court was thus obligated to draw lines with reference to the three main evils against which the establishment clause was
intended to afford protection, "sponsorship, financial support, and
active involvement of the sovereign in religious activity," the Chief
Justice ruled:

> In order to determine whether the government entanglement with religion is
> excessive, we must examine the character and purposes of the institutions
> which are benefited, the nature of aid that the state provides, and the result-
> ing relationships between the government and the religious authority. . . .
> Here we find that both statutes foster an impermissible degree of entangle-
> ment.[228]

And in concluding, he reiterated the basic dimensions of the new line:

> The merit and benefits of these schools . . . are not the issue before us in
> these cases. The sole question is whether state aid to these schools can be
> squared with the dictates of the Religious Clauses. *Under our system the
> choice has been made that government is to be entirely excluded from the
> area of religious instruction and churches excluded from the affairs of
> government.*[229]

---

[228]*Lemon v. Kurtzman*, 403 U.S. 602 (1971), at 615.
[229]*Ibid.*, at 625. (Italics supplied.) Yet in a rather grotesque postscript, the Court—
through the Chief Justice—held 5:3 two years later that Pennsylvania could and indeed

Along the way, the Chief Justice had restated the governing three-pronged "cumulative criteria" as follows: "First, the statute must have a secular legislative purpose; second, its principal or primary effect must be one that neither advances nor inhibits religion; finally, the statute must not foster an excessive entanglement with religion."[230] But Justice White disagreed; he theorized that aid to a "separable secular function" of a church-related school was *not* unconstitutional, contending that it does not matter if religious interests "may substantially benefit" from the aid.[231]

As if to underscore future problems for the "excessive entanglement" doctrine, on the very same opinion day the Chief Justice, speaking for himself and Justices Harlan, Stewart, White, and Blackmun, *upheld* 5:4 the Federal Higher Educational Facilities Act of 1963, under which $240 million in federal funds was paid for the construction of academic buildings on the campuses of private colleges—*including* religious colleges.[232] Over a sarcastic dissenting opinion by Justice Douglas—which was also signed by Justices Black and Marshall—charging that evidently "small violations of the First Amendment over the years are unconstitutional while a huge violation occurring only once is *de minimus*,"[233] the Chief Justice distinguished the federal higher education case from the two state secondary and primary school cases under three headings: that pre-college church schools are more involved in religious indoctrination than colleges; that there are fewer entanglements between Church and State in the "one-time, single purpose construction grant than in continuing salary-supplement programs"; and that what he viewed as the evil of bitter political battles,

---

should release the $24 million in special aid for those private sectarian schools which it had authorized and appropriated for the school year *preceding* the 1971 holding of unconstitutionality! (*Lemon v. Kurtzman*, 411 U.S. 192, [1973].)

[230]403 U.S. 602, at 612–13. See the editorial, "Bureaucratic Governmental Regulation of Churches and Church Institutions," 21 *Journal of Church and State* 2 (Spring 1979).

[231]Dissenting opinion in *Earley v. Dicenso*, 403 U.S. 602 (1971), at 664.

[232]*Tilton v. Richardson*, 403 U.S. 672 (1971). The Court did strike down unanimously a provision of the law which enabled the colleges to use the buildings for *any* purpose twenty years after receiving the funds. The right of states to help private colleges and universities borrow money to build *non-sectarian* facilities, even those that are owned and operated by a religious sect, was upheld 6:3 in 1973. (*Hunt v. McNair*, 412 U.S. 734.) See also *Roemer v. Maryland Public Works Board*, 426 U.S. 736 (1976), *infra*, pp. 294–95.

[233]*Ibid.*, at 692.

which he regarded as fatally damaging and divisive at the state programs' level, "is not likely to erupt" over aid to colleges. (Five years
later he would join Justice Blackmun's opinion, utilizing the same
general distinctions between college and below-college levels, in the
Court's 5:4 decision upholding Maryland's aid to higher educational
facilities program.[234]) The only Roman Catholic on the Court, Justice
Brennan, echoing Jefferson and Madison's warnings, dissented separately, deploring what he saw as the secularizing impact of public
assistance on church schools. By accepting government funds, he reasoned, not only do the religious activities of a sectarian institution
become compromised—for there must inevitably be "policing" by the
secular authorities—but there is really no way to separate out the religious and secular functions. Brennan restated his deeply held conviction
that "the establishment clause forbids the federal government to provide funds to sectarian universities in which the propagation and advancement of a particular religion is a function or purpose of the
institution."[235]

Obviously, neither the "excessive entanglement" line nor the allegedly governing "three-pronged cumulative criteria" thus settled the
establishment clause controversies—but they did serve notice to policy
makers across the land that the First Amendment contained certain basic
strictures against the commingling of Church and State—especially on
pedagogical levels *below* college. Hence when Ohio passed a law for
direct tuition grants of $90 annually to all parents of children in private
and parochial schools, the Court barred it 8:1, with once again only
Justice White in dissent.[236] And down in three 1973 cases went sundry
formidable, ambitious non–public school aid attempts by New York
and—again—Pennsylvania, the votes ranging from 8:1 to 6:3.[237]

---

[234]See pp. 294–95, 306, and 311–312, *infra*. For an interesting discussion of the
dichotomy between aid to higher and pre-college institutions, see Edward N. Leavy and
Eric Alan Raps, "The Judicial Double Standard for State Aid to Church-Affiliated Educational Institutions," 21 *Journal of Church and State* 2 (Spring 1979). See also the same
"wave length" distinction *cum* dichotomy between the Court's 1981 decisions in
Brandon v. Board of Education, 454 U.S. 1123, and in *Widmar v. Vincent*, 454 U.S. 263,
involving on-site activities of religious groups in elementary schools and universities,
respectively.

[235]403 U.S. 602, *op. cit.*, at 689.

[236]*Essex v. Wolman*, 409 U.S. 808 (1972).

[237]*Levitt v. Committee for Public Education and Religious Liberty*, 413 U.S. 427;
Committee for Public Education and Religious Liberty v. Nyquist, 413 U.S. 756; and
Sloan v. Lemon, 413 U.S. 825.

Included among them were such attempts as direct grants for mainte-nance and repair, for full and/or partial reimbursement of tuition, for non-mandatory testing and record keeping, and for tax relief. Such an endeavor, wrote Justice Powell for the Court, "advances religion in that it subsidizes directly the religious activities of sectarian elementary and secondary schools"; and he specifically viewed the programs as con-stituting a crass violation of the injunctions against any programmatic *effect* of advancing religion.[238]

The controlling Powell opinion in the above three mid-1973 decisions demonstrated clearly that, at least as of that period of history, the applicable test on separation between Church and State was the already repeatedly alluded-to "purpose-effect-entanglement" trilogy yardstick. In the five cases at issue in the New York and Pennsylvania litigation, the first ("purpose") passed muster; the third ("entanglement") was but briefly discussed; the second ("effect") became decisive. When, undismayed, undaunted, and stubborn, Pennsylvania tried once more in 1975, with a host of provisions for state aid to private and parochial schools for such services as counseling, testing, remedial classes in speech and hearing therapy, and for instructional equipment like charts, maps, records, films, tape recorders, and projectors, as well as an additional textbook loan program, all, except—predictably—the last, which survived 6:3, fell 3:6. With Justice Stewart speaking for the majority, joined wholly or partly by his colleagues Douglas, Brennan, Powell, Marshall, and Blackmun—the Chief Justice and Justices White and Rehnquist dissenting, more or less—and again zeroing in on the *effect* of the multiple legislation plus what it regarded as patent "politi-cal [and] administrative entanglement," the Court, in a stern, broadly sweeping opinion, saw grave potential for conflict between Church and State. Provision of such services, wrote Stewart, raises "the danger that religious doctrine will become intertwined with secular instruction"[239] and creates a "serious potential for divisive conflict over the issue of aid to religion"[240] as legislation providing financial support comes up in the legislature year after year. The program, which cost $12 million for non-public schools in 1972–73, "inescapably" results in the direct

---

[238]*Committee for Public Education . . . v. Nyquist, op. cit.*, at 774. For reconfirmation of Nyquist's tax relief negation, see also the Court's summary disposition in *Byrne v. Public Funds for Public Schools*, 442 U.S. 907 (1979).

[239]*Meek v. Pittenger*, 421 U.S. 349, at 370.

[240]*Ibid.*, at 372.

and substantial advancement of religious activity, Stewart held for the majority, "and thus constitutes an impermissible establishment of religion."[241]

In fine, what the Court held in that 1975 landmark decision of *Meek v. Pittenger* was—speaking somewhat oversimplifiedly but accurately—that tax-raised funds may plainly not be used to finance the operations of church schools. Few, if any, Court watchers seriously believed, however, that the determined and numerous supporters of aid to non-public schools would cease and desist. Indeed, the Court's docket for the following term contained a number of possible candidates for renewed Church-State legal strife. And one of them—to the astonishment (and dismay) of a number of close students of the Court—may have done more than "open a small crack in the 'wall' of separation," as *The New York Times* put it.[242] In a 5:4 decision in the *Roemer* case, featuring a welter of opinions, but *no* majority agreement (the five-man victorious side splitting two ways in its reasoning),[243] the Supreme Court upheld Maryland's program of *non-categorical* financial aid to church-related *colleges,* thereby, for the first time in history, approving a system of state *general purpose* subsidies benefitting church-related educational institutions. Over the troubled, fervent, often biting dissents by Justices Brennan, Stewart, Marshall, and Stevens (Justice Douglas's recent replacement), who viewed the subsidies as demonstrably involving "the disease of entanglement," the five Justices composing the high tribunal's marginal majority—Chief Justice Burger and his colleagues Blackmun, Powell, White, and Rehnquist—saw no constitutional violation for a variety of reasons. The decision seemed to be controlled by a less than totally persuasive rationale that had also governed in the 5:4 holding four years earlier in *Tilton v. Richardson*[244]—which upheld limited *federal* aid to higher educational facilities for construction purposes. The "character" of the colleges, the ability of these colleges "to separate their secular and religious functions," and the lower "impressionability" of college students[245]—as contrasted

---

[241]*Ibid.*, at 366. With respect to the described expenditure, see p. 291, footnote 229, *supra.*

[242]Sec. 4, p. 7E, June 27, 1976.

[243]*Roemer v. Maryland Public Works Board,* 426 U.S. 736 (1976).

[244]403 U.S. 672 (1971). See discussion, *supra,* pp. 291–93.

[245]For a different point of view, see Howard L. Reiter, "Do Professors Persuade Students?", *News for Teachers of Political Science* (Winter 1980), pp. 5–7.

with students on the secondary and primary levels—were held to lessen the dangers of indoctrination and thus sufficed to meet the trifold requirements of non-religious purpose, non-religious effect, and avoidance of excessive entanglement. The controlling plurality opinion by Justice Blackmun did admit "entanglement," but since he and his supporters did not deem it "excessive," it was not viewed as constitutionally fatal to the program.[246]

Needless to relate, however, the *Roemer* holding and reasoning encouraged pro–parochial aid forces on all levels of the pedagogical and political ladder. Thus, a scant year later, in the 1977 *Wolman* case, when the Justices split five ways in ruling on a welter of six "aid" issues and their votes ranged from 8:1 to 3:6, new authority to aid parochial education was established by another Blackmun opinion, which was joined in all of its aspects only by Justice Stewart. Among the *Wolman* rulings "OK" were therapeutic, remedial, and guidance counseling services, if provided on "neutral" sites off school premises (7:2); diagnostic services "on ground" (8:1); and state-mandated standardized tests and test-scoring services (6:3)—but *not* the loan to either parents or children of classroom paraphernalia like wall charts, maps, globes, science kits, and slide projectors (3:6); nor subsidized field trips (4:5).[247] The Justices' five opinions were hardly models of clarity! Indeed, they constituted a mishmash of interpretations, which naturally invited further litigation. That December, perhaps in an effort to send a message that its broadening *Wolman* decision earlier in 1977 had decidedly not pulled out all the proverbial First Amendment stops, the Court ruled unconstitutional (6:3) a New York law that had provided for *direct financial reimbursement* to parochial schools for record-keeping and testing services,[248] the Chief Justice and Justices White and Rehnquist predictably dissenting.

Although 1978 and 1979 passed without any significant new development on the Church-State litigation front, the Court returned to the fray with a major decision in 1980, spawned by the 1977 *Wolman v. Walter*

[246]And for Justices White and Rehnquist only the first two requirements were constitutionally mandated. The Court, without opinion, affirmed similar college assistance programs in North Carolina and Tennessee in 1977—although Justices Brennan, Marshall, and Stevens wanted to hear oral arguments. (*Americans United for Separation of Church and State v. Blanton*, 434 U.S. 803.)

[247]*Wolman v. Walter*, 433 U.S. 229 (1977).

[248]*New York v. Cathedral Academy*, 434 U.S. 125 (1977).

confusion.[249] The new case, *Committee for Public Education and Religious Liberty v. Regan*,[250] arose as a result of New York's revised 1974 version of its 1970 law that the Justices had struck down 3 : 6 in the 1973 *Nyquist* decision.[251] Now, however, in an opinion by Justice White—the Court's most ardent and consistent champion of widespread accommodation—the Court distinguished the latter decision (5 : 4) by pointing to the fact that the 1974 statutory revision mandated that the state-required tests and supporting procedures, for which *all* schools were to be reimbursed, were *prepared by officials of the state* rather than by the schoolteachers themselves, as had been the case under the 1970 law. White's opinion, joined by his close allies on the issue, Chief Justice Burger and Justice Rehnquist, and "swing" Justices Stewart and Powell, contained numerous *caveats* and frankly acknowledged a course that "sacrifices clarity and predictability for flexibility."[252] Not surprisingly, the four dissenters, Justices Blackmun, Brennan, Marshall, and Stevens, perceived and warned against a demonstrable primary effect on advancing religion and an entanglement patently violative of the First Amendment's strictures.

Notwithstanding the broadening of the open door implications of its *Regan* ruling,[253] the Court continued to recognize limits, such as it had done in the same term with it proscription of New Jersey's attempt to provide *special income tax deductions* for parents who send their offspring to non-public schools.[254] Its 6 : 3 *per curiam* opinion again endeavored to make clear that neither tax credits nor tax deductions nor exemptions nor rebates, nor any form of *direct* financial aid to parents or teachers, would pass muster with six (Brennan, Stewart, Marshall, Blackmun, Powell, and Stevens) of the nine members of the Court, at least not in the absence of some permissible type of federal statutory sanction. Chief Justice Burger and Justices White and Rehnquist, on the other hand, appeared to be firmly on record as finding constitutional support for almost any type of "accommodation," provided they could detect *some* kind of secular purpose. In the instance of the Chief Justice, this posture obtained only so long as he did not perceive an entangle-

---

[249]433 U.S. 229, *op. cit.*
[250]444 U.S. 646.
[251]*Committee for Public Education and Religious Liberty v. Nyquist,* 413 U.S. 476.
[252]*Reagan, op. cit.,* at 653.
[253]*Ibid.*
[254]*Byrne v. Public Funds for Public Schools,* 442 U.S. 907 (1979).

ment that was "excessive." But Justices White and Rehnquist, especially the former, seemed to be concerned not at all about either the "primary effect" of the state involvement or the attendant "entanglement." If they saw a viable *secular* purpose, they would vote to uphold the measure or action. For them, the Court's three-pronged test on the establishment front had thus been reduced to the single one of the presence of a secular purpose as perceived by them.[255]

A major late June 1983 holding not only confirmed these "line-up" assumptions, but gave demonstrable evidence of a further widening of the door on behalf of "accommodation." For that Court, on which Justice Sandra Day O'Connor had replaced the retired Justice Stewart one and a half years earlier, was now willing to sanction an across-the-board tax deduction of up to $500 for parents of *all* elementary, and up to $700 of *all* secondary, school children for *bona fide* educational expenses, identified as "tuition, secular textbooks and instructional materials, and transportation." Distinguishing *Nyquist*,[256] and gaining not only Justice O'Connor's vote but, arguably surprisingly, that of Justice Powell, the 5 : 4 ruling,[257] authored by Justice Rehnquist—and, also predictably, supported by Chief Justice Burger and Justice White—contended that the Minnesota law withstood separation of Church and State challenges because it was "neutral" in design: it enabled parents of public school children as well as those in parochial and other private schools to avail themselves of the annual deduction.

To the four dissenters, however, speaking through Justice Marshall—who was joined by Justices Brennan, Blackmun, and Stevens—that reasoning was akin to a bad joke. In their eyes, the small benefits conceivably made available to parents of public school children were a mere pittance: of 815,000 beneficiaries, only 79 paid public school tuition, for example. The dissenters insisted that the *per se* inclusion of public schools could not "alter the fact that the most substantial benefit provided by the statute is available only to those parents who send their

---

[255]For an important scholarly advocacy of that point of view, see the extensive essay by George Anastoplo, "The Religion Clauses of the First Amendment," 11 *Memphis State University Law Review* 2 (Winter 1981), pp. 151–230. His essential "line test" responds to the question whether the *community* benefits in any manner. If so, fine—no constitutional problems.

[256]*Committee for Public Education and Religious Liberty v. Nyquist*, 413 U.S. 756 (1973).

[257]*Mueller v. Allen*, 463 U.S. 388 (1983).

children to schools that charge tuition.'' Thus, Marshall saw only a ''distinction without a difference'' between the New York *Nyquist* and the Minnesota *Mueller* decisions, concluding both sadly and angrily that Minnesota's provisions for ''the tax deduction for tuition and other educational expenses necessarily results in aid to the sectarian school enterprise as a whole.''[258] There could be but little doubt now that, absent changes in the Court's membership, the constitutional tilt for a considerably greater degree of commingling of Church and State had thereby been Court-sanctioned by mid-1983.

That assumption was confirmed one year later, when the Court's line-up made it clear not only that *Mueller* was no aberration, but that an apparently firm 5 : 4 majority was now in solid control of an expanded ''accommodationist'' approach: In March 1984, the Justices, splitting 5 : 4 exactly as they had in *Mueller,* and speaking through Chief Justice Burger, upheld against a Church and State separation challenge the constitutionality of the sponsorship by the city of Pawtucket, Rhode Island, of a forty-year old practice of displaying a crèche as an integral part of a Christmas display in a park owned by a non-profit corporation in the heart of the city's shopping district.[259] Its expenses were defrayed by the city and a downtown retail merchants' association.

Seeing only an ''indirect'' religious effect by what he termed a ''passive symbol,'' the Chief Justice's brief but forthright opinion frankly stipulated that ''total separation [of Church and State] is neither ''possible'' nor ''required.'' He called for the kind of ''line drawing'' that would ''affirmatively mandate accommodation, not merely tolerance of all religions, and forbids hostility to any.'' There was little doubt that the Burger opinion's emphasis on ''accommodation'' heralded a shift in, if not perhaps a total abandonment of, the then thirteen-year-old *Lemon* ''three part test'' of constitutionality, notwithstanding his reiteration of it.[260] Indeed, Justice O'Connor's concurring opinion saw ''no government endorsement or disapproval'' of religion, but merely a ''traditional symbol of the holiday.'' She called for a ''clarification of our Establishment Clause'' doctrine so as to place at its center of constitutional gravity ''what is crucial,'' namely, ''that a government practice not have the effect of communicating a message of government

[258]*Ibid.,* at 416.
[259]*Lynch v. Donnelly,* 465 U.S. 668, at 670–74.
[260]*Lemon v. Kurtzman,* 403 U.S. 602 (1971).

endorsement or disapproval of religion. It is only practices having the effect," she continued, "whether intentionally or unintentionally, that makes religion relevant, in reality or public perception, to status in the political community."[261] But the two impassioned dissents, one penned by Justice Brennan, joined by Justices Marshall, Blackmun, and Stevens, and the other by Blackmun, in which Stevens joined, saw a clearly proscribable "primary effect. . . . that place[s] the government's imprimatur of approval on the particular religious belief exemplified by the crèche."[262] To the four dissenters, Pawtucket's action amounted to an impermissible governmental endorsement of a particular faith. But one year later, with Justice Powell not participating, a divided 4 : 4 ruling upheld a decision below that had *required* the village of Scarsdale, New York, to allow a nativity scene by a private group in a public park in the center of town, citing the *Lynch* precedent.[263]

A tabular recapitulation of the more significant Supreme Court decisions on separation of Church and State is given in Table 6.3 and Table 6.4, augmented by the subsequent textual discussion. They are designed to demonstrate that of all the questions posed by the delicate and emotion-charged issue of establishment, the leading one has been on the type, degree, and conditions under which governmental aid may be constitutionally extended to non-public schools. To all intents and purposes, this means predominantly Roman Catholic schools. Regardless of which of the three theories of separation one may regard as most appropriate, there are no easy answers—on either procedural or substantive grounds. The facts of life (1987), on the other hand, are plain: the parents of some 4,800,000 parochial school children,[264] 83 percent of them Roman Catholic, are members of the body politic and wield

[261]*Lynch v. Donnelly, loc. cit.,* at 674–76.

[262]*Ibid.,* at 676–85.

[263]*Village of Scarsdale v. McCreary,* 471 U.S. 83 (1985). But contrast *City of Birmingham v. American Civil Liberties Union,* 55 LW 3309 (1986), in which the Court affirmed 8 : 1 a lower court's ruling holding unconstitutional the display of a Christmas nativity scene on the front lawn of Birmingham's City Hall, styling it a "purely religious symbol," in isolation, and thus violating the First Amendment ban against "establishment of religion." And shortly prior to Christmas 1986, Richmond, Virginia, withdrew its sponsorship from the fifty-five-year-old Christmas Eve Nativity Pageant to avoid violating the doctrine requiring the separation of Church and State. But the city continued its support of the production of *Amahl and the Night Visitors* ([Charlottesville] *Daily Progress,* December 3, 1986, p. C6.). Similarly, see Charlottesville, Va., Christmas 1987.

[264]*Standard Educational Almanac* 1987 (Marquis Academic Media), p. 174.

Table 6.3

"Separation of Church and State" Cases* in Which the Court Found No Constitutional Violation

DATE	CASE	VOTE	CONSTITUTIONAL ISSUES RAISED	DECISION AND COMMENTARY
1872	*Watson v. Jones*, 13 Wallace 679.	5:2	Can decisions by appropriate ecclesiastical tribunals as to which of two Louisville Presbyterian church factions had the legal right to possess and operate a local church be held binding on the civil authorities as well as the churches?	The U.S. Supreme Court recognized here that the freedom and independence of churches would be in grave danger if *it* or any other organ of civil government undertook to define religious heresy or orthodoxy or to decide which of two factions was the "true faith." (Reconfirmed, more than a century later, in a 7:2 decision: *Serbian Orthodox Diocese v. Milivojovich*, 429 U.S. 873 [1976], and, but somewhat more equivocally, in the 5:4-decided case of *Jones v. Wolf*, 443 U.S. 595 [1979].)
1899	*Bradfield v. Roberts*, 175 U.S. 291.	9:0	May Congress appropriate funds ($30,000) for a District of Columbia hospital, operated by a sisterhood of the Roman Catholic Church but chartered by Congress?	Peckham held for unanimous Court that the 1st Amendment was *not* violated, since the hospital, as a corporation chartered by Congress, is a "purely secular agency" and does not become a religious one merely because its members are Catholic nuns.
1908	*Quick Bear v. Leupp*, 210 U.S. 50.	9:0	Could U.S. Government legally disburse treaty and other funds of which it was trustee for Indians (their real owners) to private religious schools, at the designation of the Indians, to defray their tuition costs?	Arrangement held constitutional on grounds that the U.S. Government is necessarily "undenominational" and cannot make any law respecting an establishment of religion. It merely held the funds in a fiduciary capacity for the Indians.

Year	Case	Vote	Issue	Holding / Commentary
1930	Cochran v. Louisiana State Board of Education, 281 U.S. 370.	8:0	Validity of a Louisiana statute providing for purchase and grant of *secular* textbooks for use by public *and* nonpublic, including parochial, school children.	Initial application of the "*child benefit*" approach. Here, through its new Chief Justice, Hughes, Court held that benefits went to the "children of the state," not to the "private schools *per se*." "Individual interests are aided only as the common interest is safeguarded." Decision based chiefly on due process.
1947	Everson v. Board of Education of Ewing Township, N.J., 330 U.S. 1.	5:4	Validity of New Jersey statute authorizing bus fare reimbursement to parents of private (non-profit) and here parochial, as well as public, school students.	Statute upheld. The famed "wall" decision. (See body of chapter, pp. 328–32, for discussion and analysis.) "Public purpose" "child benefit" doctrine applied.
1952	Zorach v. Clauson, 343 U.S. 306.	6:3	Validity of New York's "released time" program in New York City's public schools.	Upheld because of its special circumstances. (See body of chapter, pp. 348–51 for discussion and analysis.)
1968	Board of Education v. Allen, 392 U.S. 236.	6:3	Constitutionality of 1965 New York State statute requiring local school districts to *lend* books gratis to seventh- to twelfth-grade children in private and parochial schools.	Sustained on basis of broad application of the "child benefit" theory. Stinging dissents by Justices Black, Douglas, Fortas. (See discussion in text, *supra*, pp. 351–53.)
1970	Walz v. Tax Commission of the City of New York, 397 U.S. 664.	7:1	Constitutionality of tax exemption of property used exclusively for religious purposes.	Sustained on the basis of "benevolent neutrality," i.e., on grounds that *no particular* religion is singled out for favorable treatment, and partly on the historical grounds that church tax exemptions have been accepted without challenge in *all* states for most of

*Some "mixed" cases, such as *The Sunday Closing Cases*, in which the "free exercise" issues predominated, are found in Table 6.1.

(*continued*)

Table 6.3 (Continued)

DATE	CASE	VOTE	CONSTITUTIONAL ISSUES RAISED	DECISION AND COMMENTARY
				the nation's history. But there are limits, as the Court's 9:0 refusal in 1984 to review the tax fraud conviction of the Rev. Sun Myung Moon for tax fraud (and an 18-month jail sentence) demonstrates. Sun Myung Moon had alleged government interference with the internal affairs of a church. (*The Reverend Sun Myung Moon v. United States, 466 U.S. 971.*)
1971	*Tilton v. Richardson*, 403 U.S. 672.	5:4	Constitutionality of $240 million Federal Higher Education Facilities Act of 1963 which funds construction of academic buildings on private sectarian as well as secular colleges.	Narrowly sustained—except for its 20-year "quit-claim" provision, which fell 9:0—on grounds that the admitted "entanglement" of Church and State was "not enough" to invalidate (unlike that in the *Lemon* and *Earley* decisions made on the same day). Saved as a "one-time, single-purpose construction," rather than a "continuing" grant. Justices Black, Douglas, Brennan, and Marshall dissenting in two separate opinions.
1973	*Hunt v. McNair*, 413 U.S. 734.	6:3	Validity of a South Carolina state bond issue designed to aid all types of institutions of higher learning in construction, financing, and refinancing of projects of non-religious purpose buildings.	Upheld on the strength of *Tilton* precedent in the absence of any showing that the recipient Baptist College involved was "any more of an instrument of religious indoctrination" than the institutions involved in *Tilton.*

Year	Case	Vote	Issue	Holding/Comment
			Orthodox Church of control over all its Church property in New York by forceful statutory transfer to the local "Russian Church in America."	impairing the separation of Church and State. Government has no capacity to intervene in religious controversies or determine which is "the true faith."
1962	*Engel v. Vitale*, 370 U.S. 421.	6:1	Constitutionality of New York State composed 22-word non-denominational prayer administered in public schools.	"The New York laws officially prescribing the Regents' prayer are inconsistent with both the purposes of the Establishment Clause and with the Establishment Clause itself." (See text, pp. 336–38, *supra*, for full discussion.)
1963	*Abington School District v. Schempp* and *Murray v. Curlett*, 374 U.S. 203.	8:1	Validity of Pennsylvania's statutory requirement of reading of 10 verses from Holy Bible in public schools and Maryland's practice of daily Bible reading and Lord's Prayer recitation in public schools.	All three procedures held to violate the establishment clause, following *Engel*. (See text, *supra*, pp. 338–42, for discussion and analysis.)
1968	*Epperson v. Arkansas*, 393 U.S. 97.	9:0	Constitutionality of Arkansas "Monkey Law," a statute which made it unlawful to teach the theory that mankind is ascended or descended from a lower order of animals.	Law violates establishment of religion clause by embodying the idea of a particular segment of religious beliefs and proscribing all others. (In 1982 U.S. District Court Judge Wm. R. Overton declared Arkansas's "creation science" law unconstitutional. *McLean v. Arkansas Board of Education*, 723 F.2d 45.)

*Some "mixed" cases, such as *Torcaso v. Watkins*, involving *both* separation and free exercise issues, are found in Table 6.2.

(continued)

Table 6.4 (Continued)

DATE	CASE	VOTE	CONSTITUTIONAL ISSUES RAISED	DECISION AND COMMENTARY
1969	Presbyterian Church v. Mary Elizabeth Blue Hull Memorial Church. 393 U.S. 440.	9:0	May civil courts award church property to dissident congregations on the grounds that the parent church has lost the faith?	"First Amendment values are plainly jeopardized when church litigation is made to turn on the resolution by civil courts of controversies over religious doctrine and practice." (cf. first entry on p. 364, supra.)
1971	Lemon v. Kurtzman and Earley v. Dicenso, 403 U.S. 602.	8:0 / 8:1	Constitutionality of direct aid to Pennsylvania and Rhode Island parochial schools, involving state "purchase" of secular "services" from sectarian schools, including the use of public funds to pay salaries of parochial school teachers.	Both statutes struck down as involving "excessive entanglement between government and religion." Chief Justice Burger also pointed to "divisive political potential" of the laws, an "evil" the First Amendment was designed to avoid. White, in the solo dissent, saw no "excessive entanglement, finding "separable" secular functions. (See text, supra, pp.353–55.)
1972	Essex v. Wolman, 409 U.S. 808.	8:1	Constitutionality of an Ohio plan for direct tuition rebates of $90 annually per child attending a private or parochial school.	Struck down as "excessive entanglement," as a violation of the establishment clause, because "the effect of the scheme is to aid religious enterprises."
1973	Levitt v. Commission for Public Education and Religious Libery, 413 U.S. 472; Committee for Public Education and Religious Liberty v. Nyquist, 413 U.S. 756; and Sloan v. Lemon, 413 U.S. 825.	8:1 / 6:3 / 6:3	Validity of several New York and Pennsylvania programs of diversely attempted financial aid to private, chiefly parochial, schools, including tuition reimbursement, tax relief, repairs, and maintenance, non-man-	All statutes involved fell as "eroding . . . the limitations of the establishment clause now firmly implanted." Powell's opinions stressed that the programs all advanced religion in that they directly

1974	*Marburger and Griggs v. Public Funds for Public Schools*, 417 U.S. 961.	6:3	dated testing, remedial classes, instructional equipment, and counseling. Constitutionality of two New Jersey programs providing money to parents of parochial school students, and also providing supplies and auxiliary services to those schools at public expense.	subsidized "the religious activities" of sectarian schools. (See text, *supra*, pp. 356–57.) Court, *per curiam*, affirmed declaration of unconstitutionality below on basis of absence of *bona fide* child benefit theory applicability and on the basis of its own 1973 *Nyquist* rulings.
1975	*Meek v. Pittenger*, 421 U.S. 349.	6:3	Constitutionality of another Pennsylvania attempt to provide sundry auxiliary services to private and parochial as well as public schools, including counseling, testing, remedial classes, and equipment. (Textbook loan provision was upheld.)	Same majority as *Nyquist, Sloan*, and *Marburger* held such provisions raised "the danger that religious doctrine will be intertwined with the secular institutions" and created a "serious potential for divisive conflict over the issue of aid to religion." Dissents by Burger, White, and Rehnquist. (See text, *supra*, pp. 357–58).
1977	*Wolman v. Walter*, 433 U.S. 229.	6:3	Validity of certain services by Ohio to nonpublic primary and secondary schools. Some upheld (see Table 6.3); some struck down, 6:3 and 5:4.	While upholding four such services (see p. 359 and Table 6.3), Court struck down financial aid for field trips (5:4) and for certain class paraphernalia (6:3).
1977	*New York v. Cathedral Academy*, 434 U.S. 125.	6:3	Constitutionality of New York's $11 million of *direct* reimbursement to parochial schools for record-keeping and testing services.	Over dissents by Burger, White, and Rehnquist, six members held law to be unconstitutional by providing either direct aid to religion or producing "excessive state involvement in religious affairs." (But *cf.* its 1980 *Regan* holding, text, *supra*, pp. 360–361 and Table 6.3.)

(continued)

Table 6.4 (Continued)

DATE	CASE	VOTE	CONSTITUTIONAL ISSUES RAISED	DECISION AND COMMENTARY
1979	*National Labor Relations Board v. Bishop of Chicago*, 440 U.S. 490.	5:4	May a sectarian institution, such as a Roman Catholic school, be required to bargain collectively with a union?	Ducking the First Amendment's constitutional issue(s), the narrow majority ruled that there was no clear-cut affirmative Congressional intention ascertainable in the National Labor Relations Board that would extend its coverage to teachers in Church-operated schools.
1979	*Byrne v. Public Funds for Public Schools*, 442 U.S. 907.	6:3	Constitutionality of New Jersey statute providing a special income tax deduction for parents who send children to non-public schools.	In a one-sentence order, the Court here affirmed two lower federal courts that had held that the tax deduction had the "primary effect of advancing religion."
1980	*Stone v. Graham*, 449 U.S. 39.	5:4	Constitutionality of a Kentucky law requiring posting of a copy of the Ten Commandments in every public school classroom in the state.	Although paid for with private rather than tax funds, the practice fell as not being a "permissible state objective under the establishment clause."
1981	*Hall v. Bradshaw*, 450 U.S. 965.	9:0	Constitutionality of a North Carolina practice of publishing a "motorist's prayer" on its official highway map.	Denying review, the Court, without dissent, upheld a decision below that saw a patent violation of the Constitution's bar against state establishment of religion.
1981	*St. Martin's Lutheran Church v. South Dakota*, 451 U.S. 772.	9:0	Are religious schools that are "integrated into a church's structure," and have no separate identity, obliged to pay unemployment taxes for their employees?	Ducking the First Amendment's constitutional issue, the Court ruled that Congress had not intended to reach such schools, in contrast to those that are church-related but not directly church-run.

Year	Case	Vote	Question	Holding
1981	*Widmar v. Vincent*, 454 U.S. 263.	8:1	May Missouri's statute prohibiting the use of university buildings or grounds "for purposes of religious worship or religious training" be applied to regulate the *content* of religious speech by a duly registered student religious group?	Over a strange dissent by White, the Powell-led majority chose to view Missouri's regulation as a "content-based discrimination against religious speech," violative of the First Amendment's strictures against impeding freedom of speech, thereby inferentially violating the religion clauses. (In 1984 Congress responded by enacting the "Equal Access Act," which legitimizes the right of students to conduct any "political, religious, or philosophical" meeting on the school premises.)
1982	*Larsen v. Valente*, 456 U.S. 229.	5:4	May Minnesota exempt some religious groups from stringent fund-raising reporting requirements on charitable solicitations, while placing that burden on others?	No, ruled Brennan (over dissents by Burger, White, Rehnquist, and O'Connor), because the rules "do not operate evenhandedly [and are] precisely the sort of official denominational preference the framers of the First Amendment forbade."
1982	*Larkin v. Grendel's Den*, 454 U.S. 1140.	8:1	May Massachusetts statutorily allow churches to control whether nearby restaurants may have liquor licenses? The law literally allowed churches to exercise a veto.	With only Rehnquist dissenting, Burger held that giving the church the power of a government agency "enmeshes churches in the exercise of substantial governmental powers contrary to . . . First Amendment" strictures against establishment.
1985	*Wallace v. Jaffree*, 472 U.S. 38.	6:3	Can Alabama's statute authorize a one-minute period of silence in all public schools "for meditation or voluntary prayer"?	Although the law was permissive in form, the Court found it to have a clearly sectarian purpose and therefore to be the kind of enactment

(*continued*)

Table 6.4 *(Continued)*

DATE	CASE	VOTE	CONSTITUTIONAL ISSUES RAISED	DECISION AND COMMENTARY
				specifically proscribed by the seminal 1962 ruling in *Engel v. Vitale.* (See text, *supra*, pp. 336–38.)
1985	*Grand Rapids School District v. Ball,* 473 U.S. 373.	7:2 and 5:4	Are the school district's "Shared Time" and "Community Education" programs constitutional? They supplement the core curriculum offered students in private schools. School district pays personnel and furnishes supplies and materials for classes during regular school day in rooms located in and leased from the private schools. All but one of the 41 participating schools are religious schools.	Down went both programs, 5:4 and 7:2, respectively, for they were viewed as having the effect of promoting religion in several ways, indeed "primary or principal" ones, and thus violate "the dicates of the First Establishment Clause of the First Amendment." (White and Rehnquist dissent in both, Burger and O'Connor only in the second program.)
1985	*Aguilar v. Felton,* 473 U.S. 402	5:4	May New York City provide instructional services, funded under Title I of the Federal Aid to Elementary and Secondary Schools of 1965, to parochial schools on the latter's premises? Although instruction was by public school teachers, the city utilized a system for monitoring the religious content of such Title I classes.	"No," ruled the Court by a 5:4 vote (Burger, White, Rehnquist, and O'Connor dissenting), because the risk of "substantial state-sponsored indoctrination" oversteps the "constitutional line between allowable governmental accommodation of religion and direct financial aid," notwithstanding the worthy goals promoted by the federal program.
1987	*Edwards v. Aguillard,* 107 S.Ct. 2573.	7:2	May Louisiana require the teaching of "creationism" to balance that of "evolution" in its public school curriculum?	"No," held Brennan's opinion, with Scalia and Rehnquist dissenting, striking it down as a crass violation of separation.

political power. When all is said and done, the issue ultimately falls into the *policy field*, heavily surcharged with considerations of public welfare in a pluralistic society with a democratic base. The sole remaining question then becomes that of the *constitutionality* of such programs as government, be it state or federal, does choose to adopt. *Is* the program a violation of the pertinent aspects of the First and/or Fourteenth Amendments?

Obviously, the judiciary, and the Supreme Court of the United States in particular, has not provided a clear-cut response to the constitutional question. At times it has upheld certain policies; at others it has struck them down. It must never be forgotten, however, that an additional consideration at the bar of judicial decision-making is the Court's strong predisposition to exercise judicial self-restraint vis-à-vis legislative enactments. The Court's avowed purpose, given at least some doubt about a measure's legitimacy, is to *save,* not to destroy. It is a recognition of this basic maxim of judicial self-restraint that will facilitate an understanding of decisions that, at least on paper, would seem to be diametrically opposite. Thus, we have witnessed three levels of approach which the Court has utilized:

Level 1. The Court *strikes down* a measure or practice as a clearly and demonstrably unconstitutional infringement of the no establishment clause—*because,* in whole or in part, it is simply and patently unconstitutional (and usually, although not always, so regarded by a large majority of the justices). Some pertinent examples are: the *Illinois Released Time* case,[265] in which the released time programs were held on public school property (8 : 1); the *Oregon Compulsory Education Law* case,[266] in which that State *required* attendance at public schools (9 : 0); the *New York Prayer* case,[267] in which the New York State–composed and –administered public school prayer was declared unconstitutional (8 : 1); the *Pennsylvania and Maryland Bible Reading* cases,[268] in which statutes and practices requiring public school reading of Bibles and the Lord's Prayer met a like fate (8 : 1 and 8 : 1); the *Arkansas "Monkey Law"* case,[269] in which the proscription of the teaching of

[265]*Illinois ex rel. McCollum v. Board of Education,* 333 U.S. 203 (1948).
[266]*Pierce v. Society of Sisters of the Holy Names,* 268 U.S. 510 (1925).
[267]*Engel v. Vitale,* 279 U.S. 421 (1962).
[268]*Abington School District v. Schempp* and *Murray v. Curlett,* 374 U.S. 203 (1963).
[269]*Epperson v. Arkansas,* 393 U.S. 97 (1968).

evolution fell (9 : 0); the *Pennsylvania and Rhode Island "purchase of secular services and direct salary supplemental laws"*[270] and the *Ohio* direct tuition reimbursement grants statute,[271] which fell on grounds of "excessive entanglement" of Church and State (8 : 0, 8 : 1, and 8 : 1); the five *New York* and *Pennsylvania* laws,[272] providing numerous forms of financial aid to non-public schools, and the renewed 1975 *Pennsylvania* statutory endeavors[273] to attain the same end, all of which fell in 1973 as having a primary *effect* of aiding religion (8 : 1, 6 : 3, 6 : 3). The Court also struck down *Ohio's* renewed efforts to provide certain class paraphernalia (6 : 3 and 5 : 4);[274] *New York's* move *directly to reimburse* parochial schools for record-keeping and testing services (6 : 3);[275] and *New Jersey's* attempt to legislate income tax deductions for parents of parochial school students (6 : 3);[276] the *Alabama Period of Silence* law (6 : 3), which authorized a one-minute period of silence for "meditation or prayer" in all public schools;[277] and the *Louisiana* statute mandating the teaching of the creationist theory of man's origin alongside evolution in public schools.[278]

Although fully aware of the relative unpopularity of some of its decisions, especially in the third and fourth illustrations (which evoked an emotional, popular reaction that was often uninformed and sometimes absurd, given the clear limits of the decisions involved), the Court did not hesitate to do what it clearly considered its duty under the commands of the Constitution. And it did so with but 31 dissenting votes cast of the 158 cast above all together, one of the former coming on procedural rather than substantive grounds.

Level 2. The Court, perhaps somewhat uncomfortably at times, and often severely divided, *upholds* a measure or practice because it believes that it can stand under the principle of "auxiliary" or "general

[270]*Lemon v. Kurtzman* and *Earley v. Dicenso*, 403 U.S. 602 (1971).

[271]*Essex v. Wolman*, 409 U.S. 808 (1972).

[272]*Levitt v. Committee for Public Education and Religious Liberty*, 413 U.S. 472, *Committee for Public Education and Religious Liberty v. Nyquist*, 413 U.S. 756, and *Sloan v. Lemon*, 413 U.S. 825 (1973).

[273]*Meek v. Pittenger*, 421 U.S. 349.

[274]*Wolman v. Walter*, 433 U.S. 229 (1977).

[275]*New York v. Cathedral Academy*, 434 U.S. 125 (1977).

[276]*Byrne v. Public Funds for Public Schools*, 442 U.S. 907 (1979).

[277]*Wallace v. Jaffree*, 105 S.Ct. 2479 (1985).

[278]*Edwards v. Aguillard*, 107 S.Ct. 2573 (1987).

public policy" rather than as "primary" or "specific" governmental aid to a non-public school—often rationalized under the controversial "child benefit" theory. Appropriate illustrations are: the *Louisiana Textbooks to All* case,[279] which enabled use of textbooks purchased with public funds by pupils of public *and* non-public schools (8:0); although that case was actually decided on "due process" grounds rather than on the religious issue *per se,* it was confirmed and expanded (6:3) by the 1968 *New York Textbook Loan* case,[280] which did deal with the establishment issue directly; it was the only provision that escaped (6:3) unconstitutionality in the 1975 Pennsylvania *Meek v. Pittenger* holding,[281] and it was upheld (6:3) in the 1977 Ohio *Wolman v. Walter* litigation;[282] the *New Jersey Bus* case,[283] the famous "wall" decision, upholding public subventions for transportation of parochial as well as public school students (5:4); the *New York Released Time* case,[284] where religious classes were held *outside* public school buildings during the school day for those wishing to attend, with the others continuing secular education (6:3); the tax exemption of wholly church-owned property in the *New York Tax Exemption* case (7:1);[285] the *Federal Education Facilities Act* case, narrowly (5:4) upholding construction grants to both sectarian and non-sectarian colleges;[286] the 1973 *South Carolina Aid to Education* case,[287] which sanctioned (6:3) a scheme providing state bond aid to *all* educational institutions of higher learning; the 1976 *Maryland Aid to Church-Affiliated Colleges and Universities* case,[288] which upheld (5:4) a program of general grants for non-sectarian use even in institutions where religion is mandatory; the 1977 *Ohio Multiple Primary and Secondary Aid to All* case,[289] upholding such heretofore unapproved state services to non-public schools as certain mandatory testing, diagnostic, and therapeutic

[279]*Cochran v. Louisiana State Board of Education,* 281 U.S. 370 (1930).
[280]*Board of Education v. Allen,* 392 U.S. 236.
[281]*Meek v. Pittenger,* 421 U.S. 349.
[282]*Wolman v. Walter,* 433 U.S. 229.
[283]*Everson v. Board of Education of Ewing Township,* 330 U.S. 1 (1947).
[284]*Zorach v. Clauson,* 343 U.S. 306 (1952).
[285]*Walz v. Tax Commissioners of New York City,* 397 U.S. 664 (1970).
[286]*Tilton v. Richardson,* 403 U.S. 672 (1971).
[287]*Hunt v. McNair,* 413 U.S. 734.
[288]*Roemer v. Maryland Public Works Board,* 426 U.S. 736.
[289]*Wolman v. Walter,* 433 U.S. 229.

services (6 : 3, 8 : 1, and 7 : 2, respectively); and the *New York 1980 Aid
to Parochial and Other Nonpublic Schools Aid* case,[290] sanctioning
(5 : 4) reimbursement for certain state-required administration and testing services, provided these were prepared by the state rather than by
the teachers; the highly controversial 1983 *Minnesota Parental Tax
Deduction* case[291] upholding (5 : 4) that state's law permitting parents
of *all* elementary and secondary school children to deduct annually up
to $700 for educational expenses, be the schools private or public; the
practice of having ordained, taxpayer-paid clergy open legislative sessions with a prayer, upheld (6 : 3) in the 1983 *Marsh v. Chambers
Legislative Chaplains* case;[292] the 1984 *Pawtucket, R. I., Crèche*
case,[293] in which that city's financial support of a Christmas display,
including a crèche, was upheld (5 : 4), the Court viewing it as a "historic symbol" rather than as a religious practice.

Here, although much more sharply split, with 45 of 140 votes cast in
dissent (roughly one-third, compared with *circa* one-fifth in the Level 1
group), the Court believed itself justified in accommodating public
policy that raised questions about, but was not regarded as violative of,
separation of Church and State.

Level 3. The Court, on the basis of the principle of judicial self-
restraint or because it adjudges the matter *res judicata,* either refuses to
accept a case for review or simply affirms the decision below. This
judicial practice may well have the effect of sanctioning practices in one
state that are unconstitutional in another, since in each separate instance
they were so held by the state courts concerned; but considerations of
federalism are far from absent in the judicial process. Some random
instances are:

Despite its decision confirming Louisiana's, New York's, Ohio's,
and Pennsylvania's free loan of textbooks for parochial schools laws,[294]
the Court denied *certiorari* in an Oregon case,[295] thereby upholding a
6 : 1 decision by Oregon's Supreme Court that school districts must *stop*
providing free textbooks to parochial schools; it even reconfirmed that

---

[290]*Committee for Public Education and Religious Liberty v. Regan,* 444 U.S. 646.
[291]*Mueller v. Allen,* 463 U.S. 388.
[292]*Marsh v. Chambers,* 463 U.S. 783.
[293]*Lynch v. Donnelly,* 465 U.S. 688.
[294]See pp. 378–80, footnotes 279–87, *supra.*
[295]*Dickman v. School District, Oregon City,* 371 U.S. 823 (1962).

decision one year later; New Mexico's and South Dakota's highest courts ruled likewise; it affirmed (6 : 3) a New Jersey decision declaring unconstitutional two state programs that provided cash funds to parents of non-public school students for the *purchase* of textbooks, and further provided supplies and auxiliary services to such schools at public expense;[296] and the Court declined to review a Missouri Supreme Court decision invalidating a Missouri law that authorized textbook *loans* to children in church-related as well as those in public and nonsectarian private schools.[297]

Despite its decision in the *New Jersey Bus* case of 1948[298] the Court has refused to review, or has simply summarily affirmed,[299] innumerable state court decisions declaring *unconstitutional,* as violative of the respective state constitutions, free transportation provisions for parochial as well as public school children in, among other states, Alaska, Iowa, Missouri, New Mexico, Oklahoma, Washington, and Wisconsin. In fact, all of these came after the *New Jersey Bus* case—although by mid-1987 twenty-seven of the states provided some type of transportation aid to parochial schools, several of which had found state judicial approval (e.g., Connecticut)—and subsequent Supreme Court sanction by virtue of refusal to review (e.g., Pennsylvania).[300]

Despite other state precedents *to the contrary,* the Court refused to review,[301] and thereby upheld, a Vermont Supreme Court decision holding unconstitutional the use of public funds for tuition payable to children attending either public or private schools of their own choice in the instance of towns that had no high schools of their own. Again, despite other state practices to the contrary, the Court refused to review,[302] and thus upheld, a 4 : 3 Court of Appeals of Maryland decision that declared unconstitutional as a violation of the *First* Amendment the subvention of matching state grants for construction purposes to two

[296]*Marburger and Griggs v. Public Funds for Public Schools,* 417 U.S. 961 (1974).

[297]*Reynolds v. Paster,* 419 U.S. 1111 (1975).

[298]*Everson v. Board of Education of Ewing Township,* 330 U.S. 1.

[299]*Luetkemeyer v. Kaufmann,* 419 U.S. 888 (1974).

[300]See *Rhoades v. Washington,* 389 U.S. 11 (1967); and *Worrell v. Matters,* 389 U.S. 846 (1967).

[301]*Anderson v. Swart,* 366 U.S. 925 (1961).

[302]*Board of Public Works of Maryland v. Horace Mann League of U.S.,* 385 U.S. 97 (1966); and *Horace Mann League of United States v. Board of Public Works of Maryland,* 385 U.S. 97 (1966).

Maryland Roman Catholic colleges (Notre Dame and St. Joseph) and one Methodist college (Western Maryland), while upholding similar grants to Hood College. It had regarded Hood's character "essentially secular," but deemed the other three as clearly projecting a religious "image" (only to reverse itself 5 : 4 a decade later!).[303] It summarily affirmed (6 : 3) a lower federal court decision invalidating a California law that authorized state income tax reductions for parents of parochial school students,[304] yet nine years later it would sanction Minnesota's that permitted such deductions in all schools.[305] And, as noted above,[306] the Court had affirmed a decision by Maryland that *upheld* state tax *exemptions* for church buildings.)

Obviously, the issue is far from settled. Notwithstanding *constitutional* proscriptions in thirty-six states, fully forty-seven (!) provided some sort of aid to church-related schools in 1988—often in the face of these constitutional prohibitions. Thus, twenty-seven states provided pupil transportation; twenty-six, textbooks; twenty-three, health services; seven, "general auxiliary" services; and three still "purchased services" from non-public schools and paid salary supplements to teachers in these schools—notwithstanding Supreme Court holdings to the contrary in similar cases.

In terms of experience these three "levels" are readily explainable and just as readily serve to reemphasize the difficulty, if not perhaps the utter impossibility, of creating and drawing a viable, predictable line between the permissible and the impermissible in the realm of the establishment clause in general and in that of the subsection of public and private education in particular. Still, some outlines of the lines that can be drawn are perceptible in general terms—if not in specific Court judgments. They can be identified, although their application cannot be predicted safely.

Some Overall Policy Positions. A number of these outlines have clearly emerged and may be stated broadly as follows:

First, because it is intended to serve pupils of all religious faiths, a

---

[303]The issue had been revived in 1974–75, when Maryland, having reinstituted a somewhat revamped program, won a victory in a Three-Judge District Court ruling, which was appealed to the U.S. Supreme Court; the latter sustained the lower tribunal in 1976. (*Roemer v. Maryland Public Works Board,* 426 U.S. 736.) See pp. 294–95, *supra.*

[304]*Franchise Tax Board v. United Americans,* 419 U.S. 890 (1974).

[305]*Mueller v. Allen,* 463 U.S. 388 (1983).

[306]See 284, footnote 197, *supra.*

public school in democratic society is *ipso facto* a secular institution. This, of course, does not mean that the public school either is, should be, or is intended to be anti- or irreligious—and the judiciary as well as the legislature have made this amply clear.

Second, freedom of conscience in all its religious aspects and concepts must be, and is, protected.

Third, while it is axiomatic that it is incumbent upon the federal government to protect freedom of religion and to ascertain the separation of Church and State in the several states of the Union, responsibility for public school curriculum and administration lodges with the State. Just as applicable provisions of the Civil Rights Act of 1964 and the Federal Aid to Elementary and Secondary Education Act of 1965, both as amended, have had far-reaching impact in altering that tradition, so indeed have they indubitably had at the level of higher education.

Fourth, notwithstanding the contemporary changes just described, public education in the several states is controlled preeminently by duly appointed and/or elected public state officials.

Fifth, although attendance of public schools is inevitably one of the hallmarks of the body politic in the several states, no state may *compel* school-age students to attend *public* as distinct from private or parochial schools, and no state has tried to do so since Oregon's defeat at the hands of a unanimous Supreme Court in the *Pierce* case[307] in 1925.

Sixth, on the other hand, a state constitutional provision (e.g., Missouri's) that *forbids* the expenditure of public funds to church-related schools does *not* violate the religious freedom (free exercise) of parents who choose to send their children to sectarian schools.[308] This posture was firmly reiterated by Chief Justice Burger for the Court in 1973: "Even assuming that the equal protection clauses might require state aid to be granted to private nonsectarian schools in some circumstances—health care or textbooks, for example—a State could rationally conclude as a matter of legislative policy that constitutional neutrality as to certain schools might best be achieved by withholding all state assistance."[309]

Seventh, either by constitutional provision or by statute most states have endeavored to prevent the "direct" disbursement or subvention of

[307]*Pierce v. Society of Sisters of the Holy Names,* 268 U.S. 510.
[308]*Brusca v. State Board of Education of Missouri,* 405 U.S. 1050 (1972).
[309]*Norwood v. Harrison,* 413 U.S. 455 (1973), at 462. (Italics supplied.)

any funds from the public state treasury to any parochial or otherwise denominational school—although at least some states have acted to "purchase services," pay salaries, and rebate taxes, sometimes called "parochaid," devices that were declared unconstitutional severally by the Supreme Court in 1971, 1973, 1974, 1975, 1977, 1979, and 1985.[310] Most states have permitted, or even encouraged, the providing of one or more, or even all, of the following "auxiliary" services to accredited non-public schools: tax exemptions; free lunches; free medical care; free protective services; free school nurse services; free textbook loans; free bus transportation; free driver education; certain diagnostic, testing, therapeutic, and record-keeping services; and other similar governmental aid, usually termed "indirect," "general," or "auxiliary." It should be noted again here, however, that many of these practices have either been specifically forbidden in some states and/or held to be unconstitutional by their state courts, while the precise *opposite* has been held in others.[311]

Eighth, even prior to the *Illinois Released Time* case[312] the type of denominational or sectarian teaching there at issue was specifically forbidden by most states. Yet a number always did, and still do, permit the kind of "released time" practiced in New York and upheld in the *New York Released Time* case.[313]

Ninth, state-mandated religious observances in the public schools, such as prayers, Bible reading, and recitation of the Lord's Prayer, practiced widely in various states[314] and banned in a good many others[315] even *prior to* the New York, Pennsylvania, and Maryland 1962 and 1963 Supreme Court decisions,[316] are no longer legal. And as it has already demonstrated repeatedly,[317] the Supreme Court will make

[310]See discussion on preceding pages and Table 6.4.

[311]The continuing controversy is demonstrated by the successful veto by Delaware Governor Charles L. Terry, Jr., early in 1966 of a bill that would have provided free bus transportation for parochial and other private school students. At approximately the same time, Governor W. W. Scranton of Pennsylvania *signed* a similar measure. Both chief executives acted—or at least professed to act—in accordance with constitutional mandates governing such aid. Similarly diverse postures continue.

[312]*Illinois ex rel. McCollum v. Board of Education,* 333 U.S. 203 (1948).

[313]*Zorach v. Clauson,* 343 U.S. 306 (1952).

[314]E.g., Alabama, Arizona, Indiana, Idaho, Maine, New Jersey.

[315]E.g., Alaska, Illinois, Nevada, Wyoming, Washington.

[316]*Engel v. Vitale,* 370 U.S. 421 (1962); and *Abington School District v. Schempp* and *Murray v. Curlett,* 374 U.S. 203 (1963).

[317]See pp. 336 ff., footnotes 153–79, *supra.*

short shrift of any subterfuges—provided a case is appealed to it (which of course does not necessarily occur in all, or even most, instances). The collateral question of the observance *in the public schools* of Christmas and other religious holidays has not squarely reached the Supreme Court. At the state court level, this matter—which raises such emotion-charged, difficult social issues—has seen one adverse[318] and one partly favorable and partly adverse ruling by courts and at least one adverse ruling by an attorney-general.[319] But a 5 : 4 ruling by the Supreme Court in 1980 struck down a Kentucky law that required the posting of a copy of the Ten Commandments in every public classroom in the state.[320] Schools with a substantial Jewish enrollment have increasingly tried to deal with the problem either by diminishing, or even eliminating, the more theological aspects of Christmas, or by commemorating the Jewish holiday of Hanukkah, which usually falls at the same time of year.

Tenth, a reasonably predictive, albeit narrow, Court majority has continued to take a relatively "hard" line on the "secular purpose/effect/entanglement" triad, resulting in a fairly close reading of the First Amendment's injunctions for separation. But such decisions as those in the *Roemer* (1976), *Wolman* (1977), *Regan* (1980), *Mueller* (1983), *Marsh* (1983), and *Lynch* (1984) cases[321] render inevitable the conclusion that an erosion of Church-State separation has taken place. That there are limits is demonstrated by the Court's 6 : 3 interdictive rulings in the *Cathedral Academy* (1977), *Byrne* (1979), *Jaffree* (1985),

[318]Florida: *Chamberlin v. Dade County Board of Public Instruction,* 143 So. 2d 21 (Fla., 1962). Yet baccalaureate services were upheld, albeit on a procedural judicial point, in the same-named case, but recorded as 160 So. 2d 97 (1964). The Supreme Court dismissed an appeal on the issue for want of a properly presented federal question. (*Ibid.,* 377 U.S. 402 [1964].) And in late 1980 the Court affirmed summarily, with two dissents, a South Dakota ruling allowing the use of religious materials in public school observances of holidays, such as Christmas, here religious symbols, music, carol singing, and literature. (*Florey v. Sioux City School District,* 449 U.S. 987.)

[319]*Baer v. Kolmorgen,* 14 Misc. 2d 1015 (N.Y., 1960) was the court decision; the attorney-general's opinion, the first of its kind, was issued by Minnesota at the request of the Rochester (Minnesota) School district, 256 *Civil Liberties* 7 (July 7, 1968).

[320]*Stone v. Graham,* 449 U.S. 39. The unsigned 5 : 4 majority opinion observed that the "pre-eminent purpose [was] plainly religious" because the document is "undeniably a sacred text" for Jews and Christians. (The dissenters were Burger, Stewart, Blackmun, and Rehnquist.)

[321]*Roemer v. Maryland Public Works Board,* 429 U.S. 736; *Wolman v. Walter,* 433 U.S. 299; *Committee for Public Education and Religious Liberty v. Regan,* 444 U.S. 646; *Mueller v. Allen,* 463 U.S. 388; *Marsh v. Chambers,* 463 U.S. 783; and *Lynch v. Donelly,* 465 U.S. 688, all discussed in the text, *supra,* pp. 358 ff.

Grand Rapids (1985), and *Aguilar* (1985) cases.[322] Yet there is little doubt that in a host of areas, broadly describable as financial support for "auxiliary" governmental aid and services to parochial schools, a more permissive judicial attitude toward separation of Church and State appears to have become *res judicata—pace* some landmark decisions, such as the three 1985 holdings just noted. As it reached the late 1980s, the Court was closely divided on the omnipresent issue.

SEPARATION AND THE PROBLEM OF FEDERAL AID TO NON-PUBLIC SCHOOLS

The above ten guidelines to policy on the separation of Church and State vis-à-vis aid to non-public schools and/or recognition of sectarian practices therein are firmly established. But new complexities may well have been triggered with the enactment of the 1965 Federal Aid to Elementary and Secondary Educational Act, which contains controversial provisions of potentially crucial importance to the meaning of the First Amendment.

The 1965 Federal Aid to Elementary and Secondary Education Act. The concept of federal aid to education is not, of course, new. What is new is the revolutionary departure from precedent embraced in the 1965 bill. Breaking historic ground, it provided subventions of *federal money for elementary and secondary instruction for children in both public and parochial as well as all other schools.* Sundry measures in the field of education, in which private schools and colleges participated, had been passed prior to 1965, but none of these had tackled the ticklish problem of instructional federal aid to non-public schools below the college level. Among the former were the "G.I. Bill," the National School Lunch Act, the Special Milk Program, subsidized college housing, the Higher Education Facilities Act, the National Defense Education Act, the College Housing Loan Program, the National Science Foundation Program, and Atomic Energy Commission Fellowships. But because of the lasting opposition of educators, lawyers, and churchmen, instructional aid was never included—and as a result no general federal aid to education measure was put forward effectively until the

---

[322]*New York v. Cathedral Academy,* 434 U.S. 125; *Byrne v. Public Funds for Public Schools,* 442 U.S. 907; *Wallace v. Jaffree,* 472 U.S. 38; *Grand Rapids School District v. Ball,* 105 S. Ct. 3216; and *Aguilar v. Felton,* 105 S. Ct. 3232, all discussed in the text, pp. 373 ff., *supra.*

presidency of Lyndon B. Johnson, who submitted his bill in 1964 and saw it become law in 1965.

To the surprise of many, notwithstanding full recognition of the remarkable Johnson *domestic* political *savoir faire*, the bill went through both houses of Congress without a big Church-State fight, without a conservative-liberal battle, without a racial row. Indeed, it passed without a single major change after it had been first introduced for the administration by Representative Carl D. Perkins (D.-Ky.). It passed because the President managed to convince most of those either involved or interested that the entire scheme would collapse if anyone were to tinker with his bill. Although it may well have pleased no one entirely, all the traditional protagonists supported the measure, or at least did not oppose it: the National Education Association, the National Catholic Welfare Conference, the American Federation of Teachers, the American Jewish Congress, Americans for Democratic Action, Baptists, Methodists, and a coterie of other religious, educational, labor, and civil rights organizations. Heretofore, every past effort to see a general federal aid to education bill pass Congress had faltered for three overriding reasons: (1) the opposition of the hard core of anti-big-government, conservative members of Congress; (2) that of the diehard Southerners whose districts were in need of the kind of financial aid only the federal treasury could provide, but who steadfastly opposed the legislation because of the perennial "Powell Amendment"[323] that barred segregated use of funds; and (3) the controversy engendered by the delicate religious issue, with almost all Roman Catholics opposed to any bill that by-passed their parochial schools, and most Protestants and Jews opposed to any bill that did *not* by-pass aid to parochial schools.

President Johnson licked all three problems deftly. The first was eliminated by the drastic reduction of conservative senators and congressmen as a result of the landslide Johnson-over-Goldwater victory in the 1964 election. The race issue was by-passed by Title VI of the Civil Rights Act of 1964, which banned the use of federal funds for segregated activities. The religious issue was the most difficult, of course; yet the superb and experienced parliamentarian and tactician was equal to the task—one his Roman Catholic predecessor in office had been unwilling even to consider: for President Kennedy believed the inclu-

[323]Named after then Representative Adam Clayton Powell (D.-N.Y.).

sion of direct federal financial assistance to elementary and secondary schools to be unconstitutional, or at least he chose to give that impression publicly in the Administration's 1961 Ribicoff Brief.[324] And Senator Robert F. Kennedy publicly agreed with his murdered brother's posture during his tragedy-truncated presidential campaign in 1968.

Determined to get a general aid-to-education measure through the 89th Congress, and given a two-thirds Democratic majority, President Johnson, however, was not to be stopped by the religious issue. He met it in several ingenious ways. First, he drafted his program as one in line with the Supreme Court's "child benefit" approach. Second, the control of funds was to be in the hands of public authorities. Third, all aid was to be "categorical" rather than "general." Fourth, he more or less restricted the bill to the poor and needy; its primary benefits were assigned to counties and school districts with ten or more children of families with a yearly income of less than $2,000. Next, the United States Office of Education was initially authorized to allocate $100 million for grants to the states for the purchase of textbooks and library materials to go to Church-controlled and other private non-profit as well as public schools. The language of this particular provision was closely tailored to the principle of textbook *grants*-to-students, e.g., Louisiana's statute[325] that survived subsequent constitutional onslaughts, with the terms of the aid changed now to emphasize *loans* rather than grants.[326] To the irrefutable argument that some states expressly *forbid* that type of book grant or even loan, the administration's response was that *it,* rather than the states, would be the "owner" of the books and could, of course, loan them to the children concerned. The last aspect of the Johnson strategy in defeating or isolating the religious issue as a factor of opposition to the over-all program, was an on-the-record promise by the President to a number of balky, key Northern urban and

[324]See its reproduction in *The New York Times,* March 29, 1961, p. 22*l. Inter alia,* he said: "[T]he Constitution clearly prohibits aid to the . . . parochial schools. I don't think there is any doubt of that. . . . The Supreme Court made its decision in the *Everson* case by determining that the aid was to the child, not to the school. Aid to the school—there isn't any room for debate on the subject. It is prohibited by the Constitution, and the Supreme Court has made that very clear. And therefore there would be no possibility of our recommending it." Justice Douglas quoted this as "the correct constitutional position" in his dissent in *Tilton v. Richardson* in 1971. (403 U.S. 672.)

[325]Upheld in *Cochran v. Louisiana,* 281 U.S. 370 (1930).

[326]See *Board of Education v. Allen,* 392 U.S. 236 (1968), *Meek v. Pittenger,* 421 U.S. 349 (1975), and *Wolman v. Walter,* 433 U.S. 229 (1977), all discussed in the text, *supra.*

suburban members of Congress to go "all out" to alleviate the over-crowded classrooms and half-day sessions so prevalent there. In typically forceful language he assured these critical legislators in March 1965 that he would "use every rostrum and every forum and every searchlight that I can to tell the people of this country and their elected representatives that we can no longer afford over-crowded classrooms and half-day sessions."[327] On the morning following this clinching declaration, the House Committee on Education and Labor reported the bill out favorably. The House ultimately passed it by a vote of 263 : 153, and the Senate, where the bill had been entrusted to Senator Wayne Morse (D.-Ore.), followed suit early in April by a vote of 73 : 18. For the first time, both houses of Congress had thus approved a broad ($1.3 billion)[328] federal program to aid elementary and secondary education, regardless of the school's secular or non-secular character. The President triumphantly signed the bill into law on April 11, 1965.

The Constitutional Attack on the 1965 Act. Exactly two days later the first steps were taken to mount the anticipated constitutional attack on the revolutionary measure. The National Governing Council of the American Jewish Congress, which has a record of close alliance with liberal Protestant denominations on the Church-State issue, announced that it would seek a court test of the three most controversial and most innovative provisions of the Act. Urging that the "grave issues that have been raised during the long debate on the [statute] must be resolved promptly—before the church-state separation guarantee in the Bill of Rights is eroded to the point of extinction,"[329] the A.J.C. moved to ask for constitutional tests of the following:

1. The dual enrollment or "shared time" arrangements authorized under the bill—to the extent that these result in the "commingling" of public and

---

[327]*The Philadelphia Evening Bulletin,* April 9, 1965, p. 1.

[328]Predictably, this relatively modest-sounding figure had risen to $2.4 billion for the three-year budget period of 1970–73 and to over $8.3 billion for 1988. This figure does not include other types of federal grants for state and local education—the *total* approaching $20 billion by the early 1980s. Not surprisingly, votes to renew now passed with overwhelming margins—a far cry from the initial vote a decade earlier. The legislation's principle, if not all of its components, is no longer controversial. It has become a congressional bread-and-butter staple.

[329]As quoted in the *Christian Science Monitor,* April 13, 1965, p. 4. The A.J.C., as noted on p. 387, *supra,* had not opposed passage of the statute, but was eager for a rapid constitutional test.

parochial school faculties, facilities, and/or administration. (Under "shared time" programs the time of parochial school children is divided between public and parochial schools; i.e., for "religiously neutral" subjects—such as languages and physics—the child goes to the former, for the social sciences to the latter.)

2. Those provisions under which public school teachers and public school equipment may be sent into parochial schools under the bill's program of "supplementary educational centers." (Under Titles I and III, $100 million was initially allocated for remedial instruction, teaching machines, and laboratory equipment, teachers, and other services to public *and* non-profit private schools.)

3. The aforementioned provisions in Title II of the Act under which textbooks purchased with an initial $100 million of federal funds were made available to Catholic, Protestant, and Jewish parochial schools—the vast majority to the first—as well as to public schools.

But in order to be able to mount the desired Court test, it would first be necessary to obtain the kind of *federal* taxpayer standing to sue that had been consistently denied by the Supreme Court as a result of a famous 1923 decision.[330] Matters looked hardly promising for a Court reversal of that posture, especially given the delicate subject at issue— but the would-be litigants received aid from a powerful quarter: Senator Sam J. Ervin, Jr. (D.-N.C.), the Senate's leading constitutional authority and, conveniently, an implacable foe of aid to parochial schools. The Senator would *himself* argue the case for Supreme Court reversal of the "standing to sue" issue here. And he did so successfully! On June 10, 1968, the Court ruled 8:1 in a suit requesting an injunction against the 1965 statute in *Flast v. Cohen*[331] that the 1923 decision was *not* a barrier to suits, contending that the government was infringing on *specific Bill of Rights guarantees,* here the First Amendment's religion clauses.[332]

[330]There, in the case of *Frothingham v. Mellon,* 262 U.S. 447, the Supreme Court had held unanimously that a *federal* taxpayer lacked "standing" to sue and had not presented a *bona fide* "case or controversy" under the Constitution for federal court review of a challenge to appropriations under the federal Maternity Act of 1921. This holding did not then, nor has it since, applied to *state* "taxpayer suits" acting under *state* laws, but it is *res judicata* for federal cases. For a detailed examination of "standing" and "case or controversy," see my *The Judicial Process: An Introductory Analysis of the Court of the United States, England and France,* 5th ed. (New York: Oxford University Press, 1986), Chapter IX.

[331]392 U.S. 83.

[332]The opinion by Chief Justice Warren, which "distinguished" rather than overruled

Although that momentous decision did not address itself to the substantive merits of the separation of Church and State problem *per se*, it opened the door to a direct challenge of the huge federal expenditures under the 1965 law. By February 1971 fully fifty-two cases were "in the mill"—although, perhaps surprisingly, only two of significance had reached the Supreme Court's decisional stage on the merits by 1988: in 1974 it upheld 8 : 1 the Act's Title I provision for the sending of public school teachers into parochial (and other private) as well as public schools during normal school hours, a practice forbidden in Missouri, whence the case was appealed.[333] Justice Blackmun, speaking for the Court, pointed to the law's rationale, which was based on programs for special federal aid for *all* children classified as "disadvantaged," be they in public or non-public schools. Over Justice Douglas's solitary dissent, Blackmun told Missouri that a state was not required to engage in Title I programs of the kind at issue if state law prohibits same—but that a comparable program must be provided. Missouri's failure to do so triggered the statutorily mandated federal one. But in 1985, albeit by a mere 5 : 4 margin, the Court made it clear that there are limits: as noted earlier, it disallowed on separation of Church and State violation grounds New York City's practice, under Title I of the federal statute, of providing instructional services, funded by that Title, to parochial schools on their premises. The city, moreover, monitored the religious content of these Title I class services. The scheme, in the eyes of the controlling opinion, penned by Justice Brennan, rose to a level of an impermissible "excessive entanglement."[334]

As the country moved toward the last decade of the twentieth century, federal aid to education on *all levels* of schooling and to *all* schools, public or private, was an established fact. It is highly unlikely

---

the 1923 case (*Frothingham v. Mellon, op. cit.*), with only Justice Harlan in dissent, went further, however, to open the door to any taxpayer's allegation that "congressional action under the taxing and spending clause is in derogation of those constitutional provisions which operate to restrict the exercise of the taxing and spending power" (*Flast v. Cohen, op. cit.*, at 106). It did this by setting two conditions, a "two-part nexus" test: (1) the taxpayer must establish a link between his status and the statute attacked by alleging that an Act of Congress is unconstitutional under the taxing and spending power; (2) the taxpayer must allege that the challenge enactment exceeds a specific limit placed on the exercise of the taxing and spending power.

[333]*Wheeler v. Barrera*, 414 U.S. 908 (1974).

[334]*Aguilar v. Felton*, 105 S.Ct. 3232 (1985). See Table 6.4, *supra*. Brennan was joined by his colleagues Marshall, Blackmun, and Stevens, plus Justice Powell's key concurrence. The four dissenters were Burger, White, Rehnquist, and O'Connor.

that the Court would be willing to strike down provisions that form the very heart of a law such as the 1965 one at issue, which was passed, and consistently extended and renewed, by an almost two-thirds majority of the people's representatives in Congress. After all, had the latter not evidently been converted to the proposition that a price, even perhaps a questionably constitutional one, had to be paid to get the much-needed and much-sought aid to our schools as a matter of public policy? It must never be forgotten that in the long run the Court reflects even as it reveals the nature of American society; that although it is often an effective educator and teacher in the short run, there are limits to which it can go in the face of determined, overwhelming *long-run* opposition by the body politic—a body politic wedded to those pluralistic concepts of which diverse schools form such an important part. What the Supreme Court of the United States says and holds indeed "reflects not only the competing interests and values at stake, but also its own role in accommodating constitutional interpretation to the demands of a pluralistic society."[335]

To reiterate, this is not to say that there are not limits. The Court, as we have seen time and time again, does ultimately determine lines— however uncertain their future may well be. Moreover, as it has demonstrated throughout its history, no amount of popular reaction and vilification will stop the Court from speaking as it perceives the command of the basic law of the land; when, convinced of its rightful duty under our Constitution, it knows it must say "no" to government and the society which it serves—and thus says so. It is a role crucial to the survival of our constitutional system, one it must continue to exercise with resolve.

[335]Kauper, *op. cit.*, p. 79.

chapter *VII* Race—*The American Dilemma:*

The Evolving Equal Protection of the

Laws

   In theory *race,* the dominant subject of this chapter, should not present the sort of difficult line-drawing that has pervaded considerations of the topics already discussed. Surely, in the last quarter of the twentieth century race could hardly, in an enlightened democratic society, determine the outcome of an individual's quest for equality before the law and equality of opportunity—nor should gender or ethnic origin or creed or religion, or any other immutable characteristics not relevant to egalitarian and libertarian imperatives. Yet theory does not necessarily govern practice, and although—beyond any rational question—we have seen enormous strides taken toward the egalitarian goals of black Americans, both under law and in the mores of society, racial discrimination is still a fact of life. That great progress has been achieved since World War II, especially since the late 1950s, in both the private *and* the governmental sphere, is obvious to any fair-minded observer. Yet ingrained sentiments and prejudices of segments of people in the North as well as in the South die hard—if indeed they die at all. And government, under the Constitution the great line-drawer in the absence of voluntary action, has had to be cautious lest it move too far in advance of those sentiments and prejudices. For full enforcement of the civil rights of all, there must be mutual trust and respect—and although government can accomplish much to promote such trust and respect, it cannot be a finite panacea substituting for the slower processes of education. Still, as the race problem has shown well indeed, leadership by responsible public officials is not only desirable but crucial at all stages. When the race controversy attained a degree of no longer ignorable public concern at the highest governmental level in the late 1940s, it was the judicial branch of the government, with the

Supreme Court at its apex, which led the other branches in tackling the problem. While it probably did not lead eagerly or joyously, a people's rightful claims could no longer be ignored merely because the political, in particular the legislative, branches refused then to become involved beyond the most cursory of levels, and in fact consistently passed the problems on to the Court. It is an intriguing question how much strife might have been spared and how much understanding might have been engendered had the elective branches of the government provided the decisive leadership with which they are charged and, as subsequent events proved, of which they are capable when pressed.

By spring of 1988 there were some 29 million blacks in the United States—roughly 11.8 percent of a total population of about 245 million. Segregation barriers had tumbled or were tumbling everywhere; the federal government and now also state governments—whether voluntarily or as a result of enforceable orders from the judiciary—had made crystal clear that race would no longer be permitted as a valid factor of adverse classification in any public or quasi-public sphere—and even the demonstrably private sector of society found itself under intense and mounting pressure to fall into line with the spirit of the times. The tough Civil Rights Act of 1964 and the equally tough Voting Rights Act of 1965, with their numerous subsequent amendatory extensions and expansions, were being vigorously enforced; desegregation of public educational facilities, on all levels, but particularly in the deep South,[1] had advanced from the tokensim of two decades earlier to an all but complete stage—with exceptions still extant, however, largely because of housing patterns and ethnic clusters that do not readily lend themselves to rapid alterations (of which much more later in these pages); the increase in college and university enrollment of blacks had become so dramatic during the 1970s and 1980s—some 300 percent in five years—that by the late 1980s the U.S. Bureau of the Census could report that blacks were entering higher education in numbers *exceeding* their representation in the total population (although their dropout rate

[1]Generally speaking, five Southern states are usually classified as the deep South: South Carolina, Georgia, Louisiana, Alabama, and Mississippi. The six other members of the erstwhile Confederacy are commonly simply called Southern: Virginia, North Carolina, Florida, Arkansas, Tennessee, and Texas. Six are normally classified as Border states: Delaware, Kentucky, Maryland, West Virginia, Oklahoma, and Missouri (although the Bureau of the Census no longer includes Missouri).

was significantly higher than that of whites).[2] Jim Crow[3] legislation was legally dead everywhere; public accommodations were open to all; registered black voters numbered close to 10 million—almost four times as many as in 1960; and over 6,600 blacks, including 1,500 women, held elective public office—an increase from but 72 in 1965 and 480 in 1967, with almost 3,000 black officials in the South (where the most dramatic gains took place). Nationally, there were over 700 black judges, almost 15 percent of whom were appointed to the *federal* bench by President Carter between 1977 and 1981.[4]

High-ranking black officials were in evidence at all levels of government by the mid- to late 1980s—including more than 300 mayors (early 1988). Thus, among others, the important cities of Los Angeles, California; Detroit and Grand Rapids, Michigan; Chicago, Illinois; Baltimore, Maryland; Washington, D.C.; New Orleans, Louisiana; Philadelphia, Pennsylvania; Gary, Indiana; Cleveland and Dayton, Ohio; and Newark and East Orange, New Jersey, had elected black mayors, and one of them, Hartford, Connecticut, chose New England's first black female mayor in 1987. Fifty-five of these cities had white majorities, and more than one-half of them were in cities of more than 100,000 inhabitants, none of which had a black mayor as late as 1966. The year 1969 saw the election of black mayors in the Southern cities of Chapel Hill, North Carolina, and Fayette, Mississippi; and 1973 not only brought the same to Raleigh, North Carolina, but witnessed the first election of a black mayor for a Southern metropolitan center, Atlanta, Georgia, in the person of thirty-three-year-old attorney Maynard Jackson, who was succeeded by another prominent black, Andrew Young, in 1982. Birmingham, a symbol of Southern intransigence on race, elected a black mayor in 1980. Massachusetts had a black population of only 3 percent when it sent Republican Edward W. Brooke to the U.S. Senate in 1966 to replace retiring New England Brahmin Leverett Saltonstall. Brooke, the first black Senator since Reconstruction—who

[2] See the Bureau's *Annual Report* for the years of the 1970s and 1980s.

[3] A slang term applied to the black, derived from the title of a minstrel song, popularized about 1835 by F. D. Rice: "Wheel About and Turn About and Jump, Jim Crow."

[4] See statistics provided regularly by the U.S. Bureau of the Census, the U.S. Bureau of Labor Statistics, *Statistical Abstract of the United States,* the Joint Center for Political Studies, *The Christian Science Monitor, The Washington Post,* and *The New York Times.* As of January 1, 1986, Mississippi had the largest number of elected black officials, 521, followed by Louisiana's 488.

had easily defeated a distinguished Massachusetts Yankee of unquestioned civil-libertarian persuasion, Endicott Peabody—was reelected by a margin of better than 2 : 1 in 1972.[5] Douglas L. Wilder, elected as Lieutenant-Governor of Virginia in 1985, became the highest popularly elected black executive official. And Representative Mike Espy of Yazoo City became the first black to represent Mississippi since Reconstruction in Congress.

In 1967 President Johnson had appointed Thurgood Marshall to the Supreme Court—the first black ever to receive this honor. In that same year, Robert H. Lawrence became the first black astronaut. In 1976 Alabama Democrats had elected the first black ever to serve as a member of the state's regular delegation to the Democratic National Committee; and neighboring Mississippi, which now led all Southern states in the number of elected black officials, saw the installation of a black as the state's Roman Catholic Auxiliary Bishop. Vanessa Williams became the first black Miss America in 1983. There were 711 black delegates (18 percent of the total) at the 1984 Democratic Convention, many of them from the deep South. In the fall of 1986, twenty-three blacks were elected to the 100th Congress (1987–89), thrice the number (only seven then) that had served there at the height of the Reconstruction, from 1873 to 1877. (The 100th Congress also held a record twenty-one women and eleven Hispanics. Hispanics held 3,202 elective offices at all levels of government as of late 1986.) In the realm of national law enforcement, in 1963 there were 1,600 whites for every black in the F.B.I.; by 1980 the ratio had dropped to 35 : 1, and 2 of the 59 special agents in charge were black, a figure that mounted steadily through the 1980s under Director William Webster, totaling 379 black, 373 Hispanic, and 733 female agents (of a total of 9,200). Indeed, the catalogue of accomplishments was proud and impressive. Moreover, between the Civil War and the Korean War the rate of Negro illiteracy had dropped from 90 percent to less than 5 percent. There was now a rising black middle class (family incomes upward of $20,000–$25,000 annually, with more than 1,500,000 black families earning more than $25,000 as of 1984 and 264,000 more than $50,000). Despite the

---

[5]His record tainted by some questionable financial transactions, Senator Brooke was defeated in his quest for a third term in 1978 by white Democrat Paul E. Tsongas—a man with an even more liberal record, who in turn was replaced in 1984 by a still more liberal white figure, John F. Kerry, also a Democrat.

economic turndown during the mid- and late 1970s, the rise in family incomes was at a rate greater than that of whites, while—for the first time in many years—blacks generally were moving into the poverty class at a lesser rate than whites. The number of non-white professional workers had more than quintupled between the *Brown* decision[6] and mid-1987; life expectancy for blacks had commenced to increase markedly, accompanied by a striking reduction in black mortality rates under one year of age; black migration to the suburbs increased 45 percent during the 1970s and 1980s; and blacks had begun to feel sufficiently confident about the evident improvement in the South's racial climate to start to move *into* the South in greater numbers than *out* of it as of 1974—a phenomenon that has continued at an accelerated pace.[7]

Yet while there was indubitably demonstrable and truly commendable progress at every level of public and private life, the picture was not universally bright. Although the median black family income in 1984 had maintained its recent annual increase of close to 9 percent, to reach almost $15,000, that figure was still only 75 percent as much as that earned by white families. At the same time, the number of black families with a female head of household (there were *circa* three million such families in July 1987) had jumped to a total of 40 percent of all black families, as opposed to 10 percent of all white families. The majority of these fatherless families are poor, their children especially vulnerable to delinquency, crime, and premarital pregnancy. There were dramatic income gains at all age levels during the 1960s, 1970s, and 1980s, with one-quarter of the black families' earnings reaching the $25,000 threshold, and real earnings of black males increased 300 percent, compared to 163 percent for white men, during the forty-year period from 1940 to 1980. But the jobless rate for blacks in 1987 stood

[6]*Brown v. Board of Education of Topeka*, 374 U.S. 483 (1954).

[7]See *The New York Times*, June 23. 1974, Sec. 4, p. 15; the 1975 report of the U.S. Bureau of the Census; "Geographical Mobility: March 1975 to March 1977," a release by the U.S. Bureau of the Census; Bernard E. Anderson, "The Black Middle Class," *The Pennsylvania Gazette*, March 1979, p. 37; Robert Reinhold, "Progress of Blacks Traced," *New York Times* News Service; *The* (Charlottesville, Va.) *Daily Progress*, July 1, 1979, p. B9; *The Daily Progress*, June 2, 1980, p. A12, November 22, 1985, p. A5, and September 4, 1986, p. A5; United States Department of Commerce, Bureau of the Census, P-23 *Current Population Reports* 80, "The Social and Economic Status of the Black Population in the United States: An Historical View, 1790–1978" (1980); *The New York Times*, July 3, 1981; *The Washington Post*, July 27, 1986, p. A8, September 7, 1986, p. A8, and August 9, 1987, insert, p. 2. See also fn. 4, *supra*.

at 14.7 percent, versus 6.5 percent for whites. Upward of 50 percent of all food stamp purchases were being made by black families. More than twice as many black women as white women were separated or divorced. The high school dropout rate for blacks, although improving substantially as of the 1960s, was still considerably higher than that for whites.[8] Unquestionably, enormous, readily recognizable progress had been made on almost all fronts of the racial dilemma—yet much remained to be accomplished. Race continues to be a fundamental cleavage in American society.

Moreover, the demonstrable psychological toll inflicted on America's blacks over almost three centuries was clearly in evidence; impatience, however understandable, threatened to play havoc with the newly established lines of equality of opportunity. Not only was racial prejudice still a factor, but, because of the assertive and highly visible civil rights clamor, it was engulfing areas it had not hitherto reached, especially in Northern urban and suburban areas. The frightful August 1965 riots in the Watts section of Los Angeles lasted six days and resulted in 34 deaths, 1,032 injuries, the arrest of 3,952 persons, and $40 million in property damage (more than 600 buildings were damaged, 200 totally destroyed). Those around Detroit's Twelfth Street in 1967 constituted the bloodiest uprising in the country in half a century, and the costliest ever in terms of property damage: the five days of rioting, looting, burning, and killing resulted in 43 deaths, 347 injuries, 3,800 arrests, 5,000 made homeless, 1,300 buildings reduced to ashes, and $500 million in damages. Watts and Detroit—and the disorders that in subsequent years engulfed such Northern centers as Washington, Newark, Buffalo, Kansas City, Cleveland, Chicago, St. Louis, San Francisco, and many others, reaching into Miami (16 deaths) and Chattanooga again in 1980—served as shocking and costly reminders that the mere removal of legal barriers to equality was not enough. The principle of equality now not only included demands for economic and even social equality, but also included demands for compensatory, pref-

[8]For sources of statistics see those cited on p. 395, footnote 4, *supra*, and p. 397, footnote 7, *ibid.*; plus "Decade of Progress," *Time* magazine, April 16, 1973, p. 16; the Annual Economic Surveys of the National Urban League; Paul Delaney, "Economic Survey Cites Black Loss," *Time* magazine, April 16, 1973, p. 16; the Annual Economic Surveys of the National Urban League; Paul Delaney, "Economic Survey Cites Black Loss," *The New York Times*, July 29, 1975, p. 27c.; the periodic reports of the United States Commission on Civil Rights; and those of the Joint Center for Political Studies.

erential "affirmative action." Yet fear and lack of communication were still rampant, and frustration, engendered by rising expectations, could readily lead to anger and thence to blind unreasoned violence. The President's National Commission on the Causes and Prevention of Violence thus reported late in 1969 that extensive violence had occurred in 239 hostile outbreaks by blacks, which resulted in more than 8,000 casualties and 191 deaths.[9] Prejudice and poverty still stood in the way. And the bitter school-busing controversies that crested in the 1970s—of which more below—would demonstrate that resort to violence is not confined to either one race or one section of the land.

Thus, whereas the gulf of opportunity and achievement was clearly narrowing, it remained wide for a good many blacks, especially at the lower socio-economic levels. And the desire to bridge it not only fully but rapidly, coupled with a demonstrable measure of success, gave rise to insistent and greater demands, not infrequently backed by what became known as "action in the streets" rather than in the courts or in legislative halls. This action, in turn, prompted considerable feeling on the part of the white community that what had hitherto been regarded as legitimate grievances based on legitimate demands had now become unreasonable and unjustifiable demands for "special" or "privileged" treatment—increasingly characterized as "preferential treatment" or "reverse discrimination." Public authorities thus found themselves faced with the problem of drawing lines particularly between *public* and *private* action and the attendant legal and governmental responsibilities, a difficult and uncomfortable task. Just how, where, and by whom could or should such a line be established? How to find accommodations between the twin basic rights of liberty and equality—*both* being constitutionally mandated? Is it purely—is it properly—a judicial function? A summary glance into the history of racial discrimination in the United States may serve as a prolegomenon to some answers, if we can speak of answers at all.

A Glance at History

Although the Declaration of Independence had stipulated, as a self-evident truth, that "all men are created equal," it soon became obvious

[9]Chapter 5, "American Society and the Radical Black Militant," in *Law and Order Reconsidered: A Staff Report* (New York: Bantam Books, Inc., 1970), pp. 85–117.

that, in the words of George Orwell, "some men are created more equal than others." The second section of the first article of the Constitution clearly recognized the existence of slavery in the United States by directing the inclusion of "three-fifths of all other persons," i.e., the *slaves*, in the enumeration which was to form the basis for representative apportionment and taxation. True, Section 9 of Article One did make it possible to stop the "migration or importation" of slaves after 1808, provided Congress chose to do so then, and the Thirteenth Amendment was designed to settle the matter by outlawing slavery in 1865. But it was not really until the ratification of the Fourteenth Amendment in 1868, five years after Lincoln's Emancipation Proclamation, that the white-supremacy concept inherent in Article One was removed from the Constitution. In the language of the Amendment's second section: "Representatives shall be apportioned among the several States according to their respective numbers, *counting the whole number of persons in each State,* excluding Indians not taxed. . . ."[10]

Yet despite these enactments, despite the mandates of Amendment Fourteen (quoted below), and despite the language of the Fifteenth Amendment of 1870, which on its face seemed to assure to blacks the privilege of the ballot, neither the myth of white supremacy nor the fact of color prejudice was wiped out. Section 1 of the Fourteenth Amendment, now so significant but then so ineffective, would have to wait more than eight decades for its triumphs on behalf of the black:

> *All persons born or naturalized in the United States, and subject to the jurisdiction thereof, are citizens of the United States and of the State wherein they reside. No state shall make or enforce* any law which shall abridge the privileges or immunities of citizens of the United States; *nor shall any State deprive* any person of life, liberty, or property, without due process of law; *nor deny to any person within its jurisdiction the equal protection of the laws.*[11]

The Emancipation Proclamation and these three Civil War amendments intended, above all, to ameliorate the lot of blacks by attacking the constitutional silence on federal protection of civil rights, a protection that had, until then, been left wholly to the several states. They proved

---

[10]Opening sentence. (Italics supplied.)
[11]Entire section quoted. (Italics supplied.)

to be ineffective. True, Reconstruction seemed to offer genuine hope: twenty-two Southern blacks went to Congress and two became United States Senators from Mississippi. True also that in the decade following the passage of the Thirteenth Amendment, Congress enacted five major civil rights statutes, spelling out the rights of the new black freedom and providing penalties for their denial.[12] But the South proved itself equal to the challenge of restoring the *status quo ante* via a host of ingenious and disingenuous devices. By 1910 every former Confederate state, for example, had succeeded in disfranchising blacks either by state statute—e.g., the "white primary" and the "grandfather clause"[13]—by state constitutional amendment, or with the direct or indirect aid of such United States Supreme Court decisions as those in *United States v. Harris,*[14] the *Slaughterhouse Cases,*[15] and the *Civil Rights Cases.*[16] The Court's position, as noted earlier,[17] was that the Fourteenth Amendment did not place under federal protection "the entire domain of civil rights heretofore belonging exclusively to the states," and that the protection offered by the Fourteenth and Fifteenth Amendments was *against state action only,* not against private action. And in 1896 the Court upheld the convenient discriminatory concept of "separate but equal" in the case of *Plessy v. Ferguson.*[18] To all intents and purposes the black was at the mercy of the states—there was no Warren Court to redress grievances. Indeed, until World War II the federal government assumed at most a highly limited role in the protection of civil rights on the state level.

In 1900 almost 90 percent of America's blacks lived in the South and the Border (a figure that had declined to 70 percent in 1950, to 60 in 1960, and to 51 in 1978[19]); the core of racial discrimination was naturally found there, on both the public and the private level. Thus, *public*

[12]Among them were the "Anti-K.K.K." Act of 1871 and the Public Accommodation Act of 1875.

[13]See pp. 354 ff., *infra.*

[14]106 U.S. 629 (1882).

[15]16 Wallace 36 (1873).

[16]109 U.S. 3 (1883).

[17]See Chapter III, *supra.*

[18]163 U.S. 537.

[19]*United States Department of Commerce News,* October 23, 1970, p. 5, and U.S. Bureau of the Census, 1979. (See also p. 397, footnote 7, *supra.*) The decline appeared to have been arrested at the end of the 1970s; and a reversal began to take place. (See text and fn. 7, p. 397, *supra.*)

authorities at the state and local levels, usually under the guise of the Court-upheld "separate but equal" concept, enacted measures (sometimes taking the form of a constitutional provision) *permitting* or even *requiring* segregation of buses, streetcars, taxicabs, railroads, waiting rooms, comfort stations, drinking fountains, state and local schools, state colleges and universities, hospitals, jails, cemeteries, sport facilities, beaches, bath houses, swimming pools, parks, golf courses, courthouse cafeterias, libraries, dwellings, theaters, hotels, restaurants, and other similar facilities—be these public, quasi-public, or private in nature; and interracial marriages were widely proscribed.[20] *Private* individuals and groups, on their own initiative, and not infrequently encouraged by state authorities, acted to deny blacks, and often other non-Caucasians as well, access to social clubs, fraternities and sororities, private schools, colleges, universities, churches, cemeteries, funeral parlors, hospitals, hotels, dwellings, restaurants, movies, bowling alleys, swimming pools, bath houses, sporting events, comfort stations, drinking fountains, barber and beauty shops, employment agencies, and employment itself. There was nothing particularly secretive about either public or private discrimination; it was simply an accepted way of life— accepted by many blacks as well as by almost all whites.

Yet the onset of World War II—which witnessed many blacks fighting side by side with whites and saw increasing migration of blacks northward—prompted the federal government to take notice of the problem. Although his administration recommended no civil rights legislation *per se* to Congress—which, needless to say, did not act on its own—President Franklin D. Roosevelt did take two far-reaching executive actions. In 1939, at the prompting of Attorney-General Frank Murphy (who would soon be promoted to the Supreme Court), he created a Civil Liberties Unit[21] in the Criminal Division of the Department of Justice. Then, since Congress would not have passed such legislation, he established by executive order[22] the first Committee on Fair Employment Practices (to be known as the F.E.P.C.). The President

---

[20]It was not until 1967 that this particular prohibition was unanimously declared unconstitutional as a violation of both equal protection and due process guaranties under Amendment Fourteen in *Loving v. Virginia*, 388 U.S. 1. See also its 1964 precurser, *McLaughlin v. Florida*, 379 U.S. 184, also decided 9:0.

[21]Subsequently to be called the Civil Rights Section.

[22]Exec. Order 8802, *Federal Register*, Vol. VI (1941), p. 3109.

created it largely at the behest of black leaders, other civil rights advocates, and, significantly, his spouse, Eleanor Roosevelt—whose entire life was dedicated to the eradication of injustice. Although its enforcement powers were severely circumscribed, and its domain was exclusively in the federal sphere, the F.E.P.C. did make some progress toward the elimination of discriminatory employment practices in those companies and labor unions that had government contracts or were engaged in activities connected with World War II. Yet Congress abolished the Committee in 1946.

The end of the war brought increasing public pressure on the federal government to combat the various manifestations of racial discrimination. But the political power of entrenched Southern forces, both in Congress and out, often combined with Northern conservative elements, was able to prevent, or at least to delay, any meaningful legislative aid. The House of Representatives, by definition theoretically "closer to the people" and more sensitive to the currents and tides of change, did pass in 1946 and 1950 such potentially remedial measures as bills establishing a permanent F.E.P.C.; but both were rejected by the more tradition-bound Senate, in which Southern influence was still decisive in such matters. Again, the House passed legislation designed to outlaw the poll tax in 1945, 1947, and 1949, yet in no instance would the Senate accept it. (It would take another thirteen years before Congress legislated against the poll tax in *federal* elections by way of the Twenty-fourth Amendment, which was ratified in 1964.) No action at all was taken on the host of anti-lynching proposals introduced at every session of Congress.

Winds of Change: President Truman. Because Congress was unwilling or unable to make progress on the race problem, President Harry S Truman—a son of Missouri, with Confederate ancestors—determined to take matters into his own hands. In a sense, the catalyst for his first move was Congress's deliberate failure to include a widely backed antidiscrimination provision in the important Selective Service Act of 1948. Angry, the President issued a no-nonsense executive order[23] that specifically banned "separate but equal" recruiting, training, and service in the armed forces. While this did not affect the National Guard and Reserve units under state aegis, it was an important step in an area of

[23]Exec. Order 9981, *Federal Register*, Vol. XIII (1948), p. 4313.

public activity in which discrimination based on race was particularly heinous: military service for one's native land. President Truman was convinced that he had to move on his own, insofar as that was legal and possible, because of the fate that the report of his President's Committee on Civil Rights had suffered at the hands of Congress: in 1946 he had appointed a fifteen-member blue-ribbon committee[24] and charged it specifically with the careful investigation of the need for legislative and other procedures designed to further and protect civil rights and liberties. One year later, the Committee reported that although civil rights were indeed better and more generally protected than ever before, there were still alarmingly widespread violations. In its broadly distributed report, *To Secure These Rights,* the Committee made numerous recommendations designed to ensure that every violation of a civil right by any individual be treated as a criminal offense. Were these recommendations to be followed, the enforcement of civil rights would become a new and vigorous government activity on a much extended scale. Specifically, the Committee's proposals included federal laws to forbid lynching; to outlaw discrimination in voting requirements; to create a permanent Fair Employment Practices Commission and a permanent Commission on Civil Rights; and to expand into a Civil Rights Division the small, undermanned Civil Rights Section in the Department of Justice that Attorney-General Murphy had established eight years earlier.

Like all proposals for the extension of government activities, these quickly became a political issue. Still, President Truman committed himself to the implementation of the report as far as federal action was feasible—in the face of considerable risks to his party position and his campaign for reelection in 1948. Indeed, that campaign witnessed the bolting from the Democratic Party of four Southern states[25] and their formation of the Dixiecrat Party under then Democrat Strom Thurmond of South Carolina. Nonetheless, the President made *To Secure These Rights* an issue throughout his campaign. He won reelection, but he did not obtain—as already noted—congressional acquiescence. In fact, Congress took no action during the remaining four years of the Truman Administration, a hiatus that extended through the first four and a half years of the Eisenhower Presidency. But Truman attempted to salvage

---

[24]Exec. Order 9808, *Federal Register,* Vol. XI (1946), p. 14153. The Committee was headed by Charles E. Wilson ("Electric Charlie"), president of General Electric.

[25]Alabama, Louisiana, Mississippi, and South Carolina.

what he could by executive order. Shortly before his 1948 order banning segregation in the armed forces, he had issued an executive order[26] establishing a Fair Employment Board to oversee announced policy that henceforth all federal jobs were to be distributed without any regard to "race, color, religion, or national origin." Three years later the President created the Committee on Government Contract Compliance, requiring any business holding a contract with the federal government not only to pledge but to provide *bona fide* fair employment policies and practices.[27] The tenor of these several executive moves gradually began to pervade much of the executive establishment.

President Eisenhower continued his predecessor's civil rights policies. Resorting to the technique of the executive order,[28] the new Chief Executive created the President's Committee on Government Contracts, headed by Vice-President Nixon. The Committee was empowered to receive complaints alleging discrimination by government contractors, and to cancel contracts if necessary. Various cabinet departments and agencies continued the policy of earlier administrations against sundry types of obvious internal discrimination.

The Watershed. These activities were of course not lost on the several states. A good many Northern states turned to F.E.P.C. and similar devices to combat discrimination. The air was filled with the beginnings of change. Yet the South was determined not to budge, and in Congress it had a seemingly eternal ally. President Eisenhower did not recommend any new civil rights legislation until his Administration's Civil Rights Bill of 1956. It failed to be enacted, but Congress did pass a modified version, the Civil Rights Act of 1957, the first major piece of civil rights legislation since Reconstruction. It is fair to say, however, that it would never have become law had not the Supreme Court swung into the fray with its monumentally significant ruling in the *Public School Segregation Cases*[29] on May 17, 1954.

That decision was one of the most far-reaching in our history in terms of its social impact.[30] It catalyzed the issue of racial discrimination; it

[26]Exec. Order 9980, *Federal Register,* Vol. XIII (1948), p. 4311.

[27]Exec. Order 10308, *Federal Register,* Vol. XVI (1951), p. 12303.

[28]Exec. Order 10479, *Federal Register,* Vol. XVIII (1953), p. 4899.

[29]*Brown v. Board of Education of Topeka,* 347 U.S. 483 (1954); and *Bolling v. Sharpe,* 347 U.S. 497 (1954).

[30]Chief Justice Warren ranked it in second place behind *Baker v. Carr,* 369 U.S. 186 (1962)—see pp. 20–21, *supra*—in terms of the significance of cases his Court decided during the sixteen-year tenure from 1953 to 1969.

focused responsibility for remedial action on government officials everywhere; and, especially, it pointed an accusing finger at that branch of government presumably responsible for social action: the legislature. The controversy triggered by the 1954 *Public School Segregation Cases* may have subsided, but it has not died. Conscious of its position as a national moral goad as well as a teacher in a continuing national constitutional seminar, the Court had led. Recognizing the necessarily limited options open to the executive branch, and the immobility of the legislative on the issue, the Supreme Court had decided unanimously that it had to create a line. As Justice Jackson remarked laconically during oral argument in *Brown,* "I suppose that realistically the reason this case is here was [*sic*] that action could not be obtained from Congress."[31] After two and a half years of painful deliberation, the high tribunal chose to attack the concept of "separate but equal" in the field of public school education on the grounds that separate facilities are "inherently unequal," and that the very concept of "separate but equal" in matters of race violates the "equal protection of the laws" clause of the Fourteenth Amendment (on the state level) and the "due process of law" clause of the Fifth (on the federal level).[32]

"Separate but Equal": Rise and Demise

We know that the intent of the three Civil War amendments was to abolish the institution of slavery, to bestow the full benefit of American citizenship upon blacks, and to enable them to exercise the franchise. And for a brief period of roughly two decades, give or take a few years depending upon the individual state involved, blacks were indeed in a position to exercise their newly confirmed civil rights relatively effectively—backed, to be sure, by federal Reconstruction forces. But, as we also know—and as C. Vann Woodward, among others, has told us so well[33]—the dominant white elements in the old Confederacy were not about to grant blacks anything like genuine, lasting freedom and equality; indeed, they utilized every conceivable covert and overt

[31]Oral argument in the Virginia and South Carolina segments of the suit, p. 244.

[32]*Brown v. Board, op. cit.,* which involved four different states—Kansas, Virginia, Delaware, and South Carolina—and *Bolling v. Sharpe, op. cit.,* which concerned the District of Columbia only.

[33]See his *The Strange Career of Jim Crow,* rev. ed. (New York: Oxford University Press, 1966).

device to bar the one-time slaves from attaining even the semblance of first-class citizenship. As the evangelism and ferver of Northern abolitionists began to subside, especially after the Hayes Compromise of 1877 had resulted in the withdrawal of the troops from the South, Southern leadership all but restored the *status quo ante*—with the overwhelming support of the Southern constituency. By 1900, the Southern black had been pushed back into second-class citizenship. Jim Crow, with certain refinements, again reigned supreme.

THE RISE OF "SEPARATE BUT EQUAL"

Black leaders endeavored to battle this trend. Unable to expect any aid in their efforts from either the executive or legislative branches, they turned to the state judiciary. But it, too, quickly proved itself generally in sympathy with the point of view of the region's population and its leadership. The black's only hope thus hinged on the United States Supreme Court. And *it* proved for a long time to be a vain hope.[34]

An Ill Omen: Slaughterhouse. The famous *Slaughterhouse Cases*,[35] handed down by the Court in 1873, foreshadowed a bleak future for the black cause. Ironically, blacks were *not* involved in that litigation, and the Court's language even seemed to give distinct comfort to them. There were ringing phrases regarding the purposes of the Civil War amendments: the achievement of "freedom for the slave race," the "security and firm establishment of that freedom," and the protection of the "newly-made freeman and citizen from the oppressions of those who had formerly exercised unlimited dominion over him."[36] But, as noted in the earlier discussion[37] of these cases, the Court's *real* point was that there must be a careful distinction between the "privileges or immunities" of *United States* citizens and *state* (here Louisiana) citizens; that the only privileges attaching to national citizenship are those that "owe their existence to the Federal Government, its National character, its Constitution, or its laws'';[38] that, in effect, a citizen of a state derived his "privileges or immunities" from *state* citizenship, a thing

---

[34]For an engaging account of the story of the Supreme Court of the United States and black petitioners, written by the son of a black slave and his white wife, see Loren Miller's *The Petitioners* (New York: Pantheon Books, 1966).

[35]16 Wallace 36.

[36]*Ibid.*, at 71.

[37]See Chapter III, *supra,* pp. 43–49.

[38]*The Slaughterhouse Cases, op. cit.,* at 79.

quite "distinct" from federal citizenship rights, which "depend upon different characteristics or circumstances in the individual."[39] In other words, if blacks had hoped to rely on the "privileges or immunities" clause of that Amendment as a source of salvation in their struggle for equal rights, the Supreme Court's narrow construction of the clause— one never really altered to this day (1988)—rendered it of little value as a restraint upon state regulation. But what of the "due process of law" and "equal protection of the laws" clauses of the Fourteenth?

Another Hope Shattered: The Civil Rights Cases. Things seemed to look up when Congress, in an effort to aid blacks, passed the Civil Rights Act of 1875, which made it a *federal* crime for any owner or operator of, *inter alia,* a hotel, public conveyance, or theater to "deny the full enjoyments of the accommodations thereof" because of race or color. Various blacks were nonetheless denied access and brought suit in a series of five cases,[40] ultimately consolidated by the Supreme Court as *The Civil Rights Cases of 1883.*[41] The Court, in an 8:1 decision written by Justice Joseph P. Bradley, with only Justice John Marshall Harlan I in dissent, declared the Act of 1875 unconstitutional. The Court did so on the grounds that the Fourteenth Amendment applied to *state* action only and did not give Congress authority to forbid discrimination by *private* individuals (a point it had already made a few months earlier in *United States v. Harris,*[42] in which it declared unconstitutional a section of the Ku Klux Klan Act of 1871 as being inapplicable to the acts of *private* persons); that if the state did not assist the discrimination of an individual against another individual, the matter is purely between the two as private persons. Thus, not only had the Supreme Court sharply limited the "privileges or immunities" that had, seemingly, come with national citizenship, it now read the phrase "no state shall" in the Fourteenth and Fifteenth Amendments to mean solely and literally the actions of state government *officials*. The decisive Court majority refused to accept the contention that it was in fact state action when individuals and corporations *licensed by a state* to "serve all

---

[39]*Ibid.,* majority opinion by Justice Miller, at 74.

[40]One each from California, Kansas, Missouri, New Jersey, and Tennessee.

[41]109 U.S. 3. Their story is well known and well told. See, for example, Alan F. Westin, "The Case of the Prejudiced Doorkeeper," in John A. Garraty, ed., *Quarrels That Have Shaped the Constitution* (New York: Harper & Row, 1987), pp. 139–56.

[42]106 U.S. 629 (1882).

without discrimination'' used race as a criterion. As for alleged violation of the Thirteenth Amendment, it regarded restrictive public accommodations as having nothing to do with slavery or involuntary servitude. Indeed, Bradley commented in an oft-quoted dictum that blacks should cease endeavoring to obtain ''special treatment''; that there had to be a time when blacks stopped being ''the special favorite of the law,'' and adopted ''the rank of a mere citizen'' (a refrain that became highly audible again in the face of the ''affirmative action'' programs of the 1960s and beyond).[43] Harlan, however, not only flayed Bradley for these comments, but firmly voted to uphold the Civil Rights Act of 1875. He insisted that it was well settled that ''railroad corporations, keepers of inns, and managers of places of public amusement are *agents or instrumentalities of the State*''[44] and that the Act regardless could and should have been upheld under the congressional power over interstate commerce—foreshadowing the Civil Rights Act of 1964 and its quick, unanimous upholding by the Supreme Court.[45]

Gradually taking their cue from the *Slaughterhouse, Harris,* and *Civil Rights* decisions, most of the states of the old Confederacy not only closed their eyes to the steadily spreading segregation practices that either had sprung up or were revived within their borders, but in the four-year period between 1887 and 1891 alone, eight of them enacted legislation *requiring* railroads, for example, to maintain *separate* facilities for whites and blacks.

Enter Plessy v. Ferguson. There had been earlier legal skirmishes at the state level; indeed, the ''separate but equal'' concept had been heavily attacked, albeit unsuccessfully, by Charles Sumner when Massachusetts Chief Justice Lemuel Shaw adopted it almost half a century earlier in 1849 in *Roberts v. the City of Boston*[46] by ruling in favor of Boston's ''police power'' to segregate schools. But the issue was first

---

[43]*The Civil Rights Cases, op. cit.,* at 25. For an analysis of the ''affirmative action''/''reverse-discrimination'' syndrome, see Chapter VIII, *infra.*

[44]*Ibid.,* at 58. (Italics supplied.)

[45]See pp. 364–67 and 395–402, *infra.*

[46]Cush. (59 Mass.) 198 at 206. Sumner here unsuccessfully represented Sarah C. Roberts, a black child, who brought suit against the City of Boston under an 1854 statute that provided for recovery of damages from ''the city or town'' that supported instruction from which any child was unlawfully excluded. Sumner's argument—to the effect that segregated schools can never be equal—prophetically antedated the NAACP brief in *Brown v. Board of Education* (see pp. 344 ff., *infra*).

joined at the highest federal level in the case of *Plessy v. Ferguson*,[47] which was destined to remain law for fifty-eight years. Before the Court was the constitutionality of Louisiana's Jim Crow Car Act of 1890, euphemistically entitled "An Act To Promote the Comfort of Passengers." It required that railroads "provide equal but separate accommodations for the white and colored races" and that "no person be permitted to occupy seats in coaches other than the ones assigned to his race." Here then it was: "EQUAL but SEPARATE." With the exception of an 1892 decision in which the State of Louisiana Supreme Court had held the new law to be inapplicable to an *interstate* passenger—a decision the state did not appeal—all prior tests of the 1890 Act at the state level had ended in victory for the new doctrine. Now at last the Supreme Court would hear and adjudicate the problem of "separate but equal," a problem which had been brought to it through the efforts of a group of eighteen blacks who had formed a "Citizens' Committee To Test the Constitutionality of the Separate Car Law," and raised $2,982 for the litigation. As their attorney they selected Albion Winegar Tourgee of Mayville, then residing in New York, a leading carpetbagger during Reconstruction who, an Ohioan by birth, had served in the Union Army and then had moved to Greensboro, North Carolina, to practice law. There he became a leader of the Radical Republican Party, took an active part in the creation of the State's Radical Constitution, and served as a judge of the Superior Court of his adopted state for six years. Tourgee had been chosen by the Citizens' Committee even prior to the 1892 Louisiana "victory," which he obtained. That case had not met the needs and aims of the Jim Crow Act's challengers. Homer Adolph Plessy's case did.[48]

Plessy was seven-eighths white; his one-eighth "African blood" was not apparent. The Citizens' Committee had seen to it that the East Louisiana Railroad knew of his background. Selected by the Committee to test the statute, Plessy boarded in New Orleans, having purchased a ticket to Covington, Louisiana, and took a seat in the "Whites Only" coach; when the conductor requested that he move to the "Colored Only" section, Plessy refused, whereupon he was promptly arrested by

[47]163 U.S. 537 (1896).

[48]For a lively and illuminating description of the case and its setting, plus an engaging sketch of the principals, see C. Vann Woodward's "The Case of the Louisiana Traveler," in Garraty, *op. cit.*, pp. 157–74.

Detective Christopher C. Cain, and charged with violating the "Jim Crow Car Act of 1890." Tourgee's defense contended that the Louisiana statute under which Plessy had been arrested and charged was null and void as a violation of both the Thirteenth and Fourteenth Amendments. The argument turned on the latter's proscription of the denial of the "equal protection of the laws." Partly because of the fundamental requirement inherent in the judicial process that all remedies "below" must be exhausted before the Supreme Court will consider an otherwise properly qualified case, and partly because of its own work load, the high tribunal did not hand down its decision until four years later. These intervening years saw a further attrition of black post–Civil War gains—and unless the Court were to strike down the "separate but equal" doctrine, Jim Crow would be perpetuated.

The opinion of the Court—with Justice David J. Brewer not participating—upheld the statute 7 : 1. Once again, the lone dissenter was John Marshall Harlan I, whose grandson and namesake was destined to help preside over Jim Crow's judicial demise in the Court six decades later.[49] The majority opinion in *Plessy* was written by Justice Henry Billings Brown, one of seven Northerners then on the Court.[50] Brown's opinion, which, he later recalled, was "reached with little difficulty,"[51] frankly acknowledged Louisiana's action to have been "state action," thus falling under Fourteenth Amendment consideration; *but*, he held, the action was *not discriminatory* since the whites were separated just as much from the blacks as the blacks were separated from the whites! As for the charge that the basis for the separation was race, Brown ruled that was not in and of itself a violation of the Constitution's equal protection clause, for a state had every right under that document to "classify" as long as that classification[52] was not capricious, arbitrary, or unreasonable. "Separate but equal" did not run afoul of these

---

[49]He joined the Supreme Court approximately one year after the 1954 *Public School Segregation Cases, op. cit.,* and was on the bench when the Court handed down its implementation decision in the second *Public Segregation Cases* (*Brown v. Board of Education of Topeka, et al.,* 349 U.S. 294 [1955]).

[50]The Southerners were Harlan and Justice Edward D. White of Louisiana.

[51]See Charles A. Lofgren, *The Plessy Case: A Legal-Historical Approach* (New York: Oxford University Press, 1987), p. 199.

[52]For a discussion of "classification" see Jewell Cass Phillips, Henry J. Abraham, and Cortez A. M. Ewing, *Essentials of American National Government,* 3rd ed. (New York: American Book Co., 1971), Chapter VI, pp. 110 ff.

considerations, said Brown, since the claim that the concept intended to "stamp the colored race with a badge of inferiority" (a phrase that would be quoted and construed quite differently by Chief Justice Earl Warren fifty-eight years later) was "not by reason of anything found in the act, but *solely because the colored race chooses to put that construction upon it.*" And Brown could not forbear to add: "If one race be inferior to another socially, the Constitution of the United States cannot put them upon the same plane." He admitted that the Fourteenth Amendment was "undoubtedly designed to enforce the absolute equality of the two races before the law," but that "it could not have been intended in the nature of things . . . [to] abolish distinction based upon color or to enforce social, as distinct from political equality."[53]

In eloquent anger, Justice Harlan rejected what he viewed as the majority's social Darwinism. To him, as to many others who would follow, the line drawn here by his colleagues reflected "a compound of bad logic, bad history, bad sociology, and bad constitutional law."[54] Moreover, it flew in the face of recent precedent.[55] "The thin disguise of 'equal' accommodations for passengers in railroad coaches will not mislead anyone, nor atone for the wrong this day done," Harlan warned the majority. He attacked the decision as one redolent with sociological speculation: "The arbitrary separation of citizens on the basis of race, while they are on a public highway, is a badge of servitude wholly inconsistent with the civil freedom and the equality of the law established by the Constitution. It cannot be justified upon any legal grounds."[56] And in memorable language he went on to note that

in view of the Constitution, in the eye of the law, there is in this country no superior, dominant, ruling class of citizens. There is no caste here. *Our constitution is color-blind, and neither knows nor tolerates classes among*

[53]*Plessy v. Ferguson*, 163 U.S. 537 (1896), at 551, 544.

[54]Robert J. Harris, *The Quest for Equality: The Constitution, Congress, and the Supreme Court* (Baton Rouge: Louisiana State University Press, 1960), p. 101.

[55]*Strauder v. West Virginia*, 100 U.S. 303 (1880), in which the Court had struck down on Fourteen Amendment "equal protection" grounds a state law that limited jury duty to *white male* citizens—although it proved to be a Pyrrhic victory. See also *ex parte Virginia*, 100 U.S. 339 (1880), where the Supreme Court upheld the conviction of a county court judge for having excluded blacks from jury lists compiled by him, solely because of their race. He had acted in violation of a federal law specifically forbidding such discrimination. Both cases were decided 7:2, Field and Clifford dissenting.

[56]163 U.S. 537, at 562.

citizens.[57] In respect of civil rights all citizens are equal before the law. The humblest is the peer of the most powerful. The law regards man as man, and takes no account of his surroundings or of his color when his civil rights as guaranteed by the supreme law of the land are involved.[58]

But this was a *dissenting* opinion. The separate-but-equal concept had not only been adopted; now it had been judicially sanctioned.[59] It proved to be most detrimental to the blacks' cause in education, public accommodations, the franchise, the administration of justice, housing, employment, and, needless to add, social relationships. White supremacy seemed to have triumphed; assuredly this was true in most of the states below the Mason-Dixon line. For that matter, when Brown spoke in *Plessy,* not only the Southern and Border states, but a total of thirty states of the Union, including most of those in the West, as well as Indiana, Kansas, and New York, had "separate but equal" public school statutes.

CHIPPING AT THE DOCTRINE

Yet, however slowly and imperceptibly, the legal chisels were being readied; the chipping away at the "separate but equal" line probably began with the case of *Missouri ex rel. Gaines v. Canada*[60] in 1938. Actually, the *first* court-enforced admission of a black to a heretofore segregated higher institution of learning had come two years earlier, when the Maryland Court of Appeals—that state's highest tribunal—ordered Donald Murray admitted to the University of Maryland Law

[57]Almost 180 years later, with *Plessy* overruled twenty years earlier in *Brown v. Board,* Chief Justice Hale of the Supreme Court of Washington, speaking in dissent in the "reverse discrimination" case of *De Funis v. Odegaard,* 507 P. 2d 1169 (1973), at 1189, asked whether the Constitution may be color conscious in order to be color blind—an ironic dénouement. (See pp. 396 ff., *infra.*) He believed not, but events since seem to have demonstrated the contrary.

[58]*Ibid.,* at 559. (Italics supplied.) According to his colleague Brewer, Harlan "went to sleep with one hand upon the Constitution and the other on the Bible, and thus secured the untroubled sleep of the just and the righteous." Quoted in G. Edward White, *The American Judicial Tradition* (New York: Oxford University Press, 1976), p. 129.

[59]Plessy pleaded "guilty" in Louisiana Criminal District Court to the charge at issue and was fined $25. The case cost $2,762 of the $2,982 that the Citizens Committee had raised to support its challenge to Jim Crow. The Committee distributed $160 of the balance to Louisiana charities and used the remaining $60 to inscribe a "flattering testimonial" to Tourgee. (Lofgren, *op. cit.,* p. 208.)

[60]305 U.S. 337.

School.[61] But it was *Gaines* which initially gave notice to the nation that the winds of change had begun to blow. That change had its practical roots in certain attitudes, both legal and social, which were growing partly as a result of what might be called a heightened egalitarian national conscience and partly because of the imminence of war. In any event, it manifested itself chiefly in the gradual but unquestionably progressive shift in rulings of the United States Supreme Court from acceptance of the separate-but-equal doctrine to a close examination of the alleged "equality" to, ultimately, the firm rejection of the constitutionality of the doctrine. It took almost two decades to proceed from stage one to stage three. Although the Supreme Court clearly led—and it did so despite vilification and abuse—it did have an important ally, however tenuous, in what might be called the national conscience.

The Gaines Case. Lloyd Gaines was a black citizen of Missouri who sought, but was denied, admission to the School of Law of the state-owned University of Missouri after his graduation from Lincoln University, an all-black Missouri institution. There was no claim of lack of qualifications—S. W. Canada, the University's registrar, simply pointed to a Missouri statute under which the two races were to be educated "separately but equally." Mr. Canada told Gaines that he could, of course, avail himself of another feature of Missouri law applying specifically to black law school applicants, whereby state funds were made available to qualified blacks for their legal education in schools of *adjacent states* that offered unsegregated facilities—e.g., Kansas, Nebraska, Iowa, Illinois. But, encouraged in his stand by the increasingly active and influential National Association for the Advancement of Colored People (NAACP), Gaines declined. What he wanted, he said, was what was his due as a full-fledged citizen and taxpayer of his home state of Missouri: the right to attend the state law school and to practice law in Missouri. Mr. Canada again refused. The NAACP then financed Gaines's appeal through the lower courts and ultimately to the Supreme Court of the United States. Chief Justice Charles Evans Hughes wrote the opinion, speaking also for Justices Brandeis, Stone, Cardozo, Roberts, Black, and Reed; only Justices McReynolds and

---

[61]*Pearson v. Murray,* 169 Md. 478 (1936). He was admitted and ultimately graduated.

Butler—the two surviving members of the so-called Arch-Conservative Quads[62]—dissented, pleading for a continuation of a practice that, they agreed, was in the "best interests" of Missouri's people.[63]

The Chief Justice praised the state of Missouri for the financial arrangements outlined, but held that since there was no law school for blacks in the entire state—Lincoln University had none—the equal protection guarantee of the Fourteenth Amendment was in fact denied Lloyd Gaines. Hughes, continuing to give comfort to the partisans of the "separate but equal" doctrine, explicitly stated that Missouri could have fulfilled its obligation to provide legal instruction to its black citizens "by furnishing equal facilities in separate schools, a method the validity of which has been sustained by our decisions."[64] In other words, he ruled that while the Constitution did not guarantee Gaines's admission to the School of Law of the University of Missouri, it did guarantee a legal education in Missouri substantially equal to that afforded by the state to members of the white race. That Gaines happened to be the only black wishing such an education was beside the point. The state subsequently decided to set up a separate law school for blacks at Lincoln University, but Lloyd Gaines, perhaps overcome by notoriety and pressure, chose to disappear shortly before the Court's decision was handed down. While it remained for someone else then to test the "separate but equal" doctrine *per se,* the *Gaines* case had laid the foundations based on the "equal protection of the laws" clause of Amendment Fourteen. It was this clause that would bring ultimate victory to the blacks' strivings; it was this clause that cast the black into the role of the Supreme Court's "unwilling ward," its "constant petitioner."[65]

Post-Gaines. Almost ten years of pre-war, war, and post-war preoccupation elapsed before the Court dealt with the doctrine again. Inconclusively, but nonetheless pointedly, in 1948 it ordered the state of

[62]The other two were Justices Van Devanter and Sutherland, replaced by Black and Reed, in 1937 and 1938, respectively. Yet it is entirely plausible that—based on their records in the civil rights and liberties realm—the two departed justices would have joined the majority opinion.

[63]*Missouri ex rel. Gaines v. Canada,* 305 U.S. 337 (1938), dissenting opinion, at 353.

[64]*Ibid.,* majority opinion, at 344.

[65]Terms used repeatedly, and appropriately, by Judge Loren Miller in his *The Petitioners, op. cit.*

Oklahoma to provide a duly qualified, NAACP-backed black woman applicant with an equal legal education in a state institution.[66] The results were less than satisfactory in terms of the ultimate goal, but there was no longer any question that, at the very least, *equal* facilities would have to be state-provided.

Two years later, however, the Court handed down a set of decisions which made painfully clear to the South that while "separate but equal" might still not be unconstitutional, it was patently on its last legs. The two 1950 cases were announced on the same Opinion Monday, and both were decided unanimously in opinions written by Chief Justice Vinson. Although neither outlawed the "separate but equal" doctrine *per se*, the conditions posited by the Court for its continued constitutionality were now in fact unattainable. Both cases had once again been stimulated and backed by the NAACP's capable, increasingly active, legal team. One, *Sweatt v. Painter*,[67] concerned the University of Texas's statutorily sanctioned denial of H. M. Sweatt's request for admission to its law school solely because he was black. Sweatt, a Houston mail carrier aspiring to be a lawyer, had refused to attend the separate law school for blacks established by Texas as a result of the *Gaines* case. He argued that because it was inferior, it would deprive him of the equal protection of the laws. The second case, *McLaurin v. Oklahoma State Regents*,[68] dealt with an ingenious requirement by the Oklahoma legislature, which enabled qualified blacks, such as Professor G. W. McLaurin, to do graduate study (here toward a doctorate in education) at the state-owned University of Oklahoma *if* the University's authorities admitted them as candidates on a "segregated basis"—defined as "classroom instruction given in separate classrooms, or at separate times."

Sweatt's argument that the Texas State University for Negroes was simply "inferior" and hence *unequal* found willing listeners. The Chief Justice's brief but lucid opinion pointed not only to the obvious physical differences between the two schools—which alone would have made them sufficiently unequal—but, far more significantly, to those "qualities which are incapable of objective measurement but which

[66]*Sipuel v. Oklahoma*, 322 U.S. 631 (1948), and *Fisher v. Hurst*, 333 U.S. 147 (1948), both decided *per curiam*. Miss Sipuel had become Mrs. Fisher in the intervening period.
[67]339 U.S. 629 (1950).
[68]339 U.S. 637 (1950).

make for greatness in a law school."[69] Among these qualities he noted "reputation of the faculty, experience of the administration, position and influence of the alumni, standing in the community, tradition and prestige."[70] Tongue in cheek, Vinson commented that it was indeed difficult to believe that one who had a free choice between the two law schools involved would "consider the question close."[71] And he went on to identify some of the intensely practical considerations that rendered the new law school for blacks so decidedly inferior:

> The law school to which Texas is willing to admit [Sweatt] excludes from its student body members of the racial groups which number 85 per cent of the population of the State and include most of the lawyers, witnesses, jurors, judges, and other officials with whom [Sweatt] will inevitably be dealing when he becomes a member of the Texas Bar. With such a substantial and significant segment of society excluded, we cannot conclude that the education offered [Sweatt] is substantially equal to that which he would receive if admitted to the University of Texas Law School.[72]

While the Court thus held that there was simply no way to make the two schools equal and yet separate, it still had stopped short of declaring the doctrine null and void. Yet its willingness to look at socio-political, philosophical, and psychological "intangibles" of the separate-but-equal doctrine inexorably pointed the way to the 1954–55 *Public School Segregation* cases.

The circumstances surrounding McLaurin's case were just as unpropitious for the future of the separate-but-equal concept. After McLaurin had been ordered admitted to the University of Oklahoma's School of Education to work for his doctorate in education, and since he was the only black so admitted at the time, the University administration endeavored to comply with the state-mandated provisions for "segregated admission" by resorting to the following degrading devices: rather than arranging separate classes for him, the University required him to sit apart at a designated desk in what was variously described as a "hallway" or an "anteroom adjoining the classroom," where he and

---

[69]*Sweatt v. Painter, op. cit.,* at 634.
[70]*Ibid.*
[71]*Ibid.*
[72]*Ibid.,* at 634. Sweatt was duly admitted, but flunked out.

the instructor could see and hear each other, but from which vantage point he would presumably not contaminate the superior race of his fellow students. In the library he was assigned a special desk on the mezzanine floor. but told that he could not use the desks in the regular reading room. In the school cafeteria he was directed to eat at a specifically designated table and to do so at a different time than his white fellow-students. And, as the Chief Justice described it in his opinion:

> For some time, the section of the classroom in which [McLaurin] sat was surrounded by a rail on which there was a sign stating, "Reserved for Colored," but these have been removed. He is now [at the time of the litigation] assigned to a seat in the classroom in a row specified for colored students.[73]

This hocus-pocus, declared the unanimous tribunal, was neither "equal" nor constitutional—and McLaurin was promptly admitted to full student citizenship and the equal protection of the laws.

After the 1950 triumphs of Messrs. Sweatt and McLaurin, the barriers prevalent in higher education in the Border states and the South began to give way, however gradually. But it would take the death of the "separate but equal" doctrine and the employment of federal troops in Tuscaloosa, Alabama, and Oxford, Mississippi, thirteen years later, before *every* state in the heretofore segregated area would admit at least one black to at least one of its graduate or professional institutions of higher learning.

Although the effective catalyst would be the *Public School Segregation Cases* of 1954 and 1955, collateral developments[74] also assisted in chipping away at the separate-but-equal doctrine. Transportation was one of these. As early as 1946, a Virginia segregation statute, as applied to interstate buses, was declared unconstitutional 7 : 1 in a Supreme Court opinion authored by Justice Stanley F. Reed.[75] Four years later, compulsory segregation on interstate trains was outlawed—first by another Supreme Court decision,[76] then by the Interstate Commerce Commission, which particularly referred to sleeping and dining cars.

---

[73]*McLaurin v. Oklahoma State Regents, op. cit.*, at 640.
[74]See pp. 329 ff., *supra.*
[75]*Morgan v. Virginia*, 328 U.S. 373 (1946).
[76]*Henderson v. United States*, 333 U.S. 816 (1950).

Ultimately, the I.C.C. ordered the cessation of all racial segregation on interstate buses and trains and their public waiting rooms in stations and terminals. To the advocates of segregation, if there was to be an effective last stand at all, it would have to come in *intra*-state matters—of which, they hoped, public schools would be one of the most important. Then, on what would be known to arch-segregationists as "Black Monday," May 17, 1954, came *Brown v. Board of Education of Topeka, et al.*[77] Powerful rear-guard actions continued to be fought, but the separate-but-equal doctrine was lost as a legal force. When the colorful Mississippi politician and rabid segregationist James K. Vardaman cautioned at the turn of the century that "[t]his education is ruining our Negroes. They're demanding equality,"[78] he did not realize how prophetic his words would prove to be some five or six decades later.

THE DEATH OF THE "SEPARATE BUT EQUAL" DOCTRINE

The *Public School Segregation Cases* of 1954, and their implementation decision one year later, transferred, in the words of one commentator, "the legal sanction and moral authority of the nation's basic law from the segregationist forces to the civil rights advocates."[79] It marked the end of an era and the beginning of a new one. In the words of Alpheus T. Mason: "On May 17, 1954, the Court initiated the greatest social revolution of this generation."[80] Most of the considerable political, economic, and social progress blacks have been able to achieve since 1954 stems demonstrably from *Brown v. Board* and its offspring—and much of the contemporary criticism of the authority of the Supreme Court is traceable to that decision and its results. It richly deserves explanation and analysis.

Some Groundwork. Following the *Sweatt* and *McLaurin* decisions, the NAACP's now highly encouraged lawyers, headed by Thurgood Marshall, bided their time in the hope that the South might show some disposition to comply with the spirit of those two decisions and embark upon some "gradualist" program of desegregation. It is idle to specu-

---

[77]347 U.S. 483.

[78]As quoted in Walter Lord, *The Past That Would Not Die* (New York: Harper & Row, 1965), p. 43.

[79]Alan F. Westin, in Redford, Truman, Hacker, Westin, and Wood, *Politics and Government in the United States* (New York: Harcourt, Brace & World, 1968), p. 588.

[80]*The Supreme Court: Palladium of Freedom* (Ann Arbor: University of Michigan Press, 1962), p. 170.

late whether more courageous leadership by Southerners and non-Southerners, in and out of government, might have brought about the desired change. The fact is that no such leadership of any consequence was forthcoming. The evolving Southern strategy now seemed to follow the candid public statement of Governor James F. Byrnes of South Carolina that, indeed, the South had failed properly to facilitate the education of its blacks and that "to remedy a hundred years of neglect" a crash building program of fine new schools for blacks had to be started instantly. Byrnes readily admitted that the South would have to act, and act at once, to preserve the "separate but equal" concept, lest the Supreme Court, as he—once (1941–42) a member of that tribunal himself—put it, "take matters out of the state's hands." When all overt and covert entreaties for a gradualist approach were rejected, particularly by Virginia and South Carolina, Marshall and his battery of attorneys determined that the time had come to wage an all-out battle in the courts against "separate but equal." They had no difficulty in finding appropriate vehicles for the desired litigation, and five separate desegregation suits were instituted in carefully selected parts of the country. Four were begun in the states of Delaware, Kansas (Topeka), South Carolina (Clarendon County), and Virginia (Prince Edward County), and one at the federal level in the District of Columbia. Each suit, painstakingly presented by NAACP attorneys, charged not only that the several local black schools involved were *inferior* to their white counterparts, but that the "separate but equal" rule itself violated the "equal protection of the laws" clause of Amendment Fourteen.

To no one's great astonishment the suits lost everywhere, save in Delaware, where a limited victory was achieved. (The lower court adhered to the "separate but equal" precedent of *Plessy,* but ordered plaintiffs admitted to the white schools because of their superiority to their black counterparts.) However, the Supreme Court granted *certiorari* during 1952, hearing extensive oral arguments from both sides that December. According to one source, the vote to grant review came by the requisite bare minimum of four.[81] Thurgood Marshall's forces, augmented by other friendly lawyers, and buttressed by a brief *amicus*

---

[81]Fred Rodell, "It Is the Earl Warren Court," *The New York Times Magazine,* March 13, 1966, p. 93. Apparently Frankfurter, Douglas, Burton, and Minton.

curiae brought by President Truman's Attorney-General Edward T. McGranahan, were supported in their argument in what was to become a famous appendix to their brief. In it, thirty American social scientists of national and international reputation[82] not only supported the NAACP's fundamental charge of segregation as constituting discrimination but—even more significantly from the standpoint of the Court's ultimate opinion—contended at length that segregation as such was harmful to the psyche of *both* black and white children, causing irreparable damage to their development as members of a healthy heterogeneous community. Arguing—without fee—on behalf of the segregation status quo, as represented by the five cases, was one of America's foremost constitutional law experts, trial attorney John W. Davis, who had not only held numerous high-ranking jobs in government but had been the unsuccessful Democratic nominee for President in 1924. It would be the now eighty-year-old Davis's last appearance before the Court—to which he had declined a nomination by President Warren G. Harding in 1922.

Conscious of the significance of the issue at bar, the Supreme Court bided its time. In June 1953, it not only rescheduled the cases for *reargument* but submitted a set of five fundamental Frankfurter-framed questions to opposing counsel with directions for appropriate responses, questions that dealt chiefly with the meaning and intent of the Fourteenth Amendment vis-à-vis segregation and certain practical aspects of desegregation. However hypothetically they were phrased, the nature of the Court's questions caused the hopes of the NAACP and its supporters to soar. But the battle was not yet won, and Marshall, especially in view of what seemed to be the controversial historical aspect of the Court's basic *quaere*,[83] once again turned to the academic community. In September 1953 he enlisted the expertise of some 130 distinguished, chiefly academic, specialists in constitutional history, law, and interpretation. The impressive array of scholars met, chiefly in New York City, and

[82]Among them Kenneth Clark, Floyd Allport, Robert M. MacIver, Robert Redfield, and Alfred McC. Lee.

[83]The 39th Congress—the framers of the Fourteenth Amendment—denied almost to a man that its equal protection of the laws clause required the desegregation of public institutions; they applied the same reasoning to racial discrimination in the exercise of the suffrage. The latter was reached, of course, by the Fifteenth Amendment two years later.

aided Marshall and his immediate lieutenants in the preparation of the new brief.[84] It was filed on November 15, 1953, and argued orally on December 8, 1953, before a new Chief Justice, Earl Warren, Vinson having died just prior to the reargument.[85] The brief's chief historical contention was that the framers of Amendment Fourteen had *intended* to ban segregation "as a last vestige of slavery"—a contention elaborately disputed by a good many historians.[86] Davis's response was geared to judicial self-restraint as much as to contrary history; neither the Supreme Court nor any other judicial body had the power, he argued, to declare unconstitutional or *ultra vires* on sociological or psychological bases a school system, a way of life, duly enacted by the people's representatives, that "has stood for three-quarters of a century." If there was change in the offing, it would have to come either by evolution or by the legislative process. The now Republican Administration's Attorney-General, Herbert Brownell, although not quite so assertive in his support of desegregation as McGranahan had been, filed a brief *amicus curiae* in favor of desegregation. It did not accept the historical rationale of the main brief but called for a one-year transition period to permit the South to adjust its social and educational problems. Listening intently to these various arguments in the jammed Supreme Court chamber, the full bench of justices peppered counsel with searching questions.

May 17, 1954. Five months after oral argument, and four years after the *Sweatt* and *McLaurin* decisions, the Supreme Court of the United States rendered its decision.[87] It did not resort to the historical issue in which it had expressed so much interest; obviously, and quite wisely, it

[84]Among them C. Vann Woodward, John Hope Franklin, Alfred H. Kelly, Robert E. Cushman, Robert K. Carr, Milton R. Konvitz, John P. Frank, Walter Gellhorn, Horace Bond, Howard J. Graham. For an excellent description of their work see Alfred H. Kelly, "The School Segregation Cases," in Garraty, *op cit.*, pp. 307–33.

[85]"This is the first indication I have ever had that there is a God," nastily quipped Frankfurter. (See Kluger, fn. 89, *infra*, p. 656.)

[86]One of these is Raoul Berger, most of whose mammoth and controversial *Government by Judiciary: The Transformation of the Fourteenth Amendment* (Cambridge: Harvard University Press, 1977) is intended to demonstrate that the Amendment's framers and supporters specifically rejected its application to segregated schools and to the franchise. (E.g., Chapter 15, "The Rule of Law," and Chapter 20, "Conclusion.")

[87]*Brown v. Board of Education of Topeka, et al.*, 347 U.S. 483, and *Bolling v. Sharpe*, 347 U.S. 497. The "Brown" in the case was the Rev. Oliver Brown, a welder on the Rock Island Railroad, who filed suit on behalf of his daughter, Linda.

did not believe it to be either convincingly resolvable or necessary to the unanimous conclusion it would reach through its new Chief Justice, who, as he would recall two decades later, assigned himself to write the opinion, "for it seemed to me that something so important ought to issue over the name of the Chief Justice of the United States."[88] Evidently Warren had labored hard and long to get a unanimous opinion; there are reliable indications that two justices were inclined to dissent— albeit on differing grounds—for at least some time during the Court's deliberations;[89] that, indeed, the initial, tentative, Conference vote was 6 : 3.[90] Notwithstanding the complex background and the emotional impact of the issue at hand, the Warren opinion—of which, after his retirement, he said he had written "every blessed word"[91]—was

[88]Lecture, University of Virginia Legal Forum, April 18, 1973. At a celebration of his ten years on the Court, Warren noted that when the decisions were announced, "the Clerk of our Court for weeks was beset by scores of requests for copies of the 'dissenting opinion.' When told that there was no dissenting opinion, many of them demanded to know by whose order the dissenting opinion had been abolished. Others, believing that there must be a dissenting opinion, threatened to have him investigated for suppressing it." (As quoted in Jacobus ten Broek, *Equal Under Law*, new enl. ed. [New York: Collier, 1965], p. 7.)

[89]See Rodell, *op. cit.* Evidently, they were Reed and Jackson. See the account by William H. Harbaugh, *Lawyer's Lawyer: The Life of John W. Davis* (New York: Oxford University Press, 1973), Chapter 28. See especially, Richard Kluger, *Simple Justice: The History of Brown v. Board of Education and Black America's Struggle for Equality* (New York: Alfred A. Knopf, 1976), particularly pp. 678–99. Kluger reprints a draft dissenting opinion by Reed and demonstrates conclusively that Reed intended to dissent until just two days prior to the rendering of the decision—despite twenty luncheons with the Chief Justice—when he yielded in the interest of "what was best for America." (At 698.) (It ought to be noted, however, that it was Reed who had authored the 1944 and 1946 majority opinions striking down the white primary [see pp. 372–74, *infra*] and state laws requiring segregated seating on interstate buses [see p. 344, *supra*].) Jackson, while prepared to go along, insisted on writing a *concurring* opinion based on judicial self-restraint, warning that the Court "was declaring new law for a new day." But he was struck down by a severe coronary thrombosis—which seemed to be the catalyst in his agreeing to desist from penning a separate opinion.

[90]See S. Sidney Ulmer, *Courts As Small and Not So Small Groups* (New York: General Learning Press, 1971), p. 24. Ulmer's (and Harbaugh's) claim that Frankfurter was the third holdout is vigorously rebutted by Kluger—whose account of *Brown's* dénouement is the most recent, most complete, lengthiest, and most convincing. Indeed, Frankfurter was one of the architects of unanimity, second in importance only to Warren. Moreover, it was Frankfurter who staved off a potentially seriously divided or even negative vote in June 1953 by framing the five key questions for reargument. "F.F." did, however, have strong reservations regarding the judiciary's proper role here.

[91]As quoted by John F. Simon, *In His Own Image: The Supreme Court in Richard Nixon's America* (New York: David McKay Co., Inc., 1973), p. 55. The Chief Justice,

amazingly brief (just eleven pages),[92] simple, and direct—although certainly controversial! "We must look to the effect that segregation itself has on public education," he noted in nearing the heart of his Court's decision:

> In approaching this problem, we cannot turn the clock back to 1868 when the [Fourteenth] Amendment was adopted,[93] or even to 1896 when *Plessy v. Ferguson* was written. We must consider public education in the light of its full development and its present place in American life throughout the Nation. Only in this way can it be determined if segregation in public schools deprives these [Negroes] of the equal protection of the laws.
>
> Today, education is perhaps the most important function of state and local government. . . . [Education] is the very foundation of good citizenship. Today it is the principal instrument in awakening the child to cultural values, in preparing him for later professional training, and in helping him to adjust normally to his environment. . . .
>
> We come then to the question presented: *Does segregation of children in public schools solely on the basis of race, even though the physical facilities*

---

by his own account, was determined to (a) get an unanimous vote; (b) write the opinion for the Court; and (c) "use low key unemotional language." He waited more than five months before calling for a final vote in Conference; when he did he had his unanimous Court: "We took one vote, and that was it." (*The New York Times,* June 11, 1974, p. 35A.) But that did not occur until after the developments described in footnote 89, *supra.* In a letter, exhibited at Harvard (October 21, 1977), commemorating Frankfurter's ninety-fifth birthday, "F.F." noted to Reed that there would have been four dissents had *Brown* been decided just one term earlier. (Reed, Vinson, Jackson, and Clark.)

[92]Responding to a student's question, Warren recounted that he "purposely wrote such a short opinion so that any layman interested in the problem could read the entire opinion [instead of getting just] a little piece here and a little piece there. Hopefully this would not be the case with *Brown.* I think most of the major newspapers printed the entire decision." They did. (University of Virginia Legal Forum, April 18, 1973.)

[93]Kluger, a strong and avowed partisan of the *Brown* decision, acknowledges that painstaking research by Alexander M. Bickel, then Frankfurter's clerk, demonstrated that there was "no evidence that the framers of the Amendment had intended to prohibit school segregation." (Kluger, *op. cit.,* at 655.) In effect, Bickel had reported to his Justice that "it is impossible to conclude that the 39th Congress intended that segregation be abolished, impossible also to conclude that they foresaw it might be, under the language they were adopting." (*Ibid.,* at 654.) Indeed, that 39th not only segregated the District of Columbia schools, but also its own Senate gallery. Raoul Berger labeled Warren's "we cannot turn back the clock" statement as "a veiled declaration that the intention of the framers was irrelevant and that the Court was revising the Constitution to meet present day needs." (Fn. 86, *op. cit.,* at 131.)

and other "tangible" factors may be equal, deprive the children of the
minority group of equal educational opportunity? We believe that it does.[94]

The Chief Justice then asserted: "Segregation of white and colored
children in public schools has a detrimental effect upon the colored
children. . . . *A sense of inferiority affects the motivation of a child to*
learn."[95] And, as Earl Warren had explained a few sentences earlier, to
separate children in grade and high schools "from others of similar age
and qualifications *solely because of their race generates a feeling of*
inferiority as to their status in the community that may affect their
hearts and minds in a way unlikely ever to be undone."[96] Now followed
the famous and controversial "social science" footnote 11, which cited
the writings of those social scientists, chiefly psychologists and sociologists, on whose findings the Court here relied. Among them were the
noted black psychologist Kenneth B. Clark and Gunnar Myrdal, the
Swedish sociologist whose celebrated *An American Dilemma*[97] had
caused such an uproar in the South and the Border states when it first
appeared in 1944. Wrote Warren: "Whatever may have been the extent
of psychological knowledge at the time of *Plessy v. Ferguson,* this
finding is amply supported by modern authority. Any language in
Plessy v. Ferguson contrary to this finding is rejected."[98] Thus, out
went the ruling by Justice Brown for his 7 : 1 Court in 1896—and up
went the lone dissent by Justice John Marshall Harlan I. All that
remained for the decision of 1954 was the dramatic conclusion that

in the field of public education the doctrine of "separate but equal" has no
place. Separate educational facilities are inherently unequal. . . . the plain-
tiffs and others similarly situated for whom the actions have been brought

[94]*Brown v. Board of Education of Topeka, et al.,* 347 U.S. 483 (1954), at 492. (Italics
supplied.)

[95]*Ibid.,* at 494. (Italics supplied.)

[96]*Ibid.* (Italics supplied.)

[97]*An American Dilemma: The Negro Problem and Modern Democracy* (New York:
Harper and Bros., 1944). Republished in 1946, and, in a revised edition, by Harper &
Row in 1962. For a highly critical recent evaluation of the resort to "social science"
evidence, see lawyer-anthropologist John Aron Grayzel, "Using Social Science Concepts
in the Legal Fight Against Discrimination: Servant or Sorcerer's Apprentice," 64 *Ameri-*
can Bar Association Journal 1238 (August 1978).

[98]*Brown, op. cit.,* at 494. (Italics supplied.)

are, by reason of the segregation complained of, *deprived of the equal protection of the laws guaranteed by the Fourteenth Amendment.*[99]

In other words, the "equal protection of the laws" clause of the Fourteenth Amendment now forbade the racially segregated education of public school children.[100] Indeed, the strong implication of the *Brown v. Board* ruling was that *any publicly* authorized or *publicly* permitted racial segregation would henceforth be unconstitutional.[101]

The Implementation Decision. Meanwhile, the 1954 decision would have to be implemented—and here the Court bowed to the counsel of Attorney-General Brownell. Refraining from an immediate desegregation order, given the revolutionary nature of the decision, the Court stayed any enforcement mandate, and ordered supportive argument in all five cases for April 1955—almost a year later. For that purpose, the Court invited all interested parties, specifically including counsel, the *amici curiae*, the Solicitor-General of the United States, and all state attorneys-general, to file briefs and, if they so chose, participate in oral argument. Most of the Southern states refused to do so, but Florida, North Carolina, Arkansas, and Texas, joined by the Border states of Oklahoma and Maryland, did argue, dramatically and at length.[102] One month later, another unanimous Warren opinion (for the same Court members as its predecessor decision, except that John Marshall Harlan II had replaced the deceased Justice Jackson) announced the implementation or "mandate" decision.[103] Invoking an old principle of equity

[99]*Ibid.*, at 495. (Italics supplied.)

[100]Raoul Berger charges repeatedly and angrily that herewith Warren "revised the Fourteenth Amendment to mean exactly the opposite of what its framers designed it to mean, namely, to leave suffrage and segregation beyond federal control, to leave it with the states, where control over internal, domestic matters resided from the beginning." (*Op. cit.*, at 245.) See also his p. 105 for voting statistics regarding the former, demonstrating that the House and Senate, by votes of 125 : 12 and 34 : 4, respectively, specifically rejected the Amendment's application to suffrage.

[101]The District of Columbia litigation had to be decided on the "due process of law" clause of Amendment Five, of course (*Bolling v. Sharpe*, 347 U.S. 497 [1954]). In effect applying a type of "reverse incorporation," the Court read the concept of "equal protection of the laws" into the "due process of law" clause of the Fifth Amendment—a policy it has embraced ever since.

[102]The Court allowed fourteen hours of argument; the usual allotment is one hour per case.

[103]*Brown v. Board of Education of Topeka, et al.*, 349 U.S. 294 (1955), and *Bolling v. Sharpe, op. cit.* Thirty-five years later, Linda Brown Smith, now a forty-three-year-old

law,[104] and thereby avoiding any immediate problem of overall enforcement, it mandated the *local federal courts* to direct and oversee the transition to a racially non-discriminatory system of public school primary and secondary education "with all deliberate speed."[105] It directed these courts to order a "prompt and reasonable start," but clearly left the door ajar for consideration of the manifold local problems involved. In fact, "wide open door" may be a more appropriate description of the *initial* judicial attitude, compared to what would be a much stiffer attitude as the fifties turned into the sixties. Inevitably the "child of its time," the Court had carefully separated the principle of integration—a word that appears nowhere in the decisions involved—from its actual implementation.[106] Just as the Supreme Court reflected the socio-political realities of a new day and age[107] in *Brown* I, so did it reflect the judicial-limitation realities in *Brown* II.[108] As the ensuing months and years would prove, the Court can be a leader and the conscience of the country—but in the political process of which, after all, it is a part, it has only "the power to persuade: purse and sword are in other hands," as Alexander Hamilton stated so perceptively at the Republic's dawn in his *The Federalist* #78.

The Court would need immediate help from the executive branch. Overt or covert defiance became the rule rather than the exception in a

---

grandmother, took the witness stand as an intervening plaintiff in that very case, charging that the public schools of Topeka still had not purged themselves of segregation. But U.S. District Court Judge Richard D. Rogers, in a strongly worded fifty-page opinion, resolutely disagreed. (*Brown v. Board of Education of Topeka, Kansas*, 671 F. Supp. 1290 [1987].)

[104]For a capsule explanation of equity see my *The Judicial Process: An Introductory Analysis of the Courts of the United States, England, and France*, 5th ed. (New York: Oxford University Press, 1980), pp. 13–15.

[105]The "all deliberate speed" formula was suggested by Justice Frankfurter, who found it in a 1911 Holmes opinion dealing with monetary matters between states. (*Virginia v. West Virginia*, 222 U.S. 17, at 20.) Holmes identified it as "language of the English Chancery."

[106]See Ulmer, *op. cit.*, pp. 23–26, for an illuminating account of the various options the Court perceived in *Brown* I and II, and the Chief Justice's leadership in the cases.

[107]On this point see the interesting article by Charles L. Black, Jr., "The Lawfulness of the Segregation Decisions," 69 *Yale Law Journal* 421 (1960).

[108]Asked whether the Justices ever considered "busing" in any of the implementation decision conferences, the Chief Justice replied, "No, I don't think we ever did." (University of Virginia Legal Forum, April 18, 1973.) For a superb account of *Brown* II, see J. Harvie Wilkinson III, *From Brown to Bakke* (New York: Oxford University Press, 1979), especially Chapters 1–9.

good many areas, chiefly in the deep South. While the District of Columbia, under direct federal control, did integrate its public schools immediately—Congress had permitted segregated schools there from 1864 onward—the response in the affected states ran from bowing to the inevitable in more or less good faith—e.g., in the District of Columbia, Delaware, and Kansas—through reasonably delayed action, to absolute refusal to obey. There was occasionally even avowed, outright defiance, accompanied by flurries of violence, in Arkansas, Virginia, South Carolina, Georgia, Florida, Louisiana, Alabama and Mississippi. Many subterfuges were adopted by these states and others, such as the closing of all public schools in Prince Edward County, Virginia— where one of the five *Public School Segregation* cases of 1954 originated.[109] Public feeling ran high indeed over what the majority of the white population in the affected sectors regarded as a threat to their way of life and the right of the states to govern themselves, the latter more often than not being a camouflage for the former. Some 200 state segregation statutes would be enacted in the decade following the implementation decision.

Even Force. Still, a start, however halting and sullen, had been made; and enforcement of the decision continued to spread through a lengthy process of litigation, a host of patient efforts by many groups and individuals, courageous stances by the fifty-odd Southern federal jurists who in many ways must be recognized as the heroes of the desegregation battles of the decade between 1955 and 1965,[110] the repeated affirmations of the basic decisions by the United States Supreme Court,[111] and, finally, a show of federal military force when deemed necessary as a last resort. President Eisenhower, for the first three years after *Brown,* had done his best to stay out of the battle and, indeed, had done nothing either to support the Supreme Court, so heavily under fire, or to explain, let alone defend, its decisions to the

---

[109]*Davis v. County School Board of Prince Edward County, Virginia,* 347 U.S. 483.

[110]Jack W. Peltason, *Fifty-Eight Lonely Men: Southern Judges and School Desegregation,* rev. ed. (Urbana: University of Illinois Press, 1971), tells their story enlighteningly and engagingly.

[111]Thus, Justice Hugo Black wrote for a unanimous Supreme Court in 1964, ultimately striking down the Prince Edward County school closing and related subterfuges: "There has been entirely too much deliberation and not enough speed in enforcing the constitutional rights which we held . . . had been denied. . . ." (*Griffin v. Prince Edward School Board,* 377 U.S. 218, at 229).

country. In the judgment of many, the enormously popular and influential national hero could have achieved something here if *anyone* could. But in the fall of 1957 he found his hand forced by Governor Orville Faubus of Arkansas. Faubus, following a lengthy desegregation battle with federal and state authorities,[112] called out the National Guard to prevent duly scheduled federal court–ordered public school desegregation in Little Rock, an order that involved only nine black children. When he was enjoined by the appropriate United States District Court from continued interference, he removed the Guard, thereby encouraging the lawless. Riots and disorders promptly ensued. After a confrontation with Governor Faubus at Newport, Rhode Island, failed, an angry and reluctant President Eisenhower felt compelled to federalize the Arkansas National Guard and dispatch it[113] to reestablish law and order and allow desegregation to proceed as judicially directed.[114] Five years later, in the fall of 1962, President John F. Kennedy deployed 25,000 federal troops to overcome the opposition of Mississippi, led by its governor, Ross R. Barnett, to the federal court ordered admission of black James Meredith[115] to the University of Mississippi at Oxford. A bloody all-night battle was fought on and near the campus of "Ole Miss," with many wounded and two lives lost.[116] Eight months later President Kennedy again had to use troops, this time mobilizing the

[112]Well told by, among others, Wilson Record and Jane Cassels Record, *Little Rock U.S.A.* (San Francisco: Chandler Publishing Co., 1960).

[113]These forces were under the command of Brigadier-General Edwin Walker, who some years later became one of the most visible anti-integrationists and caused considerable difficulties for the federal authorities during the Oxford, Mississippi, confrontations. (See *Associated Press v. Walker*, 388 U.S. 130, [1967].)

[114]See the Court's unanimous, seminal decision—signed and authored jointly by all nine members of the tribunal—in *Cooper v. Aaron*, 358 U.S. 1 (1958) where it not only sternly ordered immediate compliance with the desegregation order by lower federal courts, but reminded one and all that it is "emphatically the province and duty of the *judicial department* to say what the law is." (Italics supplied.) (For a discussion, see my *The Judicial Process, op. cit.*, pp. 215–16.)

[115]Four years later, while on a march from Memphis to Jackson to dramatize the Negro registration drive in Mississippi, Meredith was shot and wounded in an ambush. Yet ten years later he would be the University of Mississippi's guest lecturer! (*The New York Times*, April 22, 1972, p. 32c.) And he ran, though unsuccessfully, for the Republican gubernatorial nomination in June 1972. By 1976, 475 blacks were on the Oxford campus. (*Ibid.*, October 10, p. 16m.)

[116]See University of Mississippi James W. Silver's important book *Mississippi: The Closed Society* (New York: Harcourt, Brace & World, 1966), and his colleague Russell H. Barrett's *Integration at Ole Miss* (Chicago: Quadrangle Books, 1965).

Alabama National Guard in order to overcome Governor George C. Wallace's defiance of the federal court–ordered admission of blacks Vivian Malone and James Hood to the University of Alabama at Tuscaloosa.[117]

Although even token integration was often resisted in the deep South, mixed classes eventually became a reality on all levels of the public school system. "Mixed," of course, sometimes meant the presence of only one black student in an otherwise all-white classroom, but the principle was being established, and the tough financial penalties provided by Title VI of the Civil Rights Act of 1964 served to spur compliance in all but the most adamant situations. These last would be left to the judicial process; yet it was clear that in some instances, such as in Wallace-led Alabama, a course of "legal defiance," including a rejection of federal funds, would be at least temporarily pursued. In any event, on August 14, 1964, Mississippi became the *last* state to desegregate at least one school district when the Biloxi District bowed to a federal court order decreeing the desegregation of its first-grade classes. Less than six months later, the Greenville, Mississippi, School Board, facing the loss of $272,000 in federal aid-to-education funds if it failed to comply with the provisions of the Civil Rights Act of 1964 affecting such federal aid, voted unanimously to prepare a desegregation plan. Providing the first instance of non-court-ordered compliance by that state's authorities, Greenville's Mayor Pat Dunne endorsed the Board's action, pointing out that there was no alternative: "Repugnant as the law is to all of us, it's a Federal law and it's either a case of comply or close the schools."[118]

Enter Busing

Notwithstanding the very real and continuing desegregation progress described, the line between genuine and token *integration* has proved to

[117]Ten years later Wallace "crowned" the first black Homecoming Queen at the same University. Twenty years later he was reelected Governor of Alabama, with the decisive vote margin coming from the black community!

[118]*The New York Times*, January 16, 1965, p. 18*l*. (At the level of higher public education, the last bastions, Alabama and South Carolina, had already fallen two years earlier. Harvey Gantt, the first black to enter Clemson, became mayor of Charlotte, N.C., in 1983.)

be extremely difficult to draw[119]—even given such a clear mandate as that contained in the landmark October 1969 decision in the *Holmes County* case,[120] which announced the death of the "deliberate speed" concept in an 8 : 0 opinion, *per curiam,* highlighted by: " 'All deliberate speed' for desegregation is no longer constitutionally permissible. . . . [T]he obligation of every school district is to terminate dual school systems at once and to operate now and hereafter only unitary school systems."[121] But even assuming good faith—not always a viable assumption—how much *busing* of students does the Constitution require in order to achieve the mandated "unitary" system?[122] How much, how far, at what cost? What of housing patterns, of fatigue factors, of the relationship of ghetto and suburb, of the right of states to create administrative subdivisions?

In the face of a host of these vexatious questions, with their manifold political, economic, social, and psychological components, the Supreme Court considered the busing-to-integrate issue on its merits in an April 1971 decision of momentous significance for the entire country. Now thrust center stage, busing became—and continues to be—*the* cardinal bone of contention in the continuing and expanding efforts to implement *Brown* I and II.

[119]Thus, in May 1968, obviously having reached the end of its patience, a unanimous Court ruled that the so-called freedom of choice desegregation plans are inadequate if they do not undo Southern school desegregation as rapidly as other available methods would. In what was its first detailed review of the adequacy of the *means* being used to implement the 1954 and 1955 *Brown* decisions, the Court—commencing a firm embrace of statistical evidence—declared that "delays are no longer tolerable"; that the "burden on a school board today is to come forward with a plan that promises realistically to work . . . *now.*" (Italics in original.) (*Green v. School Board of New Kent County,* 391 U.S. 430 [1968], at 439.) And in 1969, acting on the *first* school desegregation suit filed by the federal government in the *North,* United States District Court Judge Julius J. Hoffman (destined to become the much-embattled presiding judge in the "Chicago Eight" trial) ordered a suburban Chicago school district to desegregate its faculties and student bodies "forthwith." (*United States v. School District 151 of Cook County, Ill.,* 301 F. Supp. 201.)

[120]*Alexander v. Holmes County Board of Education,* 396 U.S. 19 (1969), at 20. Authorship has been attributed to Justice Brennan.

[121]*Ibid.* For a copy of the text of the Supreme Court's order, see *The New York Times,* October 30, 1969, p. 34. (Italics supplied.)

[122]As early as 1869, Massachusetts had authorized the expenditure of public funds to send children to and from school in horse-drawn wagons and carriages. (See Wilkinson, *From Brown to Bakke, op. cit.,* Chapters 6–9, for a thorough discussion of the busing issue.)

The 1971 *Swann* or *Charlotte-Mecklenburg* case,[123] as it became known popularly, headed a series arising from desegregation orders to a large school district covering the Charlotte, North Carolina, metropolitan area that had a long history of maintaining two sets of segregated schools. By 1969, under court orders, half of the 30 percent of black students in the district were in formerly all-white schools, the others remaining in virtually all-black schools. The case squarely raised the seminal question, posed by attorneys for a group of white *and* black North Carolina parents, whether the *Brown* ruling required "color-blind" assignment of students and, if so, whether busing to achieve integration was in effect unconstitutional. "We plead the same rights here that the plaintiffs pleaded in *Brown,*" asserted the lawyers opposing busing—leaving to the Court another particularly complicated line-drawing problem, one charged with deep emotions.

These were not vitiated by the fact that, when the high tribunal handed down its decision on that April 20, it was unanimous—one of the last times all nine Justices would be in agreement on racial matters.[124] Speaking for his Court, Chief Justice Burger's controversial opinion—which reportedly went through several drafts—confounded Court watchers and the Nixon Administration alike: for it specifically upheld not only *busing* but also *racial quotas, pairing* or *grouping* of schools, and *gerrymandering* of attendance zones as well as other devices designed to remove "all vestiges of state-imposed segregation. . . . *Desegregation plans cannot be limited to the walk-in school,*" he declared.[125] The Court stopped short of ordering the elimination of all-black schools or of requiring racial balance in the schools (and it made clear that its decision did *not* apply to Northern-style segregation, commonly based on *de facto* neighborhood patterns). But it said that the

[123]*Swann v. Charlotte-Mecklenburg Board of Education,* 402 U.S. 1.

[124]That long-standing unanimity—of almost two decades—ended on June 22, 1972, when the four Nixon appointees (Burger, Blackmun, Powell, and Rehnquist) dissented from a Supreme Court ruling that they characterized as *requiring* the imposition of "racial balance" rather than "desegregation." They protested that the majority of five (Douglas, Brennan, Stewart, White, and Marshall) had in effect equated racial balance with desegregation. (*Wright v. Council of the City of Emporia,* 407 U.S. 451.) According to one insider's account, the Court's unanimity in *Swann* was in fact deceptive: that the initial vote had actually been 6 : 3 *against* forced busing. (See Wilkinson, *op. cit.,* pp. 146–50.) See also Bernard Schwartz, *Swann's Way: The School Busing Cases and the Supreme Court* (New York: Oxford University Press, 1986).

[125]*Swann, op. cit.,* at 15, 30. (Italics supplied.)

existence of all-black schools created a presumption of discrimination and held that federal district judges—to whom it gave extremely broad discretion—may indeed use *racial quotas*[126] as a guide in fashioning desegregation decrees. On the busing issue, the Chief Justice, in a nod to that large element among the populace favoring the neighborhood school concept, admitted that "all things being equal, with no history of discrimination, it might well be desirable to assign pupils to schools nearest their homes. But all things are not equal," he continued, "in a system that has been deliberately constructed and maintained to enforce racial segregation."[127] The sweeping *Charlotte-Mecklenburg* ruling represented a landmark along the road to full desegregation, yet there was little doubt that the problem remained unsettled.

That it was indeed not settled would promptly be demonstrated by two landmark decisions—the first school desegregation cases to reach

[126]This notwithstanding the on-its-face prohibition by §2000c-6 of Title IV of the Civil Rights Act of 1964, which *specifically* would seem to *bar* racial quota assignments. But the Chief Justice brushed that argument aside, invoking the judiciary's "historic equitable remedial powers" in the quest of attaining what he viewed as full compliance with the spirit as well as the letter of the equal protection of the laws clause of Amendment Fourteen. In another portent of the Court's future posture on racial quotas, in 1977 it ruled 7 : 1—over a sharp dissent by Chief Justice Burger—in a "multiple plurality" decision that a state (here New York), drawing up a reapportionment plan in an effort to comply with the federal Voting Rights Act of 1965, as amended, may sometimes use racial quotas that are designed to assure that blacks and other non-whites have majorities in certain legislative districts. (*United Jewish Organizations of Williamsburg v. Carey*, 430 U.S. 144.) But the Court refused (6:3) three years later to impose election by district in Mobile, Alabama, where the long-standing practice of at-large election of the three-member City Commission had failed to produce a black commissioner, finding no *intent* to discriminate on racial grounds. (*City of Mobile v. Bolden*, 466 U.S. 55.) Yet in 1982 that same Court ruled 6 : 3 that Burke County, Georgia, could be lower-court-required to switch to an election system using single-member districts, based on a finding that the erstwhile at-large system of electing its Board of Commissioners had been maintained for the purpose of discriminating against blacks. (*Rogers v. Lodge*, 458 U.S. 613.) See also the one-sentence upholding of a Mississippi-drawn district on *purely* racial lines to ensure black hegemony, based on the Court's reading of the Voting Rights Act, as amended in 1982. (*Mississippi Republican Committee v. Brooks*, 469 U.S. 1002 [1984].) And note especially the 1986 North Carolina decision in *Thornburg v. Gingles*, 54 LW 4877, in effect embracing (5 : 4) the *results*-oriented concept, indeed coming perilously close to reading the Civil Rights Act of 1982 as requiring proportional representation in the realm of racial composition.

[127]*Swann, op. cit.,* at 28. During the controversy surrounding the Charlotte-Mecklenburg school district, the North Carolina legislature enacted a law flatly forbidding any "busing assignment of any student on account of race or for the purpose of creating a racial balance or ratio in the schools." That provision, too, fell 9:0 on the same day *Swann* was decided. (*North Carolina State Board of Education v. Swann*, 402 U.S. 43.)

the Court involving a major city outside the South. One came in a Denver, Colorado, case that squarely raised the crucial issue of "Northern-style segregation," which—unlike *segregation by law*, typical of the South—was the product of *economic and social patterns*. In a surprisingly decisive 7 : 1 holding[128] (or 6½ : 1½, depending upon one's analysis) and speaking through Justice Brennan—with only Justice Rehnquist in full dissent—the Court refused to discard the *de facto–de jure* distinction, as urged upon it by concurring Justices Douglas and, espeically, Powell, who also took pains to abjure forced busing. But it demonstrably expanded the *de jure* scope by making it clear that even in the absence of statutorily authorized segregation policies—and none such existed in Denver or, for that matter, in Colorado, where in fact it had been statutorily *forbidden* since 1895—it was provable that the Denver school board had in fact practiced segregation by manipulating school attendance zones and school sites and favoring a "neighborhood school" policy. The Court held it was necessary to demonstrate neither total or overall segregation nor the presence of a dual school system in order to find impermissible discrimination: it was sufficient to be able to point to segregation of "a substantial portion" of the school district, with the Court thus strongly hinting that pockets of intentional segregation, be they such as a result of law, custom, or neglect, would be regarded as constituting cause for judicial proscription applicable to the *entire* district. This, of course, would mean busing—as an increasing number of cities in the North as well as the South were experiencing.

The Denver litigation had confined itself to a *single* school district, as had that involving Charlotte-Mecklenburg. But what of the manifold situations, particularly extant in the North, in which integration is in effect not accomplishable without *busing across district lines*, usually involving black cities and white suburbs? The *Charlotte-Mecklenburg* case had involved such cross-county (city-suburb) busing, but it dealt with a *single* school district. The explosive issue was joined in 1972, when U.S. District Court Judge Robert R. Merhige, Jr., sitting in Richmond, Virginia, in a momentous 325-page (!) opinion,[129] ordered a merger of that city's predominantly black public schools with those of two predominantly white suburban counties, Henrico and Chesterfield.

---

[128]*Keyes v. School District #1, Denver, Colorado*, 413 U.S. 189 (1973), rehearing denied, 423 U.S. 1066 (1976).

[129]*Bradley v. School Board of the City of Richmond*, 338 F. Supp. 67.

A similarly contentious order was subsequently issued by U.S. District Court Judge Stephen J. Roth and was to involve the cross-county busing of 300,000 Detroit area children between that city and its suburbs.[130] There the similarity ended, for while the U.S. Circuit Court of Appeals for the Fourth Circuit *overruled* Judge Merhige 5 : 1,[131] Judge Roth's order was sustained 6 : 3 by the Sixth Circuit's Court of Appeals.[132] To the surprise of no one, both decisions were appealed to a somewhat less than eager U.S. Supreme Court.

Down came the Court, first with a "no-answer" answer in the Richmond case in a 4 : 4 one-sentence *per curiam* ruling, with Virginia's Justice Powell not participating: "The judgment is affirmed by an equally divided Court."[133] All eyes then turned toward Detroit, about which a decision was made in 1974. Speaking through the Chief Justice, the Court ruled (5 : 4) that whatever the situation in the city of Detroit itself might be or have been, the school systems in the surrounding suburbs had not been accused of unlawful segregation; that, absent proof of the latter, no constitutional power exists in the courts to decree relief balancing the racial composition of one community-wide segregated district (Detroit) with those of surrounding districts (the suburbs).[134] In bitter dissent Justices Douglas, Brennan, White, and Marshall accused the majority of taking "a giant step backward."[135]

What the Detroit landmark decision thus evidently conveyed was that the Court—recognizing the "deeply rooted" public education tradition of local control—would refuse to order cross-county or city-suburb integration, *unless* it could be proved that *intentional* segregation in one district leads to a "significant segregative effect in another district." Not surprisingly, numerous cross-county merger cases subsequently began to reach the Court, involving, among others, the areas around Louisville, Kentucky; Indianapolis, Indiana; Wilmington, Delaware;

[130]*Bradley v. Milliken,* 338 F. Supp. 582 (1972).

[131]*School Board of the City of Richmond v. Bradley,* 462 F. 2d 1058 (1972). Judge Harrison Winter dissented.

[132]*Bradley v. Milliken,* 484 F. 2d 215 (1973).

[133]*Bradley v. State Board of Education of the Commonwealth of Virginia,* 411 U.S. 913 (1973).

[134]*Milliken v. Bradley,* 418 U.S. 717. In the concurring Justice Stewart's words, "the multidistrict remedy contemplated by the desegregation order was an erroneous exercise of equitable authority of the federal courts." (At 756.) Joining Mr. Chief Justice Burger in the majority were Justices Stewart, Blackmun, Powell, and Rehnquist.

[135]*Ibid.,* at 782.

Atlanta, Georgia; Little Rock, Arkansas; and Buffalo, New York. In its actions, the Supreme Court adhered to its announced test of whether proof of deliberate, intentional segregation had been provided. In a number of instances it so found and, for example, upheld lower-court orders mandating inter-district busing between the cities of Wilmington and Louisville and their respective suburbs, but it struck down an order directed to Atlanta and its suburbs.[136]

The busing issue[137] continued to smolder—and to create controversy of a magnitude rarely seen in the body politic. To illustrate: consistently having defied—or at least having but mildly obeyed—U.S. District Court orders to bus its children, the Boston community, led by South Boston (heavily white ethnic, very few blacks), was confronted with a series of drastic ultimata handed down by Judge W. Arthur Garrity, Jr. Rejecting or downplaying these, the Boston School Committee, an elected, popular body, subsequently found itself deprived of many of its powers in December 1975; e.g., some of its schools were placed in the hands of a court-appointed receiver. Widespread and intense pressures began to mount among the electorate: along with abortion, the busing issue became a key concern of the 1976 presidential primary races in Massachusetts; around the nation segregationist George C. Wallace was emerging victorious in the Democratic race almost entirely on the busing issue. But Boston's strife-torn public school system continued in effect to be administratively directed by Judge Garrity[138]—whose stern

---

[136]*Evans v. Buchanan*, 423 U.S. 963 (1975), *Board of Education v. Newburg Area Council*, 421 U.S. 931 (1975), and *Armour v. Nix*, 446 U.S. 930 (1980), respectively. The Wilmington order was narrowly reconfirmed twice (4:3 in 1977 and 6:3 in 1980); (see *Delaware State Board of Education v. Evans*, 429 U.S. 973 and, *ibid.*, 447 U.S. 916 rehearing denied.) See also *Pulaski County v. Little Rock*, 54 LW 3823, and *Arkansas State Board of Education v. Little Rock*, 54 LW 3824 (1986).

[137]For some post-1970 literature on busing, see the following: Robert H. Bork, *Constitutionality of the President's Busing Proposals* (Washington, D.C.: American Enterprise Institute, 1972); "The Agony of Busing Moves North," *Time* magazine, November 15, 1971, pp. 57–64; John A. Morsell, "Busing is not the Issue," *Freedom at Issue*, May–June, 1972, pp. 12 ff.; Nicolaus Mills (ed.), *The Great School Bus Controversy* (New York: Thomas Y. Crowell, 1973); James Bolner and Robert Shanley, *Busing: The Political and Judicial Process* (New York: Praeger, 1974); Christopher Jencks, "Busing—The Supreme Court Goes North," *The New York Times Magazine*, November 19, 1972, pp. 38 ff.; and Lino A. Graglia, *Disaster by Decree* (Ithaca: Cornell University Press, 1976).

[138]Judge Garrity created a "permanent Department of Implementation (administration of racial desegregation)," with an annual payroll of $473,559 for salaries alone (as of 1977). Note his April 2, 1987, comment about the role of the courts: "The honored place

desegregation order was twice denied review, and thus upheld, by the United States Supreme Court.[139] Even stronger measures were taken by United States District Judge Frank J. Battisti in connection with his desegregation orders affecting the Cleveland, Ohio, school system. His orders included a citation for civil contempt of court in August 1980 for "incompetently administering" his program, and the appointment of an "administrator for desegregation" with power over every aspect of public education in Cleveland. The opposition to forced busing cannot simply be interpreted as merely *prima facie* evidence of racial discrimination or as racism; if it were that simple, evaluation as well as remedial action might be simpler. These labels do, of course, apply in the case of a good many opponents; but it is unquestionably also true that a good many other opponents of forced busing are neither racists nor anti-desegregation obstructionists. They are opposed to busing *qua* busing for their children on understandable human grounds, and they do indeed prefer to embrace the thrust of Chief Justice Burger's *Swann* "all things being equal" hope: "assignment to schools nearest [the children's] homes"[140]—as do sizable segments of the black, the Hispanic, and almost all of the Chinese communities.

In what was indubitably a recognition of and response to majoritarian public sentiment on the issue, the congressional hoppers have been replete with legislation endeavoring either to amend or to strike down busing practices and orders. Most failed of passage; but a number of "riders" to annual appropriation bills prohibiting the executive departments from using federal funds "to require, directly or indirectly, the transportation of any student to a school other than the school which is nearest the student's home, except for a student requiring special education,"[141] did become law—the judiciary making it quite clear, however, that it would continue to invoke its perceived powers of judicial equity in the contentious issue. A constitutional amendment to ban

in our legal tradition has not been judicial restraint, but rather, its bedrock antecedent, judicial review." (*The New York Times,* April 3, 1987, p. A 1.)

[139]*White v. Morgan,* 426 U.S. 935 (1975), and *McDonough v. Morgan,* 429 U.S. 1042 (1976). In 1988 school officials finally regained some control. (*Morgan v. Nucci.*)

[140]*Swann v. Charlotte–Mecklenburg School of Education,* 402 U.S. 1 (1971), at 28.

[141]Sec. 208 of the Health, Education and Welfare–Labor Appropriations Act for fiscal year 1978. (See *The New York Times,* March 31, 1978, p. A14.) When a lower federal court upheld the rider, the Supreme Court refused to review the decision in 1978. (*Carroll v. Department of Health, Education and Welfare,* 435 U.S. 904.)

busing as a desegregation/integration tool failed 216 : 109 in the House in 1979; but late in 1980 both houses of Congress voted over-whelmingly to prohibit the Justice Department from using appropriated funds to pursue legal cases that would result in busing orders. Presidents Nixon and Ford had repeatedly called for remedial statutory or amen-datory action; President Carter, however, firmly opposed such moves, and when he pointedly threatened to veto the 1980 measure Congress bowed reluctantly. Since the Republican Platform for 1980 again con-tained a plank against forced busing, it was a foregone conclusion that the issue had been postponed, not resolved. A plethora of anti-busing bills were introduced early in 1981, with at least tacit backing by the Reagan Administration. One, the Helms-Johnston measure passed the Senate 57 : 37 in 1982, only to die in the House, and a similar fate met a 1986 Helms bill, which had passed the Senate 50 : 45.

How did the Court view the volatile issue as the divided land entered the 1980s? Any response would be tentative at best; indeed, to employ a vernacular but apposite term, the Justices' holdings have been perilously close to being "as clear as mud" on the dilemmas created by forced busing. Thus, they held (6 : 2) that if school authorities initially complied with a busing plan and thereby achieved a racially neutral student assignment scheme, the school authorities cannot be judicially com-pelled to readjust busing zones each subsequent year in an effort to maintain the same initial racial mix in the face of changing population patterns.[142] Concurrently, the Court unanimously declined to review, and thus in effect upheld, a lower federal appellate court ruling that school authorities in Chattanooga, Tennessee, need not redraft a desegre-gation plan to reflect population shifts that had taken place *after* busing and other desegregation measures had been duly and constitutionally adopted.[143] The justices also ruled unanimously that federal tribunals may order school districts to provide costly, far-reaching, broader-than-ever *remedial* educational programs—such as remedial reading classes, teaching training, counseling, and career guidance[144]—thus seemingly embracing a compensatory approach that would avoid the busing issue *per se*. When the Court also remanded three system-wide busing order

[142]*Pasadena City Board of Education v. Spangler*, 427 U.S. 424 (1976).
[143]*Mapp v. Board of Education of Chattanooga*, 427 U.S. 911 (1976).
[144]*Milliken v. Bradley II*, 433 U.S. 267 (1977).

cases[145] for reconsideration because they did not meet the "purpose and intent" standard it had developed in 1976–77 as a requirement for specific findings regarding alleged violations of equal protection of the laws, the Court seemed to have embarked upon a course that required proof of *de jure* rather than *de facto* segregation for judicially ordered redress. Yet such expectations of either a predictable or consistent course were in vain (despite the fact that the same justices sat on the Court between 1975 and 1981), for 1979 and 1980 brought a series of bitterly divided compulsory-busing decisions.[146] They ranged in votes from 7 : 2 to 5 : 4 in upholding lower-court busing plans and orders. Led by Justices Brennan, White, Marshall, and Blackmun, the Court had now developed a dramatic new test *cum* approach to the question of desegregation/integration, namely, that henceforth the test of compliance would not be a school board's *purpose* in acting to liquidate a dual system of education dating from pre-*Brown* days, but its *effectiveness*. In the words of Justice White, the author of the Court's sweeping decisions on school busing orders for Dayton, Ohio (5 : 4), and Columbus, Ohio (7 : 2), there is an "affirmative duty" to eliminate the *effects* of *past* discrimination, even if there is no longer any discrimination practiced. Perhaps even more significantly, the Court adopted, albeit narrowly, a new test of the burden of proof in these school desegregation cases. Traditionally, a plaintiff alleging unlawful conduct has the burden of proof; but in accordance with the 5 : 4 Columbus holding, the burden of proof has now been shifted to the defendant school board—which in effect thus has to prove its innocence, rather than have the plaintiff prove a board's guilt. Yet in what the NAACP styled as "we won one and lost one," the Court seemed to signal more sympathy with anti-busing forces shortly thereafter: while it narrowly struck down (5 : 4) a 1976 State of Washington initiative that barred busing beyond neighborhood schools,[147] it upheld

[145]*Dayton Board of Education v. Brinkman* (I), 433 U.S. 406 (1977).

[146]*Columbus Board of Education v. Penick*, 443 U.S. 449 (1979); *Dayton Board of Education v. Brinkman*, 443 U.S. 526 (1979); *Estes v. Metropolitan Branches of Dallas NAACP*, 444 U.S. 437 (1980); *Cleveland Board of Education v. Reed*, 445 U.S. 935 (1980); and *Austin Independent School District v. United States*, 443 U.S. 915 (1980). Justice Powell's separate dissenting opinion in the first two cases cited represents a masterful analysis of the basic issue involved, including that of burdens of proof and the nature of the judicial function.

[147]*Washington v. Seattle School District #1*, 458 U.S. 457 (1982).

(8 : 1) a 1979 California initiative that limited mandatory busing to the federal standard of intentional violation.[148] The Court's quizzicality was reconfirmed in two 1986 decisions, one of which went "pro" and the other "con" school board contentions of compliance.[149]

Much of the thrust toward school desegregation implementation had been provided by a famed report written in 1966 by the distinguished University of Chicago sociologist James S. Coleman, who had then demonstrated with convincing statistical evidence that while home background tended to have a greater impact than the school on children's performance, the integration of a minority of disadvantaged youngsters (chiefly non-white) in classrooms dominated by middle-class children (chiefly white) tended to raise the poor children's achievements without hurting those of their more affluent peers.[150] The Coleman Report, widely distributed and meeting with general approbation in the academic and governmental communities, thus became a genuine catalyst in the desegregation-integration efforts that soon began to reach a crescendo. But in mid-1975—almost a decade later—Professor Coleman issued a bombshell "second thoughts" report in which he concluded that "programs of desegregation have acted to further separate blacks and whites rather than bringing them together"; that court-ordered busing and the instability created by the assignment of great numbers of disadvantaged children to middle-class schools in the big cities "have accelerated the white flight into the suburbs and have thus led to greater racial segregation in the schools." Still firmly committed to desegregation-integration, Dr. Coleman laid the blame at the doorstep of the judiciary, concluding that "it is ludicrous to attempt to *mandate* an integrated society. Integration must come through other means."[151] Primary attention, he pointed out, must focus on both education and environment; lack of special educational preparation and

---

[148]*Crawford v. Board of Education*, 458 U.S. 527 (1982).

[149]*Riddick v. School Board of Norfolk*, 55 LW 3311 and *Board of Education of Oklahoma v. Dowell*, 55 LW 3311.

[150]*Equality of Educational Opportunity* (Washington, D.C.: U.S. Government Printing Office, 1966).

[151]*The New York Times*, June 15, 1975, Sec. 4, p. 16e, and *Time* magazine, June 23, 1975, p. 60. The Court's 8 : 0 ruling in 1976 that federal courts are empowered to order the Department of Housing and Urban Development (HUD) to provide low-cost housing in a city's white suburbs to relieve racial segregation in housing within the city would prove to be a significant counterforce. (*Hills v. Gautreaux*, 425 U.S. 284.) In writing for the Court, Justice Stewart noted: "The critical distinction between HUD and the suburban

failure to maintain discipline would bring about, as he had warned in his 1966 report, a white backlash that had now taken the form of flight to the suburbs. As he concluded, "a large portion of that white flight has to do with the unresponsiveness of large school systems [in the inner cities], with the whole question of order and discipline in the schools, and with an undifferentiated sense of fear and disorder."[152] Readdressing the issue of "beneficial" versus "destructive" desegregation at the end of 1978, he cited "mandatory busing in large cities" as its "most destructive method" and called for its cessation forthwith.[153] In the final analysis, society must find an answer to the basic problem of the elimination of inferior schools—it is *that* goal upon which the strategies of desegregation-integration must concentrate.

SOME OTHER POST-BROWN DEVELOPMENTS

To revert to the days following *Brown* I and II, implementing the spirit of the *Public School Segregation Cases* beyond their specific educational substance became the foremost concern and task of a host of public and private groups, agencies, and individuals. In general, it was a painfully slow process. Gradualism characterized most progress. Even at the national level, the legislature and executive would thus wait, for all intents and purposes, until 1957, although President Eisenhower did move on the employee-hiring front in 1955 by issuing an executive order[154] to create the Committee on Government Employment Policy. This Committee was charged with hearing individual complaints of alleged racial or religious discrimination in hiring or promotion by federal agencies. It became quite active and, on President Kennedy's assumption of office, merged with the Committee on Government Contracts (which had been created by President Truman in 1951), to become the Equal Employment Opportunities Committee (E.E.O.C.).[155] With Vice-President Johnson as its first chairman, it proved to be a far more significant body than its predecessor.

Civil Rights Act of 1957. By far the most important *legislative* action

---

school districts in *Millikin* [pp. 341–42 *supra*] is that HUD has been found to have violated the Constitution." (At 297.)

[152]*The* [Charlottesville, Va.] *Daily Progress,* June 1, 1975, p. 1.

[153]*The Washington Post,* December 8, 1978, p. A19.

[154]Exec. Order 10590, *Federal Register,* Vol. XX (1955), p. 409.

[155]Exec. Order 10925, *Federal Register,* Vol. XXVI (1961), p. 1977.

of the Eisenhower Administration in civil rights, however, was the passage of the Civil Rights Act of 1957, the first major legislation of its kind since Reconstruction. Enacted largely owing to the bipartisan cooperation of Congress's Democratic leaders, House Speaker Sam Rayburn and Senate Majority Leader Lyndon B. Johnson (both from Texas), it contained three or four significant provisions. One created the United States Commission on Civil Rights, which became a busy and assertive unit in the governmental struggle against racial discrimination. A second transformed the small and weak Civil Rights Section in the Department of Justice into the more effective Civil Rights Division, headed by an Assistant Attorney-General.[156] A third and fourth not only authorized the federal government to obtain federal civil injunctions against actual or threatened interference with the right to vote (with or without the individual's consent) and to pay the costs for the litigation but also gave the appropriate United States District Courts jurisdiction over such suits without the normal requirement that all state judicial and administrative remedies be first "exhausted below."

Civil Rights Act of 1960. Despite considerable activity by the new Civil Rights Commission, however, the 1957 statute proved to be of only marginal value. Nevertheless, it served to focus and popularize aspects of the problem; and its weaknesses did prompt the Eisenhower Administration to call for a new statute, which became the Civil Rights Act of 1960. No longer did the Southern members of Congress have the necessary number of votes and allies to block such measures. The Act of 1960 promised to be a far-reaching piece of legislation chiefly because, in an elaborate provision for appointment of federal "voting referees," it undertook to safeguard the black citizen's right to vote freely and without discrimination. The measure authorized federal district courts, through appointment of these referees, to enroll qualified voters for *all* state as well as federal elections in areas where local officials systematically denied them the right to register or to vote. And it enabled the federal Department of Justice to file suit to bring about this desired result. More than fifteen times as many suits were brought during the Act of 1960's first three years of life as had been brought during any similar span of time under the previous statute.

[156]From a staff of 29 lawyers and 30 clerical workers in 1957 the C.R.D. had grown to a staff of more than 400 by 1982, and its case load increased from 143 in December 1957 to 2,300 in July 1982. (*The Washington Post*, January 16, 1983, p. A11.)

Still, black leaders and other civil rights spokesmen regarded the Act of 1960 as too slow, too costly to administer, and too cumbersome. Black restlessness and impatience—assuredly understandable, if not inevitably justifiable in all instances—were intensified; 1963 saw the peak of visible public protest movements. Reiterating their "loss of faith in the white power structure," blacks took to the streets in ever-increasing numbers throughout the United States. The summer of 1963 became known as the "long, hot summer," culminating late in August in a massive, peaceful, interracial march by some 20,000 people in Washington, D.C., billed as the "March on Washington for Jobs and Freedom." Other demonstrations were not so peaceful and orderly, especially some of those that took place in scattered cities in the deep South where feelings ran high. Although not necessarily directly connected with the demonstrations, reprisals by white extremists resulted in forty-four violent deaths during 1963, 1964, and 1965.[157] The black riots in Northern cities in the summer of 1966 led to a score more. Against this background of mounting anger, threats, and sporadic violence, President Kennedy had asked Congress twice in 1963 for new, strong, and expanded civil rights legislation. President Johnson again requested it when he first addressed Congress as the nation's new Chief Executive following the tragic assassination of President Kennedy on November 22. In the following June, Congress passed the Civil Rights Act of 1964.

Civil Rights Act of 1964. Demonstrably, that statute was the most comprehensive piece of legislation to be enacted by the federal legislature since the ill-fated measures of the 1870s. It cleared the House with relative ease, 290 : 130. But its success in the Senate, by a bipartisan vote of 73 : 27, was delayed until the breaking of a seventy-five-day Southern filibuster by the application of the Senate's debate-limiting

[157]*The Southern Regional Council Report*, released on January 30, 1966. Among these murders were those of Mississippi NAACP leader Medgar Evers near his Jackson home; a pro–civil rights white Baltimore postman, William L. Moore, in northeast Alabama; the bomb-murder of four black girls, eleven to fourteen years old, in the 16th Street Birmingham Baptist church (eleven years later, Chris McNair, the father of one of the murdered girls, was elected chairman of the Jefferson County, Birmingham, delegation to the Alabama House of Representatives); and, almost on the day of the passage of the 1964 Act, the murder of three young civil rights workers, two white and one black, near Philadelphia, Mississippi. According to the S.R.C.'s report, eighty civil rights murders were committed between 1956 and 1966.

cloture rule on the eighty-third day of debate by a vote of 71 : 29.[158] It was the first time that cloture had been attained on a civil rights filibuster since the adoption of the cloture rule in 1917.

The principal provisions of the Civil Rights Act of 1964 extended the heretofore sharply limited life of the Civil Rights Commission for four years, to 1968 (extended periodically since then), and broadened both its duties and powers; established a Community Relations Service to aid in the conciliation of racial disputes; forbade, in its crucial Title VII, discrimination because of race, color, sex, religion, or national origin either by employers or by labor unions in business concerns with 100 employees or more, this number to drop by stages until it reached 15[159]—public employees were covered as of a 1972 amendment—and created an Equal Economic Opportunity Commission (E.E.O.C.) to administer that aspect of the Act; prohibited voting registrars from applying different standards to white and black applicants, required all literacy tests to be in writing, and rendered a sixth-grade education a "rebuttable assumption" of literacy; permitted the Attorney-General to bring suit, upon written complaint by aggrieved individuals, to secure

[158]On the bill's final roll call, 46 Democrats and 27 Republicans voted in favor of it; 21 Democrats and 6 Republicans against. Voting to invoke cloture were 44 Democrats and 27 Republicans; opposed were 23 Democrats and 6 Republicans.

[159]In the first interpretation of this provision as it relates to racial bias, the Supreme Court ruled 8 : 0 in March 1971 that it bars job tests by employers that screen out blacks without realistically measuring their qualifications to do the work. (*Griggs v. Duke Power Co.*, 401 U.S. 424.) On the other hand, the Court ruled 7 : 2 five years later, in the absence of proof of "racially discriminatory purpose," a statute or an official act is *not* unconstitutional just because it places a "substantially disproportionate" burden on one race. (*Washington v. Davis*, 426 U.S. 229 [1976], involving a written qualifying test for members of the District of Columbia Police Department.) Also, the Court refused to review an unsuccessful challenge by blacks of the Georgia bar exam, which blacks had traditionally failed in greater numbers than whites. (*Tyler v. Vickey*, 426 U.S. 940 [1976].) Just prior to the end of its 1975–76 term, the Supreme Court held 7 : 2 and 9 : 0, in opinions written by its only black member, Justice Marshall, that §1981 of the Civil Rights Act of 1866 as well as Title VII of that of 1964 prohibit employers from discrimination against whites on the basis of their race in and to the same extent they prohibit racial discrimination against blacks. (*McDonald v. Santa Fe Transportation Co.*, 427 U.S. 273 [1976].) And in 1978 it upheld 5 : 2 the use of the National Teacher Examination Test to determine hiring and promotion in a state, although the test results disqualified more than four times as many blacks as whites. (*National Education Association v. South Carolina*, 434 U.S. 1026.) See also the related, unanimous 1981 decision in *Texas Department of Community Affairs v. Burdine*, 450 U.S. 248.

desegregation of facilities owned, operated, or managed by state and local governments; authorized, in its tough Title VI, the executive to halt any federal aid funds to either public or private programs "or activities" in which discrimination on grounds of race, color, or national origin (sex and age were added in 1972 and 1978, respectively[160]—note that "religion" is not included; it *is* in Title VII) is allowed to continue (a provision used since with considerable success—and increasingly accompanied by serious, and not inevitably rebuttable, charges of "preferential treatment" and "*reverse* discrimination"[161]—by governmental agencies,[162] coupled with Title IV grants available to state and local agencies to help them cope with problems stemming from school desegregation); outlawed, in its Public Accommodation Title II, discrimination because of race, religion, color, or national origin in hotels, restaurants, theaters, gas stations, and all other public accommodations that affect interstate commerce, as well as in all public facilities (Title II was specifically held constitutional in December 1964, the first test of any provision of the Act of 1964 to reach the United States Supreme Court);[163] and empowered the Attorney-General to file enforcement suits against any owners of public accommodations who discriminate, and on behalf of any persons whose con-

[160]Broadly interpreted by the Department of Health, Education, and Welfare, for example, to *require* special assistance to non-English-speaking Chinese students—who were far from eager for such help—with the Court upholding the requirement in a multiple-opinion decision in 1974. (*Lau v. Nichols*, 414 U.S. 563.)

[161]E.g., see Justice Douglas's remarkable dissenting opinion in *De Funis v. Odegaard*, 416 U.S. 312 (1974)—the University of Washington "reverse discrimination" case, in which a majority of five ducked the delicate issue by ruling the case "moot." Douglas wrote there: "The Equal Protection Clause commands the elimination of racial barriers, not their creation in order to satisfy our theory as to how society ought to be organized." (*De Funis*, at 342.) See also Mary K. Hammond, "May the Constitution be Color Conscious to Remain Color Blind?", I *Ohio Northern University Law Review* 81 (1973), and the extensive discussion of the "affirmative action"/"reverse discrimination" issue, *infra*, pp. 396 ff.

[162]Until 1980 the latter two were part and parcel of the erstwhile Department of Health, Education and Welfare.

[163]*Heart of Atlanta Motel v. United States*, 379 U.S. 241, and *Katzenbach v. McClung*, 379 U.S. 294. Justice Clark's opinion for the unanimous Court rested the case for Title II's constitutionality on the congressional power over interstate commerce—although Justices Douglas and Goldberg, in concurring, contended that the "equal protection of the laws" clause of Amendment Fourteen and the latter's §5 (the "enforcement by appropriate legislation" power) also applied.

stitutional rights are deemed violated in school segregation or other instances.[164]

Understandably, the two most controversial provisions of the Civil Rights Act of 1964, both prior to and during the national debate that attended its conception and birth, were the two then most obviously concerned with delicate "line-drawing": those dealing with fair employment practices[165] and with public accommodations. For here the basic issues of individual rights and of societal obligations were patently joined. No other sections of the statute, not even its voting and educational segments, stirred so much controversy and debate or attracted so many negative votes. However, Title VI, too, was bitterly attacked and its application questioned even by such staunch Northern liberals as Senate Majority Leader Mike Mansfield.[166] Indeed, given the implications of the aforementioned "preferential treatment" and "reverse dis-

[164]For a table excerpting, comparing, and contrasting the Acts of 1957, 1960, and 1964, see John H. Ferguson and Dean E. McHenry, *The American System of Government*, 13th ed. (New York: McGraw-Hill Book Co., 1977), pp. 193–94.

[165]With the recently sworn-in Justice John Paul Stevens not participating, the Court addressed itself, albeit obviously somewhat uncomfortably, to the long-smoldering inherent seniority issue in a landmark decision in 1976. Speaking through Justice Brennan, the 5:3 majority (consisting also of Justices Stewart, White, Marshall, and Blackmun) ruled that blacks who were denied jobs in violation of Title VII (see p. 364, *supra*) of the 1964 statute must be awarded *retroactive seniority* once they succeeded in obtaining those jobs. The majority held that blacks must thus be given the same seniority they would have had if they had been hired initially, with all accompanying rights, including pension benefits—even if this means that some whites, hired *after* the blacks' initial job applications, but *before* the blacks entered the jobs, would thereby now have less security and job protection. (*Franks v. Bowman Transportation Co.*, 434 U.S. 747.) Partly dissenting, together with Justices Powell and Rehnquist, Chief Justice Burger saw a clear-cut case of reverse discrimination, commenting that "I cannot join in judicial approval of 'robbing Peter to pay Paul.'" (*Ibid.*, at 4366.) But *cf.* the 1977 *Teamster* rulings (*Teamsters v. United States* and *T.I.M.E.-D.C., Inc. v. United States*, 431 U.S. 324). Their gist was that unless a seniority plan *intentionally* discriminates among workers it is *not* illegal under Title VII. The Court reconfirmed this posture 4:3 in 1980 in the instance of the California brewing industry system. (*California Brewers Association v. Bryant*, 444 U.S. 598.) Thus, "neutral" seniority systems might legally perpetuate favored employment for white males where, as in these cases, the seniority systems had been operative *before* the Civil Rights Act of 1964 took effect in 1965. In 1982 the Court came full cycle when it ruled 5:4 in *American Tobacco Co. v. Patterson*, 456 U.S. 63, that even those seniority systems emplaced *after* the Civil Rights Act of 1964, as a result of collective bargaining, may withstand racial or gender challenges, absent a showing of discriminatory *intent*. See also the 1984 *Stotts* and 1986 *Wygant* holdings, affirming *bona fide* seniority systems, discussed *infra*, pp. 435 ff. Of course, seniority systems that *deliberately*, i.e., intentionally, discriminate are illegal, whether they date from pre- or post-1964 days.

[166]See John Herber's article in *The New York Times*, September 29, 1966, p. 1L.

crimination,'' it was destined to become the focus of major national controversy during the early 1970s and into the 1980s, centering on legal and constitutional implications of the governmental role against the backdrop of the twin constitutional guarantees of liberty and equality.[167] After all, *both* are guarantees that are seminal to our society—and they do not readily lend themselves to facile line-drawing.

Toward the Civil Rights Act of 1968. Still more legislation was to come, legislation replete with provisions that promised to cause lively debate in and out of Congress. While conceding that the fruits of the 1964 Act—and the Voting Rights Act of 1965 (see pp. 449 ff., *infra*)—were already ''impressively apparent,'' President Johnson sent Congress his third civil rights bill in three years in 1966, noting the obvious: that discriminatory practices ''still exist in many American communities.'' In a tough attempt to further egalitarian goals, the Civil Rights Bill of 1966's most contentious provision would have outlawed discrimination on either racial or religious grounds in the ''purchase, rental, lease, financing, use and occupancy'' of *all housing*. Chiefly because of the so-called open housing provision, the bill, although it had passed the House in a watered-down version by a vote of 259 : 157, died on the floor of the Senate[168]—against a backdrop of black riots and demonstrations in cities throughout the land, now predominantly in the North, and the rise of resentment to the new ''black power'' slogan that began to characterize much of the civil rights activity of that year.

Undaunted, President Johnson submitted a new bill in 1967, emphasizing the controversial housing issue. It failed to pass, but became law

[167]E.g., see the critical book-length treatments by Nathan Glazer, *Affirmative Discrimination* (New York: Basic Books, 1976); George C. Roche, III, *The Balancing Act: Quota Hiring in Higher Education* (La Salle, Ill.: Open Court Publishing Company, Inc., 1974); and Thomas Sowell, *Affirmative Action Reconsidered: Was It Necessary in Academia?* (Washington, D.C.: American Enterprise Institute, 1975). For supportive works, see Boris I. Bittker, *The Case for Black Reparations* (New York: Random House, 1973); Ronald Dworkin, *Taking Rights Seriously* (Cambridge: Harvard University Press, 1977); and Robert M. O'Neil, *Discriminating Against Discrimination* (Bloomington: Indiana University Press, 1975). More or less ''neutral'' are works such as M. Cohen, T. Nagel, and T. Scanlon (eds.), *Equality and Preferential Treatment* (Princeton: Princeton University Press, 1977); Allan P. Sindler, *Bakke, De Funis, and Minority Admissions: The Quest for Equal Opportunity* (New York: Longman, Inc., 1978); and Ralph A. Rossum, *Reverse Discrimination: The Constitutional Debate* (New York: Marcel Dekker, Inc., 1980). See the discussion of the issue, *infra,* pp. 517 ff.

[168]Twice the Senate refused to shut off debate on the measure that September; the votes were 54 : 42 and 54 : 41—both short of the needed two-thirds.

on April 10, 1968—six days after the assassination of Dr. Martin Luther King, Jr., and one day after his burial. Styled "a memorial to the fallen leader" by the President, the 1968 Act significantly broadened existing federal criminal laws dealing with civil rights, cataloguing a whole range of federally protected activities; articulated Indian rights; and addressed itself to the rising tide of rioting and civil disobedience. But its most notable provision, certainly in terms of the yearnings of most blacks, was that on fair housing, which, with certain limited exemptions,[169] outlawed discrimination in the *sale or rental of all housing*—not just in public or public-aided housing—because of race, color, religion, or national origin. As if to confirm its legitimacy, even in advance of any litigation involving it on its docket, the Supreme Court, just two months later, ruled 7 : 2 that, under the almost-forgotten 102-year-old Civil Rights Act of 1866—enacted under the enforcement provisions of the Thirteenth Amendment—racial discrimination in the purchase, lease, sale, holding, and conveyance of real and personal property was expressly forbidden.[170] And in 1980 Congress moved to toughen and speed the 1968 statute's available administrative enforcement powers.

The Quest for Suffrage

A good many sincere as well as fair-weather friends of black equality prior to the decision to concentrate on education had insisted that it would be wiser to direct the thrust of the movement toward suffrage, arguing that effective suffrage would almost automatically rectify most, if not all, of the black grievances in the public sector, the private sector ultimately following. The feeling that NAACP strategists and their supporters committed a fundamental error persists in many circles to this day. Whatever the argument's merit, the suffrage problem was not really tackled until the Civil Rights Acts of 1957, 1960, and 1964 had

---

[169]See §§8803 (b) and 807 of Title VIII of Public Law 90-284, 82 Stat. 73.

[170]*Jones v. Alfred H. Mayer Co.*, 392 U.S. 409 (1968). In a stinging dissenting opinion, joined by Justice White, Justice Harlan flayed the majority for proceeding "with such precipitous and insecure strides." He doubted that the 1866 law's "goals could constitutionally be achieved under the Thirteenth Amendment." (At 476.) In that connection, see the Court's 1976 decisions in *Hills v. Gautreaux*, p. 440, footnote 151, *supra*, and, especially, in *Runyon v. McCrary*, pp. 495 ff., *infra*.

become law—and not effectively until the passage of the Voting Rights Act of 1965.

ANTECEDENTS TO THE VOTING RIGHTS ACT OF 1965

Our nation's history is replete with systematic disfranchisement of blacks, particularly in the South and the Border states. Although prior to the Civil War, especially in the early decades following the adoption of the Constitution, other groups, too, had experienced considerable difficulty in their quest for suffrage—e.g., Quakers, Catholics, and Jews— blacks more than any other single minority group suffered second-class political citizenship. And, as we have seen, despite the enactment of the Civil War Amendments—in particular the Fifteenth, which specifically and expressly provided, as the Fourteenth had not,[171] that the "right of citizens of the United States to vote shall not be denied or abridged by the United States or by any State on account of race, color, or previous condition of servitude"—blacks continued to find access to the ballot box difficult, and often impossible, in much of the old Confederacy. That access had been all but closed by the turn of the century, if not directly then indirectly by resort to assorted devices such as the "grandfather clause," the "white primary," the poll tax, interpretation clauses, understanding clauses, and sundry other registration requirements— a seemingly inexhaustible array of covert as well as overt tools of discrimination.[172]

Until the legislative activity in the 1950s, much of this discrimination was rendered feasible by our federal structure. An important distinction existed between the legal right to vote for *federal* officials and the legal right to vote for *local* and *state* officials. The latter vote stems from state constitutions and laws and is thus not on its face a federal right in the same sense and to the same degree as the right to vote for federal officers, such as members of Congress and Presidential electors. Hence, at least until enactment of the four recent Civil Rights Acts and, more pertinently, the Voting Rights Act of 1965 and its subsequent strengthening amendments of 1970, 1975, 1982, and 1987, states were free to define their own qualifications for voting for state and local officials,

[171]See the discussion in Berger, *op. cit.*, Chapters 4 and 5.

[172]For data on black registration and the denial of voting rights to blacks, see, among others, the 1959 *Report* and the 1961 voting study of the United States Commission on Civil Rights; subsequent annual *Reports;* and those by the U.S. Bureau of the Census.

and in part also for their federal representatives. This state power was subject only to the limitations of Amendments Fourteen, Fifteen, Nineteen, and Twenty-Four and that intriguing Article One, Section 4. The latter, while granting the "Times, Places, and Manner" of holding elections for federal officials to the states, also contains a clause that would become an important tool in the judicial arsenal of aid to blacks: "but the Congress may at any time by Law make or alter such Regulations, except as to the Places of chusing Senators."

When access to the ballot remained foreclosed to blacks because they continued to be denied their rightful influence in Southern politics, and when Congress failed to come to their aid, they turned to the federal *courts* for redress. Initially they found little because of a then unsympathetic judiciary and the absence of appropriate precedent. When the Supreme Court rejected a promising challenge to the Mississippi literacy test in 1898,[173] matters looked bleak indeed. As recently as 1959, the literacy device was upheld unanimously by the Court in a North Carolina case,[174] in an opinion written by no less firm an exponent of black equality than Justice Douglas!

Light Ahead. Moving toward the 1950s and 1960s when blacks were to win equal rights at least on paper and at the bar of the judiciary in all parts of the land, an important judicial tool proved to be the Fifteenth Amendment—although the crucial one, as in the education struggles, became the "equal protection of the laws" clause of Amendment Fourteen, notwithstanding its legislative history of excluding black suffrage from its intended reach.[175] Still, in 1915 the Supreme Court had based its decision on the clear-cut language of the Fifteenth Amendment when in a unanimous opinion by Chief Justice Edward D. White it struck down the Oklahoma "grandfather clause."[176] This transparent device, adopted in several Southern and Border states, provided a convenient loophole through which illiterate whites could escape the provisions of literacy tests. It exempted from those tests all "persons and their lineal descendants" who were qualified to vote as of January 1, 1866, or any similarly convenient date prior to Amendments Fourteen and Fifteen, which would not apply to blacks. The words "Negro," "black," and

[173]*Williams v. Mississippi,* 170 U.S. 213 (1898).
[174]*Lassiter v. Northampton Election Board,* 360 U.S. 45.
[175]See Berger, *op. cit.,* data in Chapters 4 and 5.
[176]*Guinn v. United States,* 238 U.S. 347.

"colored" did not appear anywhere in the various grandfather clauses, because practically no blacks, if any, had voted or been able to vote before the Civil War.

After the failure of an attempt to resuscitate its spirit, if not its letter, in 1939,[177] the grandfather clause was indeed gone. But the poll tax, the "white primary," and a number of other devices remained available to those state officers bent upon the perpetuation of a pure or almost-pure white suffrage. A windfall came their way in 1921 when a narrowly divided Supreme Court ruled—in a messy Michigan Senatorial primary case, involving Henry Ford and Truman H. Newberry[178]—that Congress had no power, or at best highly dubious power, to regulate *primary* elections in the states, be they for federal or state or local office. Although the litigation itself dealt with fraud rather than racial discrimination, the decision was tailor-made for the devotees of the white primary. Hence, Texas went to work at once and passed the blatant Texas White Primary Law of 1924, which read: "In no event shall a negro be eligible to participate in a Democratic primary election in the State of Texas, and should a negro vote in a Democratic primary election, such ballot shall be void and election officials shall not count the same."

A black physician from El Paso, Dr. L. A. Nixon, took up the fight. Denied participation in the Democratic Party's primary under the terms of the Texas law, Dr. Nixon challenged its constitutionality. In a 9 : 0 opinion, written by Justice Holmes in 1927, the Supreme Court agreed. Without passing on the matter of primaries *versus* general elections, so importantly present in the Michigan decision,[179] the Court declared the Texas White Primary Law unconstitutional as a "direct and obvious infringement" of the "equal protection of the laws" clause of the Fourteenth Amendment. Here, then, that important clause entered the fray in the voting field—fully a decade prior to its first meaningful utilization in the area of educational segregation.[180]

Texas was not so easily discouraged, however: it repealed the 1924 statute and substituted a measure authorizing the State Executive Committee of every political party to "prescribe the qualifications of its own

[177]*Lane v. Wilson*, 307 U.S. 268.
[178]*Newberry v. United States*, 256 U.S. 232.
[179]*Newberry v. United States*, ibid.
[180]*Nixon v. Herndon*, 273 U.S. 536.

members.'' The state's Democratic Party then promptly "prescribed" that "only whites" shall be eligible in *its* primaries. When Dr. Nixon thus again was denied participation in the party of his choice, he returned to court with a constitutional challenge to Texas's enabling statute. The Supreme Court, speaking through Justice Cardozo, soon struck down this latest Texas device (albeit this time by the narrowest of margins, 5 : 4) on the grounds that by setting qualifications the Democratic Party was usurping state law and that, consequently, the State of Texas had in fact *acted through* the Party as its agent, thereby violating once again the "equal protection of the laws" clause of the Fourteenth Amendment.[181] Not to be outdone, Texas then (1932) *repealed* the authorizing clause of the above legislation. Its Democratic Party, in turn, acting through the *Democratic State Convention*, on its own authority and without any statutory sanction, adopted a resolution to render itself a "private group," permitting as members of this *private group* only *white* persons. When this arrangement also was challenged at the bar of our highest tribunal, the Court unanimously (9 : 0) accepted the constitutionality of this new loophole on the ground that the *State of Texas was not involved:* that the private group referred to was not a "creature of the state" but a *voluntary association* that had acted on its own. This appeared to settle the matter at issue, for, as Justice Roberts wrote for the Court, "private persons or groups cannot violate the Fourteenth Amendment," in the absence of state action *per se.*[182]

But this seeming triumph of the disfranchisers was short-lived. In 1941, just six years after the *"Private Group"* decision, the Supreme Court was confronted with a case of fraud in a Louisiana *federal* primary. A Louisiana election official, one Patrick B. Classic, had crudely transferred ninety-seven votes cast validly for two candidates in that primary to a third candidate—his own choice. In its 5 : 3 holding the Court, through Justice Stone, ruled that the above-mentioned Section 4 of the Constitution's Article One in fact authorized Congress to regulate *primaries* as well as *elections* because "primaries" in the words of the Constitution were tantamount to "elections" and, being "an integral part of the election machinery," were subject to congressional regulations.[183] This decision did not, to be sure, settle the question whether

---

[181]*Nixon v. Condon*, 286 U.S. 73 (1932).

[182]*Grovey v. Townsend*, 295 U.S. 45 (1935), at 52.

[183]*United States v. Classic*, 313 U.S. 299 (1941), at 318.

whites were legally at liberty to exclude blacks from primaries for state and local officials, for the race question was not involved. What the *Classic* decision did do—and it was a truly significant accomplishment in constitutional interpretation—was pave the way for federal regulation by overruling the *Newberry* (Michigan) holding, which had separated the concept of federal "primaries" from "elections."[184] The *Grovey v. Townsend "Private Group"* case[185] still stood, however.

The White Primary Falls. Yet three years later, in the case of *Smith v. Allwright,*[186] the Supreme Court in an 8 : 1 opinion written by Justice Reed—a Border state Democrat from Kentucky[187]—declared the Texas white primary unconstitutional as a violation of the *Fifteenth Amendment.* Smith, a black, had been denied participation by a Texas election judge, Allwright, who relied on the "voluntary association" concept developed by the Court in the *Grovey* decision. But now that tribunal ruled that, in effect, the Democratic Party of the State of Texas was acting as an *agent of the state* because of the character of its duties—such as providing election machinery—and was thus subject to the pertinent provisions of Amendments Fourteen and Fifteen, here the latter. In the *Classic* case,[188] the Court had set up two alternate or complementary "tests" to determine whether or not a primary was validly affected, and thus regulatable, by the provisions of federal authority under the Constitution: (a) had the state law made the primary an integral part of the election machinery; and/or (b) did the primary "effectively control the choice."[189] Now in *Allwright both* tests applied. The Court admonished Texas and the nation that the constitutional right to be free from racial discrimination in voting

is not to be nullified by a state through casting its electoral process in a form which permits a private organization to practice racial discrimination in the election. . . . It may be taken as a postulate that the right to vote in . . . a

[184]*Newberry v. United States,* 256 U.S. 232 (1921).

[185]*Grovey v. Townsend, op. cit.*

[186]321 U.S. 649 (1944).

[187]For a fascinating account, demonstrating that the case had originally been assigned to Justice Frankfurter but then reassigned for "strategic" reasons to Justice Reed, see Alpheus T. Mason, *Harlan Fiske Stone: Pillar of the Law* (New York: Viking Press, 1956), p. 615. (It is also related in my *The Judicial Process, op. cit.,* pp. 218–19.)

[188]*United States v. Classic, op. cit.*

[189]*Ibid.,* at 318.

primary . . . without discrimination by the State . . . is a right secured by the Constitution.[190]

As had been true of the *Grovey "Private Group"* case,[191] the controlling issue had to be the answer to the basic question: had the black claimant involved thereby been barred from the primary by *state* action? The Supreme Court held that he had—and *Grovey* was thus overruled, nine years after it had become law. Only Justice Roberts dissented from the *Allwright* decision—and he did so as much on grounds of judicial "self-restraint" *cum stare decisis* as on the merits of the controversy, grumbling that "Supreme Court decisions are becoming in the same class as a restricted railroad ticket, good for this day and train only."[192]

The *Smith v. Allwright* decision did much to stimulate black participation in primary elections in the South and the Border states; but the forces of exclusion were far from ineffective, and ingenuity was not lacking. For example, in an attempt to perpetuate white hegemony at the polls and, concurrently, to test the *Allwright* ruling further, South Carolina promptly *repealed* all of its 147 laws and one constitutional provision relating to the conduct of primaries. But a courageous United States District Court jurist, J. Waties Waring—a tenth-generation member of the South Carolina aristocracy—held in 1947 in *Rice v. Elmore*[193] that the South Carolina primaries, though denuded of state authorization *per se*, "effectively control the choice" of candidates for public office. This finding satisfied test (b) of the *Classic* case,[194] and Waring ruled, consequently, that the denial to blacks of their right to vote in primaries was *prima facie* evidence of a violation of both the Fourteenth and Fifteenth Amendments. On appeal, the United States Court of Appeals for the Fourth Circuit sitting in Richmond, Virginia, sustained Judge Waring.[195] That opinion was written by Chief Judge John J. Parker—ironically, the same man who had been rejected as President Hoover's nominee to the United States Supreme Court in

---

[190]*Smith v. Allwright*, 321 U.S. 649 (1944), at 661, 664.
[191]*Grovey v. Townsend, op. cit.*
[192]*Smith v. Allwright, op. cit.*, at 669.
[193]72 F. Supp. 516 (1947).
[194]*United States v. Classic, op. cit.*
[195]*Rice v. Elmore*, 165 F. 2d 387 (1947).

1930, by a 41 : 39 vote, in part because of his alleged anti-black bias.[196] And the Supreme Court refused to review the *Elmore* case,[197] thus letting Waring's holding stand. As a result, 35,000 blacks came to the polls in South Carolina's Democratic primary in 1948. Judge Waring, now harassed, pilloried, and isolated, found it necessary five years later to leave his old home and his beloved bench to move with his family to New York. "My ostracism was total," he recalled wistfully in a 1963 interview. "After my racial cases it got very lonely."[198]

Yet, undeterred by the decision in *Rice v. Elmore,* South Carolina sought to evade it by vesting control of primaries in private clubs to which blacks were not admitted. As a prerequisite to voting in primaries, these clubs required the taking of an oath that was particularly odious to blacks. Among other things, it was necessary to swear to a belief in the social and educational separation of the races. Predictably, this effort to continue disfranchisement of non-whites also ran afoul of effective judicial vetoes in 1948 and 1949.[199] And in 1953 a much more elaborate and less obvious device used to keep blacks from voting in Ford Bend County, Texas, fell: the "pre-primary primary," conducted by a group known as the "Jaybird Democratic Association."[200] Few could continue to doubt that the federal authorities really meant business in the voting field. Still, the various shenanigans continued, often taking the form of "understanding" and "interpreting" clauses, which were destined to fall too, sooner or later.[201] Then, of course, there was

[196]See my *The Judicial Process, op. cit.,* pp. 80–81. The next rejectees were President Nixon's 1969 and 1970 nominations of Clement H. Haynsworth and G. Harrold Carswell, by votes of 55 : 45 and 51 : 45, respectively. See my *Justices and Presidents: A Political History of Appointments to the Supreme Court,* 2nd ed. (New York: Oxford University Press, 1985). The most recent rejection was President Reagan's 1987 nomination of Robert H. Bork, 58 : 42.

[197]*Rice v. Elmore,* 333 U.S. 875 (1948), *certiorari* denied.

[198]*The Greenwich* (Conn.) *Times,* Aug. 30, 1963, p. 13—interviewed by Charles L. West. When he died in 1968, his Charleston, South Carolina, burial was attended by two hundred blacks and fewer than a dozen whites. See the sympathetic biography by T. E. Yarbrough, *A Passion for Justice: J. Waties Waring and Civil Rights* (New York: Oxford University Press, 1987).

[199]*Brown v. Baskin,* 78 F. Supp. 933 (1948) and 174 F. 2d 391 (1949).

[200]*Terry v. Adams,* 345 U.S. 461 (1953). For an explanatory article, see Luther A. Huston, "High Court Upsets a Limited Primary," *The New York Times,* May 5, 1953, p. 19*l*.

[201]E.g., *Schnell v. Davis,* 336 U.S. 933 (1949).

the poll tax—a device more difficult to indict: it had been specifically *upheld* by the Supreme Court both in 1937[202] and 1951.[203] While it was perhaps the best-known of the several devices, it was the least important. When it was outlawed for *federal* elections by the Twenty-fourth or Holland Amendment,[204] ratified in January 1964, its Southern presence was confined to Alabama, Arkansas, Mississippi, Texas, and Virginia. But even for *state* elections its days were numbered: when the question of the constitutionality of the Virginia state poll tax, as applied to state elections, reached the Supreme Court in 1966, the tax was given a prompt judicial burial.[205] Appropriately, it was Justice Douglas, the sole dissenter when the Court had upheld the Virginia tax fifteen years before,[206] who spoke for the six-man majority. Avoiding the First Amendment issue urged upon the Court by the then Solicitor-General Thurgood Marshall, Douglas leaned heavily on the Court's newly developed "one man, one vote" doctrine[207] for his authority that Virginia's $1.50 tax as a prerequisite for voting in state elections violated the "equal protection of the laws" guarantee of the Fourteenth Amendment. Interestingly, although the plaintiffs in the two cases before the Court were black, the majority's holding was based on *economic* rather than on racial discrimination. "To introduce wealth or payment of a fee as a measure of a voter's qualifications," wrote Douglas, "is to introduce a capricious or irrelevant factor. The degree of the discrimination is irrelevant."[208] Justices Black, Harlan, and Stewart, on the other hand, while dissenting on varying grounds, all agreed that "non-discriminatory and fairly applied" payment of a poll tax *could* be a reasonable basis for determining the right to vote.[209]

[202]*Breedlove v. Suttles,* 302 U.S. 277, involving a *white* male Georgian.

[203]*Butler v. Thompson,* 341 U.S. 937.

[204]Named after U.S. Senator Spessard Holland (D.-Fla.), who "fathered" it.

[205]*Harper v. Virginia State Board of Elections,* 383 U.S. 663 (decided March 25, 1966).

[206]*Butler v. Thompson, op. cit.*

[207]*Gray v. Sanders,* 372 U.S. 368 (1963), at 381. See pp. 19–20, *supra.* (Justice Stewart preferred the term "one voter, one vote"; Chief Justice Warren often used "one man, one vote," the most commonly employed terminology; Justice Douglas alternated between the nouns "person" and "man.")

[208]*Harper v. Virginia Board of Elections, op. cit.,* at 668.

[209]See the separate dissenting opinions by Justices Black and Harlan, *ibid.,* at 670 and 680. The former objected to what he viewed as the majority's "natural law" approach vis-à-vis "reasonableness"; the latter believed a constitutional amendment to be necessary.

The problem with the literacy test—in itself neither unreasonable nor discriminatory (something that could be said, at least in theory, of several of the devices used to disfranchise)—was its *application;* it was frequently used for gross discrimination against blacks. Its "non-discriminatory" principle was upheld by the United States Supreme Court as late as 1959,[210] and, as we shall see, when the Voting Rights Act of 1965 launched a selective assault upon the literacy test, almost one-half of the states of the Union were using a variety of such tests. Although it is perhaps easier to attack the concept of the literacy test as a necessary and desirable suffrage requirement than it is to attack the more essential requirements of residence[211] and registration, it would be unfair to condemn it on its face. There are other causes for non-voting than racial discrimination; apathy, for example, is the chief cause of low participation by the American electorate—averaging barely 50 percent of those eligible to vote even in presidential elections. However, the privilege of voting also contains the privilege of abstinence, of course.[212]

The Voting Rights Act of 1965. Regardless of the weight one might assign to any one of the various factors that caused the demonstrably low black suffrage, mid-twentieth-century statistics serve well as an indictment of a state of affairs that cried out for government action above and beyond the Civil Rights Acts of 1957, 1960, and 1964. The presidential election year of 1948 saw barely 600,000 blacks registered in the eleven states of the South, a mere 12 percent of those of voting age; 1952 saw close to 1,000,000, some 20 percent; and 1956 roughly 1,250,000, or 25 percent. Sixty percent of the eligible whites were registered in the same region. Although the percentage of blacks *registered* continued to climb—reaching 27 percent by 1961 and 40 percent just prior to the enactment of the Voting Rights Act of 1965—the diehard resistance to *any* registration in widespread and important areas of the South, particularly in most of Mississippi, much of Alabama, and a good many counties of Louisiana, continued to rankle civil rights leaders. As late as the summer of 1965, a mere 6.8 percent of eligible blacks had been registered in Mississippi, an increase of scarcely 2

---

[210]*Lassiter v. Northampton Election Board,* 360 U.S. 45 (a North Carolina case).
[211]Affirmed by the Court in a Maryland (one-year) test case in 1965 (*Deueding v. Devlin,* 380 U.S. 125). But see the 1970 federal statute, p. 380, *infra.*
[212]For a discussion of the problem of participation, including the issue of compulsory voting, see my *Compulsory Voting* (Washington, D.C.: Public Affairs Press, 1955).

percent after more than four years of activity and three federal statutes.[213]

Counsels of patience were now clearly falling on deaf ears; the civil rights movement had begun to take to the streets in 1960; and then, in early 1965, the town of Selma, Alabama, became the catalyst for the new voting law. Civil rights leaders, headed by Dr. Martin Luther King, organized a well-advertised fifty-mile march from Selma to Montgomery in support of efforts to obtain greater black voter registration in the face of continued difficulty, defiance, and procrastination. The march began on March 7, only to be brutally broken up by Alabama state troopers, under orders of Governor George C. Wallace,[214] while it was still close to Selma. Employing whips, night sticks, cattle prods, and tear gas, the troopers injured at least forty of the marchers. The scene flashed on the television screens of homes throughout the nation and the world. Widespread revulsion set in at once, and hundreds of additional civil rights supporters, many of them white clergy of all faiths, poured into the Selma area. Tragedy was not long in coming: a white Unitarian minister from Boston, the Reverend James J. Reeb, was fatally clubbed down on a Selma street by irate white natives. Civil rights leaders then rescheduled the march, and President Johnson ordered the Alabama National Guard into federal service to protect the marchers. Again led by Dr. King, the march was completed peacefully on the twenty-fifth, with a crowd of 30,000 gathering on the steps of the Alabama capitol in Montgomery. But on the same night a white woman from Detroit, Mrs. Viola Liuzzo, who was shuttling blacks back to Selma from Montgomery in her car, was shot and killed by a trio of white ambushers.

Ten days later, responding to public clamor for action following the Selma outrages,[215] President Johnson addressed Congress in an extraor-

[213]Statistics are obtainable from numerous sources, among them the Southern Regional Council, the *Race Relations Reporter*, various almanacs, the daily press, the *Statistical Abstract of the United States*, and annual compendia by the United States Commission on Civil Rights, the American Civil Liberties Union, the American Jewish Congress, and numerous other groups.

[214]Twenty years later, the very same Governor George C. Wallace cordially received the leaders of a 3,000-member, peaceful Selma-to-Montgomery march in his Capitol office. Times had changed indeed. (See *The Stars and Stripes*, March 9, 1985, p. 5.) And in mid-1987 Selma's City Council had its first black voting majority.

[215]It is poetic justice that the 1972 elections—just seven years after Selma—would show that the greatest political gains for Southern blacks had come in Alabama, generally,

dinary Joint Session, calling for the enactment of the strongest voting rights legislation proposed in nine decades. "The time for waiting is gone," the President told his hushed audience, "outside this chamber is the outraged conscience of a nation—the grave concern of many nations—and the harsh judgment of history on our acts."[216] Against this background his administration submitted the Voting Rights Bill of 1965, based on the Fifteenth Amendment's exhortation that no person shall be denied the right to vote because of "race, color, or previous condition of servitude," and giving Congress the power to enforce its provisions "by appropriate legislation."

The bill became law in August, and it was a tough one. It had passed the Senate by a vote of 79 : 18 and the House of Representatives by 328 : 74—an even more decisive margin than in the enactment of the Civil Rights Act of 1964—and contained these key provisions: It barred literacy and other tests for voting deemed to be discriminatory, based on a rather complicated formula that affected six Southern states: Alabama, Georgia, Mississippi, Louisiana, South Carolina, and Virginia; thirty-four counties in North Carolina; all of Alaska; and single counties in Maine, Arizona, and Idaho. (The formula concerning literacy tests extended only to those states where such tests were in force November 1, 1964, *and* where less than 50 percent of the voting-age population voted, or were registered to vote, in the 1964 presidential election.) It set up new criminal penalties for attempts to keep qualified persons from voting or to threaten or harm civil rights workers assisting potential voters. It directed the U.S. Department of Justice to begin court suits challenging the constitutionality of poll taxes still used in *state and local* elections. (Arkansas having by then abandoned the poll tax, this provision was directed at Alabama, Mississippi, Texas, and Virginia.)

Clearly, the fundamental purpose of the Voting Rights Act of 1965, the passage of which President Johnson termed a "proud moment for this nation," was to facilitate black registration and voting by the elimination, in those states where discrimination had been proved to be both

---

and in Selma, in particular: that year 117 blacks were elected to Alabama offices, and in Selma—where the black registration had risen from 2.3 percent in 1965 to 67 percent (!) in 1972—five of the ten city council seats were won by blacks. Over 200 blacks held elective office in Alabama in 1976; double that number in 1986.

[216]As quoted in *The New York Times*, March 16, 1965, p. 1*l*.

most rampant and most persistent, of all requirements but the basic ones of age, residence, mental competence, and absence of a criminal record. Needless to say, this and some other provisions[217] of the Act raised serious problems of constitutionality, given the somewhat murky division of responsibility for suffrage between the federal and state governments. South Carolina quickly brought suit, though it seemed hardly likely that the Supreme Court would strike down legislation that, however marginal in constitutional interpretation in some of its aspects, was still clearly based upon the letter and spirit of the Fifteenth Amendment, adopted some ninety-five years before. The Court's answer came rapidly and, as anticipated, approvingly: with Justice Black dissenting in part (on the law's Section 5 appeals *cum* clearance procedure, which he viewed as treating the South as little more than a conquered province) and concurring in part, the Court upheld the seven major provisions of the Act in a thirty-one-page opinion written by Chief Justice Warren. He based his ruling squarely on the Act's constitutionality and, predictably, on the power of Congress to act under the provisions of the Fifteenth Amendment. The Chief Justice wrote that two points "emerge vividly" from the voluminous legislative history of the Act: (1) that Congress felt itself "confronted by an insidious and pervasive evil which had been perpetuated in certain parts of our country by unremitting and ingenious defiance of the Constitution"; and (2) that Congress demonstrably concluded that the unsuccessful remedies which it had prescribed in the past would have to be replaced by "sterner and more elaborate measures."[218] "We may finally look for-

---

[217]One of the most contentious was the Kennedy (Robert F.) amendment to the statute, which specifically granted the right to vote to Puerto Ricans, of whom 750,000 then lived in New York City, provided they had a sixth-grade education from a Puerto Rican school—in which Spanish is the principal language, of course. In effect, the amendment circumvented the then otherwise legal New York literacy test. A three-judge federal district court, one judge dissenting, declared that section of the Voting Rights Act unconstitutional in November 1965 (247 F. Supp. 196). However, in a 7:2 opinion, written by Justice Brennan with Justices Harlan and Stewart dissenting (they believed that *the Court* rather than Congress should have determined the constitutionality of the New York literacy law), the Supreme Court reversed the lower tribunal, concluding that Congress in passing the special Spanish literacy amendment to the bill had acted legally because it was "appropriate legislation . . . plainly adapted" to the enforcement of the equal protection of the laws clause of the Fourteenth Amendment and otherwise consistent with the letter and spirit of the "positive grant of legislative power" to Congress inherent in that amendment to the Constitution. (*Katzenbach v. Morgan*, 384 U.S. 641 [1966].)

[218]*South Carolina v. Katzenbach*, 383 U.S. 301 (1966). Black's statement is at p. 359, Warren's at 309.

ward to the day,'' summarized the Chief Justice, quoting verbatim the commands of Amendment Fifteen, ''when truly the right of citizens of the United States to vote shall not be denied or abridged by the United States or by any state on account of race, color, or previous condition of servitude.''[219]

The Voting Rights Act of 1965 had hardly become law when the Johnson Administration commenced its enforcement with two steps. First, literacy tests were suspended as a prerequisite to voting in seven states (Alabama, Alaska,[220] Georgia, Louisiana, Mississippi, South Carolina, and Virginia), twenty-six counties of North Carolina, and one in Arizona; second, the Department of Justice, true to its mandate under the Act, filed suits to abolish the poll tax in the four states that still had one: Alabama, Mississippi, Texas, and Virginia. Moreover, under the provisions of the law, some forty-five *federal voting examiners,* all employees of the United States Civil Service Commission, were standing by in the deep South, waiting to move into fifteen to twenty counties that had a history of resistance to black voting. The examiners, working in teams, began to register eligible blacks that August within a matter of days. Results were almost immediately apparent: on the first supervised registration day under the new statute, 1,144 blacks were enrolled in nine counties with a history of rampant discrimination in Alabama, Louisiana, and Mississippi—an increase of 65 percent! Extending their work to four other counties, the federal voting examiners had registered almost 20,000 blacks within ten days. In the first two months after the enactment of the new voting law, about 110,000 blacks were registered voluntarily by *local officials* and more than 56,000 by the federal examiners sent to areas designated by Attorney-General Nicholas Katzenbach. It was in the May 1966 primaries that, for the first time, blacks voted in large numbers in the deep South—and in six Southern states they elected some of their candidates to office.

By March 1966, under pressure of the new law, federal examiners

---

[219]*Ibid.,* at 337.

[220]On May 24, 1966, Alaska became the first state to be exempted from the Act's literacy test suspension provisions when it convinced the Department of Justice that its literacy test had never been used to deny the right to vote on the basis of race or color. Virginia requested repeatedly to be exempted. Unsuccessful, it ultimately went to the Supreme Court (*Virginia v. United States,* 420 U.S. 901), which, however, without hearing oral argument, in 1975 affirmed 6:3 a lower federal court's decision denying Virginia's plea. (Dissenting were Chief Justice Burger and Justices Powell and Rehnquist.)

had enrolled 101,370 blacks; local registrars another 201,000. That November, the percentage of eligible blacks registered to vote in the South ranged from 27.8 percent in Mississippi and 48.9 in Alabama to 71.7 percent in Tennessee, averaging 50.1 percent. Although the apathy and fear by blacks about voting, which had been so firmly established by decades of white exclusionary rule, could not be eradicated overnight, Southern black registration had now reached 2,671,514, fully 1,200,000 more than as of July 1960.[221]

The 1970 Amendments. The success of the 1965 statute heralded a fierce legislative battle to extend and amend it upon its termination five years later. Predictably, pro and con forces jockeyed to broaden and gut it, respectively. The resultant legislation was a compromise; but, by and large, the line was drawn in favor of the aspirations of the still unfranchised or underfranchised. Continued for five years, the amended statute, in its main provisions: extended the franchise in both federal *and* state elections to 18-year-olds;[222] extended the 1965 prohibition against the use of literacy tests as a condition to voting registration to *all* fifty states until 1975 (thus removing the "selective stigma" of the 1965 provision);[223] established a thirty-day limit for *residency* requirements in *Presidential* elections.[224] By fall 1971, the new voting laws had added 1.5 million blacks and 6 million of the 11 million eighteen- to twenty-one-year-old voters. By Presidential election time 1972 the figures for Southern blacks had risen to 3,448,565,[225] reaching well above

---

[221]*The New York Times*, July 27, 1966, p. 25*l*, and November 27, 1966, p. 74*l*. By September 1, 1966, a total of 1,147,236 blacks had registered in the five "black belt" states of Mississippi, Alabama, Georgia, Louisiana, and South Carolina, compared with 687,000 when the Voting Rights Act of 1965 became law one year earlier. (*Ibid.*, October 21, 1966, p. 1*l*.) An additional 210,000 had been added to the rolls three years later. (*Ibid.*, December 14, 1969, p. 1*l*.)

[222]Late in December 1970 the Supreme Court upheld (5:4) the provision's *federal* applicability, but struck down (5:4) the *state* aspect. (*Oregon v. Mitchell*, 400 U.S. 112), Justice Black, the decision's author, providing the swing vote in both instances.

[223]Upheld by the Court (8:1) in *United States v. Arizona*, 400 U.S. 112 (1970).

[224]Upheld by the Court (9:0) in *United States v. Idaho*, 400 U.S. 112 (1970). In 1972 it extended this interpretation (6:1) to reach *state* and local elections. (*Dunn v. Blumstein*, 405 U.S. 330.) On the other hand, it upheld (6:3) the fifty-day pre-election registration requirements for state and local elections in Arizona and Georgia. (*Marston v. Lewis* and *Burns v. Fortson*, 410 U.S. 679.) It also upheld (5:4) a New York State requirement of a *pre-primary* registration period of eight to eleven months. (October 22, 1974.)

[225]Charles V. Hamilton, *The Bench and the Ballot: Southern Federal Judges and Black Voters* (New York: Oxford University Press, 1973), p. vii.

entitlement to "proportional representation" based on race—and perhaps other group concepts—the judiciary commenced to strike down at-large and other multi-member electoral systems in favor of single-member or single-unit district systems. When the Supreme Court applied the new standard, albeit by the narrowest of division (5 : 4), in the 1986 North Carolina case of *Thornburg v. Gingles,* there remained little doubt that the 1982 changes effected in Section 2 had demonstrably embraced the *result* test and that, arguably, something very close to an expection of proportional representation based upon race had been judicially sanctioned. As Justice O'Connor, speaking also for Chief Justice Burger and Justices Powell and Rehnquist, saw the matter in dissent:

> Although the Court does not acknowledge it expressly, [the ruling] results in the creation of a right to a form of proportional representation in favor of all geographically and politically cohesive minority groups that are large enough to constitute majorities if concentrated within one or more single-member districts. . . . [The ruling] has disregarded the balance struck by Congress [in amending the Voting Rights Act of 1982]. That compromise was not designed to assure safe seats for minorities.[232]

But Justice Brennan's controlling opinion pointed to the "totality of the circumstances" and found in each district

> racially polarized voting; the legacy of official discrimination in voting matters, education, housing, employment, and health services; and the persistence of campaign appeals to racial prejudice [all of which] acted to impair the ability of black voters to participate equally in the political process and to elect candidates of their choice.[233]

Whatever one's perception may be, it became rapidly apparent that the 1982 law, as interpreted and applied, gave blacks a powerful tool to challenge and change election practices in cities and counties across the land, particularly in the South. Indeed, as if in response to that fact, the U.S. Department of Justice, in an abrupt reversal of earlier statements, issued new regulations in 1987 allowing its civil rights lawyers to reject

[232]*Thornburg v. Gingles,* 54 LW 4877, at 4892–98, concurring opinion.
[233]*Ibid.,* at 4878–91, majority opinion.

proposed election changes simply on the basis of discriminatory *results,* rather than having to prove that local officials intended to discriminate against blacks or other minorities.

New Tactics for Old Problems and New Ones

The evolving desegregation process, described in the preceding pages, underwent a major change following that Opinion Monday on May 17, 1954, when Chief Justice Warren announced the Court's decision in *Brown v. Board of Education.*[234] The change in tactics began with the Montgomery bus boycott in December 1955, although it became most dramatically evident with the Greensboro "sit-ins" early in 1960. Whatever its genesis, the protest movement was now clearly tired of delays, frustrated by creeping gradualism, angered by physical outrages. Militancy came to the forefront.

Thus, the initiative for change shifted from a relatively few professional desegregationists, in such traditional organizations as the NAACP and the Urban League, to large numbers of average citizens who concluded that they had no choice but to do battle against "The System" by direct action "in the streets." This development both stemmed from and gave rise to a coterie of new, formally organized protest groups,[235] particularly the Southern Christian Leadership Conference (SCLC), which had been created in 1956–57 under the leadership of Dr. Martin Luther King, Jr.[236]

[234]347 U.S. 483.

[235]See the illuminating article by James H. Laue, "The Changing Character of Negro Protest," in 357 *The Annals of the American Academy of Political and Social Science* 119 (January 1965).

[236]Others were the Congress of Racial Equality (CORE), established in 1943; the Student Non-violent Coordinating Committee (SNCC), an "action" group founded in 1960; and the National Welfare Rights Organization (NWRO), established in 1968 (but dissolved after its founder, George Wiley, drowned in a boating accident in 1973). While SCLC under Dr. King's guidance steadfastly maintained its dedication to non-violence, CORE and especially SNCC proved to be not averse to violent action, as demonstrated from 1965 on under the direction of such fiery young leaders as CORE's Floyd McKissick and SNCC's Stokely Carmichael and H. Rap Brown. But after having been the pace-setter in the civil rights movement for eight years, SNCC, with a rural Southern origin, was largely displaced as of 1968 by the slum-born Black Panthers, a militant "black liberation" group: violence-prone, and small but potent. Additional groups were organized, with varying degrees of success, throughout the 1970s, some featuring the rise of highly visible, influential leaders, such as the Rev. Jesse Jackson, head of the Chicago-based PUSH, who would become a candidate for President of the United States in 1984 and again in 1988. More than a thousand delegates from thirty-four states formed a new

The "sit-in" movement of 1960 had first illustrated the belief that only *action* would obtain results, a belief that became a firm conviction of these groups and their followers—action as a supplement or complement to the educational and legal means heretofore predominantly employed. Although the educational, and especially the legal, tools had produced significant results since World War II, they were nevertheless for Dr. King, other protest movement leaders, and their vast number of followers too slow in producing change. Turning then to "action," the black leadership rapidly discovered that the development of community "crisis situations," such as economic boycotts by black protest movements, was usually at least partly successful simply because the crises demanded a speedy resolution by community decision makers. Yet "activism" was certain to raise serious problems in and for society— problems of the limits of civil disobedience: problems, once again, of where to draw the line.

Illustrations of New Tactics. Of course, some "action" had accompanied the movement for quite a while: there were sporadic rallies, marches, boycotts, and picket lines; but almost none really attained major significance.

Yet the Montgomery, Alabama, bus boycott, eighteen months after *Brown* I, did. It was a stubborn, year-long boycott of the city's buses in protest against Montgomery's continued segregated seating practices. The action began when a black seamstress, Mrs. Rosa Parks—who was to become a symbol of the civil rights movement—refused to give up her front row black section seat to a white rider and was fined $10. Led by Dr. King, Montgomery's entire black community participated in the boycott. No longer willing to sit in the "Jim Crow" section, something they had done all their lives, they were ready to walk miles or wait hours for car pools. As one seventy-two-year-old weary black woman said with ungrammatical profundity: "My feets is tired but my soul is at rest."[237] The boycott did not end until, one entire year later, segregation was outlawed by a federal court injunction, followed quickly by a Supreme Court decision that struck down as a violation of equal protec-

---

organization, the National Black United Front, in mid-1980 "to pull together the diverse elements within black America, most of which have not succeeded." (*The New York Times,* June 30, 1980, p. B-13.)

[237]As quoted by Martin Luther King, Jr., "Letter From Birmingham Jail," in *Why We Can't Wait* (New York: Harper and Row, 1963), p. 99.

tion of the laws the Montgomery statute that had required segregation on motor buses operated within the city.[238] It is not astonishing that the successful Montgomery boycott set a precedent for similar actions in cities throughout the South, extending to retail stores, produce markets, and a host of other sales and service facilities.

Yet a boycott destined to be far more militant and far more controversial began on February 1, 1960, when four black freshmen[239] at North Carolina Agricultural and Technical College began what at first was a spontaneous "sit-in" demonstration at the lunch counter of F. W. Woolworth's dime store in Greensboro. They had asked for cups of coffee, and had done so politely, but were refused service. They then simply continued to sit at the counter in protest—notwithstanding cursing, pushing, spitting, and catsup-throwing by their white neighbors. Ultimately, the four filed out, formed a tight circle on the sidewalk, and recited the Lord's Prayer—and another group took over for them inside.

This example of non-violent protest spread to six more North Carolina and forty-eight other cities as well as eight additional Southern states within four weeks. Not only did the Greensboro sit-in set a precedent,[240] it led directly to the organization of the Student Non-violent Coordinating Committee. SNCC quickly began to serve both in the South and in the North as an organizer and backer for "sit-ins" and a large variety of other "ins," such as "stand-ins," "read-ins," "pray-ins," "wade-ins," "sleep-ins," and "lie-ins."[241] Thousands

---

[238]*Gayle v. Browder*, 352 U.S. 903 (1956).

[239]Joseph McNeil, David Richmond, Franklin McCain, and Ezell Blair, Jr. (who later changed his name to Jibreel Khazan). Exactly twenty years to the day later (February 1, 1980) the four met triumphantly at the same counter to commemorate the historic event—which was widely covered by the media. A plaque on a downtown street near the site reads:

SIT-INS
Launched the national
drive for integrated
lunch counters, Feb. 1, 1960,
in Woolworth
store 2 blocks south.

[240]The first "sit-in" was reenacted on the same spot by David Richmond on February 1, 1985, a quarter of a century later.

[241]The developing record of sit-in demonstrations in Southern cities during the fourteen months from February 1, 1960, to March 27, 1961, was as follows (adapted from the

who had never before taken an active part in the protest movement now joined. Variously successful, the movement also gave rise to an intricate set of legal problems stemming from the action by the protesters themselves or by the local authorities, who, either by request or on their own initiative, would often arrest the "ins" for such common law offenses as "breach of the peace" or "trespassing." When *statutes* compelling, permitting, or forbidding segregation were present, the legal setting was tailor-made for litigation, of course. But when the actions of the "ins" constituted action against *private* inhospitable hosts acting in their *private* capacity, line-drawing would naturally be far more difficult; here, indeed, the Supreme Court's usually unanimous opinion on race discrimination issues would be bitterly split.

Other participants in "ins" movements, mounted largely by CORE, were the "freedom riders." Their chief target was transportation, supposedly desegregated for some time. The "rides" not only pinpointed but actually tested, often at the cost of imprisonment and violence, the still prevalent segregation practices in almost all interstate travel and terminal facilities in the deep South. In general, these rides accomplished their purpose: the exposure of continued, rampant violation of what was now the declared law of the land.

The Birmingham Trigger. Yet it was Birmingham, Alabama, that

---

special report of the Southern Regional Council, *The Freedom Ride,* published in Atlanta in May 1961):

				DEMONSTRATORS	ARRESTS
Feb.	1, 1960	North Carolina	Greensboro	4,200	268
Feb.	11	Virginia	Hampton	11,000	235
Feb.	12	South Carolina	Rock Hill	4,000	947
Feb.	12	Florida	Deland	2,500	243
Feb.	13	Tennessee	Nashville	16,000	692
Feb.	25	Alabama	Montgomery	5,500	86
Feb.	27	Kentucky	Lexington	6,000	374
March	5	Texas	Houston	6,500	317
March	10	Arkansas	Little Rock	50	20
March	15	Georgia	Atlanta	7,000	292
March	28	Louisiana	Baton Rouge	10,000	71
March	27, 1961	Mississippi	Jackson	1,600	40
			Totals	74,350	3,585

For further illustrative aspects of the matter, see Table 4, "Peaceful Rights Demonstrations, 1954–1968," in Jonathan W. Casper, *The Politics of Civil Liberties* (New York: Harper and Row, 1972), p. 90.

was destined to become the center of the militant black activism of
April–May 1963, with vast implications for the years to follow. Having
failed to make headway in the quest for desegregation in the state's
largest and most highly industrialized city, mass street demonstrations,
involving thousands, including schoolchildren, were staged there by
Dr. King and his faithful allies, the Reverends Ralph D. Abernathy and
Fred L. Shuttlesworth. Some 150 demonstrators were arrested on the
first day, but the protests continued with a march and a "kneel-in" in
the face of a court injunction. When the three leaders were also arrested,
the street demonstrations daily grew larger. So did the prison populace,
reaching 2,500 in a matter of days. Failing to obtain any concessions,
the blacks continued to demonstrate, and were now met by high-pres-
sure water hoses, police dogs, and cattle prods. The entire nation was
outraged, and the Birmingham authorities, under pressure from both the
Kennedy Administration and local business leaders, agreed to a
"truce," promising alleviation of black grievances in public accommodation, employment opportunities, and interracial committees. But
Governor Wallace promptly denounced the agreement, and on May 11,
after a series of bomb blasts directed against, among others, Dr. King
and his brother, thousands of irate blacks resumed demonstrations.
Within hours the streets were filled with uncontrollable rioters battling
with the police. At this juncture President Kennedy, having experienced
nothing but defiance from Wallace, dispatched 3,000 federal troops to
the area—but not to Birmingham itself. This seemed to achieve results;
racial tensions gradually subsided. And although they were revived by
Governor Wallace's infamous "schoolhouse door stand," which
unsuccessfully tried to prevent the court-ordered admission of two
blacks to the University of Alabama at Tuscaloosa, an important corner
had been turned. After Wallace's interference with court-ordered desegregation of certain public schools was blocked by the federalization of
the Alabama National Guard that September, a tenuous peace finally
came to Birmingham. Tragically, it did so only after four little black
girls had died in the wreckage of the bombed Sixteenth Street Baptist
Church[242] and two black teen-agers had been gunned down by white
terrorists.

[242]See the retrospective essay by Howell Raines, "The Birmingham Bombing," *The
New York Times Magazine*, July 24, 1983, pp. 12 ff.

These 1963 events set off chain reactions throughout the country. In the seventy days following the Birmingham "truce," almost 800 racial demonstrations took place in the nation. They culminated in the mammoth, orderly Washington march of August 1963, in which, as already noted, more than 200,000 blacks and whites participated. Racial demonstrations continued during the ensuing six summers throughout Northern cities.[243] Not even the new federal civil rights and voting statutes would lessen the now determined, often militant and impatient drive for black equality. It had obtained results! For most Southerners and, indeed increasingly, Northerners as well, adaptation to change had become a fact of daily life for state and local governments; racial incidents had to be avoided; and resistance to federal authority was, in the long run, futile. Still, the Southern leadership was allowed to move slowly and, with some exceptions, to do nothing more than the bare minimum. "Tokenism" was still the rule of the day.

This attitude, however understandable it might be in terms of the practices and traditions of generations, continued to incite militancy on the part of the increasingly restive blacks—and now particularly those in the ghettos of the *Northern* cities. They were tired of waiting, tired of gradualism, tired of tokenism. In effect, they demanded what was patently impossible: full equality "here and now"—and if that meant "favored treatment," so be it! But black poverty, both of means and of opportunity, and prejudice—always prejudice—could not be eradicated so quickly. The resultant frustration frequently generated overt belligerency, often referred to by the participants as "direct action," which was frequently, although by no means inevitably, counterproductive to the aims of the black cause and which, as indicated, provoked a serious split in the Supreme Court,[244] which heretofore had been supporting civil rights causes with unanimity.

While it is feasible to offer explanations for the wave of questionable and tragic actions, such as the riots that swept so many Northern cities between 1963 and 1969, there could be no excuse for the looting, the

---

[243]See pp. 327–28, *supra,* for statistics and details. Few, if any, of the large centers, were spared.

[244]See, among others, *Bell v. Maryland,* 378 U.S. 226 (1964); *Hamm v. City of Rock Hill,* 379 U.S. 306 (1964); *Elton v. Cox,* 379 U.S. 536 (1965); *Brown v. Louisiana,* 383 U.S. 131 (1966); *Adderley v. Florida,* 385 U.S. 39 (1966); and *Cameron v. Johnson,* 390 U.S. 611 (1968).

burning, the destruction, the loss of lives—the reckless dedication to manifestations of hate. As a result, there was mounting fear among civil rights leaders and supporters that the days of wide national support for civil rights had come to an end, at least temporarily. It would ultimately prove to be a groundless fear, but the failure of Congress to pass the 1966 Civil Rights bill seemed to confirm it at the time. And as President Johnson—who had done so much for blacks—told a group of visiting bishops from the all-black African Methodist Episcopal Church in October of that year:

> We have entered a new phase. . . . What if the cry for freedom becomes the sound of a brick cracking through a store window, turning over an automobile in the street, or the sound of the mob? If that sound should drown out the voices of reason, frustration will replace progress and all of our best work will be undone.[245]

In any event, it was now clear that, even in the non-violent sector of black protest, lines were becoming increasingly blurred: had not the limits of civil disobedience in a free representative democracy now been reached, and sometimes exceeded? There is a difference between the exercise of constitutional rights that are inherent in the freedoms of speech, press, assembly, and petition and the kind of militant, often lawless, activities that were becoming frequent. The basic issues of racial discrimination, of the injustices of generations, were obvious; there could no longer be any doubt of the need for the acknowledgment, both legally and morally, of full egalitarianism. Yet, it was also obvious that it would still take a long time to achieve it in the public sphere—and it would take infinitely longer in the *private* sector.

Since the means of amelioration of injustice in a representative democracy are patently lodged in the public sector, one of the great issues of the day thus became: just what constitutes that "public" sphere, which *is* reachable by the authority of government under law? Just when does an action become "state action"—an action subject to the commands and sanctions of the Constitution in general and Amendment Fourteen in particular?

---

[245]As quoted in *Time*, October 7, 1966, p. 17. Appropriately, indeed, did leading civil rights activist Clarence M. Mitchell, Jr., say of L.B.J.: "He was the greatest American President on civil rights." (As quoted in *The New York Times*, April 15, 1979, p. 28.)

State Action and Beyond: A True Dilemma

The words of the famed second sentence of Section 1 of the Fourteenth Amendment concerning "state action" would seem to be quite clear:

> *No State shall make or enforce any law* which shall abridge the privileges or immunities of citizens of the United States; *nor shall any State deprive* any person of life, liberty, or property without due process of law; *nor deny to any person within its jurisdiction the equal protection of the laws.*[246]

What is proscribed here is *discriminatory state action* only; it does *not* extend to *private action* (unless, of course, it has been legislatively covered to extend to the private sector—as is significantly true, for example, of segments of the Civil Rights Acts of 1964 and 1968 and their progeny). And this is the interpretation the judiciary has quite naturally and appropriately given to the Amendment. But at what point has a State, or its "agent," deprived an individual of life, liberty, or property without due process of law; or, more appropriately since black litigants have relied predominantly upon the "equal protection of the laws" clause, when has a State, or its "agent," denied an individual that equal protection? The important question is not so much "state action" *per se,* but whether, as Court opinions have demonstrated increasingly, "state action" denies "equal protection."

THE DILEMMA

Technically, *state action* is any action taken by legislative, executive, or judicial instrumentalities of the state. *Private action* is any act or action engaged in or perpetrated by any individual in his private capacity and association.[247] But six Supreme Court justices, in a highly sig-

---

[246]Italics supplied.

[247]One expert, Professor Louis Henkin, suggests three bases for holding the state legally responsible *when private discrimination is involved:* (1) "The state is responsible for what it could prevent, and should prevent, and fails to prevent." (2) "The state is responsible for discrimination which it encourages or sanctions." (3) "The state is responsible when its courts act to render discrimination effective." See his *"Shelley v. Kraemer:* Notes for a Revised Opinion," 110 *University of Pennsylvania Law Review* 481–87 (February 1962). Yet some of his arguments in this important and scholarly article would seem to cast doubt on his own tests.

nificant set of racial violence cases in 1966,[248] warned that they would feel bound to uphold any appropriate law aimed at punishing *private* individuals who use violence to deny persons their Fourteenth Amendment rights. Of course, *state* activity causing or abetting racial discrimination would, under present-day interpretations by the courts, be regarded as patently violating the Fourteenth Amendment injunctions against discriminatory state action. It is thus that the "separate but equal" concept met its doom, along with the manifold instances of state-authored or state-enforced racial discrimination in education, transportation, housing, employment, voting, and a vast array of other areas. But *private* discrimination, or so it might be assumed, would be entirely legal, even though neither democratic nor just. Hence, until the passage of the federal Civil Rights Act of 1964, it was not considered illegal to refuse to serve or admit blacks in privately owned establishments, such as restaurants, hotels, motels, or theaters, so long as the owner was *really* a *private* person, acting in his *private* capacity, and, of course, provided that *state* law did not forbid such discrimination.

Even before the Civil Rights Act of 1964 extended the reach of governmental proscription of discrimination on racial, religious, ethnic and other related grounds to such contentious areas as public accommodations and employment, however, the distinction between "public" and "private" under certain conditions had been legally questioned, although never really effectively challenged. Perhaps the first such instance to raise and at the same time to befuddle the basic issue at the bar of the judiciary was the *Restrictive Covenant* decision, *Shelley v. Kraemer*.[249] Briefly, in the lead case, J. D. and Ethel Lee Shelley, black citizens from St. Louis, Missouri, had "for valuable consideration" received in 1945 from one Josephine Fitzgerald a warranty deed to a parcel of land situated in an area restricted by common agreement of some thirty resident-owners to persons of "the Caucasian race." The restrictive covenant, originally scheduled to run from 1911 to 1961, specifically barred "people of the Negro or Mongolian race." Louis

---

[248]*United States v. Price*, 383 U.S. 688 (1966), and *United States v. Guest*, 383 U.S. 746 (1966). Expressed in two concurring opinions, severally joined by Chief Justice Warren and Associate Justices Black, Douglas, Clark, Brennan, and Fortas. *Griffin v. Breckenridge*, 403 U.S. 88 (1971), unanimously confirmed and expanded the two earlier holdings via Amendment Thirteen.

[249]334 U.S. 1 (1948). A similar question was raised by a Detroit group and was decided concurrently.

and Fern E. Kraemer, for the restrictive covenanters, attempted to block the Fitzgerald-to-Shelley sale in the appropriate Missouri State Circuit Court, but they lost—more or less on an interpretative technicality. The Supreme Court of Missouri, however, reversed the lower court's ruling and directed it to order the Shelleys to vacate their property.

Yet with Justices Reed, Jackson, and Rutledge taking no part in either the consideration or the decision of the case, the Supreme Court of the United States unanimously *reversed* the highest Missouri tribunal. Speaking through Chief Justice Vinson, the Court affirmed that orders by state courts *enforcing* restrictive covenants based on race and color are violative of the "equal protection of the laws" clause of the Fourteenth Amendment. Restrictive covenants drawn up by private individuals, reasoned the Court, are not in themselves a violation of the Amendment's commands so long as they are completely private and voluntary, and, of course, do not breach some federal or state law or state ordinance (which restrictive covenants in the housing field would have done in a number of states even in the late 1940s; and since the enactment of the federal fair housing law of 1968 and the Supreme Court's decision in *Jones v. Alfred H. Mayer Co.*,[250] such covenants would be illegal anywhere in the country). "Here, however," the Chief Justice pointed out, "there was more," because the State of Missouri, through its judicial branch, not only *aided in the enforcement* of the restrictive covenant—which would in itself have constituted forbidden state action—but, in effect, rendered the agreements workable. "We have no doubt," concluded America's highest jurist, "that there has been *state action* in the full and complete sense of the phrase."[251]

In other words, *Shelley* presented the intriguing dichotomy of permitting private discrimination so long as no state aid in its implementation or enforcement was sought: the judicial aid desired by Kraemer and his supporters *was* regarded as such state aid. The implications of the *Shelley* case became quickly apparent, and the decision evoked a flood of favorable, unfavorable, and tentative commentary by laymen and professionals alike.[252] But whatever one's feelings regarding either the

---

[250]392 U.S. 409 (1968). See the discussion regarding the statute and the *Mayer* decision on p. 352, *supra*, and p. 384. *infra*.

[251]*Shelley v. Kraemer, op. cit.*, at 13, 19.

[252]For example, Herbert Wechsler, "Toward Neutral Principles of Constitutional Law," 73 *Harvard Law Review* 1 (1959); Louis Henkin, "Some Reflections on Current

equity of the decision or the viability of the dichotomy it enunciated, the decision brought the state action problem to the fore. In brief, the problem comes down to the crucial question of a free democratic society: how to reconcile the competing rights and claims of *equality and liberty*—a question as old as the ages. Where *does* the Constitution draw the line between the right to legal equality and to equality of opportunity, and the rights of liberty, property,[253] privacy, and voluntary association? Where *do* we draw it? Where *should* we draw it? Where *can* we draw it? It is, of course, a balancing problem. Yet "balancing" is a delicate matter, often regarded as "nasty," even unconstitutional in some quarters—particularly when applied to the Bill of Rights. Thus, notwithstanding his avowedly absolutist position on the First Amendment,[254] Justice Black was deeply disturbed over the implications of the broad interpretation of "state action" under the Fourteenth Amendment; in fact, he came to "balance" *here*—most notably in some of the sit-in and demonstration cases,[255] although he did *not* in the cases concerning *bona fide* freedom of expression under the First Amendment. A few additional illustrations of the problem of private and state action and rights may be helpful (although it ought to be noted that the problem is assuredly not confined to matters of race).

Popular Referenda and State Action. The housing field provides a number of fascinatingly complex state action cases—particularly when "state action" involves a linkage to what, presumably, is *the* most democratic expression of a free participating electorate: the "direct democracy" instrumentalities of initiative and/or the referendum. What if a state's electorate, in a free and open election, approves a constitutional amendment to a state constitution, duly initiated by that state's

---

Constitutional Controversy," 109 *University of Pennsylvania Law Review* 637 (1961); Henkin, "*Shelley v. Kraemer:* Notes for a Revised Opinion," *op. cit.;* and Louis Pollak, "Racial Discrimination and Judicial Integrity: A Reply to Professor Wechsler," 108 *University of Pennsylvania Law Review* 1 (1959).

[253]In that connection see the interesting 5 : 4 Supreme Court decision in *San Antonio Independent School District v. Rodriguez,* which dealt, among other things, with the matter of "state action" and "equal protection" regarding the singular use of the property tax to fund public education (411 U.S. 1 [1973]). For a 5 : 4 holding on the other side of the entitlement scale, see the "Children of Illegal Aliens" case of *Plyler v. Doe,* 457 U.S. 202 (1982).

[254]See the explanation and analysis of his position throughout the pages of this book, particularly in Chapters II, III, and V, *passim*.

[255]See p. 471, footnote 244, *supra*, and p. 481, footnotes 271–76, *infra*.

electorate, that was designed to repeal fair housing legislation previously passed by the state legislature? This is precisely what occurred in the case of "Proposition 14" in California in 1964, when that state's voters, by the almost 2 : 1 margin of 4.5 to 2.4 million votes, adopted the following seemingly neutral provision: "Neither the state nor any subdivision or agency thereof shall deny . . . the right of any person . . . to decline to sell, lease, or rent [real] property to such person or persons as he, in his absolute discretion, chooses." Approved by an overwhelming majority, the provision became Section 26 of the California Constitution. *But* when a challenge to the newly adopted provision reached the California Supreme Court in 1966, that tribunal ruled it unconstitutional (5 : 2) as a violation of the "equal protection of the laws" clause of the Fourteenth Amendment, reasoning that "when the electorate assumes to exercise the law-making function [as it had done here by initiating and subsequently approving Proposition 14], then the electorate is as much a state agency as any of its elected officials."[256] This interpretation of the equal protection clause bewildered many observers, and predictably went to the United States Supreme Court— which, by the narrowest of margins, 5 : 4, upheld the California tribunal. Justice White's opinion, joined by Chief Justice Warren and Justices Douglas, Brennan, and Fortas, held that the amendment went beyond a mere repeal of the state's fair housing legislation and created "a constitutional right to discriminate on racial grounds in the sale and rental of real property."[257] He concluded that, in effect, the electorate's action constituted "state action"—state action that would impermissibly involve the state in private racial discrimination to an unconstitutional degree. In other words, both the state and the federal judiciary rejected the contention that the electorate's action had merely restored *neutrality;* they instead held that the "in his absolute discretion" clause *ipso facto* legislated discrimination. But in an angry dissenting opinion, joined by Justices Black, Clark, and Stewart, Justice Harlan pronounced Section 26 unquestionably "neutral" and "inoffensive on its face," that the "state action" required to bring the Fourteenth Amend-

[256]*Reitman v. Mulkey,* 64 Cal. 2d 529, at 542.

[257]*Reitman v. Mulkey,* 387 U.S. 369 (1967), at 376. For an excellent commentary on the case see R. E. Wolfinger and F. I. Greenstein, "The Repeal of Fair Housing in California: An Analysis of Referendum Voting," LXII *American Political Science Review* 753 (September 1968).

ment into operation must be "affirmative and purposeful"; and he warned, in what constitutes an intriguing exhortation of appropriate institutional roles, that

> By refusing to accept the decision of the people of California, and by contriving a new and ill-defined constitutional concept to allow Federal judicial interference, I think the court has taken to itself powers and responsibilities left elsewhere by the Constitution.[258]

The *Reitman* holding, notwithstanding its far-reaching implications concerning the range of state action under Amendment Fourteen, seemed to leave the door open, however, for straightforward "neutral" repealers of anti-discrimination legislation. Not only did the White opinion so hint, but during oral argument before the Supreme Court, A. L. Wirin, counsel for the Los Angeles chapter of the American Civil Liberties Union, which sponsored the challenge to Proposition 14, conceded during a colloquy with Justices Black and White that a referendum merely repealing California's fair housing statutes would *not* have been unconstitutional.[259] Yet along came the Court's 1969 decision in *Hunter v. Erickson*,[260] in which it held, with only Justice Black dissenting, that an Akron, Ohio, charter provision, adopted by the voters in a city-wide referendum, violated the equal protection of the laws clause. That provision not only repealed a "fair housing" law that had been shortly prior thereto enacted by Akron's City Council but, moreover, required that before any fair housing law could be restored to the books, it would have to be readopted *by a referendum vote*.[261] Speaking for the eight-man Court majority, Justice White reasoned that, by singling out fair housing laws as the only ones subject to such referendum votes— whereas the City Council regularly and routinely legislates on such other housing matters as rent control and urban renewal—the voters of Akron in effect engaged in constitutionally proscribed state action; that the referendum requirement here "makes an explicitly radical classifi-

---

[258]*Reitman v. Mulkey, op. cit.,* at 396.

[259]*The New York Times,* March 22, 1967, p. 1e, and oral argument at the Supreme Court, March 21, 1967.

[260]393 U.S. 385.

[261]That provision of the charter (§137) required that any ordinance regulating real estate transactions "on the basis of race, color, religion, national origin or ancestry must first be approved by a majority of the electors voting on the question at a regular or general election before said ordinance shall be effective."

cation.'' The majority denied Black's contention that it had made even a simple repealer impossible—and it not only proved that point in a 1971 case, but it gave Black an opportunity to write the opinion. At issue was the constitutionality of a California referendum law—similar to that of a good many states—permitting a majority of the voters in a community to block the construction of low-cost housing. A lower federal court had declared it unconstitutional as a violation of the equal protection of the laws clause. Justice Black's majority opinion, joined by Chief Justice Burger and Justices Harlan, Stewart, and White, reversed (5:3) the decision below, declaring that the thrust of the Fourteenth Amendment was to outlaw legal distinction based on race; that there was no evidence that the California law was aimed at any racial minority; and that this ''procedure for democratic decision making gives the people a voice in decisions that would raise their taxes, dilute the tax base, and affect the future development of the community.''[262] But the dissenting opinion by Justice Marshall, joined by his colleagues Brennan and Blackmun, charged that the statute ''explicitly singles out low-income persons'' for unequal treatment. ''It is far too late in the day,'' the Court's black member noted, ''to contend that the 14th Amendment prohibits only racial discrimination; and to me, singling out the poor to bear a burden not placed on any other class of citizens tramples the values that the 14th Amendment was designed to protect.''[263] Yet in a 6:3 ruling in 1976 the Court again sustained a referendum requirement—this time that of a city charter provision in Eastlake, Ohio, requiring land use changes to be ratified by a 55 percent referendum majority as well as the city council.[264] And in 1977 it held (5:3) that it was not inherently unconstitutional for a suburb to refuse to change zoning restrictions, the practical effect of which is to block construction of racially integrated housing for persons with low and moderate income; that to be unconstitutional there must also be an ''intent'' or ''purpose'' to discriminate—which, however, does not mean that under no circumstances could a village, such as Arlington Heights, be *statutorily* required to rezone so as to provide such housing.[265]

Aspects of the ''In'' Syndrome. What of ''private'' versus ''public''

[262]*James v. Valtierra,* 402 U.S. 137 (1971), at 143.
[263]*Ibid.,* at 144.
[264]*Eastlake v. Forest City Enterprises, Inc.,* 426 U.S. 668.
[265]*Village of Arlington Heights v. Metropolitan Housing Development Corp.,* 429 U.S. 252.

action inherent in the spate of "sit-in" demonstration cases that reached the Court prior to the Civil Rights Act of 1964?[266] The Act settled the matter in terms of the constitutionality of the pertinent section, based on congressional power over interstate commerce, *provided* the establishment concerned came under the provisions of the statute governing "public accommodations"; but did it really settle the problem of liberty *versus* equality in philosophical terms? Justice Black had joined in the unanimous opinion in the two late 1964 cases upholding the law's public accommodations section,[267] yet obviously he did so only because he believed Congress to have had the power to legislate as it had *because* it *expressly* invoked its authority over interstate commerce. But, as he had noted orally from the bench in conjunction with his dissenting opinion in one of the sit-in cases a few months earlier in 1964, "this Court has never said, in the school segregation decisions or any before or since, that the prejudice of individuals could be laid to the state."[268] And again, from the bench on the last day of the Court's 1963–64 term, Black commented that the idea that the Fourteenth Amendment *itself* prohibited segregation in public accommodations made "the last six months' struggle in Congress a work of supererogation"[269]—a reference to the prolonged debate that preceded passage of the legislation. As his long-time jurisprudential "adversary," the retired Justice Frankfurter, had done so often, Black then again admonished his country that "The worst citizen no less than the best is entitled to equal protection of the laws of his state and of his nation."[270] And it was Black again, this time joined by Harlan, Stewart, and White, who, having all voted to uphold the constitutionality of the contentious provision of the Civil Rights Act of 1964, took pains to emphasize on the very same Opinion Monday what should be obvious to all believers in law, order, justice, and the dignity of liberty: that the passage of the Act did *not* authorize persons "who are unlawfully refused service a 'right' to take the law into their own hands by sitting down and occupying the

[266]For example, *Edwards v. South Carolina*, 372 U.S. 229 (1963); *Peterson v. Greenville*, 373 U.S. 244 (1963); *Lombard v. Louisiana*, 373 U.S. 267 (1963); *Griffin v. Maryland*, 378 U.S. 130 (1964); *Robinson v. Florida*, 378 U.S. 153 (1964); *Barr v. City of Columbia*, 378 U.S. 146 (1964); and *Bell v. Maryland*, 378 U.S. 226 (1964).

[267]*Heart of Atlanta Motel v. United States*, 379 U.S. 241 (1964) and *Katzenbach v. McClung*, 379 U.S. 294 (1964).

[268]*Barr v. City of Columbia, op. cit.*

[269]As quoted in *The New York Times*, June 23, 1964, p. 16*l*.

[270]*Bell v. Maryland*, 378 U.S. 226 (1964), dissenting opinion, at 328.

premises for as long as they choose to stay."[271] Black's deep concern—one steeped in his high dedication to what he regarded as the prerogatives of home privacy and local control—continued to make itself known, albeit in the minority. Yet he carried three other justices—Clark, Harlan, and Stewart—with him when, in a public library "stand-in" case in 1966, he asked impassionedly:

> Can any provision of the United States Constitution tell any citizens—white or colored—they can march with impunity into a public library and demonstrate against some public policy? . . . It has become automatic for people to be turned loose as long as whatever they do has something to do with race. That is not the way I read the Constitution.[272]

A few pages earlier he had vigorously challenged the majority's position with the exhortation that

> It is high time to challenge the assumption in which too many people have too long acquiesced, that groups that think they have been mistreated have a constitutional right to use the public streets, buildings, and property to protest whatever, wherever, whenever they want, without regard to whom such conduct may disturb.[273]

That spring the Court summarily *upheld* the conviction of twenty-five New York City racial demonstrators at a housing project[274] and the conviction of a CORE "stand-in" at the office of the police chief of Syracuse[275]. And on the last day of the 1965–66 term, Justice Clark formally provided the fifth vote for that point of view, and thus a Court majority. He joined his colleagues Black, Harlan, Stewart, and White in holding that twenty-nine persons arrested on various local charges arising from civil rights movements in 1964 in Leflore County, Mississippi, could not have their trials transferred from state to federal courts merely upon their contention that their rights of free speech might be infringed by prejudicial treatment in state courts.[276]

Lest that decision be regarded as a procedural "fluke," or one based

---

[271]*Hamm v. City of Rock Hill*, 379 U.S. 306 (1964), dissenting opinion, at 318.
[272]*Brown v. Louisiana*, 383 U.S. 131 (1966), dissenting opinion, at 168.
[273]*Ibid.*, at 162.
[274]*Penn v. New York*, 383 U.S. 969 (1966).
[275]*Baer v. New York*, 384 U.S. 154 (1966).
[276]*Greenwood v. Peacock*, 384 U.S. 808 (1966).

on a wavering majority, the same five justices again agreed late in 1966 in a case of particular significance in the fundamental freedom-*versus*-order clash because the civil rights demonstrations involved were directed against *public* rather than *private* property. Speaking through Justice Black, the five-man majority upheld the "willful-trespass" conviction of Harriet Adderley and thirty-one other Florida A & M University Negro students who had demonstrated outside the Leon County jail in Tallahassee, Florida.[277] The earlier decisions had involved prosecutions for *breach of the peace* rather than trespass. In attempting to draw the line between speech and *conduct,* Black wrote:[278]

> [N]othing in the Constitution of the United States prevents Florida from even-handed enforcement of its general trespassing statute against those refusing to obey the sheriff's order to remove themselves. . . . *The state, no less than a private owner of property, has power to preserve the property under its control for the use to which it is lawfully dedicated.*[279]

But to Justice Douglas, dissenting in a vigorously worded opinion in which he was joined by Warren, Brennan, and Fortas, the Black holding represented "a great break with the traditions of the Court." Now, he said, trespass laws could be used as a "blunderbuss" to suppress civil rights; the Court has, he concluded, "now set into the record a great and wonderful police-state doctrine."[280] Although two subsequent decisions intensified the concern voiced by Douglas and his supporting colleagues,[281] the Court unanimously made it clear in 1968 that it is unconstitutional for tribunals to delay public meetings—even when violence is threatened—without hearing testimony from those who wish to meet; that, in other words, there could be no *ex parte* injunctions.[282] And, also unanimously, it reversed in 1969 the 1965 conviction of civil rights leaders King and Shuttlesworth for parading without a permit in

---

[277]*Adderley v. Florida,* 385 U.S. 39 (1966). The Florida statute reads: "Every trespass on the property of another, committed with a malicious and mischievous intent . . . shall be punished."

[278]See his discussion of that vexatious line in his *A Constitutional Faith* (New York: Alfred A. Knopf, 1968), pp. 53–56.

[279]*Adderley v. Florida, op. cit.,* at 47. (Italics supplied.)

[280]*Ibid.,* extemporaneous remark from the bench, November 14, 1966.

[281]*Walker v. Birmingham,* 388 U.S. 307 (1967), and *Cameron v. Johnson,* 390 U.S. 611 (1968).

[282]*Carroll v. President and Commissioners of Princess Anne County,* 393 U.S. 175.

Birmingham in 1963 because that city's ordinance gave its commissioners "unfettered discretion" to reject permits.[283] Moreover, in a
1972 decision (*not* involving race) the Court unanimously declared
unconstitutional a federal 1882 law that banned all "unauthorized"
demonstrations on the grounds of the United States capitol,[284] and in
1983 it invalidated a part of one that banned picketing or the distribution
of leaflets on the *sidewalks* surrounding the U.S. Supreme Court.[285]
Clearly, then, the line is drawn on the basis of each case's facts.

State Action or Routine Service? What of such services rendered by
the state as *licensing* or the *probation of wills* that do involve the state,
but which had heretofore been regarded as *routine services* rather than
as state action? If these services were to be construed as "state action,"
would not almost *everything* then be state action? Would anything
remain in the private sphere at all?

Girard College. The matter of probation of discriminatory wills (of
which there are innumerable examples) underwent its first important
post-*Brown* litigation in the *Girard College* cases,[286] involving Philadelphia's famed Girard College (actually a private elementary and high
school for "male, white orphans," as provided in the generous will of
Stephen S. Girard, an early-nineteenth-century Philadelphia merchant).
The trust, established by Girard's will, was being administered by the
Board of Directors of the City of Philadelphia when in 1957 the
Supreme Court of the United States, citing the precedent of the *Public
School Segregation Cases,*[287] ruled unconstitutional as a violation of
the "equal protection of the laws" clause of Amendment Fourteen the
municipality's described participation in the Girard trust's administra-
tion.[288] It was deemed "state action." But then an interesting turn of
events took place: the Board of Directors of City Trusts asked the
Orphans Court—the appropriate tribunal of jurisdiction—to *remove the*

[283]*Shuttlesworth v. Birmingham,* 394 U.S. 147.

[284]*Chief of Capitol Police v. Jeannette Rankin Brigade,* 409 U.S. 972.

[285]*United States v. Grace,* 461 U.S. 171.

[286]*Pennsylvania v. Board of Directors of City Trusts of the City of Philadelphia,* 353
U.S. 230 (1957) and 357 U.S. 570 (1958), *certiorari* denied. (These two citations are
confined to *Supreme Court* action. There was a host of lower federal and state case
dispositions, of course.)

[287]*Brown v. Board of Education of Topeka,* 347 U.S. 483 (1954).

[288]*Pennsylvania v. Board of Directors of City Trusts of the City of Philadelphia,* 353
U.S. 230.

municipal trustees and to *substitute private trustees.* This the Orphans Court promptly did, and the Supreme Court of Pennsylvania upheld the action as not being violative of the equal protection clause's "state action" concept. In other words, the state judiciary did not regard either the administration of the trust by private individuals or the role of the two courts in facilitating it to be constitutionally proscribed. On the Pennsylvania Attorney-General's petition for a writ of *certiorari,* the United States Supreme Court denied review,[289] thus upholding the state tribunals.

The Girard issue continued to bubble, however, and became acute again fully eight years later when, following lengthy sparring between the NAACP and the school's board of trustees, U.S. District Court Judge Joseph S. Lord III ruled that blacks could not be excluded from Girard College *under Pennsylvania law.* Specifically *refusing to pass on the probate problem,* Judge Lord simply held that the Pennsylvania Public Accommodations Act of 1939—which threw open all *public* institutions and accommodations—applied to Girard College, for he classified it as a "public institution."[290] Shortly thereafter, he ordered the admission of seven black orphans if they were otherwise found to qualify.[291] The trustees appealed his decision to the U.S. Third Circuit Court of Appeals, which first stayed Judge Lord's order and then reversed him on the ground that the 1939 statute did *not* apply to Girard College.[292] The plaintiffs, armed with a different strategy, returned to Judge Lord in 1967. The latter, eschewing the Pennsylvania law as well as any probation of wills consideration, now ruled that Girard's refusal to admit the black applicants constituted a violation of the "equal protection of the laws" clause by virtue of being proscribable *state action* under the Constitution, since the College was sufficiently "public" (e.g., tax-exempt) to invoke the Fourteenth Amendment's state action strictures.[293] This time the United States Court of Appeals, in a three-opinion 5 : 0 decision, affirmed Judge Lord's ruling. The principal opinion, written by Judge Gerald McLaughlin, turned predominantly on the quasi-public nature of the institution—which constituted sufficient

[289]*Ibid.,* 357 U.S. 570 (1958).
[290]*Commonwealth of Pennsylvania v. Brown,* 260 F. Supp. 323 (1966).
[291]*Commonwealth of Pennsylvania v. Brown,* 360 F. Supp. 358 (1966).
[292]*Ibid.,* 373 F. 2d 771 (1967).
[293]*Ibid.,* 270 F. Supp. 782 (1967).

"state action."[294] The Supreme Court refused to review,[295] and thus another attempt to make distinctions in the realm of racial discrimination sector had succeeded. But could the distinction hold? What of "private" parks, deeded in a bequest, for example?

Bacon's Park. The Court soon confronted the question of whether such a privately owned park, here one in Macon, Georgia, could discriminate racially because of the terms of the original donor's will. In 1914, the 100-acre park had been left in trust to the City of Macon by the will of a former Confederate general, Senator Augustus Octavius Bacon, stipulating that the park's use be reserved for "white women and children." As did parts of the Girard will, Bacon's bequest contained a number of features that were ultimately branded "state action" by civil rights leaders. The will had been drawn up under a Georgia law that, unlike Pennsylvania's, *specifically permitted segregation* in charitable trusts. But, like Philadelphia, Macon appointed the trustees and, like Girard College, Bacon's Park was considered an eleemosynary institution and therefore tax-exempt. Similar to the Philadelphia actions regarding Girard, Macon withdrew as trustee in 1963 and transferred the fiduciary authority to private trustees after lower federal courts had ruled unmistakably that a municipality could not constitutionally operate a segregated park.

Six blacks, successful in getting the trustee transfer question before the Supreme Court, contended that Macon had become so intimately involved in the operations of Bacon's Park that to permit private individuals to take over and continue to discriminate racially would be tantamount to "unconstitutional state action." In a 6 : 3 decision, with Justice Douglas delivering the Court's opinion, the Supreme Court agreed with the six petitioners.[296] It held that Macon had become so "entwined" in the park's operation that the mere change of trustees could not constitutionally remove the command to desegregate. Joined by the Chief Justice and Associate Justices Brennan, Clark, and Fortas, Douglas held that park services are "municipal in nature" and in the "public domain." Under the circumstances, he ruled, "we cannot but

---

[294]*Ibid.*, 392 F. 2d 120 (1968).

[295]*Brown v. Commonwealth of Pennsylvania*, 391 U.S. 921 (1968). For an engaging, albeit not unflawed, summary of the *Girard* case (and the eccentric Stephen S. Girard) see John Keats, "Legacy of Stephen Girard," 29 *American Heritage* 38 (June to July 1978).

[296]*Evans v. Newton*, 382 U.S. 296 (1966).

conclude that the public character of this park requires that it be treated as a public institution" and therefore subject to the commands of the "equal protection of the laws" clause of the Fourteenth Amendment. As opposed to golf clubs, social centers, *private schools*,[297] and other similar organizations, a park, Douglas explained, "is more like a fire department or police department that traditionally serves the community. Mass recreation through the use of parks is plainly in the public domain."[298]

Justices Harlan and Stewart dissented, as did Black, but the latter did so on separate and largely jurisdictional grounds. To Harlan and Stewart, the Douglas contention was at best dubious. Noting that Douglas had specifically excepted private schools, Harlan was nonetheless alarmed, contending that the Douglas theory could "be spun out to reach *privately owned* orphanages, libraries, garbage collection companies, detective agencies, and a host of other functions *commonly regarded as nongovernmental though paralleling fields of governmental activity.*"[299] As for private schools, Harlan argued cogently that the "public function" of privately established schools and privately established parks is assuredly similar. If, Harlan continued, the majority really believed that its ruling left "unaffected the traditional view that the Fourteenth Amendment does *not* compel private schools to adapt their admission policies to its requirements," he certainly could not agree with their interpretation in the light of the *Bacon's Park* case. He regarded it as indeed difficult

to avoid the conclusion that this decision opens the door to reversal of these basic constitutional concepts. . . . The example of schools is, I think, sufficient to indicate the pervasive potentialities of this "public function" theory . . . a catch phrase as vague and amorphous as it is far reaching.[300]

But, in one of those unpredictable Court actions, the Supreme Court ruled (5:2) four years later that Baconsfield (as Senator Bacon had called it) could be returned to the donor's heirs despite a federal court

[297]See the discussion of burgeoning private school developments in 1976, pp. 406–410, *infra*.

[298]*Ibid.*, at 302.

[299]*Ibid.*, at 322. (Italics supplied.)

[300]*Ibid.*, at 322.

order to admit blacks to its use.[301] In thus siding with the Georgia Supreme Court, Justice Black—speaking also for Chief Justice Burger and Justices Harlan, Stewart, and White—concluded that no constitutionally forbidden state action was involved here; that the Georgia courts had merely carried out Senator Bacon's wishes and had not themselves acted to discriminate against Macon's blacks; and that the Fourteenth Amendment's crucial equal protection of the laws clause had not therefore been violated. Dissenting, Justices Brennan and Douglas, however, asserted that making the park private to frustrate desegregation *did* amount to discriminatory state action.[302] In any event, at least as of this writing (mid-1988)—and buttressed by a 1975 holding, with only Justice Douglas in dissent[303]—it seems clear that the mere probation of a will falls outside the realm of the kind of "state action" governed by constitutional commands—which is not to say that a future Court may not read the Constitution differently.

Jackson's Pool. Demonstrating its capability of "surprises" and the dangers of attempting predictions as to its course of action, the Court, dividing 5 : 4, held in a contentious 1971 Mississippi litigation that public officials may close all of a city's public swimming pools rather then comply with a court order to desegregate them—the city having desegregated its public parks, golf courses, auditoria, and the City Zoo.[304] Thus the majority opinion, written by Justice Black—who was joined by his colleagues Harlan, Stewart, Blackmun, and Chief Justice Burger—upheld the right of the City Council of Jackson to shut its five community pools on the claimed grounds that to integrate them would be "uneconomical" and create a threat of violence. Refusing to be drawn into attempts to "ascertain the motivation, or collection of different motivations, that lie behind a legislative enactment," Black ruled:

Neither the 14th Amendment nor any act of Congress purports to impose an affirmative duty on a state to begin to operate or to continue to operate

---

[301]*Evans v. Abney,* 396 U.S. 435 (1970).

[302]The Court's sole black member, Justice Thurgood Marshall, disqualified himself from sitting in the case because he was once chief counsel for the NAACP Legal Defense and Educational Fund, Inc., which represented the blacks who began legal proceedings challenging the segregated park in 1963.

[303]*Sutt v. First National Bank of Kansas City,* 421 U.S. 992. The Court here let stand a bequest to Protestant Christian hospitals in a single county to help care for native-born, white patients.

[304]*Palmer v. Thompson,* 403 U.S. 217.

swimming pools. . . . It is not a case where a city is maintaining different sets of facilities for blacks and whites and forcing the races to remain separate in recreational or educational activities.[305]

But in his heated dissenting opinion, Justice White, joined by his colleagues Brennan, Marshall, and Douglas—who also issued a separate one, based on his reading of the Ninth Amendment—accused the majority of turning back the clock seventeen years on racial equality, of adopting a policy tantamount to "apartheid." In White's words, "a State may not have an official stance against desegregating public facilities . . . implemented by closing those facilities in response to a desegregation order."[306] At the least, "an honest difference of opinion about what the Constitution says,"[307] as Black put it, underlay the Court's majority opinion—one replete with broad implications for future policy judgments and decisions (irrespective of the fact that Jackson *voluntarily* reopened its pools on an integrated basis in 1975).

Private Clubs. Perhaps not one of the most important on the scale of basic bread-and-butter values, but assuredly an intriguing one, and one replete with considerations of dignity and egalitarianism as well as freedom of association and liberty, is the matter of the exclusionary policies of private clubs. Even the tough provisions of the Civil Rights Act of 1964, which, among others, forbid places of public accommodation—and these have been broadly defined and construed by the courts[308]—to discriminate because of race, color, religion, or national origin, leave a specific loophole (in Title II) by *expressly* permitting private clubs to do so, thus testifying to Congress's belief that private clubs can, indeed, discriminate without violating the Constitution. But the courts, of course, are not ultimately bound by the beliefs and/or enactments of Congress, and they have been faced increasingly with difficult questions. When is a "club" a club; i.e., when is a "club" a place of public entertainment or public "business" rather than a private club exempt under the C.R.A.? At what point, if at all, do the prerogatives the Court "found" in the Civil Rights Act of 1866 as of its 1968

[305]*Ibid.*, at 220.
[306]*Ibid.*, at 240.
[307]*Ibid.* Oral comment from bench, June 14, 1971.
[308]E.g., *Heart of Atlanta Motel v. United States*, 379 U.S. 241 (1964) and *Katzenbach v. McClung*, 379 U.S. 294 (1964). See also pp. 392 ff., *supra*.

fair-housing law decision[309] vitiate prevailing concepts of the rights of private clubs? And, finally, and most importantly, at what point, if any, do a club's actions, and the services it receives, constitute proscribable "state action"? In the 1970s the Supreme Court began to face each of these questions.

Thus, as to when is a "club" a club, the Court ruled (7 : 1) in 1969 that so-called private recreational clubs cannot resort to subterfuge to bar blacks from membership when in fact they are *not* private.[310] The case involved a swimming, boating, and picnicking club near Little Rock, Arkansas (Lake Nixon); the establishment widely advertised that it charged but twenty-five cents for "membership," and had 100,000 "members" in a single year. While the lower federal courts, to whom two excluded blacks had appealed, found the "club" arrangements to be a sham, they held that blacks could nonetheless be excluded because Lake Nixon was a private, local activity, not covered by the Civil Rights Act's public accommodations provision. It took a bit of imaginative stretching, but the Supreme Court, speaking through Justice Brennan, with only Justice Black in dissent, found that the establishment *did* affect commerce and therefore came under the statute's reach.[311] How? Well, it solicited business where interstate travelers might respond; it leased canoes from an Oklahoma company; it used a jukebox and records manufactured outside of Arkansas; and ingredients of three out of four items served at the snack bar were shipped interstate. This reasoning was simply too much for Black,[312] but he had no supporters.

In 1969, too, the Court reached the question of whether those provisions of the Civil Rights Act of 1866 which, as explained earlier,[313]

[309]*Jones v. Alfred H. Mayer Co.*, 392 U.S. 409 (1968). See p. 448, footnote 169, *supra*, for the Act's key provision on housing. See also the Court's important 1967 *Gautreaux* decision, p. 440, footnote 151, *supra*.

[310]For example, in 1976 the Court upheld a lower tribunal's ruling that health spas are "places of entertainment" within the meaning of the C.R.A. of 1964 and thus subject to the Act's prohibition against racial discrimination. (*Shape Spa for Health & Beauty, Inc. v. Rousseve*, 425 U.S. 911, [1976].)

[311]*Daniel v. Paul*, 395 U.S. 298 (1968).

[312]As he put it: "This would be stretching the commerce clause so as to give the federal government complete control over every little remote country place of recreation in every nook and cranny of every precinct and county in every one of the fifty states. This goes too far for me."

[313]See pp. 368 ff., *supra*. The Act's pertinent provision (42 U.S.C.A. §1982) reads:

outlawed racial discrimination against anyone who wishes to *contract* to buy or lease real estate, extended to any "private club" rights. In a 5 : 3 decision, written by Justice Douglas—who was joined by his colleagues Black, Brennan, Marshall, and Stewart, with Justices Harlan, White, and Chief Justice Burger dissenting—the Court ruled that the 1866 statute prevented the exclusion of a black family, which had moved into a certain neighborhood housing development, from a swimming pool and a park owned by residents of the suburban community involved.[314] The excluded black applicant for membership, Dr. R. Freeman, Jr., an official of the Department of Agriculture, had obtained a share in the pool and park with the lease of his house from its owner-member, Paul E. Sullivan. Not only did the development's board of directors refuse to admit Dr. Freeman, it also expelled Mr. Sullivan from membership when he protested the action. The Douglas opinion did not decide whether a club membership is "personal property" under the 1866 Act, since the share in the development (Little Hunting Park) was part of the lease itself. The three dissenters objected that the majority unnecessarily propounded grave constitutional questions and that the fair housing provisions of the Civil Rights Act of 1968 would have provided the same relief without reliance upon the vaguely worded 1866 law. The majority left undecided the broader question of whether private clubs that admit white applicants without selectivity may legally exclude blacks when *no* lease is involved—an issue it again dodged, perhaps quite understandably, four years later.[315]

But what of a private club or lodge that discriminates on racial—or, for that matter, on sexual or religious—grounds and *holds a state liquor*

"All citizens of the United States shall have the same right, in every State and Territory, as is enjoyed by white citizens thereof to inherit, purchase, lease, sell, hold, and convey real and personal property."

[314]*Sullivan v. Little Hunting Park, Inc.*, 396 U.S. 229 (1969).

[315]Relying heavily on its 1969 decision, the Court, speaking through Justice Blackmun, held unanimously: "When an organization links membership benefits to residency in a narrow geographical area, that decision infuses those benefits into the bundle of rights for which an individual pays when buying or leasing within the area." *Tillman v. Wheaton-Haven Recreation Association*, 410 U.S. 431 (1973), at 437. The Association drew *all* of its members from *whites* living within three-quarters of a mile from its swimming pool, and barred all *non-whites* living in the same area. The Court refused to recognize the Association as a "private club on any level." See also a similar stance in 1980 by the United States Court of Appeals for the Fourth Circuit, by overturning a lower court ruling that had dismissed a charge of racial discrimination. (*Wright v. Salisbury Country Club, Ltd.*, 632 F. 2d and 479 F. Supp. 378, respectively.)

license? In the absence of "state action," even the tough provisions of the Civil Rights Act of 1964 specifically exempt *private* organizations from its non-discrimination mandates. Is the grant of a state liquor license the sort of "state action" at issue, or is it, like probating of wills, merely a "service" that does not constitute proscribable state action? The judicial response to date has been rather equivocal but, on the whole, the answer would appear to be negative—at least of this writing (mid-1988)—so long as a law does not specifically bar such discrimination as a condition for obtaining either a license or tax exemption—as Boston's Licensing Board, for one, did in 1987.

Thus, could the Loyal Order of Moose, for example, limit membership in its 2,000 lodges to white adult Caucasian males—who, if married, are married to "white Caucasians," and are of "good moral character" and "mentally normal" and "express a belief in a supreme being"? If it is a truly private organization, receives no governmental aid, and pays its taxes, the answer would presumably be "yes"—for the liberty to associate privately, even if it be on a discriminatory basis, would appear to outweigh egalitarian commands, especially since the First and Fourteenth Amendments guarantee freedom of association and liberty as well as equality. The Harrisburg, Pennsylvania, Lodge #107 of the Moose, possessor of a state liquor license, refused to serve a meal and drinks to K. Leroy Irvis, the black Majority Leader of the Pennsylvania State House of Representatives, who had gone to the Lodge as a guest of a Moose member. Evidently, the Lodge did not discriminate selectively in its discrimination against blacks! After losing in Pennsylvania Commonwealth Court—which called the Lodge's refusal to serve Irvis "morally indefensible and deficient in good manners and common sense,"[316] but held the Lodge to be a private club exempt on grounds of privacy and association—Representative Irvis brought suit before a three-judge Federal District Court, contending that state regulation of liquor was "so detailed and pervasive" that to license a club that discriminated was tantamount to licensing discrimination. Unanimously, the three-judge tribunal ruled in Mr. Irvis's favor, agreeing that the holder of a liquor license was, indeed, clothed with "state action" under the Fourteenth Amendment.[317] Blurring the issues somewhat, however, the court added that the Lodge could continue to dis-

---

[316]*Commonwealth v. Loyal Order of Moose*, 92 Dauph. 234 (1970), at 239.
[317]*Irvis v. Scott and Moose Lodge #107*, 318 F. Supp. 1246 (1970), at 1251.

criminate on the basis of religion and national origin—it said nothing about sex—because it did not regard these characteristics to be protected by that Civil War Amendment—which had been adopted primarily to prevent discrimination against blacks.

The Lodge, in its resultant appeal to the U.S. Supreme Court, called that distinction "clearly fallacious," and pointed to the stipulated exemption of private clubs under the public accommodations provision of the Civil Rights Act of 1964. Moreover, it invoked freedom of association concepts under the First (and Fourteenth) Amendment. The high tribunal evidently agreed, at least in part: in a 6 : 3 opinion, written by Justice Rehnquist—Justices Douglas, Brennan, and Marshall dissenting—it ruled that *mere liquor regulation* does *not* involve the state in the kind of discriminatory state action forbidden by the Fourteenth Amendment's equal protection clause—"the State," in Rehnquist's words, "must have significantly involved itself with invidious discriminations . . . in order for the discriminatory action to fall within the ambit of constitutional prohibition."[318] However, the *Moose Lodge* decision did *not* mean that states could not make the receipt of a liquor license, or its continued retention, contingent upon the eschewing of racial discrimination—as fifteen Maine "Elk" lodges soon found out.[319] On the other hand, in the absence of state laws prohibiting discrimination on the basis of *sex* as well as race in places of public accommodation—and in the absence of the adoption of an "Equal Rights Amendment"—the Court consistently refused, until the mid-1980s, to overturn lower tribunal rulings upholding the right of *private* clubs or other *private* organizations that were "male only" to obtain and/or retain liquor licenses, *provided* that they were *genuinely* private.[320]

---

[318]*Moose Lodge #107 v. Irvis,* 407 U.S. 163 (1972). But it ought to be noted, that when—just two months after the Court's decision—the Pennsylvania State Human Relations Commission ruled that Lodge #107 had in fact turned itself into a *"public accommodation"* because it freely allowed guests, and thus could not ban blacks under state law, the State Supreme Court affirmed, and the U.S. Supreme Court dismissed the Lodge's appeal, thus upholding the Commission's ruling. (*Loyal Order of Moose v. Pennsylvania Human Relations Commission,* 409 U.S. 1052 (1972).

[319]*B.P.O.E. Lodge #2043 v. Ingraham,* 412 U.S. 913 (1973). Later that year the Elks dropped their "whites-only" rule.

[320]E.g., *Millenson v. New Hotel Monteleone,* 414 U.S. 1011 (1973), *Junior Chamber of Commerce of Rochester v. U.S. Jaycees,* 419 U.S. 1026 (1974), and *Junior Chamber of Commerce of Philadelphia v. U.S. Jaycees,* 419 U.S. 1026 (1974). See also the 1977

Yet, to the delight of many women's organizations and civil rights and liberties groups, an alteration in the Court's stance on "all-male" clubs came clearly into view. Thus, in 1984 it applied Minnesota's public accommodation statute making it "an unfair discriminatory practice" to discriminate in public accommodations because of "race, color, creed, religion, disability, national origin, or sex" to the restrictive membership policies of the Jaycees, whose national organization by-laws limited that membership to young men between the ages of eighteen and thirty-five. While Justice Brennan's opinion for the unanimous (7:0) Court[321] conceded that "there can be no clearer example of an intrusion into the internal structure or affairs of an association than a regulation that forces the group to accept members it does not desire," and that freedom of association, protected by the First and Fourteenth Amendments, "plainly supposes a freedom not to associate," Brennan pointed out that "the right to associate for expressive purposes is not absolute." He rejected the Jaycees' contention that the Minnesota law posed "any serious burden on the male members' freedom of expressive association," and he seemed to set the constitutional parameters for future litigation of this nature by apparently distinguishing large associational groups like the Jaycees from those characterized by "relative smallness, a high degree of selectivity in decisions to begin and maintain the affiliation, and seclusion from others." Justice O'Connor, who concurred separately, as did Justice Rehnquist (Chief Justice Burger and Justice Blackmun recused themselves because of their Minnesota ties), wanted to create a distinction resting solely between rights of *commercial* association and rights of *expressive* association. Because she

---

ruling by federal Judge W. C. Conner, upholding the right of the politically influential Town Club of Scarsdale, New York, to continue to bar women as it has done since 1905 (440 F. Supp. 607). The U.S. Supreme Court also refused to review a lower ruling upholding the right of the international Kiwanis organization to withdraw the charter of an affiliate for having admitted women to its membership. (*Kiwanis Club v. Board of Trustees*, 434 U.S. 859 [1977].) In the same year the Illinois Appellate Court, under Illinois's Liquor Control Act, which specifically sanctions "exclusionary policy" for private clubs, held that private clubs may exclude women and members of minority groups as guests. (*The New York Times*, December 25, 1977, p. A27.) But compare *Iron Arrow Honor Society v. Heckler*, 464 U.S. 67 (1983). The tax exemption issue remains murky in this connection: private non-profit fraternal clubs can evidently still enjoy that exemption, even if they discriminate, but all earned income becomes taxable. (*McGlotten v. Connally*, 338 F. Supp. 448, 1972.)

[321]*Roberts v. U.S. Jaycees*, 465 U.S. 455.

viewed the Jaycees as primarily commercial, she concurred in regarding the associational challenge to be without merit.

Evidently the Court found its only female member's argument persuasive, for a major 1987 holding on the issue in a case involving California's Rotary Clubs was based upon Justice O'Connor's dichotomy. She, together with Justice Blackmun, recused herself because of a conflict of interest, but their seven brethren agreed unanimously, in an opinion written by Justice Powell, that the Constitution does not protect sex discrimination by most all-male private clubs, and in particular not by those that are often used for business purposes or by non-members.[322] The Court did not define with precision how private and selective a club would henceforth have to be to mount a successful constitutional prerogative to exclude women—thus leaving the door open for other clubs to argue that they are indeed more private than the Rotary Clubs or the Jaycees.[323] But as for the 19,000 Rotary Clubs, with their 900,000 members in 157 countries, the Powell ruling made clear that in the Court's considered judgment the evidence in the case indicated that the relationship among their members "is not the kind of intimate or private relation that warrants constitutional protection."

Private Schools. Perhaps the most significant and most emotion-charged area of the "private"-"public" dichotomy is that of the Fourteenth Amendment "state action" status, if any, of genuine *private schools.* We know, of course, that those otherwise private institutions of higher and lower learning who receive funds from the federal government have had to toe the proverbial "no discrimination" line in accordance with the mandates of Titles IV, VI, VII, and IX of the Civil Rights Act of 1964, and that the rules laid down by the Departments of Labor, Education, and Health and Human Services have been so adamant and persistent that many aspects of compliance have arguably been justifiably characterized as "reverse discrimination" (of which much more below). But what of the status of governmentally *non*-aided *private* schools? Because they are not covered by the Civil Rights Act of

[322]*Board of Directors of Rotary International v. Rotary Club of Duarte,* 55 LW 4606 (1987).

[323]This argument promised to become a key aspect of putative litigation involving such presumably private clubs as New York City's Century Club, Bethesda, Maryland's Burning Tree Club, and Washington, D.C.'s Cosmos Club. Late in 1987 the Supreme Court agreed to review New York's law aimed at banning sex and race discrimination by all-male private clubs.

1964 (and provided they do not fall under state civil rights statutes), may they not, being indeed private, discriminate in their admissions on whatever basis they may determine? In particular, on the basis of race?

That issue reached the highest court in the land in 1976, when it heard oral arguments in the case of *Runyon v. McCrary*, with the nation a fascinated and interested witness. The Court's decision was almost certain to lead to one of the most far-reaching judgments involving the clash between the private and public realms. Involved were two all-white private Virginia schools in the suburbs of Washington, the Fair-fax-Brewster School and the Bobbe's School, organized in 1955 and 1958, respectively. Neither had ever admitted a black student. When two black youngsters, Michael McCrary and Colin M. Gonzales, were rejected in 1973, their parents filed suit in federal district court, citing §1981 of the now more than a century-old Civil Rights Act of 1866, which was enacted to provide for blacks the same right "to make and enforce contracts . . . as is enjoyed by white citizens." Judge Albert V. Bryan, Jr., ruled firmly that private all-white schools cannot legally bar blacks from admission on the basis of race. No "state action" need be shown, he held: the cited provision of the 1866 Civil Rights Act amply covered the quest for redress.[324]

The schools appealed to the United States Circuit Court of Appeals for the Fourth Circuit, which, in a 4:3 decision, authored by Chief Justice Clement F. Haynsworth, Jr.—of 1969 Supreme Court nomination-rejection fame[325]—narrowly affirmed Judge Bryan's holding.[326] A private school, he wrote, "may not refuse with impunity to accept an otherwise qualified black applicant simply because it declines to admit unqualified white applicants." In the bare majority's view, the pertinent provision of the 1866 law simply prohibited private schools from barring students solely because of their race. The two schools now took their case to the U.S. Supreme Court, where the U.S. Department of Justice submitted a brief *amicus curiae* on the side of the black applicants. The Court's answer came quickly in a historic 7:2 (5:2:2) decision[327] written by Justice Stewart, who was joined by his col-

---

[324]*McCrary v. Runyon*, 363 F. Supp. 1200 (1973).

[325]See my *Justices and Presidents: A Political History of Appointments to the Supreme Court*, 2d ed. (New York: Oxford University Press, 1985), especially Chapter II.

[326]*McCrary v. Runyon*, 515 F 2d 1052 (1975).

[327]*Runyon v. McCrary*, 427 U.S. 160 (1976).

leagues Burger, Brennan, Marshall, and Blackmun—Justices Powell and Stevens concurring separately and with considerable misgivings.[328] The Supreme Court upheld the lower courts, ruling that "private, commercially operated, non-sectarian schools" may not deny "admission to prospective students because they are Negroes." Over a strongly worded dissenting opinion by Justice White, who was joined by Justice Rehnquist, the Court majority based its ruling on the aforementioned section (§1981) of the Civil Rights Acts of 1966—passed to enforce the Thirteenth Amendment's ban on slavery—which accords "all persons the same rights to make and enforce contracts as is enjoyed by white citizens." In response to the schools' contention that this interpretation and application of the statute violate constitutional guarantees of freedom of association, the right to privacy, and parental rights, the controlling opinion found no invasions of any of these safeguards, holding that they "do not provide easy or ready escapes" through which whites "can contravene laws enacted by Congress to enforce the Constitutional right to equality."

But Justice White viewed the legislative history and intent of the section of the 1866 statute at issue utterly differently than did the five-member majority. It confirms, he wrote in his dissenting opinion,

> that the statute means what it says and no more, *i.e.*, that it outlaws any legal rule disabling any person from making or enforcing a contract, but does not prohibit private racial motivated refusals to contract. . . . What is conferred by [the disputed section of the law] is the right—which was enjoyed by whites—"to make contracts with other willing parties and to enforce those contracts in court." . . . The statute by its terms does not *require* any *private* individual or institution to enter into a contract or perform any other act under any circumstances, and it consequently fails to supply a cause of action by respondent students against petitioned schools based on the latter's racially motivated decision not to contract with them.[329]

---

[328]*Ibid.*, at 186, 189. Their reluctant concurrences came almost solely because of what they viewed as the binding 1968 precedent of the *Mayer* decision (footnote 309, p. 402, *supra*), also citing the "*mores* of the day." Powell admitted that he would have sided with the dissenters "if the slate were clean," and Stevens, while acknowledging an almost certain misinterpretation of the Act of 1866 by the majority, pointed to the Court's need for and "interest in stability in orderly development of the law." The all-white Prince Edward Academy in Farmville, Virginia, which had been established in 1959 to avoid integration, admitted its first black students in the fall of 1986.

[329]*Ibid.*, at 195–96. In 1988 the Court ordered the case reargued! (*Patterson v. McLean.*)

In language and philosophy reminiscent of Justices Harlan, II and Frankfurter, he concluded by flaying his colleagues for undertaking the political task of "construing a statute. . . . a task appropriate for the legislature, not the judiciary." Nonetheless, a bit more than a decade later the Court ruled unanimously that the 1866 Civil Rights Act protects not only racial groups—as it had blacks in the above private school case—but also what are now considered ethnic groups, namely Jews and Arabs.[330]

Left intriguingly unanswered until a future day and Court by Justice Stewart's majority opinion were such tantalizing questions as the right of *sectarian* schools to discriminate on the basis of race and, conceivably, the application of the 1866 statute to *private clubs*. What was not difficult to predict is that there would be future litigation involving that fascinatingly vexatious line between liberty and equality. And an answer to the first issue came in mid-1983: two fundamentalist Christian educational institutions, one Bob Jones University, the other Goldsboro Christian School, had long practiced racial discrimination in admissions policy or internal rules of conduct or both—based on their professed religious creed and customs. Ultimately, the Internal Revenue Service withdrew their tax-exempt status, and the two schools, losing in lower federal courts on their First Amendment contentions, appealed to the Supreme Court. In an 8 : 1 opinion, authored by Chief Justice Burger, with only Justice Rehnquist in dissent on grounds of the absence of congressional action on the issue, the high tribunal ruled that the governmental interest in eradicating racial discrimination "substantially outweighs whatever burden denial of tax benefits places on petitioners' exercise of their religious beliefs."[331] Although he concurred with the Court's judgment that Congress had determined that the policy against racial discrimination in education should "override the countervailing interest in permitting unorthodox private behavior," he wrote separately to emphasize that "the balancing of these substantial interests is for *Congress* to perform. . . . It is not appropriate to leave the IRS 'on the cutting edge of developing national policy.' The contours of public

---

[330]*Shaare Tefila Congregation v. Cobb*, 55 LW 4629 (1987), and *Saint Francis College v. Al-Khavraji AKA Allan*, 55 LW 4626 (1987).

[331]*Bob Jones University and Goldsboro Christian School v. United States*, 461 U.S. 574. (Emphasis in original.)

policy should be determined by Congress, not by judges or the IRS."[332]

Thus we return to the basic question of establishing a viable line between "private" and "state" action. Does the line *really* serve the desired purpose when it is applied to such utterly routine governmental services as business registration, licensing,[333] contract enforcement, or probation of wills? One may question the choice of the adjective "utterly" in conjunction with "routine services" yet still acknowledge that when services such as those indicated are categorized as "state action" the private sector becomes an anomaly. Perhaps this has happened, but it is doubtful that a majority of the American polity would subscribe to such a conclusion. In the second Justice Harlan's observation, "[t]he times have changed [but] perhaps it is appropriate to observe that . . . the equal protection clause of [the Fourteenth] Amendment [does not] rigidly impose upon America an ideology of unrestrained egalitarianism."[334] For, as he had commented on an earlier occasion: "Freedom of the individual to choose his associates or his neighbors, to use and dispose of his property as he sees fit, to be irrational, arbitrary, capricious, even unjust in his personal relations, are things all entitled to a large measure of protection from governmental interference."[335] And as Professor Joseph Tussman, a proved and dedicated partisan of the cause of civil rights and liberties, put the matter of the private-public distinction:

> Do we really want, in the end, to make impossible an Armenian or Jewish Home for the Aged? Do we really wish to deny to the harassed ethnocentric commuter to the polyglot city the solace of spending the evenings of his life in the bosom of a monochromatic suburb? Must the Black Muslims admit White Christians? Must the Far Eastern Cafe hire blond waiters? Cannot the

[332]*Ibid.*, concurring opinion, at 612. (Emphasis in original.) For an intriguing *quaere* on tax exemption involving the *Bob Jones* issue(s), see Dean M. Kelley's "Guest Editorial: A New Meaning for Tax Exemption," 25 *Journal of Church and State* 415 (Autumn, 1983).

[333]See *Jackson v. Metropolitan Edison Co.*, 419 U.S. 345 (1974), in which the Court, dividing 6 : 3, held that a Pennsylvania electric company was not related closely enough to the state government merely because it held a license to service, and that consumers were hence unable to raise "due process of law" claims.

[334]*Harper v. Virginia Board of Elections*, 383 U.S. 663 (1965), dissenting opinion, at 678.

[335]*Lombard v. Louisiana*, 373 U.S. 267 (1963), dissenting opinion, at 250.

Cosmos Club be silly without losing its liquor license? Is there not some point of saying that much must wait on the slow process of education and maturation?[336]

One can wholly support, encourage, fight for, and even die for the eradication of the fundamental injustices in the realm of racial discrimination; equality before the law and of economic, educational, and cultural opportunity; the suffrage; access to the rewards and responsibilities of public office; the end of state-supported or state-permitted or state-enforced segregation—these are the aspects of the problem that should, and do matter! Indeed, a general consensus exists here. But there is less agreement on wills, clubs, and societies. There *is* something to be said for privacy of association, no matter how silly, undemocratic, or puerile. While, generally, the "equal protection" clause does preclude state enforcement of private discrimination, there may thus well be, in the words of Professor Louis Henkin, one of the foremost students of the field—and a devoted libertarian—"a small area of liberty favored by the Constitution even over claims to equality. Rights of liberty and property, of privacy and voluntary association, must be balanced, in close cases, against the right not to have the state enforce discrimination against the victim. In the few instances in which the right to discriminate is protected or preferred by the Constitution, the state may enforce it."[337] Unquestionably, this stance raises as many problems as it professes to solve, but a dogmatic approach is no answer either. In part, of course, such legislation as the public accommodations title of the Civil Rights Act of 1964, enacted by the nation's legislative representatives, and subsequently upheld by the Supreme Court, settles the matter in an orderly and legal fashion. So does the "open housing" section of the Civil Rights Act of 1968—whatever one's view of its wisdom.

Yet not all aspects of the vexatious public versus private problem can be conclusively settled by legislative action, nor should they be. There will always be gray areas that should be treated with common sense—a common sense cognizant of our responsibilities as well as our ideals, a common sense that is conscious both of constitutional commands and of the need to strike a balance between liberty and equality. When all other

[336]Ed., *The Supreme Court on Racial Discrimination* (New York: Oxford University Press, 1963), p. 5. Reprinted by permission.
[337]"*Shelley v. Kraemer*, Notes for a Revised Opinion," *op. cit.*, p. 496.

avenues fail, the last word may well have to be given by the judiciary, that branch of our government that has proved itself more capable than any other of guarding our basic civil rights and liberties. As Justice Douglas once wrote: "The people should know that when filibusters occupy other forums, when oppressions are great, when the clash of authority between the individual and the State is severe, they can still get justice in the courts."[338] But in the final analysis all judicial actions must be grounded in constitutional authority.

[338]*Bell v. Maryland*, 378 U.S. 226 (1964), concurring opinion, at 242–45.

chapter *VIII* *Gender and Race Under the New Equal Protection*

In a host of ways, although superficially differing in kind, degree, and genesis, discrimination on the basis of sex—or, perhaps more appropriately termed, gender-based discrimination—is part and parcel of the American dilemma. Such discrimination is now constitutionally impermissible. Although there has long been a "women's movement," the issue of invidious discrimination in the realm of gender did not really impress itself upon the public conscience in majoritarian contemplation until the desegregation movement in the racial sphere evolved close to its crescendo in the mid- to late 1960s. And, as has been so true of invidious racial discrimination, it would again preeminently be the judiciary that was called upon initially to articulate and to mandate the parameters of egalitarianism and equal opportunity in the realm of sex, broadly based upon the implicit and explicit commands of the "equal protection of the laws"—in its "new" model—and the "due process of law" clauses of the basic document.[1]

A Glance at the Evolving History of Gender Discrimination

That women have faced special obstacles deriving from their historically *subordinate* role in American society is axiomatic: sexually stereotyped, their economic, educational, and political opportunities subordinated to that of males—even their legal position suffered from a double standard. Moreover, while the strivings of blacks were directed against a legal tradition designed to retain them in a *subservient* status, women had to direct their struggle against a deeply ingrained tradition that was patently designed to accord them a *protective* as well as a

[1]See Chapter II, *supra*.

subordinate status. Thus, in 1908, in a constitutional landmark decision that upheld a 1903 Oregon statute limiting female workers in mechanical establishments, factories, and laundries to a ten-hour work day, the State's victory came clearly because of attorney—and future United States Supreme Court Justice—Louis D. Brandeis's brilliant brief (which, incidentally, heralded the utilization of social science data in the judicial process). Here, in what would become known as the "Brandeis Brief," the scholarly Boston lawyer attained a unanimous Court victory by disposing of the constitutional issues and precedents (chiefly apposite to the Fourteenth Amendment's due process of law clause) in two pages, but devoting more than one hundred pages to statistical data on hours of labor, health, morals, and factory legislation abroad—all emphasizing the protective status of women. Accepting Brandeis's contentions, Justice David Brewer, speaking for the Court, justified its decision, *inter alia,* as follows:

> The two sexes differ in structure of body, in the functions to be performed by each, in the amount of physical strength, in the capacity for long-continued labor, particularly when done standing, . . . the self-reliance which enables one to assert full rights, and in the capacity to maintain the struggle for subsistence. This difference justifies a difference in legislation and upholds that which is designed to compensate for some of the burdens which rest upon her.[2]

Today's jurists would hardly be likely to employ such language!

Women's egalitarian movements existed prior to our days, but they were not generally or overridingly successful at any of the governmental branches, and especially not at the federal level, despite isolated victories such as Wyoming's grant of the right to vote to women in 1869, while still a territory. When Congress made noises about "this petticoat provision" in Wyoming's application for statehood in 1890, the territory's legislature responded that it would stay out of the Union a hundred years rather than enter it without women's suffrage.[3] Indeed, led by the pioneering West, more than one-half of the states had granted women the suffrage by the end of World War I. Yet, in the pithy comment by

---

[2]*Muller v. Oregon,* 208 U.S. 412.

[3]James McGregor Burns, J. W. Peltason, and Thomas E. Cronin, *Government by the People,* 11th ed. (Englewood Cliffs, N.J.: Prentice-Hall, Inc., 1981), p. 114.

United States Circuit Court Judge Ruth Bader Ginsburg, except for the Nineteenth Amendment—which, in 1920, granted women the right to vote in *all* federal and state elections—"the Constitution remained an empty cupboard for sex equality claims."[4] It would take another fifty years before the Supreme Court would bite the proverbial bullet and begin to strike at invidious gender discrimination. Surprisingly, it was *not* the Warren Court, which did so much, and so decisively, to attack racial discrimination, but the Burger Court that would recognize women's rightful constitutional claims as of the beginning of the 1970s. The Warren Court had maintained a passive stance, generally inclining to uphold gender-based legislative classifications by invoking the "reasonable man" or "rational person"[5] standard of adjudication—and women continued to be denied equal rights, equal pay, and a host of *a priori* justifiable legal claims. Disabilities imposed by both federal and state laws were endemic and rampant.

But, perhaps inevitably, the 1960s would witness a significant degree of legislative action on the federal level to commence the changes which many now take for granted. One of the catalysts in the now-no-longer-to-be-denied egalitarian movement on the gender front was feminist activist Betty Friedan's highly influential, widely noted, and eagerly read *The Feminine Mystique,* which was published in 1963.[6] There is simply no doubt that her work served to raise women's consciousness far beyond the once so commonly accepted notion that a woman's place was essentially in the home, that by and large the proper and appropriate role was that of wife, mother, and housekeeper. That same eventful year saw some long-overdue action by Congress with the adoption of the Equal Pay Act as an amendment to the Fair Labor Standards Act, embracing the basic principle of equal pay for equal work, regardless of sex. And just one year later Congress enacted the seminal Civil Rights Act of 1964, Title VII of which prohibited discrimination on the ground of sex by employer, labor unions and organizations, and employment agencies. Its Title V was amended in 1972 to include gender discrimination as a trigger for the denial of federal aid funds to any public or private program or activity, and Title IX, also adopted in 1972, made a

---

[4]"Employment of the Constitution to Advance the Equal Status of Men and Women," unpublished paper delivered at Hebrew University, Jerusalem, May 19, 1987, p. 4.
[5]See Chapter II, *supra.*
[6](New York: W. W. Norton & Co.)

point of ascertaining that equal athletic facilities opportunities were available to women—amidst anguished wails by male coaches, especially those in contact sports. They appear to have survived, however.

The E.R.A. Struggle. The indisputable accretion and extension of rights to women, by both judicial and legislative action, seemed to herald relatively easy sailing for an "Equal Rights Amendment" (E.R.A.). In fact, such an amendment had been in the congressional hoppers since 1923, but it had never garnered the necessary two-thirds majority for passage in both houses. Its operative clause read: "Equality of rights under the law shall not be denied by the United States or any State on account of sex." Resuscitated amidst widespread support, led by the increasingly visible and influential National Organization for Women (NOW) and the National Women's Political Caucus, founded in 1966 and 1971, respectively, the E.R.A. passed Congress overwhelmingly in 1972, by votes of 84 : 8 in the Senate and 354 : 24 in the House. Its future looked bright indeed.

That optimism seemed wholly justified when the legislatures of twenty-two states ratified the E.R.A. within twelve months of its passage, almost always by huge margins. But three years later that enthusiastic reception had obviously slowed markedly, and two of the erstwhile ratifiers, Nebraska and Tennessee, voted to rescind their initial "aye" actions. By 1978, while thirty-five states had ratified, three had changed their minds; even not counting the recissions, the E.R.A. still lacked three votes; and March 22, 1979, the deadline for ratification, loomed on the horizon. In what was indubitably an action of highly questionable constitutionality, Congress, by simple majority vote, extended the ratification deadline to June 30, 1982—but none of the fifteen state refusers would change their minds. The E.R.A. was dead. In view of the significant progress of the women's movement and the Court's generous rulings in its favor, it may well be doubted that the E.R.A., or a similar measure, will become constitutional law. As James Q. Wilson succinctly summarized the reasons for its failure to do so: "The ERA became an issue that symbolized the conflict over a broad range of cultural values in the United States."[7] Since it is always difficult to obtain ratification by three-fourths of the states—and,

[7]*American Government: Institutions and Policies,* 3rd ed. (Lexington, Mass.: D. C. Heath and Co., 1986), p. 560.

except for unicameral Nebraska, both houses of each state legislature had to vote affirmatively—it was not surprising that well-organized, confirmed opposition groups such as the Mormons, the National Council of Catholic Women, other important segments of orthodox religions, and tireless crusading individuals, such as Phyllis Schlafly and her Eagle Forum, would triumph in blocking the E.R.A.'s enactment. But the Supreme Court proved to be a sympathetic interpreter of the Fifth and Fourteenth Amendments and, arguably, the Court may well have achieved what the E.R.A. was expected to accomplish (as the following text and Table 8.1 demonstrate).

The Court's Attack on Gender Discrimination. Two years after President Nixon had appointed Warren Earl Burger Chief Justice of the United States, the latter wrote an opinion on the gender discrimination front that heralded a new day for egalitarianism. As the front page of the *New York Times* announced in large type on November 23, 1971: "Court, for First Time, Overrules a State Law That Favors Men." Indeed, not since the Fourteenth Amendment's birth in 1866 and its ratification in 1868 had the Supreme Court of the United States provided a victory for women on the ground that a state had violated its equal protection of the laws mandate. Here, in the now memorable case of *Reed v. Reed,*[8] the Court *unanimously* struck down an Idaho statute that accorded men preference over women in administering deceased persons' estates. It marked the first time that the Court had invalidated a state law on grounds of sex discrimination.

In doing so the Justices applied the traditional "rationality" test, which merely requires a judicial judgment whether or not rational or reasonable legislators could constitutionally enact legislation of the type under attack. Not wisdom, fairness, intelligence, or even democracy is thus an issue: the key is the law's "reasonableness." In the Idaho case, however, the Court, applying that test, found that its legislature had made an "arbitrary" decision to favor men over women, in order to spare trial judges from having to decide in each case who was best suited to administer each contested estate. The result, wrote the Chief Justice of the United States, was to divide men and women into separate classes "on the basis of criteria wholly unrelated" to the objective of efficient distribution of estates. And he thus concluded that, plainly,

[8]404 U.S. 71 (1971).

Idaho's women had been denied equal legal rights—even under the otherwise so deferential-to-legislative-action test of "reasonableness" or "rationality." But as the anti-gender-discrimination movement grew and matured, the judiciary was soon persuaded also to utilize tests that would be more generous to aggrieved plaintiffs. Soon the scrutiny the Court extended to allegation of gender discrimination thus commenced to embrace stricter standards, with the scrutiny ranging from "close" to "heightened," stopping just short of adopting the "suspect" plane standard that the Court had adopted for claims of racial discrimination.[9] The latter became a live issue with the Court's significant 8 : 1 ruling in the important 1973 case of *Frontiero v. Richardson*.[10]

In that litigation, Air Force Lieutenant Sharron Frontiero objected to a federal statute under which male officers automatically qualified for benefits for their wives, whereas female officers could obtain the same benefits only upon profiding proof that their husbands were dependent upon them for support. Recognizing this injustice, the court, in the plurality opinion written by Justice Brennan, with Justice Rehnquist in solitary dissent, declared that the federal government had failed to demonstrate the necessary "compelling interest" to justify the law's distinction between men and women; that laws such as the instant one "in practical effect . . . put women, not on a pedestal, but in a cage."[11] Indeed, joined by his colleagues Douglas, White, and Marshall, Brennan now wanted to establish the application of the "suspect" category test to gender discrimination—just as it had already been judicially embraced for the realms of race, alienage, and nationality. But he fell short of securing the necessary fifth vote, the other four concurring Justices—Stewart, Powell, Blackmun, and the Chief Justice—contending in two separate opinions that it was "unnecessary . . . to characterize sex as a suspect classification"; that *Frontiero* should be decided on the basis of the "rationality" test utilized in *Reed;* and that "any expansion of its rationale" should be reserved for the future.[12] Although more than fifteen years have passed at this writing (mid-1988), and although the Court's membership changed by four in

[9]See Chapter II, *supra.*
[10]411 U.S. 677.
[11]*Ibid.*
[12]See the concurring opinion by Justice Powell, joined by Chief Justice Burger and Justice Blackman. Justice Stewart concurred separately.

the interim, including the appointment of the first woman, the Court has declined to embrace the "suspect" test for gender discrimination.

What it has done, on the other hand, is to adopt a "heightened" or "intermediate" scrutiny standard test, one it developed with considerable aplomb in *Craig v. Boren*[13] in 1976. There, Oklahoma's 3.2 percent beer regulation law prohibited the beverage's sale to males under the age of twenty-one, but to females only under eighteen. Over dissents by Chief Justice Burger and Justice Rehnquist, who regarded the state law as entirely sustainable under the "rationality" test, Justice Brennan's opinion struck it down as invidiously discriminatory under the equal protection of the laws clause of the Fourteenth Amendment. In therewith adopting its new "heightened scrutiny" test, the Court let it be known that it would no longer sustain differential treatment of men and women that was merely *rationally* related to some *permissible* government objective; that, instead, the Court would henceforth strike down any gender classification absent a *substantial* relationship to an *important* government objective.[14] Thus we see that, while the Court has neither totally abandoned the "rationality" test nor embraced the "suspect category" test, it has, in general, embraced the "heightened or 'intermediate' level of scrutiny" test developed in *Craig v. Boren* in 1976. And it is noteworthy that the victors in that case were *male,* just as Justice O'Connor's opinion of the 5:4 majority in *Mississippi University for Women v. Hogan*[15] in 1982 held in favor of *male* registered nurse Joe Hogan, who had been denied admission to MUW's School of Nursing solely because of his sex. "That this statute discriminates against males rather than females," lectured the Court's first woman member, "does not exempt it from scrutiny or reduce the standard of review." Chief Justice Burger, Justice Blackmun, and Justices Powell and Rehnquist dissented in three separate opinions, each of which in one degree or other maintained that Mississippi's policy of single-sex admission for what was the oldest state-supported all-female university in the nation was both "benign" and "compensatory" and was readily sustainable under the "rationality" test. Many commentators agreed— but five votes beat four!

Table 8.1 (below) demonstrates that the Court has, in general, fol-

[13]429 U.S. 190.
[14]Ginsburg, *op. cit.,* fn. 4, p. 15.
[15]458 U.S. 718.

Table 8.1

REPRESENTATIVE DECISIONS BY THE UNITED STATES SUPREME COURT IN RECENT GENDER-BASED DISCRIMINATION CASES

CASE	YEAR DECIDED	ISSUE AND DISPOSITION	VOTE	DISSENTS
Reed v. Reed, 404 U.S. 71	1971	State of Idaho gave preference to males in intestate administration. Declared a violation of the equal protection clause of the Fourteenth Amendment, based on the Court's "rationality" test.	9:0	None
Frontiero v. Richardson, 411 U.S. 677	1973	Federal law that automatically qualified male service personnel for spousal benefits but that required female personnel to show proof of dependency. Declared unconstitutional infringement of due process clause of the Fifth Amendment, since Court found no "compelling" state interest.	8:1	Rehnquist
Kahn v. Shevin, 416 U.S. 351	1974	Florida law granting widows but not widowers $500 property-tax exemption. Declared constitutional because a woman's loss of spouse imposed greater financial disability usually than a man's loss of spouse.	6:3	Douglas Brennan Marshall
Geduldig v. Aiello, 417 U.S. 484	1974	State of California disability insurance payments to private employees not covered by workmen's compensation, *excluding* normal pregnancies, among other disabilities. Upheld as a rational choice by state.	6:3	Douglas Brennan Marshall
Schlesinger v. Ballard, 419 U.S. 498	1975	Federal law on mandatory Navy discharges: women guaranteed 13 years of service; men automatically discharged after failing twice to be promoted. Upheld as rational because women have less opportunity for promotion.	5:4	Douglas Brennan Marshall White
Taylor v. Louisiana, 419 U.S. 522	1975	Louisiana statutory and constitutional provisions excluded women from juries unless they manifest a desire to serve via a written request. Declared unconstitutional as violation of equal protection clause of the Fourteenth Amendment.	8:1	Rehnquist
Stanton v. Stanton, 421 U.S. 7	1975	Utah law that provides for lower age of majority for girls than for boys in connection with parental obligation to pay child support. Struck down as "irrational" legislative action.	8:1	Rehnquist

Case	Year	Description	Vote	
Weinberger v. Wiesenfeld, 420 U.S. 636	1975	U.S. Social Security Act provision for payment of death benefits to surviving spouse and minor children in case of husband's death, but only to the latter in case of wife's demise. Struck down as violative of Fifth Amendment's due process of law guarantees.	8:0	None
General Electric Co. v. Gilbert, 429 U.S. 125	1976	Private employer's disability plan excluded pregnancies from coverage. Upheld as not invidiously discriminatory under due process of law clause of the Fifth Amendment. (Later overturned in corrective legislation by Congress.)	6:3	Brennan Marshall Stevens
Craig v. Boren, 429 U.S. 190	1976	Oklahoma statute prohibiting sale of 3.2 percent beer to males under 21 years of age but to females only under 18. Held to be invidiously discriminatory under equal protection clause of the Fourteenth Amendment, the Court here introducing the "heightened scrutiny" test.	7:2	Burger Rehnquist
Califano v. Webster, 430 U.S. 313	1977	Section of federal Social Security Act providing that wives may exclude three more of their lower earning years in computing average wage for retirement benefits than husbands may. Upheld as "benign," not illogical, and thus not constitutionally defective. Cf. Califano v. Goldfarb, 430 U.S. 199 (1977).	9:0	None
Vorchheimer v. School District of Philadelphia, 430 U.S. 703	1977	Philadelphia's existence of some "all-boy" and some "all-girl" public schools is permissible, provided enrollment is voluntary and quality is equal.	4:4	Brennan Marshall Blackmun Stevens
Nashville Gas Co. v. Satty, 434 U.S. 136	1977	Distinguishing Gilbert, supra, Court holds that losing all accumulated seniority when returning to work after pregnancy violates Title VII of C.R.A. of 1964.	9:0	None
City of Los Angeles Department of Water v. Manhart, 435 U.S. 702	1978	Municipal regulation that required female employees to pay 15 percent more into pension fund than male employees because women expect statistically to live longer than men. Declared unconstitutional as violation of equal protection of the laws clause of Amendment Fourteen.	6:2	Burger Rehnquist

(continued)

Table 8.1 *(Continued)*

CASE	YEAR DECIDED	ISSUE AND DISPOSITION	VOTE	DISSENTS
Orr v. Orr, 440 U.S. 268	1979	Alabama law providing that husbands but not wives are liable to pay post-divorce alimony. Struck down as violation of equal protection clause of Fourteenth Amendment.	6:3	Burger Powell Rehnquist
Califano v. Westcott, 443 U.S. 76	1979	Section of federal Social Security Act providing benefits to needy dependent children only because of father's unemployment, not because of mother's. Struck down as violation of the due process clause of the Fifth Amendment.	9:0	None
Wengler v. Druggists Mutual Insurance Co., 446 U.S. 142	1980	Section of Missouri's workmen's compensation law that requires a husband to prove actual dependence on his spouse's earnings but does not require wife to prove such dependence. Declared unconstitutional as violation of the equal protection clause of the Fourteenth Amendment.	8:1	Rehnquist
Michael M. v. Superior Court, 450 U.S. 464	1981	California statutory rape law punishing males, but not females, for sexual intercourse with an underage partner of the opposite sex upheld as not irrational because "only women may become pregnant." Law defines unlawful sexual intercourse as "an act of sexual intercourse accomplished with a female not the wife of the perpetrator where the female is under the age of 18."	5:4	Brennan White Marshall Stevens
Rostker v. Goldberg, 453 U.S. 57	1981	Draft Registration Act of 1980, confined to males. See text, *supra,* for discussion.	6:3	Brennan White Marshall
McCarty v. McCarty, 453 U.S. 210	1981	Federal law to preserve regular and reserve commissioned officers' military pensions as the service member's "personal entitlement" *not* subject to being considered for anyone else's benefit in a property or divorce settlement. (Later overturned by corrective legislation by Congress.)	6:3	Brennan Stewart Rehnquist

Case	Year		Vote	
Kirchberg v. Feenstra, 450 U.S. 455	1981	Louisiana law giving husband the unilateral right to dispose of property jointly owned by husband and wife declared unconstitutional as invidious discrimination by gender.	9 : 0	None
Mississippi University for Women v. Hogan, 458 U.S. 718	1982	Single-sex public institution of higher learning discriminates against males. See text, *supra*, for discussion.	5 : 4	Blackmun Powell Rehnquist Burger
Arizona v. Norris, 464 U.S. 808	1983	Title VII of Civil Rights Act of 1964, which outlaws employment discrimination on the basis of both race and sex, requires employees to be treated as individuals rather than as members of a group (here women's level of pensions).	5 : 4	Burger Blackmun Powell Rehnquist
Roberts v. U.S. Jaycees, 465 U.S. 555	1984	Rejecting freedom of association argument by the Jaycees, Court rules through Brennan that the "large and basically unselective" nature of the organization could not vitiate Minnesota's law forbidding discrimination in "public accommodations." (See text, *supra*, for discussion.)	7 : 0	None
Hishon v. King & Spaulding, 467 U.S. 69	1984	The no-gender-discrimination mandate of Title VII of the Civil Rights Act of 1964 reaches the issue of promotion of lawyers to the status of *partners* in a law firm. Burger's opinion overturns two lower federal court holdings to the contrary, rejects the argument that "partners" are not "employees" under Title VII and should therefore not be covered by its terms. Also turned aside freedom-of-association claims.	9 : 0	None
Grove City College v. Bell, 465 U.S. 555	1984	Title IX of the Federal Education Act of 1972 subjects non-compliant institutions to federal fund cut-offs, since any aid to students constitutes aid to their colleges. However, the law's verbiage "any educational program or activity receiving federal financial assistance" means *only* the *specific* program of a college and *not the entire* institution. The holding was re-affirmed 6 : 3 in 1986 in *Department of Transportation v. Paralyzed Vets of America*, 55 LW1004. (But Congress took corrective action in 1988 over President Reagan's veto.)	6 : 3	Brennan Marshall Stevens

(continued)

Table 8.1 (Continued)

CASE	YEAR DECIDED	ISSUE AND DISPOSITION	VOTE	DISSENTS
Board of Directors of Rotary International v. Rotary Club of Duarte, 55 LW 4606	1987	Decision similar to *Roberts, supra*: states may outlaw gender discrimination by certain types of private clubs. See text, *supra*, for discussion.	7:0	None
California Savings & Loan Association v. Guerra, 55 LW 4077	1987	Upheld a California law requiring employers to grant up to four months of unpaid leave to women "disabled" by pregnancy and childbirth, even if similar leaves are not granted for other disabilities. Dissenters saw a violation of the 1978 federal law prohibiting employers from treating pregnant employees differently from other employees who are "similar in their ability or inability to work."	6:3	White Rehnquist Powell
Johnson v. Transportation Agency of Santa Clara County, 55 LW 4379	1987	C.R.A. of 1964 permits employers to promote a woman over a more qualified man. See text, *infra*, for discussion.	6:3	Rehnquist White Scalia

lowed the test developed in *Craig v. Boren;* but it has not been unwilling to apply the *Reed* rationale when it has seemed appropriate. Consequently, as the plethora of successive decisions amply manifests, while the vast majority of holdings in the cascading number of cases on the gender discrimination front has favored claims of invidious gender discrimination, rulings *permitting* differences based on sex are not unknown. Among them have been the following: Florida (1974) may grant widows but not widowers a $500 tax exemption, because a woman's loss of a husband normally imposes a greater financial disability than a man's loss of a wife;[16] the U.S. Navy (1975) may guarantee female officers thirteen years of service, whereas men are automatically discharged after twice failing of promotion, because women have less opportunity for promotion;[17] Philadelphia (1977) may have "all-boy" and "all-girl" public schools, provided that enrollment is voluntary and the quality of instruction is equal;[18] the federal Social Security Act (1977) may permit wives to exclude three more of their lower-earning years in computing the average wage for retirement benefits than may husbands, because of the "historical disparity in earning power";[19] a California law (1981) that punishes males but not females for statutory rape (under eighteen) is considered permissible and not irrational, because "only women may become pregnant."[20] But a glance at Table 8.1 will quickly indicate that, especially of late, few differences based on sex have been Court-sanctioned. One that was, and deserves special notice, is the Draft Registration Act of 1980.

Draft Registration: Rostker v. Goldberg.[21] The contentious enactment of the draft-registration statute of 1980, which specifically *excluded* women, created natural controversy by friend and foe of sexual equality alike, all of which tended to blur lines between otherwise predictable supporters and opponents of legislative classification by gender. A major class-action suit was filed almost instantly in federal court by a group of *male* registrants, alleging invidious sex discrimination. *Either,* so their argument went, the exclusion of women con-

[16]*Kahn v. Shevin,* 416 U.S. 351.
[17]*Schlesinger v. Ballard,* 419 U.S. 498.
[18]*Vorchheimer v. School District of Philadelphia,* 430 U.S. 703.
[19]*Califano v. Webster,* 430 U.S. 213.
[20]*Michael M. v. Superior Court,* 450 U.S. 464.
[21]453 U.S. 57 (1981).

stitutes a violation of their Fifth Amendment constitutional rights of due process of law ("equal protection" *per se* not being applicable because it is confined to *state* infractions under the Fourteenth Amendment) *or* it constitutes a violation of the rights of *males* because they are being "singled out." The Court's answer came in June 1981. Speaking through Justice Rehnquist, who applied the heightened scrutiny test developed in *Craig v. Boren,* it ruled 6 : 3 that the registration provisions excluding women do not violate the Fifth Amendment; that Congress acted well within its constitutional authority to raise and regulate armies and navies. Noting that Congress had already acted to bar women from combat roles, the majority insisted that the "customary deference" accorded Congress's judgments is "particularly appropriate" in national defense and military affairs. Dissenting, Justices Brennan, White, and Marshall contended that the *complete* exclusion of women was not a valid governmental objective and thus violated the due process of law guarantees of both sexes.

Brennan and Marshall were the only dissenters when the Court ruled 6 : 2 three years later that a much-debated law, which required male college students to register for the draft if they wish to obtain federal financial aid, was constitutional as "a plainly rational means to improve compliance with the registration requirements" (which had been flouted by a sizable number of potential registrants).[22] The application of the registration statute itself and prosecution thereunder was upheld 7 : 2 in early 1985, again with Justices Brennan and Marshall in dissent, here on grounds of First Amendment freedom of expression as well as Fifth Amendment due process of law.[23]

The 1973 Abortion Decisions

If any Supreme Court ruling lies at the center of gravity of the success of the feminist movement, it is that tribunal's seminal holding in the now legendary *Abortion* cases of *Roe v. Wade* and *Doe v. Bolton.*[24] Already analyzed briefly in connection with the developing law of privacy,[25] the two decisions did not, like the vast majority of the afore-

---

[22]*Selective Service System v. Minnesota Public Interest Resource Group,* 468 U.S. 841 (1984).

[23]*Wayte v. United States,* 470 U.S. 598.

[24]410 U.S. 113 and 410 U.S. 179, respectively.

[25]See Chapter III, *supra,* pp. 74–78.

mentioned or analyzed gender discrimination, turn on claims of violation of the equal protection of the laws. Rather, the basic rights they
created on that Opinion Day in 1973 were based upon the newly articulated—largely Justice Douglas–developed—right of privacy in the
Ninth Amendment, coupled with the due process of law commands of
the Fourteenth (and, by implication, of the Fifth on the federal level).
When the two controversial decisions were handed own, abortion law
was already in a state of flux and change throughout the several states of
the nation. Liberalization of state abortion laws, as the Court's opinion,
written by Justice Blackmun, recognized, had been well under way for
some time. However, a well-organized, highly vocal "right-to-life"
movement had begun to succeed in either delaying or even reversing
that tide, and criminal abortion statutes remained on the books of many
a state.

The *Roe* and *Doe* decisions, which instantly became and remain a
veritable constitutional, legal, medical, sociological, anthropological,
social, religious, moral, psychological, and—markedly—political
storm center, personify women's civil rights strivings. Justice
Blackmun's opinion for the 7 : 2 Court—which took two years to com-
pose—frankly recognized "the sensitive and emotional nature of the
abortion controversy, of the vigorous opposing views, even among
physicians, and of the deep and seemingly absolute convictions that the
subject inspires." Indeed, six of the nine Justices were moved to pen
opinions, four on the side of the majority (Blackmun, Burger, Stewart,
and Douglas) and two in dissent (White and Rehnquist). Justice
Blackmun's controlling opinion for the Court held that the right to
personal privacy includes the abortion decision; but he acknowledged
that this right is not unqualified and must be considered against important state regulatory interests. On the other hand, he made it clear that
such a "fundamental right" as abortion may be limited by the state only
in the face of a "compelling state interest" and that "legislative enactments must be narrowly drawn to express only the legitimate state
interests at stake. . . ." He concluded that the Texas and Georgia abortion control statutes in front of the Court failed that basic test by
"sweeping too broadly." Over Justice White's outcry that the decisions
constituted "an exercise of raw judicial power," and that by Justice
Rehnquist that there is no such thing as the right of "privacy" involved
in the matter at issue, the lengthy Blackmun opinion, replete with
references to medical science, biology, psychology, and history, ulti-

mately neatly summarizes the pioneering constitutional holding as follows:

> (a) For the stage prior to approximately the end of the first trimester [of the pregnancy], the abortion decision and its effectuation must be left to the medical judgment of the pregnant woman's physician.
>
> (b) For the stage subsequent to approximately the end of the first semester, the State, in promoting its interest in the health of the mother, may, if it chooses, regulate the abortion procedure in ways that are reasonably related to maternal health.
>
> (c) For the stage subsequent to viability the State, in promoting its interest in the potentiality of human life, may, if it chooses, regulate, and even proscribe, abortion except where it is necessary, in appropriate medical judgment, for the preservation of the life or health of the mother.[26]

That the creation of what opponents have called a "national abortion code created by judicial fiat rather than by legislative action" would spawn a torrent of attacks on a host of judicial, legislative, and executive fronts[27] is hardly astonishing. Yet, in essence, the gravamen of the 1973 *Abortion* cases remains intact, notwithstanding a plethora of cases before the Court, three new Justices on it, and the passage of fifteen years. While it is entirely conceivable that the Court may approve some legislative forays in the second or third trimester, it seems highly unlikely that the crucial first trimester will be subjected to a decisive change, let alone an overruling. But nothing is impossible in the judicial process.

Not all of the goals of the feminist movement have been achieved, yet enormous strides have been taken toward the eradication of invidious gender discrimination. Much remains to be done, but the improvements that have characterized the past two decades are proof positive of genuine achievements on the egalitarian agenda. The absence of the Equal Rights Amendment has not stifled or truncated the continuing commitment to the enhancement of women's rights, and a glance at the demonstrably significant gains achieved on a host of fronts—economic, social, legal, and political—underscores that fact. Such visible political triumphs as, for example, a Vice-Presidential candidate in 1984 (Geraldine Ferraro); a United States Supreme Court Justice in 1981

---

[26]*Roe v. Wade*, 410 U.S. 113, at 164.
[27]See Chapter III, *supra*, especially footnotes 202–209 and accompanying text.

(Sandra Day O'Connor); seven members of cabinets under Presidents Carter and Reagan; several Governors; mayors of a number of our largest cities (e.g., Dallas and Houston); 25 members of Congress (1988); some 1,200 state legislators (1988); 2,200 women jurists (1988), up from 600 in 1980; numerous college and university presidencies (including the University of Chicago and the University of Wisconsin), deanships of prestigious law schools (e.g., Columbia University)—all point to genuine amelioration. The latter will unquestionably continue. And it is clear that in considerable measure the nation's commitment to "affirmative action" programs, however controversial and embattled they may be, has played a major role in the quest for equality in the universes of both gender and race.

The Wrench of "Affirmative Action" and "Reverse Discrimination"

As the history of the post–World War ll period, especially the post–Brown I and II[28] days, has demonstrated incontestably, the advances in the desegregation-integration and gender realms have been as widespread and evident as they have been gratifying. The nation, led by the judiciary, then joined by the executive and legislative branches, acknowledged the injustices of the past and proceeded, however gradually at first, to make amends.

Yet much remains to be done, in particular on the economic frontier. It is thus hardly surprising that the 1960s and, more insistently, the 1970s and 1980s would bring demands from blacks, as well as other minority groups and, of course, women that programs be established, both in and out of government, that would go well beyond "mere" equality of opportunity and provide compensatory treatment for the injustices of three centuries by commitments not only to remedial action but to outright preferment on a host of fronts, headed by employment and education. Known as "affirmative action" to bring about increased employment opportunities, promotions, and admission to colleges and universities for minorities and women, the programs soon became controversial because of their use of *quotas,* particularly racial quotas, also

---

[28]*Brown v. Board of Education of Topeka,* 347 U.S. 483 (1954) and 349 U.S. 294 (1955)—commonly referred to as "*Brown* I" and "*Brown* II."

called "goals" and/or "guidelines." In other words, the basic plea, along with the philosophy of the *proponents* of "affirmative action," was (and is) that it is not enough to provide a full measure of absolute equality of opportunity, based upon individual merit. Given the ravages of the past, preferential treatment must be accorded through affirmative action that, in effect, all but guarantees numerically targeted slots or posts based upon membership in racial (and sexual) groups. The *opponents* of such a course of public and, to a lesser degree, private policy do not necessarily object to affirmative action *per se*—such as aggressive recruiting, remedial training (no matter what the expense), and perhaps even what Justice Powell in the *Bakke* case styled a "plus" consideration of race along with other equitable factors.[29] But they do object to policies that may be regarded as "reverse discrimination," generally comprehending the *numerus clausus* (rigid quotas set aside to benefit identifiable racial or other groups), as in the *Weber* case;[30] double standards in grading, rating, ranking, admissions, job placement, promotions, and similar requirements on the employment, educational, and other pertinent thresholds of opportunity; and so-called setaside laws that guarantee specified percentages of contracts to minority groups, as in the *Fullilove* case.[31]

The Bakke Case. It was a foregone conclusion that, sooner or later, the "reverse discrimination" issue(s) would reach the Supreme Court—especially in view of what seems to be the proscriptive intent of the Fourteenth Amendment with respect to race; judicial precedents pointing to "color blindness"; and, perhaps most clearly, the ringing mandates of both the language and the intent of the seminal Civil Rights Act of 1964, in general, and Titles VI and VII, in particular.[32] As described earlier, the high tribunal was far from eager to come to grips with this explosive, emotion-charged, delicate, and vexatious issue, and it had managed to moot it in its non-decision *De Funis* decision of 1974.[33] But events would not be denied, and the nine Justices confronted on its merits—more or less—the "reverse discrimination" aspect of "affirmative action" for the first time in the now historic

[29]*Regents of the University of California v. Bakke,* 438 U.S. 265 (1978), at 317.
[30]*United Steelworkers of America v. Weber,* 443 U.S. 193 (1979).
[31]*Fullilove v. Klutznick,* 448 U.S. 448 (1980).
[32]See pp. 443–47, *supra,* for the Act's main titles and commentary.
[33]See p. 413, footnote 57, and p. 445, footnote 161, *supra.*

Bakke case of 1978. Yet the long-in-coming ruling provided neither clear-cut "winners" nor clear-cut "losers"—and that may well be precisely what the Justices intended. Still, disappointment by friends, foes, and neutrals was widespread; for very little was in fact finally settled by *Bakke*. The verbose opinions that were handed down were seriously divided—a stark contrast to the brief, unanimous decision in the seminal *Brown* I and II cases[34] a quarter of a century earlier. Still, the multiple, seven-opinion, 154-page judgments did spell out some basics, although the case neither settled, nor did it pretend to settle, the ongoing controversy at issue.

Essentially, and summarily, three identifiable groups of Justices rendered at least three different opinions; the two controlling ones were fashioned by the swing vote of the key Justice in the case, Lewis F. Powell, Jr. In one of these, joined by Justices Stevens, Stewart, Rehnquist, and Chief Justice Burger, Powell's 5:4 stewardship affirmed the California judiciary's decision ordering the University of California's Medical School at Davis to admit Allan Bakke, a white applicant who had twice been rejected by Davis, notwithstanding the University-acknowledged fact that he was more highly qualified than any of the admittees from the sixteen-member minority group. These students had entered the Medical School under a special program that had set aside, on an *admitted* quota basis, sixteen of the hundred openings at the school for "minorities." Justice Powell held the University's action to be an unconstitutional violation of the equal protection of the laws clause of the Fourteenth Amendment, whereas the other four regarded *any* racial quota systems utilized by government-supported programs (such as higher education) to be an obvious violation of the explicit language of Title VI of the Civil Rights Act of 1964. The four dissenters, Justices Brennan, White, Marshall, and Blackmun, on the other hand, saw neither a constitutional nor a statutory infraction; they called for the permissive use of race as a justifiable "compensatory" action to redress past wrongs generally. (No racial discrimination against blacks or any other minorities had ever been charged against the University of California at Davis.) While refusing to join these four in so expansive a constitutional stance, Justice Powell nevertheless also held for them and himself (5:4) that the California courts had been

[34]See pp. 344–51, *supra*.

wrong in ruling that race could *never* be a factor in admissions decisions (the state's judiciary had been *adjudging* such a practice to be *both* illegal *and* unconstitutional); that a state university had "a substantial interest" in a diverse student body "that legitimately may be served [here pointing to Harvard] by a properly devised admission program involving the competitive consideration of race and ethnic origin."[35]

What the Supreme Court did, then, in *Bakke* was: (1) disallow (5:4) the kind of explicit, specific, rigid racial quota established by California; and (2) uphold (5:4) the use of "race" as a tool of affirmative action programs in the absence of Davis-like quota arrangements; but— at least for the time being—(3) reject (4:5) the interpretation by the Stevens, Stewart, Rehnquist, Burger group that found the use of race in *any* programs benefiting from statutorily provided federal financial assistance to be illegal; and also (4) reject (4:5), at least by implication, the position of the Brennan, White, Marshall, Blackmun group that any benign "affirmative action" use of race, far from being constitutionally or legally proscribed, was permitted. In a sense, then, the *Wall Street Journal* was justified in headlining the *Bakke* verdict as "The Decision Everyone Won"[36]—although, *de minimis,* that statement needs both considerable explication and qualification. In fine, the Court's long-awaited decision left intact the bulk of affirmative action programs that give special consideration to statutorily identified minority groups (and women), while running up a *caveat* flag on obvious, *rigid* racial (and, by implication, probably sexual and other) quotas. The controversial matter at issue in *Bakke*—confined, as it was, to higher education— hardly settled the overall "reverse discrimination" problem. In 1979 a string of cases winding their way through the judicial structure toward the highest court of the land were headed by a number of potentially seminal "quota cases" in education[37] and, particularly and naturally, in employment.

Weber. Among the cases in the "judicial mill" was the *Weber*

[35]*Bakke, op. cit.,* at 321–24.

[36]June 29, 1978, p. 1.

[37]By the margin of one vote the Court declined in 1979 to review the "Italian Bakke" case of an Italian-American New Yorker whose application under the University of Colorado Law School's special admissions program for blacks, Chicanos, and American Indians had been refused consideration because he did not belong to any of the eligible groups. (*DiLeo v. Board of Regents,* 441 U.S. 927.)

case,[38] decided by the Supreme Court one year after *Bakke*. Together with the latter and the forthcoming 1980 *Fullilove* decision,[39] it would become one of the triad of "reverse discrimination" cases that, in effect, provided a green light, or at least a green-and-yellow one, for the widespread affirmative action programs pushed aggressively by the Carter Administration—and ultimately cemented in the 1980s by the Court, despite strong opposition by the Reagan Administration.

At issue in *Weber* was an allegedly "voluntary" and "temporary" affirmative action plan devised by the Kaiser Aluminum and Chemical Corporation and the United Steelworkers of America for Kaiser's Gramercy, Louisiana, plant, under which at least one-half of the available thirteen positions in an on-the-job training program had been reserved for blacks. Finding himself excluded solely because he was white, Brian Weber filed suit in federal district court, claiming a *prima facie* violation of Title VII of the Civil Rights Act of 1964, which categorically bans any racial discrimination in employment, no matter whether the individual's race be black, white, or any other color, and which specifically states that its provisions are not to be interpreted "to require any employer . . . to grant preferential treatment to any individual or to any group because of the race . . . of such individual or group." Moreover, the congressional history of the statute's enactment made it crystal clear that Congress meant precisely what it said, and that the Civil Rights Act's proponents had so assured the doubters during the exciting eighty-three days of floor debate in 1964.[40] Basing their decisions on *both* the language of Title VII and that of the congressional debates, enshrined in the *Congressional Record,* the two lower federal

---

[38]*United Steelworkers of America v. Weber*, 443 U.S. 193 (1979).

[39]*Fullilove v. Klutznick*, 448 U.S. 448 (1980).

[40]Thus, in an exchange between the C.R.A.'s floor manager, Senator Hubert H. Humphrey (D.-Minn.), and a principal opponent, Senator Willis Robertson (D.-Va), Humphrey insisted: "If the Senator can find in Title VII . . . any language which provides that an employer will have to hire on the basis of percentage or quota related to color . . . I will start eating the pages, one after another, because it is not in there." (110 *Cong. Rec.* 7420.) Senator Edmund Muskie (D.-Me.) said that the provision calls for "not equal pay, not 'racial balance.' Only equal opportunity." (*Ibid.*, at 12617.) Senator Leverrett Saltonstall (R.-Mass.) avowed that 703(j) "provides no preferential treatment for any group of citizens. In fact, it specifically forbids it." (*Ibid.*, at 12691.) Senator Joe Clark (D.-Pa) noted: "The bill establishes no quotas. It leaves an employer free to select whomever he wishes to employ." (*Ibid.*, at 13080.)

courts that had ajudicated the case[41] upheld Weber's contentions and ruled the affirmative action plan at issue to be illegal under Title VII.

But in an astonishing decision, handed down during the last week of its 1978–79 term, the Supreme Court reversed the courts below in a 5 : 2 holding, Justices Powell and Stevens abstaining (although it is fair to conjecture that, based upon their votes *up to that point,* they would have dissented). Writing for the majority, Justice Brennan (joined by Justices Marshall, Stewart, White, and, with reservations, Blackmun) frankly conceded that the rulings by the lower courts had *followed the letter* of the Civil Rights Act of 1964 but not its *spirit.* He conjectured that Congress's primary concern had been with "the plight of the Negro in our economy," and that it would be "ironic indeed" if Title VII would be used to prohibit "all voluntary private, race-conscious efforts to abolish traditional patterns" of discrimination.[42]

Chief Justice Burger and Justice Rehnquist dissented vehemently, charging that the majority had engaged in the crassest kind of judicial activism, which amounted to blatant judicial legislation; that it had, in fact, "totally rewritten a crucial part" of the law. As a member of Congress, the Chief Justice admonished, he "would be inclined to vote for" the views expressed by the majority; but as a judge he had no business in writing legislation. "Congress," he explained with feeling, "expressly *prohibited* the discrimination against Brian Weber" that the five-member majority now approved.[43] And in what may well constitute one of the angriest dissenting opinions in recent times, Justice Rehnquist accused the Court majority of acting like Harry Houdini, the escape artist.[44] Congress sought to require racial equality in government, Rehnquist contended, and "there is perhaps no device more destructive to the notion of equality than . . . the quota. Whether described as 'benign discrimination' or 'affirmative action,' the racial quota is nonetheless a creator of castes, a two-edged sword that must demean one in order to prefer the other." He concluded:

> With today's holding, the Court introduces . . . a tolerance for the very evil that the law was intended to eradicate, without offering even a clue as to

---

[41]415 F. Supp. 761 and 563 F. 2d 216 (1977).
[42]*Weber, op cit.,* at 201.
[43]*Ibid.,* at 218. (Italics in original.)
[44]*Ibid.,* at 222.

what the limits on that tolerance may be. . . . The Court has sown the wind. Later courts will face the impossible task of reaping the whirlwind.[45]

Fullilove. Since the *Weber* majority held that, notwithstanding prohibitory statutory language, racial quotas were neither illegal nor unconstitutional if adopted by a private employer (and later extended to governmental employment, too)[46] on a "voluntary" and "temporary" basis, the Court's six-opinion "reverse-discrimination" decision in *Fullilove v. Klutznick*[47] one year later did not come as a major surprise. For at issue in the latter case was the constitutionality of a 1977 congressional law that, in a floor amendment, adopted without prior hearings, had set aside 10 percent of a $4 billion public works program for "minority business enterprises." The latter were defined in the statute as companies in which blacks, Hispanic-Americans, Oriental-Americans, American Indians, Eskimos, or Aleuts controlled at least a 50 percent interest. It was noteworthy that the governing plurality opinion was written by the Chief Justice, who had so sternly dissented in *Weber*.[48] But speaking also for Justices White and Powell—with the latter additionally filing a separate concurring opinion[49]—and joined on far more expansively permissive grounds in another concurrence by Justice Marshall, who in turn was joined by Justices Brennan and Blackmun,[50] Chief Justice Burger found warrant for his ruling that the program did "not violate the equal protection component of the Due Process Clause of the Fifth Amendment"[51] in the power of Congress "to enforce by appropriate legislation" the equal protection guarantees of the Fourteenth Amendment.[52] Rejecting the contention by the nonminority business enterprises that Congress is obligated to act in a "color blind" fashion, and is in fact forbidden to employ racial quotas under the Constitution's mandates, he referred repeatedly to what he viewed as the temporary nature of the "narrowly tailored" program, one designed by the national legislature to remedy long-standing past

[45]*Ibid.*, at 225.
[46]*Bushey v. New York State Civil Service Commission*, 469 U.S. 1117 (1985).
[47]448 U.S. 448.
[48]*United Steelworkers of America v. Weber*, 443 U.S. 193 (1979).
[49]*Fullilove v. Klutznick, op. cit.*, at 495–517.
[50]*Ibid.*, at 517–21.
[51]*Ibid.*, at 450, 473.
[52]*Ibid.*, at 476.

wrongs.[53] (In fact, the policy became permanent and, in 1987, controversially added "*women*" to the "M.B.E." entitlees.)

There were three vocal dissenters, their leading opinion being written by Justice Stewart, who had joined the majority in *Weber*—he never explained his *Weber* vote—but had been on the other side in *Bakke*. This dissenting opinion was also signed by Justice Rehnquist, who consistently opposed racial quotas in all three cases. The other dissent was filed by Justice Stevens, who did not sit in *Weber*, but whose views were in accord with Rehnquist in *Bakke* as well as now in *Fullilove*. Bristling with anger, Stewart accused his colleagues on the other side of the decision of having rendered a "racist" decision,[54] an adjective he veritably spit out while reading his dissent in full from the bench on that 1980 July Opinion Day. Styling the "set-aside law" an "invidious discrimination by government," he pleaded that the Constitution permits no discrimination of any kind between the races; that the

Fourteenth Amendment was adopted to ensure that every person must be treated equally by each State regardless of the color of his skin . . . that it would honor no preference based on lineage. . . .[55]

and he concluded:

Today the Court derails this achievement and places its imprimatur on the creation once again by government of privileges based on birth.[56]

In his even more scathing dissenting opinion, which he read aloud from the bench on the day of the decision, Justice Stevens charged that the "minority set-aside law"—which had been written on the House floor through the efforts of the Black Caucus, and had not been sent to committee—represents a "perverse form of reparation," a "slapdash" law that rewards some who may not need rewarding and hurts others who may not deserve hurting.[57] Suggesting that such a law could be

53*Ibid.*, at 482, 490.
54*Ibid.*, at 532.
55*Ibid.*, at 531.
56*Ibid.*, at 532.
57*Ibid.*, at 534, 539–40.

used simply as a patronage tool by its authors, he warned that it might breed more resentment and prejudice than it corrects,[58] and he asked what percentage of "oriental blood or what degree of Spanish-speaking skill is required for membership in the preferred class?"[59] Sarcastically, he said that now the government must devise its version of the Nazi laws that defined who was a Jew, musing that "our statute books will once again have to contain laws that reflect the odious practice of delineating the qualities that make one person a Negro and make another white."[60]

Stotts. However, after having upheld several racial quota affirmative action arrangements in employment, the Supreme Court, to the pleasant surprise of some observers, and the consternation of others, appeared to shift gears in a case reaching it from Memphis, Tennessee, in 1984.[61] A lower federal court had forced the layoff or demotion of senior white firefighters in that city in order to protect black hiring and promotion gains achieved under a court-approved affirmative action plan in 1980. The latter required that at least 50 percent of all new employees be black until two-fifths of the department was black. Responding to long-term pressure that generated the arrangement, Memphis increased the proportion of black firefighters from 4 percent in 1974 to 11.5 percent in 1980.

As a result of a 1981 budget crunch, however, the city announced that it would abide by a "last-hired-but-first-fired" seniority system negotiated with the union. It thus began to lay off those who had most recently been hired, a group that included many of the new black firefighters. A federal district court denied the city's right to reduce the proportion of blacks in the department, and as a result three whites lost their jobs to three blacks who had less seniority. Both the city of Memphis and the union appealed to the United States Supreme Court.

In a 6:3 opinion, written by Justice White—who had been on the "other" side in *Bakke*, *Weber*, and *Fullilove*—the Court held that Title VII of the Civil Rights Act of 1964 clearly "protects bona fide seniority systems," unless the plans are *intentionally discriminatory* or black

---

[58]*Ibid.*, at 545.
[59]*Ibid.*, at 552, fn. 30.
[60]*Ibid.*, at 534.
[61]*Firefighters Local Union v. Stotts*, 467 U.S. 561 (1984).

workers can demonstrate that they were *individually* victimized by hiring discrimination.[62] Joined in dissent by Justices Brennan and Marshall, Justice Blackmun—perhaps loath to reach the merits of the case—contented himself by voting to throw out the controversy as being legally irrelevant to those involved because the layoff orders had since been rescinded.

Wygant. The Court continued to receive affirmative action/reverse discrimination cases, and two years after *Stotts* it handed down a decision in which it seemed to say both "yes" *and* "no" to racial preferences, while evidently promising to return to the fray in yet other cases then still on its 1985–86 docket. In the former, *Wygant v. Jackson Board of Education,*[63] the Court held unconstitutional as a violation of the equal protection of the laws clause of the Fourteenth Amendment a Michigan school board's plan for laying off teachers that gave preference to members of minority groups. Under that plan the school district had sought to protect minority hiring gains by laying off white teachers ahead of blacks who had *less* seniority. But the six-opinion 5:4 holding, written by Justice Powell, was so diverse in reasoning that it seemed to provide a bit of triumph for both foes *and* friends of affirmative action. The Reagan Administration could take solace from the majority's view that the mere fact of discrimination in American life is not in and of itself a constitutionally sufficient reason for resorting to the type of affirmative action remedy propounded by the Jackson school board. On the other hand, the supporters of affirmative action *per se* could and did find much satisfaction in Justice O'Connor's concurring opinion, which appeared to be *the* controlling one in terms of the practice's future.

The Court's junior Justice professed to see a forging of "a degree of unanimity" in rejecting a central contention of the Administration, namely, that affirmative action is appropriate only as a device to remedy discrimination *against specific individual victims.* But as Justice O'Connor saw the gravamen of the issue, "a carefully constructed affirmative-action program . . . need not be limited to the remedying of specific instances of identified discrimination" and the Court would be prepared to approve such a course. The Jackson school board, however,

[62]*Ibid.*
[63]106 S.Ct. 1842 (1986).

had ever held—the victorious Brennan opinion also marked the first time that the Court unambiguously held that *without any proof of past discrimination* against women or minorities by a particular employer, the latter may use racial and sexual preferences in hiring and promotions to bring the work force into line with the local population or labor market. Building on his controversial *Weber* opinion of 1979,[77] Justice Brennan—who was joined in full by Justices Marshall, Blackmun, and, perhaps surprisingly, Powell, and in part by Justices Stevens and O'Connor (who both wrote separate concurrences)—insisted that the Santa Clara Transportation Agency's plan was "consistent with Title VII's purpose of eliminating the effects of employment discrimination." He concluded: "Given the obvious imbalance in the skilled craft division and given the agency's commitment to eliminating such imbalances . . . it was appropriate to consider as one fact the sex of Ms. Joyce in making its decision."[78]

Justice O'Connor, distinctly uncomfortable with her senior colleague's reasoning, yet agonizingly opting to vote in favor of the Agency's action, scolded the majority for having gone too far in taking "an expansive and ill-defined approach to voluntary affirmative action . . . despite limitations imposed by the Constitution and by the provisions of Title V."[79] But she resolved to go along "with the reality of the course that the majority of the Court has determined to follow . . . in light of our precedents."[80] Established precedents, as she viewed these, thus became decisive in casting her vote.

There were three dissenters, who wrote two opinions. The leading one was authored by Justice Scalia, joined in full by Chief Justice Rehnquist and in part by Justice White, who also wrote a separate dissent. Like his colleague, White called for the overruling of *Weber,* as now broadened by the *Johnson* holding, as a perversion of Congress's intent in Title VII.[81] White had been in the majority in *Weber,* but he now concluded that the Court had impermissibly overextended it. It was Justice Scalia's opinion, however, that manifested the fundamental disagreement between the two—or arguably three—camps then on the

---

[77]*Supra,* pp. 431–33.
[78]*Johnson v. Transportation Agency, Santa Clara County, op. cit.,* at 4385.
[79]*Ibid.,* at 4388.
[80]*Ibid.*
[81]*Ibid.,* at 4391.

Court. In harsh, blistering, forceful language he contended that the *Johnson* decision now "effectively requires employers, public as well as private, to engage in intentional discrimination on the basis of race or sex." He charged that the decision will insulate employers who adopt affirmative action plans against "reverse discrimination" suits, and that, accordingly, it would be "economic folly" in many cases for employers *not* to engage in reverse discrimination.[82] He was particularly critical of that part of the *Johnson* holding permitting statistical imbalance to constitute criteria for justifying an affirmative action program, rather than requiring that there be evidence of past discrimination. "This is an enormous expansion," he wrote, "undertaken without the slightest justification or analysis."[83] With deep feeling he concluded:

> A statute designed to establish a color-blind and gender-blind work place has thus been converted into a powerful engine of racism and sexism, not merely permitting intentional race- and sex-based discrimination but often making it, through operation of the legal system, practically compelled. . . .
>
> The only losers in the process are the Johnsons of the country, for whom Title VII has been not merely repealed [by the Court] but actually inverted. The irony is that these individuals—predominantly unknown, unaffluent, unorganized—suffer this injustice at the hands of a court fond of thinking itself the champion of the politically impotent. I dissent.[84]

Where, then, do we now stand on the so deeply troubling issue as the Court addressed its 1987–1988 workload? No one would be so sanguine—or so foolhardy—as to conclude that the broad sweep of the 1986–87 rulings, especially those in *Paradise* and *Johnson*, represent the last word. However, as a good many students of both issue and Court hazarded after these two early 1987 decisions, absent dramatic changes in Court personnel and Court *Weltanschauung*—and the utterly unlikely event of definitive legislative action by Congress—*Paradise* and *Johnson*, and particularly the latter, may have anchored the permissible parameters on the affirmative action/reverse discrimination front for the foreseeable future.[85] Thus, it would seem quite clear that

[82]*Ibid.*, at 4396.
[83]*Ibid.*, at 4394.
[84]*Ibid.*, at 4396.
[85]See, for example, the excellent summary by *Time* magazine, April 6, 1987, p. 20.

both public and private companies and agencies now have the option of adopting more or less voluntary programs to hire and promote *qualified* minorities and women to correct a "manifest imbalance" in their representation in various job categories, *even* when better qualified other candidates are available, and *even* when there is *no* evidence of past discrimination. Race or sex may accordingly be legally, and presumably constitutionally, weighed in the balance as a primary "plus"—to use Justice Powell's terminology in *Bakke* II. However, job layoffs and firings fall into a different category, as *Stotts* and *Wygant* demonstrated. In the realm of inaction by employers, federal courts now possess incontrovertible authority to impose involuntary affirmative action plans in the face of strong evidence of previous discrimination against women, blacks, and other minorities. Moreover, executive orders may—and indeed do—require evidence of minority employment for federal contractors. Finally, and notwithstanding Court demurrers and protestations to the contrary in erstwhile decisions, such as *Bakke* I, the Justices are prepared to sanction rigid court-imposed numerical quotas for the employment of minorities, as the 1986 *Cleveland* firefighters and *New York* sheet metal workers and the 1987 Alabama *Paradise* state troopers cases demonstrated. Thus, some lines have indubitably been drawn. How certain their future will prove to be remains necessarily at least somewhat conjectural.

Coda

The several affirmative action/reverse discrimination rulings once again underscore not only the wrench of the quest for equal justice under law but also the omnipresent question of the judicial role—of how to draw that line between judicial restraint and judicial activism, between the judiciary's presumed role of finding rather than making the law and its other assumed role of being the country's "conscience."[86] As for the so divisive issue of affirmative action/reverse discrimination itself, the words of Philip B. Kurland, one of the country's foremost experts on constitutional law and history, are worth keeping in mind. In his view the entire syndrome will almost certainly be with us for years to come, given what he regards as the troublesome "fundamental shift

[86]See my *The Judicial Process,* 5th ed. (New York: Oxford University Press, 1985), Chapters VII, VIII, and IX.

of constitutional limitations from protection of individual rights to protection of class rights . . . to the measurement of equality of opportunity to equality of condition or result."[87]

To the Supreme Court of the United States we have thus turned again and again to help us in our unending need to draw lines. Despite the storms of controversy that have engulfed it, with some notable exceptions it has remained true to its assumed role as our national conscience and our institutional common sense. In the long run, if not always in the short, the Court has served us well in maintaining that blend of change and continuity that is so necessary to the stability of the governmental process of a democracy. It has seemed to adhere to the basic American value so beautifully phrased by Thomas Jefferson and inscribed around the ceiling of the rotunda of the Jefferson Memorial: "I have sworn upon the altar of God eternal hostility against every form of tyranny over the mind of man."

[87]"The Private I . . . ," X, *The University of Chicago Record* 4 (July 19, 1976).

Bibliographical Note

The nature of the relationship of the judicial process to civil rights and liberties has been the subject of a profusion of pertinent writings. In the first edition of my *The Judicial Process: An Introductory Analysis of the Courts of the United States, England, and France* (Oxford University Press, 1962), I compiled four separate bibliographies of constitutional law totaling some 1,200 books. The fifth, which appeared in 1986, featured some 6,500 entries; not all of these apply here, of course, but a good many do, at least tangentially. Yet specific works on the problem of "line-drawing" itself are scarce indeed; most of the published material treats the problem implicitly, rather than explicitly, and within the context of the particular publication's theme. On the other hand, there are some trenchant and stimulating works, generally relatively brief and topical, that do address themselves to line-drawing in a few selected fields. Among these are Sidney Hook's thoughtful *The Paradoxes of Freedom* (University of California Press, 1962), which deals with "intelligence and human rights," "democracy and judicial review," and "intelligence, conscience, and the right to revolution"; David Fellman's *The Limits of Freedom* (Rutgers University Press, 1959), an incisive consideration of religious freedom, "the right to communicate," and "the right to talk politics"; Arthur M. Okun's intriguing study, *Equality and Efficiency: The Big Tradeoff* (Brookings, 1975), in which he analyzes the timely aspect of current line-drawing with insight and perception; and J. M. Buchanan's *Between Anarchy and Leviathan: The Limits of Liberty* (University of Chicago Press, 1975), which deals engagingly with the rule of law, the judicial process, and certain rights of the citizen in democratic society. Milton R. Konvitz's *Expanding Liberties* enjoys a telling designated subtitle, "The Emergence of New Civil Liberties and Civil Rights in Postwar America" (Viking, 1967). The reader, *New Dimensions of Freedom in America* (Chandler, 1969), ably edited by Frederick M. Wirt and Willis D. Hawley, is a useful compendium of "position" essays. So is the sophisticated array edited by Gary L. McDowell, *Taking the Constitution Seriously* (Kendall/Hunt, 1981), and Francis Graham Lee's recent *Neither Conservative Nor Liberal: The*

535

Burger Court on Civil Rights and Liberties (Krieger, 1983). Intriguingly critical of aspects of the contemporary civil rights revolution is Richard E. Morgan's *Disabling America: The "Rights Industry" in Our Time* (Basic Books, 1984). A different viewpoint is presented by R. K. Fullinwiden and C. Mills, *The Moral Foundation of Civil Rights* (Rowman & Littlefield, 1986). A useful compendium is G. A. Phelps and R. A. Poirier, *Contemporary Debates on Civil Liberties* (Heath, 1985). And there is the magnificent little gem by that great American, Justice Hugo LaFayette Black, *A Constitutional Faith* (Alfred A. Knopf, 1968), which shines with first principles.

The "double standard," discussed in my second chapter, has absorbed and troubled many students of the judicial process. Paul A. Freund outlines its difficulties in his *The Supreme Court of the United States: Its Business and Purposes* (Meridian Press, 1961); Judge Learned Hand opposes it in—among other works—*The Bill of Rights* (Harvard University Press, 1958); Justice Hugo L. Black upholds it in many of his opinions and, most dramatically perhaps, in his famous essay "The Bill of Rights," 35 *New York University Law Review* 866 (April 1960); Loren P. Beth favors it in "The Case for Judicial Protection of Civil Liberties," 17 *The Journal of Politics* 112 (February 1955); Robert G. McCloskey is critical of it in "Economic Due Process and the Supreme Court: An Exhumation and Reburial," in Philip B. Kurland, ed., *The Supreme Court Review* 1962 (University of Chicago Press, 1962), pp. 34–62; and so is Bernard H. Siegan in his *Economic Liberties and The Constitution* (University of Chicago Press, 1980). A significant "think-piece" is Judge Richard A. Posner's *The Federal Courts: Crisis and Reform* (Harvard, 1985). An exchange between Richard Funston and me on the justifiability of its existence appeared in 90 *Political Science Quarterly* 2 (Summer 1975). Important analyses and evaluations of the "new" double standard, linked to the "new" or "substantive" equal protection *cum* "suspect categories" approach to the problem, are, among many others: Gerald Gunther, "The Supreme Court: 1971 Term; In Search of Evolving Doctrine on a Changing Court: A Model for a Newer Equal Protection," 86 *Harvard Law Review* 1 (1972); J. Harvie Wilkinson III, "The Supreme Court, the Equal Protection Clause, and the Three Faces of Constitutional Equality," 61 *Virginia Law Review* 945 (1975); and Robert G. Dixon, Jr., "The 'New' Substantive Due Process and the Democratic Ethic: A Prolegomenon," 1 *Brigham Young Law Review* 1 (1976). A good historical "period" work is Arnold M. Paul, *Conservative Crisis and the Rule of Law, 1889–1895*, rev. ed. (Harper & Row, 1969).

Further reading on "The Bill of Rights and Its Applicability to the States," the topic of Chapter III, may be done in a number of works. Robert A. Rutland's *The Birth of the Bill of Rights, 1776–1791*, rev. ed. (Northeastern, 1983), provides valuable background to the document's purpose and framing.

The elusive intentions of the framers of the Fourteenth Amendment, which have been interpreted and reinterpreted from all points of view, often with diametrically opposed conclusions, should not be considered without some reference to the records of the actual debates in the 39th Congress during 1866. *The Globe* will help. The major protagonists in the controversy over "incorporation" of the Bill of Rights are identified and evaluated both in the text and in the footnotes in Chapter III, especially between pages 35 and 43, so that there is no need to cite them here. While there is very little material available on the evolution of "incorporation" or "absorption" and the position of the justices, a host of writings, chiefly journal articles, exist on specific clauses of the Bill of Rights and on the attitudes of the justices. A perusal of the *Index to Legal Periodicals*, the *Public Affairs Information Service*, and the *Reader's Guide to Periodical Literature* will provide a good many citations. The leading Supreme Court decisions themselves are rich natural fare for analysis and debate. Thus, *Palko v. Connecticut*, 302 U.S. 319 (1937), *Adamson v. California*, 332 U.S. 46 (1947); *Griswold v. Connecticut*, 381 U.S. 479 (1965); and *Duncan v. Louisiana*, 391 U.S. 145 (1968), to name just four, feature numerous opinions on the question of applying the Bill of Rights to several states of the Union. A good summary of its evolution is available in Arthur A. North, S.J., *The Supreme Court: Judicial Process and Judicial Politics* (Appleton-Century-Crofts, 1966). Justice Black's essay, "The Bill of Rights," and his *A Constitutional Faith* are again pertinent here; and a sophisticated analysis of the position is presented by Norman G. Rudman in "Incorporation Under the Fourteenth Amendment—The Other Side of the Coin," in 3 *Law in Transition Quarterly* 3 (Spring 1966). An excellent full-length study is Richard C. Cortner's *The Supreme Court and the Second Bill of Rights* (University of Wisconsin Press, 1981). Howard N. Meyer's *The Amendment That Refused to Die* (Beacon, 1978) ably traces the history of the Fourteenth Amendment in thirty-three short chapters. Two recent pro-incorporation book-length studies are Roald Y. Mykkeltvedt, *The Nationalization of the Bill of Rights: Fourteenth Amendment Due Process and Procedural Rights* (Associated Faculty Press, 1983), and Michael K. Curtis, *No State Shall Abridge: The Fourteenth Amendment and the Bill of Rights* (Duke, 1986). A much-quoted essay by Justice William J. Brennan, Jr., exhorting incorporation acceptance by state judiciaries, is "State Constitutions and the Protection of Individual Rights," 90 *Harvard Law Review* 489 (1977).

"Due process" and questions of criminal justice are ever timely and are treated in many media. The Supreme Court's "liberalizing" decisions in this field, beginning about 1961, gave rise to a stream of commentaries in the daily press, the weeklies, and sundry journals. That stream became a flood after the Warren Court's opinions in the landmark cases of *Escobedo v. Illinois*, 378

U.S. 478 (1964), and *Miranda v. Arizona*, 384 U.S. 436 (1966); the end is not in sight. Some fine books on procedural due process generally are David Fellman's *The Defendant's Rights Today* (University of Wisconsin Press, 1976), a superb reference work; Roscoe Pound's still pertinent *Criminal Justice in America* (Holt, 1945); an excellent, fairly recent volume by an active participant in the pursuit of criminal justice, Arnold S. Trebach, *The Rationing of Justice: Constitutional Rights and the Criminal Process* (Rutgers University Press, 1964); and Fred P. Graham's book-length study of the Warren Court's rulings on criminal law, *The Self-Inflicted Wound* (Macmillan, 1970), a major contribution to the debate. Necessary reading, at least *passim,* are the 1969 and 1970 reports of the National Commission on the Causes and Prevention of Violence (Bantam paperbacks). To cite just a few of the many important books available in specific areas of due process: for two opposite views on the meaning and application of the Fifth Amendment's self-incrimination clause, we have Erwin N. Griswold's *The Fifth Amendment Today* (Harvard University Press, 1955), and Sidney Hook's *Common Sense and the Fifth Amendment* (Criterion Books, 1957); and Leonard W. Levy won a Pulitzer prize for his superb *Origins of the Fifth Amendment* (Oxford University Press, 1968). J. W. Landynski's *Search and Seizure and The Supreme Court* (The Johns Hopkins University Press, 1966), is an important work in constitutional interpretation, and Alan F. Westin tries to find middle ground in the eternally puzzling field of wire-tapping in his *Privacy and Freedom* (Atheneum, 1967); David M. O'Brien's *Privacy, Law, and Public Policy* (Praeger, 1979) deals ably between concepts of privacy and information. There is no better book extant on the right to counsel than Anthony Lewis's justly praised study of the travail of Clarence Earl Gideon, *Gideon's Trumpet* (Random House, 1964); the much neglected problem of bail is persuasively criticized by Ronald Goldfarb in *Ransom* (Harper & Row, 1965); L. G. Miller and J. A. Sigler are on different sides in the continuing controversy on the range of double jeopardy in our federal system in their, respectively, *Double Jeopardy and the Federal System* (University of Chicago Press, 1968) and *Double Jeopardy: The Development of a Legal and Social Policy* (Cornell University Press, 1969); and Judge Marvin E. Frankel makes a thoughtful contribution with his *Criminal Sentences: Law Without Order* (Hill and Wang, 1973). James Q. Wilson, in *Thinking about Crime* (Basic Books, 1975), and Charles Silberman, in *Criminal Violence, Criminal Justice* (Random House, 1978) present masterful, no-nonsense analyses about the nature, causes, prevention, and control of crime; George F. Cole provides a useful reader with his *Criminal Justice: Law and Politics,* 3d ed. (Duxbury, 1980); Vincent Blasi makes a commendable contribution with his anthology, *The Burger Court: The Counter-Revolution That Wasn't* (Yale, 1983); and Chief Justice Warren E. Burger's annual "State of the Judiciary" message always contained useful data and exhortations on crime and criminal justice.

There is probably more material available in the area of freedom of expression than in any of the others that I have treated in the book; much of it is mentioned in Chapter V. The classic study is still Zechariah Chafee, Jr., *Free Speech in the United States* (Harvard University Press, 1954); his contributions to the comprehension and appreciation of freedom of expression are towering. The writings, both on and off the bench, of such steadfast supporters of free speech as Justices Holmes, Brandeis, Hughes, Stone, Cardozo, Black, and Douglas deserve the same respect. Other important works are *Free Speech and Its Relation to Self-Government* (Harper, 1948) and *Political Freedom: The Constitutional Powers of the People* (Oxford University Press, 1965) by Alexander Meiklejohn, who taught Chafee but outlived him. Meiklejohn's thesis goes beyond Chafee's limits, but remains a fine testament to freedom of speech and press. Chafee's review of this book in 62 *Harvard Law Review* 891 (1949) is necessary reading for anyone interested in line-drawing on the frontiers of freedom of expression. A timely, if wistful, evaluation of the Meiklejohn position is presented by Justice William J. Brennan, Jr., in his "The Supreme Court and the Meiklejohn Interpretation of the First Amendment," 79 *Harvard Law Review* 1 (November, 1965). An insightful, albeit questionably successful, endeavor to find and draw that elusive "line" for freedom of expression in relation to proscribable conduct is Thomas I. Emerson's fascinating *Toward a General Theory of the First Amendment* (Vintage, 1967). A dramatically diverse point of view is presented by Walter Berns in his *Freedom, Virtue and the First Amendment* (Louisiana State, 1957) and *The First Amendment and the Future of American Democracy* (Basic, 1976). A long-time student of the free press, John Lofton, has given us a fine treatment of it in his *The Press as Guardian of the First Amendment* (The University of South Carolina Press, 1980), and Charles E. Rice does equally well for association and assembly in *Freedom of Association* (New York University Press, 1962). The nine (!) opinions rendered by the justices in the 1971 *New York Times* and *Washington Post* cases make for a fascinating study of differing approaches to the First Amendment's posture with respect to governmental national security claims. Civil disobedience is examined from varying points of view by such diverse libertarians as Abe Fortas, *Concerning Dissent and Civil Disobedience* (New American Library, 1968); Sidney Hook, *Academic Freedom and Academic Anarchy* (Cowles, 1969); William O. Douglas, *Points of Rebellion* (Random House, 1970); and Howard Zinn, *Disobedience and Democracy* (Random House, 1968). Among important works on the issues of obscenity, morals, and censorship, which are so closely related to freedom of expression, are: Harriet F. Pilpel's *Obscenity and the Constitution* (Bowker,

1973); a superb study by Alexander Meiklejohn's son, Donald, *Freedom and the Public: Public and Private Morality in America* (Syracuse University Press, 1965); an interesting conservative approach by Harry M. Clor, *Obscenity and Public Morality: Censorship in a Liberal Society* (University of Chicago Press, 1969); a concise, realistic monograph by Lane V. Sunderland, *Obscenity: The Court, the Congress and the President's Commission* (American Enterprise Institute, 1974); a controversial behavioral study, *Pornography and Sexual Deviance* (University of California Press, 1974) by Michael J. Goldstein *et al.;* and an overview of a burgeoning contemporary issue, edited by D. C. Knutson, *Homosexuality and the Law* (Haworth Press, 1980). A trio of recent general works: Eric Barendt, *Freedom of Speech* (Oxford University, 1986), Joseph J. Hemmer, *The Supreme Court and the First Amendment* (Praeger, 1986), and D. F. B. Tucker, *Law, Liberalism and Free Speech* (Rowman & Littlefield, 1986). And an engaging new study of the *Abrams* case is Richard Polenberg's *Fighting Faiths: The Abrams Case, the Supreme Court and Free Speech* (Viking, 1987).

There is no dearth of works in the realm of religion, and there is a particularly heavy output on the question of the separation of Church and State. Here Leo Pfeffer's excellent one-volume condensation of Anson Phelps Stokes's monumental *Church and State in the United States* (Harper, 1950), published by Harper and Row in 1964 under the same title, is the key work for both its historical account and its sound analysis—although the author and editor hold controversial points of view. Representative Roman Catholic stances on the matter of separation of Church and State may be found in Robert F. Drinan, *Religion, the Courts, and Public Policy* (McGraw-Hill, 1963); Jerome G. Kerwin, *Catholic Viewpoint on Church and State* (Hanover House, 1959); Neil G. McCluskey, *Catholic Viewpoint on Education* (Hanover House, 1959); and D. M. Kelly, *Why Churches Should Not Pay Taxes* (Harper and Row, 1977). The other side is ardently presented in, for example, Paul Blanshard's *Religion and the Schools: The Great Controversy* (Beacon Press, 1963); Leo Pfeffer's *God, Caesar, and Constitution* (Beacon Press, 1975); and in J. M. Swomley, Jr.'s *Religion, the State and the Schools* (Pegasus, 1969). An excellent collection of diverse viewpoints is *The Wall Between Church and State,* edited by Dallin H. Oaks (University of Chicago, 1963); and a nicely done volume by a political scientist and prominent church layman is Murray S. Stedman's *Religion and Politics in America* (Harcourt, Brace & World, 1964). Among other scholarly works that evaluate the establishment problem ably are Paul G. Kauper, *Religion and the Constitution* (Louisiana State University Press, 1964); Robert Gordis, *Religion and the Schools* (Fund for the Republic, 1959); Robert T. Miller and Ronald B. Flowers, *Toward Benevolent Neutrality: Church, State and the Supreme Court,* 3d. ed. (Baylor, 1987); Wilbur G. Katz, *Religion and American Constitutions* (Northwestern University Press, 1964); and Philip B. Kurland, *Religion and the Law: Of Church and State and the Supreme Court*

(Aldine Publishing Co., 1962). Richard E. Morgan's *The Politics of Religious Conflict: Church and State in America*, 2d ed. (University Press of America, 1980), posits some intriguingly unorthodox suggestions. Interesting case studies are Theodore Powell, *The School Bus Law: A Case Study in Education, Religion, and Politics* (Wesleyan University Press, 1960); Albert N. Keim, *Compulsory Education and the Amish: The Right Not to Be Modern* (Beacon Press, 1975); E. F. Frazier, *The Negro Church in America* (Schocken, 1969); and Victor E. Blackwell, *O'er the Ramparts They Watched* (Carlton, 1976), a work by one of the leading attorneys for the Jehovah's Witnesses. The best historical work extant on the controversial problem of the free exercise of religion and conscientious objection is still Mulford Q. Sibley and Philip E. Jacob, *Conscription of Conscience: The American State and the Conscientious Objector, 1940–1947* (Cornell University Press, 1952), though it must now be supplemented with readings of recent significant Supreme Court decisions, such as *United States v. Seeger*, 380 U.S. 163 (1965); *Welsh v. United States*, 398 U.S. 333 (1970); and *Gillette v. United States* plus *Negre v. Larsen*, 401 U.S. 437 (1971). Also notable is Milton R. Konvitz's *Religious Liberty and Conscience: A Constitutional Inquiry* (Viking, 1969). Gordon W. Allport's *The Individual and His Religion* (Macmillan, 1950) blends philosophical with pragmatic considerations; William H. Marnell's *The First Amendment: The History of Religious Freedom in America* (Doubleday, 1964) is a valuable account; and Davis R. Manwaring's *Render Unto Caesar: The Flag-Salute Controversy* (University of Chicago Press, 1962) gives us the exciting, engagingly written story of the *Flag Salute* cases of the early 1940s—cases that tell us much about line-drawing and the judicial process. The complete legal briefs, court proceedings, and decisions in the heart-rending, fascinating case of *Karen Ann Quinlan* are available in a handy publication by University Publishers of America, 1975. A very useful anthology is Francis Graham Lee's *Wall of Controversy: Church-State Conflict in America* (Krieger, 1986).

Lastly, some suggested further readings on egalitarianism, on race, and on gender, especially race. Gunnar Myrdal's epic *An American Dilemma: The Negro Problem and Modern Democracy*, rev. ed. (Harper, 1962), is still an essential introduction to the problem. C. Vann Woodward's informative and purposeful work, *The Strange Career of Jim Crow*, 3d ed. (Oxford University Press, 1974), explains definitively the origin and development of "Jim Crow." Loren Miller, son of a Negro slave and his white wife, has a highly useful work on the story of the Court and the Negro, *The Petitioners* (Pantheon Books, 1966). Betty Friedan's *The Feminine Mystique* (Norton, 1963) and Kate Millet's *Sexual Politics* (Doubleday, 1970) provided *the* literary impetus for the rising women's movement. A thorough overview of the latter's dénouement may be found in Leslie F. Goldstein's *The Constitutional Rights of Women: Cases in Law and Social Change* (Longman, 1979). Paul Lewinson's *Race*,

Class, and Party: A History of Negro Suffrage and White Politics in the South (Russell and Russell, 1963) illustrates well the rocky road that led to the successful Voting Rights Act of 1965. To understand that other road, which—at least on paper—reached its destination faster by a decade, the road to the desegregated schoolhouse, one could do no better than to read some of the pertinent key Supreme Court decisions: *The Civil Rights Cases*, 109 U.S. 3 (1883); *Plessy v. Ferguson*, 163 U.S. 537 (1896), which made "separate but equal" king for almost six decades; *Missouri ex rel. Gaines v. Canada*, 305 U.S. 337 (1938); *Sweatt v. Painter*, 339 U.S. 629 (1950); and, of course, the *Public School Desegregation* cases of 1954 and 1955 (see Chapter VII), which heralded the death of "separate but equal"—not only in education but elsewhere. *Plessy* is reexamined by Charles A. Lofgren in his 1987 work, *The Plessy Case: A Legal-Historical Interpretation* (Oxford University Press). A handy and factual description of the last decisions is Daniel M. Berman's *It Is So Ordered: The Supreme Court Rules on School Segregation* (Norton, 1966); but the best work to date on *Brown* is Richard Kluger's mammoth *Simple Justice: The History of Brown v. Board of Education and Black America's Struggle for Equality* (Knopf, 1975). Literally thousands of books have appeared on the subject of race; among those that stand out are J. Harvie Wilkinson III's ably analytical and historical *From Brown to Bakke* (Oxford University Press, 1979); Walter Lord's *The Past That Would Not Die* (Harper and Row, 1965); Robert J. Harris's eloquent activist plea, *The Quest for Equality: The Constitution, Congress, and the Supreme Court* (Louisiana University Press, 1960); and Charles E. Silberman's *Crisis in Black and White* (Random House, 1964), an important analysis of fundamentals. Also outstanding are Lerone Bennett, Jr., *Confrontation: Black and White* (Penguin Books, 1966); James W. Silver's courageous analysis, *Mississippi: The Closed Society*, enl. ed. (Harcourt, Brace & World, 1966), which became a classic example of the basic problem that existed in certain areas of the Deep South; Pat Watters's excellent analysis and exposition, *The South and the Nation* (Pantheon, 1970); the important statistical study by W. Brink and L. Harris, *Black and White: A Study of U.S. Racial Attitudes Today* (Simon & Schuster, 1967); the patently unduly sanguine tome by W. J. Wilson, *The Declining Significance of Race* (University of Chicago Press, 1978); and the realistic tome by Margaret Edds, *Free At Last: What Really Happened When Civil Rights Came to Southern Politics* (Adler & Adler, 1987). The continuing emotion-charged issue of "affirmative action"–"reverse discrimination," highlighted by the non-decision in *De Funis v. Odegaard*, 417 U.S. 532 (1974), that of the "balancing" one of *Regents of the University of California v. Bakke*, 438 U.S. 265 (1978), and that of the perhaps most contentious one of *United Steel Workers v. Weber*, 442 U.S. 193 (1979), ultimately leading inexorably to *Johnson v. Transportation Agency of Santa Clara County*, 107 S. Ct. 1442 (1987), is the subject of an increasing number of diverse-in-viewpoint works on what, together with forced busing, turned into the most volatile civil rights issue of the 1970s and 1980s. Among them are: Nathan Glazer's pointed *Affirmative Discrimination* (Harvard University Press, 1987); Ralph A. Rossum, *Reverse Discrimination: The Constitutional Debate* (Dekker, 1980); Robert M. O'Neil, *Discriminating Against Discrimination* (Indiana University Press, 1975); George Roche, *The Balancing Act: Quota Hiring in Higher Education* (Open Court, 1974); Ronald Dworkin, *Taking Rights Seriously* (Harvard University Press, 1977); Kent Greenawalt, *Discrimination and Reverse Discrimination* (Knopf, 1983); T. J. O'Neill, *Bakke and the Politics of Equality* (Harper & Row, 1985); J. J. Thompson, *Rights, Restitution, and Risks* (Harvard, 1986); and Abigail M. Thernstrom, *Whose Votes Count? Affirmative Action and Minority Voting Rights* (Harvard University Press, 1987).

The volatile *busing* issue, dramatically brought to the fore in the seminal Supreme Court decision in *Swann v. Charlotte-Mecklenburg Board of Education*, 402 U.S. 1 (1971), has been addressed widely in the literature: e.g., L. Rubin's *Busing and Backlash* (University of California Press, 1972); Robert H. Bork, *Constitutionality of the President's Busing Proposals* (American Enterprise Institute, 1972); Nicolaus Mills (ed.), *The Great School Bus Controversy* (Texas Christian Press, 1973); James Bolner and Robert Shanley, *Busing: The Political and Judicial Process* (Praeger, 1974); R. R. Diamond, *Beyond Busing: Inside the Challenge to Urban Segregation* (University of Michigan, 1985); "Busing—The Supreme Court Goes North," a prophetic article by Christopher Jencks, *The New York Times Magazine*, November 19, 1972, pp. 40ff; Lino A. Graglia's potent *Disaster by Decree: The Supreme Court Decisions on Race and the Schools* (Cornell University Press, 1976); and Bernard Schwartz, *Swann's Way: The School Busing Case and the Supreme Court* (Oxford University Press, 1986).

For works on the evolving techniques of the black civil rights movement, which have led to serious line-confrontations in both a physical and a legal sense, important treatises are: Estelle Fuchs, *Pickets at the Gates* (Free Press, 1966), which deals with difficulties inherent in New York City; W. Haywood Burns, *The Voices of Negro Protest in America* (Oxford University Press, 1963), an excellent historical and analytical study of Negro pressure groups, especially the Muslims; Everett C. Ladd, Jr., *Negro Political Leadership in the South* (Cornell University Press, 1966), an important analysis of an all-too-neglected aspect of the problem; Howard Zinn's description and evaluation of the "energetic young radicals" in *SNCC: The Abolitionists* (Beacon Press, 1964); Arthur I. Waskow's overview, *From Race Riot to Sit-in: 1919 and the 1960's* (Doubleday, 1966); the intelligent political analysis of the rising influence of the Negro voter by Donald R. Matthews and James W. Prothro, *Negroes and the New Southern Politics* (Harcourt, Brace & World, 1966); L. S. Foster's informative anthology, *The Voting Rights Act: Consequences and*

Implications (Praeger, 1985); P. S. Foner's study of the increasingly visible Black Panthers, *The Black Panthers Speak* (Lippincott, 1970); Martin Oppenheimer's *The Urban Guerilla* (Quadrangle, 1969); J. H. Cone's *Black Theology and Black Power* (Seabury Press, 1969); Thomas Wagstaff's *Black Power: The Radical Response to White America* (The Glencoe Press, 1969); Alan Altshuler's *Community Control: The Black Demand for Participation in Large American Cities* (Pegasus, 1970); the influential Saul Alinsky's *Rules for Radicals: A Pragmatic Primer for Realistic Radicals* (Random House, 1971); W. D. Wynn's *The Black Protest Movement* (Philosophical Library, 1974); E. Patterson's *Black City Politics* (Dodd, Mead, 1975); W. H. Chafe's *Civilities and Civil Rights: Greensboro, North Carolina, and the Black Struggle for Freedom* (Oxford University Press, 1980); and Paul Burstein's realistic *Discrimination, Jobs, and Politics* (University of Chicago, 1985).

Finally in this brief bibliography, the vexatious "state action" problem, which has dominated so many facets of the race issue, is discussed in several excellent works. Among them are Paul G. Kauper's penetrating chapter "Private and Governmental Actions: Fluid Concepts," in his *Civil Liberties and the Constitution* (University of Michigan Press, 1962); Jerre Williams's "Twilight of State Action," 4 *Texas Law Review* 374 (February 1963); the already listed book by Robert J. Harris; and Morrow Berger's *Equality by Statute: The Revolution in Civil Rights,* rev. ed. (Doubleday, 1967). Among several, two distinguished scholars have raised basic issues of the state action problem that will probably always be with us in some form even though the legislative and judicial processes have to some extent passed them by: Herbert Wechsler, "Toward Neutral Principles of Constitutional Law," 73 *Harvard Law Review* 1, which appeared in November 1959 and is still widely discussed; and Louis Henkin, "Shelley v. Kraemer: Notes for a Revised Opinion," 110 *University of Pennsylvania Law Review* 473 (February 1962), a searching, troubled, and honest essay. A host of fascinating cases involving the state-action/private-action dichotomy point to what will indubitably be a continuing source of constitutional controversy—among them: *Reitman v. Mulkey,* 387 U.S. 369 (1967), the California Fair Housing Ban Proposition case; *Jones v. Alfred H. Mayer Co.,* 392 U.S. 409 (1968), the first contemporary Civil Rights Act of *1866* case; *Palmer v. Thompson,* 403 U.S. 217 (1971), the Mississippi Pool Closing case; *Moose Lodge #107 v. Irvis,* 407 U.S. 163 (1972), the Private Club Ban of Blacks case; *Tillman v. Wheaton-Haven Recreation Association,* 410 U.S. 431 (1973), the Montgomery County, Maryland, Swimming Facilities case; and, perhaps most contentiously, *Runyon v. McCrary,* 427 U.S. 160, the 1976 Virginia Private School Segregation case, coupled with its philosophical companion duo a decade later, *Bob Jones University & Goldsboro Christian School v. United States,* 461 U.S. 574 (1983).

It would be easy to continue—but here too, lines must be drawn.

Appendix A

Statistical Data on Supreme Court Justices

APPOINTING PRESIDENT	PRESIDENT'S POLITICAL PARTY	DATES OF PRESIDENT'S SERVICE	NAME OF JUSTICE	DATES OF BIRTH & DEATH	JUSTICE'S NOMINAL PARTY ALLEGIANCE ON APPOINTMENT	STATE FROM WHICH JUSTICE WAS APPTD. #	DATES OF SERVICE ON SUPREME COURT
Washington	Federalist	1789–1797	1. Jay, John*	1745–1829	Federalist	N.Y.	1789–1795
"	"	"	2. Rutledge, John	1739–1800	"	S.C.	1789–1791‖
"	"	"	3. Cushing, William	1732–1810	"	Mass.	1789–1810
"	"	"	4. Wilson, James	1724–1798	"	Pa.	1789–1798
"	"	"	5. Blair, John	1732–1800	"	Va.	1789–1796
"	"	"	6. Iredell, James	1750–1799	"	N.C.	1790–1799
"	"	"	7. Johnson, Thomas	1732–1819	"	Md.	1791–1793
"	"	"	8. Paterson, Wm.	1745–1806	"	N.J.	1793–1806
"	"	"	9. Rutledge, John*	1739–1800	"	S.C.	1796‡
"	"	"	10. Chase, Samuel	1741–1811	"	Md.	1796–1811
"	"	"	11. Ellsworth, Oliver*	1745–1807	"	Conn.	1796–1800
Adams	"	1797–1801	12. Washington, Bushrod	1762–1829	"	Va.	1798–1829
"	"	"	13. Moore, Alfred	1755–1810	"	N.C.	1799–1804
"	"	"	14. Marshall, John*	1755–1835	"	Va.	1801–1835
Jefferson	Republican	1801–1809	15. Johnson, Wm.	1771–1834	Republican	S.C.	1804–1834
"	"	"	16. Livingston, H. Brockholst	1757–1823	"	N.Y.	1806–1823
"	"	"	17. Todd, Thomas	1765–1826	"	Ky.	1807–1826
Madison	"	1809–1817	18. Duval, Gabriel	1752–1844	"	Md.	1811–1835
"	"	"	19. Story, Joseph	1779–1845	"	Mass.	1811–1845
Monroe	"	1817–1825	20. Thompson, Smith	1768–1843	"	N.Y.	1823–1843
Adams	"	1825–1829	21. Trimble, Robert	1777–1828	"	Ky.	1826–1828
Jackson	Democrat	1829–1837	22. McLean, John	1785–1861	Democrat	Ohio	1829–1861
"	"	"	23. Baldwin, Henry	1780–1844	"	Pa.	1830–1844
"	"	"	24. Wayne, James M.	1790–1867	"	Ga.	1835–1867

Appointing President	Term	Party	No. Justice	Birth–Death	Party	State	Service
"		"	25. Taney, Roger B.*	1777–1864	"	Md.	1836–1864
"		"	26. Barbour, Philip P.	1783–1841	"	Va.	1836–1841
Van Buren	1837–1841	"	27. Catron, John§	1778–1865	"	Tenn.	1837–1865
"		"	28. McKinley, John	1780–1852	"	Ala.	1837–1852
"		"	29. Daniel, Peter V.	1784–1860	"	Va.	1841–1860
Tyler	Whig / 1841–1845		30. Nelson, Samuel	1792–1873	"	N.Y.	1845–1872
Polk	Democrat / 1845–1849		31. Woodbury, Levi	1789–1851	"	N.H.	1845–1851
"			32. Grier, Robert C.	1794–1870	"	Pa.	1846–1870
Fillmore	Whig / 1850–1853		33. Curtis, Benjamin R.	1809–1874	Whig	Mass.	1851–1857
Pierce	Democrat / 1853–1857		34. Campbell, John A.	1811–1889	Democrat	Ala.	1853–1861
Buchanan	1857–1861		35. Clifford, Nathan	1803–1881	"	Me.	1858–1881
Lincoln	Republican / 1861–1865		36. Swayne, Noah H.	1804–1884	Republican	Ohio	1862–1881
"	"		37. Miller, Samuel F.	1816–1890	"	Iowa	1862–1890
"	"		38. Davis, David	1815–1886	"	Ill.	1862–1877
"	"		39. Field, Stephen J.	1816–1899	Democrat	Cal.	1863–1897
"	"		40. Chase, Salmon P.*	1808–1873	Republican	Ohio	1864–1873
Grant	1869–1877		41. Strong, William	1808–1895	"	Pa.	1870–1880
"	"		42. Bradley, Joseph P.	1803–1892	"	N.J.	1870–1892
"	"		43. Hunt, Ward	1810–1886	"	N.Y.	1872–1882
"	"		44. Waite, Morrison R.*	1816–1888	"	Ohio	1874–1888
Hayes	1877–1881		45. Harlan, John M.	1833–1911	"	Ky.	1877–1911
"	"		46. Woods, William B.	1824–1887	"	Ga.	1880–1887
Garfield	Mar.–Sept.		47. Matthews, Stanley	1824–1889	"	Ohio	1881–1889
Arthur	1881–1885		48. Gray, Horace	1828–1902	"	Mass.	1881–1902
"	"		49. Blatchford, Samuel	1820–1893	"	N.Y.	1882–1893
Cleveland	Democrat / 1885–1889		50. Lamar, Lucius Q. C.	1825–1893	Democrat	Miss.	1888–1893
"	"		51. Fuller, Melville*	1833–1910	"	Ill.	1888–1910
Harrison	Republican / 1889–1893		52. Brewer, David J.	1837–1910	Republican	Kans.	1889–1910
"	"		53. Brown, Henry B.	1836–1913	"	Mich.	1890–1906
"	"		54. Shiras, George, Jr.	1832–1924	"	Pa.	1892–1903
"	"		55. Jackson, Howell E.	1832–1895	Democrat	Tenn.	1893–1895

(continued)

APPOINTING PRESIDENT	PRESIDENT'S POLITICAL PARTY	DATES OF PRESIDENT'S SERVICE	NAME OF JUSTICE	DATES OF BIRTH & DEATH	JUSTICE'S NOMINAL PARTY ALLEGIANCE ON APPOINTMENT	STATE FROM WHICH JUSTICE WAS APPTD. #	DATES OF SERVICE ON SUPREME COURT
Cleveland	Democrat	1893–1897	56. White, Edward D.	1854–1921	"	La.	1894–1910
"	"	"	57. Peckham, Rufus W.	1838–1909	"	N.Y.	1895–1909
McKinley	Republican	1897–1901	58. McKenna, Joseph	1843–1926	Republican	Cal.	1898–1925
Roosevelt	"	1901–1909	59. Holmes, Oliver W., Jr.	1841–1935	"	Mass.	1902–1932
"	"	"	60. Day, William R.	1849–1923	"	Ohio	1903–1922
"	"	"	61. Moody, William H.	1853–1917	"	Mass.	1906–1910
Taft	"	1909–1913	62. Lurton, Horace	1844–1914	Democrat	Tenn.	1909–1914
"	"	"	63. Hughes, Charles E.	1862–1948	Republican	N.Y.	1910–1916
"	"	"	64. White, Edward D.†*	1845–1921	Democrat	La.	1910–1921
"	"	"	65. Van Devanter, Willis	1859–1941	Republican	Wyo.	1910–1937
"	"	"	66. Lamar, Joseph R.	1857–1916	Democrat	Ga.	1910–1916
"	"	"	67. Pitney, Mahlon	1858–1924	Republican	N.J.	1912–1922
Wilson	Democrat	1913–1921	68. McReynolds, J. C.	1862–1946	Democrat	Tenn.	1914–1941
"	"	"	69. Brandeis, Louis D.	1856–1941	Republican**	Mass.	1916–1939
"	"	"	70. Clarke, John H.	1857–1945	Democrat	Ohio	1916–1922
Harding	Republican	1921–1923	71. Taft, William H.*	1857–1930	Republican	Conn.	1921–1930
"	"	"	72. Sutherland, George	1862–1942	"	Utah	1922–1938
"	"	"	73. Butler, Pierce	1866–1939	Democrat	Minn.	1922–1939
"	"	"	74. Sanford, Edward T.	1865–1930	Republican	Tenn.	1923–1930
Coolidge	"	1923–1929	75. Stone, Harlan F.	1872–1946	"	N.Y.	1925–1941
Hoover	"	1923–1933	76. Hughes, Charles E.*	1862–1948	"	N.Y.	1930–1941
"	"	"	77. Roberts, Owen J.	1875–1955	"	Pa.	1930–1945
"	"	"	78. Cardozo, Benjamin	1870–1938	Democrat	N.Y.	1932–1938
Roosevelt	Democrat	1933–1945	79. Black, Hugo L.	1886–1971	"	Ala.	1937–1971
"	"	"	80. Reed, Stanley F.	1884–1980	"	Ky.	1938–1957
"	"	"	81. Frankfurter, Felix	1883–1965	Independent	Mass.	1939–1962

President	Party	Term	No.	Justice	Born–Died	Party	State[#]	Service
"			82.	Douglas, William	1898–1980	Democrat	Conn.	1939–1975
"			83.	Murphy, Frank	1893–1949	"	Mich.	1940–1949
"			84.	Byrnes, James F.	1879–1972	"	S.C.	1941–1942
"			85.	Stone, Harlan F.†*	1872–1946	Republican	N.Y.	1941–1946
"			86.	Jackson, Robert H.	1892–1954	Democrat	N.Y.	1941–1954
"			87.	Rutledge, Wiley B.	1894–1949	"	Iowa	1943–1949
Truman	"	1945–1953	88.	Burton, Harold H.	1888–1965	Republican	Ohio	1945–1958
"			89.	Vinson, Fred M.*	1890–1953	Democrat	Ky.	1946–1953
"			90.	Clark, Tom C.	1899–1977	"	Tex.	1949–1967
"			91.	Minton, Sherman	1890–1965	"	Ind.	1949–1956
Eisenhower	Republican	1953–1961	92.	Warren, Earl*	1891–1974	Republican	Cal.	1953–1969
"			93.	Harlan, John M., Jr	1899–1971	"	N.Y.	1955–1971
"			94.	Brennan, Wm. J.	1906–	Democrat	N.J.	1956–
"			95.	Whittaker, Charles	1900–1973	Republican	Mo.	1957–1962
"			96.	Stewart, Potter	1915–1985	"	Ohio	1958–1981
Kennedy	Democrat	1961–1963	97.	White, Byron R.	1917–	Democrat	Colo.	1962–
"			98.	Goldberg, Arthur	1908–	"	Ill.	1962–1965
Johnson	"	1963–1969	99.	Fortas, Abe	1910–	"	Tenn.	1965–1969
"			100.	Marshall, Thurgood	1910–	"	N.Y.	1967–
Nixon	Republican	1969–1974	101.	Burger, Warren E.*	1907–	Republican	Va.	1969–
"			102.	Blackmun, Harry A.	1908–	"	Minn.	1970–
"			103.	Powell, Lewis F., Jr.	1907–	Democrat	Va.	1972–
"			104.	Rehnquist, William H.†*	1924–	Republican	Ariz.	1972–
Ford	"	1974–1977	105.	Stevens, John Paul	1920–	"	Ill.	1975–
Reagan	Republican	1981–	106.	O'Connor, Sandra D.	1930–	Republican	Ariz.	1981–
"			107.	Scalia, Antonin	1936–	"	Va.	1986–
"			108.	Kennedy, Anthony M.	1936–	"	Cal.	1988–

*Chief Justice.   ‖Resigned without sitting.
‡Unconfirmed recess appointment, rejected by Senate, Dec. 1795.
#Not necessarily, but often, state of birth.
§Catron was nominated by Jackson but he was not confirmed until Van Buren had assumed the presidency.
†Promoted from Associate Justice.
**Many—and with some justice—consider Brandeis a Democrat; however, he was in fact a registered Republican when nominated.

Appendix B. Civil Rights and Liberties in the Constitution

First Ten Amendments (Adopted in 1791)

AMENDMENT I

Congress shall make no law respecting an establishment of religion, or prohibiting the free exercise thereof; or abridging the freedom of speech, or of the press; or the right of the people peaceably to assemble and to petition the Government for a redress of grievances.

AMENDMENT II

A well-regulated militia being necessary to the security of a free State, the right of the people to keep and bear arms, shall not be infringed.

AMENDMENT III

No soldier shall, in time of peace, be quartered in any house without the consent of the owner, nor in time of war but in a manner to be proscribed by law.

AMENDMENT IV

The right of the people to be secure in their persons, houses, papers, and effects, against unreasonable searches and seizures, shall not be violated, and no warrants shall issue but upon probable cause, supported by oath or affirmation, and particularly describing the place to be searched, and the persons or things to be seized.

AMENDMENT V

No person shall be held to answer for a capital, or otherwise infamous crime, unless on a presentment or indictment of a Grand Jury, except in cases arising in the land or naval forces, or in the militia, when in actual service in time of war or public danger; nor shall any person be subject for the same offense to be twice put in jeopardy of life or limb; nor shall be compelled in any criminal case to be a witness against himself, nor be deprived of life, liberty or property, without due process of law; nor shall private property be taken for public use, without just compensation.

Amendment VI

In all criminal prosecutions, the accused shall enjoy the right to a speedy and public trial, by an impartial jury of the State and district wherein the crime shall have been committed, which districts shall have been previously ascertained by law, and to be informed of the nature and cause of the accusation; to be confronted with the witnesses against him; to have compulsory process for obtaining witnesses in his favor, and to have the assistance of counsel for his defense.

Amendment VII

In suits at common law, where the value in controversy shall exceed twenty dollars, the right of trial by jury shall be preserved, and no fact tried by a jury, shall be otherwise re-examined in any court of the United States, than according to the rules of the common law.

Amendment VIII

Excessive bail shall not be required, nor excessive fines imposed, nor cruel and unusual punishments inflicted.

Amendment IX

The enumeration in the Constitution of certain rights shall not be construed to deny or disparage others retained by the people.

Amendment X

The powers not delegated to the United States by the Constitution, nor prohibited by it to the States, are reserved to the States respectively, or to the people.

Other Amendments

AMENDMENT XIII (Ratified in 1865)

Section 1. Neither slavery nor involuntary servitude, except as a punishment for crime whereof the party shall have been duly convicted, shall exist within the United States, or any place subject to their jurisdiction.

Section 2. Congress shall have power to enforce this article by appropriate legislation.

AMENDMENT XIV (Ratified in 1868)

Section 1. All persons born or naturalized in the United States, and subject to the jurisdiction thereof, are citizens of the United States and of the State wherein they reside. No State shall make or enforce any law which shall abridge the privileges or immunities of citizens of the United States; nor shall any State deprive any person of life, liberty, or property, without due process of law; nor deny to any person within its jurisdiction the equal protection of the laws. . . .

Section 5. The Congress shall have power to enforce by appropriate legislation the provisions of this article.

AMENDMENT XV (Ratified in 1870)

Section 1. The right of citizens of the United States to vote shall not be denied or abridged by the United States or by any State on account of race, color, or previous condition of servitude.

Section 2. The Congress shall have power to enforce this article by appropriate legislation.

AMENDMENT XIX (Ratified in 1920)

Section 1. The right of citizens of the United States to vote shall not be denied or abridged by the United States or by any State on account of sex.

Section 2. Congress shall have power to enforce this article by appropriate legislation.

AMENDMENT **XXIV** (Ratified in 1964)

Section 1. The right of citizens of the United States to vote in any primary or other election for President or Vice-President, for electors for President or Vice-President, or for Senator or Representative in Congress, shall not be denied or abridged by the United States or any State by reason of failure to pay any poll tax or other tax.

Section 2. The Congress shall have power to enforce this article by appropriate legislation.

AMENDMENT **XXVI** (Ratified 1971)

Section 1. The right of citizens of the United States, who are 18 years of age or older, to vote shall not be denied or abridged by the United States or by any State on account of age.

Section 2. The Congress shall have power to enforce this article by appropriate legislation.

Provisions from the Original Constitution

ARTICLE I

Section 9. . . .

2. The privilege of the writ of habeas corpus shall not be suspended, unless when in cases of rebellion or invasion the public safety may require it.

3. No bill of attainder or ex post facto law shall be passed.

Section 10.

1. No State shall . . . pass any bill of attainder, ex post facto law, or law impairing the obligation of contracts. . . .

ARTICLE III

Section 2. . . .

3. The trial of all crimes. except in cases of impeachment, shall be by jury. . . .

Section 3.

1. Treason against the United States shall consist only in levying war against them, or in adhering to their enemies, giving them aid and comfort. No Person shall be convicted of treason unless

on the testimony of two witnesses to the same overt act, or on confession in open court.

ARTICLE IV

Section 2.

1. The citizens of each state shall be entitled to all privileges and immunities of citizens in the several States.

ARTICLE VI

3. . . . . no religious test shall ever be required as a qualification to any office or public trust under the United States.

General Index

abortion, 9, 30
"Affirmative Action," 337, 463–66, 518
Alien and Sediton Acts (1978), 234
American Bar Association
  report on Fair Trial and a Free Press,
    224
American Jewish Congress
  recommendations for constitutional test
    of Federal Aid to Education Act
    (1965), 387
Amicus curiae, brief, 85, 420
Anti-Ku Klux Klan Act (1871), 401
appeal, writ of, 7
Assize of Clarendon, 99
Awake!, 297

bad tendency test, 200, 201. *See also*
  expression, freedom of
  Gitlow v. New York, 200, 201
bail, 107
basic freedoms
  crucial nature of, 28–30
Bill for Establishing Religious Freedom
  (Disestablishment Bill), 326
Bill of Rights, 23, 38–117, 279, 348.
  See also enumerated amendments
  applicability to states, 38–117
  Barron v. Baltimore, 16, 39–41, 51,
    52, 55, 63
  historical background, 38–39
Birmingham (Ala.), 469–71
Black Panthers, 466
"blue ribbon" jury, 171

"blue laws," 319–25
Boston (Mass.), 436
boycotting. *See* race
Brandeis brief, 13
British Privy Council, 6
Buffalo (N.Y.), 398
busing. *See* race

capital punishment, 83
carpetbagger, 56
Central Intelligence Agency, 23
certiorari, writ of, 7
Chambre de Droit Public of the *Tribunal
  Federal Suisse* (Switzerland), 255
Chicago (Ill.), 398
child benefit theory, 351, 354–55
Christian Scientists, 317
citizenship
  defined in *Slaughterhouse Cases,*
    55–62
  and the Fourteenth Amendment, 55–62
civil disobedience, 5
Civil Rights Act (1866), 42, 49, 444,
  448, 489–95
Civil Rights Act (1871), 8, 408–9
Civil Rights Act (1875), 408–413
Civil Rights Act (1957), 405, 441–48,
  457
Civil Rights Act (1960), 442, 448, 454,
  457, 460, 481–82
Civil Rights Act (1964), 42, 430, 433,
  442–43, 457, 473, 488, 491–92,
  494, 503

Name Index

Case Index

572

Case Index • 573

Baltimore and Ohio Railroad v. United
    States, 34
Bantam Books, Inc. v. Sullivan, 258
Barenblatt v. United States, 216, 239
Barker v. Wingo, 100
Barnette, v. W.Va. State Board of
    Education, 304
Barr v. City of Columbia, 480
Barron v. Baltimore, 39, 40, 51, 52, 55,
    63, 103
Bartkus v. Illinois, 106
Bates v. Arizona State Bar, 209
Beal v. Doe, 96
Bell v. Maryland, 4, 471, 480, 500
Bellotti v. Baird, 96
Benton v. Maryland, 105, 106, 144
Berger v. New York, 180, 184
Berger v. United States, 171
Berkemer v. McCarty, 168
Bernal v. Fainter, 20
Berry v. Cincinnati, 85
Bethel School District v. Fraser, 215
Betts v. Brady, 70, 84, 85
Bible Reading Cases. See Abington
    School District v. Schempp;
    Chamberlain v. Dade County Board
    of Public Instruction; Murray v.
    Curlett
Bigelow v. Virginia, 233
Birmingham v. A.C.L.U., 363
Bivens v. Six Unknown Named Agents,
    171
Blevins v. United States, 100
Blount v. Rizzi, 257
Board of Directors of Rotary
    International v. Rotary Clubs of
    Duarte, 494, 512
Board of Airport Commissioners v. Jews
    for Jesus, 210
Board of Education v. James, 215
Board of Education v. Newburg Area
    Council, 436
Board of Education of Central School
    District #1 v. Allen, 348, 351, 353,
    365, 379, 388

Board of Education of Netcong, N.J. v.
    State Board of Education, 342
Board of Education of Oklahoma v.
    Dowell, 440
Board of Public Works of Maryland v.
    Horace Mann League of United
    States, 381
Bob Jones Univeristy and Goldsboro
    Christian Schools v. United States,
    312, 497
Bodde v. Connecticut, 137
Bolling v. Sharpe, 405, 406, 422, 426
Bond v. Floyd, 205
Boorda v. Subversive Activities Control
    Board, 251
Bowen v. Roy, 312
Bowers v. Hardwick, 97, 265, 271
B.P.O.E. #2043 v. Ingraham, 492
Braden v. United States, 239
Bradfield v. Roberts, 364
Bradley v. Milliken, 435
Bradley v. School Board of the City of
    Richmond, 434
Bradley v. State Board of Education of
    the Commonwealth of Virginia, 435
Bradshaw v. Hall, 374
Brandenburg v. Ohio, 202, 205, 275
Brandon v. Board of Education of
    Guilderland School District, 342, 356
Branti v. Finkel, 210
Branzburg v. Hayes, 231
Braunfeld v. Brown, 310, 319, 320–22
Breard v. City of Alexandria, 310
Breedlove v. Suttles, 456
Breithaupt v. Abram, 140
Brewer v. Williams, 167
Bridges v. California, 24, 218
Brown v. Baskin, 455
Brown v. Board of Education of Topeka
    I, 163, 397, 405, 406, 409, 411,
    413, 419, 422, 425–27, 483, 517
Brown v. Board of Education of Topkea
    II, 426, 427, 517
Brown v. Commonwealth of
    Pennsylvania, 485

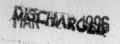